W9-DDZ-871

SOCIOLOGY

INTRODUCTORY READINGS IN
MASS, CLASS, AND BUREAUCRACY

Edited by Joseph Bensman and Bernard Rosenberg

PRAEGER PUBLISHERS
New York

Published in the United States of America in 1975
by Praeger Publishers, Inc.
111 Fourth Avenue, New York, N.Y. 10003

© 1975 by Praeger Publishers, Inc.

All rights reserved

LIBRARY OF CONGRESS CATALOGING IN PUBLICATION DATA
Main entry under title:

Sociology.

    Includes bibliographical references.
    1. Sociology—Addresses, essays, lectures.   I. Bensman, Joseph, ed.
II. Rosenberg, Bernard, 1923–   ed.
HM51.S66343   301   74–1719
ISBN 0–275–51590–7
ISBN 0–275–88800–2   pbk.

Printed in the United States of America

Contents

Introduction

Sociology is not only a broad discipline with many specializations and subdivisions; it is also a field full of conflicting or apparently unrelated approaches, theories, and methods. To describe this field in its entirety would be tantamount to analyzing all the institutions of modern and promodern society. We may console ourselves that in an introduction a complete summary of theoretical and empirical sociology is no more desirable than it is possible. Writers and editors who attempt to cover everything cover nothing—such an attempt ensures that no single aspect of a complex subject is treated with the kind of attention it deserves. A superficial report of thousands of studies, innumerable topics, endless data, various theories, and incompatible methods would do little more than confuse and discourage the student for whom we propose to open an exciting new world.

Every field of knowledge is always in process of changing, adding new ideas and revising old ones. In putting together a collection of introductory readings, it is difficult to avoid presenting a more unified image of a subject than ongoing research may warrant. As editors, simply by selecting and organizing certain points of view into a representative whole, we provide an overall vision of contemporary society. However, no editor or writer who goes by the name of sociologist can claim to give definitive answers. Instead, we must be content with satisfying the more realistic (and sufficiently ambitious) objectives of raising pertinent question about our society and giving students some sense of scholarly and intellectual direction in the discipline.

In undertaking this project we have limited ourselves to several central themes and concepts, among them: culture, society, stratification, race and ethnicity, bureaucracy, and mass communications. While some reflect the turmoil of our particular age, most of them are perennial themes. The basic concern of sociology is an old one, namely, to illuminate the human situation. Nowadays this means interaction between the individual in his personal environment and a host of functionaries representing anonymous institutions. Many technical sociologists focus on either the former or the latter. It is fashionable to call one emphasis *microsociology* and the other, *macrosociology*. This schematic distinction is important; it pertains to separate frames of reference, to different levels of abstraction, to small and large aggregates. Analytically, they may be kept strictly differentiated. But no overview is valuable to students that does not cause them to see the vast collectivity in the individual or the individual in the vast collectivity. Accordingly, readings in this book that deal with the family, the peer group, and the community as "primary groups" and "agencies of socialization" suggest how deeply these institutions are affected by large-scale societal development. Similarly, the readings on urbanism, mass, class, race, bureaucracy, economics, and politics suggest how macrostructures affect and are yet constrained by the distributive culture of individuals in society.

Our task would be impossible if we did not draw upon the rich reservoir of ideas developed by our great predecessors. Thus we have included writings by Spencer, Simmel, Marx, and Weber; they are indispensable. Those who followed have applied, amplified, modified, or rebutted the work of the "masters"; they too are duly included.

The first two sections of the book deal with the fundamental themes of culture and methodology, thus laying the intellectual groundwork for the sections that follow. Culture, language, and symbols are the primary data of sociology—concepts that provide a substructure for many of the essays on specific social practices and institutions. This is especially true where socialization, mass culture, or the arts are considered. The essays on methodology deal with the tools of sociology, a thorough understanding of which is necessary for evaluating the work of any sociologists. The various methodological approaches we have presented are inherently controversial and continue to generate conflict within the discipline. We hope to have made their strengths and weaknesses as clear as possible, the better to foster fruitful dialogue both inside and outside the classroom.

If one reads the book carefully and consecutively, its cumulative impact will become apparent. For, despite differences in viewpoint, all the essays are concerned with one aspect or another of the evolution of large-scale society, whether in economics and politics or mass communications, and the effect of that evolution on class, race, ethnicity, the family, the peer group, and the process of socialization.

Anthologists are always unhappy—they have to omit so much. We are only too keenly aware of how many more concepts and methods might have been included but for lack of space. Yet even without such constraints, the scope of our effort to produce a reasonably coherent image of society, and of sociology, would still have been less than encyclopedic because of our preference for readable, self-contained selections.

We hope that beginners will acquire enough knowledge from this book so that they can gain their bearings in sociology and in the labyrinth of society that at first bewilders all of us. May it also encourage undergraduates who concentrate in sociology or related disciplines to move on and do better.

Thanks to Jim Bergin, editor par excellence; James Latimore, researcher, for his help in obtaining permissions; our wives, who are also our colleagues; and our teachers, one or two alive, many dead, who are more with us than ever.

I. The Cultural Basis of Sociology

As much as any man, Herbert Spencer was the founder of Anglo-American sociology. In 1873 he wrote *The Study of Sociology*, one of his least ambitious and most durable books. In it he sought to explain and justify the new discipline. Spencer succeeded in presenting his ideas with such consummate clarity that, despite an archaic ring to some of the illustrative matter, we know of no better general introduction to the field. Spencer entitled his first chapter "Our Need of It." The need for the scientific study of society, as a counterweight to the deceptions of "common sense" and heedless human intervention, is as great as ever. So are the overall reasons as they were originally set forth by this pioneer sociologist. The contemporary student should have no trouble finding more up-to-date examples. The principles stand firm more than a century after they were first enunciated.

It is but a step in time and space from Spencer to another great English scholar, Edward B. Tylor, best known as the author of *Primitive Culture*. We begin our selection from that work with the best known passage in it, namely Tylor's definition of culture. For if sociology or anthropology is a legitimate enterprise, the main reason may well be that its practitioners have developed the culture concept. Tylor's definition of culture can be usefully memorized (our own shorthand version is "the totality of everything made by *Homo sapiens*"). But it would be well to follow him beyond that point, to note the modesty with which he sees his subject as susceptible to or "on the threshold of" science, his impatience with "speculative dogmatism," and perhaps most strikingly, his perception of constancy and change in human affairs.

If culture is central to an understanding of our species, one must ask how it is created, accumulated, and perpetuated. Few can tell us

1

better than a professional linguist like Charlton Laird or the "culturologist" Leslie A. White. Together they affirm the primary dictum of sociology—that is, that man is an organism in symbolic communication with his fellows. If so, we need to learn much about the nature of language. It is, in the final analysis, what distinguishes us from all other species. Human beings learn like other animals, but conserve and transmit what they learn. This is their distinctive trait. We are all able to *endow* objects with meaning and value, as White points out, and it is this gift that makes each of us a dynamic culture-carrier, absorbing and building on traditions handed down to us. But for "the emission and comprehension" of sounds, of words uttered and understood, there would be no culture, and but for the written word there would be no civilization. It is impossible to exaggerate the importance of this fact, which Laird and White go far toward illuminating, never more so than in their agreement that language is always changing. The same may be said for human society, to which language is the indispensable key.

1.   From *The Study of Sociology:* Our Need of It

Herbert Spencer

The material media through which we see things, always more or less falsify the facts: making, for example, the apparent direction of a star slightly different from its real direction, and sometimes, as when a fish is seen in the water, the apparent place is so far from the real place, that great misconception results unless large allowance is made for refraction; but sociological observations are not thus falsified: through the daily press light comes without any bending of its rays, and in studying past ages it is easy to make allowance for the refraction due to the historic medium. The motions of gases, though they conform to mechanical laws which are well understood, are nevertheless so involved, that the art of controlling currents of air in a house is not yet mastered; but the waves and currents of feeling running through a society, and the consequent directions and amounts of social activities, may be readily known beforehand. Though molecules of inorganic substances are very simple, yet prolonged study is required to understand their modes of behavior to one another, and even the most instructed frequently meet with interactions of them producing consequences they never anticipated; but where the interacting bodies are not molecules but living beings of highly-complex natures, it is easy to foresee all results which will arise. Physical phenomena are so connected that between seeming probability and actual truth, there is apt to be a wide difference, even where but two bodies are acting: instance the natural supposition that during our northern summer the Earth is nearer to the Sun than during the winter, which is just the reverse of the fact; but among sociological phenomena, where the bodies are so multitudinous, and the forces by which they act on one another so many, and so multiform, and so variable, the probability and the actuality will of course correspond. Matter often behaves paradoxically, as when two cold liquids added together become boiling hot, or as when the mixing of two clear liquids produces an opaque mud, or as when water immersed in sulphurous acid freezes on a hot iron plate; but what we distinguish as Mind, especially when massed together in the way which causes social action, evolves no paradoxical results—always such results come from it as seem likely to come.

The acceptance of contradictions like these, tacitly implied in the beliefs of the scientifically cultivated, is the more remarkable when we consider how abundant are the proofs that human nature is difficult to manipulate; that methods apparently the most rational disappoint expectation; and that the best results frequently arise from courses which common sense thinks unpractical. Even individual human nature shows us these startling anomalies. A man of leisure is the man naturally fixed upon if something has to be done; but your man of leisure cannot find time, and the man most likely to do what is wanted, is the man who is already busy. That the boy who studies longest will learn most, and that a man will become wise in proportion as he reads much, are propositions which look true but are quite untrue; as teachers are now-a-days finding out in the one case, and as Hobbes long ago found out in the other. How obvious it appears that when minds go deranged, there is no remedy but replacing the weak internal control by a strong external control. Yet the "non-restraint system" has had far more success than the system of strait-waistcoats. Dr. Batty Tuke, a physician of much experience in treating the insane, has lately testified that the desire to escape is great when locks and keys are used, but almost disappears when they are disused: the policy of unlocked doors has had 95 per cent of success and 5 per cent of failure. And in further evidence of the mischief often done by measures supposed to be curative, here is Dr. Maudsley, also an authority on such questions, speaking of "asylum-made lunatics." Again, is it not clear that the repression of crime will be effectual in proportion as the punishment is severe? Yet the great amelioration in our penal code, initiated by Romilly, has not been followed by increased criminality but by decreased criminality; and the testimonies of those who have had most experience—Maconochie in Norfolk Island, Dickson in Western Australia, Obermier in Germany, Montesinos in Spain—unite to show that in proportion as the criminal is left to suffer no other penalty than that of maintaining himself under such restraints only as are needful for social safety, the reformation is great: exceeding, indeed, all anticipation. French schoolmasters, never questioning the belief that boys can be made to behave well only by rigid discipline and spies to aid in carrying it out, are astonished on visiting England to find how much better boys behave when they are less governed: nay more—among English boys themselves, Dr. Arnold has shown that more trust is followed by improved conduct. Similarly with the anomalies of incorporated human nature. We habitually assume that only by legal restraints are men to be kept from aggressing on their neighbors; and yet there are facts which should lead us to qualify our assumption. So-called debts of honor, for the non-payment of which there is no legal penalty, are held more sacred than debts that can be legally enforced; and on the Stock-Exchange, where only pencil memoranda in the respective note-books of two brokers guarantee the sale and purchase of many thousands, contracts are safer than those which, in the outside world, are formally registered in signed and sealed parchments.

Multitudes of cases might be accumulated showing how, in other directions, men's thoughts and feelings produce kinds of conduct which, *à priori*, would be judged very improbable. And if, going beyond our own society and our own time, we observe what has happened among other races, and among the earlier generations of our own race, we meet, at every step, workings-out of human nature utterly unlike those which we assume when making political forecasts. Who, generalizing the experiences of his daily life, would suppose that men, to please their gods, would swing for hours from hooks drawn through the muscles of their backs, or let their nails grow through the palms of their clenched hands, or roll over and over hundreds of miles to visit a shrine? Who would have thought it possible that a public sentiment and a private feeling might be as in China, where a criminal can buy a substitute to be executed in his stead: the substitute's family having the money? Or, to take historical cases more nearly concerning ourselves—Who foresaw that the beliefs in purgatory and priestly intercession would cause one-half of England to lapse into the hands of the Church? or who foresaw that a defect in the law of mortmain would lead to bequests of large estates consecrated as graveyards? Who could have imagined that robber-kings and bandit-barons, with vassals to match, would, generation after generation, have traversed all Europe through hardships and dangers to risk their lives in getting possession of the reputed burial place of one whose injunction was to turn the left cheek when the right was smitten? Or who, again, would have anticipated that when, in Jerusalem, this same teacher disclaimed political aims, and repudiated political instrumentalities, the professed successors of his disciples would by and by become rulers dominating over all the kings of Europe? Such a result could be as little foreseen as it could be foreseen that an instrument of torture used by the Jews would give the ground-plans to Christian temples throughout Europe; and as little as it could be foreseen that the process of this torture, recounted in Christian narratives, might come to be mistaken for a Christian institution, as it was by the Malay chief who, being expostulated with for crucifying some rebels, replied that he was following "the English practice," which he read in "their sacred books."

Look where we will at the genesis of social phenomena, we shall similarly find that while the particular ends contemplated and arranged for have commonly not been more than temporarily attained if attained at all, the changes actually brought about have arisen from causes of which the very existence was unknown.

How, indeed, can any man, and how more especially can any man of scientific culture, think that special results of special political acts can be calculated, when he contemplates the incalculable complexity of the influences under which each individual, and *à fortiori* each society, develops, lives, and decays? The multiplicity of the factors is illustrated even in the material composition of a man's body. Every one who watches closely the course of things, must have observed that at a single meal he may take in bread made from Russian wheat, beef from Scotland, potatoes from the midland counties, sugar from the Mauritius, salt from Cheshire, pepper from Jamaica, curry-powder from India, wine from France or Germany, currants from Greece, oranges from Spain, as well as various spices and condiments from other places; and if he considers whence came the draught of water he swallows, tracing it back from the reservoir through the stream and the brook and the rill, to the separate rain-drops which fell wide apart, and these again to the eddying vapors which had been mingling and parting in endless ways as they drifted over the Atlantic, he sees that this single mouthful of water contains molecules which, a little time ago, were dispersed over hundreds of square miles of ocean swell. Similarly tracing back the history of each solid he has eaten, he finds that his body is made up of elements which have lately come from all parts of the Earth's surface.

And what thus holds of the substance of the body, holds no less of the influences, physical and moral, which modify its actions. You break your tooth with a small pebble among the currants, because the industrial organization in Zante is so imperfect. A derangement of your digestion goes back for its cause to the bungling management in a vineyard on the Rhine several years ago; or to the dishonesty of the merchants at Cette, where imitation wines are produced. Because there happened a squabble between a consul and a king in Abyssinia, an increased income-tax obliges you to abridge your autumn holiday; or because slave-owners in North America try to extend the "peculiar institution" further west, there results here a party dissension which perhaps entails on you loss of friends. If from these remote causes you turn to causes at home, you find that your doings are controlled by a *plexus* of influences too involved to be traced beyond its first meshes. Your hours of business are pre-determined by the general habits of the community, which have been slowly established no one knows how. Your meals have to be taken at intervals which do not suit your health; but under existing social arrangements you must submit. Such intercourse with friends as you can get, is at hours and under regulations which everybody adopts, but for which nobody is responsible; and you have to yield to a ceremonial which substitutes trouble for pleasure. Your opinions, political and religious, are ready moulded for you; and unless your individuality is very decided, your social surroundings will prove too strong for it. Nay, even such an insignificant event as the coming-of-age of grouse affects your goings and comings throughout life. For has not the dissolution of Parliament direct reference to the 12th of August? and does not the dissolution end the London season? and does not the London season determine the times for business and relaxation, and so affect the making of arrangements throughout the year? If from co-existing influences we turn to influences that have been working through past time, the same general truth becomes still more conspicuous. Ask how it happens that men in England do not work every seventh day, and you have to seek through thousands of past years to find the initial cause. Ask why in England, and still more in Scotland, there is not only a cessation from work, which the creed interdicts, but also a cessation from amusement, which it does not interdict; and for an explanation you must go back to successive waves of ascetic fanaticism in generations long dead. And what thus holds of religious ideas and usages, holds of all others, political and social. Even the industrial activities are often permanently turned out of their normal directions by social states that passed away many ages ago: witness what has happened throughout the East, or in Italy, where towns and villages are still perched on hills and eminences chosen for defensive purposes in turbulent times, and where the lives of the inhabitants are now made laborious by having daily to carry themselves and all the necessaries of life from a low level to a high level.

The extreme complexity of social actions, and the transcendent difficulty which hence arises of counting on special results, will be still better seen if we enumerate the factors which determine one simple phenomenon, as the price of a commodity—say, cotton. A manufacturer of calicoes has to decide whether he will increase his stock of raw material at its current price. Before doing this, he must ascertain, as well as he can, the following data: whether the stocks of calico in the hands of manufacturers and wholesalers at home, are large or small; whether by recent prices retailers have been led to lay in stocks or not; whether the colonial and foreign markets are glutted or otherwise; and what is now, and is likely to be, the production of calico by foreign manufacturers. Having formed some idea of the probable demand for calico, he has to ask what other manufacturers have done, and are doing, as buyers of cotton—whether they have been waiting for the price to fall, or have been buying in anticipation of a rise. From cotton-brokers' circulars he has to judge what is the state of speculation at Liverpool—whether the stocks there are large or small, and whether many or few cargoes are on their way. The stocks and prices at New Orleans, and at other cotton-ports throughout the world, have also to be taken note of; and then there come questions respecting forthcoming crops in the Southern States, in India, in Egypt, and elsewhere. Here are sufficiently numerous factors, but these are by no means all. The consumption of calico, and therefore the consumption of cotton, and therefore the price of cotton, depends in part on the supplies and prices of other textile fabrics. If, as happened during the American Civil War, calico rises in price because its raw material becomes scarce, linen comes into more general use, and so a further rise in price is checked. Woollen fabrics, also, may to some extent compete. And, besides the competition caused by relative prices, there is the competition caused by fashion, which may or may not presently change. Surely the factors are now all enumerated? By no means. There is the estimation of mercantile opinion. The views of buyers and sellers respecting future prices, never more than approximations to the truth, often diverge from it very widely. Waves of opinion, now in excess now in defect of the fact, rise and fall daily, and larger ones weekly and monthly, tending, every now and then, to run into mania or panic; for it is among men of business as among other men, that they stand hesitating until some one sets the example, and then rush all one way, like a flock of sheep after a leader. These characteristics in human nature, leading to these perturbations, the far-seeing buyer takes into account—judging how far existing influences have made opinion deviate from the truth, and how far impending influences are likely to do it. Nor has he got to the end of the matter even when he has considered all these things. He has still to ask what are the general mercantile conditions of the country, and what the immediate future of the money market will be; since the course of speculation in every commodity must be affected by the rate of discount. See, then, the enormous complication of causes which determine so simple a thing as the rise or fall of a farthing per pound in cotton some months hence!

If the genesis of social phenomena is so involved in cases like this, where the effect produced has so concrete persistence but very soon dissipates, judge what it must be where there is produced something which continues thereafter to be an increasing agency, capable of self-propagation. Not only has a society as a whole a power of growth and development, but each institution set up in it has the like—draws to itself units of the society and nutriment for them, and tends ever to multiply and ramify. Indeed, the instinct of self-preservation in each institution soon becomes dominant over everything else; and maintains it when it performs some quite other function than that intended, or no function at all. See, for instance, what has come of the "Society of Jesus," Loyola set up; or see what grew out of the company of traders who got a footing on the coast of Hindostan.

To such considerations as these, set down to show the inconsistency of those who think that prevision of social phenomena is possible without much study, though much study is needed for prevision of other phenomena, it will doubtless be replied that time does not allow of systematic inquiry. From the scientific, as from the unscientific, there will come the plea that, in his capacity of citizen, each man has to act—must vote, and must decide before he votes—must conclude to the best of his ability on such information as he has.

In this plea there is some truth, mingled with a good deal more that looks like truth. It is a product of that "must-do-something" impulse which is the origin of much mischief, individual and social. An amiable anxiety to undo or neutralize an evil, often prompts to rash courses, as you may see in the hurry with which one who has fallen is snatched up by those at hand; just as though there were danger in letting him lie, which there is not, and no danger in incautiously raising him, which there is. Always you find among people in proportion as they are ignorant, a belief in specifics, and a great confidence in pressing the adoption of them. Has some one a pain in the side, or in the chest, or in the bowels? Then, before any careful inquiry as to its probable cause, there comes an urgent recommendation of a never-failing remedy, joined probably with the remark that if it does no good it can do no harm. There still prevails in the average mind a large amount of the fetishistic conception clearly shown by a butler to some friends of mine, who, having been found to drain the half-emptied medicine-bottles, explained that he thought it a pity good physic should be wasted, and that what benefited his master would benefit him. But as fast as crude conception of diseases and remedial measures grow up into Pathology and Therapeutics, we find increasing caution, along with increasing proof that evil is often done instead of good. This contrast is traceable not only as we pass from popular ignorance to professional knowledge, but as we pass from the smaller professional knowledge of early times to the greater professional knowledge of our own. The question with the modern physician is not as with the ancient—shall the treatment be blood-letting? shall cathartics, or shall diaphoretics be given? or shall mercurials be administered? But there rises the previous question—shall there be any treatment beyond a wholesome regimen? And even among existing physicians it happens that in proportion as the judgment is most cultivated, there is the least yielding to the "must-do-something" impulse.

Is it not possible, then—is it not even probable, that this supposed necessity for immediate action, which is put in as an excuse for drawing quick conclusions from few data, is the concomitant of deficient knowledge? Is it not probable that as in Biology so in Sociology, the accumulation of more facts, the more critical comparison of them, and the drawing of conclusions on scientific methods, will be accompanied by increasing doubt about the benefits to be secured, and increasing fear of the mischiefs which may be worked? Is it not probable that what in the individual organism is improperly, though conveniently, called the *vis medicatrix naturæ*, may be found to have its analogue in the social organism? and will there not very likely come along with the recognition of this, the consciousness that in both cases the one thing needful is to maintain the conditions under which the natural actions have fair play? Such a consciousness, to be anticipated from increased knowledge, will diminish the force of this plea for prompt decision after little inquiry; since it will check this tendency to think of a remedial measure as one that may do good and cannot do harm. Nay more, the study of Sociology, scientifically carried on by tracing back proximate causes to remote ones, and tracing down primary effects to secondary and tertiary effects which multiply as they diffuse, will dissipate the current illusion that social evils admit of radical cures. Given an average defect of nature among the units of a society, and no skillful manipulation of them will prevent that defect from producing its equivalent of bad results. It is possible to change the form of these bad results; it is possible to change the places at which they are manifested; but it is not possible to get rid of them. The belief that faulty character can so organize itself socially, as to get out of itself a conduct which is not proportionately faulty, is an utterly-baseless belief. You may alter the incidence of the mischief, but the amount of it must inevitably be borne somewhere. Very generally it is simply thrust out of one form into another; as when, in Austria, improvident marriages being prevented, there come more numerous illegitimate children; or as when, to mitigate the misery of foundlings, hospitals are provided for them, and there is an increase in the number of infants abandoned; or as when, to insure the stability of houses, a Building Act prescribes a structure which, making small houses unremunerative, prevents due multiplication of them, and so causes overcrowding; or as when a Lodging-House Act forbids this overcrowding, and vagrants have to sleep under the Adelphi-arches, or in the Parks, or even, for warmth's sake, on the dungheaps in mews. Where the evil does not, as in cases like these, reappear in another place or form, it is necessarily felt in the shape of a diffused privation. For suppose that by some official instrumentality you actually suppress an evil, instead of thrusting it from one spot into another—suppose you thus successfully deal with a number of such evils by a number of such instrumentalities; do you think these evils have disappeared absolutely? To see that they have not, you have but to ask—Whence comes the official apparatus? What defrays the cost of working it? Who supplies the necessaries of life to its members through all their gradations of rank? There is no other source but the labor of peasants and artizans. When, as in France, the administrative agencies occupy some 600,000 men, who are taken from industrial pursuits, and, with their families, supported in more than average comfort, it becomes clear enough that heavy extra work is entailed on the producing classes. The already-tired laborer has to toil an additional hour; his wife has to help in the fields as well as to suckle her infant; his children are still more scantily fed than they would otherwise be; and beyond a decreased share of returns from increased labor, there is a diminished time and energy for such small enjoyments as the life, pitiable at the best, permits. How, then, can it be supposed that the evils have been extinguished or escaped? The repressive action has had its corresponding reaction; and instead of intenser miseries here and there, or now and then, you have got a misery that is constant and universal.

When it is thus seen that the evils are not removed, but at best only re-distributed, and that the question in any case is whether re-distribution, even if practicable, is desirable; it will be seen that the "must-do-something" plea is quite insufficient. There is ample reason to believe that in proportion as scientific men carry into this most-involved class of phenomena, the methods they have successfully adopted with other classes, they will perceive that, even less in this class than in other classes, are conclusions to be drawn and action to be taken without prolonged and critical investigation.

Still there will recur the same plea under other forms: "Political conduct must be matter of compromise." "We must adapt our measures to immediate exigencies, and cannot be deterred by remote considerations." "The data for forming scientific judgments are not to be had: most of them are unrecorded, and those which are recorded are difficult to find as well as doubtful when found." "Life is too short, and the demands upon our energies too great, to permit any such elaborate study as seems required. We must, therefore, guide ourselves by common sense as best we may."

And then, behind the more scientifically-minded who give this answer, there are those who hold, tacitly or overtly, that guidance of the kind indicated is not possible, even after any amount of inquiry. They do not believe in any ascertainable order among social phenomena—there is no such thing as a social science.

---

2. Culture Defined

Edward B. Tylor

Culture or civilization, taken in its wide ethnographic sense, is that complex whole which includes knowledge, belief, art, morals, law, custom, and any other capabilities and habits acquired by man as a member of

Reprinted from *Primitive Culture* by Edward B. Tylor, vol. 1, pp. 1–6, John Murray, London, 1891.

society. The condition of culture among the various societies of mankind, in so far as it is capable of being investigated on general principles, is a subject apt for the study of laws of human thought and action. On the one hand, the uniformity which so largely pervades civilization may be ascribed, in great measure, to the uniform action of uniform causes; while on the other hand its various grades may be regarded as stages of development or evolution, each the outcome of previous history, and about to do its proper part in shaping the history of the future. . . .

Our modern investigators in the sciences of inorganic nature are foremost to recognize, both within and without their special fields of work, the unity of nature, the fixity of its laws, the definite sequence of cause and effect through which every fact depends on what has gone before it, and acts upon what is to come after it. They grasp firmly the Pythagorean doctrine of pervading order in the universal Kosmos. They affirm, with Aristotle, that nature is not full of incoherent episodes, like a bad tragedy. They agree with Leibnitz in what he calls "my axiom, that nature never acts by leaps (*la nature n'agit jamais par saut*)," as well as in his "great principle, commonly little employed, that nothing happens without its sufficient reason." Nor, again, in studying the structure and habits of plants and animals, or in investigating the lower functions even of man, are these leading ideas unacknowledged. But when we come to talk of the higher processes of human feeling and action, of thought and language, knowledge and art, a change appears in the prevalent tone of opinion. The world at large is scarcely prepared to accept the general study of human life as a branch of natural science, and to carry out, in a large sense, the poet's injunction to "Account for moral as for natural things." To many educated minds there seems something presumptuous and repulsive in the view that the history of mankind is part and parcel of the history of nature, that our thoughts, wills, and actions accord with laws as definite as those which govern the motion of waves, the combination of acids and bases, and the growth of plants and animals.

The main reasons of this state of the popular judgment are not far to seek. There are many who would willingly accept a science of history if placed before them with substantial definiteness of principle and evidence, but who not unreasonably reject the systems offered to them, as falling too far short of a scientific standard. Through resistance such as this, real knowledge always sooner or later makes its way, while the habit of opposition to novelty does such excellent service against the invasions of speculative dogmatism, that we may sometimes even wish it were stronger than it is. But other obstacles to the investigation of laws of human nature arise from considerations of metaphysics and theology. The popular notion of free human will involves not only freedom to act in accordance with motive, but also a power of breaking loose from continuity and acting without cause,—a combination which may be roughly illustrated by the simile of a balance sometimes acting in the usual way, but also possessed of the faculty of turning by itself without or against its weights. This view of an anomalous action of the will which it need hardly be said is incompatible with scientific argument, subsists as an opinion patent or latent in men's minds, and strongly acting their theoretic views of history, though it is not, as a rule, brought prominently forward in systematic reasoning. Indeed the definition of human will, as strictly according with motive, is the only possible scientific basis in such enquiries. Happily, it is not needful to add here yet another to the list of dissertations on supernatural intervention and natural causation, on liberty, predestination, and accountability. We may hasten to escape from the regions of transcendental philosophy and theology, to start on a more hopeful journey over more practicable ground. None will deny that, as each man knows by the evidence of his own consciousness, definite and natural cause does, to a great extent, determine human action. Then, keeping aside from considerations of extra-natural interference and causeless spontaneity, let us take this admitted existence of natural cause and effect as our standing ground, and travel on it so far as it will bear us. It is on this same basis that physical science pursues, with ever-increasing success, its quest of laws of nature. Nor need this restriction hamper the scientific study of human life, in which the real difficulties are the practical ones of enormous complexity of evidence, and imperfection of methods of observation.

Now it appears that this view of human will and conduct, as subject to definite law, is indeed recognized and acted upon by the very people who oppose it when stated in the abstract as a general principle, and who then complain that it annihilates man's free will, destroys his sense of personal responsibility, and degrades him to a soulless machine. He who will say these things will nevertheless pass much of his own life in studying the motives which lead to human action, seeking to attain his wishes through them, framing in his mind theories of personal character, reckoning what are likely to be the effects of new combinations, and giving to his reasoning the crowning character of true scientific enquiry, by taking it for granted that in so far as his calculation turns out wrong, either his evidence must have been false or incomplete, or his judgment upon it unsound. Such a one will sum up the experience of years spent in complex relations with society, by declaring his persuasion that there is a reason for everything in life, and that where events look unaccountable, the rule is to wait and watch in hope that the key to the problem may some day be found. This man's observation may have been as narrow as his inferences are crude and prejudiced, but nevertheless he has been an inductive philosopher "more than forty years without knowing it." He has practically acknowledged definite laws of human thought and action, and has simply thrown out of account in his own studies of life the whole fabric of motiveless will and uncaused spontaneity. It is assumed here that they should be just so thrown out of account in wider studies, and that the true philosophy of history lies in extending and improving the methods of the plain people who form their judgments upon facts, and check them upon new facts. Whether the doctrine be wholly or but partly true, it accepts the very condition under which we search for new knowledge in the lessons of experience, and in a word the whole course of our rational life is based upon it.

"One event is always the son of another, and we must never forget the parentage," was a remark made by a Bechuana chief to Casalis the African missionary. Thus at all times historians, so far as they have aimed at being more than mere chroniclers, have done their best to show not merely succession, but connection, among the events upon their record. Moreover, they have striven to elicit general principles of human action, and by these to explain particular events, stating expressly or taking tacitly for granted the existence of a philosophy of history. Should any one deny the possibility of thus establishing historical laws, the answer is ready with which Boswell in such a case turned on Johnson: "Then, sir, you would reduce all history to no better than an almanack." That nevertheless the labors of so many eminent thinkers should have as yet brought history only to the threshold of science, need cause no wonder to those who consider the bewildering complexity of the problems which come before the general historian. The evidence from which he is to draw his conclusions is at once so multifarious and so doubtful, that a full and distinct view of its bearing on a particular question is hardly to be attained, and thus the temptation becomes all but irresistible to garble it in support of some rough and ready theory of the course of events. The philosophy of history at large, explaining the past and predicting the future phenomena of man's life in the world by reference to general laws, is in fact a subject with which, in the present state of knowledge, even genius aided by wide research seems but hardly able to cope. Yet there are departments of it which, though difficult enough, seem comparatively accessible. If the field of enquiry be narrowed from History as a whole to that branch of it which is here called Culture, the history, not of tribes or nations, but of the condition of knowledge, religion, art, custom, and the like among them, the task of investigation proves to lie within far more moderate compass. We suffer still from the same kind of difficulties which beset the wider argument, but they are much diminished. The evidence is no longer so wildly heterogeneous, but may be more simply classified and compared, while the power of getting rid of extraneous matter, and treating each issue on its own proper set of facts, makes close reasoning on the whole more available than in general history. This may appear from a brief preliminary examination of the problem, how the phenomena of Culture may be classified and arranged, stage by stage, in a probable order of evolution.

3. The Miracle of the Desart

Charlton Laird

The Lonesome Land

To most of us a desert is a place with too little water and too much sand, but to our ancestors a "desart" was any wild place where no one lived, presumably because no one would want to.

Imagine that you live in such a place. No other human being is near, and you have never seen anything human except the reflection of yourself in a pool. You suppose you are as unique as the sun and the moon.

You live in a world of sight and sound, but sounds of a limited sort. You know the rushing wind, the pattering sleet. You know the lonesome and terrifying howls of the wolves, the insane laughter of the loons, the chattering of chipmunks and squirrels. You can extract meaning from these sounds. You know that after the wind may come rain or snow or hail to beat upon you. You know that with the wolves abroad you want a good fire at night, and that with the loons crying a certain season of the year has come. You can guess that if the chipmunk chatters and jerks his tail with uncommon violence he is probably either hungry or angry. But to none of these sound makers, wind or wolf or chipmunk, can you say anything. Nor do they mean to say anything to you; not even the loon, in whose voice there is a human note, means to discuss the weather. You are living in a world almost devoid of communication.

And so one evening you are lonely and empty because the moon is shining and there is a strange beauty over the land. Being sad, you imagine the nicest thing that could happen to you—that there might be another creature such as you, such as you are though a little different, for there seem to be two chipmunks and numerous loons. Except that this creature, since it would be like you, would not scurry off to hide in a hole, nor disappear with a whirring of wings. It would come and want to live with you, and the two of you could do everything together. And if you happened to like each other very much—well, you could look at each other in the moonlight and feel good inside. You might even touch each other, very intimately. Beyond that you could not go, for how can any creature, you would assume, let another know how he is feeling or what he is thinking?

Oh, you could rub your belly if you were hungry, smile and nod your head if you wanted to agree, and bellow if you were angry or got

Copyright 1953 by Charlton Laird. From *The Miracle of Language* by Charlton Laird, with the permission of Thomas Y. Crowell Company, Inc.

burned. But if you looked at another creature and felt very loving, how could you let the other creature know it? Or how could you find out if the other creature felt the same way? Or maybe a little bit different?

Since you have already imagined the impossible, and in the moonlight with the strange shapes and shadows everywhere it is very pleasant and strangely comforting to imagine nice and impossible things, you imagine something more. You imagine that by some sort of magic, whenever you want the other creature to know what you are thinking, your thoughts will appear in the other person. This creature, too, can give you his thoughts just by wanting you to have them. Then, if you love each other, you can tell each other all about it, only by wanting the other one to know.

But that could not happen. That would be a miracle and, being a practical fellow who takes little stock in miracles, you go off and try to drown your lonely feeling in fermented goat's milk.

Far from being fantastic, this miracle is occurring at the moment. Anyone reading this page knows essentially what I was thinking when I wrote it. Wherever this page goes, to Denver or Dublin, people will know what I was thinking, and if by some waywardness in fashion this book should have more than momentary life, people as yet unheard of will know. Similarly if any of these people were here in this room, and instead of writing I were to start creating, with my tongue and my teeth and the holes in my head, the intermittent sounds which we call speech, they would know immediately what I ám thinking. Furthermore, for all or any of this to occur, neither you nor I need be conscious of the way it occurs. I need only want you to know, and you need only refrain from leaving the room or throwing down the book.

In short "the miracle of the desert" can and does occur; it occurs so commonly that most of us never give it a thought. The very babes learn to take advantage of it, just as they learn to walk or to hold a spoon. The miracle is the subject of this book. We call it language.

The Mechanics of a Miracle

The miracle of speech does not grow less if we examine it. Let us consider what happens. At first let us take the simplest sort of instance, in which one person speaks a word and another hears it. Any word would do, but let us use the word *wrist*.

What has the speaker done when he utters this word? By gentle pressure of the diaphragm and contractions of the intercostal muscles he has emitted a little air, scrupulously controlled, although the muscles which expelled the air are so strong they could shake his whole body if they were used vigorously. He has slightly tightened some membranes in his throat so that the column of air has forced the membranes to vibrate. Meanwhile a number of minute movements, especially of the tongue, have caused the center of vibration to spread sideways across the tongue, move suddenly forward, concentrate just back of the upper teeth, and then cease. With the cessation of this voiced sound, the column of air hisses against the upper teeth and gums, and is suddenly and momentarily stopped by a flip of the tongue. The tongue strikes the roof of the mouth with the portion just back from the tip, and spreads so that the whole column of air is suddenly dammed up and then released. All this must be done with the muscles of the throat relatively relaxed, and when the little explosion has taken place, everything must stop at once.

Now the word *wrist* has been spoken, only a word, but the whole operation is so complex and delicately timed that nobody could do this by thinking about it. It can be done successfully, in the main, only when it is done unconsciously. In part it can be learned, and people having speech defects sometimes learn part of the practice by laborious study, but good speech is always mainly unconscious speech. Any tennis player, even if he could not explain this enigma, could provide an analogy for it. When he sees a rapidly flying tennis ball coming toward him, he knows what he must do. He must maneuver himself into the proper position, be poised with his weight properly distributed, meet the ball with the proper sweep of his arm and with his racket held at just the right pitch, and all this must be timed to stop the flying ball at a precise point. But if the tennis player pauses to think of all these things which must be done and how he will do them, he is lost. The ball will not skim back over the net, building air pressure as it goes until it buzzes down into the opponent's corner. If the tennis player thinks about anything except where he wants the ball to go and what he plans for the next stroke, he will probably become so awkward that he will be lucky to hit the ball at all. Rapid, precise muscular actions can be successfully carried out only by the unconscious part of the brain. And so with the speaker. He cannot speak well unless he speaks unconsciously, for his movements are as precise, as complicated, and as exactly timed as those of the tennis player. Anyone who doubts it need only observe the distress of a speaker who has not learned English as a child trying to say the word *clothes*.

So much for the speaker. Now for the hearer. Sound waves which are set in motion by humming, purring, and hissing in the speaker's throat and head penetrate to the listener's inner ear, and there set up kindred vibrations. At once that marvelous agglomeration of nerves, nuclei, and whatnot which we call the brain makes the hearer aware that a familiar sound has been produced, and presents him with various concepts associated with the sound. And here we are in the presence of meaning.

THE END AND MEANS OF MEANING

How is it possible that two people who may never have seen each other before, or who may not even live on the same continent, or be alive in the same century have immediate, similar, and complicated ideas in the presence of a sound? Especially is this event amazing when we consider that there are hundreds of thousands of these sounds with millions of meanings and still more millions of implications so delicate that they cannot be defined. Somehow hundreds of millions of people have agreed, at least roughly, as to the meaning of the word *wrist* and the other countless words in the language, and this in spite of the fact that the human animal is so varied, and contentious a creature that seldom will two human beings agree about anything, whether the subject be religion, politics, or what will "go" with that hat.

Of course when the word *wrist* is spoken by one person and heard by another, communication has not as yet taken place in any very elaborate or precise way. The single word raises almost as many questions as it answers. Is the speaker thinking that his wrist is arthritic, or that certain brush strokes can best be made with the wrist? These questions can be partially answered by adding a few more words, but in spite of anything he can do the speaker is likely to remain to a degree ambiguous. He cannot be precise because the syllable he is uttering has no precise meaning.

Thus "the miracle of the desart" is far enough from the divine to exhibit a human flaw. Exact communication is impossible among men. Gertrude Stein may have felt that "a rose is a rose is a rose," but our speaker, if he considers the matter carefully, must know that a wrist is not necessarily a wrist. It may be some bones hung together by ligaments. It may be the skin outside these bones. It may be the point which marks the end of the sleeve. If the speaker is a tailor, *wrist* may be a command to hem a glove. But even granted that both speaker and hearer agree that *wrist* is here associated with the bones, flesh, and skin at the juncture of the human hand and arm, they may still associate highly varied feelings with this part of the body. The speaker may have big, bony wrists, and have hated them all her life. The hearer may have been forced out of an Olympic skiing contest when he fell and broke a wrist. There is no one thing which *wrist* calls up in exactly the same form to everyone; there are not even areas of meaning which are the same for everybody. Meanings exist only in minds, and minds result from beings and experiences; no two of them are alike, nor are the meanings they contain. Still, granted that meaning is not and never can be exact, there remains a body of agreement as to the association to be connected with certain sounds which is staggering to anyone who will contemplate it.

But we have only begun, for we started with the simplest sort of example of spoken language. A word like *no* can mean *no, damn it,* or *yes,* or dozens of things between and among these meanings, depending upon the way in which the word is pronounced and the sounds modulated. The emission and comprehension of words, furthermore, become immeasurably complicated as soon as a speaker starts running them together into sentences. But let us ignore those possible ramifications and complicate the situation only slightly by making the speaker also a writer, and let him make a few marks on any sort of impressionable object. These marks can now take the place of sound and can call up the concepts associated with *wrist* wherever they go. They can continue calling up these concepts long after the man who made them is dead; they can do so for hundreds, even thousands, of years. Clay cones and slabs of stone, scratched with marks which were long indecipherable, were still able to produce something like their original meaning when their language was rediscovered, although no living man had known how to speak or write or think the language for thousands of years.

Man, then, can be defined, if one wishes, as a languagized mammal. A cow may be able to communicate in a cowlike way by bawling and dogs may be able to express themselves to a degree by looking soulfully from one end while wagging the other, but man is probably more significantly distinguished from his fellow creatures by his complicated means of communication than by any other difference. In short, man as we know him could not exist without language and until there was language. Civilization could not exist until there was written language, because without written language no generation could bequeath to succeeding generations anything but its simpler findings. Culture could not be widespread until there was printed language.

In the beginning was the word. Or, if in the beginning was the arboreal ape, with the word and an opposable thumb he scrambled down from the trees and found his way out of the woods.

The Miracle and the Nature of Man

Now having said so much, we have implied a great deal more. If language is intimately related to being human, then when we study language we are, to a remarkable degree, studying human nature. Similarly we may expect language to be what it is because human beings are what they are. But we should not expect to study language by making inferences from other fields of study. That way madness lies—or at the least, monumental blunders. For instance, in the nineteenth century, students of society assumed that since the theory of evolution revealed new truths about human anatomy the same theory working in the same way should reveal new truths about human society. It did not. It led folklorists and anthropologists into one misbegotten generalization after another, and scattered the pages of a monumental work like *The Golden Bough* with errors which must now be patiently corrected. Any field of study which does not have principles of its own is a poor study, and surely no one can accuse language of paucity. We must expect language, however it is rooted in mankind and civilization, to have principles of its own, and we shall doubtless find ourselves in trouble unless we respect them.

Men have not always done so. There was, for instance, a serious group of enthusiasts for language who hoped to reform national conduct and international manners, to harden sloppy thinking and to clear muddy expression by reforming our vocabulary. These people were well intentioned, and certainly their ends were desirable. If we could stop an international gangster with a few well-chosen words, that would be an admirable stroke. But it does seem a good bit to achieve with nothing more tangible than a refurbished vocabulary, particularly since a large number of learned and eloquent people have been laboring for a long time, using the excellent disciplines of grammar, rhetoric, and lexicography, to encourage the precise use of language, and in spite of them national and international hoodlums are still with us. But let us see what these people proposed by way of method.

They recognized, first, that words have many usages, and that unless we are sure in what sense a word is being used we are likely to misunderstand one another. Furthermore, they recognized that many serious arguments, even fights and wars, grow out of misunderstandings, and that these misunderstandings may rest on various usages of words. Our language is so lacking in precision, they felt, that communication with any exactitude is impossible. Could exact communication be achieved, they trusted, we should find ourselves in complete harmony.

To follow their reasoning we might take a simple sentence like the following: *Civilized man cannot live without religion.* Obviously this sentence means many things depending upon the definition of the words. When is a man civilized? When can he be said to live? What degree of withoutness is *without?* By *religion* do you mean belief in a supernatural and omnipotent being, adherence to a recognized church, the practice of an abiding faith, a conviction that there is order and purpose in the universe, or what? A word like *religion* can have a score of meanings, or more, and even seemingly unequivocal words like *can* and *not* have various uses. Accordingly, some of the reformers decided to make American diction so precise that words could be used with mathematical exactness, and to do this they planned a dictionary. In this work all words would be defined in all uses and each would be given a label. To be clear, one need only affix the label.

According to the New Dictionary, the sentence above would read something like the following: $Civilized_{10}$ man_8 can_2 not_1 $live_{14}$ $without_3$ $religion_9$. Now the statement has become clear and precise. As soon as the reader has looked up each of these words in the New Dictionary and learned that *religion* here means "conviction of the existence of a supreme being," and that *live* means "enjoy one's powers to the fullest," he will be approaching some certainty as to the meaning of the sentence, and be the readier either to agree with it or to dispute it more violently than before.

The Miracle Will Have No Nostrums

Undoubtedly if this method were feasible it would promote the precise use of language. But the procedure has faults and they are pretty obvious. Not the least of them are these: nobody would be willing to use this method, and nobody could use it if he wanted to, because it ignores human nature and because it defies fundamental principles of human language.

It ignores, for instance, the fundamental principle that language constantly changes. So far as we know, it always has changed; it is changing now, and we have good reason to suppose it will continue to change in spite of handbooks on usage, the grade school teacher, and the National Broadcasting Company. A dictator like Hitler can influence language considerably; if he wishes to jail everybody caught using the Greek roots in the word *telephone* and let them out only if they will use the equivalent German roots in *Fernsprecher*, most of them will say *Fernsprecher*. But not even a dictator with a concentration camp can keep language from changing, because it changes in more ways than any dictator could detect. The guards in the concentration camp themselves would be changing it unconsciously. So would the dictator. Before we could decide which was $religion_{21}$ and which $religion_{22}$ and print a dictionary with those decisions, the language would have changed.

No writer would use this language and no speaker could speak it. Would Mr. Hemingway consent to write about an old man and the sea, looking up in his dictionary every time he used the word *sea* to discover whether this was sea_{15} or sea_{18}? Would the president of the National City Bank require all his letters to be written with it? I doubt it. Bankers, as far as I have observed them, are even more conservative with their language than with their loans.

In short, this system could not be used for many reasons, but mainly because it ignores the nature of the human mind, as the mind expresses itself in language. We have no difficulty distinguishing between the words *religion* and *theology* because we have differences in form and sound with which to associate differences in meaning, but if *theology* were $religion_{21}$, we never could remember whether it was religion-sub-twenty-one, religion-sub-twenty-two, or religion-sub-twelve.

If a language like this is unusable in writing, it is worse than unusable in speaking. The new language might reduce gossip, but ordinary conversation would cease altogether and that would be a pity. To speak at all in the new language, all of us would have to wheel monumental dictionaries about with us, using something like a self-serve grocery cart. Talk would however die in a good cause, for it would carry this artificial language along with it. No language has ever been able to survive unless rooted in common speech. Language is a product of the human mind and the human vocal organs; it follows the ways of the human mind and the human larynx. For the moment, let us postpone consideration of larynxes and speculate a little about brains and language.

DIALECT: THE MIRACLE IN THE MAKING

We have already agreed that every speaker or writer uses words as they exist for him; figuratively, he picks them out of his own brains. The

Anglo-Saxons had a fine phrase for speaking, "to unlock the word-hoard," just as though each person about to speak his mind would first go to his great safe-deposit box of words, and pick out those he wanted to present to you on this occasion. Many of these jewels and pieces of old linguistic treasure would be similar to other word-jewels in other people's word-hoards, but each is an individual piece with its own background and character, made anew though on a familiar model. Quite literally each of us has his own word-hoard, be it large or small, and every word in that treasury is a little different from any word owned by anyone else, different in meaning, in pronunciation, and in the manner in which its owner uses it.

Now, since each of us owns his own words and uses them in his own way, it follows that each of us speaks a dialect. More properly, each of us participates in a number of ways of speaking and has what is sometimes called an *idiolect*. Each of us has an individual way of speaking, shares family speech habits, shares also a neighborhood dialect or several neighborhood dialects, and has occupational speech peculiarities, perhaps of several sorts. For instance, an old lady of my acquaintance was fond of the word *pesky* and unconsciously bequeathed it to all her children, along with a good many other words she had made her own when she was a girl. These children grew up with their family peculiarities, but added to them the community speech common in Iowa. They say *goin'* and *doin'*. One left home early and his speech is tinged with pronunciations from San Antonio, Texas. One became an engineer and his language is spattered with *pylons* and *safety factors*. Another became a labor leader and the jargon of his job is all over his talk. That is, each of these children of the old lady now speaks a dialect which reflects his home, his family and acquaintances, his occupation, and dozens of other things.

Some people, of course, suppose that dialects are shameful, or at least unfortunately conspicuous like a large Adam's apple, and they try to "correct" their dialectal peculiarities. But how can we decide which is the "correct" dialect? It used to be easy. We used to assume that the New England dialects were better than the others, because most of the lexicographers came from New England, and they put their own pronunciations into the dictionaries. Noah Webster, in prescribing a pronunciation, remarked that he knew the word was pronounced differently in the South. "But in Connecticut," he added, "we pronounce it this way." Apparently he assumed that in matters of speech, a New Havenite could do no wrong; a Yankee was born a linguistic standard. But lexicographers are no longer so provincial—besides, a considerable number of them come from the Middle West and the South. They are inclined to ask why is it better to pronounce *idea* with the sound of an *r* at the end and *mother* without it, than to change one nasal for another at the end of *going*? Students of language now tend to find all dialects equally interesting, and to write those into dictionaries which incline to be central.

When people try to "correct" their speech, they often succeed only in mixing up their dialects more than they were mixed before, or they develop a stilted pronunciation. A friend of mine was born in a little community of Latter Day Saints, and acquired the dialect peculiar to that group, in which the sounds customarily heard in *harm* and *warm* are transposed. My friend discovered to his horror that he was saying *form* where other people said *farm*. This was a serious matter, for he had to work with agricultural people, and he carefully taught himself to say *farm* with a fine, broad *a*. But he did not learn the related words; he still says *farmer formers* when he means *former farmers,* and he talks about the *business of forming* on farms. Personally, I preferred the speech of another of my Mormon friends, who was more forthright. She was a dean of women and, feeling responsible for the conduct of the students, was outraged when they stormed, shouting, into the college dining hall. "Why," she said, "they act as if they were barn in a born." We all liked her, more so because her speech was redolent of her background and character.

Basically all speech is dialectal. It exists as dialects, and if it is to be understood, it must be studied as dialects. This is one reason that there are, at this writing, at least two zealous efforts to study local American speech. One program is dedicated to preparing a linguistic atlas of the country, tracing dialects and their movements by careful study of a relatively small number of locutions. Dialect maps have already been prepared for New England, and are in process elsewhere; they are modeled upon some excellent European dialect maps. A second project envisages a monumental dialect dictionary. Both works will be fascinating, if and when they can be finished. Meanwhile anyone interested in language can have fun with two excellent albums of dialect records; one for the United States, *The Linguaphone Language Records,* and one for the British Isles, *British Drama League Dialect Records,* both available through the Linguaphone Institute, RCA Building, New York City.

Miracle with Dual Controls

We may now observe a curious paradox, a paradox embodied in the apparently diametric statements in the earlier and later parts of this chapter. First we noticed that language relies upon a body of human agreement bewildering in its complexity. Human beings can speak, and can be understood, only because they have at their call millions of meanings and countless ways of putting these meanings together to produce larger and more exact meanings. These meanings and means of meaning, although they may eventually become codified, rest in reality upon an agreement unconsciously entered into, signed, and sealed by all of us. Language is language only because it has currency; the giving of currency is an act of social faith, the utilizing of the common by-product of many minds busy with their own affairs. Thus looked at from one point of view, language is a common product made by all of us, in process of being remade by all of us, existing in any real sense because it is made by all of us, and understandable only if studied as the commonality of many minds over many generations.

On the other hand we have seen that language as it exists is always the possession of individuals. Vocabularies are individual vocabularies, and ways of speaking are always the ways of individuals. A man's speech is as peculiar to him, as inseparable from him, as is his own shadow. It has grown with him, and most of it will die with him; like his shadow, it is to a degree made anew every day. He inevitably speaks a dialect, his own dialect, which is in turn compact of many regionalisms, a sort of linguistic goulash, made of many ingredients and stewed in a man's own way. Looked at from this point of view, language becomes a pattern of dialects, myriads of dialects infinitely blending into one another.

Philosophically, here is a dualism strange indeed. Like the higher forms of life, language results from engendering by opposites. But unlike mammalian life, it never becomes either male or female; it carries always with it the impress of this curious duality, and it must always be studied as at once general and particular, common and individual. This is not the least of the curiosities of language.

Nor is it the only one.

---

4. The Symbol: The Origin and Basis of Human Behavior

Leslie A. White

I

In July, 1939, a celebration was held at Leland Stanford University to commemorate the hundredth anniversary of the discovery that the cell is the basic unit of all living tissue. Today we are beginning to realize and to appreciate the fact that the symbol is the basic unit of all human behavior and civilization.

Reprinted with the permission of the author and Farrar, Straus & Giroux, Inc. from *The Science of Culture* by Leslie A. White. Copyright 1949 by Leslie A. White.

All human behavior originates in the use of symbols. It was the symbol which transformed our anthropoid ancestors into men and made them human. All civilizations have been generated, and are perpetuated, only by the use of symbols. It is the symbol which transforms an infant of homo sapiens into a human being; deaf mutes who grow up without the use of symbols are not human beings. All human behavior consists of, or is dependent upon, the use of symbols. Human behavior is symbolic behavior; symbolic behavior is human behavior. The symbol is the universe of humanity.

II

The great Darwin declared that "there is no fundamental difference between man and the higher mammals in their mental faculties," that the difference between them consists "solely in his [man's] almost infinitely larger power of associating together the most diversified sounds and ideas," (chap. 3, *The Descent of Man*). Thus the difference between the mind of man and that of other mammals is merely one of degree, and it is not "fundamental."

Essentially the same views are held by many present day students of human behavior. Professor Ralph Linton, an anthropologist, writes in *The Study of Man:*[1] "The differences between men and animals in all these [behavior] respects are enormous, but they seem to be differences in quantity rather than in quality" (p. 79; the same idea is also expressed on p. 68). "Human and animal behavior can be shown to have so much in common," Professor Linton observes, "that the gap [between them] ceases to be of great importance" (p. 60). Dr. Alexander Goldenweiser, likewise an anthropologist, believes that "In point of sheer psychology, mind as such, man is after all no more than a talented animal" and "that the difference between the mentality here displayed [by a horse and a chimpanzee] and that of man is merely one of degree."[2]

That there are numerous and impressive similarities between the behavior of man and that of ape is fairly obvious; it is quite possible that even chimpanzees in zoos have noted and appreciated them. Fairly apparent, too, are man's behavioral similarities to many other kinds of animals. Almost as obvious, but not easy to define, is a difference in behavior which distinguishes man from all other living creatures. I say "obvious" because it is quite apparent to the common man that the non-human animals with which he is familiar do not and cannot enter, and participate in, the world in which he, as a human being, lives. It is impossible for a dog, horse, bird, or even an ape, ever to have *any* understanding of the meaning of the sign of the cross to a Christian, or of the fact that black (white among the Chinese) is the color of mourning. But when the scholar attempts to *define* the mental difference between animal and man he sometimes encounters difficulties which he cannot surmount and, therefore, ends up by saying that the difference is merely one of degree:

man has a bigger mind, "larger power of association," wider range of activities, etc.[3]

There is a *fundamental* difference between the mind of man and the mind of non-man. This difference is one of kind, not one of degree. And the gap between the two types is of the greatest importance—at least to the science of comparative behavior. Man uses symbols; no other creature does. A creature either uses symbols or he does not; there are no intermediate stages.

III

A symbol is a thing the value or meaning of which is bestowed upon it by those who use it. I say "thing" because a symbol may have any kind of physical form; it may have the form of a material object, a color, a sound, an odor, a motion of an object, a taste.

The meaning, or value, of a symbol is in no instance derived from or determined by properties intrinsic in its physical form: the color appropriate to mourning may be yellow, green, or any other color; purple need not be the color of royalty; among the Manchu rulers of China it was yellow. The meaning of the word "see" is not intrinsic in its phonetic (or pictorial) properties. "Biting one's thumb at"[4] someone might mean anything. The meanings of symbols are derived from and determined by the organisms who use them; meaning is bestowed by human organisms upon physical forms which thereupon become symbols.[5]

All symbols must have a physical form otherwise they could not enter our experience.[6] But the meaning of a symbol cannot be perceived by the senses. One cannot tell by looking at an x in an algebraic equation what it stands for; one cannot ascertain with the ears alone the symbolic value of the phonetic compound *si;* one cannot tell merely by weighing a pig how much gold he will exchange for; one cannot tell from the wave length of a color whether it stands for courage or cowardice, "stop" or "go"; nor can one discover the spirit in a fetish by any amount of physical or chemical examination. The meaning of a symbol can be communicated only by symbolic means, usually by articulate speech.

But a thing which in one context is a symbol is, in another context, not a symbol but a sign. Thus, a word is a symbol only when one is concerned with the distinction between its meaning and its physical form. This distinction *must* be made when one bestows value upon a sound-combination or when a previously bestowed value is discovered for the first time; it *may* be made at other times for certain purposes. But after value has been bestowed upon, or discovered in, a word, its meaning becomes identified, in use, with its physical form. The word then functions as a sign,[7] rather than as a symbol. Its meaning is then perceived with the senses. This fact that a thing may be both symbol (in one context) and non-symbol (in another context) has led to some confusion and misunderstanding.

Thus Darwin says: "That which distinguishes man from the lower animals is not the understanding of articulate sounds, for as everyone knows, dogs understand many words and sentences" (chap. 2, *The Descent of Man*).

It is perfectly true, of course, that dogs, apes,[8] horses, birds, and perhaps creatures even lower in the evolutionary scale, can be taught to respond in a specific way to a vocal command. But it does not follow that no difference exists between the meaning of "words and sentences" to a man and to a dog. Words are both signs and symbols to man; they are merely signs to a dog. Let us analyze the situation of vocal stimulus and response.

A dog may be taught to roll over at the command "Roll over!" A man may be taught to stop at the command "Halt!" The fact that a dog can be taught to roll over in Chinese, or that he can be taught to "go fetch" at the command "roll over" (and, of course, the same is true for a man) shows that there is no necessary and invariable relationship between a particular sound combination and a specific reaction to it. The dog or the man can be taught to respond in a certain manner to *any* arbitrarily selected combination of sounds, for example, a group of nonsense syllables, coined for the occasion. On the other hand, any one of a great number and variety of responses may become evocable by a given stimulus. Thus, so far as the *origin* of the relationship between vocal stimulus and response is concerned, the nature of the relationship, that is, the meaning of the stimulus, is not determined by properties intrinsic in the stimulus.

But, once the relationship has been established between vocal stimulus and response, the meaning of the stimulus becomes *identified with the sounds;* it is then *as if* the meaning were intrinsic in the sounds themselves. Thus, "halt" does not have the same meaning as "hilt" or "malt." A dog may be conditioned to respond in a certain way to a sound of a given wave length. Sufficiently alter the pitch of the sound and the response will cease to be forthcoming. The meaning of the stimulus has become identified with its physical form; its value is perceived with the senses.

Thus we see that in *establishing* a relationship between a stimulus and a response the properties intrinsic in the stimulus do not determine the nature of the response. But, *after the relationship has been established* the meaning of the stimulus is *as if* it were *inherent* in its physical form. It does not make any difference what phonetic combination we select to evoke the response of terminating self-locomotion. We may teach a dog, horse, or man to stop at any vocal command we care to choose or devise. But once the relationship has been established between sound and response, the meaning of the stimulus becomes identified with its physical form and is, therefore, perceivable with the senses.

So far we have discovered no difference between the dog and the man;

they appear to be exactly alike. And so they are as far as we have gone. But we have not told the whole story yet. No difference between dog and man is discoverable so far as learning to respond appropriately to a vocal stimulus is concerned. But we must not let an impressive similarity conceal an important difference. A porpoise is not yet a fish.

The man differs from the dog—and all other creatures—in that *he can and does play an active role in determining what value the vocal stimulus is to have, and the dog cannot.* As John Locke has aptly put it, "All sounds [that is, in language] . . . have their signification from the arbitrary imposition of men." The dog does not and cannot play an active part in determining the value of the vocal stimulus. Whether he is to roll over or go fetch at a given stimulus, or whether the stimulus for roll over be one combination of sounds or another is a matter in which the dog has nothing whatever to "say." He plays a purely passive role and can do nothing else. He learns the meaning of a vocal command just as his salivary glands may learn to respond to the sound of a bell. But man plays an active role and thus becomes a creator: Let *x* equal three pounds of coal and it does equal three pounds of coal; let removal of the hat in a house of worship indicate respect and it becomes so. This creative faculty, that of freely, actively, and arbitrarily bestowing value upon things, is one of the most commonplace as well as *the* most important characteristic of man. Children employ it freely in their play: "Let's pretend that this rock is a wolf."

The difference between the behavior of man and other animals then, is that the lower animals may receive new values, may acquire new meanings, but they cannot create and bestow them. Only man can do this. To use a crude analogy, lower animals are like a person who has only the receiving apparatus for wireless messages: He can receive messages but cannot send them. Man can do both. And this difference is one of kind, not of degree: a creature can either "arbitrarily impose signification," to use Locke's phrase, can either create and bestow values, or he cannot. There are no intermediate stages.[9] This difference may appear slight, but, as a carpenter once told William James in discussing differences between men, "it's very important." All *human* existence depends upon it and it alone.

The confusion regarding the nature of words and their significance to men and the lower animals is not hard to understand. It arises, first of all, from a failure to distinguish between the two quite different contexts in which words function. The statements, "The meaning of a word[10] can not be perceived with the senses," and "The meaning of a word can be perceived with the senses," though contradictory, are nevertheless equally true. In the *symbol* context the meaning cannot be perceived with the senses; in the *sign* context it can. This is confusing enough. But the situation has been made worse by using the words "symbol" and "sign" to label, not the *different contexts,* but *one and the same thing:* the word.

Thus a word is a symbol *and* a sign, two different things. It is like saying that a vase is a *doli* and a *kana*—two different things—because it may function in two contexts, esthetic and commercial.[11]

That which is a *symbol* in the context of origination becomes a *sign* in use thereafter. Things may be either signs or symbols to man; they can be only signs to other creatures.

IV

Very little indeed is known of the organic basis of the symbolic faculty: we know next to nothing of the neurology of symbolizing.[12] And very few scientists—anatomists, neurologists, physical anthropologists—appear to be interested in the problem. Some, in fact, seem to be unaware of the existence of such a problem. The duty and task of giving an account of the organic basis of symbolizing does not fall within the province of the sociologist or the cultural anthropologist. On the contrary, he should scrupulously exclude it as irrelevant to his problems and interests; to introduce it would bring only confusion. It is enough for the sociologist or cultural anthropologist to take the ability to use symbols, possessed by man alone, as given. The use to which he puts this fact is in no way affected by his, or even the anatomist's, inability to describe the symbolic process in neurological terms. However, it is well for the social scientist to be acquainted with the little that neurologists and anatomists do know about the structural basis of "symboling." We, therefore, review briefly the chief relevant facts here.

The anatomist has not been able to discover why men can use symbols and apes cannot. So far as is known the only difference between the brain of man and the brain of an ape is a quantitative one: ". . . man has no new kinds of brain cells or brain cell connections" (A. J. Carlson, *op. cit.*). Nor does man, as distinguished from other animals, possess a specialized "symbol-mechanism." The so-called speech areas of the brain should not be identified with symbolizing. These areas are associated with the muscles of the tongue, larynx, etc. But symbolizing is not dependent upon these organs. One may symbolize with the fingers, the feet, or with any part of the body that can be moved at will.[13]

To be sure, the symbolic faculty was brought into existence by the natural processes of organic evolution. And we may reasonably believe that the focal point, if not the locus, of this faculty is in the brain, especially the forebrain. Man's brain is much larger than that of an ape, both absolutely and relatively.[14] And the forebrain especially is large in man as compared with ape. Now in many situations we know that quantitative changes give rise to qualitative differences. Water is transformed into steam by additional quantities of heat. Additional power and speed lift the taxiing airplane from the ground and transform terrestrial locomotion into flight. The difference between wood alcohol and grain alcohol is a qualitative expression of a quantitative difference in the proportions of carbon and hydrogen. Thus a marked growth in size of the brain in man may have brought forth a *new kind* of function.

V

All culture (civilization) depends upon the symbol. It was the exercise of the symbolic faculty that brought culture into existence and it is the use of symbols that makes the perpetuation of culture possible. Without the symbol there would be no culture, and man would be merely an animal, not a human being.

Articulate speech is the most important form of symbolic expression. Remove speech from culture and what would remain? Let us see.

Without articulate speech we would have no *human* social organization. Families we might have, but this form of organization is not peculiar to man; it is not per se, *human*. But we would have no prohibitions of incest, no rules prescribing exogamy and endogamy, polygamy or monogamy. How could marriage with a cross cousin be prescribed, marriage with a parallel cousin proscribed, without articulate speech? How could rules which prohibit plural mates possessed simultaneously but permit them if possessed one at a time, exist without speech?

Without speech we would have no political, economic, ecclesiastic, or military organization; no codes of etiquette or ethics; no laws; no science, theology, or literature; no games or music, except on an ape level. Rituals and ceremonial paraphernalia would be meaningless without articulate speech. Indeed, without articulate speech we would be all but toolless: we would have only the occasional and insignificant use of the tool such as we find today among the higher apes, for it was articulate speech that transformed the nonprogressive tool-using of the ape into the progressive, cumulative tool-using of man, the human being.

In short, without symbolic communication in some form, we would have no culture. "In the Word was the beginning" of culture—and its perpetuation also.[15]

To be sure, with all his culture man is still an animal and strives for the same ends that all other living creatures strive for: the preservation of the individual and the perpetuation of the race. In concrete terms these ends are food, shelter from the elements, defense from enemies, health, and offspring. The fact that man strives for these ends just as all other animals do has, no doubt, led many to declare that there is "no fundamental difference between the behavior of man and of other creatures." But man does differ, not in *ends* but in *means*. Man's means are cultural means: culture is simply the human animal's way of living. And, since these means, culture, are dependent upon a faculty possessed by man alone, the ability to use symbols, the difference between the behavior of man and of all other creatures is not merely great, but basic and fundamental.

VI

The behavior of man is of two distinct kinds: symbolic and nonsymbolic. Man yawns, stretches, coughs, scratches himself, cries out in pain, shrinks with fear, "bristles" with anger, and so on. Nonsymbolic behavior of this sort is not peculiar to man; he shares it not only with the other primates but with many other animal species as well. But man communicates with his fellows with articulate speech, uses amulets, confesses sins, makes laws, observes codes of etiquette, explains his dreams, classifies his relatives in designated categories, and so on. This kind of behavior is unique; only man is capable of it; it is peculiar to man because it consists of, or is dependent upon, the use of symbols. The nonsymbolic behavior of man is the behavior of man the animal; the symbolic behavior is that of man the human being.[16] It is the symbol which has transformed man from a mere animal to a human animal.

As it was the symbol that made mankind human, so it is with each member of the race. A baby is not a human being so far as his behavior is concerned. Until the infant acquires speech there is nothing to distinguish his behavior qualitatively from that of a young ape.[17] The baby becomes a human being when and as he learns to use symbols. Only by means of speech can the baby enter and take part in the human affairs of mankind. The questions we asked previously may be repeated now. How is the growing child to know of such things as families, etiquette, morals, law, science, philosophy, religion, commerce, and so on, without speech? The rare cases of children who grew up without symbols because of deafness and blindness, such as those of Laura Bridgman, Helen Keller, and Marie Heurtin, are instructive.[18] Until they "got the idea" of symbolic communication they were not human beings, but animals, they did not participate in behavior which is peculiar to human beings. They were "in" human society as dogs are, but they were not *of* human society. And, although the present writer is exceedingly skeptical of the reports of the so-called "wolf children," "feral men," etc., we may note that they are described, almost without exception, as without speech, "beastly," and "inhuman."

VII

Summary. The natural processes of organic evolution brought into existence in man, and man alone, a new and distinctive ability: the ability to use symbols. The most important form of symbolic expression is articulate speech. Articulate speech means communication of ideas; communication means preservation—tradition—and preservation means accumulation and progress. The emergence of the organic faculty of symbol-using has resulted in the genesis of a new order of phenomena: a superorganic, or cultural, order. All civilizations are born of, and are perpetuated by, the use of symbols. A culture, or civilization, is but a particular kind of form (symbolic) which the biologic, life-perpetuating activities of a particular animal, man, assume.

Human behavior is symbolic behavior; if it is not symbolic, it is not human. The infant of the genus homo becomes a human being only as he is introduced into and participates in that superorganic order of phenomena which is culture. And the key to this world and the means of participation in it is—the symbol.

NOTES

1. (New York, 1936).
2. *Anthropology* (New York, 1937), p. 39.
3. We have a good example of this in the distinguished physiologist, Anton J. Carlson. After taking note of "man's present achievements in science, in the arts (including oratory), in political and social institutions," and noting "at the same time the apparent paucity of such behavior in other animals," he, as a common man "is tempted to conclude that in these capacities, at least, man has a qualitative superiority over other mammals" ("The Dynamics of Living Processes," in *The Nature of the World and Man*, H. H. Newman, ed. [Chicago, 1926], p. 477). But, since, as a scientist, Professor Carlson cannot *define* this qualitative difference between man and other animals, since as a physiologist he cannot explain it, he refuses to admit it—". . . the physiologist does not accept the great development of articulate speech in man as something qualitatively new; . . ." (p. 478)—and suggests helplessly that some day we may find some new "building stone," an "additional lipoid, phosphatid, or potassium ion," in the human brain which will explain it, and concludes by saying that the difference between the mind of man and that of non-man is "probably only one of degree" (*op. cit.*, pp. 478–79).
4. "Do you bite your thumb at us, sir?"—*Romeo and Juliet*, Act I, Sc. 1.
5. "Now since sounds have no natural connection with our ideas, but have all their signification from the arbitrary imposition of men . . . ," John Locke, *Essay Concerning the Human Understanding*, Bk. III, chap. 9.
   "When *I* use . . . [a] word, it means just what I choose it to mean," said Humpty Dumpty to Alice (*Through the Looking Glass*).
6. This statement is valid regardless of our theory of experiencing. Even the exponents of "Extra-Sensory Perception," who have challenged Locke's dictum that "the knowledge of the existence of any other thing [besides ourselves and God] we can have only by sensation" (Bk. IV, chap. 11, *Essay Concerning the Human Understanding*), have been obliged to work with physical rather than ethereal forms.
7. A *sign* is a physical form whose function is to indicate some other thing, object, quality, or event. The meaning of a sign may be intrinsic, inseparable from its physical form and nature, as in the case of the height of a column of mercury as an indication of temperature; or it may be merely identified with its physical form, as in the case of a hurricane signal displayed by a weather bureau. But in either case, the meaning of the sign is perceived with the senses.
8. "Surprising as it may seem, it was very clear during the first few months that the ape was considerably superior to the child in responding to human words," W. N. and L. A. Kellogg, *The Ape and the Child* (New York, 1933).
9. Professor Linton speaks of "the faintest foreshadowing of language . . . at the animal level" (*op. cit.*, p. 74). But precisely what these "faintest foreshadowings" are he does not say.
10. What we have to say here would, of course, apply equally well to gestures (e.g., the "sign of the cross," a salute), a color, a material object, etc.
11. Like a word, the value of a vase may be perceived by the senses or imperceptible to them depending upon the context in which it is regarded. In an esthetic context its value is perceived with the senses. In the commercial context this is impossible; we must be *told* its value—in terms of price.

12. Cf. "A Neurologist Makes Up His Mind," by C. Judson Herrick, *Scientific Monthly* (August, 1939). Professor Herrick is a distinguished one of a not too large number of scientists who are interested in the structural basis of symbol using.

13. The misconception that speech is dependent upon the so-called (but mis-called) organs of speech, and, furthermore, that man alone has organs suitable for speech, is not uncommon even today. Thus Professor L. L. Bernard lists "The fourth great organic asset of man is his vocal apparatus, also characteristic of him alone," *Introduction to Sociology,* J. Davis and H. E. Barnes, eds. (New York, 1927), p. 399.

The great apes have the mechanism necessary for the production of articulate sounds: "It seemingly is well established that the motor mechanism of voice in this ape [chimpanzee] is adequate not only to the production of a considerable variety of sounds, but also to definite articulations similar to those of man," R. M. and A. W. Yerkes, *The Great Apes* (New Haven, 1929), p. 301. Also: "All of the anthropoid apes are vocally and muscularly equipped so that they could have an articulate language if they possessed the requisite intelligence," E. A. Hooton, *Up from the Ape* (New York, 1931), p. 167.

Furthermore, the mere production of articulate sounds would not be symbolizing any more than the mere "understanding of words and sentences" (Darwin) is. John Locke made this clear two and a half centuries ago: "Man, therefore had by nature his organs so fashioned, as to be *fit to frame articulate sounds,* which we call words. But this was not enough to produce language; for parrots, and several other birds, will be taught to make articulate sounds distinct enough, which yet, by no means, are capable of language. Besides articulate sounds, therefore, it was further necessary, that he should be *able to use these sounds as signs of internal conceptions;* and to make them stand as marks for the ideas within his own mind, whereby they might be made known to others . . . ," Book III, chap. 1, secs. 2, 3, *Essay Concerning the Human Understanding.*

And J. F. Blumenbach, a century later, declared in his *On the Natural Variety of Mankind,* "That speech is the work of reason alone, appears from this, that other animals, although they have nearly the same organs of voice as man, are entirely destitute of it" (quoted by R. M. and A. W. Yerkes, *op. cit.,* p. 23).

14. Man's brain is about two and one-half times as large as that of a gorilla. "The human brain is about 1/50 of the entire body weight, while that of a gorilla varies from 1/150 to 1/200 part of that weight" (Hooton, *op. cit.,* p. 153).

15. "On the whole, however, it would seem that language and culture rest, in a way which is not fully understood, on the same set of faculties . . . ," A. L. Kroeber, *Anthropology* (New York, 1923), p. 108. It is hoped that this essay will make this matter more "fully understood."

16. It is for this reason that observations and experiments with apes, rats, etc., can tell us nothing about human behavior. They can tell us how ape-like or rat-like man is, but they throw no light upon human behavior because the behavior of apes, rats, etc., is nonsymbolic.

The title of the late George A. Dorsey's best seller, *Why We Behave Like Human Beings,* was misleading for the same reason. This interesting book told us much about vertebrate, mammalian, primate, and even man-animal behavior, but virtually nothing about symbolic, i.e., human, behavior. But we are glad to add, in justice to Dorsey, that his chapter on the function of speech in culture (Ch. II) in *Man's Own Show: Civilization* (New York, 1931), is probably the best discussion of this subject that we know of in anthropological literature.

17. In their fascinating account of their experiment with a baby chimpanzee, kept for nine months in their home and treated as their infant son was treated, Professor and Mrs. Kellogg speak of the "humanization" of the little ape: "She may thus be said to have become 'more humanized' than the human subject . . ." (p. 315).

This is misleading. What the experiment showed so strikingly was *how like an ape* a child of homo sapiens is *before he learns to talk.* The boy even employed the ape's "food bark"! The experiment also demonstrated the ape's utter inability to learn to talk, which means an inability to become humanized at all.

18. The reader will find a resume of the more significant facts of these cases in W. I. Thomas, *Primitive Behavior* (New York, 1937), pp. 50–54, 776–77.

II. Modern Approaches to Sociology

Since its inception in the nineteenth century, sociology has been an arena in which practitioners of the new discipline compete, debate, argue, and polemicize, and the end is nowhere in sight. Sociologists continue to differ over the very meaning of their field and the direction it should take. Some, like August Comte and George Lundberg, maintain that sociology is actually social physics, a branch of the natural sciences. As such, it makes use of techniques similar or identical to those of the natural sciences in order to isolate and solve the problems of human society. Comte and his successors called this position positivism.

The positivist viewpoint provokes two basic questions: (1) Are natural science techniques appropriate to the study of culture and human interaction? and (2) Is sociology primarily a field designed to reform the world, or is it a "pure science" like theoretical physics?

Lundberg argues for a quantitative, problem-solving natural science. Embracing positivist methods, even he, however, recognized the need for an *a priori* theory and value system underlying those methods. So far such a consensus had yet to be reached.

Reflecting the whole tradition of classical sociology, Hans Gerth, the brilliant German-American sociologist, and Saul Landau, his disciple, take an entirely different position. They hold that sociology was born out of profound change in the social structure of Western civilization. The great classical sociologists sought an understanding of their own disruptive times—times of revolutionary change, different from other times only in the rate of the change. History provides the raw material for sociology of which the primary task is to focus upon significant large-scale social changes. By contrast, positivist sociology in this century tended to focus upon microscopic segments of society *in situ* —and they were to be studied solely by application of "scientific," mostly mathematical, techniques. Gerth and Landau, with their concentration upon history, argue that sociology cannot fulfill its promise without immersing itself in the dynamic, macroscopic dimensions of society. The science of society is not social physics. Consequently, mathematical techniques do not exhaust its methodological resources.

Alvin Gouldner, a prominent contemporary sociologist, addresses himself to the question of "value-free" sociology. He is implicitly concerned with the basic values through which social science views society and its problems. He uses Max Weber, the German genius, as a convenient target for his attack on the "scientific" or positivistic sociologists of our day. Gouldner claims that these sociologists pretend to be value-free, that they take on an attitude of neutrality in order to conceal their own value system or the value system of those they serve. Many scholars, including ourselves, believe that Gouldner has misrepresented Max Weber's position. They understand Weber to be saying that all important sociological questions are posed precisely because they are relevant to certain values. But Weber insisted on neutrality and technical competence in the *means* by which those questions were handled. And he fought against heavy odds to preserve the classroom from ideological contamination. Weber feared that the academy would be ruined by preaching and special pleading. A university should be devoted to the disinterested pursuit of the truth. Weber had seen too much that distressed him in the German university. He would not have been surprised by the destruction of higher learning in Hitler's Germany by self-righteous men who claimed to know a higher truth.

Weber aside, Gouldner does indeed make a case for political and moral commitment among sociologists. He realized that values cannot be avoided. In this, Lundberg, Gerth, Landau, and Gouldner agree. They disagree only about which values to espouse. And there the dispute remains.

---

5. The Transition to Science in Human Relations

George A. Lundberg

I   Consensus on Methods

The best hope for man in his present social predicament lies in a type of social science strictly comparable to the other natural sciences. . . . It is generally agreed, even by those who differ most radically as to the

Copyright © 1961 by George Lundberg. From the book *Can Science Save Us?*, second edition. Published by Longmans Green and Company. Used with permission of the David McKay Company, Inc.

proper approach, that our first need is a unified, coherent theory on which to proceed. A society cannot achieve its adjustments by mutually incompatible or contradictory behavior, any more than can an individual organism. However we may differ on details and on ends, we must agree on certain broad means, certain principles of action toward whatever ends we do agree upon.

In short, we all apparently agree with Comte's appraisal of the situation as he saw it a hundred years ago. Speaking of the theological, the metaphysical, and the positive scientific approaches, he said: "Any one of these might alone secure some sort of social order: but, while the three co-exist, it is impossible for us to understand one another upon any essential point whatever."

Of course there are some who find in our present predicament merely further evidence of the futility of the scientific approach in human affairs. They overlook the fact that, actually, science has as yet not been tried on social problems. Consequently, they advocate a return to theology, or "the" classics, either in their historic forms or in new versions in which the advocates of these approaches personally can play the role of major prophets. If I could see any chance of bringing about a return to theology or "the" classics, I might give it serious consideration, because any one unified approach might be better than two or more contradictory ones. But I see no such possibility in the long run. The commitments we have already made to science, chiefly in our technological culture, are of such character that we can neither go back nor stand still.

Our technological developments and our methods of communication have resulted in a fundamental interdependence which dominates our lives. This state of affairs requires, as we shall see, that we bring our social arrangements into line with this basic technological pattern, rather than vice versa. This basic technological pattern unquestionably rests upon natural science. On this ground, rather than on any assumption of absolute or intrinsic superiority of science as a philosophy of life, I think the following conclusion is inescapable: *In our time and for some centuries to come, for better or for worse, the sciences, physical and social, will be to an increasing degree the accepted point of reference with respect to which the validity (Truth) of all knowledge is gauged.*

If we accept this conclusion, then a number of questions arise. (1) What are some examples of what the social sciences have done or might do in furthering sound and orderly adjustments in human relations? (2) What are some of the requirements and the costs of a transition to a social order in which science is the final court of appeal? (3) What would be the effect of such a transition upon democratic institutions?

The present chapter will deal with these questions.

II WHAT CAN BE DONE—SOME EXAMPLES

What are some examples of types of work by social scientists that are of vast importance in managing human relations?

When we speak of *types* of work by social scientists, we are obviously announcing an undertaking so large as to prevent even a summary within the confines of this book. There are at least five well-recognized social sciences, and if we use the larger category of "behavioral science," the number rises to twelve or more. The social sciences are well-recognized in the sense that they are firmly established as departments in nearly all leading universities and colleges as well as in professional, industrial, and governmental circles. Over a hundred journals publish every year hundreds of research reports of studies large and small, designed to yield new knowledge or to test and refine previous conclusions and to predict behavior under stipulated conditions. We shall confine ourselves to a few illustrations[1] selected chiefly because they are individually of interest to more than one of the social sciences. Readers interested in more comprehensive accounts, including methodological details, will find a large literature readily available.[2]

For our present purpose we shall not here become involved in the question, touched in preceding chapters, of the degree of scientific refinement attained in the different sciences. My argument in previous chapters has been based in large part on what appears to me to be warranted anticipations regarding *future developments* of the social sciences. Here, and throughout the rest of the book, I shall rather take the view that, *even with their present shortcomings,* the social sciences must be taken seriously. The recent (1960) elevation of the Office of Social Sciences to full divisional status in the National Science Foundation[3] is an indication of this growing recognition.

The work of such agencies at the Census Bureau is known to all and is more or less taken for granted. Without the data and the analyses which it provides, the administration of public affairs would certainly dissolve in chaos and perhaps in civil war. It is equally certain that no international organization can function without an elaborate organization of this kind to provide the essential facts regarding people and their characteristics and activities. Perhaps the most permanently valuable contribution of the ill-fated League of Nations was its establishment of an international statistical bureau which managed to survive until taken over by the larger information agencies of the United Nations. The Office of Population Research at Princeton University has engaged in detailed studies of local and international population trends in various parts of the world and has predicted the future areas of population pressure. This knowledge is of the utmost practical importance in the administration of national and international organization of any kind. The Scripps Foundation, the Milbank Memorial Fund, and many others are engaged in similar or related work of a character that measures up very well to the standards of the physical sciences.

Social scientists have also been prominent in pointing out one of the most serious of the world's *problems,* namely, the problem of overpopulation. As a result of the drastic decline in the death rate resulting from the application of medical science, world population is increasing at an unprecedented rate. For example, although it took thousands of years for the human species to reach the number of one billion of living people (about 1830) it required only one century to add the second billion. It is now taking less than thirty-five years for the world population to add a third billion—probably before 1965. The United Nations' population experts estimate that it will take only fifteen years to add a fourth billion, and another ten years to add the fifth billion if present rates should continue. The idea that any expansion of the food supply could do more than temporarily alleviate the starvation of people under such rates of population increase is merely a confusion of wishful thinking with stern realities.

However, just as the application of science to health and sanitation has produced this situation, science has provided the means for its control. Further improvements in the latter are highly likely and imminent. The distinctively social problem of securing the widespread adoption of known methods of control involve a number of problems of a type not yet fully solved, but under extensive inquiry by social scientists. In the meantime we have an example of successful population control in the case of postwar Japan. We are not here concerned with these problems in themselves, but with the role of scientifically gathered and analyzed human social data in the prediction of future population, and the solution of a problem which some regard as more dangerous than nuclear war. Also in other ways, statistics of individual countries, and the data collected by the United Nations organization, are of fundamental importance to the work of many scientists engaged in a wide variety of particular projects. Human ecology, which cuts across the conventional boundaries of demography, geography, sociology, economics, political science (and perhaps others), has produced very impressive work both of applied and theoretical significance.

Reliable and objective knowledge of other peoples and cultures constitutes another field in which social scientists have made distinguished contributions. This knowledge has thrown a flood of light on our own civilization and permits the formulation and test of hypotheses regarding human behavior patterns in general. The Human Relations Area Files contain, systematically filed and indexed, virtually all present reliable knowledge regarding some two hundred cultures. To make a long story short, if a researcher happens to be interested in some subject as, for example, divorce, crime, education, law (and about a thousand other topics), in other cultures, he can go to one of the twenty or more libraries which subscribe to the File, and find all the known information on any or all of these subjects for each of about two hundred cultures. The information is neatly filed away in a separate drawer for each subject. Information which it might take years to locate as scattered in hundreds of books in a library can be secured in a few hours from the File. The importance of this kind of knowledge and its ready availability in facilitating our contacts with people of other lands and cultures became very evident during and after World War II.

We mentioned in the preceding chapter the importance of instruments and methods of observation and measurement in the social as well as in the physical sciences. Social scientists have produced revolutionary developments in this field in the last thirty years. Thousands of such instruments have been invented by means of which vocational aptitudes, success in college and other undertakings, and social behavior of great variety can be accurately measured and predicted. Instruments and scales for the measurement of attitudes have opened vast new fields for investigation.

Perhaps the best known, but by no means the only one, of these devices is the public opinion poll. We have in this technique an illustration of how a development in the social sciences may be as significant for the future of social organizations as many physical inventions have been in our industrial development. The mechanisms by which the "public will" can make itself reliably felt in government and community action have always been in the foreground of political discussion. With the expansion of the areas in which public opinion must operate, many students of the problem have despaired of the capacity of the town meeting technique adequately to make operative the "public will." In the face of this situation, the scientific public opinion poll constitutes an instrument which cheaply and accurately permits us to learn the beliefs, the attitudes, and the wishes of the rank and file of the population. Public opinion polls are at present frequently thought of as interesting devices mainly for predicting the outcome of elections. They do permit such predictions, but this is a very minor aspect of their full possible importance. Polls were extensively used in the armed forces in World War II as a guide to the administration of the invaded areas, the return of the armed forces after the war, and in many other ways.

Public opinion polling may be a device through which can be resolved one of the principal impasses of our time, namely, the apparent irreconcilability of authoritarian control on the one hand and the "public will" on the other. It may be that through properly administered public opinion polls professionalized public officials can give us all the efficiency now claimed for authoritarian centralized administration and yet have that administration at all times subject to the dictates of a more delicate barometer of the peoples' wills than is provided by all the technologically obsolete paraphernalia of traditional democratic processes. In short, it is not impossible that as the advancing technology in the physical adjustments of our lives leads to a threatened breakdown of democracy, so an improved social research instrument may restore and even increase the dominance of the people's voice in the control of human society.

The time may come when the reliable polling of public opinion will be a science comparable to meteorology. Charts of all kinds of social weather, its movements and trends, whether it be anti-Semitism, anti-

Negro sentiment, or mob-mindedness will be at the disposal of the administrators of the people's will in every land. A barometer of international tension has been designed to detect reliably and early the tensions that lead to war.[4] It is true that mere knowledge of these tensions does not necessarily operate to alleviate them. But it is also true that a reliable diagnosis of the tension and an understanding of the feelings and sentiments that underlie tensions is essential for an effective approach to the problem.

"Statesmen" will doubtless continue for some time to value their intuitions more highly than scientific prediction. Pious platitudes doubtless will continue to be heard about the "unpredictability" of human behavior. It remains a fact that social scientists predicted within a fraction of 1 per cent the actual voting behavior of sixty-eight million voters in the U.S.A. in the presidential election of 1960. The pollsters have been doing so regularly since 1936 with a maximum error of 6 per cent. Nor are such results limited to voting behaviors. The late Professor Stouffer of Harvard predicted, also within a fraction of 1 per cent, the number of discharged soldiers after World War II who would take advantage of the educational privileges of the G.I. Bill of Rights. Hundreds of other cases could be reported from a great variety of fields of human social behavior, including the vast areas of market research.

To those who constantly have their minds on quick and dramatic solutions to the world's troubles this type of research is likely to seem offensively trivial—a kind of fiddling while Rome burns. "Writers" are fond of referring contemptuously to basic scientific work as an "ivory tower" and as "lecturing on navigation while the ship sinks." Navigation today is what it is because some people were willing to study the *principles* of their subject while their individual ships went down, instead of rushing about with half-baked advice as to how to save ships that could not be saved, or were not worth saving anyway. As A. J. Carlson has recently said: "The failure of bacteria to survive in close proximity to certain moulds looked trivial at first, but few informed people would label the discovery of that initial fact *trivial* today."

So much, then, for a few illustrations, rather than a summary, of the type of work that is being done and that needs to be done in the social sciences. Is there enough of it being done? Clearly not, or we would not need to flounder as we are in national and international affairs, pursuing diametrically opposite courses within the same decade. Can the social sciences ever hope to catch up with the other sciences, the increasingly rapid advance of which constantly creates new social problems? Certainly we can, if we devote ourselves to the business with something like the seriousness, the money, and the equipment that we have devoted to physical research. Consider how the physical scientists are today given vast resources to concentrate on the invention of a new submarine detector or a new bomb, not to mention the peacetime occupations of these scientists with penicillin and sulpha drugs. Obviously,

I am not criticizing this action. On the contrary, it is the way to proceed if you want results. Is there anything like that going on regarding the world organization and its numerous subsidiary problems, all of them important to peace and prosperity?

Comparatively speaking, there is almost nothing that could be called fundamental research into the basic nature of human relations. To be sure, there are endless petty projects, surveys, conferences, oratory, and arguments by representatives of pressure groups, as if argument ever settled any scientific questions. Of basic social research there is very little.[5] Why isn't there more? As we pointed out in the first chapter, it is not yet realized that scientific knowledge is relevant to successful world organization. We still think that common sense, good will, eloquent leaders, and pious hopes are sufficient when it comes to management of social relations.

NOTES

1. For a longer list, see Stuart Chase, *The Proper Study of Mankind* (New York: Harper & Bros., 1948), pp. 50–51. Chase lists some twenty "outstanding accomplishments" as of 1948.
2. See, for example, Gardner Lindzey, *Handbook of Social Psychology*, 2 vols., (Reading, Mass.: Addison-Wesley, 1954). Also, R. K. Merton, L. Broom, L. S. Cottrell, Jr. (eds.), *Sociology Today* (New York: Basic Books Inc., 1959).
3. The other divisions are: (1) Mathematical, Physical, and Engineering Sciences; (2) Biological and Medical Sciences; and (3) Scientific Personnel and Education.
4. S. C. Dodd, "A Barometer of International Security," *Public Opinion Quarterly*, Summer, 1945.
5. For an excellent brief summary of the recent trend toward more adequate moral and financial support of the social sciences by the federal government, see H. A. Alpert, "The Government's Growing Recognition of Social Science," *Annals of the American Academy of Political and Social Science*, January, 1960, pp. 59–67.

6. The Relevance of History to the Sociological Ethos

Hans Gerth and Saul Landau

Sociological thought emerged in response to the crisis of a newly dynamic European society, fresh from industrial and political revolution. The aim of this new thought process was to forge intellectual tools which would make the complex web of social relations more transparent. So-

From *Studies on the Left* 1, no. 1 (Fall 1959): 7–14. Copyright © 1959 by *Studies on the Left*. Reprinted by permission of the authors.

ciology was born and grew in a rapidly changing world, a world that
seemed to be drifting, and in which man was again and again surprised
and frightened by experiencing the unforeseen and unintended consequences of his actions. From the Enlightenment, the wars for revolution
and independence on the European and American continents, the
Napoleonic conquests and defeats, the czarist and Metternichean reaction, and the explosion of British industrial and commercial energies,
emerged sociology—the intellectual quest pursued by a new type of
scholar.

In 1816, Friedrich Buchholz, in Germany, saw this quest as "the advent
of a science of which former centuries could not dream; namely, the
science of society in its necessary and fortuitous relations." Buchholz did
not have a name for these new scholars, but he described them as special
minds whose "entire endeavor aims at bringing science nearer the state
of society, as it actually is, and adjusting science to it.[1] Later, Auguste
Comte, the disciple of Saint Simon, named the new intellectual approach
"sociology," and sloganized its ethos as "*Savoir pour prévoir, prévoir pour
pouvoir.*" This new science of society, as its originators thought of it was
designed to overcome blind drift, fate, or the unforeseen and unintended
consequences of man's action. The end of knowledge was to be prediction, the end of prediction, control.

The great founders of sociology were not traditional academicians in
any sense. Men like Buchholz, Comte, and Spencer were academic outsiders; Ferdinand Tönnies and, later, Max Weber were at least relative
outsiders.[2] Those that were in the academy did not behave like the
average college professor, for they would not, and could not, be confined
to one academic discipline. Buchholz, a pastor's son from Brandenburg,
was a free-lance writer and critic. Karl Marx, the "non-Jewish Jew,"[3]
was an economist, philosopher, sociologist, historian, and social revolutionary. And not only was he obviously outside traditional academic
life, but, as an exile who did not assimilate, he was a cultural outsider
as well. Certainly for Tönnies and Simmel, Spencer, Weber, and Durkheim (a Jew in Paris in the days of Dreyfus and Zola), the narrow confines of the traditional professor were intolerable.

This fact is related to the nature of the contribution which these men
made; for to probe deeper into the analysis of society, to see society in
its transition toward a world market, supported by world-wide industrialization, required a sense of time and reality, and a breadth of vision, that
could only be possessed by men outside, or at least partially outside
academic walls. Most of the older academicians were involved in a
process of division of labor which increasingly tended to confine their
scholarship to expertness (the expert has rightly been defined as a man
who knows more and more about less and less), and the court historian
of old, the biographer of kings and captains, was giving way, in an age
of high-pitched nationalism, to the national historian concerned with the

heroes and martyrs of his nation. But at the same time, and in opposition to this tendency to contraction, the great minds were developing a sense of world history. Men like Adam Smith, Hegel and Marx, Burckhardt, Ranke, and Mommsen all tried to see the world as a whole.

To the sociologists, seeing the world in totality involved the concrete comprehension of historical causality, not to be explained by reference to "the spirit of the times." For to them, "spirit of the times" seemed a handy phrase that begged the real issues, a slogan substituted for real knowledge. Interestingly, Goethe, who coined the term "world literature," spoke through Faust on the same subject:

> The spirit of the times,
> At bottom merely the spirit of the gentry
> In whom each time reflects itself,
> And at that it often makes one weep
> And at the first glance run away,
> A lumber room and a rubbish heap,
> At best an heroic puppet play
> With excellent pragmatical Buts and Yets
> Such as are suitable to marionettes.[4]

From the inception of sociology as a way of thinking, its practitioners conceived of decision making as a property of all men and women. History was made by all men, albeit some contributed minutely and some grandly. But each individual in his society meant something, and, since he was a maker of history, all parts of his life had to be studied and analyzed. His vocational life and his political life were inseparable; and so, for the sociologist, history and biography merged in the analysis of society.

The case study was born as a steppingstone to the construction or documentation of *types*.[5] It was the use of these types that helped the sociologist to conceptualize society as a whole. Each individual was important, but for the purposes of analysis he had to be seen with reference to a type construct, whether it was "intellectual" or "yeoman farmer," Marx's "bourgeois" or "lumpen proletariat," or Max Weber's heroic Puritan. The heroic individual and unique individual of historical biography was now replaced on the analytical pedestal by the type. The individual could be measured as an approximation of, or deviation from what was typical. Type man enabled the sociologist to broaden the intellectual horizon by making comparative studies of societies and groups of men. Thus, the study of "Caesarism" replaced the study of Caesar, so that Alexander the Great and Napoleon could now be studied comparatively as "Caesarists." The type approach did not deny the importance of great historical personages, but rather, it made for analysis of the great man in a different way, concretely and comparatively. Men like Jay Gould and John D. Rockefeller might be used to study economic supermen, or "robber barons"[6] as they were called by the muckrakers.

These Promethean bourgeois, in turn, could be compared with the English merchant capitalist from Sir Walter Raleigh to Smythe and his cohorts on the Muscovy, East India, and Virginia companies.

Thus, whatever the limitations of the great social analysis, it is apparent that they attempted to see things in their interconnections, and on a world scale. They all consciously worked within a dynamic social structure, and each saw his own age as one of crisis and transition. For Marx it was an age of transition from capitalism to socialism; for Spencer it was an age of conflict between peaceful industrial society running according to natural law, and despotic military society which threatened chaos. For Max Weber, the revival of imperialism spelled disaster for Germany, which he feared would be divided, along with the rest of Europe, between the "rule of the Russian official's ukase and Anglo-Saxon conventionality with a dash of Latin *raison* thrown in."[7]

II

The coming of the twentieth century saw America's emergence as a world power. The nineteenth century sociologist's schematization of the past, whether in terms of evolutionism, or progress toward national efficiency and/or "virtuous perfection," seemed to have been outgrown. By 1919, the Kaiser and his armies were no more. The world should now have been safe for democracy, and the War had supposedly ended all wars. The obstacle to the Wilsonian mission—the guilty Germans and the stubborn Bolsheviks—were placed in the diplomatic dog house where they belonged for not cooperating. The prophet of the Western world, President Wilson, sailed to Paris with a proposal for a League that would usher in a new age of mankind. The United States sat on top of the world. Its age in world history had been reached.

Just as United States leaders began to realize their dream of a world economic empire headed by American corporate power, the American sociologist dispensed with world concepts. He dismissed, as metaphysics, all thought and theory that dealt with world or total structures. The world simply was taken for granted. To be sure, there was still work to be done, but it was no more than a scattering of problems that remained to be solved, involving industrial efficiency and the rational adjustment of certain immigrant-alien milieus to the American system. The integration of the world was left to the businessmen and politicians. The sociologist wanted to routinize the functioning of the good society at home, focusing on industrial problems, the family, and the behavior of groups in their natural setting.

To do this, statistical and survey techniques, and small precision group work had to be perfected. Robert Park, in Chicago in the 1920's, contributed more than any other man to the origination of milieu sociology. Park was fascinated by the cultural hybrid, the bilingual immigrant, the marginal man.[8] As a journalist, he offered rich descriptive techniques, in the tradition of Balzac's realism, to help conceptualize the changing milieus in the post-World War I United States. Sociologists became intrigued by this kind of study. Following the old maxim that "nothing human is alien to me," but without the "let's go slumming attitude" of the debutante, sociologists descended upon the slums and studied the sex codes of slum dwellers. They also associated with café society to study the behavior patterns of the night-life set. Humanity was studied in the raw, and in its environment—Chinese peasants in their villages, bandits of the Robin Hood type in forests, gunmen in the old West, and Al Capone and Anastasia types in American gangland. Salesladies at Macy's, schoolteachers, Chicago and New York street gangs, POW's—all were studied in their respective roles in their respective settings.

This analysis of society into segments for separate study, necessarily led to specialization. Comte and Spencer, the nineteenth-century mainstays of United States sociology, gave place to the empirical scholars, who proceeded to tackle problems, small and smaller, of milieu, families, and small groups in general, until a sociologist was no longer just a sociologist, but a specialist in family sociology, public opinion, criminology, statistics, small groups, methodology and methods, race relations, and so on, *ad infinitum*. The "experts" and "specialists" emerged and conquered. Fame went to the innovating specialist, the more so if his new specialty fed material into IBM statistical machines. The kind of material fed into the machines came to matter less and less. The synthesizing minds, both past and present, that possessed what C. Wright Mills calls the "sociological imagination," began to be berated as impractical and unscientific. Karl Mannheim and Pitirim Sorokin were dismissed by many of the new "expert specialists" as out of date. The questions that Marx, Comte, Spencer, Ross, and Weber had wrestled with, and the great theoretical legacy they had bequeathed were cast into limbo. Their works were largely unread: in some academic circles they were unknown; in others they were sanctified as classics, and so did not have to be read. And one result of this intense division of labor was that sociologists failed to predict anything. Meanwhile, the war that had ended all wars generated steam for a second war to end war, while bolshevism, fascism, and nazism made a mockery of the Wilsonian dream.

Certainly, society had to be broken down and studied in its units. Certainly, too, milieu sociology refined and broadened the tools of the trade, developing advanced techniques of inquiry and scientific methods of analysis. The closeup-microcosmic lens was utilized with admirable pictorial results, and observations were made with millimetric exactitude. But all this was achieved at the expense of total structure; that is, by disjoining history and sociology. And such exactitude, even when applied to a society as a whole, cannot be a substitute for the examination of social movements in terms of their roots and far-reaching consequences.

The impact of the Bolshevik revolution on the structure of the Western world, to say nothing of the Asian world, cannot be revealed through milieu studies, no matter how thorough. The history of czarist Russia, in the context of world history, must be analyzed in order that the sociologist may see the roots of the upheaval and its future direction. A study of Russian workers or peasants, while valuable, could not reveal much more than some aspects of worker and peasant attitudes. Even if several milieu studies were put together, they would only form an incomplete compilation of some of the clues. Without a view of the total structure, from a historical bridge, only narrow currents can be analyzed, and much of their content will necessarily remain unknown. Similarly, to take a less revolutionary example, the far-reaching results of the long Slavonic migration to Prussian Junker labor barracks, or of immigrants arriving in boatloads from Poland, and heading to the mines, mills, and factories of the New World in Pennsylvania, Chicago, and Milwaukee, cannot be grasped through the close-up camera, or attitude studies of changes in Old World patriarchalism. While such studies by Thomas and Znaniecki[9] and other milieu sociologists greatly enriched the tool kit of the profession, the more basic issues were neglected: the analysis of *structures*, which *cause* milieu changes, was forsaken for more "empirical" investigation.

Thus, compartmentalization and the confinement of precision work to milieu and industrial sociology have threatened to smother the original sociologists' ethos. Interest in sterile verbal systems and faddist professional jargon have often replaced the concern with the substance of society. The fact that "all the facts are not in" has been used as an excuse for the failure to examine important problems, and the failure to examine important problems has, of course, resulted in the failure to predict. It was not until 1940, after the hot war was underway, that the *American Journal of Sociology* decided to publish an article on the Nazi Party.[10] In all, from 1933 to 1947, only two articles on National Socialism appeared in the *Journal*.[11] A fifty-year index of the *Journal* shows exactly three listings under Marx or Marxism, and under Lenin (or Leninism) there are no citations.[12] By and large, the sociologists of today have shut the world crisis out of their vision, focusing their intellectual energy on the crisis of the family, while the Chinese revolution, involving 600,000,000 people—perhaps the greatest mass movement of mankind— is totally neglected.

III

Hot and cold wars have tortured the earth since the beginning of this century. No one has escaped the horrors of the age of imperialism and its wars, or the effects of the rapid bureaucratization of industrial societies and their empires, and of the movement toward centralized control in almost all areas of the world. The effects of all this on the social sciences are hard to measure. Bureaucracy of all sorts has built high walls of "necessary secrecy" (official secrecy classified from confidential to top secret), and has befogged the human mind with the "necessary" vapors of publicity and rival propagandas. Mass media, themselves products of the age of total warfare and bureaucratization, have transformed the journalist of old into an adjunct of a state and/or business bureaucracy (who sees him any more as a crusader and fighter for truth, except in grade B movies?). Likewise, the academician, although one step removed from the market place and the political arena, does not escape, and does not want to escape, his obligation to state and corporate power. "Science in uniform" is the other of the day, and the sociologist, along with his colleagues, has become an auxiliary of the bureaucracies, in an age in which bureaucracies have become almost universal.

But there are hopeful signs. Among the newer sociologists, C. Wright Mills demonstrates in his work a fresh concern with the important questions of modern society. His *White Collar* and *The Power Elite* represent important and challenging attempts to analyze the nature and direction of American society. His work has something relevant to say to an intelligent reading public that is concerned about the future of American society and of the world.

This concern of Mills and others with the drift of social structures and the concatenation of institutional orders and social strata accounts, in part, for the recently greater receptivity on the part of sociologists to the work of Max Weber, who epitomizes the former sociological concern with the totality of man's social life and future. Weber, who practiced what Comte preached as a motto for sociology, wrote comparatively little on the methodology of prediction, but he predicted much, fusing history with sociology. The death of czarism in Russia and the subsequent rise of bolshevism did not surprise Weber, who had devoted twelve hundred pages to the study of Russia since Admiral Togo sank the Czar's Baltic navy in the Tsushima straits and General Nogi's troops killed 90,000 Russian soldiers and took 40,000 prisoners of war in 1906, in the battle of Mukden. And in his study of Confucian China, its village and agrarian problems, he expressed his awareness of what lay ahead by apprehending the attraction that agrarian bolshevism might have for the Chinese peasantry.[13] On the basis of his study of Chinese society, Weber was able to predict the future of China. The same professor, who accompanied the German peace delegation to Versailles, had no Wilsonian illusions. He warned his students about the "polar night of icy darkness" that lay ahead for Germany after World War I.[14]

The notion that the development of mankind can be formulated in terms of a single law of evolution has been almost unanimously rejected.

Social scientists have learned to appreciate the relativity of cultural contexts and the diversity of developments in simultaneously existing cultures. Yet, though we no longer refer to "backward nations," we nevertheless recognize the existence of "underdeveloped areas" (that is, pre-industrial areas such as India and a large part of Africa) side by side with the United States and the Soviet Union. But when the most educated of the Indian electorate, the people of the state of Kerala (47 per cent are literate, as against 16 per cent for the whole of India), returned a Communist majority in 1957, in a democratic election, not only Prime Minister Nehru was shocked.

The revolutionary transitions of large parts of the world since World War I make it urgent for sociologists to study the historical backgrounds of value systems and social structures other than those of the United States, and it is in this direction—with the aid of Fulbright grants— that we hope to see a reorientation of American sociology in the postwar generation, in an age in which the maintenance of peace is a more urgent necessity than ever before. Historiography offers a great storehouse of facts and ideas to the sociologist in quest of insight into total social structures, their phases of growth, decline, and destruction. Only in this way, with one eye on history and one on the future, can the sociologist broaden his scope to meet the obligations of the contemporary world.

And the contemporary world certainly imposes obligations. Today, the planning bureaucracy of bolshevism speaks for almost one billion people (a fact which was hardly expressed in U.N. votes); so that it is perhaps time for the sociologist to begin to ponder the success of industrialization processes under the new system of planning. It is in addressing ourselves to this situation that Weber's work may be of invaluable help, for it is permeated with a keen sense of the historicity of social structures and ideas. And just as Weber devoted a great part of his life's work to the study of the rise and spread of capitalism, we must now turn our attention to the spread of bolshevism to Thuringia and China. Only by read-dressing ourselves to the big questions, and by analyzing character formation and social structures in historical perspective, may we perhaps, at long last, overcome the blind drift and arrive at the level of development where Comte's *savoir pour prévoir, prévoir pour pouvoir* becomes a fact rather than a pious hope for sociologists.

NOTES

1. Hans Gerth, "Friedrich Buchholz: Auch Ein Anfang der Soziologie," *Zeitschrift für die gesamte Staatswissenschaft* CX (1954), pp. 665–92.
2. Ferdinand Tönnies became a professor more than thirty years after his great work, *Community and Society,* had been published. He received a chair in 1918, but was ousted in 1933 with the advent of National Socialism in Germany. Weber, although technically on the faculty of Heidelberg, did not teach for nineteen years. Prince Max of Badeniea appreciated Weber's essays in the

Frankfurter Zeitung, and exerted his influence to keep Weber on the faculty.

3. See Isaac Deutcher, "The Wandering Jew as Thinker and Revolutionary," *Universities and Left Review* I (Summer 1958), pp. 9–13.

4. Stephen Spender, ed., *Great Writings of Goethe* (A Mentor Book, 1958), p. 76.

5. For the best single exposition on the use of the type see Max Weber, *The Methodology of the Social Sciences,* Edward A. Shils, ed. (Glencoe, Ill.: Free Press, 1949), pp. 50–112; for a good example of a type study monograph see Frederic M. Thrasher, *The Gang; a Study of 1313 Gangs in Chicago* (Chicago: University of Chicago Press, 1936).

6. Mathew Josephson, *The Robber Barons* (New York: Harcourt, Brace & World, Inc., 1934).

7. Max Weber, *Gesammelte Politische Schriften,* Johannes Winckelman, ed. (Tübingen: J. C. B. Mohr, 1958), p. 164.

8. Robert E. Park, "Human Migration and the Marginal Man," *American Journal of Sociology* XXXIII (1928), pp. 881–93; Everett V. Stonequist, *The Marginal Man: A Study in Personality and Conflict* (New York: Charles Scribner's Sons, 1937).

9. William Isaac Thomas and Florian Znaniecki, *The Polish Peasant in Europe and America* (Chicago: University of Chicago Press, 1918).

10. Hans H. Gerth, "The Nazi Party: Its Leadership and Composition," *American Journal of Sociology,* XLV (1940), pp. 517–41. This article was later incorporated into the *Civil Affairs Handbook* published by the War Department in 1943.

11. *American Journal of Sociology: Index to Volumes I-LII,* 1895–1947, p. 70, p. 83; see Nazism, National Socialism, and Germany.

12. *Ibid.,* pp. 78, 77.

13. Max Weber, *The Religion of China; Confucianism and Taoism,* Hans H. Gerth, trans. (Glencoe, Ill., Free Press, 1956), p. 76.

14. Max Weber, "Politics as a Vocation," in *From Max Weber,* Hans Gerth and C. Wright Mills, eds. (New York: Oxford University Press, 1958), p. 128.

7. Anti-Minotaur: The Myth of a Value-free Sociology

Alvin W. Gouldner

This is an account of a myth created by and about a magnificent minotaur named Max—Max Weber, to be exact; his myth was that social science should and could be value-free. The lair of this minotaur, although reached only by a labrynthian logic and visited only by a few who never return, is still regarded by many sociologists as a holy place. In particular, as sociologists grow older they seem impelled to make a pilgrimage to it and to pay their respects to the problem of the relations between values and social science.

From an address delivered at the annual meetings of the Society for the Study of Social Problems, August 28, 1961. Copyright © by *Social Problems* and the Society for the Study of Social Problems. Reprinted by permission of the publisher and author. Originally appeared in *Social Problems* 9, no. 3 (1962):199–213.

Considering the perils of the visit, their motives are somewhat perplexing. Perhaps their quest is the first sign of professional senility;
perhaps it is the last sigh of youthful yearnings. And perhaps a concern
with the value problem is just a way of trying to take back something
that was, in youthful enthusiasm, given too hastily.

In any event, the myth of a value-free sociology has been a conquering
one. Today, all the powers of sociology, from Parsons to Lundberg, have
entered into a tacit alliance to bind us to the dogma that "Thou shalt
not commit a value judgment," especially as sociologists. Where is the
introductory textbook, where the lecture course on principles, that does
not affirm or imply this rule?

In the end, of course, we cannot disprove the existence of minotaurs
who, after all, are thought to be sacred precisely because, being half man
and half bull, they are so unlikely. The thing to see is that a belief in
them is not so much untrue as it is absurd. Like Berkeley's argument for
solipsism, Weber's brief for a value-free sociology is a tight one and,
some say, logically unassailable. Yet it is also absurd. For both arguments
appeal to reason but ignore experience.

I do not here wish to enter into an examination of the *logical* arguments involved, not because I regard them as incontrovertible but because I find them less interesting to me as a sociologist. Instead what I
will do is to view the belief in a value-free sociology in the same manner
that sociologists examine any element in the ideology of any group. This
means that we will look upon the sociologist just as we would any other
occupation, be it the taxi-cab driver, the nurse, the coal miner, or the
physician. In short, I will look at the belief in a value-free sociology as
part of the ideology of a working group and from the standpoint of the
sociology of occupations.

The image of a value-free sociology is more than a neat intellectual
theorem demanded as a sacrifice to reason; it is, also, a felt conception
of a role and a set of (more or less) shared sentiments as to how sociologists should live. We may be sure that it became this not simply because
it is true or logically elegant but, also, because it is somehow useful to
those who believe in it. Applauding the dancer for her grace is often the
audience's way of concealing its lust.

That we are in the presence of a group myth, rather than a carefully
formulated and well validated belief appropriate to scientists, may be
discerned if we ask, just what is it that is believed by those holding
sociology to be a value-free discipline? Does the belief in a value-free
sociology mean that, in point of fact, sociology is a discipline actually free
of values and that it successfully excludes all non-scientific assumptions
in selecting, studying, and reporting on a problem? Or does it mean that
sociology *should* do so? Clearly, the first is untrue and I know of no one
who even holds it possible for sociologists to exclude completely their
non-scientific beliefs from their scientific work; and if this is so, on what

grounds can this impossible task held to be morally incumbent on sociologists?

Does the belief in a value-free sociology mean that sociologists cannot, do not, or should not make value judgments concerning things outside their sphere of technical competence? But what has technical competence to do with the making of value judgments? If technical competence does provide a warrant for making value-judgments then there is nothing to prohibit sociologists from making them within the area of their expertise. If, on the contrary, technical competence provides no warrant for making value judgments then, at least sociologists are as *free* to do as anyone else; then their value judgments are at least as good as anyone else's, say, a twelve year old child's. And, by the way, if technical competence provides no warrant for making value judgments, then what does?

Does the belief in a value-free sociology mean that sociologists are or should be indifferent to the moral implications of their work? Does it mean that sociologists can and should make value judgments so long as they are careful to point out that these are different from "merely" factual statements? Does it mean that sociologists cannot logically deduce values from facts? Does it mean that sociologists do not or should not have or express *feelings* for or against some of the things they study? Does it mean that sociologists may and should inform laymen about techniques useful in realizing their own ends, if they are asked to do so, but that if they are not asked to do so they are to say nothing? Does it mean that sociologists should never take the initiative in asserting that some beliefs that laymen hold, such as the belief in the inherent inferiority of certain races, are false even when known to be contradicted by the facts of their discipline? Does it mean that social scientists should never speak out, or speak out only when invited, about the probable outcomes of a public course of action concerning which they are professionally knowledgeable? Does it mean that social scientists should never express values in their roles as teachers or in their roles as researchers, or in both? Does the belief in a value-free sociology mean that sociologists, either as teachers or researchers, have a right to covertly and unwittingly express their values but have no right to do so overtly and deliberately?

I fear that there are many sociologists today who, in conceiving social science to be value-free, mean widely different things, that many hold these beliefs dogmatically without having examined seriously the grounds upon which they are credible, and that some few affirm a value-free sociology ritualistically without having any clear idea what it might mean. Weber's own views on the relation between values and social science, and some current today are scarcely identical. While Weber saw grave hazards in the sociologist's expression of value judgments, he also held that these might be voiced if caution was exercised to distinguish them from statements of fact. If Weber insisted on the need to maintain scientific objectivity, he also warned that this was altogether different from moral indifference.

Not only was the cautious expression of value judgments deemed permissible by Weber but, he emphasized, these were positively mandatory under certain circumstances. Although Weber inveighed against the professorial "cult of personality" we might also remember that he was not against all value-imbued cults and that he himself worshipped at the shrine of individual responsibility. A familiarity with Weber's work on these points would only be embarrassing to many who today affirm a value-free sociology in his name. And should the disparity between Weber's own views and many now current come to be sensed, then the time is not far off when it will be asked, "Who now reads Max Weber?"

What to Weber was an agonizing expression of a highly personal faith, intensely felt and painstakingly argued, has today become a hollow catechism, a password, and a good excuse for no longer thinking seriously. It has become increasingly the trivial token of professional respectability, the caste mark of the decorous; it has become the gentleman's promise that boats will not be rocked. Rather than showing Weber's work the respect that it deserves, by carefully re-evaluating it in the light of our own generation's experience, we reflexively reiterate it even as we distort it to our own purposes. Ignorance of the gods is no excuse; but it can be convenient. For if the worshipper never visits the altar of his god, then he can never learn whether the fire still burns there or whether the priests, grown fat, are simply sifting the ashes.

The needs which the value-free conception of social science serves are both personal and institutional. Briefly, my contention will be that, among the main institutional forces facilitating the survival and spread of the value-free myth, was its usefulness in maintaining both the cohesion and the autonomy of the modern university, in general, and the newer social science disciplines, in particular. There is little difficulty, at any rate, in demonstrating that these were among the motives originally inducing Max Weber to formulate the conception of a value-free sociology.

This issue might be opened at a seemingly peripheral and petty point, namely when Weber abruptly mentions the problems of competition among professors for students. Weber notes that professors who do express a value-stand are more likely to attract students than those who do not and are, therefore, likely to have undue career advantages. In effect, this a complaint against a kind of unfair competition by professors who pander to student interests. Weber's hope seems to have been that the value-free principle would serve as a kind of "Fair Trades Act" to restrain such competition. (At this point there is a curious rift in the dramatic mood of Weber's work; we had been listening to a full-throated Wagnerian aria when suddenly, the singer begins to hum snatches from Kurt Weill's "Mack the Knife.")

This suggests that one of the latent functions of the value-free doctrine is to bring peace to the academic house, by reducing competition for students and, in turn, it directs us to some of the institutional peculiarities of German universities in Weber's time. Unlike the situation in the American university, career advancement in the German was then felt to depend too largely on the professor's popularity as a teacher; indeed, at the lower ranks, the instructor's income was directly dependent on student enrollment. As a result, the competition for students was particularly keen and it was felt that the system penalized good scholars and researchers in favor of attractive teaching. In contrast, of course, the American system has been commonly accused of over-stressing scholarly publication and here the contrary complaint is typical, namely, that good teaching goes unrewarded and that you must "publish or perish." In the context of the German academic system, Weber was raising no trivial point when he intimated that the value-free doctrine would reduce academic competition. He was linking the doctrine to guild problems and anchoring this lofty question to academicians' *earthy* interests.

Another relation of the value-free principle to distinctively German arrangements is also notable when Weber, opposing use of the lecture hall as an arena of value affirmation, argues that it subjects the student to a pressure which he is unable to evaluate or resist adequately. Given the comparatively exalted position of the professor in German society, and given the one-sided communication inherent in the lecture hall, Weber did have a point. His fears were, perhaps, all the more justified if we accept a view of the German "national character" as being authoritarian, that is, in Nietzsche's terms a combination of arrogance and servility. But these considerations do not hold with anything like equal cogency in more democratic cultures such as our own. For here, not only are professors held in, shall I say, more modest esteem, but the specific ideology of education itself often stresses the desirability of student initiative and participation, and there is more of a systematic solicitation of the student's "own" views in small "discussion" sections. There is little student servility to complement and encourage occasional professorial arrogance.

When Weber condemned the lecture hall as a forum for value-affirmation he had in mind most particularly the expression of *political* values. The point of Weber's polemic is not directed against all values with equal sharpness. It was not the expression of aesthetic or even religious values that Weber sees as most objectionable in the university, but, primarily, those of politics. His promotion of the value-free doctrine may, then, be seen not so much as an effort to amoralize as to depoliticize the university and to remove it from the political struggle. The political conflicts then echoing in the German university did not entail comparatively trivial differences, such as those now between Democrats and Republicans in the United States. Weber's proposal of the value-free doctrine was, in part, an effort to establish a *modus vivendi* among academicians whose political commitments were often intensely felt and in violent opposition.

Under these historical conditions, the value-free doctrine was a proposal for an academic truce. It said, in effect, if we all keep quiet about our political views then we may all be able to get on with our work. But if the value-free principle was suitable in Weber's Germany because it served to restrain political passions, is it equally useful in America today where, not only is there pitiable little difference in politics but men often have no politics at all. Perhaps the need of the American university today, as of American society more generally, is for more commitment to politics and for more diversity of political views. It would seem that now the national need is to take the lid off, not to screw it on more tightly.

Given the historically unique conditions of nuclear warfare, where the issue would not be decided in a long-drawn out war requiring the sustained cohesion of mass populations, national consensus is no longer, I believe, as important a condition of national survival as it once was. But if we no longer require the same degree of unanimity to *fight* a war, we do require a greater ferment of ideas and a radiating growth of political seriousness and variety within which alone we may find a way to *prevent* war. Important contributions to this have and may further be made by members of the academic community and, perhaps, especially, by its social science sector. The question arises, however, whether this group's political intelligence can ever be adequately mobilized for these purposes so long as it remains tranquilized by the value-free doctrine.

Throughout his work, Weber's strategy is to safeguard the integrity and freedom of action of both the state, as the instrument of German national policy, and of the university, as the embodiment of a larger Western tradition of rationalism. He feared that the expression of political-value judgments in the university would provoke the state into censoring the university and would imperil its autonomy. Indeed, Weber argues that professors are not entitled to freedom from state control in matters of values, since these do not rest on their specialized qualifications.

This view will seem curious only to those regarding Weber as a liberal in the Anglo-American sense, that is, as one who wishes to delimit the state's powers on behalf of the individual's liberties. Actually, however, Weber aimed not at curtailing but at strengthening the powers of the German state, and at making it a more effective instrument of German nationalism. It would seem, however, that an argument contrary to the one he advances is at least as consistent; namely, that professors are, like all others, entitled and perhaps obligated to express their values. In other words, professors have a right to profess. Rather than being made the objects of special suspicion and special control by the state, they are no less (and no more) entitled than others to the trust and protection of the state.

In a *realpolitik* vein, Weber acknowledges that the most basic national questions cannot ordinarily be discussed with full freedom in government universities. Since the discussion there cannot be completely free and all-sided, he apparently concludes that it is fitting there should be no discussion at all, rather than risk partisanship. But this is too pious by far. Even Socrates never insisted that all views must be at hand before the dialogue could begin. Here again one might as reasonably argue to the contrary, holding that one limitation of freedom is no excuse for another. Granting the reality of efforts to inhibit unpopular views in the university, it seems odd to prescribe self-suppression as a way of avoiding external suppression. Suicide does not seem a reasonable way to avoid being murdered. It appears, however, that Weber was so intent on safeguarding the autonomy of the university and the autonomy of politics, that he was willing to pay almost any price to do so, even if this led the university to detach itself from one of the basic intellectual traditions of the West—the dialectical exploration of the fundamental purposes of human life.

Insofar as the value-free doctrine is a mode of ensuring professional autonomy note that it does not, as such, entail an interest peculiar to the social sciences. In this regard, as a substantial body of research in the sociology of occupations indicates, social scientists are kin to plumbers, house painters, or librarians. For most if not all occupations seek to elude control by outsiders and manifest a drive to maintain exclusive control over their practitioners.

Without doubt the value-free principle did enhance the autonomy of sociology; it was one way in which our discipline pried itself loose—in some modest measure—from the clutch of its society, in Europe freer from political party influence, in the United States freer of ministerial influence. In both places, the value-free doctrine gave sociology a larger area of autonomy in which it could steadily pursue basic problems rather than journalistically react to passing vents, and allowed it more freedom to pursue questions uninteresting either to the respectable or to the rebellious. It made sociology—as Comte had wanted it to be—to pursue all its own theoretical implications. In other words, the value-free principle did, I think, contribute to the intellectual growth and emancipation of our enterprise.

There was another kind of freedom which the value-free doctrine also allowed; it enhanced a freedom from moral compulsiveness; it permitted a partial escape from the parochial prescriptions of the sociologist's local or native culture. Above all, effective internalization of the value-free principle has always encouraged at least a temporary suspension of the moralizing reflexes built into the sociologist by his own society. From one perspective, this of course has its dangers—a disorienting normlessness and moral indifference. From another standpoint, however, the value-free principle might also have provided a *moral* as well as an intellectual *opportunity*. For insofar as moral reactions are only suspended and not aborted, and insofar as this is done in the service of knowledge and intellectual discipline, then, in effect, the value-free principle strengthened Reason (or Ego) against the compulsive demands of a merely traditional morality. To this degree, the value-free discipline provided a foundation for the development of more reliable knowledge about men and, also, established a breathing space within which moral reactions could be less mechanical and in which morality could be reinvigorated.

The value-free doctrine thus had a paradoxical potentiality: it might enable men to make *better* value judgments rather than *none*. It could encourage a habit of mind that might help men in discriminating between their punitive drives and their ethical sentiments. Moralistic reflexes suspended, it was now more possible to sift conscience with the rod of reason and to cultivate moral judgments that expressed a man's total character as an adult person; he need not now live quite so much by his past parental programming but in terms of his more mature present.

The value-free doctrine could have meant an opportunity for a more authentic morality. It could and sometimes did aid men in transcending the morality of their "tribe," to open themselves to the diverse moralities of unfamiliar groups, and to see themselves and others from the standpoint of a wider range of significant cultures. But the value-free doctrine also had other, less fortunate, results as well.

Doubtless there were some who did use the opportunity thus presented; but there were, also, many who used the value-free postulate as an excuse for pursuing their private impulses to the neglect of their public responsibilities and who, far from becoming more morally sensitive, became morally jaded. Insofar as the value-free doctrine failed to realize its potentialities it did so because its deepest impulses were—as we shall note later—dualistic; it invited men to stress the separation and not the mutual connectedness of facts and values: it had the vice of its virtues. In short, the conception of a value-free sociology has had *diverse* consequences, not all of them useful or flattering to the social sciences.

On the negative side, it may be noted that the value-free doctrine is useful both to those who want to escape *from* the world and to those who want to escape *into* it. It is useful to those young, or not so young men, who live off sociology rather than for it, and who think of sociology as a way of getting ahead in the world by providing them with neutral techniques that may be sold on the open market to any buyer. The belief that it is not the business of a sociologist to make value-judgments is taken, by some, to mean that the market on which they can vend their skills is unlimited. From such a standpoint, there is no reason why one cannot sell his knowledge to spread a disease just as freely as he can to fight it. Indeed, some sociologists have had no hesitation about doing market research designed to sell more cigarettes, although well aware of the implications of recent cancer research. In brief, the value-free doctrine of social science was sometimes used to justify the sale of one's talents to the highest bidder and is, far from new, a contemporary version of the most ancient sophistry.

In still other cases, the image of a value-free sociology is the armor of the alienated sociologist's self. Although C. Wright Mills may be right in saying this is the Age of Sociology, not a few sociologists and Mills included, feel estranged and isolated from their society. They feel impotent to contribute usefully to the solution of its deepening problems and, even when they can, they fear that the terms of such an involvement require them to submit to a commercial debasement or a narrow partisanship, rather than contributing to a truly public interest.

Many sociologists feel themselves cut off from the larger community of liberal intellectuals in whose spitty satire they see themselves as ridiculous caricatures. Estranged from the larger world, they cannot escape except in fantasies of posthumous medals and by living huddled behind self-barricaded intellectual ghettoes. Self-doubt finds its anodyne in the image of a value-free sociology because this transforms their alienation into an intellectual principle; it evokes the soothing illusion, among some sociologists, that their exclusion from the larger society is a self-imposed duty rather than an externally imposed constraint.

Once committed to the premise of a value-free sociology, such sociologists are bound to a policy which can only alienate them further from the surrounding world. Social science can never be fully accepted in a society, or by a part of it, without paying its way; this means it must manifest both its relevance and concern for the contemporary human predicament. Unless the value-relevances of sociological inquiry are made plainly evident, unless there are at least some bridges between it and larger human hopes and purposes, it must inevitably be scorned by laymen as pretentious word-mongering. But the manner in which some sociologists conceive the value-free doctrine disposes them to ignore current human problems and to huddle together like old men seeking mutual warmth. "This is not our job," they say. "And if it were we would not know enough to do it. Go away, come back when we're grown up," say these old men. The issue, however, is not whether we know enough; the real questions are whether we have the courage to say and use what we do know and whether anyone knows more.

There is one way in which those who desert the world and those who sell out to it have something in common. Neither group can adopt an openly critical stance toward society. Those who sell out are accomplices; they may feel no critical impulses. Those who run out, while they do feel such impulses, are either lacking in any talent for aggression, or have often turned it inward into noisy but essentially safe university politics or into professional polemics. In adopting a conception of themselves as "value-free" scientists, their critical impulses may no longer find a target in society. Since they no longer feel free to critcize society, which always requires a measure of courage, they now turn to the cannibalistic criticism of sociology itself and begin to eat themselves up with "methodological" criticisms.

One latent meaning, then, of the image of a value-free sociology is this: "Thou shalt not commit a critical or negative value-judgment—especially of one's own society." Like a neurotic symptom this aspect of the value-free image is rooted in a conflict; it grows out of an effort to compromise between conflicting drives: On the one side, it reflects a conflict between the desire to criticize social institutions, which since Socrates has been the legacy of intellectuals, and the fear of reprisals if one does criticize—which is also a very old and human concern. On the other side, this aspect of the value-free image reflects a conflict between the fear of being critical and the fear of being regarded an unmanly or lacking in integrity, if uncritical.

The doctrine of a value-free sociology resolves these conflicts by making it seem that those who refrain from social criticism are acting solely on behalf of a higher professional good rather than their private interests. In refraining from social criticism, both the timorous and the venal may now claim the protection of a high professional principle and, in so doing, can continue to hold themselves in decent regard. Persuade all that no one must bell the cat, then none of the mice need feel like a rat.

Should social scientists affirm or critically explore values they would of necessity come up against powerful institutions who deem the statement or protection of public values as part of their special business. Should social scientists seem to compete in this business, they can run afoul of powerful forces and can, realistically, anticipate efforts at external curbs and controls. In saying this, however, we have to be careful lest we needlessly exacerbate academic timorousness. Actually, my own firsthand impressions of many situations where sociologists serve as consultants indicate that, once their clients come to know them, they are often quite prepared to have sociologists suggest (not dictate) policy and to have them express their own values. Nor does this always derive from the expectation that sociologists will see things their way and share their values. Indeed, it is precisely the expected difference in perspectives that is occasionally desired in seeking consultation. I find it difficult not to sympathize with businessmen who jeer at sociologists when they suddenly become more devoted to business values than the businessmen themselves.

Clearly all this does not mean that people will tolerate disagreement on basic values with social scientists more equably than they will with anyone else. Surely there is no reason why the principles governing social interaction should be miraculously suspended just because one of the parties to a social relation is a social scientist. The dangers of public resentment are real but they are only normal. They are not inconsistent with the possibility that laymen may be perfectly ready to allow social scientists as much (or as little) freedom of value expression as they would anyone else. And what more could any social scientist want?

The value-free image of social science is not consciously held for expedience's sake; it is not contrived deliberately as a hedge against public displeasure. It could not function as a face-saving device if it were. What seems more likely is that it entails something in the nature of a tacit bargain: in return for a measure of autonomy and social support, many social scientists have surrendered their critical impulses. This was not usually a callous "sell-out" but slow process of mutual accommodation; both parties suddenly found themselves betrothed without a formal ceremony.

Nor am I saying that the critical posture is dead in American sociology; it is just badly sagging. Anyone who has followed the work of Seymour Lipset, Dennis Wrong, Leo Lowenthal, Bennett Berger, Bernard Rosenberg, Lewis Coser, Maurice Stein, C. Wright Mills, Arthur Vidich, Philip Rieff, Anselm Strauss, David Riesman, Alfred McClung Lee, Van den Haag and of others, would know better. These men still regard themselves as "intellectuals" no less than sociologists: their work is deeply linked to this larger tradition from which sociology itself has evolved. By no means have all sociologists rejected the legacy of the intellectual, namely, the right to be critical of tradition. This ancient heritage still remains embedded in the underground culture of sociology; and it comprises the enshadowed part of the occupational selves of many sociologists even if not publicly acknowledged.

III. Socialization and Social Character

Socialization is a generic term for the process by which the biological organism *Homo sapiens* absorbs culture, that is, those aspects of a culture with which one comes into contact. At birth we are incomplete organisms, unable to sit up, turn over, or focus our eyes. The period of infantile dependency is inordinately prolonged, but with care and luck we become healthy, growing organisms. This physical *maturation* is a necessary but not a sufficient condition of *socialization* —which is, after all, equivalent to "humanization." We are socialized by encounters with those who are already socialized, either through direct interaction with them or via exposure to our arts and the mass media.

No social scientist can ignore socialization, and none has apprehended its nature more fully than the great philosopher and psychologist, George Herbert Mead. Most sociologists rely heavily on the Meadian outlook, which is variously classified as social behaviorism (not to be confused with Watsonian behaviorism or animal psychology), symbolic interactionism, or role theory. Our distinguished colleague Walter C. Bailey gives us an excellent account of Mead's approach. Bailey skillfully disentangles certain complexities of what Mead meant by the self as a product of social action and how Mead visualized individuals responding to themselves and to their environment. In being socialized we take over the attitudes of others, particularly "significant others." How so? For Mead, as for others, symbolic communication is decisive. In speech, by meaningful expulsions of air, we "listen" to ourselves as we respond to others. Small children learn the meaning of their "vocal gestures" by relating the response they prompt in others to the response they evoke in themselves. In time, they are able to anticipate the response and modify their gestures accordingly.

Mead divided human personality into the "I," the "Me," and the "Generalized Other." Insofar as we internalize responses and images of the "Generalized Other," we are nothing but "Me"s. And we are all more than that—else we would just be carbon copies of one another, interminably duplicating ourselves. There is another side to personality, a naive, unreflective, ungovernable, and spontaneous side. Mead dubbed it the "I." In accumulating a succession of attitudes and values, we take over an already existing culture as exemplified by other individuals in our society. That culture is presented in more or less stable *roles* or sets of expectancies. One can study society and all its institutions as an elaborate organization of roles. But to do so would hardly satisfy Mead, who was more interested in the actual performance of these roles. Given the unpredictable "I" plus the variability of human experience (no two persons interact in the same sequence with exactly the same others), we constantly redefine, reinterpret and re-create the culture that imperfectly creates us.

Mead focused on the "knowing," or cognitive and intellectual aspects of socialization. More psychologically oriented theorists have emphasized the "feelings," or affective and emotive aspects. Among these theorists, the incomparable Sigmund Freud stands first and highest. Freud spent many years perfecting a theory of personality formation (and deformation). Out of it he evolved a volatile theory of socialization. Freud started with primal or "libidinal" energy, picturing its flow in the distribution of basic biological drives and human emotions. He envisaged a state of perpetual warfare between biology and civilization, sure that if the former were not contained it would subdue the latter. Freud never stopped tinkering with this theory. Disciples, neo-Freudians and anti-Freudians—all beholden to the master—have continued to refine his work. Many stress organized society more than Freud did. Of these, Erik Erikson towers above the others.

James Latimore, a young sociologist, clearly and accurately summarizes Erikson's thought while cogently relating it to the "orthodox" Freudian psychology. Latimore's synopsis helps us to understand those elements of socialization added by Erikson.

History is yet another element. For the process of socialization is inseparable from its shifting content. The literature provides no better example than that of "childhood" as analyzed by a gifted social historian, Philippe Ariès. In his masterly *Centuries of Childhood,* Ariès traces radical changes in the very idea of childhood (as contrasted with "little man"-hood and "miniature woman"-hood.) He illustrates the varied definitions and cultural prescriptions of that category and the norms of work, play, freedom and responsibility that go with it. Ariès covers five hundred years of Western history, resurrecting the past through literature, religion, art, and a dazzling display of iconography. Not the least of his accomplishments for our purposes is to have shown that culture content, the ideas, symbols and values communicated, is an intrinsic ingredient in the process of socialization.

For brilliance and insight few living sociologists can be compared with Georg Simmel. Nevertheless, Erving Goffman comes to mind as a kind of American Simmel. Goffman's earliest books leaned heavily on Mead, but they also contained many flashes of originality. Goffman concentrated on techniques by which the individual projects images of his self to others and thereby manages his own identity. Roles are nearly all-encompassing in Mead's and Goffman's conception of society. Indeed, the concept of roles, including such auxiliary concepts as role performance, role-set, and role commitment, is crucial to the analysis of socialization. Goffman softens the role concept somewhat in his important little book *Encounters,* in which he allows for somewhat more freedom than he had previously conceded.

Hans Gerth and C. Wright Mills, two major figures in modern sociology, while strongly drawn to Mead and Freud, were even more impressed with the effect of history on "social character." Programmatically at least they anticipated scholars like Ariès. Gerth and Mills probably did more than any of their peers to demonstrate how social action at the interpersonal level can be linked with large-scale societal action at the macroscopic level. The final selection in this section, "The Person," appears in their durable text *Character and Social Structure.* It illustrates their general point of view as well as the specifically sociological point of view that takes socialization to be a lifelong process.

8. George Herbert Mead's Theories of Socialization

Walter C. Bailey

George Herbert Mead (1863–1931) may, with some justification, be called the "father of American sociological social psychology." Mead chose to call this social psychology *social behaviorism.* "The point of approach that I wish to suggest is that of dealing with experience from the standpoint of society, at least from the standpoint of communication as essential to the social order." [1] Apparently, he wished to distinguish between his conceptual frame of reference and that of Watsonian radical behaviorism. [2] However, he wished to call attention to both the similarities *and* the differences. Like Watsonian behaviorism, Mead starts with *observable* actions, but unlike Watson, he included in social behaviorism a concep-

"George Herbert Mead's Theories of Socialization" has been written expressly for this volume.

tion of behavior broad enough to include *covert* activity as well.[3] Mead wanted to understand the uniquely human aspects of human behavior that he considered to be qualitatively different and, in fact, emergent from animal behavior (infrahuman behavior). So Mead began his conceptual scheme with *society* as the basic point of reference and "worked down" to the individual, while Watson began with the individual (and even infrahuman forms) and "worked up" to society. Thus, the natural, logical order of Mead's thinking seems to have been in terms of *society, self,* and *mind*—rather than Mind, Self and Society.

Society

Mead's entire social psychological framework is based upon *society* as the primary and pivotal construct from which all else is derived. For him, again in the pragmatic tradition, the concept of society should be viewed as a verb rather than a noun because it really denotes a certain kind of activity or, more precisely, interaction that goes on among human beings. The kind of interaction he is talking about is, essentially, *cooperative* behavior. Mead, like many before and since, is therefore addressing himself to the most fundamental question facing sociological theorists—the Hobbesian question: How and why is society possible?[4] In answering this question, Mead posits society as *cooperative interaction* among persons whose type of behavior, although uniquely human, emerged within the biological process of evolution. Instead of looking for the biological "missing link," Mead looks for and "finds" the "missing link" of infrahuman interaction that, through the adaptive process, evolved into the distinctly human kinds of social interaction meant by the term *society*. Thus, he resolved the age-old "chicken or the egg?" problem of the priority of the individual or society as follows:

> Human society . . . could not exist without minds and selves, since all its most characteristic features presuppose the possession of minds and selves by its individual members; but its individual members would not possess minds and selves if these had not arisen within or emerged out of the human social process in its lower stages of development—those stages at which it was merely a resultant of, and wholly dependent upon, the physiological differentiations and demands of the individual organisms implicated in it. There must have been such lower stages of the human social process, not only for physiological reasons, but also (if our social theory of the origin and nature of minds and selves is correct) because minds and selves, consciousness and intelligence, could not otherwise have emerged; because, that is, some sort of ongoing social process in which human beings were implicated must have been there in advance of the existence of minds and selves in human beings, in order to make possible the development, by human beings, of minds and selves within or in terms of that process.[5]

Society seen as *prior* in the above context is, for Mead, simply the organization of *social acts* or, in Blumer's terminology, "joint action,"[6] which human beings have evolved in the process of resolving the peculiar problems presented by the needs, demands, and unique abilities of their physiological organisms. The social act ("joint action") refers to the "larger collective form of action that is constituted by the fitting together of the lines of behavior of the separate participants."[7] Blumer gives illustrations of joint action as follows: a trading transaction, a family dinner, a marriage ceremony, a shopping expedition, a game, a convivial party, a debate, a court trial, a war.[8] Everywhere we look in a society we see people involved in a great variety of such social acts—organized forms of interaction characterized by the integrated activities of one or more persons that (1) has *meaning* for the participants and (2) may be characterized by either consensus or conflict, or both.

If a society is thought of as organized action or process, there must be a corresponding structure. The structure of society is conceptualized as being composed of a system of interrelated institutions that for Mead are simply *social habits*. Institutions or social habits, then, are complex systems of social acts ("joint actions") that take on what Mead calls an *institutional form*.[9] In this sense an institution represents a complex of social acts ("joint actions") that represent common responses and expectations of all members of a community to a particular situation. For example, to return to Blumer's illustrations of joint action (social acts), the *trading transaction* represents a social act involved in the "pivotal institution," the economic system; the *family dinner* represents, among other things, the "pivotal institution," the family; the *convivial party* represents the expressional institution; and so on.

How then did society, in the Meadian sense, emerge within the process of biological evolution to become the cardinal characteristic of all that is uniquely human? Ignoring, because of limitations of space, the complex evolutionary processes occurring at the strictly physiological level discussed by Mead as necessary conditions for the development of society, we may consider his general theory of communication in terms of the "conversation of gestures" as the key to this important development.

Mead developed the notion that human beings can "communicate" with physical objects. But, as he emphasized, this kind of communication was itself predicated on the priority of society and the intelligent "minded" behavior of the individual derived from his incorporation of common meanings and self-reflexive behavior.

In discussing rudimentary forms of "social" organization and communication, Mead selects insects as illustrative of the difference between infrahuman society and human society[10] and points to the "conversation of gestures" at the infrahuman level[11] as crucial in the evolution of nonsymbolic, subhuman kinds of communication to symbolic human communication.

According to Mead, *all* group life involves varying degrees of cooperative behavior. He distinguishes, however, between infrahuman society and human society. Insects present what appears to be a complex social organization, but, as far as can be established, they act together in complicated ways because of their biological makeup. Here cooperative behavior is biologically determined.[12] This is evidenced by many facts, including those of fixity and stability, and of the constancy of the relationships of insect society that go on and on for countless generations without any marked differences in their *patterns* of association.[13] Human interactions are qualitatively different. Human cooperation is not brought about by mere physiological factors and cannot be explained in the same terms as the cooperative life of insects and other "lower" animals.

Human cooperation and communication, according to Mead, can only be explained in terms of evolutionary processes that resulted in a most flexible and adaptive organism—this versatility being based on the development of the ability to communicate (particularly verbally) in a *meaningful* way.

Mead uses several illustrations of primitive, infrahuman communication in terms of the conversation of gestures. In one, he describes the kind of communication that goes on between a mother hen and her chicks.[14] When a mother hen clucks, her chicks will respond by running to her. Although the chicks respond to this signal, the mother hen does not cluck with the self-conscious *intention* of guiding them to her. In other words, the "clucking" is a natural sign rather than a meaningful or *significant symbol*—that is, the hen does not cluck with the *intention* of guiding her chicks; she does not take the role or the viewpoint of the chicks toward its own gesture and respond to it, in her imagination, as they do. In this sense, hens and chicks are not sharing the same experience.[15]

Similarly, in the case of the "dog fight," Mead describes how two hostile dogs may approach each other utilizing a non-symbolic conversation of gestures.[16] In the prefight stage, the two hostile dogs approach each other, growling and snapping. They may go through an elaborate conversation of gestures—snarling, growling, baring fangs, walking stiff legged around each other, and so on. "There the stimulus which one dog gets from the other is to a response which is different from the response of the stimulating form." [17] This is a conversation of gestures—a reciprocal shifting of the dogs' positions and attitudes. The dogs are adjusting themselves to one another by responding to each other's gestures. (The gesture is the portion of an act that represents the initial, overt phases of the entire act—such as shaking one's fist at someone.)[18] Again, as in the case of the mother hen and her chicks, neither dog is dealing with the *intentions* of the other dog. Rather, the response of each dog is sequentially determined by pre-established tendencies to respond in certain ways. Neither dog, as he makes a gesture, is responding imaginatively to itself in the same way he would anticipate the other dog to respond to the gesture (taking the role of the other). Thus, animal interaction is devoid of conscious, self-conscious, deliberate meaning—the *significant symbol*.[19] A significant symbol is a gesture that not only elicits a response in the other but, of greater importance, tends also to elicit the same response in the person making the gesture. The most effective of such gestures is the vocal gesture that has meaning.[20]

Mead hypothesizes that the process of infrahuman conversation of gestures provided the evolutionary basis for the emergence of the significant symbol, real language behavior. The significant symbol is a necessary condition for the development of the social act; the social act is a necessary condition (and integral part of) for the development of society in the Meadian sense. Given the biological structure of the human form—the hand[21] (ability to hold and manipulate things), erect posture (increased agility in adjusting to the environment), the enormous increase in size and complexity of the brain[22] (central nervous system), and the unique construction of the larynx (the "voice box")—meaningful vocal gestures (the significant symbol) arose in the interaction between human forms incidental to the evolution of social organization (*society*).

For the purpose of logical and analytical description, Mead assumed that society existed prior to, and was a necessary condition for, the development of the self.

THE SELF

The second major building block in Mead's social behaviorism was his notion of the *self*. For Mead, the self is a hypothetical construct that denotes the organization of certain kinds of human activities. These activities, subsumed under the term self, are socially learned and therefore a product of social interaction—the kind of interaction that can occur only *in society*.[23] More specifically, it refers to those social activities of individuals that are *reflexive* in the sense that the person is self-consciously both subject and object in his social relations. In other words, it refers to the capacity of man to act socially toward himself, just as toward others. For example, he may praise, blame, or encourage himself; he may become disgusted with himself, he may seek to punish himself, he may try to kill himself, and so forth. "Thus, the human being may become the object of his own actions. The self is formed in the same way as other objects—through the 'definitions' made by others."[24]

The self, then, develops in a social situation, that is, in meaningful communication with others who are representatives of society. As the individual learns to use and react to symbols that have a common meaning to all individuals involved (the significant symbol), he develops self-consciousness and the "beginnings" of a self.

Mead described the evolvement of the self in terms of three developmental stages, and a fourth stage that is only implied in his writings. These developmental stages are:

1. *The Preparatory Stage.* This stage was not explicitly identified by Mead, but is inferable from various fragmentary essays.[25] It is one of "meaningless imitation," seen in the infant who imitates various activities of the parents or other *significant others*. The infant "reads the newspaper," "watches television," and so on. This form of activity is essentially imitation of actions performed by others around the child, but the child

does them without any real understanding of what he or she is doing. Nevertheless, the child is incipiently taking the roles of others around it, that is, "on the verge of putting itself in the position of others and acting like them."[26]

2. *The Play Stage.* In this stage the actual playing of roles begins. The child "plays" at being mother, teacher, policeman, postman, cowboy, etc. In such playacting the child is "forced" to "act back toward itself" in such roles as mother, cowboy, and so on. In this stage the child begins to form a self—that is, direct activity back toward itself by "taking the roles of others."[27]

3. *The Game Stage.* This is the stage in which, eventually, the child finds himself in social situations in which he is "forced," not simply to take the specific roles of others sequentially, but rather to take the roles of a number of "others" simultaneously and in an organized fashion. Mead's classic example is that of the baseball game. Here, the child, in assuming one specific role such as *"the pitcher,"* must be ready to take the role of everyone else involved in that total situation—such as the other members of his own team, the members of the opposing team, the umpire, and so forth, and even the audience, if any.[28] As Mead puts it: "If he gets in a ball nine he must have the responses of each position involved in his own position. He must know what everyone else is going to do in order to carry out his own play. He has to take all of these roles."[29]

In this process, the game stage, the child must take the roles of groups of individuals over the role of a single individual. This is accomplished by means of *abstracting* a "composite" role out of the concrete roles of particular persons. It is in this kind of process (The Game) that he begins to build up a *generalized other*—a generalized role or point of reference from which he views himself and *controls* his behavior in terms of these generalized expectations of the social group.[30] As Mead pointed out: "We get then an 'other' which is an organization of the attitudes of those involved in the same process."[31]

4. *The "Mature Adult" Stage.* This stage is not explicitly described by Mead but is implicit in his writings and elaborated by Sullivan.[32] It requires a transition from the simple *game stage* of the "generalized other" to the incorporation of a generalized other of maximum scope and depth. "The organized community . . . which gives to the individual his unit of self may be called the 'generalized other.' The attitude of the generalized other is the attitude of the whole community."[33] This *mature adult* is, of course, an "ideal construct." No person is ever so totally "socialized" or so completely incorporates the *generalized other* of the whole community that his behavior is entirely controlled by the attitudes, values, and norms of that community. There are two major reasons for this situation, one of which Mead touched upon only tangentially, and the other he explained in some detail in terms of the "structure of the self" (the "I" and the "Me"). The former, to which Mead refers only in passing, is the fact that all larger, heterogeneous societies are characterized by a number of *sub-*

cultures and even *contracultures*. Thus, for most (if not all) of us the "Meadian community" is a restricted one, dependent on our own specific membership groups and reference groups.

In his discussion of the structure of the self, Mead accounts for both the predictable and unpredictable (problematic) aspects of individual behavior as well as social order (consensus) and social change (conflict). According to Mead, the self is composed of two analytically distinguishable social processes going on "within" the individual. These are termed the "I" and the "Me." Mead gives us a general definition of both concepts as follows:

> The "I" is the response of the organism to the attitudes of the others, the "me" is the organized set of attitudes of others which one himself assumes. The attitudes of the others constitute the organized "me," and then one reacts toward that as an "I."[34]

In a very real way, the notions of the "I" and "Me" correspond with our common sense distinctions. The "I" is used to designate the *acting* part of the self; the "Me" is used to refer to the reflexive, controlling aspects of the self. The "I" represents our impulsive tendencies to act in any given situation. It represents "the undirected tendencies of the individual."[35] The "Me" represents the incorporated "generalized other" within the individual—the organized set of attitudes, definitions, understandings, expectations, and meanings common to the group. "In any given situation, the "Me" comprises the generalized other, and often, some particular other."[36]

These subsidiary constructs provide additional heuristic devices for handling the active and reflexive, the unpredictable and predictable aspects of conduct. The "Me," as the individual's organized set of attitudes and roles, is that portion of the self of which the person is consciously aware. It is the self that exists in immediate awareness. It is the introjected "generalized other" that provides stability, predictability, and unity to the self. It is predictable because it is composed of the social situation incorporated in conduct. It is the presence of these organized sets of attitudes, the "Me," to which the "I," as the actor, is responding.

The "I" as the self in immediate action is, however, uncertain and unpredictable. According to Mead, we may know the nature of the individual's organized attitudes (the "Me") and the nature of the stimulus situation, but "what the response will be he does not know and nobody else knows."[37] The "I" is the self in action "in the specious present."[38] Since it represents the self in action, is also movement into a future that always contains some elements of novelty and is something not given by the "Me."

Since the "Me" represents the incorporation and organization of past experiences, and the "I" involves "the immediate present moving into the future," there is a continuous process in which the "I" is becoming a part of the "Me." Mead sums it up as follows:

> The two are separated in experience but they belong together in the sense of being a part of a whole. They are separated and yet they belong together.

The separation of the "I" and "me" is not fictitious. They are not identical, for, as I have said, the "I" is something that is never calculable. The "me" does call for a certain sort of an "I" in so far as we meet the obligations that are given in conduct itself, but the "I" is always something different from what the situation itself calls for. So there is always that distinction, if you like, between the "I" and the "me." The "I" both calls out the "me" and responds to it. Taken together they constitute a personality as it appears in social experience. The self is essentially a social process going on with these two distinguishable phases. If it did not have these two phases there would not be conscious responsibility, and there would be nothing novel in experience.[39]

THE MIND

The *mind,* in Mead's pragmatic tradition, is considered as a hypothetical construct used to refer to a certain kind of self-conscious, intelligent interaction between the individual and the objects in his environment that is mediated by language (significant symbols). This is the third, and final, basic building block in Mead's conceptual frame of reference, social behaviorism.

Mead posited an evolutionary progression from infrahuman to human behavior in which, at the distinctly human level, the linear sequence involved the development of: (1) *society,* (2) *the self,* and (3) *the mind.* The almost simultaneous emergence of the mind ("intelligent activity") from the self was dependent upon (as previously noted) the hand as the organ of "contact manipulation," and a central nervous system capable of *delayed reaction,* selection of stimuli, implicit initiation of a number of alternative responses with reference to any given stimulus-object for the completion of an already initiated act, distance perception, and speech as significant symbolization.

In terms of the development and functioning of the mind ("minded behavior"), Mead used the "delayed act" as a crucial heuristic concept. He discussed the relation between human intelligence, a primary aspect of the self, and the physiological organism as follows:

Delayed reaction is necessary to intelligent conduct. The organization, implicit testing, and final selection by the individual of his overt responses or reactions to social situations which confront him and which present him with problems of adjustment, would be impossible if his overt responses or reactions could not in such situations be delayed until this process of organizing, implicitly testing, and finally selecting is carried out; that is, would be impossible if some overt response or other to the given environmental stimuli had to be immediate. Without delayed reaction, or perhaps in terms of it, no conscious or intelligent control over behavior could be exercised; for it is through this process of selective reaction—which can be selective only because it is delayed—that intelligence operates in the determination of behavior. Indeed, it is this process which constitutes intelligence. The central nervous system provides not only the necessary physiological mechanism for this process, but also the necessary physiological conditions of delayed reaction which this process presupposes.[40]

The self then emerges when the individual is able to respond to himself in ways in which he imagines others would respond to him. In anticipating this response, he can decide *not* to act. He may decide that his anticipated action would produce negative consequences for himself or for the other, and he thus "delays" or avoids action. In doing so, he has "taken over the attitude of the other"; he has "internalized" the other's probable response; and he has made that response a part of his "me."

In being able to imagine the response of the other and respond selectively to that response, the individual becomes a thinking, self-aware person. But the process by which one becomes a differentiated individual is a social process.

The individual emerges in the process of social action, but that process is, in total, the operation of society: The very operation of society creates individuals. The central element that produces individuals (and culture) is language: for in the use of language, symbolic interaction, the individual is able to respond to himself as he responds to others. Through that process, he also shares in, and is socialized to the ongoing culture.

To the extent that his response to the roles or expectancies of others is spontaneous, "novel" or unstereotyped—that is, to the extent that his "I" is operative—the individual may make a contribution to culture. For his purely individual, subjective responses may enter the objective social stream through the process of symbolic social interaction. That process is endless, constantly changing but always has an objective, social character that expresses in content the culture of society and in form the structure of society.

NOTES

1. George Herbert Mead, *Mind, Self and Society* (Chicago: University of Chicago Press, 1943), p. 1.
2. Watson rejected all "mentalistic concepts" and insisted that all behavior (human and animal) is analyzable in terms of stimulus and response; cf John B. Watson, *Behavior: An Introduction to Comparative Psychology* (New York: Holt, Rinehart & Winston, 1914).
3. Bernard N. Meltzer, "Mead's Social Psychology," in Jerome G. Manis and Bernard N. Meltzer, eds., *Symbolic Interaction: A Reader in Social Psychology* (Boston: Allyn & Bacon, 1967), pp. 5–24.
4. Thomas Hobbes, *Leviathan* (New York: Macmillan, 1947); originally published in 1651.
5. Mead, *Mind, Self and Society*, p. 227.
6. Herbert Blumer, "Sociological Implications of the Thought of George Herbert Mead," *American Journal of Sociology* 71 (March 1966):535–44.
7. *Ibid.*
8. *Ibid.*
9. Mead, *Mind, Self and Society*, pp. 167, 261.
10. *Ibid.*, pp. 227–37.
11. *Ibid.*, p. 63.
12. Meltzer, "Mead's Social Psychology," p. 6.
13. *Ibid.*, p. 7.
14. Mead, *Mind, Self and Society*, p. 253.
15. Meltzer, "Mead's Social Psychology," p. 7.
16. Mead, *Mind, Self and Society*, pp. 14, 63.
17. *Ibid.*, p. 63.
18. Meltzer, "Mead's Social Psychology," p. 7.

19. Mead, *Mind, Self and Society*, p. 71.
20. *Ibid.*, pp. 71–82.
21. Mead, *Mind, Self and Society*, p. 237.
22. *Ibid.*, p. 236.
23. *Ibid.*, pp. 135–226.
24. Meltzer, "Mead's Social Psychology," p. 10.
25. *Ibid.*
26. *Ibid.*
27. Mead, *Mind, Self and Society*, p. 150.
28. *Ibid.*, p. 151.
29. *Ibid.*
30. *Ibid.*, p. 154.
31. *Ibid.*
32. Harry Stack Sullivan, *The Interpersonal Theory of Psychiatry* (New York: W. W. Norton, 1953), p. 28.
33. Mead, *Mind, Self and Society*, p. 154.
34. *Ibid.*, p. 175.
35. Meltzer, "Mead's Social Psychology," p. 11.
36. *Ibid.* (Sullivan's "significant other.")
37. Mead, *Mind, Self and Society*, p. 175.
38. *Ibid.*, p. 176.
39. *Ibid.*, p. 178.
40. *Ibid.*, pp. 99–100.

9.　Erik Erikson's Concept of the Psycho-Socialization of Man

James Latimore

Erik Erikson's work enjoys widespread acceptance these days—and not only in psychoanalytic and academic circles. As one who preaches historical and cultural relativism, Erikson himself might be the first to appreciate that, aside from whatever truth lies in his work, one reason for his popularity and influence is that historically he is at the right place at the right time. Placing himself between biological and social determinism, and stressing individual responsibility rather than individual "victimization," Erikson, in *Childhood and Society*, offers a body of contemporary ideas that are especially appealing in the United States.

In doing so, Erikson provides a theory of socialization. He demonstrates how the biological organism, under the force of social and cultural con-

"Erik Erikson's Concept of the Psycho-Socialization of Man" has been written especially for this anthology.

trols, begins to reshape itself to comply with those controls. But he also shows how biological bases—mini-drives—assert themselves and remain present in the social and cultural life of the individual. In reasserting themselves they are of course transformed and sometimes blocked by social and cultural forces in society. Erikson attempts to suggest the interplay of biology and culture by describing precise processes and stages that occur in the life history of the individual. Personality and culture, character and social organization intersect and merge.

Basing his work on Freud's, Erikson might be said to have saved Freud from the Freudians—that is, from a scriptural reverence for every thought of the Master, and from an overemphasis on biological factors—the instincts and drives often referred to in much of Freud's work. Erikson was himself trained in Freudian psychoanalysis by Anna Freud and August Aichorn.

But this has not kept Erikson from adapting and interpreting Freud's work in his own version of contemporary man's psychological dynamics.

The emphasis on *contemporary* man (and, in specific cultures) is important in reading and understanding Erikson's work. It is this emphasis that leads Erikson, in *Childhood and Society*, to characteristically reinterpret and build upon Freud's work, rather than to disavow or attack it as other former disciples of Freud have done.[1] Erikson recognizes that Freud's perspective, for all the man's brilliant creativity, was limited by his time and culture, and he is inclined to attribute whatever mistakes Freud made to these limitations. In stressing man's ego, identity, ideology, and culture, Erikson's view of man may sometimes seem as "one-sided" as Freud's was thought to be earlier in this century, but it is actually quite different. Though his description of the eight *psychosocial* ages of man includes the Freudian stages of orality, anality, genitality, and so on, as coexisting *psychosexual* stages, there is a decided emphasis on cultural and egoistic components. And though he does not fail to mention the unconscious, it is the conscious, integrating, coping aspects of man with which he is most concerned. Gone are the dark tales of man's unconscious life. Even instincts are played down, at least the sexual instincts. Erikson substitutes fragmentary instincts that are highly modifiable. Fidelity, for example, is treated almost as an instinct by Erikson.

Erikson's view is that psychoanalysis must be alert to the changing as well as the changeless elements contributing to man's personality. The very existence of psychoanalysis—or more importantly, its incorporation in popular thinking and behavior—may well change the appearance or the content of psychic development and conflict. In time, psychoanalytic concepts may be more influential in this way than when used in the treatment of individual patients. If certain unconscious wishes become accepted as "normal," this "resolution" may shift the psychic drama to another stage of development. Eriksons' view is that problems of identity, rather than "sexual" problems, are the primary source of development and conflict for contemporary technological man.

In *Childhood and Society,* Erikson characterizes the "eight ages" in the life cycle of man as "a list of ego qualities which emerge from critical periods of development." These "qualities" must develop to permit the ego to integrate the developmental scheme of the organism and the social institutions and cultural forces to which the individual is exposed. The emergence of the ego qualities is a sign that the ego has developed the necessary strength.

The biological organism, the ego, and the social external world are the three main factors of personality development for Erikson. Included under "organism" are the Freudian psychosexual stages: oral, anal, genital, latency, and puberty. Erikson adds *stages of bodily development* to the first three of these. That is, the first, or oral stage, is also the stage of sensory development and primacy in the infant. The anal stage is coincident with the development of essential muscular-control skills. The genital stage is also marked by the growth of locomotor skills. Erikson does not say so specifically, but it seems that the stages of bodily development he adds actually include the Freudian stages, rather than merely coexist with them. The early predominance of oral gratification is but one part of a sensory stage. Anality, involving control of the sphincters, is but one facet of a stage characterized by a growth of muscular control. Similarly, genitality for boys is part of "being on the make," a "pleasure in attack and conquest" that goes with the ability to move around, to "intrude" on others—that is, a locomotor stage. For girls, the mode is that of catching or attracting rather than attacking.

Erikson presents the eight "ages" in the life cycle of man as a sequence of "positive" and "negative" polarities characteristic of that age. These are identified by Erikson as follows:

1. Basic Trust vs. Mistrust
2. Autonomy vs. Shame and Doubt
3. Initiative vs. Guilt
4. Industry vs. Inferiority
5. Identity vs. Role Confusion
6. Intimacy vs. Isolation
7. Generativity vs. Stagnation
8. Ego Integrity vs. Despair

In the oral-sensory stage (roughly the first year of infancy), the ego develops its crucial sense of trust (or mistrust) according to how well the (primarily mother-centered) world is coordinated with the biological needs and temperamental characteristics of the infant organism.

Pleasure and pain (or discomfort) are the primary motivators—seeking one and avoiding the other. The dependent infant learns to associate maternal activities with the relief of bodily discomfort. The pains of hunger are balanced by a growing experience and trust that the mother will respond to signals of discomfort in an appropriate way. Cumulative, remembered experiences of relief are associated with an outer world of "familiar and predictable things and people." This is simple learning theory (stimulus and response). But it enables the infant to anticipate responses before the existence of stimuli, and thus to attain his first social achievement: the "willingness to let the mother out of sight without undue rage or anxiety." The mother's dependability and predictability have become trustworthy. Erikson notes, incidentally, that the quantity of trust developed depends more on the *quality* of the mother's care than on the sheer *quantity* of food, affection, and so on, given to the child. Even prohibitions in child care contribute to the ego's strength if they convey "an almost somatic conviction" that there is a societal meaning to them. Erikson is not exactly clear about what he means by this. Presumably, it refers to the quality of inner conviction that the parent conveys, based on internalization of relevant parts of the culture. Erikson says that children become neurotic not from frustrations, but from the lack or loss of societal meaning in these frustrations.

It is important to note that the infant develops neither a sense of trust *nor* a sense of mistrust. To Erikson, it is a matter of *ratio*. The ratio of trust to mistrust is what counts. Moreover, mistrust is not all "bad." We must learn those things that may not be innocently and always trusted—for example, strangers. We might say (although Erikson does not do so explicitly) that this implies a need for the infant to develop a generalized sense of trust in its world as a predictable, even-keeled, gratifying place, and at the same time to mistrust certain specific things in that world as a matter of survival. Problems occur when a generalized trust does not develop (infantile schizophrenia in children and depression and schizoid states in adults are some of the problems).

The matter of the *ratio* of ego qualities applies to all the later ages as well. The growing personality is composed of both positive and negative qualities. Erikson expresses several times his frustration and annoyance over the tendency of others to use the ego qualities that he describes as the basis of a scale of achievement to measure ego development. Those who do so, he says, miss the point about the ratio of qualities, and furthermore, do not grasp the meaning of an epigenetic model. There are some important, complex features of such a model:

1. Each psychosocial age (and the ego strength typical of it) is related to all the others.
2. The development of each ego strength is dependent upon the proper sequential development of the preceding ones.
3. The blueprint of the whole exists from the beginning—"each item (ego strength) exists in some form before its critical time normally arrives."

To complicate matters further, once each level of the ego develops, it does not necessarily retain forever its initial content or form. The interaction of one quality with another leads to further development. Erikson notes that *basic trust* may evolve into a *mature faith* in our culture and historical period by the time we arrive at the last of the eight ages. What do we call the form of each *ego strength* at each succeeding *psychosocial age?* Erikson does not know; the model he proposes "suggests a global form of thinking and rethinking which leaves details of methodology and terminology to further study."

The various ages are often described in terms of a "nuclear conflict" or a "crisis." Erikson makes it clear, toward the end of his essay on the eight ages, that he does not consider crisis to be the whole of development. What he has in mind instead is the idea of "critical steps—'critical' being a characteristic of turning points, of moments of decision between progress and regression, integration and retardation." Nevertheless, what appears to be critical is that conflict between one or another tendency be resolved toward a favorable ratio of positive to negative. The "critical step" in the first age, for example, is the development of a higher ratio of trust than mistrust. There is a conflict, but in the sense of an unknown outcome rather than a direct conflict. Forces capable of producing either outcome may be present. Thus, the real conflict is between those forces. Discomfort (including hunger) is "in conflict" with the culturally shaped maternal practices of child care. The outcome is a sense of basic trust or basic mistrust of the external world and the people who inhabit it. In the second age, "Autonomy vs. Shame and Doubt," the infant's muscular development is accompanied by a "sudden violent wish to have a choice, to appropriate demandingly, and to eliminate stubbornly." This is a move towards autonomy, a move that is usually supported by his culture. At the same time, the infant must be protected against "his as yet untrained sense of discrimination, his inability to hold on and let go with discrimination." It is this age that Freud labeled the anal phase—that phase in which the primary sexual gratification is focused on the anal region. In both theories, Freud's and Erikson's, a significant and crucial element of social control is exerted on the infant. For Erikson, this control must be "firmly reassuring" so that the "basic faith in existence" derived from the first stage will not be threatened. Simultaneous with encouraging autonomy, the environment must protect the infant against "meaningless and arbitrary experiences of shame and early doubt."

Erikson seems to imply that shame (as a means of control) and doubt (as an outcome) are not always to be avoided. Perhaps "meaningful" and "planned" experiences of shame and early doubt are unavoidably part of the socialization of children. The danger, however, is that shame and doubt will come to dominate the person rather than develop his sense of autonomy.

Shame and doubt appear at first glance to be intimately related; one might regard them as two aspects of the same basic attribute, or as cause and effect—that is, perhaps shame causes doubt. Actually they represent two separate developments, two different schemes. Erikson traces shame through guilt to superego and conscience. Shame is "visual" in essence. It "supposes that one is completely exposed and conscious of being looked at. One is visible and not ready to be looked at." Shame is not sufficiently studied in our civilization because "it is so early and easily absorbed by guilt." Guilt, which is "auditory" (the voice of the conscience), succeeds "visual" shame. There is no biological basis for shame, as there is for doubt. Shame is social in origin.

Erikson describes doubt as "the brother of shame." Shame is "dependent on the consciousness of being upright and exposed." Doubt "has much to do with a consciousness of having a front and a back—and especially a 'behind.'" But it seems more like an in-law than a brother, for the "behind" leads to an explanation based on anality. This "reverse area of the body, with its aggressive and libidinal focus in the sphincters and in the buttocks . . . can be dominated by the will of others . . . and effectively invaded by those who would attack one's power of autonomy and who would designate as evil those products of the bowels which were felt to be all right when they were being passed." A "basic sense of doubt" ensues from this and forms "a substratum for later and more verbal forms of compulsive doubting."

It is a highly complex phase of development. There is an interaction among the developing, functioning organism, the relative size and vulnerability of the organism and its ego, and external elements of social control. The infant's muscular development leads it toward a beginning autonomy. The environment supports the infant's growing autonomy while at the same time subjecting it to certain controls. The small size and limited power of the infant make it vulnerable to shame. At the same time, the existence of cultural values and practices contribute a basic doubt to the ego by attaching a new, conflicting, and nonsensory value to the products of the infant's bowels: They are defined by others as evil or dirty. The dynamics of all this are not specified in detail by Erikson, but are assumed as part of the tradition of Freudian psychology.

"From a sense of self-control without loss of self-esteem comes a lasting sense of good will and pride; from a sense of loss of self-control and of foreign over-control comes a lasting propensity for doubt and shame." The key seems to be the application of a sufficient degree of control and guidance so as to promote autonomy characteristic of a normal, healthy ego. Over-control through shaming and doubt leaves shame and doubt as its product.

The third age, "Initiative vs. Guilt," has an Eriksonian and a Freudian component. It coincides with the development of locomotor skills and the onset of the genital (and Oedipal) phase. Initiative appears to derive from the very existence of the newly developed abilities to move about. In Erikson's words, it "adds to autonomy the quality of undertaking, planning and 'attacking' a task for the sake of being active and on the move." These skills open new horizons for action and virtually demand to be used; in combination with genitality, they create a new basic mode of social behavior. Erikson calls it "'making,' first in the sense of 'being on the make.'" Boys exhibit "phallic-intrusive modes" of behavior. Girls turn to modes of "catching," either aggressively in the form of "snatching" or, less aggressively, in the form of snaring (luring, "making oneself attractive and endearing"). Erikson chooses the term "making" with care, in order to convey the sense of "pleasure in attack and conquest" found here. There is in this mode of behavior, besides the obvious sexual overtones, an element of aggression. Erikson does not use aggression in the sense of instinct, though; he disavows instincts in humans. There are only "instinct fragments" that are highly modifiable. What appears to be crucial in this age is a certain form of learning: One learns toward what one may or may not employ initiative; one learns what is forbidden. Guilt is both the means of accomplishing this and the "danger of this stage." The objects desired may be out of bounds, and the acts that are initiated in the child's "exuberant enjoyment" of his developing abilities may be beyond the child's capabilities. They may "call for an energetic halt on one's contemplated initiative."

Guilt becomes generalized—that is, not exclusively sexual—through the superego. But the superego is sexual in origin. The child usually recognizes that he or she cannot have the parent of the opposite sex as a sexual partner and identifies with the parent of the same sex. In Erikson's words, "the child must turn from an exclusive, pregenital attachment to his parents to the slow process of becoming a parent, a carrier of tradition." There is really no reconciliation of initiative—based on the combination of locomotor skills and infantile genitality—and this "parental set" as internalized in the superego. The child becomes "forever divided in himself." The "infantile set" of instinct fragments is associated with exuberance and growth potentials. The "parental set" resides in the superego, supporting and increasing "self-observation, self-guidance and self-punishment." This conflict then, is not resolved. It continues throughout life. The problem, Erikson notes, is "one of mutual regulation" by the ego. A sense of initiative is essential, but so is the "sense of moral responsibility" and the "insight into the institutions, functions, and roles" of his culture that the child ultimately gains from guilt and identification. What Erikson means when he says that the danger of the third age is a sense of guilt is that guilt embedded too deeply in the superego can pose a danger both to the individual's own ego as well as to others. "Naturally," he says, "the parental set is at first infantile in nature; the fact that human conscience remains partially infantile throughout life is the core of human tragedy." The superego in its infantile state, with its all-or-nothing quality, can be so harsh and primitive that it may lead to self-obliteration. It can also be turned against others "in the form of persistent moralistic surveillance" and moralistically grounded aggression. It is the ego's task to utilize both initiative and guilt within culturally prescribed limits. This third age appears to be crucial in a way different from the first two. In the first age trust is primarily an outcome of parental care. In the second, a favorable ratio and sense of autonomy is normally developed—but largely as a result of "firmly reassuring" parental control. Now, in this third age, the ego begins to make use of its autonomy in allocating and regulating personality processes. It becomes an active instrument of personality in a real sense.

The fourth age, which Erikson calls "Industry vs. Inferiority," coincides with the latency phase described by Freud. Sexual drives are usually dormant. Thus there is no pattern of "inner upheaval" followed by the ego's resolution and integration of the conflicting forces. After the monumental discovery in the preceding age that there are distinct limits in his function and future within the family, the child's attention is turned to the outer world. At the same time, the "wider society" turns its attention more to the child, preparing the child for an understanding of "meaningful roles in its technology and economy." "In all cultures, at this age," Erikson notes, "children receive some *systematic instruction.*" It may be aimed at teaching hunting skills, or it may be the kind of education we are accustomed to—based on literacy—with salaried professional teachers. Regardless of form and content, learning during this period is focused on the tool world and the educational requirements of the culture's technology. The imagination and wishes of the child are "harnessed to the laws of impersonal things."

Erikson again borrows directly from Freud in explaining the dynamics and processes of this age. "With the oncoming latency period," he says, "the normally advanced child forgets, or rather *sublimates,* the necessity to 'make' people by direct attack or to become papa and mama in a hurry: He now learns to win recognition by producing things." [Italics added.] In Freudian theory, sublimation involves the diversion of libido—sexualized energy—away from a forbidden object to a socially approved object. It is Freud's fundamental explanation of the higher achievements of culture—art, music, philosophy, and so on. Erikson has elsewhere [2] stated that while the concept of libido was a notable achievement in Freud's time, it was basically a reflection of nineteenth-century physics. If Freud had had access to modern developments in biology, chemistry, and physics, he would have arrived at a different concept. But as we see, Erikson himself falls back on the libido-based process of sublimation. This observation only serves to demonstrate the Freudian substructure of Erikson's work. Dynamic explanations ultimately go back to "the old man."

The danger in this fourth age is a sense of inferiority and inadequacy. If the child comes to believe that his tools and skills are inadequate or his status among his peers not sufficient, he may have difficulty in identifying with peers or in visualizing himself as capable of occupying a meaningful place in the tool world of the culture. Erikson notes that these difficulties may cause him to pull back to the "familial rivalry of the Oedipal time." The child, in that case, may see himself as inadequate, both anatomically and with regard to tool skills, and consider himself "doomed to mediocrity or inadequacy." On the other hand, if the child over-internalizes the work principle, and accepts " 'what works' as his only criterion of worthwhileness," he may end up as a rigid conformist, susceptible to exploitation by others. The ego's—and the culture's—task in regulating and "balancing" these tendencies is apparent.

The fifth age of man, "Identity vs. Role Confusion," marks the end of childhood and the beginning of youth. It occurs during puberty. The "samenesses and continuities" developed in earlier ages are no longer adequate; they are "questioned again," owing to the rapid body growth and the "new addition of genital maturity." In the quest for continuities, Erikson says, "adolescents have to refight many of the battles of earlier years." The age of identity is marked by a concern with seeing oneself through the eyes of others—not only through those of one's peers and heroes, but through the eyes of everyone with whom one is involved.

How does one appear to others, compared with what one feels one is? How do the roles and skills one has developed connect one with the occupational structure and requirements of one's culture? Erikson notes that the integration now taking place in the form of ego identity "is more than the sum of the childhood identifications." It is really a new testing of those identifications against the "vicissitudes of the libido," one's abilities and skills, and the opportunities offered in social roles. A sense of ego identity emerges when the ego can integrate these factors, confident that the continuities of the earlier stages are consistent and more or less harmonious with the meaning one has for others—that is, that others see you as you see yourself. And not just particular others, but societal others. This connection between past and present, with its implications for the future, affords a good illustration of the epigenetic character of Erikson's scheme.

The search for identity emerges both from earlier continuities—things previously accepted and internalized—and from the emerging need to see oneself through new eyes. The latter visualization would not be as crucial were it not for the former. The age would seem to be marked by a great reduction in primary narcissism—whatever remains of it—as a result of the concern with oneself *as seen by others,* and by the *direction of libido toward others,* such as girl and boy friends, heroes and idols. Erikson regards falling in love and adolescent hero worship as means of developing and clarifying one's identity. Falling in love aids by "projecting one's diffused ego image on another and by seeing it thus reflected and gradually clarified." Over-identification associated with "the heroes of cliques and crowds" is a defense against a sense of identity confusion, especially confusion relating to occupational identity. The danger in this stage is of either sexual or occupational *role confusion.* Identity, then, is a role. It is, on the one hand, social certification of who one is; and on the other hand, it is the integration of who one thinks one is with who (or what) others think one is. Ideology, rituals, and creeds are important in this age for their identity-forming capacities, The ideological aspect of the culture "speaks most clearly to the adolescent." But while trying out different cultural ideologies, adolescents are also helping one another through this period by forming cliques, thus stereotyping themselves and the world around them by in-group and out-group adherence and disaffiliation. Clannishness, cruelty, pettiness, iron-bound fidelity—those things that adults usually see as the less desirable and less lovable features of adolescents, Erikson sees as playing a crucial part in the formation and emergence of their identity.

Once a sense of identity is achieved, it too must be tested and transcended in the next stage. The sixth age, "Intimacy vs. Isolation," is dependent on a well-formed sense of identity in order for the individual to face the possibility and fear of ego loss in intimate relations with others. It is a highly "social" age. Erikson says that "the young adult, emerging from the search for and the insistence upon identity, is now eager to fuse his identity with that of others." Intimacy is defined as the capacity to commit oneself to "concrete affiliations and partnerships" and to discover and test the "ethical strength to abide by such commitments," even when such commitments may call for "significant sacrifices and compromises." Intimate relations include, for example, friendships and sexual relations and all manner of "close affiliations" where a feeling of solidarity can be found. It even includes "experiences . . . of intuition from the recesses of the self"—a kind of self-intimacy. The inability to achieve intimate relations with others, or the avoidance of such relations due to a fear of ego loss, may result in "a deep sense of isolation and consequent self-absorption."

A counterpart to intimacy, a carry-over from the struggle for identity, is the readiness to differentiate between "the familiar and the foreign." The prejudices thus developed, Erikson says, "are a more mature outgrowth of the blinder repudiations" occurring in the adolescent struggle for identity noted earlier. The danger is that intimate, competitive, and combative relationships are attempted with the same others. However, these are normally differentiated in time; examples are the competitive encounter and the sexual embrace. Eventually these social relations become ruled by what Erikson calls "that *ethical sense* which is the mark of the adult."

The "ethical sense" refers to an internalization of the culture's rules governing behavior—goals as well as means. It is this ethical sense that permits a *"true genitality"* to develop. As we observed before, sex life in the earlier identity stage was closely related to the search for identity, or was dominated by "phallic or vaginal strivings" that gave sex life a rather combative quality. But "true genitality," to Erikson, is not expressed merely by sexual union, not even orgasm. Physically and emotionally, it means sexual union unhindered by remnants of pregenitality. The "genital libido . . . is expressed in heterosexual mutuality." This is an important word in Erikson's work—mutuality—but it is not always clear just what he means by the term. He talks about the "mutual regulation of two beings," for example, without attempting to pin down the concept precisely. It contains ideas of being "more than oneself" and of complementarity.

Sexuality acquires a "spiritual" or ethical component. The *relationship* is a unitary one rather than one based on the sum of the *individual's* experiences.

Erikson seems to accept Freud's notion of the inherent hostility between male and female; for he says that satisfactory sexual relations "takes the edge off the hostilities and potential rages caused by the oppositeness of male and female," making sex "less obsessive, overcompensation less necessary, and sadistic controls superfluous."

To be of "lasting social significance," Erikson lists six goals of genitality. Breaking with the usual psychoanalytic prescription, which focused on satisfaction in the sexual relationship, Erikson's "utopia of genitality" includes, in addition to "mutuality of orgasm," a loving, heterosexual, trusting relationship accompanied by a commitment to mutual regulation of the major adult activities of work, procreation, and recreation. A major goal is "to secure to the offspring, too, all the stages of a satisfactory development." The end is thus the beginning. Erikson embraces a traditionalistic, societal orientation that both helps to explain and confuses the problem of Erikson's reputation in an individualistic age, where pleasure for its own sake appears to be increasingly legitimate and sought after.

Beginning with this age (intimacy), there is no longer a close correspondence between the Freudian psychosexual phases and Eriksonian psychosocial ages. Freud's work emphasized the early years, up to the age of puberty. Erikson shows how they contribute to personality development through the age of identity. In his writings, especially the later ones, Freud was not unmindful of the importance of ego psychology and the possibility of personality development beyond adolescence. But there are no "Freudian phases" beyond adolescence. Freud, of course, postulated a genital phase, but that phase is undifferentiated. Beginning with the age of intimacy, Erikson then is "beyond Freud." Though he includes genitality as an important component of intimacy, we have seen that it is a "true genitality" with a good many social overtones.

The seventh age, "Generativity vs. Stagnation," is a further step in constructing the full life cycle. But Erikson does not forget Freud. In his discussion of intimacy, Erikson quotes Freud's response to the question, What did he think a normal person should be able to do well? Freud reportedly said, "To love and to work." Erikson comments: "It pays to ponder on this simple formula; it gets deeper as you think about it." And, indeed, it forms the basis for two of the three remaining ages that Erikson adds to the Freudian structure. Intimacy, then, is on the theme of loving. Generativity is on the theme of working and caring about productivity and creativity.

Generativity begins in wanting and having children, but later involves a "concern in establishing and guiding the next generation." It involves a "belief in the species" that makes a child a "welcome trust of the community." It includes a consciousness of the future, as well as the acceptance of responsibility for the provision of a future for the young, and thus the species. Erikson says:

> At this stage one begins to take one's place in society, and to help in the development and perfection of whatever it produces. And one takes responsibility for that. I know that generativity is not an elegant word, but it means to generate in the most inclusive sense. . . . I use the word 'generativity' because I mean everything that is generated from generation to generation: children, products, ideas, *and* works of art.[3]

While sexual elements are not directly present as the bases of this phase, Erikson sees this age (as he did the age of intimacy) as a psychosexual stage because there is a "libidinal investment in that which is being generated." This comes about through the individual's ability to love himself "in the meeting of bodies and minds," leading to an expansion in number and depth of ego interests. Where this expansion does not occur, one regresses to obsessive pseudointimacy and an accompanying sense of standing still—"stagnation"—and of feeling a sense of "personal impoverishment," or that something is missing.

The eighth age, "Ego Integrity vs. Despair," is above all the integration of all the ego qualities developed in the earlier ages. As we observed earlier, each ego quality continues to develop after emerging from the "nuclear conflict" central to the appropriate age. In the eighth age the various ego qualities reach their most mature development. "Only in him who in some way has taken care of things and has adapted himself to the triumphs and disappointments adherent to being, the originator of others or the generator of products and ideas—only in him may gradually ripen the fruit of these seven stages." The age of ego integrity is thus a culmination of all the earlier stages of development.

The "fruit" of which Erikson speaks is not only a complete personality with which to face life; it is, perhaps more significantly—for by now life has, to a considerable extent, gone by—a way of facing death. A philosophical spirit pervades this age. The individual in the bodily stage that Erikson calls "maturity" is at one with his culture and its history, and with biological reality. He sees "that an individual life is the accidental coincidence of but one life cycle with but one segment of history." There is an acceptance of one's "one and only life cycle as something that had to be and that, by necessity, permitted of no substitutions." The hard factuality of this view is conditioned by an acceptance of the facts, leading away from despair. Moreover, the individual in a sense puts his faith in his culture and in humanity itself. For him, "all human integrity stands or falls with the one style of integrity of which he partakes." Erikson also speaks of a feeling of "comradeship" with the continuities of the culture—"the ordering ways of distant times and different pursuits." Beyond that, man transcends his self-love in a "post-narcissistic love of the human ego," thus experiencing a feeling of "world order and spiritual sense."

And what is despair? It is signified by the fear of death. It manifests the feeling that there is no longer enough time to have another go at it, "to try out alternate roads to integrity." The life cycle that one has lived "is not accepted as the ultimate of life." Death does not lose its sting. Erikson makes no mention of religion. It has no place in his scheme. The ultimate mystery and meaning of life are not in question. There is no mystery. The proximate meaning of life is personality survival and playing one's part, as follower as well as leader, in the ongoing continuity of one's culture, and thus the human species.

Erikson has commented that the life cycle he describes is an attempt to represent normal personality development within a specific cultural and historical framework. The last age may be more an ideal than a normal reality; that question, however, must be taken up elsewhere. For present purposes, the discussion of the eighth age is concluded by noting how Erikson causes it to feed back into the beginning. Webster's Dictionary, he notes, defines *trust*, the first of his ego qualities, as "the assured reliance on another's integrity," which is the last of his ego qualities. Webster was, of course, thinking of business rather than human psychology. Erikson paraphrases the definition, however, seeking to describe the relationship between adult integrity and infantile trust. Healthy children, he says, "will not fear life if their elders have integrity enough not to fear death."

We may wonder if the integrity of the ego, with its philosophical wisdom, comes too late to influence significantly the values of children, especially in a culture such as ours, which seems more and more willing to accede to the values of childhood and youth. We may wonder whether these eight ages are strictly chronological or if, for example, integrity may overlap or even precede generativity in some cases. We may be curious about the data basis for Erikson's work. How did he arrive at his conclusions? What cases? What patterns? Why do they work that way? Good works usually raise as many good questions as they answer. They provide broad conceptual outlines, but do not always provide detailed answers. In this respect, the "Eight Ages of Man" qualifies as better than a good work. It does not present the problem and the findings with the same creativity and extraordinary detail as did Freud in the whole of his work, or even some of the single works. Erikson himself notes that the "foregoing conception of the life cycle . . . awaits systematic treatment." But he is in mighty company. Erikson does not provide that wrenching of thought, that same conceptual blast. He is a builder upon existing frameworks, adding some architectural refinements of his own. He is a linker of thought, a synthesizer, one who "adds to."

Perhaps for this reason, the "eight ages" are remarkable for the complexity of the model. Erikson links together the Freudian psychosexual stages, the cognitive stages of Piaget, which he mentions only in passing, and bodily development—treating the latter in a more inclusive sense than Freud. The theory attempts to encompass the full range of experience that the individual encounters in his culture, as well as the changes inherent in history and the differences inherent in culture and in the institutions of society. Erikson makes connections at each age between the age and particular social institutions relevant to that age. It is a suggestive and interesting—if highly speculative—list. Each successive age and crisis, he notes, has a special relation to one of the basic elements of society, because "the human life cycle and man's institutions have evolved together." The remnants of our "infantile mentality and youthful fervor" are contributors to specific institutions, and in turn our "infantile gains" at each age are supported by the institution. The faith in parents characteristic of the "Age of Trust," for example, finds its institutional safeguard in *religion*. Religion, too, involves a "childlike surrender to a Provider," signs of man's smallness, his misdeeds, and so on. The "Age of Autonomy" has a relationship to the *principle of law and order*. The individual's need to have both his own will and that of others "reaffirmed and delineated within an adult order of things" is the link.

The other ages, and their institutional counterparts are as follows:

Age	Institution
Initiative	economic ethos
Industry	fundamentals of technology
Identity	ideology and aristocracy
Intimacy	an ethical sense
Generativity	all institutions

The eighth age represents an integration of all the others, and has no institutional counterpart.

Most of the connections may be apparent from our discussion of the different ages. The list strongly suggests a unity between and an interpenetration of personality and culture, which is a central aspect of Erikson's thought. It is this concept that seems most striking in the essay. The idea seems most exciting and most frustrating in its complexity, especially since unity and interpenetration are so rarely achieved in actual life—a fact attested to by the turbulence, violence, and instability of both personality and social institutions not only in the present, but in the near and distant past as well.

NOTES

1. Erik Erikson, *Childhood and Society*, 2d ed. (New York: W. W. Norton, 1963).
2. For example, see Richard I. Evans, *Dialogue with Erik Erikson* (New York: Harper & Row, 1967).
3. Erikson, *Childhood and Society*, pp. 50–51.

10. The Discovery of Childhood

Philippe Ariès

Medieval art until about the twelfth century did not know childhood or did not attempt to portray it. It is hard to believe that this neglect was due to incompetence or incapacity; it seems more probable that there was no place for childhood in the medieval world. An Ottonian miniature of the twelfth century provides us with a striking example of the deformation which an artist at that time would inflict on children's bodies.[1] The subject is the scene in the Gospels in which Jesus asks that little children be allowed to come to Him. The Latin text is clear: *parvuli*. Yet the miniaturist has grouped around Jesus what are obviously eight men, without any of the characteristics of childhood; they have simply been depicted on a smaller scale. In a French miniature of the late eleventh century the three children brought to life by Saint Nicholas are also reduced to a smaller scale than the adults, without any other difference in expression or features.[2] A painter would not even hesitate to give the naked body of a child, in the very few cases when it was exposed, the musculature of an adult: this in a Psalter dating from the late twelfth or early thirteenth century, Ishmael, shortly after birth, has the abdominal and pectoral muscles of a man.[3] The thirteenth century, although it showed more understanding in its presentation of childhood, remained faithful to this method.[4] In Saint Louis's moralizing Bible, children are depicted more often, but they are still indicated only by their size. In an episode in the life of Jacob, Isaac is shown sitting between his two wives, surrounded by some fifteen little men who come up to the level of the grown-ups' waists: these are their children.[5] When Job is rewarded for his faith and becomes rich once more, the illuminator depicts his good fortune by placing Job between an equal number of cattle on the left and children on the right: the traditional picture of fecundity inseparable from wealth. In another illustration in the Book of Job, some children are lined up in order of size.

In the thirteenth-century Gospel-book of the Sainte-Chapelle, in an illustration of the miracle of the loaves and fishes, Christ and one of the Apostles are shown standing on either side of a little man who comes up

From *Centuries of Childhood* by Philippe Ariès, translated by Robert Baldick. Copyright © 1962 by Jonathan Cape Ltd. Reprinted by permission of Alfred A. Knopf, Inc.

to their waists: no doubt the child who carried the fishes.[6] In the world of Romanesque formulas, right up to the end of the thirteenth century, there are no children characterized by a special expression but only men on a reduced scale. This refusal to accept child morphology in art is to be found too in most of the ancient civilizations. A fine Sardinian bronze of the ninth century B.C. shows a sort of Pietà: a mother holding in her arms the somewhat bulky body of her son.[7] The catalogue tells us: "The little masculine figure could also be a child which, in accordance with the formula adopted in ancient times by other peoples, had been represented as an adult." Everything in fact would seem to suggest that the realistic representation of children or the idealization of childhood, its grace and rounded charms, was confined to Greek art. Little Eroses proliferated in the Hellenistic period, but childhood disappeared from iconography together with the other Hellenistic themes, and Romanesque art returned to that rejection of the special features of childhood which had already characterized the periods of antiquity before Hellenism. This is no mere coincidence. Our starting-point in this study is a world of pictorial representation in which childhood is unknown; literary historians such as Monsignor Calvé have made the same observation about the epic, in which child prodigies behave with the courage and physical strength of doughty warriors. This undoubtedly means that the men of the tenth and eleventh centuries did not dwell on the image of childhood, and that that image had neither interest nor even reality for them. It suggests too that in the realm of real life, and not simply in that of aesthetic transposition, childhood was a period of transition which passed quickly and which was just as quickly forgotten.

Such is our starting-point. How do we get from there to the little imps of Versailles, to the photographs of children of all ages in our family albums?

About the thirteenth century, a few types of children are to be found which appear to be a little closer to the modern concept of childhood.

There is the angel, depicted in the guise of a very young man, a young adolescent: a *clergeon*, as Père du Colombier remarks.[8] But how old is this "little clerk"? The *clergeons* were children of various ages who were trained to make the responses in church and who were destined for holy orders, seminarists of a sort in a period when there were no seminaries and when schooling in Latin, the only kind of schooling that existed, was reserved for future clerks. "Here," says one of the *Miracles de Notre-Dame*, "there were little children who had few letters and would rather have fed at their mother's breast [but children were weaned very late at that time: Shakespeare's Juliet was still being breast-fed at three] than do divine service."[9] The angel of Reims, to take one example, is a big boy rather than a child, but the artists have stressed the round, pretty, and somewhat effeminate features of youths barely out of childhood. We have already come a long way from the small-scale adults of the Ottonian miniature. This type of adolescent angel was to become extremely common in the fourteenth century and was to last to the very end of the Italian *Quattrocento*: the angels of Fra Angelico, Botticelli and Ghirlandajo all belong to it.

The second type of child was to be the model and ancestor of all the little children in the history of art: the Infant Jesus, or the Infant Notre-Dame, for here childhood is linked to the mystery of motherhood and the Marian cult. To begin with, Jesus, like other children, is an adult on a reduced scale: a little God-priest in His majesty, depicted by Theo-tokos. The evolution towards a more realistic and more sentimental representation of childhood begins very early on in painting: in a minia-ture of the second half of the twelfth century, Jesus is shown wearing a thin, almost transparent shift and standing with His arms round His mother's neck, nestling against her, cheek to cheek.[10] With the Virgin's motherhood, childhood enters the world of pictorial representation. In the thirteenth century it inspires other family scenes. In Saint Louis's moralizing Bible,[11] there are various family scenes in which parents are shown surrounded by their children with the same tender respect as on the rood-screen at Chartres: thus in a picture of Moses and his family, husband and wife are holding hands while the children (little men) sur-rounding them are stretching out their hands towards their mother. These cases, however, remained rare: the touching idea of childhood remained limited to the Infant Jesus until the fourteenth century, when, as is well known, Italian art was to help to spread and develop it.

A third type of child appeared in the Gothic period: the naked child. The Infant Jesus was scarcely ever depicted naked. More often than not, like other children of His age, He was chastely wrapped in swaddling-clothes or clad in a shift or a dress. He would not be undressed until the end of the Middle Ages. Those few miniatures in the moralizing Bibles which depicted children showed them fully dressed, except in the case of the Innocents or the dead children whose mothers Solomon was judging. It was the allegory of death and the soul which was to introduce into the world of forms the picture of childish nudity. Already in the pre-Byzan-tine iconography of the fifth century, in which many features of the fu-ture Romanesque art made their appearance, the bodies of the dead were reduced in scale. Corpses were smaller than living bodies. In the *Iliad* in the Ambrosian Library the dead in the battle scenes are half the size of the living.[12] In French medieval art the soul was depicted as a little child who was naked and usually sexless. The Last Judgments lead the souls of the righteous to Abraham's bosom in this form.[13] The dying man breathes the child out through his mouth in a symbolic representation of the soul's departure. This is also how the entry of the soul into the world is depicted, whether it is a case of a holy, miraculous conception—the Angel of the Annunciation presenting the Virgin with a naked child, Jesus's soul[14]—or a case of a perfectly natural conception: a couple rest-ing in bed apparently quite innocently, but something must have hap-pened, for a naked child can be seen flying through the air and entering the woman's mouth—"the creation of the human soul by natural means."[15]

In the course of the fourteenth and particularly the fifteenth century, these medieval types would develop further, but in the direction already indicated in the thirteenth century. We have already observed that the angel-cum-altar-boy would go on playing its part, without very much change, in the religious painting of the fifteenth century. On the other hand the theme of the Holy Childhood would never cease developing in both scope and variety from the fourteenth century on—its popularity and fecundity bearing witness to the progress, in the collective consciousness, of that idea of childhood which only a keen observer can distinguish in the thirteenth century and which did not exist at all in the eleventh century. In the group of Jesus and His mother, the artist would stress the graceful, affectionate, naive aspects of early childhood: the child seeking its mother's breast or getting ready to kiss or caress her, the child playing the traditional childhood games with fruit or a bird on a leash, the child eating its pap, the child being wrapped in its swaddling-clothes. Every gesture that could be observed—at least by somebody prepared to pay attention to them—would henceforth be reproduced in pictorial form. These features of sentimental realism would take a long time to extend beyond the frontiers of religious iconography, which is scarcely surprising when one remembers that this was also the case with landscape and genre painting. It remains none the less true that the group of Virgin and Child changed in character and became more and more profane: the picture of a scene of everyday life.

Timidly at first, then with increasing frequency, the painters of religious childhood went beyond that of Jesus. First of all they turned to the childhood of the Virgin, which inspired at least two new and popular themes: the theme of the birth of the Virgin—people in Saint Anne's bedroom fussing over the new-born child, bathing her, wrapping her in swaddling-clothes and showing her to her mother—and the theme of the Virgin's education: a reading lesson, with the Virgin following the words in a book held by Saint Anne. Then came other holy childhoods: those of Saint John, the Infant Jesus's playmate, Saint James, and the children of the holy women, Mary Zebedee and Mary Salome. A completely new iconography thus came into existence, presenting more and more scenes of childhood, and taking care to gather together in similar groups these holy children, with or without their mothers.

This iconography, which generally speaking started with the fourteenth century, coincided with a profusion of priors' tales and legends, such as those in the *Miracles de Notre-Dame*. It continued up to the seventeenth century and its development can be followed in painting, tapestry and sculpture. We shall in any case have occasion to return to it with regard to the religious practices of childhood.

From this religious iconography of childhood, a lay iconography eventually detached itself in the fifteenth and sixteenth centuries. This was not yet the portrayal of the child on its own. Genre painting was developing at this time by means of the transformation of a conventional allegorical iconography inspired by the antiquo-medieval concept of Nature: ages of life, seasons, senses, elements. Subject pictures and anecdotal paintings began to take the place of static representations of symbolic characters. We shall have cause to deal with this evolution at some length later on. Let us merely note here that the child became one of the characters most frequently found in these anecdotal paintings: the child with his family; the child with his playmates, who were often adults; the child in a crowd, but very definitely "spotlighted" in his mother's arms, or holding her hand or playing or even piddling; the child among the crowds watching miracles or martyrdoms, listening to sermons, or following liturgical rites such as presentations or circumcisions; the child serving as an apprentice to a goldsmith or a painter or some other craftsman; or the child at school, an old and popular theme which went back to the fourteenth century and would go on inspiring subject paintings up to the nineteenth century.

These subject paintings were not as a general rule devoted to the exclusive portrayal of childhood, but in a great many cases there were children among the characters depicted, both principal and secondary. And this suggests the following ideas: first, children mingled with adults in everyday life, and any gathering for the purpose of work, relaxation or sport brought together both children and adults; secondly, painters were particularly fond of depicting childhood for its graceful or picturesque qualities (the taste for the picturesque anecdote developed in the fifteenth and sixteenth centuries and coincided with the appreciation of childhood's charms), and they delighted in stressing the presence of a child in a group or a crowd. Of these two ideas one now strikes us as out of date, for today, as also towards the end of the nineteenth century, we tend to separate the world of children from that of adults; the other foreshadows the modern idea of childhood.

The origins of the themes of the angel, the holy childhoods, and their subsequent iconographical developments date as far back as the thirteenth century; two new types of child portrayal appeared in the fifteenth century: the portrait and the *putto*. The child, as we have seen, was not missing from the Middle Ages, at least from the thirteenth century on, but there was never a portrait of him, the portrait of a real child, as he was at a certain moment of his life.

In the funeral effigies listed in the Gaignières Collection,[16] the child appeared only at a very late date, in the sixteenth century. Curiously enough, his first appearance was not on his own tomb or that of his parents but on that of his teachers. On the tombs of the masters of Bologna, the teacher was shown surrounded by his pupils.[17] As early as 1378, Cardinal de La Grange, the Bishop of Amiens, had the two princes he had tutored portrayed at the ages of ten and seven on a "handsome pillar" in his cathedral.[18] No one thought of keeping a picture of a child if that child had either lived to grow to manhood or had died in infancy. In the first case, childhood was simply an unimportant phase of which there was no need to keep any record; in the second case, that of the dead child, it was thought that the little thing which had disappeared so soon in life was not worthy of remembrance: there were far too many children whose survival was problematical. The general feeling was, and for a long time remained, that one had several children in order to keep just a few. As late as the seventeenth century, in *Le Caquet de l'accouchée*, we have a neighbor, standing at the bedside of a woman who has just given birth, the mother of five "little brats," and calming her fears with these words: "Before they are old enough to bother you, you will have lost half of them, or perhaps all of them."[19] A strange consolation! People could not allow themselves to become too attached to something that was regarded as a probable loss. This is the reason for certain remarks which shock our present-day sensibility, such as Montaigne's observation: "I have lost two or three children in their infancy, not without regret, but without great sorrow,"[20] or Molière's comment on Louison in *Le Malade imaginaire*: "The little girl doesn't count." Most people probably felt, like Montaigne, that children had "neither mental activities nor recognizable bodily shape." Mme de Sévigné records without any sign of surprise[21] a similar remark made by Mme de Coetquen when the latter fainted on receiving the news of her little daughter's death: "She is greatly distressed and says that she will never again have one so pretty."

Nobody thought, as we ordinarily think today, that every child already contained a man's personality. Too many of them died. "All mine die in infancy," wrote Montaigne. This indifference was a direct and inevitable consequence of the demography of the period. It lasted until the nineteenth century in the depths of the country, in so far as it was compatible with Christianity, which respected the immortal soul in every child that had been baptized. It is recorded that the people of the Basque country retained for a very long time the custom of burying children that had died without baptism in the house, on the threshold, or in the garden. Here we may perhaps see a survival of ancient rites, of sacrificial offerings, or rather it may be that the child that had died too soon in life was buried almost anywhere, much as we today bury a domestic pet, a cat or a dog. He was such an unimportant little thing, so inadequately involved in life, that nobody had any fears that he might return after death to pester the living. It is interesting to note that in the frontispiece to the *Tabula Cebetis* Mérian has placed the little children in a sort of marginal zone, between the earth from which they have emerged and the life into which they have not yet entered, and from which they are separated by a portico bearing the inscription *Introitus ad vitam*.[22] This feeling of indifference towards a too fragile childhood is not really very far removed from the callousness of the Roman or Chinese societies which practiced the exposure of new-born children. We can now understand the gulf which separates our concept of childhood from that which existed before the demographic revolution or its preceding stages. There is nothing about this callousness which should surprise us: it was only natural in the community conditions of the time. On the other hand, there are grounds for surprise in the earliness of the idea of childhood, seeing that conditions were still so unfavorable to it. Statistically and objectively speaking, this idea should have appeared much later. True, there was the taste for the picturesque, pleasing aspects of the little creatures, the idea of the charms of childhood and the entertainment to be derived from the ingenuous antics of infancy: "puerile nonsense," as Montaigne said, in which we adults take an interest "for our amusement, like monkeys."[23] But this idea could quite easily go hand in hand with indifference towards the essential, definitive personality of the child: the immortal soul. The new taste for the portrait indicated that children were emerging from the anonymity in which their slender chance of survival had maintained them. It is in fact quite remarkable that at that period of demographic wastage anyone should have felt a desire to record and keep the likeness of a child that would go on living or of a child that was dead. The portrait of the dead child in particular proves that that child was no longer generally considered as an inevitable loss. This solicitous attitude did not exclude or eliminate the opposite attitude, that of Montaigne, the neighbor at the mother's bedside, and Molière: down to the eighteenth century they coexisted. It was only in the eighteenth century, with the beginning of Malthusianism and the extension of contraceptive practices, that the idea of necessary wastage would disappear.

The appearance of the portrait of the dead child in the sixteenth century accordingly marked a very important moment in the history of feelings. This portrait was a funeral effigy to begin with. The child was not at first portrayed alone, but on his parents' tomb. Gaignières's records show the child by his mother's side and very tiny, or else at his parents' feet.[24] These tombs all date back to the sixteenth century: 1503, 1530, 1560. Among the interesting tombs in Westminster Abbey, let us note that of the Marchioness of Winchester, who died in 1586.[25] The recumbent figure of the Marchioness is life-size; represented on the front of her tomb on a smaller scale are her husband the Marquess, kneeling, and the tiny tomb of a dead child. At Westminster too, on a tomb dating from 1615 to 1620, the Earl and Countess of Shrewsbury are represented in a pair of recumbent figures, with their little daughter kneeling at their feet, her hands folded in prayer. It should be noted here that the children who surround the dead are not always dead themselves: the whole family is gathered round the heads of that family, as if it were at the time when they breathed their last. But beside the children who are still alive the sculptor has portrayed those who are already dead; there is always an indication to distinguish them: they are smaller and they hold a cross in their hands (as on John Coke's tomb at Holkham, 1639) or else a skull (on Cope of Ayley's tomb at Hambledon, 1633, there are four boys and three girls around the dead parents, and one boy and one girl are holding a skull).

At Toulouse in the Musée des Augustins there is an extremely interesting triptych that comes from the Du Mège Collection.[26] The volets are dated 1610. On either side of a "Descent from the Cross" the donors, a husband and wife, are depicted on their knees, together with their ages. Both are sixty-three. Next to the man there is a child, wearing what was then the fashion for very little children, under five years of age: a girl's dress and pinafore and a big bonnet with feathers. The child is dressed in bright, rich colors, green brocaded in gold, which throw into relief the severity of the donors' black clothes. This woman of sixty-three cannot possibly have a child of five. It is clearly a dead child, no doubt an only son whose memory the old couple treasured and whom they wanted to show beside them in his best clothes.

It was a pious custom in the old days to present churches with a picture or a stained-glass window, and in the sixteenth century the donor had himself portrayed with his whole family. On the walls and pillars of German churches one can still see a great many pictures of this kind which are in fact family portraits. In Saint Sebastian's in Nürnberg, in a portrait from the second half of the sixteenth century, the father is shown in the foreground with two full-grown sons behind him and then a scarcely distinguishable bunch of six boys crowded together, hiding behind each other so that some of them are barely visible. Surely these must be dead children.

A similar picture, dated 1560, and kept in Bregenz Museum, has the children's ages recorded on the banderoles: three boys, aged one, two and three; five girls, aged one, two, three, four and five. But the eldest girl of five has the same size and dress as the youngest of one. She has been given her place in the family group just as if she had gone on living, but she has been portrayed at the age when she died.

These family groups are naive, clumsy, monotonous works without style; their painters, like their models, remain unknown or obscure. It is a different matter when the donor has obtained the services of a celebrated painter: in such instances art historians have carried out the research required to identify the figures in a famous painting. This is the case with the Meyer family which Holbein portrayed in 1526 at the Virgin's feet. We know that of the six people in the picture three had died in 1526: Jacob Meyer's first wife and her two boys, one of whom were dead at the age of ten and the other, who is shown naked, at an earlier age.

Here in fact we have a custom which became widespread in the sixteenth century and remained so until the mid-nineteenth century. Versailles Museum has a picture by Nocret portraying the families of Louis XIV and his brother; this painting is famous because the King and the princes are half-naked—the men at least—like gods of Olympus. We would draw attention to one detail here: in the foreground, at Louis

XIV's feet, Nocret has placed a framed picture showing two little children who had died in infancy.

Gaignières's records note as early as the end of the sixteenth century some tombs bearing effigies of children on their own: one dates from 1584, the other from 1608. The child is shown in the costume peculiar to his age, in a dress and bonnet, like the child in the Toulouse "Descent from the Cross." When within the two years of 1606 and 1607 James I lost two daughters, one when she was three days old and the other at two years of age, he had them portrayed fully dressed on their tombs at Westminster, and he gave instructions that the younger should be shown lying in an alabaster cradle in which all the accessories—the lace of her swaddling-clothes and her bonnet—should be faithfully reproduced to create the illusion of reality. The inscription on the tomb gives a good idea of the pious feeling which endowed this three-day-old child with a definite personality: *Rosula Regia prae-propero Fato decerpta, parentibus erepta, ut in Christi Rosario reflorescat.*

Apart from these mortuary effigies, portraits of children shown separately from their parents were a rarity until the end of the sixteenth century: witness the painting of the Dauphin, Charles Orlando, by the Maître de Moulins, another instance of the pious regard felt for children who had died at an early age. On the other hand, they became very common at the beginning of the seventeenth century; it is clear that it had become customary to preserve by means of the painter's art the ephemeral appearance of childhood. In the portraits of this period the child parted company with the family, just as a century earlier, at the beginning of the sixteenth century, the family had parted company with the religious section of the presentation portrait. Henceforth he would be depicted by himself and for himself: this was the great novelty of the seventeenth century. The child would be one of its favorite models. There are countless examples among the leading painters of the period: Rubens, Van Dyck, Franz Hals, Le Nain, Philippe de Champaigne. Some of these painters portray little princes, as in the picture of Charles I's children by Van Dyck or that of James II's children by Largillière; others, the offspring of great lords, such as the three children painted by Van Dyck, the eldest of whom is wearing a sword;[27] and others, well-to-do bourgeois such as those depicted by Le Nain or Philippe de Champaigne. Sometimes there is an inscription giving the child's name and age, as used to be the custom for adults. Now the child is all alone (see Philippe de Champaigne's work at Grenoble), now the painter gathers together several children from the same family. This last is a popular type of portrait, favored by a great many anonymous painters, and often to be found in provincial art-galleries or in antique-shops. Henceforth every family wanted portraits of its children, and portraits painted while they were still children. The custom originated in the seventeenth century and is still with us. Photography took over from painting in the nineteenth century: the idea remained the same.

Before finishing with the portraits, we must mention the pictures of children on *ex-votos*, the plaques placed in churches to record the making or granting of a prayer. There are some in the museum of Puy Cathedral, and the Eighteenth Century Exhibition of 1958 in Paris revealed an astonishing portrait of a sick child which must also be an *ex-voto*.

Thus, although demographic conditions did not greatly change between the thirteenth and seventeenth centuries, and although child mortality remained at a very high level, a new sensibility granted these fragile, threatened creatures a characteristic which the world had hitherto failed to recognize in them: as if it were only then that the common conscience had discovered that the child's soul too was immortal. There can be no doubt that the importance accorded to the child's personality was linked with the growing influence of Christianity on life and manners.

This interest shown in the child preceded by more than a century the change in demographic conditions which can be roughly dated from Jenner's great discovery. Correspondences such as that of General de Martange[28] show that certain families insisted at that time on having their children vaccinated; this precaution against the smallpox reveals a state of mind which must have favored other hygienic practices at the same time, producing a reduction in the death-rate which was counter-balanced to some extent by an increasingly widespread control of the birth-rate.

NOTES

1. Gospel-book of Otto III, Munich.
2. "Vie et miracle de saint Nicolas," Bibliothèque Nationale.
3. Psalter of Saint Louis of Leyden.
4. Compare the scene, "Suffer the little children to come to me," in Otto's Gospel-book and in the *Bible moralisée de saint Louis*, f° 505.
5. *Bible morelisée de saint Louis*, f° 5. A. de Laborde, *Bibles moralisées illustrées*, 1911–21, 4 vols. of plates.
6. Gospel-book in the Sainte-Chapelle; scene reproduced in H. Martin, *La Miniature française*, plate VII.
7. *Exposition des bronzes sardes*, Bibliothèque Nationale, 1954, no. 25, plate XI.
8. P. du Colombier, *L'Enfant au Moyen Age*, 1951.
9. *Miracles de Notre-Dame*, edited by G. F. Warner, 1885.
10. *Manuscrits à peinture du VIIe au XIIe siècle*, exhibition at the Bibliothèque Nationale, 1954, no. 330, plate XXX.
11. See note 5.
12. *Iliad*, Ambrosian Library, Milan.
13. Rampilly.
14. See note 5.
15. *Miroir d'humilité*, Valenciennes, f° 18, early fifteenth century.
16. Gaignières, *Les Tombeaux*.
17. G. Zaccagnini, *La vita dei maestri e degli scolari nella studio di Bologna*. Geneva, 1926, plates IX, X.
18. Before this, the representation of children on tombs was rare.
19. *Le Caquet de l'accouchée*, 1622.
20. Montaigne, *Essais*, II, 8.
21. Mme de Sévigné, *Lettres*, August 19, 1671.

22. Mérian, *Tabula Cebetis*, 1655. Cf. Lebègue, "Le Peintre Varin et le Tableau de Cebes," *Arts*, 1952, pp. 167–71.
23. Montaigne, *Essais*, II, 8.
24. Gaignières, *Les Tombeaux*.
25. F. Bond, *Westminster Abbey*, London, 1909.
26. Musée des Augustins, no. 465 in the catalogue.
27. Van Dyck, K. d. K., plate CCXIV.
28. *Correspondence inédite du général de Martange*, 1756–82, edited by Bréard, 1898.

---

11. Role Concepts
Erving Goffman

The classic formulation of role concepts comes from the social-anthropological tradition[1] and has led to the development of a conceptual framework sometimes called "role theory." A *status* is a position in some system or pattern of positions and is related to the other positions in the unit through reciprocal ties, through rights and duties binding on the incumbents. *Role* consists of the activity the incumbent would engage in were he to act solely in terms of the normative demands upon someone in his position. Role in this normative sense is to be distinguished from *role performance* or role enactment, which is the actual conduct of a particular individual while on duty in his position. (Accordingly, it is a position that can be entered, filled, and left, not a role, for a role can only be performed; but no student seems to hold to these consistencies, nor will I.) In describing a role there is, of course, a problem of how much detail to give, the amount sometimes being tacitly determined unsystematically by the degree of familiarity the reader is assumed to have with the role in question.

The individual's role enactment occurs largely through a cycle of face-to-face social situations with *role others,* that is, relevant audiences. These various kinds of role others for an individual in role, when taken together, have recently been termed a *role-set.*[2] The role-set for a doctor, for example, contains colleagues, nurses, patients, and hospital administrators. The norms relating the individual to performers of one of the roles in his role-set will have a special and non-conflictful relation to one another—more so than the norms relating the individual to different kinds of role others. The over-all role associated with a position falls into *role sectors*[3] or subroles, each having to do with a particular

From *Encounters* by Erving Goffman, copyright © 1961 by The Bobbs-Merrill Company, Inc., reprinted by permission of the publisher.

kind of role other. Doctor-nurse is a role sector of the doctor role; doctor-patient, another. Social changes in a role can be traced by the loss or gain to the role-set of types of role other. However, even within the special sector of a role relating the performer to one type of role other, the activities involved may themselves fall into different, somewhat independent parcels or bundles, and through time these may also be reduced or added to, a bundle at a time. In any case, we ought not to be embarrassed by the fact that what is handled from one kind of position in one organization may be apportioned to two or three kinds of positions in another organization. We need only claim to know how a role is likely to be broken up should it come to be divided—the points of cleavage—and what roles are likely to be combined at times of organizational retrenchment.

The elementary unit of role analysis, as Linton was at pains to point out,[4] is not the individual but the individual enacting his bundle of obligatory activity. The system or pattern borrows only a part of the individual, and what he does or is at other times and places is not the first concern. The role others for whom he performs similarly represent only slices of these others. Presumably his contribution and their contribution, differentiated and interdependent, fit together into a single assemblage of activity, this *system* or pattern being the real concern of role analysis.

The role perspective has definite implications of a social-psychological kind. In entering the position, the incumbent finds that he must take on the whole array of action encompassed by the corresponding role, so role implies a social determinism and a doctrine about socialization. We do not take on items of conduct one at a time but rather a whole harness load of them and may anticipatorily learn to be a horse even while being pulled like a wagon.[5] Role, then, is the basic unit of socialization. It is through roles that tasks in society are allocated and arrangements made to enforce their performance.

Recruitment for positions is restrictively regulated in some way, assuring that the incumbents will possess certain minimal qualifications, official and unofficial, technically relevant and irrelevant.[6] Incumbency tends to be symbolized through status cues of dress and manner, permitting those who engage in a situation to know with whom they are dealing. In some cases there will also be a role term of reference and address. Each position tends to be accorded some invidious social value, bringing a corresponding amount of prestige or contamination to the individual who fills it.

For this paper, it is important to note that in performing a role the individual must see to it that the impressions of him that are conveyed in the situation are compatible with role-appropriate personal qualities effectively imputed to him: a judge is supposed to be deliberate and sober; a pilot, in a cockpit, to be cool; a bookkeeper to be accurate and neat in doing his work. These personal qualities, effectively imputed and effectively claimed, combine with a position's title, when there is one, to provide a basis of *self-image* for the incumbent and a basis for the image that his role others will have of him. A self, then, virtually awaits the individual entering a position; he need only conform to the pressures on him and he will find a *me* ready-made for him. In the language of Kenneth Burke, doing is being.

Sociologists have added several concepts to round out the Lintonian perspective; these can be introduced here, along with some effort at clarification.

It can be useful to distinguish between the *regular performance* of a role and a *regular performer* of a role. If, for example, a funeral parlor is to stay in business, then the role of the director, of the immediately bereaved, and of the deceased must be performed regularly; but, of these regularly performed roles, only the director will be a regular performer. The immediately bereaved may play the same role on a few other occasions, but certainly the role of the deceased is played but once by any one individual. We can now see that to speak in common-sense terms of an "irregular" performer is to refer to someone performing only a few times what is usually performed by a regular performer.

The *function* of a role is the part it plays in the maintenance or destruction of the system or pattern as a whole, the terms *eufunction* and *dysfunction* sometimes being employed to distinguish the supportive from the destructive effects.[7] Where the functional effect of a role is openly known and avowed, the term *manifest* function is sometimes employed; where these effects are not regularly foreseen and, especially, where this foresight might alter effects, the term *latent* is sometimes used.[8]

A concept that is often employed in the discussion of roles is that of *commitment*. I propose to restrict this term to questions of impersonally enforced structural arrangements. An individual becomes committed to something when, because of the fixed and interdependent character of many institutional arrangements, his doing or being this something irrevocably conditions other important possibilities in his life, forcing him to take courses of action, causing other persons to build up their activity on the basis of his continuing in his current undertakings, and rendering him vulnerable to unanticipated consequences of these undertakings.[9] He thus becomes locked into a position and coerced into living up to the promises and sacrifices built into it. Typically, a person will become deeply committed only to a role he regularly performs, and it is left to gallants, one-shot gamblers, and the foolhardy to become committed to a role they do not perform regularly.

The self-image available for anyone entering a particular position is one of which he may become affectively and cognitively enamored, desiring and expecting to see himself in terms of the enactment of the role and the self-identification emerging from this enactment. I will speak here of the individual becoming *attached* to his position and its role, adding only that in the case of larger social units—groups, not positions—attachment is more likely to have a selfless component.[10] An appreciation can grow up concerning how attached an individual ought properly to be to a particular role, giving rise to the possibility that, compared to this moral norm, a performer may be overattached to his role or alienated from it. For example, it is said that a new capitalist of the seventeenth century in Europe who entered and left an area of trade according to the temporary profit in it was felt by members of crafts and guilds to be sinfully unattached to what he dealt in.[11] Currently, it is felt to be sound mental hygiene for an individual to be attached to the role he performs, especially if he is a committed and regular performer of it. In all this there may be a middle-class bias, with our understanding of attachment coming from the learned professions, where attachment traditionally is great, to the neglect of the many roles that persons play with detachment, shame, or resentment.

In describing individuals' attachment to a role, it is sometimes said that they have committed their self-feelings to it, but in this paper I shall try to restrict the concept of commitment to the forced-consequence sense previously suggested.[12] We will then be able to see that while attachment and commitment are often found together, as virtue doth cover necessity, there may also be discrepancies. Adoption agencies, for example, deal with two kinds of couples, the too fertile and the insufficiently fertile, the first being committed to the parent role without being attached to it, and the second being attached to the role without yet being committed to it.

Although traditional role analysis starts by focusing on the pattern or system arising from the differentiation and integration of roles, a second concern has emerged, related to, but analytically quite different from, the first, with the individual as the central unit. It is a basic assumption of role analysis that each individual will be involved in more than one system or pattern and, therefore, perform more than one role. Each individual will, therefore, have several selves, providing us with the interesting problem of how these selves are related. The model of man according to the initial role perspective is that of a kind of holding company for a set of not relevantly connected roles; it is the concern of the second perspective to find out how the individual runs this holding company.

While manifestly participating in one system of roles, the individual will have some capacity to hold in abeyance his involvement in other patterns, thus sustaining one or more dormant roles that are enacted roles on other occasions. This capacity supports a life cycle, a calendar cycle, and a daily cycle of role enactments; such scheduling implies some jurisdictional agreements as to where and what the individual is to be when. This *role-segregation* may be facilitated by *audience-segregation,* so that those who figure in one of the individual's major role-sets do not figure in another, thereby allowing the individual to possess contradictory qualities. Nevertheless, a person such as a surgeon, who keeps his surgical tools off his kitchen table and his wife off his other table, may someday find himself with the role dilemma of treating an other both as a kinsman and as a body. The embarrassment and vacillation characteristic of *role conflict* presumably result. The identification of this kind of trouble is not a limitation of role analysis but one of its main values, for we are led to consider mechanisms for avoiding such conflict or dealing with unavoidable conflict.[13]

Given the role perspective, it is of course possible to have a clinical, historical, or biographical interest, and to be concerned with all the roles performed by a particular concrete individual. Uusally, however, role analysis is pitched in terms of the roles of some particular category of person, such as doctor or female. Often, in addition, concern is narrowed to some sphere of life, such as a formal organization, a social establishment, an occupational group, or a task activity. It may be added that while these distinctions in focus are easy enough to stipulate, it is apparently much less easy to keep within one focus once it has been selected.[14]

NOTES

1. Principally Ralph Linton, *The Study of Man* (New York: Appleton-Century, 1936), especially Chap. 8, "Status and Rôle."
2. R. K. Merton, "The Role-Set: Problems in Sociological Theory," *British Journal of Sociology*, 8 (1957), pp 106–20. Presumably, a term will be needed to refer to the complement of individuals within *one* element in the role set, so that we can discuss the fact that some role others, such as wife, contain only one performer, while other role others, such as patient, contain many.
3. Neal Gross, Ward Mason, and Alexander McEachern, *Explorations in Role Analysis* (New York: Wiley, 1958), especially p. 62. This book provides a very useful treatment of role. See also the helpful article by F. L. Bates, "Position, Role, and Status: A Reformulation of Concepts," *Social Forces*, 34 (1956), pp. 313–21.
4. Linton, *op. cit.*, p. 113.
5. See Orville Brim, unpublished paper, "Socialization as Role Learning."
6. E. C. Hughes, "Dilemmas and Contradictions of Status," *American Journal of Sociology*, 50 (1945), pp. 353–59.
7. M. J. Levy, Jr., *The Structure of Society* (Princeton: Princeton University Press, 1952), pp. 76–79. It sometimes seems to be the hope of so-called functional analysis to transform all role analysis into role-function analysis.
8. R. K. Merton, *Social Theory and Social Structure* (revised ed.; Glencoe: The Free Press, 1957), Chap. 1, "Manifest and Latent Functions," pp. 19–84, especially definitions, p. 51.
9. This last point is based on the thorough statement by Philip Selznick, *TVA and the Grass Roots* (Berkeley: University of California Press, 1953), pp. 255–59. A general consideration of the term commitment may be found in Howard S. Becker, "Notes on the Concept of Commitment," *American Journal of Sociology*, 66 (1960), pp. 32–40.
10. Strictly speaking, while it is possible for an individual to become attached to a position (as when a Queen becomes convinced of the public value of monarchical government), to be attached to a position usually means to be attached to one's own incumbency of it.
11. See, for example, Werner Sombart, *The Jews and Modern Capitalism* (Glencoe: The Free Press, 1951), Chap. 7, "The Growth of a Capitalistic Point of View in Economic Life."

12. K. T. Erikson, in an interesting paper, "Patient Role and Social Uncertainty—A Dilemma of the Mentally Ill," *Psychiatry*, 20 (1957), pp. 263–74, suggests a different pairing of terms: "commitment" to refer to the process by which an individual comes to take a role to heart, and "validation" to refer to the process by which the community comes to accord a given role to the individual, ratifying his right to perform it.
13. For example, see S. E. Perry and L. C. Wynne, "Role Conflict, Role Redefinition, and Social Change in a Clinical Research Organization," *Social Forces*, 38 (1959), pp. 62–65.
14. A very useful treatment of these issues can be found in Gross, *op. cit.*, pp. 56–57, under the heading "situational specifications."

---

12. The Person

Hans Gerth and C. Wright Mills

In discussing the psychic integration of emotion, impulse, and perception, we found it necessary to consider man as a person as well as man as an animal organism. The conception of the psychic structure is closely linked to that of the person, and the person as such, in turn, is predominantly a creature of interpersonal situations. Indeed, this integration of person with others—that is to say, the roles that persons play—is the key to the understanding of the concept: the person is composed of the combination of roles that he enacts.

Awareness, or consciousness, is a reference to the field of our experiences at any given waking moment; it is *what* we are aware of. Thus we may experience a crowd of people, or a forest of trees; or we may experience a certain body tone, a diffuse feeling of tiredness, the localized pangs of hunger, or a knife cutting our left hand. To be conscious of external events in just the way that we are, requires an organism with certain kinds of sense organs; the anatomy and physiology of these organs are as necessary for our consciousness of a brown dog as is the dog as a brown physical thing. Anyone who is equipped with the appropriate kind of eyes can be aware of the dog. But awareness of our toothache, hunger pangs, or body tone of buoyancy is restricted to each of us individually. Yet, our awareness of external and of internal events, is primarily rooted in the organism and the psychic structure.

In *self*-consciousness, or *self*-awareness, however, the person is also involved. Although our bodily feelings and our awareness of our toes, hands, and noses are involved in our image of self, or at least often color

From *Character and Social Structure* by Hans Gerth and C. Wright Mills, copyright, 1953, by Harcourt Brace Jovanovich, Inc., and reprinted with their permission.

it with feelings and sensitivities, our total self-image involves our relations to other persons and their appraisals of us.

I Language, Role, Person

The use of language is the most important mechanism of interpersonal conduct, and the major source of knowledge of our selves.

The speech apparatus of the organism is a necessary condition for the acquisition and use of language. As an organism, man can make a wider variety of articulate noises than any other animal. Moreover, he can control his noises, varying them according to tone, pitch, percussion, inflection, and intervening silences; he can gurgle, goo, squeak, and grunt in a wonderfully flexible manner. From this wide variety of sounds, certain patterns of articulate sounds are selected and socially fixed as units with definite meanings. Strictly speaking, there are no "organs of speech"; rather, as Edward Sapir put it, there are "organs that are incidentally useful in the production of speech sounds."[1] The controlled sounds of speech require delicate co-ordinations of an elaborate muscle and nervous structure; they involve the teeth, tongue and lips, the larynx and the lungs, as well as the auditory senses.

Yet these organic conditions are not sufficient for human speech. The human organism isolated from all other human beings probably would not develop intelligible speech, even though it had all the organically required equipment.

All men are biologically similar in their speech equipment, yet they learn variously to speak Chinese, Portuguese, Brooklynese, or English, according to which is spoken in the community in which they grow up. No doubt the larynx of a North Chinese peasant is not very different from the larynx of an East End Londoner, but the language they come to understand and use is quite different. When we say that the Londoners and the Chinese cannot "understand" the different articulate noises they have respectively learned to make, we refer to the fact that the sounds which one makes do not "mean" the same thing to the other. Now, what is meant by "mean the same thing"?

When a sound which one person utters calls out similar responses in those who hear it as in those who utter it, then the sound has a common meaning. It is then, as George Mead terms it, a significant symbol. When a given symbol means similar things to a group of persons, we may say that these persons make up a community of discourse. In general, symbols will mean similar things to this community in so far as they are used by persons acting in co-ordination. If one person interprets a symbol differently from another, the common behavior in which they are involved may become unco-ordinated. This mixup of conduct, arising from the symbol's failure to co-ordinate the actions of two or more persons, will check the wrong interpretation—that is, the one which is not usual and common to most of the participants. In this way, the meaning of a symbol, the response which it typically calls out in various persons, is kept common.

A community of discourse thus normally coincides with a community of co-ordinated activities. For the prime function of language is to co-ordinate social conduct. Very little truly human conduct could be successfully performed if for even a single day we could not speak or understand the speech of others.

Traditional theorists of language have held that the primary function of language is the "expression" of some "idea," or some feeling already within the individual. Although it is true that language enables the mature person to express ideas and feelings, modern theorists no longer agree that the prime function of language is expressive. It has been found more fruitful to approach linguistic behavior, not by referring it to prior states or elements in the psychic structure or even in the person, but by observing its objective function of co-ordinating social behavior.[2]

Language is primarily a system of signs which are responded to by other persons as indicators of the future actions of the person speaking. A given symbol can thus mediate conduct only if it calls out a similar response in the one as in another, that is, if it has a common meaning. This point of view toward the function of language invites us to pay attention to the social context of language behavior, for the same sound may have different meanings when uttered in different contexts.

Words take on meanings from the other words with which they are associated. The United States Senate has been known to argue for several days over the insertion of the word "an" in a formal document.

But the context which lends meaning to words is social and be-havioral, as well as linguistic. This is indicated by the meaninglessness of words which we hear without being aware of the context in which they are uttered or written. Most language situations carry unseen and unspoken references which must be known if the utterances are to be meaningful. In the case of the Senate debate, the full meaning of the inclusion or omission of "an" may require an understanding of the connections of various senators with their respective state organizations, and of pronouncements previously made by Republican and Democratic party officials.

A person is composed of an internalization of organized social roles; language is the mechanism by which these internalizations occur. It is the medium in which these roles are organized. Now, we have defined role as a conduct pattern of a person which is typically expected by other persons. It is an expected pattern of conduct. The roles a person plays thus integrate one segment of his total conduct with a segment of the conduct of others. And this integration of persons, and of the roles they expect of one another, occurs by means of language. For it is largely by a language of vocal gestures that we know what is expected of us. We meet the expectations of others by calling out in ourselves a response similar to the response which the other person has called out in himself . . . that is, both respond similarly to the same vocal gesture.

When we are learning a new role and do not know what is expected of us, our correct and incorrect moves are indicated to us by the approval and disapproval of others. By their vocal expectations they guide us into the conduct pattern. Various nonvocal gestures may also guide our performance: The frown and the smile deter or encourage us. But the vocal gesture is more explicit, for the gesturer himself is more readily affected by speech than by any other kind of gesture he can make. We can hear ourselves talk more easily than we can feel our eyes blink or our foreheads wrinkle. This means that we can manage the performance of our own roles by our own vocal gestures.

When we have internalized the vocal gestures of others, we have internalized, so to speak, certain key features of an interpersonal situation. We have taken over into our own person the gestures which indicate to us what others expect and require. And then, we can make certain expectations of ourselves. The expectations of others have thus become the self-expectations of a self-steering person. The social control and guidance which the gestures of others provide have thus become the basis for self-control—and for the self-image of the person.

II   IMAGES OF SELF

The self-image develops and changes as the person, through his social experiences, becomes aware of the expectations and appraisals of others. He acts one way, and others reward him with food, warmth, and attention; he acts in another way and they punish him with inattention; when he fails to meet their durable expectations, they deny him satisfaction and give him their disapproval. "The approbation of the important person is very valuable," Harry Stack Sullivan has written, "since disapprobation denies satisfaction [psychic structure] and gives anxiety [person], the self becomes extremely important."[3]

If, as a child, the person does not meet the roles expected of him, he may be faced with two results: (1) Such impulses as impel him will not be satisfied, for other persons will not cater to his needs unless he meets the requirements they exact. He is dependent upon these others for nutrition and warmth and other bodily requirements. (2) He may also, in the course of his experience, know anxiety or insecurity, for he is dependent upon others for approval of himself as a person.

As he matures, the person's image of self is taken over from the images of him which others present to him, by their gestures of approval and of disapprobation. This general statement, however, must be qualified in two ways:

For the adult, it is more accurate to say that the attitudes and expectations of others facilitate or restrain the self-image. For by the time the person is adult, the image of self, although dependent in varying degrees upon the current appraisals of others, is normally strong enough to exist autonomously. This is possible because the person has already built his self-image on the basis of a long sequence of previous appraisals and expectations which others have presented to him.

The person learns to follow models of conduct which are suggested to him by others; in addition, as he comes to read, he chooses such models from the store of socially organized memory. These latter models, as well as those he imagines for himself, may be at variance with those whom others immediately around him appraise favorably. His own expectations and appraisals of self thus acquired may enable him to *accept, refract, ignore,* or *reject* the expectations and appraisals of the current others. Indeed, if this is not the case, if there is not some autonomy of self-image and the adult person is completely and immediately dependent for his own self-image upon what others may currently think of him, he is considered an inadequate person.[4] The self-image which we have at any given time is a reflection of the appraisals of others as modified by our previously developed self.

The social idea of the self must be qualified in a second way: by consideration of who the "others" to whom we respond are. Only the appraisals of those others who are in some way significant to the person count for much in the building and maintenance of his self-image. In some societies and families "the mother" is the most significant other to the infant and child, since she caters most directly to the bodily needs and by her actions completes the impulsive beginnings of the child's activities. In such cases, the image which the child has of himself is perhaps at first the image which his mother has of him. But as the person grows up, a variety of significant others begins to operate. If we know who has been and who is thus significant to the person's image of self, we know a very great deal about that person.

Three general principles seem important in determining this *selection of significant others:*

1. *Cumulative Confirmations.* The image of self which a person already possesses and which he prizes leads him to select and pay attention to those others who confirm this self-image, or who offer him a self-conception which is even more favorable and attractive than the one he possesses. This principle leads the person to ignore, if he can, others who do not appreciate his prized or aspired-to self-image, or who debunk his image or restrain the development of it. A circle of friends is typically made up of those who further, or who at least allow the other persons to retain, their respective self-images. As the ancients put it, "The friend is my other self." One avoids as best he can the enemies of the self-images one prizes. The cumulative selection of those persons who are significant for the self is thus in the direction of confirming persons, and the more he succeeds in limiting his significant others to those who thus confirm his prized self-image, the more strongly he will seek such

persons as significant in the future. So there is a tendency in the biography of the person for a sequence of confirming persons to accumulate.

Now if this were the only principle involved in the selection of significant others, life might perhaps be a happy and spontaneous affair; but other considerations do interfere with its single action: a person cannot choose all his relationships. The child, for example, is less selective than the adult of the others to whom he pays attention— which is one reason that children are so easily "hurt."

Trusting children frequently experience disappointments, rebuffs, and slights, until they learn to stem their confident approach with some degree of "shyness." If the balance tips in the direction of withdrawal, a scale of orientations and traits are observable, from reserve through suspicion toward the friendliest guest; anyone and anything that is new may become fearsome, until the child is frequently misunderstood as "insensitive." In fact, he may not have learned how to deal with the new, and hence be relying upon total avoidance of all new challenges.

The image of self built up during childhood may thus contain negative elements so firmly integrated that they are never gotten rid of. During adolescence in Western societies, the child is "catching on" to the selection of confirming others as significant, and this involves the development of sensitivities to little cues which other persons present and which warn the person whether or not someone is likely to confirm or to threaten prized self-images. Between the polar opposites of the fear of always being "left out" and of "never being left alone," the maturing person seeks to win and move in his own "elbow room." The adult often sees a man and immediately "takes a dislike to him." Other persons he immediately likes; they are felt to be "considerate," which means that they defer to him in the direction of his desired self-image. They treat him as he would like to be treated: they are confirming others. But the child may not be so aware of those often unspoken cues which aid the strategic adult in his selection of significant others according to the principle of the confirmation of his desired self-image.

2. *Selection by Position and Career.* In the construction and maintenance of a prized self-image, the selection of significant others is limited by the institutional position of the person and by the course of his career from one institutional position to another. This selection is not, of course, a simple mechanical process; in most positions there are various possibilities. The position of a nobleman within the status levels of a feudal society in revolt, and of a factory worker within the occupational hierarchy of modern capitalism may each be examined in this connection:

A nobleman may be (a) insulated against the harsh and negative appraisals of serfs or peasants by childhood segregation in which a strong and exalted self-image was built—an image which later enables him to deem the peasants' approval and disapproval as equally irrelevant. Only the judgments of his status peers count. (b) The noble may interpret the peasants' negative appraisals in a way wholly different from the way they are intended. He may have become aware of the peasants' attitudes only from other nobles, and thus his self may refract and modify the appraisals before they are incorporated into his self-image. He may, indeed, force the obedience of the peasants to him, and then interpret their obedient gestures as confirming and facilitating his honorable image of self. (c) Under certain conditions, the noble may not be able to stand the real or imaginary disapprovals of the peasants. He may then change his own self-image, and the conduct which it involves, so as to permit kindness to the peasants, which his previous self-image permitted only to other nobles. He thus seeks to modify their negative appraisals and in the process of doing so, he gets from their appraisals another image of himself. In turn, he will now strive "to live up to it": the line of his confirming other has shifted, and the strategies employed by him to win such confirmation from persons who become significant have shifted. So did certain Russian noblemen in the nineteenth century "humble themselves," go among the peasants, and, on humanitarian grounds, seek to co-operate with them politically.

The class and status positions of a person may thus be restrictions upon his *selection* of significant others, as well as determinants of the *degree and kind of significance* and of the *angles of refraction* which other persons of differing status may possess for the person of a given status position.

If a factory worker rejects, on ideological or other grounds, the appraisals of members of the employing class, his image of self may not directly reflect their appraisals of him. If working-class parents proudly tell their children tales of how they, and their parents before them, were imprisoned for heroic violence "against the capitalists and their state apparatus," then upper-class appraisals are less likely to be positively significant to the construction and retention of a self-image of the child of the workers. Under such conditions we may speak of "class consciousness." Such class tradition and consciousness may be said to have considerable weight when it restricts to one's own economic class the community of others who are significant for the self-image.

On the other hand, if the upper classes monopolize the means of communication and fill the several mass media with the idea that all those at the bottom are there because they are lazy, unintelligent, and in general inferior, then these appraisals may be taken over by the poor and used in the building of an image of their selves. The appraisal of the wealthy, privileged children may then be internalized by underprivileged children and facilitate negative self-images. Such images, if impressed early enough and continually enough by all persons who are significant to these children may cripple their chances to better their social position and thus obtain economic and social bases for more favorable self-images. An outstanding example of such restriction in the selection of significant others as determined by class and ethnic position is found in the self-images of many American Negroes. If, on the other hand, the Negro child is able to exclude the appraisals of various public others, he may build up a more favorable self-image on the social basis of the more intimate others of his ingroup of fellow Negroes.

It is worth noting that there are several ways in which self-respect and social respect may be related:

Self-valuation and valuation by others may be in positive agreement. For example, a proud group of rulers may also be admired by others—the feudal lords of the Middle Ages or the Roman emperors come to mind.

The self and the other may be in agreement—but negatively; an inferior group may accept the negative images imposed on it by their status superiors. All ruling groups seek to impose such sentiments upon subject groups. Stereotyped images and unwarranted generalizations from the worst case, which make him "representative" for all, are among the means used to breed inferiority feelings. Exacted deference is another. Thus, the despised serf comes to think lowly of himself and of his fellows. The slave is despised as chattel and, being powerless, seeks to hold his own by fraud, which is despicable to those who esteem only violence.

Self-respect may be high, but the social esteem of others may be low. Thus, the posturing of the "misunderstood" or "unknown" genius and the dictum that the prophet is not known in his own home town. In such cases, an invented or imaginary other may be used to compensate for the denial of respect by a public and thus high self-valuation be maintained. The misunderstood genius assures himself that "posterity," if not his present colleagues, will surely come to honor and respect him and his work. Behind such a secularized theology of martyrdom there is often religious imagery of various sorts. Such sentiment may be entirely adequate to the situation—as it was for Schopenhauer, who published in 1819, but gained esteem only after 1848; or for Arnold Schönberg whose works for long years were not fully appreciated. On the other hand, a mere megalomanic, and hence groundless and spurious, attitude is also possible.

Finally there are situations in which, despite the great esteem of others, a man deprecates his own worth, and, in the eyes of his God he may—as did young Luther—go to extraordinary length in his sense of humility and his moods of penance.

3. *The Confirming Use of the Intimate Other.* Thwarted in his public search for a confirming other, the person may restrict his search for confirming others to a few intimate others. Perhaps this is especially true of persons who occupy inferior institutional positions, who thus try to build durable, intimate relations with which to counteract public depreciation. The number of intimate others may even become drastically restricted and at times become a sole significant other. The persons may then attempt to derive the image of his or her self entirely from the appraisals

of this one particular other. These two withdraw socially: as far as other people are concerned, they are "in a daze." They integrate themselves in a situation of intimacy, and together face the broad and alien world which "does not understand." Fed by the warmth and security of such intimate closure, they have this larger world at their mercy and can discuss, debunk, and ignore it. This strategy may be temporarily success- ful—and in fact, expected—during certain phases of adolescence, when many others crowd in upon the person with new and less favorable appraisals than his family and school have offered.

Such a condition cannot usually last forever. Nevertheless, in the modern industrial metropolis in which private and public roles are rigorously segregated, a certain degree of such exclusion and refraction of public appraisals by intimate circles, and a more or less exclusive acceptance of the desired approval of intimate others, may be integrated into a rather enduring basis for personal images of self.

These three principles involved in the selection of significant others may be linked in this way: the social position and career of the person set limits, more or less broad, for the selection of significant others. Within these limits, the selection will proceed in the direction of those others who are believed to confirm the prized or aspired-to image of self. If the institutional position and career prohibits the selection of such others from public life, the quest for such confirmation of self-image by significant others may be narrowed down to a sequence of intimate others.

These principles do not, of course, exhaust the determinants of the process of selection. We shall encounter others, and further examples of these, in their proper institutional contexts. For it is, in some major part, through the line-up of significant others that institutions form personalities in often intricate ways.

NOTES

1. *Language* (New York: 1939), pp. 7–9.
2. The shift in the general approach to language has been summarized by Edwin Esper in "Language," *Handbook of Social Psychology*, Carl Murchison, ed. (2d ed., rev.; Worcester: Clark Univ. Press, 1935). The shift is part of the larger drift to a sociological psychology, a connection traced by John F. Markey, *The Symbolic Process and Its Integration in Children* (New York: Harcourt, Brace, 1928). From a philosophical viewpoint, the neatest and most useful analytic scheme for the study of language is probably C. W. Morris, *Foundations of the Theory of Signs*, International Encyclopedia of Unified Science, Volume 1, No. 2 (Chicago: 1938). Among the many scholars responsible for the newer viewpoint toward language, see: Grace De Laguna, *Speech: Its Function and Development* (New Haven: Yale Univ. Press, 1927); Bronislaw Malinowski, Appendix in Ogden and Richards's, *The Meaning of Meaning* (New York: Harcourt, Brace, 1927) and *Coral Gardens and Their Magic* (New York: American Book Co., 1935), Vol. II; George H. Mead, *Mind, Self and Society* (Chicago: Univ. of Chicago Press, 1934); and John Dewey, *Experience and Nature* (Chicago: Open Court, 1925), Chapter 4.
3. *Conceptions of Modern Psychiatry* (Washington: W. A. White Psychiatric Foundation, 1947).

4. Erich Fromm has aptly called such a person "the automaton": being completely dependent upon the appraisals of others the person conforms to their expectations in a compulsive manner; he does not have "a center in himself." Both Fromm and Karen Horney attempt to resolve the problem by invoking components of the psychic structure as "the real self." This does not seem to us an adequate solution: The psychic structure, if it is to operate in a manner harmonious to a social order, must itself be quite socialized in specific directions, even stereotyped in some. The answer to the "façade self" and the "real self" dichotomy is found not by trying to jump past the socialized portions of the personality and finding something more "genuine" in the psychic or organic "foundations," but by viewing the social process of the self in a longitudinal way, and "finding" a "genuine self" that is buried by later socializations. See Erich Fromm, *Escape from Freedom* (New York: Farrar & Rinehart, 1941).

IV. The Family

The family, out of which all other institutions have materialized, is as old as the human species. For most people it remains the institution that encapsulates them in their infancy, leaving an impress that can never be wholly effaced. The greater part of one's character and personality is formed within its confines. By the time an individual gains some distance from his original family (the family of orientation), he or she is most likely forming another family (the family of procreation).

Indeed, the family looms so large over time and space (including inner space), that too many of us think of it as somehow isolated from society at large. In his brilliant critique of that misperception, Bernard Greenblatt, a very gifted social scientist, pinpoints major relationships between the family and other social institutions. For instance, where the state is weak, the family has to be strong; and where the state is strong, it regulates or absorbs various family functions. The state is not alone in this "usurpation." Corporate, proprietary, educational, philanthropic, and commercial institutions all act to some degree *in loco parentis*. They achieve a kind of "social parenthood."

Actual parents retain no more than a fraction of their historical role. Even in playing that role, they may be subject to strict supervision or to somewhat subtler economic and social pressures that deflect them from performing family functions. Greenblatt does not argue that this trend is necessarily harmful; in some cases, state and other supervision and regulation of the family can be beneficial. At times, social and welfare regulations place a premium on fatherless families. Low income drastically reduces the possibility of escaping social parentage. Only the well-to-do can really choose how much and what kind of surrogate parentage they will allow for their children.

Alice Rossi, a major American sociologist, wrote *the* breakthrough article on sex roles, published in 1964. It is an examination of problems related to parenthood, with special emphasis on the middle-class mother. Rossi's perspective is historical. She points out something we tend to forget, namely, that full-time motherhood is an exceedingly *recent* phenomenon. The economic duties of women in an agricultural society precluded the full-time motherhood that educated middle-class urban women were required to assume. Total preoccupation with children has its drawbacks. Rossi proposes ways in which women's careers might be combined with extended social parenthood to the possible advantage of all concerned.

Steven Goldberg, the controversial young social scientist and author of a book whose title, *The Inevitability of Patriarchy*, has understandably upset many feminists, does not deny the right or the ability of women to do so-called man's work. He contends, however, that radical feminists are mistaken when they attempt to obliterate basic biological differences between the sexes. In his view, women are closer than men not only to the nurturance of life, but to its biological sources as well; they have greater stamina and endurance; they are indispensable to the emotional development of their children and of other adults; they are less aggressive and less brilliant than men. Goldberg marshals his evidence as the radical feminists marshal theirs. His assertions cannot be tested, confirmed, or refuted until men and women have for a long time enjoyed equal opportunity in all disciplines. Then habituation and tradition will tell the tale. Meanwhile, Goldberg's point that none of us can lead satisfying lives by ideology alone seems to be well taken.

13. The Family and the Social Structure

Bernard Greenblatt

On the basis of historical research of the medieval period, the French historian Georges Duby arrived at a theoretical generalization of the relationship of the family to a dominant component of the social structure, the State.

> In fact, the family is the first refuge in which the threatened individual takes shelter when the authority of the State weakens; but as soon as political

"The Family and the Social Structure" has been written especially for this anthology.

institutions afford him adequate guarantees, he shakes off the constraint of the family and the ties of blood are loosed. The history of lineage is a succession of contractions and relaxations whose rhythm follows the modifications of the political order.[1]

With some exceptions, the history of the American family from the early colonial period to the twentieth century conforms substantially to that generalization. First, the state in a society with a continental-wide frontier began as a weak political institution, the family as a relatively authoritative one. Second, the revolution and democratic sentiment, except for the South, obstructed the development of landed estates that would be passed intact down the family line. But the inverse relationship Duby posited otherwise fits well enough. Life on the frontier, for example, brought about unconventional, legally irregular, or even illegal marriage relations—marriages consummated without a legal license or without officiation by authorized officials, and sometimes even without ministerial ceremony. This freedom to marry exemplifies the way in which family matters were decided on the frontier in the absence of a strong political institution. The range of family discretion continued to narrow in America as the authority of the state increased: Firmer rules for marriage formation were established; divorce fell under legal regulation; the state began its intrusion upon bedroom sexual relations—marital or not—via the Comstock Act, which itself has fallen by the wayside and been superseded by other laws regulating birth control. Child labor was regulated and the family was surrounded by countless regulations, supports, and so on. So, during the two hundred years in which the federal and state governments expanded, consolidated, and centralized their authority to become the dominant political institutions, familial and parental authority fragmented and shrank. The decentralization of government in frontier society favored the autonomous family; the decline of the frontier and growth of government centralization helped to weaken the autonomous family, even when that weakening was described as providing support.

On the basis of both theory and fact, it seems a plausible prediction that the continued or heightened strength of the state would sustain past, or even lead to future encroachments on the family. For example, the likelihood of some form of public regulation of family size—such as sterilization, particularly of poor families—no longer seems preposterous. However, several qualifications and comments must be made regarding that prediction. The first concerns the stratified impact of the state—the differential effects on families in the several social strata.

Bertrand Russell has illustrated the relationship between the state and families of the lower social strata. Six years before the passage of the Social Security Act in the United States, Russell correctly predicted the probable outcome of a government policy of financial assistance to mothers of illegitimate children: "The family would probably cease after a time to be bi-parental."[2] Schorr more recently assessed such a policy in a similar fashion: "The provision that ADC is available only if a parent is absent or incapacitated operates precisely counter to any cohesive forces in the family."[3] Such a policy, he pointed out, produces children who are "socially orphaned."[4]

Welfare laws and rules since 1962 sharply illuminate policies which increasingly restrict families on welfare. More precisely, as the above illustration of ADC provisions indicates, the effects of these laws and rules depend upon the specific conditions and qualifications enacted by legislators or required by administrators. In 1967, day care services and funds were extended, but also, "a large measure of choice about working was removed from [AFDC] mothers."[5] In 1971, the degree of freedom to choose "suitable" child care available to welfare mothers when at work or training was reduced.[6] And in 1972, eligibility for mandatory registration for work or work-training was extended to physically well mothers.[7] These and other measures suggest a trend toward a level of economic and political dependency of AFDC families regressing to that of the English Poor Laws, or progressing to that of totalitarian regimes.

The families most exposed to the policies of the state are those which are economically dependent and politically powerless. This usually results in a decrease of the recipients' opportunities to make effective choices. Families in the non-poor classes are in a socio-economic position that shields them considerably from the merciful or merciless embrace of the state.

One possible inference which may be drawn from the prediction of continuing or increased state assumption of familial functions must be explicitly rejected: Not all the effects of the state on the family are negative. In fact, many state policies have been beneficial. Political imposition upon parental authority eliminated child labor, the cruelty to children described so movingly by Charles Dickens. In abolishing child labor, the state enacted the humanitarian impulse that many parents, employers, and even some clerics had sublimated. Public education, at least until recently, has in general been favorably regarded, as have public health measures. Adequate social security benefits permit many elderly people to select living arrangements by choice, not compulsion. Even today it seems difficult to reject in principle Russell's assessment of forty years ago: "The substitution of the state for the father, so far as it has yet gone in the West, is in the main a great advance. It has immensely improved the health of the community and the general level of education."[8]

In general terms, the social legislation adopted by the state has principally benefited children from the poorer strata. Middle- and upper-class fathers were able to afford most of these and other benefits for their own children. But progress in this regard has been far from steady, sufficient, or consistent. The health and nutritional deficiencies of poor families account for their higher rates of perinatal and infant mortality, their shorter life span, and a host of harmful medical conditions that afflict them during their lifetime. If the publicity currently given to the decrease in the number of families at the poverty level and the increase in the number of black middle-class families and welfare chiselers serves to further eliminate or reduce to minuscule proportions the allocation of public funds to health programs for the poor, it will mark a weakness and shortness of humanitarian sentiment and/or fiscal self-serving by wealthy and respectable families.

Yet another qualification must be placed on the general prediction of increased dominance of the state over family relationships. Stable working-class, middle-class, and probably to some extent, upper-class mothers and fathers may not be as increasingly supplanted by the state as have the poor. This does not mean a lessening of the "social parenthood" of their children. The sharing of familial responsibilities by formal and informal social agencies and organizations continues. The strata of the non-poor, too, cannot fully escape the collectivization of life brought on by the proliferation and expansion not only of public, semi-public, and "public-private" bureaucracies, but also of private corporate entities.

Toward the end of the nineteenth century, Samuel Dike, one of the first sociologists to focus on the family, noted the increasing transfer of family prerogatives to larger social institutions. His observations, to be sure, were stated in moralistic terms of the *surrender* of familial function. A diverse range of public organizations and private corporations, profit and non-profit, began to proliferate, expand, and densely pack the social space between the individual, family, and state, pushing aside the small voluntary associations that Weber considered such significant components of the nineteenth-century American social structure.[9] The small farms and businesses, nascent corporations, local unions and small federations, local charities, and other voluntary associations of the nineteenth century have been succeeded as significant forms today by agri-business, chain stores, franchised businesses, corporate giants (including conglomerates and multi-national firms), and national unions—the battery of economic organizations constituting the prevailing and countervailing powers in our society. The hope of effectively dealing with the producer firms calls for the organization of consumer-interest groups, such as Nader's Raiders. The corporate perspective suggests an important modification of Duby's or Russell's view of the simple institutional juxtaposition of family and state.

The main point here is not simply that private corporate entities, like the state, are growing in institutional power, but that they surrogate family responsibilities. These organizations join the state as surrogates for fathers and, thus far to a lesser extent, mothers, by exercising authority and paying for services that were formerly parental options. By transferring the husband from one office or plant to another, they dictate the location and movement of families. An increasing range of fringe benefits bears directly and indirectly upon the family: sale of an employee's home upon transfer, or purchase of the home; education for the employee;

educational loans and scholarships for the children; recreational facilities or opportunities for the family; health and life insurance; pensions; and in a small but possibly growing number of instances, day care. The expanding concern of these incorporated entities with the family gained symbolic, but suggestive expression, at least before the current rise of the women's liberation movement, in such phrases of titular possession as "corporation wife," "army wife," "faculty wife," and so forth.

Professions and the mass media play a significant part in social parenthood. The theories developed and articulated within several disciplines serve as the conceptual supply from which are taken "ideas whose time has come." From those ideas, professional statesmen, moralists, and policy-makers derive cultural images that are then disseminated by the media. The images serve to guide parents and children whose behavior can again be described and conceptualized. Of course, the results or rationality of these processes are not necessarily realistic. The conceptualization may be valid, contrived, and so on; the internalization by parents and children, appropriate, futile, and so on.

The incorporated entities present an interesting day-care facet of their own. Some organizations have established essentially subsidized day-care programs for their employees or clients. The industrial day-care centers of World Wars I and II have recently been emulated by a small but not unimpressive number of hospitals, unions, federal agencies, and private organizations (for example, the Ford Foundation). Other firms operate day-care locator services for interested employees, enter into contracts with day-care centers to reserve a specified number of places for employees' children, or may participate in joint labor-management trust funds for the establishment of child-care centers for the member-employees' children.[10] Beginning in the late 1960's, a considerable number of colleges and universities succumbed to pressure from students to establish day-care centers on their campuses. They primarily cater to children of students, but attendance by faculty and staff children is not uncommon.[11] The conduct of or direct payment for day care of employees' children by corporations, however, departs from a wider pattern of corporate avoidance in this field, presumably for reasons of cost.

The families that reap the corporate benefits thereby obtain desired services or coverage at social—that is, corporate—expense and unburden themselves of anxieties, chores and expenses, but in exchange give up various degrees of freedom: freedom to decide on such things as location, mobility, other benefits not covered by insurance plans, choice of participating practitioners, and so on. Only a minority escape from or can avoid the corporate network even if the exchange is beneficial. But even more devastating than the restriction or loss of freedom of choice are the critical effects of unemployment. For the victims of corporate cutbacks, the loss of organizational security benefits in addition to wages or salary is the functional equivalent of being devastated by a tornado. In the face of the impersonal power of these incorporated entities, the ordinary individual and family are as defenseless as the medieval peasant against the arbitrariness of the feudal lord.

More than a decade ago Barrington Moore, Jr., speculated in an interesting essay on the prospect of the bureaucratization of familial functions. Growth of the large, formal organizations that accompanied industrialization might develop, he noted,

> . . . from such contemporary forms as the creche, play school and boarding school. . .[and] assume a much larger share of the burden of child-rearing. . . .
>
> Though a considerable part of the task of raising children is not routine, a very great portion is repetitive. For these reasons one may expect that semi-bureaucratic arrangements will continue to encroach on the traditional structure of the family. No doubt many individual variations, combinations, and compromises will remain for some time to come. Yet one fine day human society may realize that the part-time family, already a prominent part of our social landscape, had undergone a qualitative transformation into a system of mechanized and bureaucratized child-rearing, cleansed of the standardized overtone these words now imply.[12]

The fine day of bureaucratized residential facilities with mechanized feeding and waste disposal has not yet arrived. Conceivably, it might arrive, joining other "strange" historical forms of child-rearing—such as the medieval British pattern of having the family send its child of seven or nine to be reared and trained for another seven or nine years by another family, and taking in a stranger's child;[13] the later British, French, and American practice of sending one's children to private boarding school, which also starts at age seven to ten; or the Israeli kibbutz. Meanwhile the expectation of "semi-bureaucratic arrangements" has been further realized in the form of commercially franchised, standardized feeding stations, such as McDonald's; franchised day care centers have already been developed.

While bureaucratized child-rearing, even residential, appears possible, a bureaucratic system "cleansed of the standardized overtone" seems less plausible. Moore bases his belief in the prospect of nonstandardized arrangements on (1) a viewpoint similar to Russell's—that a good institutional setting may be better than a harmful family, and (2) that "any first-class hotel knows how to cope" with the problem of individualized attention. While such hotels do exist and provide a basis for thinking that corporate child-care residences of quality are possible, that possibility offers little assurance that first-class bureaucratic service would be the norm. Flexible organizations with resources to "satisfy variations in the human temperament" would most likely be available to those high on the social ladder or otherwise with influence.

Whether or not Moore's expectations will ever come to pass, social parentage by the state, private organizations, mass media, and peer influence can only continue to spread. Only a major social transformation, nuclear war, or natural calamity can stem that tide. It would be, however, both inaccurate and misleading to attribute only negative qualities to the corporate society. Social parenthood produces benevolent as well as malevolent effects. Several relative or even outright gains may be mentioned. The material gains from educational, health, recreational, and other such benefits from corporate security are well understood. What may be less recognized, however, is the moral division of benefits in society. The families of workers in the skilled and strongly organized unions, and the families of employees in large business, nonprofit, and governmental organizations receive from corporate membership a range and level of benefits exceeding in quantity and quality the comparable help provided by the state to the impoverished.

Collectivization by pluralistic, corporate units allows the ordinary individual and family more freedom than does totalitarian control, that is, thoroughgoing dominance by one of the incorporated entities. Indeed, authoritarian control may be greater in some noncollectivized societies of the so-called Third World than in the United States. But social parenthood means an attenuation of the direct, personal dependence of the child upon the parents. Measured by the Weberian conception of freedom, "making deliberate choices among open alternatives,"[14] social parentage allows for the *possibility* of the earlier emancipation of the child. To realize this possibility, however, we would require better ways of making the child's choices deliberate, such as by making available sensible school counseling in place of the superficial variety usually encountered and, above all, by loosening those social structures and procedures that restrict rather than expand the choice of alternatives. The relationship between the family and other social structures depends upon the chances of freedom coexisting with equality.

<h2 style="text-align:center">NOTES</h2>

1. Georges Duby, *La société aux XIe et XIIe siècles dans la région maconnaise,* 1953, quoted in Philippe Ariès, *Centuries of Childhood: A Social History of Family Life* (New York: Alfred A. Knopf, 1962), p. 355.
2. Bertrand Russell, *Marriage and Morals* (New York: Bantam Books, 1959), p. 144.
3. Alvin L. Schorr, *Explorations in Social Policy* (New York: Basic Books, 1968), p. 36.
4. *Ibid.*, p. 58.
5. *Ibid.*, p. 11.
6. " . . . when there is only one source [of child care] available the [mother] must accept it unless [she] can show that it is unsuitable for [her] child." *Federal Register,* Vol. 37, 155 (August 10, 1972), Title 45, Chapter II, Part A, Section 220.18, p. 1358.
7. More than 1.2 million mothers were estimated as affected. Mothers of children under 6 are *not* required to sign up. " 'But even some who are not required to sign up under the new law will do so anyhow,' Secretary Richardson said, 'because they want to go to work.' An estimated 300,000 mothers with children under six will make up the bulk of these 'volunteers,' he said." [Quotes around "volunteers" in the original; the basis for predicting that 300,000 mothers of preschool children "will make up the bulk of these 'volunteers' " was not provided.] U.S. Department of Health, Education and Welfare, *HEW News,* for release in A.M. papers, Tuesday, June 20, 1972.
8. Russell, *Marriage and Morals,* p. 146. He went on to make explicit the hesitancy in his muted qualification (" . . . so far . . . "). Education by militaristic states,

he feared in 1929, might intensify "what is called patriotism, i.e., a willingness to indulge in mutual extermination without a moment's hesitation, whenever the governments feel so inclined." (p. 147).

9. Weber's observation derived from a visit in 1904, when the corporate organizations were on the rise and the smaller voluntary units at their apex. We see here another illustration of "theory lag." See Hans Gerth and C. Wright Mills, *From Max Weber: Essays in Sociology* (New York: Oxford University Press, 1946), p. 17.

10. U.S. Department of Labor (Women's Bureau), *Child Care Services Provided by Hospitals*, Bulletin 295, 1970; and *Day Care Services: Industry's Involvement*, Bulletin 296, 1971.

11. B. Greenblatt and L. Eberhard, *Children on Campus* (Washington, D.C.: Day Care Council of America, 1973).

12. Barrington Moore, Jr., "Thoughts on the Future of the Family," in Maurice Stein *et al.*, eds., *Identity and Anxiety* (Glencoe, Ill.: The Free Press, 1962), pp. 399–401.

13. Ariès, *Centuries of Childhood*, p. 365.

14. Gerth and Mills, *From Max Weber*, p. 70.

14. Equality Between the Sexes: An Immodest Proposal

*Alice S. Rossi**

Introduction

When John Stuart Mill wrote his essay on "The Subjection of Women" in 1869, the two major things he argued for with elegance and persuasion were to extend the franchise to women, and to end the legal subordination of married women to their husbands. The movement for sex equality had already gathered considerable momentum in England and the United States by 1869, reaching its peak fifty years later, when the franchise was won by American women in 1920. In the decades since 1920, this momentum has gradually slackened, until by the 1960's American society has been losing rather than gaining ground in the growth toward sex

* I wish to express my gratitude to Peter H. Rossi for his critical assessment of several drafts of this essay; to the Social Science Research Committee at the University of Chicago for a research grant that supported part of the research on which this essay is based; and to Stephen R. Graubard for his generosity of time and editorial skill.

Reprinted by permission of *Daedalus*, Journal of the American Academy of Arts and Sciences, Boston, Massachusetts, from *Daedalus* 93, no. 2, *The Woman in America* (Spring 1964).

equality. American women are not trying to extend their claim to equality from the political to the occupational and social arenas and often do not even seem interested in exercising the rights so bitterly won in the early decades of the twentieth century in politics and higher education. The constitutional amendment on equal rights for men and women has failed to pass Congress for seventeen consecutive years, and today a smaller proportion of college graduates are women than was true thirty years ago.

There is no overt antifeminism in our society in 1964, not because sex equality has been achieved, but because there is practically no feminist spark left among American women. When I ask the brightest of my women college students about their future study and work plans, they either have none because they are getting married in a few months, or they show clearly that they have lowered their aspirations from professional and research fields that excited them as freshmen, to concentrate as juniors on more practical fields far below their abilities. Young women seem increasingly uncommitted to anything beyond early marriage, motherhood and a suburban house. There are few Noras in contemporary American society, because women have deluded themselves that the doll's house is large enough to find complete personal fulfillment within it.

It will be the major thesis of this essay that we need to reassert the claim to sex equality and to search for the means by which it can be achieved. By sex equality I mean a socially androgynous conception of the roles of men and women, in which they are equal and similar in such spheres as intellectual, artistic, political and occupational interests and participation, complementary only in those spheres dictated by physiological differences between the sexes. This assumes the traditional conceptions of masculine and feminine are inappropriate to the kind of world we can live in in the second half of the twentieth century. An androgynous conception of sex role means that each sex will cultivate some of the characteristics usually associated with the other in traditional sex role definitions. This means that tenderness and expressiveness should be cultivated in boys and socially approved in men, so that a male of any age in our society would be psychologically and socially free to express these qualities in his social relationships. It means that achievement need, workmanship and constructive aggression should be cultivated in girls and approved in women so that a female of any age would be similarly free to express these qualities in her social relationships. This is one of the points of contrast with the feminist goal of an earlier day: rather than a one-sided plea for women to adopt a masculine stance in the world, this definition of sex equality stresses the enlargement of the common ground on which men and women base their lives together by changing the social definitions of approved characteristics and behavior for both sexes.

It will be an assumption of this essay that by far the majority of the differences between the sexes which have been noted in social research are socially rather than physiologically determined. What proportion of these sex differences are physiologically based and what proportion are socially based is a question the social and physiological sciences cannot really answer at the present time. It is sufficient for my present purposes to note that the opportunities for social change toward a closer approximation of equality between the sexes are large enough within the area of sex differences now considered to be socially determined to constitute a challenging arena for thought and social action. This is my starting point. I shall leave to speculative discourse and future physiological research the question of what constitutes irreducible differences between the sexes.

There are three main questions I shall raise in this essay. Why was the momentum of the earlier feminist movement lost? Why should American society attempt to reach a state of sex equality as I have defined it above? What are the means by which equality between the sexes can be achieved?

Why Feminism Declined

I shall discuss three factors which have been major contributors to the waning of feminism. The chief goals of the early leaders of the feminist movement were to secure the vote for women and to change the laws affecting marriage so that women would have equal rights to property and to their own children. As in any social reform movement or social revolution, the focus in the first stage is on change in the legal code, whether this is to declare independence from a mother country, establish a constitution for a new nation, free the slaves, or secure the right of women to be equal citizens with men. But the social changes required to translate such law into the social fabric of a society are of a quite different order. Law by itself cannot achieve this goal. It is one thing to declare slaves free or to espouse a belief in racial equality; quite another matter to accept racial integration in all spheres of life, as many northern communities have learned in recent years. In a similar way, many people accept the legal changes which have reduced the inequality between men and women and espouse belief in sex equality, but resist its manifestation in their personal life. If a social movement rests content with legal changes without making as strong an effort to change the social institutions through which they are expressed, it will remain a hollow victory.

This is one of the things which occurred in the case of the feminist movement. Important as the franchise is, or the recent change in Civil Service regulations which prevents the personnel specification of "male only," the new law or regulation can be successful only to the extent that women exercise the franchise, or are trained to be qualified for and to aspire for the jobs they are now permitted to hold. There is no sex equality until women participate on an equal basis with men in politics, occupations and the family. Law and administrative regulations must permit such participation, but women must want to participate and be able to participate. In politics and the occupational world, to be able to participate depends primarily on whether home responsibilities can be managed simultaneously with work or political commitments. Since women have had, and probably will continue to have, primary responsibility for child-rearing, their participation in politics, professions or the arts cannot be equal to that of men unless ways are devised to ease the combination of home and work responsibilities. This is precisely what has not occurred; at the same time, since fewer women today choose a career over marriage, the result has been a reduction in women's representation in the more challenging and demanding occupations.

By itself, the stress on legal change to the neglect of institutional change in the accommodations between family and work does not go very far in explaining why the feminist movement has lost momentum. There is an important second factor which must be viewed in conjunction with this first one. The feminist movement has always been strongest when it was allied with other social reform movements. In the nineteenth century its linkage was with the antislavery movement, and in the early twentieth century it was allied to the social welfare movement. There is an interesting and a simple explanation of this: unlike any other type of social inequality, whether of race, class, religion or nationality, sex is the only instance in which representatives of the unequal groups live in more intimate association with each other than with members of their own group. A woman is more intimately associated with a man than she is with any woman.[1] This was not the case for lord-serf, master-slave, Protestant-Roman Catholic, white-Negro relationships unless or until the social groups involved reach a full equality. By linking the feminist cause to the antislavery or social welfare movement, women were able to work together with men of similar sympathies and in the process they enlisted the support of these men for the feminist cause. To a greater extent than any other underprivileged group, women need not only vigorous spokesmen and pacesetters of their own sex, but the support of men, to effect any major change in the status of women, whether in the personal sphere of individual relationships or on the level of social organization.[2] The decline of political radicalism and the general state of affluence and social conservatism in American society since World War II have contributed in subtle ways to the decline of feminism, for women are not joined with men in any movement affecting an underprivileged group in American society. At the present time, marriage remains the only major path of social mobility for women in our society.

The general conservatism of the total society has also penetrated the academic disciplines, with side effects on the motivation and ability of women to exercise the rights already theirs or to press for an extension of them. Feminism has been undermined by the conservatism of psychology and sociology in the postwar period. Sociologists studying the family have borrowed heavily from selective findings in social anthropology and from psychoanalytic theory and have pronounced sex to be a universally necessary basis for role differentiation in the family. By extension, in the larger society women are seen as predominantly fulfilling nurturant, expressive functions and men the instrumental, active functions. When this viewpoint is applied to American society, intellectually aggressive women or tender expressive men are seen as deviants showing signs of "role conflict," "role confusion," or neurotic disturbance. They are not seen as a promising indication of a desirable departure from traditional sex role definitions.[3] In a similar way, the female sphere, the family, is viewed by social theorists as a passive, pawnlike institution, adapting to the requirements of the occupational, political or cultural segments of the social structure, seldom playing an active role either in affecting the nature of other social institutions or determining the nature of social change.[4] The implicit assumption in problem after problem in sociology is that radical social innovations are risky and may have so many unintended consequences as to make it unwise to propose or support them. Although the sociologist describes and analyzes social change, it is change already accomplished, seldom anticipated purposive social change.[5] When the changes are in process, they are defined as social problems, seldom as social opportunities.

Closely linked to this trend in sociology and social anthropology, and in fact partly attributable to it, is the pervasive permeation of psychoanalytic thinking throughout American society. Individual psychoanalysts vary widely among themselves, but when their theories are popularized by social scientists, marriage and family counselors, writers, social critics, pediatricians and mental health specialists, there emerges a common and conservative image of the women's role. It is the traditional image of woman which is popularized: the woman who finds complete self-fulfillment in her exclusive devotion to marriage and parenthood. Women who thirty years ago might have chosen a career over a marriage, or restricted their family size to facilitate the combination of family and work roles, have been persuaded to believe that such choices reflect their inadequacy as women. It is this sense of failure as a woman that lies behind the defensive and apologetic note of many older unmarried professional women, the guilt which troubles the working mother (which I suspect goes up in direct proportion to the degree to which she is familiar with psychoanalytic ideas), the restriction of the level of aspiration of college women, the early plunge into marriage, the closed door of the doll's house.

Our society has been so inundated with psychoanalytic thinking that any dissatisfaction or conflict in personal and family life is considered to require solution on an individual basis. This goes well with the general American value stress on individualism, and American women have increasingly resorted to psychotherapy, the most highly individualized solution of all, for the answers to the problems they have as women. In the process the idea has been lost that many problems, even in the personal family sphere, cannot be solved on an individual basis, but require solution on a societal level by changing the institutional contexts within which we live.

The consequences of this acceptance of psychoanalytic ideas and conservatism in the social sciences have been twofold: first, the social sciences in the United States have contributed very little since the 1930's to any lively intellectual dialogue on sex equality as a goal or the ways of implementing that goal. Second, they have provided a quasi-scientific underpinning to educators, marriage counselors, mass media and advertising researchers, who together have partly created, and certainly reinforced, the withdrawal of millions of young American women from the mainstream of thought and work in our society.[6]

Why Seek Equality Between the Sexes

This brings us to the second question: why should American society attempt to reach a state of sex equality? If women seem satisfied with a more narrowly restricted life pattern than men would be, why should we seek to disturb this pattern? To begin with, I do not think this question is really relevant to the issue. There have been underprivileged groups throughout history which contained sizable proportions of contented, uncomplaining members, whether slaves, serfs or a low status caste. But the most enlightened members of both the privileged and underprivileged groups in such societies came to see that inequality not only depressed the human potential of the subject groups but corrupted those in the superordinate groups. The lives of southern whites are as crippled by racial inequality as the lives of southern Negroes are impoverished. In the same way, many men spend their daytime hours away from home as vital cognitive animals and their nights and weekends in mental passivity and vegetation. Social and personal life is impoverished for some part of many men's lives because so many of their wives live in a perpetual state of intellectual and social impoverishment.

A second reason why American society should attempt to reach a state of full sex equality is that at the level our industrial society has now reached, it is no longer necessary for women to confine their life expectations to marriage and parenthood. Certain of the reasons for this have been increasingly stressed in recent years: with increased longevity, and smaller sized families, the traditional mother role simply does not occupy a sufficient portion of a woman's life span to constitute any longer the exclusive adult role for which a young woman should be prepared.[7] American girls spend more time as apprentice mothers with their dolls than they will as adult women with their own babies, and there is half a lifetime still ahead by the time the youngest child enters high school. Although studies have shown that women today are working in the home roughly the same number of hours a week as their mothers did,[8] this is not because they have to do so: technological innovations in the production and distribution of food, clothing and other household equipment have been such that homemaking no longer requires the specialized skills and time-consuming tasks it did until early in our century. Contemporary women often turn what should be labor-saving devices into labor-making devices. In the light of the many time-consuming tasks the American mother fifty years ago had to perform, and the much longer work day for those in the labor force then, the woman in 1964 who holds down a full-time job will probably have as much or more time with her children as her grandmother had. Furthermore, most of the skills needed for adulthood are no longer taught within the family: child socialization is increasingly a shared enterprise between the parent and teachers, doctors, nurses, club leaders and instructors in an assortment of special skills.

These are perhaps all familiar points. What has not been seen is the more general point that *for the first time in the history of any known society, motherhood has become a full-time occupation for adult women.* In the past, whether a woman lived on a farm, a Dutch city in the seventeenth century, or a colonial town in the eighteenth century, women in all strata of society except the very top were never able to be full-time mothers as the twentieth-century middle class American woman has become. These women were productive members of farm and craft teams along with their farmer, baker or printer husbands and other adult kin. Children either shared in the work of the household or were left to amuse themselves; their mothers did not have the time to organize their play, worry about their development, discuss their problems. These women were not lonely because the world came into their homes in the form of customers, clients or patients in villages and towns, or farmhands and relatives on the farm; such women had no reason to complain of the boredom and solitude of spending ten-hour days alone with babies and young children because their days were peopled with adults. There were no child specialists to tell the colonial merchant's wife or pioneer farmer's wife that her absorption in spinning, planting, churning and preserving left her children on their own too much, that how she fed her baby would shape his adult personality, or that leaving children with a variety of other adults while she worked would make them insecure.

There are two important questions this analysis raises: why has full-time motherhood been accepted by the overwhelming majority of American women, and how successful has been the new pattern of full-time motherhood of the past forty years or so? I believe the major answer to the first question is that the American woman has been encouraged by the experts to whom she has turned for guidance in child-rearing to believe that her children need her continuous presence, supervision and care and that she should find complete fulfillment in this role. If, for example, a woman reads an article by Dr. Spock on working mothers, she is informed that any woman who finds full-time motherhood produces nervousness is showing a "residue of difficult relationships in her own childhood"; if irritability and nervousness are not assuaged by a brief trip or two, she is probably in an emotional state which can be "relieved through regular counseling in a family social agency, or, if severe, through psychiatric treatment"; and finally, "any mother of a preschool child who is considering a job should discuss the issues with a social worker before making her decision."[9] Since the social worker shares the same analytic framework that Dr. Spock does, there is little doubt what the advice will be; the woman is left with a judgment that wanting more than motherhood is not natural but a reflection of her individual emotional disturbance.

The fundamental tenet of the theory underlying such advice is that the physically and emotionally healthy development of the infant requires the loving involvement of the mother with the child. If an infant does not receive stable continuous mothering there is almost invariably severe physical and emotional disturbance. There is apparently ample clinical evidence to support these points. Studies have suggested that prolonged separation from parents, and particularly from the mother, has serious effects upon infants and young children.[10] However, practitioners make unwarranted extrapolations from these findings when they advise that *any* separation of mother and child is risky and hazardous for the healthy development of the child.[11] Despite the fact that the empirical evidence stems from instances of prolonged, traumatic separation caused by such things as the death or serious illness of the mother, or the institutionalization of the child, this viewpoint is applied to the situation of an employed mother absent from the home on a regular basis. No one predicts that any dire consequences will flow from a woman's absence from home several afternoons a week to engage in a shopping spree, keep medical appointments or play bridge; nor is a father considered to produce severe disturbance in his young children even if his work schedule reduces contact with them to the daylight hours of a weekend. But women who have consulted pediatricians and family counselors about their resuming work are firmly told that they should remain at home, for the sake of their children's emotional health.[12]

What effect *does* maternal employment have upon children? Many sociologists of the family have raised this question during the past fifteen years, expecting to find negative effects as psychoanalytic theory predicted. In fact, the focus of most maternal employment studies has been on the effect of mothers' working upon the personalities of their children, somewhat less often on the tensions and strains between the mother role and the occupational role,[13] seldom on the question of how maternal employment affects the woman's satisfactions with herself, her home and marriage. To date, *there is no evidence of any negative effects traceable to maternal employment;* children of working mothers are no more likely than children of non-working mothers to become delinquent, to show neurotic symptoms, to feel deprived of maternal affection, to perform poorly in school, to lead narrower social lives, or the like.[14] Many of the researchers in the 1950's frankly admitted surprise at their negative findings. In a study reported in 1962,[15] the only significant difference found between working and non-working mothers was the mother's confidence about her role as mother: 42 per cent of the working mothers but only 24 per cent of the non-working mothers expressed concern about their maternal role, "often by explicit questioning and worry as to whether working is interfering with their relationships and the rearing of their children." Yet these working women did not actually differ from the at-home mothers in the very things that concerned them: there were no differences between these women in the emotional relationships with their children, household allocation of responsibilities, principles of child-rearing, and so on. The working mothers appeared to share the prevailing view that their children would suffer as a result of their employment, though in fact their children fare as well as those of non-working mothers.[16]

It would appear, therefore, that the employment of women when their children are eight years of age or older has no negative effect on the children. What about the earlier years, from infancy until school age? In the American literature, there is little to refer to as yet which bears directly upon the effect of maternal employment on the infant or toddler, partly because employment of mothers with preschool children is so negligible in the United States, partly because the measurement of "effects" on young children is difficult and cannot be done with the research tools which have been used in most studies of maternal employment effects—questionnaires administered to mothers and to their schoolage children.[17]

There is, however, one significant body of data which is of considerable relevance to the question of the effect of maternal employment upon infants and very young children. Maternal employment is a regular pattern of separation of mother and child: the Israeli kibbutzim are collective settlements with several decades of experience in precisely this pattern. On the kibbutz, infants live in children's houses where their physical care and training are largely handled. During the infancy months the mother visits the house to feed the infant; as toddlers, children begin a pattern of visiting with their parents for a few hours each day, living in the children's houses for the remaining portions of their days and nights. A number of studies have been conducted to investigate the effect of this intermittent multiple mothering on the young child.[18] They all point to essentially the same conclusion; the kibbutz child-rearing practices have no deleterious effects upon the subsequent personality development of the children involved. In fact, there are a number of respects in which the kibbutz-reared Israeli children exceed those reared in the traditional farm family: the kibbutz children showed a more accurate perception of reality, more breadth of interest and cultural background, better emotional control and greater overall maturity.

Continuous mothering, even in the first few years of life, does not seem to be necessary for the healthy emotional growth of a child.[19] The crux of the matter appears to be in the nature of the care which is given to the child.[20] If a child is reared by a full-time mother who is rejecting and cold in her treatment of him, or if a child is reared in an institutional setting lacking in warmth and stimulation and with an inadequate staff, both children will show personality disturbances in later years. If the loving care of the biological mother is shared by other adults who provide the child with a stable loving environment, the child will prosper at least as well as and potentially better than one with a good full-time mother.[21] In the section below on child care and careers, I shall suggest institutional innovations which would ensure good quality care for children and ease the combination of work and child-rearing for women.

Turning now to the second question raised above: how successful has the new pattern of full-time motherhood been? Are women more satisfied with their lives in the mid-twentieth century than in the past? Does motherhood fulfill them, provide them with a sufficient canvas to occupy a lifetime? Are contemporary children living richer lives, developing greater ego strength to carry them through a complex adulthood? Are children better off for having full-time mothers?

I think the answer to all the questions posed above is a firm *no*. Educators, child psychologists and social analysts report an increasing tendency for American middle-class children to be lacking in initiative, excessively dependent on others for direction and decision, physically soft.[22] Our children have more toys and play equipment than children in any other society; yet they still become bored and ask their mothers for "something to do." No society has as widespread a problem of juvenile delinquency and adolescent rebellion as the United States. Alcoholism, compulsive sex-seeking and adolescent delinquency are no longer social problems confined to the working-class, socially disorganized sections of our cities, but have been on the increase in the middle-class suburb in the past twenty years, and involve more women and girls than in the past. There is a strong strand of male protest against the mother or "matriarch" in both our beatnik culture and our avant-garde literature: social and artistic extremes are seldom fully deviant from the middle range in a society, but show in an exaggerated heightened way the same though less visible tendencies in the social majority.

In a large proportion of cases, the etiology of mental illness is linked to inadequacy in the mother-child relationship. A high proportion of the psychoneurotic discharges from the army during World War II was traced to these young soldiers' overly dependent relationships to their mothers.[23] This has been the subject of much earnest discussion in the years since the war, but the focus has remained on the mother-*son* relationship, I suspect only because as a fighter, a professional man or a worker, male performance is seen to be more crucial for society than female performance. But dependence, immaturity and ego diffusion have been characteristic of daughters as well as sons. The only difference is that, in the case of daughters, this less often reaches the overt level of a social problem because young women move quickly from under their mothers' tutelage into marriage and parenthood of their own: female failures are therefore not as socially visible, for they are kept within the privacy of family life and psychoanalytic case records. It is a shortsighted view indeed to consider the immature wife, dominating mother or interfering mother-in-law as a less serious problem to the larger society than the male homosexual, psychoneurotic soldier or ineffectual worker, for it is the failure of the mother which perpetuates the cycle from one generation to the next, affecting sons and daughters alike.

Disturbing trends of this sort cannot all be traced to the American woman's excessive and exclusive involvement with home and family. We live in turbulent times, and some part of these trends reflects the impact of world tension and conflict. But there is no reason to assume that world tension is relevant to many of them. Emotional and physical difficulties after childbirth or during the menopause years, the higher incidence of college girl than college boy breakdowns, the shrunken initiative and interdependence of children, are clearly not explained by world conflict. Besides, vast sections of American society remain totally unmoved and unaffected by international political and military events until they directly impinge on their own daily lives. Since history is both written and produced more by men than by women, the fact that our writers are preoccupied with the relationship to the mother points to difficulties in our family system more than the course of world events.

It is a paradox of our social history that motherhood has become a full-time occupation in precisely the era when objectively it could, and perhaps should, be a part-time occupation for a short phase of a woman's life span. I suspect that the things women do for and with their children have been needlessly elaborated to make motherhood a full-time job. Unfortunately, in this very process the child's struggle for autonomy and independence, for privacy and the right to worry things through for himself are subtly and pervasively reduced by the omnipresent mother. As a young child he is given great permissive freedom, but he must exercise it under supervision. As an adolescent he is given a great deal of freedom, but his parents worry excessively about what he does with it. Edgar Friedenberg has argued that there is entirely too much parental concentration on adolescent children, with the result that it has become increasingly difficult to *be* an adolescent in American society.[24] He suggests that parents are interested in youth to the extent that they find their own stage of life uninteresting. Middle-class children are observed and analyzed by their mothers as though they were hothouse plants psychologically, on whose personalities any pressure might leave an indelible bruise. If a woman's adult efforts are concentrated exclusively on her children, she is likely more to stifle than broaden her children's perspective and preparation for adult life. Any stress or failure in a child becomes a failure of herself, and she is therefore least likely to truly help her child precisely when the child most needs support.[25] In myriad ways the mother binds the child to her, dampening his initiative, resenting his growing independence in adolescence, creating a subtle dependence which makes it difficult for the child to achieve full adult stature without a rebellion which leaves him with a mixture of resentment and guilt that torments him in his mother's declining years.

It seems to me no one has linked these things together adequately. Psychiatric counselors of college students frequently have as their chief task that of helping their young patients to free themselves from the entangling web of dependence upon their parents, primarily their mothers, and encouraging them to form stable independent lives of their own. In other words, if the patient is 18 years old the analyst tries to help her free herself from her mother, but if the next patient is 25 years old with young children at home, the analyst tells her the children would suffer emotional damage if she left them on a regular basis to hold down a job. The very things which would reduce the excessive dependency of children before it becomes a critical problem are discouraged by the counselor or analyst during the years when the dependency is being formed. If it is true that the adult is what the child was, and if we wish adults to be assertive, independent, responsible people, then they should be reared in a way which prevents excessive dependence on a parent. They should be cared for by a number of adults in their childhood, and their parents should truly encourage their independence and responsibility during their youthful years, not merely give lip service to these parental goals. The best way to encourage such independence and responsibility in the child is for the mother to be a living model of these qualities herself. If she had an independent life of her own, she would find her stage of life interesting, and therefore be less likely to live for and through her children. By maintaining such an independent life, the American mother might finally provide her children with something she can seldom give when she is at home—a healthy dose of inattention, and a chance for adolescence to be a period of fruitful immaturity and growth.[26] If enough American women developed vital and enduring interests outside the family and remained actively in them throughout the child-bearing years, we might then find a reduction in extreme adolescent rebellion, immature early marriages, maternal domination of children, and interference by mothers and mothers-in-law in the lives of married children.

There remains one further general characteristic of our industrial society which has relevance to the question of why American society should achieve full sex equality. Our family unit is small, for the most part geographically if not socially isolated from its kin. This small family unit is possible because of the increased longevity in highly industrialized societies. In agricultural societies, with their high rate of mortality, many parents die before they have completed the rearing of their young. The extended family provided substitutes for such parents without disturbing the basic lines of kin affiliation and property rights of these children. In our modern family system it is an unusual event for women or men to be widowed while they have young dependent children. This also means, however, that American families must fend for themselves in the many emergencies less critical than the death of a spouse: army service, long business or professional trips, prolonged physical or emotional illness, separation or divorce often require that one spouse carry the primary responsibility for the family, even if this is cushioned or supplemented by insurance, government aid, paid helpers or relatives. The insurance advertisements which show fathers bending over a cradle and begin "what would happen if?" evoke a twinge of fear in their readers precisely because parents recognize the lonely responsible positions they would be in if serious illness or death were to strike their home. In our family system, then, it is a decided asset if men and women can quickly and easily substitute for or supplement each other as parents and as breadwinners. I believe these are important elements in the structure of our economy and family system which exert pressure toward an equality between men and women. It is not merely that a companionate or equalitarian marriage is a desirable relationship between wife and husband, but that the functioning of an urban industrial society is facilitated by equality between men and women in work, marriage and parenthood.

The conclusions I have drawn from this analysis are as follows: full-time motherhood is neither sufficiently absorbing to the woman nor beneficial to the child to justify a contemporary woman's devoting fifteen or more years to it as her exclusive occupation. Sooner or later—and I think it should be sooner—women have to face the question of who they are besides their children's mother.

A major solution to this question would be found in the full and equal involvement of women in the occupational world, the culmination of the feminist movement of the last one hundred and fifty years. This is not to overlook the fact that involvement as a volunteer in politics or community organizations or a serious dedication to a creative art can be a solution for many women. These areas of participation and involvement provide innumerable women with a keen sense of life purpose, and women are making significant and often innovative contributions in these pursuits. A job *per se* does not provide a woman, or a man either, with any magical path to self-fulfillment; nor does just any community volunteer work, or halfhearted dabbling in a creative art.

Women are already quite well represented in volunteer organizations in American communities. However, broadening the range of alternatives open to women and chosen by women for their life patterns is still to be achieved in the occupational world. It is also true that at the most challenging reaches of both political and community volunteer work, the activities have become increasingly professionalized. Thus while many women have and will continue to make innovative contributions to these fields as volunteers, such opportunities have become limited. Furthermore, many such women often find themselves carrying what amounts to a full-time job as a "volunteer executive"; yet neither the recognition nor the rewards are equivalent to what they would receive in comparable positions in the occupational system.[27] Hence, the major focus in this essay will be on the means by which the full and equal involvement of well-educated women in the occupational world may be achieved. For reasons which will become clear later, I believe that the occupational involvement of women would also be the major means for reducing American women's dominance in marriage and parenthood, and thus for allowing for the participation of men as equal partners in family life.

Of course there have already been changes in the extent and the nature of women's participation in the American labor force. Indeed, this is sometimes cited as proof that sex equality has been achieved in the United States. There are roughly twenty-three million American women in the labor force, and it is predicted that this will swell to thirty million by 1970. About three-fifths of these women are married, an increase of well over 20 per cent since 1940. It should be noted that this increase came predominantly from women between the ages of 35 and 54 years, after the child-rearing years and before the usual retirement age for workers. This is a major social change, to be sure, and people who still raise the question of whether married women should work are arguing after the fact, for such women are doing so at increasing rates. The point is, however, that most American women—65 per cent—do *not* work outside the home, and those who do are found largely in blue collar or low-skill white collar occupations. Men fill roughly 85 per cent of the very top professional and technical jobs in the United States. Furthermore, only a very small proportion of American wives work if their husbands are in the middle and top income brackets, or if they have young children. Finally, the distribution of the female labor force by age shows two major peaks of female participation, before and for a short time after marriage, and then for the fifteen years from their early forties through middle fifties. Withdrawal and re-entry many years later is now a common female work pattern in the United States. As long as this pattern continues, women will not increase their representation in the top professional and technical occupations.[28]

Over the past twenty years, women in many European countries have doubled or more their representation in the professional occupations. By comparison, American women constitute a smaller proportion of the professional world today than they did twenty years ago. That this reflects a lowering of ambition among American women is suggested by the fact that of all the women capable of doing college work, only one out of four do so, compared to one out of two men. This is the point at which we begin to tap a deeper root of women's motivations in the United States. Whether a woman works steadily throughout her marriage or returns to work after the child-rearing period, no significant increase of women in the professional and high-skill job categories will occur unless American women's attitude toward education and work is changed.[29] To study and to prepare for a future job "in case I have to work" is just as poor a preparation for occupational participation as the postponement of learning domestic skills "until I have to" is a poor preparation for the homemaker role. Both views reflect a digging in of the heels into the adolescent moment of a lifetime. In many ways the middle-class girl considers only the present, the here-and-now, as do most members of the working class, and not the future, as do her father, brothers and male friends. There is evidence to suggest that such an emphasis on the present is characteristic not only of the American woman at college age, but also more generally throughout her life span. Thus, Gallup's portrait of the American woman shows the same characteristic at all points during the younger half of the life cycle: young unmarried women as well as mature women with their children now entering high school give little thought to and no preparation for their life over 40 years of age.[30]

The middle-class wife of a successful business executive or professional man has a special problem. To earn a salary in the occupational world, she will be judged by her own achieved merits without regard to her social position or her husband's influence. Unless she has had the education and experience necessary to hold a position of some prestige, she will experience social and personal barriers to entering the labor force. In the absence of such education and experience, she is qualified to be only the occupational subordinate of men who are her equals socially, a status incongruity few women are likely to tolerate. By contrast, no matter how menial, her service as a volunteer will be socially approved. Unless such women secure specialized training before marriage, or acquire it after marriage, there will be little increase in the proportion of working wives and mothers in the upper half of the middle class. Many such women with a flair for organization have found full scope for their independent fulfillment in volunteer work in politics, education, social welfare and the arts. Unfortunately, there are innumerable other women for whom such outlets have little attraction who realize they have missed their chance for independent self-fulfillment, and who have little opportunity for a second chance by their late forties.

It has been argued by some sociologists that the American marriage is already too fragile to sustain competition at comparable skill levels between spouses.[31] If this were true, and women are also reluctant to work at lower prestige jobs than their husbands, this would effectively freeze most middle-class women out of the occupational world. I would raise three points concerning this assumption. First, husbands and working wives are usually found in different segments of the occupational system, which makes comparison of success a difficult matter. For example, is an architect working for a large firm and earning $20,000 a year more or less successful than his wife who directs a large family welfare agency and earns $15,000 a year? Second, even were such achievements in non-family roles to provoke some competitive feeling between husband and wife, I think the consequences of this competition are far less potentially harmful to the marriage or to the children than the situation of the well-educated able women who is not working and engages instead in a competition with her husband for the affections and primary loyalties of the children. If a woman is markedly more successful than her husband, it would probably create difficulty in the marriage, particularly if there are residues of traditional expectations of male breadwinner dominance on the part of either partner to the marriage. But competition does not necessarily mean conflict. It can be a social spice and a source of pride and stimulation in a marriage of equals. Last, one must face up to the fact that a new social goal exacts a price. A change toward sex equality may cause some temporary marital dislocations, but this is not sufficient reason to expect all women to remain enclosed in the past.

NOTES

1. This is one among many points of crucial and still relevant significance to be found in John Stuart Mill's essay "The Subjection of Women" (London, 1869).
2. In recent years of acute manpower shortages in scientific, professional and technical fields, there has been a growing awareness of the fact that women constitute the only sizable remaining reservoir of such talent. Many men whose administrative or policy responsibilities alert them to this fact have been eagerly exploring the ways by which female brainpower could be added to the national pool of skilled manpower. The contemporary period is therefore ripe with opportunities for talented women, and women can anticipate a welcome from male colleagues and employers. I shall not discuss any further the current societal need for women in the labor force, because I would argue for an extension of female participation in the higher levels of occupations even in an era with *no* pressing manpower shortages, on the grounds of the more general principles to be developed in this essay.
3. Often the conclusion that sex differentiation is a basic and universal phenomenon is buttressed by pointing to a large number of societies, all of which manifest such sex differentiation. Since Americans are easily impressed by large numbers, this does indeed sound like conclusive evidence against the likelihood of any society's achieving full sex equality. Closer examination of such samples, however, reveals two things: very little representation of numerous African societies in which the instrumental-expressive distinction is simply *not* linked to sex in the predicted direction, and second, they are largely primitive societies, a half dozen of which might equal the size of a very small American city. Such cultural comparisons assume every possible kind of societal arrangement is represented, but this is not the case: Sweden, China, Yugoslavia, the Soviet Union, Israel, are not represented on such a continuum. I believe we may learn more that is of relevance to a future America by studying family patterns in these societies than from a study of all the primitive societies in the world. Unfortunately, most of contemporary sociology and social anthropology is far less concerned with the future than the present as molded by the past.
4. A rare exception is the recent work by William J. Goode, who has focused precisely on the active role of the family in determining the course of social change in the non-family segments of social structure. See his *World Revolution and Family Patterns* (Glencoe, Ill.: The Free Press, 1963).
5. When the sociologist finds, for example, that the incidence of divorce is higher for those who marry outside their religion than for those who do not, he con-

cludes that intermarriage is "bad" or "risky"; he does not say such marital failures may reflect the relative newness of the social pattern of intermarriage, much less suggest that such failures may decline once this pattern is more prevalent. In fact, the only aspect of intermarriage which is studied is the incidence of its failure. Sociologists have not studied *successful* intermarriages.

6. A full picture of this post-World War II development is traced in Betty Friedan's *The Feminine Mystique* (New York: Norton, 1963). See particularly Chapters 6 and 7 on the "Functional Freeze" and the "Sex-Directed Educators."

7. Demographic changes in the family life cycle between 1890 and 1950 are shown in great detail in Paul Glick's *American Families* (New York: Wiley, 1957). It should also be noted that even in contemporary families with four or five children, child-bearing occupies a far shorter portion of a woman's life span than it did to achieve this size family fifty years ago, because infant mortality has been so drastically reduced.

8. Cowles and Dietz, Myrdal and Klein, and Jean Warren have shown that there has been very little change in the past quarter century in the total working time per week devoted to homemaking activities. May L. Cowles and Ruth P. Dietz, "Time Spent in Homemaking Activities by a Selected Group of Wisconsin Farm Homemakers," *Journal of Home Economics,* 48 (January 1956), 29–35; Jean Warren, "Time: Resource or Utility," *Journal of Home Economics,* 49 (January 1957), 21 ff.; Alva Myrdal and Viola Klein, *Women's Two Roles: Home and Work* (London: Routledge and Kegan Paul, 1956).

9. Benjamin Spock, "Should Mothers Work?" *Ladies' Home Journal,* February 1963.

10. See Anna Freud and Dorothy T. Burlingham, *Infants without Families* (New York: International Universities Press, 1944); William Goldfarb, "Psychological Deprivation in Infancy and Subsequent Adjustment," *American Journal of Orthopsychiatry,* 15 (April 1945), 247–55; John Bowlby, *Maternal Care and Mental Health* (Geneva: World Health Organization, 1952); John Bowlby, *Child-Care and the Growth of Love* (London: Pelican Books, 1953); and James Bossard, *The Sociology of Child Development* (New York: Harper, 1954).

11. A few authors have seen this claim that all separation of the child from the biological mother or mother surrogate, even for a few days, is inevitably damaging to the child as a new and subtle form of anti-feminism, by which men, under the guise of exacting the importance of maternity, are tying women more tightly to their children than any real clinical or cultural evidence indicates is necessary. See Hilde Bruch, *Don't Be Afraid of Your Child* (New York: Farrar, Straus, and Young, 1952); and Margaret Mead, "Some Theoretical Considerations on the Problem of Mother-Child Separation," *American Journal of Orthopsychiatry,* 24, (1954), 471–83.

12. It is interesting in this connection that studies concerning the separation of the mother and child are frequently cited as cases of *maternal deprivation,* but those concerning the separation of the father and child are cited more neutrally as cases of *father absence,* never as *paternal deprivation.*

13. Social scientists raise the question of whether there are not such diametrically opposed requirements of an occupational role from the mother role as to involve great strain between the two. It is argued that because of this contrast between the two spheres, one or the other role must "suffer": there will be "role conflict." The researchers were not prepared to find either that woman could slip back and forth between these two spheres just as men have done for decades without any of the same difficulty predicted for women, or that the mother role may be subtly changed in the direction of more rationality, greater stress on independence and autonomy in children than is found in the child-rearing values of non-working mothers (See Faye VonMehring, "Professional and Non-Professional Women as Mothers," *Journal of Social Psychology,* 42 [August 1955], 21–34). Rather, the researcher expected to find maternal neglect, negative effect on children's personality, or inadequacy in occupational roles, such as absenteeism, overly personal view of work relationships, and so on. As in many areas in which role conflict has been predicted, human beings have a greater tolerance for sharp contrasts in role demands than social scientists credit them with.

14. Burchinal and Rossman found no significant relationships between any kind of employment and personality characteristics or social interaction of children in

the seventh and eleventh grades in school—Lee G. Burchinal and Jack E. Rossman, "Relations among Maternal Employment Indices and Developmental Characteristics of Children," *Marriage and Family Living*, 23 (November 1961), 334–
40. Nye administered questionnaires to over two thousand high school students
and found no significant relationships between maternal employment and educational achievement or neurotic symptoms—F. Ivan Nye, "Employment Status of
Mothers and Adjustment of Adolescent Children," *Marriage and Family Living*,
21 (August 1959), 240–44. Using scales to tap nervous symptoms, antisocial and
withdrawing tendencies, Perry found no significant differences between children
with working and non-working mothers—Joseph B. Perry, "The Mother Substitutes of Employed Mothers: An Exploratory Inquiry," *Marriage and Family
Living*, 23 (November 1961), 362–67. Kligler found that employed mothers reported their maternal role suffered least from their occupations—Deborah S.
Kligler, "The Effects of the Employment of Married Women on Husband and
Wife Roles," unpublished doctoral dissertation, Department of Sociology, Yale
University, 1954. Roy found no consistent effects of maternal employment on the
social life and participation of children or their academic performance, or the af-
fection, fairness of discipline, and cooperation in the family—Prodipto Roy,
"Maternal Employment and Adolescent Roles: Rural-Urban Differentials," *Marriage and Family Living*, 23 (November 1961), 340–49. Peterson found no significant differences on employment of mothers and maternal interest in the
supervision of their adolescent daughters—Evan T. Peterson, "The Impact of
Maternal Employment on the Mother-Daughter Relationship," *Marriage and
Family Living*, 23 (November 1961), 355–61. In Eleanor Maccoby's reanalysis of
data from the Gluecks' study of working mothers and delinquency, she shows
that working or not working has little effect once the quality of child care is
taken into account—Eleanor Maccoby, "Effects upon Children of their Mothers'
Outside Employment," in National Manpower Council, *Work in the Lives of
Married Women* (New York: Columbia University Press, 1958), pp. 150–72.
General reviews of the literature are found in: Lois M. Stolz, "Effects of
Maternal Employment on Children: Evidence from Research," *Child Develop-
ment*, 31 (December 1960), 749–82; Henry David, "Work, Women and Children,"
in Eli Ginzberg (ed.), *The Nation's Children*, Vol. 3, *Problems and Prospects*
(New York: Columbia University Press, 1960), pp. 180–98; and Elizabeth Herzog,
Children of Working Mothers (Washington, D.C.: U.S. Department of Health,
Education, and Welfare, Children's Bureau Publication No. 382, 1960); and most
recently, a volume of research papers on the employed mother by F. Ivan Nye
and Lois W. Hoffman, *The Employed Mother in America* (Chicago: Rand Mc-
Nally, 1963).

15. Marian Radke Yarrow *et al.*, "Child-rearing in Families of Working and Non-
working Mothers," *Sociometry*, 25 (June 1962), 122–40.

16. Only in recent years has there been a shift in the discussion and research on
maternal employment: investigators have begun to explore the *positive* effects of
maternal employment. For example, Urie Bronfenbrenner has suggested that
employed mothers may have a positive effect upon adolescent children by giving
them a chance to develop responsibility for their own behavior—Urie Bronfenbrenner, "Family Structure and Personality Development: Report of Progress"
(Ithaca: Cornell University, Department of Child Development and Family Relationships, 1958, mimeographed). Ruth Hartley has suggested that the working
mother may have "stretching effects" upon a child's perceptions and social concepts—Ruth E. Hartley, "What Aspects of Child Behavior Should Be Studied in
Relation to Maternal Employment," in *Research Issues Related to the Effects of
Maternal Employment on Children* (New York: Social Science Research Center,
Pennsylvania State University, 1961), p. 48.

17. The Burchinal-Rossman research cited previously did give special attention to
employment of mothers during the child's early years. Their seventh- and
eleventh-grade students were divided according to when the maternal employment
occurred—i.e., whether during the first three years of the child's life, second three,
between the ages of 1 and 6, only within the previous 30 months or for the
child's entire life. How long the mother had been working, or when in the
growth of the child she began work, showed no significant effect upon the

children's development: those whose mothers were working when they were under three years of age did not differ from those whose mothers began working when they were adolescents.

18. A. I. Rabin, "Infants and Children under Conditions of 'Intermittent' Mothering in the Kibbutz," *American Journal of Orthopsychiatry*, 28 (1958), 577–84; Rabin, "Personality Maturity of Kibbutz and Non-Kibbutz Children as Reflected in Rorschach Findings," *Journal of Projective Techniques*, 21 (1957), 148–53; Rabin, "Attitudes of Kibbutz Children to Family and Parents," *American Journal of Orthopsychiatry*, 29 (1959), 172–79; Rabin, "Some Psychosexual Differences between Kibbutz and Non-Kibbutz Israeli Boys," *Journal of Projective Techniques*, 22 (1958), 328–32; H. Faigin, "Social Behavior of Young Children in the Kibbutz," *Journal of Abnormal and Social Psychology*, 56 (1958), 117–29. A good overview of these studies can be found in David Rapaport, "The Study of Kibbutz Education and Its Bearing on the Theory of Development," *American Journal of Orthopsychiatry*, 28 (1958), 587–99.

19. There are, of course, other instances of infant and toddler care by persons supplementing the biological mother, notable among them being the crèche and nursery school systems in the Soviet Union. What effect these early experiences of crèche care have upon the subsequent personality development of Soviet young people is not known. Western observers who have visited them during the past several years have been impressed with the facilities, quality of staff personnel, and general happy mood of the children seen in them, but there is no rigorous evidence to substantiate these impressions or assess the effect of such early separation from the mother upon personality.

20. In this analysis, I am placing primary emphasis on the quality of the care given to the children. Another specification of maternal employment involves introducing the motivations and satisfactions of working and non-working mothers: many women work who do not wish to work, and many women are at home who do not wish to be at home. One recent study which took these factors into consideration found that the non-working mothers who are dissatisfied with not working (who want to work but, out of a sense of "duty," do not work) show the greatest problems in child rearing—more difficulty controlling their children, less emotional satisfaction in relationships to their children, less confidence in their functioning as mothers. Cf. Marian Radke Yarrow *et al.*, *op. cit.*

21. This shifts the ground of the problem of maternal employment to a very different level from the one on which it is usually discussed. As a research problem, the crucial question is not whether the mother is employed or not, but what is the quality of the care given to the children—whether by the mother alone or a combination of other adults. Since full-time mothers vary from loving care to rejecting neglect, and mother substitutes may be presumed to vary in the same way, it is scarcely surprising that maternal employment *per se* shows very little effect upon the personality of children. Social scientists have uncritically borrowed the assumption of the psychoanalysts that the mental health of the child is possible only with continuous care by the biological mother. What is clearly called for is a shift in research definition from maternal employment vs. full-time motherhood to the quality of the care the child receives under conditions of full- and part-time working or non-working mothers. There is also a need for research based on a clear conceptualization of the variables of both "maternal care" and "maternal deprivation." For a careful review of crucial dimensions of maternal care and their effect upon infants, see Leon J. Yarrow, "Research in Dimensions of Early Maternal Care," *Merrill-Palmer Quarterly*, 9 (April 1963), 101–14. The same author has written a careful re-evaluation of the concept of maternal deprivation: "Maternal Deprivation: Toward an Empirical and Conceptual Re-evaluation," *Psychological Bulletin*, 58 (1961), 459–90.

22. This passivity and softness in American young people has been noted in the following works: David Riesman, Introduction to Edgar Friedenberg, *The Vanishing Adolescent* (Boston: Beacon, 1959); Paul Goodman, *Growing Up Absurd* (New York: Random House, 1960); Marjorie K. McCorquodale, "What They Will Die for in Houston," *Harper's*, October 1961; the *Dædalus* issue on *Youth: Change and Challenge*, Winter 1962. The White House attempt in recent years

to revitalize physical education has been in part a response to the distressing signs of muscular deterioration and physical passivity of American youth.

23. Edward A. Steeker, *Their Mothers' Sons* (Philadelphia: Lippincott, 1946).
24. Friedenberg, *op. cit.*
25. Numerous authors have analyzed the effect of women's focus on their children as their chief achievement: John Spiegel, "New Perspectives in the Study of the Family," *Marriage and Family Living*, 16 (February 1954), 4–12; Bruno Bettelheim, "Growing Up Female," *Harper's*, October 1962. The effects of such exclusive maternal focus on children upon relations with married children are shown in: Marvin Sussman, "Family Continuity: Selective Factors Which Affect Relationships between Families at Generational Levels," *Marriage and Family Living*, 16 (May 1954), 112–30; Paul Wallin, "Sex Differences in Attitudes toward In-Laws," *American Journal of Sociology*, 59 (1954), 466–69; Harvey Locke, *Predicting Adjustment in Marriage* (New York: Holt, 1951); Evelyn M. Duvall, *In-Laws: Pro and Con* (New York: Associated Press, 1954); and Frances Jerome Woods, *The American Family System* (New York: Harper, 1959), pp. 265–66. These authors discuss the strains with mothers-in-law stemming from a too exclusive focus of women on their children and their subsequent difficulty in "releasing" their children when they are grown.
26. This has been argued by Eric Larrabee, though he does not suggest the employment of the mother as the way to make the older woman's life more interesting. See Eric Larrabee, "Childhood in Twentieth Century America," in Ginzberg, *op. cit.*, III, pp. 199–216.
27. See Margaret Cussler's profile of the "volunteer executive" in her study *The Woman Executive* (New York: Harcourt, Brace, 1958), pp. 111–18.
28. Viola Klein's study of English working women shows the same pattern: withdrawal and return to work at a later age is paid for by a loss of occupational status. See Viola Klein, *Working Wives*, Occasional Papers No. 15 (London: Institute of Personnel Management, 1960), pp. 21–24.
29. Myrdal and Klein, *op. cit.*, pp. 33–64; National Manpower Council, *Womanpower* (New York: Columbia University Press, 1957); Florence Kluckhohn, *The American Family: Past and Present and America's Women* (Chicago: Delphian Society, 1952), p. 116; and Rose Goldsen *et al.*, *What College Students Think* (Princeton: Van Nostrand, 1960), pp. 46–59, 81–96.
30. Florence Kluckhohn, "Variations in Basic Values of Family Systems," in Norman W. Bell and Ezra F. Vogel, *A Modern Introduction to the Family* (Glencoe, Ill.: The Free Press, 1960), pp. 304–16; and George Gallup and Evan Hill, "The American Woman," *Saturday Evening Post*, December 22, 1962, pp. 15–32.
31. Talcott Parsons, *Essays in Sociological Theory Pure and Applied* (Glencoe, Ill.: The Free Press, 1949), pp. 222–24, 243–46.

15. Male and Female

Steven Goldberg

No doubt there are many reasons why some women will accept the illogic of feminism. Anyone wishing to explore this area should examine a contemporary America in which the rage of young women protesting

Reprinted by permission of William Morrow & Co., Inc., from *The Inevitability of Patriarchy* by Steven Goldberg. Copyright © 1973 by Steven Goldberg.

professional discrimination is complemented by a revulsion toward professional roles by the men who are "supposed" to fill them. For an understanding of the forces that lead to the feelings of meaninglessness that so many men and women now seem to attach to their traditional roles perhaps one should begin not with the content of roles that were formerly capable of providing meaning, but with the failure of contemporary American society to inculcate in the society's members the feeling that the society's value system, its way of defining reality, is correct and meaningful. It is this ability, rather than the specific characteristics of the value system or the value system's "humaneness," that is the precondition for the society's survival and that is relevant to the members' present feeling of meaninglessness and the feelings of aloneness that are inevitable if the members have no meaning to share. When a society loses its ability to inculcate values its members fall into the abyss. Here traditions evaporate, as they must when the values on which they were founded seem meaningless, and they take all sense of continuity with them. Children no longer provide a sense of future, for values are the link we have with our children, and if we have no values—values based on intelligence infused with experience, not ideological proclamations supported by utopian fantasy—then we sacrifice our future for their contempt. In the abyss some will have the strength to become "the calm in the center of the whirlwind," but many will lack the faith, the strength, the courage, the will, and the imagination to create their own meaning. Having received no values from their society and having themselves created nothing worthy of passing on to their children, they will rail against everything in sight save the image in the mirror.

Liberation is an experience of personal salvation that implies power over oneself. It is far more than the attainment of social and economic freedom. One who has found a well of pure meaning will have no need to drown everyone in it. The priest does not frantically ignore biological evidence by arguing that the "sex drive" is merely an arbitrary social value or that we could expect many people to choose celibacy; he acknowledges the power of this drive while himself answering a more compelling call. Likewise, any woman who feels that her sense of meaning is satisfied in areas not usually considered feminine need not explain to anyone. She can never hope to live in a society that does not attach feminine expectations to women, but if she has the courage she will overcome the attitudinal discrimination that she will, undeniably, face. Certainly such discrimination is less threatening to one's liberation than the obsessive hatred of an enemy who serves only to symbolize one's inner turmoil, the avoidance of the battles for one's own existence, or the inevitably futile attempt to substitute group strength for individual psychic weakness. No one is denying the value of the woman who devotes her life to career rather than to children; there is no need for her to rewrite physiology, anthropology, and psychology in order to rationalize an unnecessary defense.

Ultimately every examined life can be interpreted as a disaster; looking closely enough we can always discover psychological and social forces that could provide fuel for unlimited rage. For every intelligent and creative woman there are ten men who must stumble through life without the aid of intelligence or creativity. But no life can transcend its own disasters unless it celebrates its uniqueness and contributes that which only it can contribute. Life is perverted if one is constantly reacting, never initiating, but always allowing rage to define it.

Too often such a definition shapes the lives of contemporary middle-class radicals in general and feminists in particular. Too often we fail to ask men and women to face the battles of their own existence; we merely inquire as to which form of societal oppression it is that is causing their desperation and accept their exaggeration of external oppressions, oppressions that they use to camouflage the terrors that one must face alone because such terrors are inherent in existence. This is not only sad, but dangerous. When a moral urgency is superimposed on an emotional immaturity, as it is when an affluent, educated generation grows up without ever being forced to learn that life's choices offer rewards that are mutually exclusive, fanaticism is more probable than altruism. The alacrity with which feminists invent some "facts" and reject or accept others on the basis of their emotional appeal is illusion in the guise of intellectual investigation. Invocation of this illusion as rationalization is self-indulgence parading as virtue. There is no doubt that American society demands some new answers quickly. But the readiness of increasingly large numbers of radicals to translate nearly any new idea immediately into action does not demonstrate rational response nor even pragmatic desperation but betrays an emotional development so stunted that they are forced to navigate life on one engine; the intellect is twisted to serve the stabilizing function of inculcating meaning usually served in part by the emotions. Who but the children of the forties and fifties could believe that evolution would do an about-face this very year just because they did not like the way it was going? Who but children, who combine an intellectual egalitarianism (which views every individual's ideas as equally valid and accepts one idea over another on the basis of its ideological value and its perceived sincerity) with an emotional elitism which derides as delusory false consciousness the emotional satisfactions of all the world's men and women, could be so petulant as to attempt to justify their longing contempt for the eternal sources of joy with an analysis built of ignorance and held together by fallacy? Who but children whose lifelong nurturance on material things has cursed them with the inability to discover the small joys which define happiness could have failed to learn that human imperfection will be grafted onto any institution? To confuse this inevitable imperfection with the causes that render the institution inevitable is unintelligent. To hope for the perfection of any institution or the disappearance of the institution because imperfection is inevitable is utopian.

Both men and women, even the feminist who rails against such a feeling, feel that the husband "allows" and "protects." Here the difference between those who strive for equal pay for equal work and those who reject the validity of their own feelings and observations and accept the feminist analysis is seen in bold relief. For the former, the question of patriarchy and dominance is unimportant. For the latter, it is crucial; the feminist's philosophical aversion to the possibility of the inevitability of male dominance stems from her finding this possibility psychologically intolerable. Indeed, feminist literature emphasizes this area far more than it does real economic discrimination. Economic discrimination is abhorrent because it is artificial. When we speak of male dominance we are speaking of the feelings of both men and women that the man selected by the woman "allows" and "protects," feelings motivating the actions and determining the institutions of every society without exception. It is these masculine and feminine feelings, the emotional manifestations of our biologies and the emotional prerequisites of political power, that prescribe the limits of sexual roles and social possibility. As long as societies are composed of human beings these feelings will be inevitable. To judge them is not merely stupid, it is blasphemous.

The central role will forever belong to women; they set the rhythm of things. Women everywhere are aware that sublimation is an ignorance of the center, one of the most stunning regularities one notices as he studies the cross-cultural data closely is the extent to which women in all societies view male preoccupation with dominance and suprafamilial pursuit in the same way the American wife views her husband's obsession with professional football—with a loving condescension and an understanding that men embrace the surrogate and forget the source. Nature has bestowed on women the biological abilities and biopsychological propensities that enable the species to sustain itself. Men must forever stand at the periphery, questing after the surrogate powers, creativity, and meaning that nature has not seen fit to make innate functions of *their* biology. Each man knows that he can never again be the most important person in another's life for long and all know that they must reassert superiority in enough areas often enough to justify nature's allowing them to stay. There is no alternative; this is simply the way it is. At the bottom of it all man's job is to protect woman and woman's is to protect her infant; in nature all else is luxury. There are feminists who try to have it both ways; they deny the importance of the biological basis of the behavior of the sexes, yet blame the world's woes on the male characteristics of its leaders. The latter hypothesis is correct, and we find that we are trapped in what could be the final irony: the biological factors that underlie women's life-sustaining abilities—the qualities most vital to the survival of our species—preclude women's ever manifesting the psychological predisposition, the obsessive need of power, or the abilities necessary for the attainment of significant amounts of political power.

It is not merely that the line is thin that separates the male's aggression from the child's demandingness; the aggression is inseparable from its childish component. What is lacking in the male is an acceptance that radiates from all women save those few who are driven to deny their greatest source of strength. Perhaps this female wisdom comes from resignation to the reality of male aggression; more likely it is a harmonic of the woman's knowledge that ultimately she is the one who matters. As a result, while there are more brilliant men than brilliant women, there are more good women than good men. Women are not dependent on male brilliance for their deepest sources of strength, but men are dependent on female strength. Few women have been ruined by men; female endurance survives. Many men, however, have been destroyed by women who did not understand or did not care to understand male fragility.

In any case the central fact is that men and women are different from each other from the gene to the thought to the act and that emotions that underpin masculinity and femininity, that make reality as experienced by the male eternally different from that experienced by the female, flow from the biological natures of man and woman. This is the one fact that the feminist cannot admit. For to admit this would be to admit that the liberations of men and women must proceed along different and complementary lines and that the women of every society have taken the paths they have not because they were forced by men but because they have followed their own imperatives. Neither I, nor, I gather, the vast majority of women can imagine why any woman would *want* to deny the biological basis of the enormous powers inherent in women's roles as directors of societies' emotional resources; doing so demands that one accept the male belief that power has to do with action rather than feeling. But whatever the reasons, denial does not indicate that there was a choice. If we have learned nothing else from the wisdom of every culture, we should have learned by now that one cannot transcend his fate until he accepts it. Women who deny their natures, who accept men's secondhand definitions and covet a state of second-rate manhood, are forever condemned—to paraphrase Ingrid Bengis's wonderful phrase—to argue against their own juices. For all the injustices committed in attempts to enforce bogus biological laws, roles associated with gender have been primarily the result rather than the cause of sexual differences. Sex is the single most decisive determinant of personal identity; it is the first thing we notice about another person and the last thing we forget. Just as it is criminal for others to limit one's identity by invoking arbitrary limitations in the name of nature, so it is terribly self-destructive to refuse to accept one's own nature and the joys and powers it invests.

V. The Peer Group

The peer group is a collectivity of individuals who associate with one another because of a certain similarity in age, interest, and social situation. They share a common culture or subculture, or, as the sociologically sophisticated J. Milton Yinger points out, they share a common contraculture. Although peer groups flourish at every point in the life cycle, the term usually pertains to adolescence and young adulthood. The groups formed may be perfectly conventional; if so, they are less likely to be studied than deviant and delinquent ones. Peer groups exist at all class levels, but again, lower-class ethnic gangs receive more attention than middle- and upper-class cliques.

In his classic essay on subcultures and contracultures, Yinger makes a number of distinctions that are especially useful, if only because they turn our attention to the norms of middle-class culture and to the society at large.

Bernard Rosenberg and Harry Silverstein delineate three ethnically, racially, and geographically distinct peer groups. In this selection the authors concentrate on dating, sex and marriage. Each economically impoverished group turns out to be markedly different from the others. Not only do their patterns of association vary, but so do their values and their actions. Each bears a distinctive mark of subcultural and contracultural variation.

William J. Chambliss, a gifted criminologist, covers the relatively neglected area of class differences in peer groups. Whether the "Saints" are lawbreakers or not, their class background protects them from being stigmatized as delinquents. The "Roughnecks," because of *their* class background, are automatically labeled delinquents. Chambliss makes clear that this difference in designation is traceable to biases in perception by teachers, police officers, and school administrators. As a result, the Saints are able to escape the punitive response to delin-quency while Roughneck delinquency is reinforced. Chambliss suggests that the Saints, who can pretend conventionality because of their middle-class origins, will be defined as normatively acceptable. The Roughnecks, lacking virtuosity in dissimulation, are destined to lead less acceptable, less reputable, and less remunerative lives.

16. Contraculture and Subculture

J. Milton Yinger

In recent years there have been widespread and fruitful employment of the concept of subculture in sociological and anthropological research. The term has been used to focus attention not only on the wide diversity of norms to be found in many societies but on the normative aspects of deviant behavior. The ease with which the term has been adopted, with little study of its exact meaning or its values and its difficulties, is indica-tive of its utility in emphasizing a sociological point of view in research that has been strongly influenced both by individualistic and moralistic interpretations. To describe the normative qualities of an occupation, to contrast the value systems of social classes, or to emphasize the con-trolling power of the code of a delinquent gang is to underline a socio-logical aspect of these phenomena that is often disregarded.

In the early days of sociology and anthropology, a key task was to document the enormous variability of culture from society to society and to explore the significance of the overly simplified but useful idea that "the mores can make anything right." In recent years that task has been extended to the study of the enormous variability of culture *within* some societies. It is unfortunate that "subculture," a central concept in this process, has seldom been adequately defined.[1] It has been used as an *ad hoc* concept whenever a writer wished to emphasize the normative aspects of behavior that differed from some general standard. The result has been a blurring of the meaning of the term, confusion with other terms, and a failure frequently to distinguish between two levels of social causation.

Reprinted with permission of author and publisher from *American Sociological Re-view* 25 (October 1960):625–35.

Few concepts appear so often in current sociological writing. In the course of twelve months, I have noted over 100 books and articles that make some use, from incidental to elaborate, of the idea of "subculture." The usages vary so widely, however, that the value of the term is severely limited. If chemists had only one word to refer to all colorless liquids and this led them to pay attention to only the two characteristics shared in common, their analysis would be exceedingly primitive. Such an analogy overstates the diversity of ideas covered by "subculture," but the range is very wide. Nevertheless three distinct meanings can be described.

In some anthropological work, subculture refers to certain universal tendencies that seem to occur in all societies. They underlie culture, precede it, and set limits to the range of its variation. Thus Kroeber writes: "Indeed, such more or less recurrent near-regularities of form or process as have to date been formulated for culture are actually subcultural in nature. They are limits set to culture by physical or organic factors."[2] In *The Study of Man*, Linton uses subculture to refer to various pan-human phenomena that seem to occur everywhere. Thus good-natured and tyrannical parents may be found in societies that differ widely in their family patterns.[3] This use shades off into other concepts that are similar but not identical: Edward Sapir's "precultural" and Cooley's "human nature" refer to biological and social influences that underlie all cultures.[4] Since subculture is only rarely used today to refer to this series of ideas, I shall exclude them from further consideration, with the suggestion that the use of Sapir's term "precultural" might well clarify our thinking.

Two other usages of subculture represent a much more serious confusion. The term is often used to point to the normative systems of groups smaller than a society, to give emphasis to the ways these groups differ in such things as language, values, religion, diet, and style of life from the larger society of which they are a part. Perhaps the most common referent in this usage is an ethnic enclave (French Canadians in Maine) or a region (the subculture of the South), but the distinctive norms of much smaller and more temporary groups (even a particular friendship group) may be described as a subculture. Kluckhohn, for example, refers to "the subculture of anthropologists" and Riesman to "subcultures among the faculty."

This second meaning, which itself contains some ambiguities, as we shall see, must be distinguished from a third meaning associated with it when the reference is to norms that arise specifically from a frustrating situation or from conflict between a group and the larger society. Thus the emergent norms of a delinquent gang or the standards of an adolescent peer group have often been designated "subcultural." In addition to a cultural dimension, this third usage introduces a social-psychological dimension, for there is direct reference to the personality factors involved in the development and maintenance of the norms. Specifically, such personality tendencies as frustration, anxiety, feelings of role ambiguity, and resentment are shown to be involved in the creation of the subculture. The mutual influence of personality and culture is not a distinctive characteristic of this type of subculture, of course, for they are everywhere interactive. . . .

Yet the nature of the relation is not the same in all cases. The term subculture, when used in the third way described here, raises to a position of prominence one particular kind of dynamic linkage between norms and personality: the creation of a series of inverse or counter values (opposed to those of the surrounding society) in face of serious frustration or conflict. To call attention to the special aspects of this kind of normative system, I suggest the term *contraculture*. Before exploring the relationship between subculture and contraculture, however, the range of meanings given subculture even when it is limited to the second usage requires comment.

SUBCULTURE AND ROLE

The variety of referents for the term subculture is very wide because the normative systems of sub-societies can be differentiated on many grounds. The groups involved may range from a large regional subdivision to a religious sect with only one small congregation. The distinctive norms may involve many aspects of life—religion, language, diet, moral values—or, for example, only a few separate practices among the members of an occupational group. Further distinctions among subcultures might be made on the basis of time (has the subculture persisted through a number of generations?), origin (by migration, absorption by a dominant society, social or physical segregation, occupational specialization, and other sources), and by the mode of relationship to the surrounding culture (from indifference to conflict). Such wide variation in the phenomena covered by a term can be handled by careful specification of the several grounds for subclassification. Confusion has arisen not so much from the scope of the term subculture as from its use as a substitute for "role." Only with great effort is some degree of clarity being achieved in the use of the role concept and the related terms "position" and "role behavior." Were this development retarded by confusion of role with subculture it would be unfortunate. All societies have differentiating roles, but only heterogeneous societies have subcultures. Role is *that part of* a full culture that is assigned, as the appropriate rights and duties, to those occupying a given position.[5] These rights and duties usually interlock into a system with those of persons who occupy other positions. They are known to and accepted by all those who share the culture. Thus the role of a physician is known, at least in vague outline, by most persons in a society and it is seen as part of the total culture. (This is not to prejudge the question of role consensus, for there may be many non-role aspects of being a physician.) But subculture is not tied in this way into the larger cultural complex: it refers to norms that set a group apart from, not those that integrate a group with, the total society. Subcultural norms, as contrasted with role norms, are unknown to, looked down upon, or thought of as separating forces by the other members of a society. There are doubtless subcultural aspects of being a physician—normative influences affecting his behavior that are not part of his role, not culturally designated rights and duties. But the empirical mixture should not obscure the need for this analytic distinction.

Along with confusion with the role concept, subculture carries many of the ambiguities associated with the parent concept of culture. In much social scientific writing it is not at all clear whether culture refers to norms, that is, to expected or valued behavior, or to behavior that is widely followed and therefore normal in a statistical sense only. This dual referent is particularly likely to be found in the work of anthropologists. Perhaps because their concepts are derived largely from the study of relatively more stable and homogeneous societies, they draw less sharply the distinction between the statistically normal and the normative. Sociologists are more apt to find it necessary to explore the tensions between the social order and culture, to be alert to deviations, and they are therefore more likely to define culture abstractly as a shared normative system. Yet much of the commentary on subculture refers to behavior. In my judgment this identification is unwise. Behavior is the result of the convergence of many forces. One should not assume, when the members of a group behave in similar ways, that cultural norms produce this result. Collective behavior theory and personality theory may also help to account for the similarities.

CONTRACULTURE

Failure to distinguish between role and subculture and vagueness in the concept of culture itself are not the only difficulties in the use of the idea of subculture. Perhaps more serious is the tendency to obscure, under this one term, two levels of explanation, one sociological and the other social-psychological, with a resulting failure to understand the causal forces at work. On few topics can one get wider agreement among sociologists than on the dangers of reductionism. If a psychologist attempts to explain social facts by psychological theories, we throw the book (probably Durkheim) at him; we emphasize the "fallacy of misplaced concreteness." In view of the widespread neglect of sociocultural factors in the explanation of behavior, this is a necessary task. It makes vitally important, however, keen awareness by sociologists that they also deal with an abstract model. Perhaps we can reverse Durkheim's dictum to say: Do not try to explain social psychological facts by sociological theories; or, more adequately, do not try to explain *behavior* (a product of the interaction of sociocultural and personality influences) by a sociological theory alone. Yablonsky has recently reminded us that an excessively sociological theory of gangs can result in our seeing a definite group structure and a clear pattern of norms where in fact there is a "near-group," with an imprecise definition of boundaries and limited agreement on norms.[6] Carelessly used, our concepts can obscure the facts we seek to understand.

To see the cultural element in delinquency or in the domination of an individual by his adolescent group, phenomena that on the surface are non-cultural or even "anti-cultural," was a long step forward in their explanation. But it is also necessary to see the non-cultural aspects of some "norms"—phenomena that on the surface seem thoroughly cultural. Our vocabulary needs to be rich enough to help us to deal with these differences. The tendency to use the same term to refer to phenomena that share *some* elements in common, disregarding important differences, is to be content with phyla names when we need also to designate genus and species.

To sharpen our analysis, I suggest the use of the term contraculture wherever the normative system of a group contains, as a primary element, a theme of conflict with the values of the total society, where personality variables are directly involved in the development and maintenance of the group's values, and wherever its norms can be understood only by reference to the relationships of the group to a surrounding dominant culture.[7] None of these criteria definitely separates contraculture from subculture because each is a continuum. Sub-societies fall along a range with respect to each criterion. The values of most subcultures probably conflict in some measure with the larger culture. In a contraculture, however, the conflict element is central; many of the values, indeed, are specifically contradictions of the values of the dominant culture. Similarly, personality variables are involved in the development and maintenance of all cultures and subcultures, but usually the influence of personality is by way of variations around a theme that is part of the culture. In a contraculture, on the other hand, the theme itself expresses the tendencies of the persons who compose it. Finally, the norms of all subcultures are doubtless affected in some degree by the nature of the relationship with the larger culture. A subculture, as a pure type, however, does not require, for its understanding, intensive analysis of interaction with the larger culture; that is, its norms are not, to any significant degree, a product of that interaction. But a contraculture can be understood only by giving full attention to the interaction of the group which is its bearer with the larger society. . . .

Empirically, subcultural and contracultural influences may be mixed, of course. Delinquency and adolescent behavior almost certainly manifest both influences. The need, however, is to develop a clean analytic distinction between the two in order to interpret the wide variations in their mixture. . . .

DELINQUENT CONTRACULTURE

The usefulness of separating subcultural and contracultural influences is seen particularly clearly in the analysis of delinquency and of criminality generally. Perhaps in no other field were there more substantial gains in understanding made possible by the introduction of a sociological point of view to supplement and to correct individualistic and moralistic interpretations. There is little need to review the extensive literature, from *Delinquent Gangs* to *Delinquent Boys*, to establish the importance of the normative element in criminal and delinquent behavior. It is a mistake, however, to try to stretch a useful concept into a total theory. A "complex-adequate" analysis[8] may seem less sharp and definitive than one based on one factor, but it is likely to be far more useful. Cohen's excellent work,[9] although labelled as a study of the culture of the gang, does not overlook the psychogenic sources of delinquency. In fact, his explanation of the origins of the subculture (contraculture) and its functions for the lower class male makes clear that the norms of the gang are not learned, accepted, and taught in the same way that we learn what foods to eat, what clothes to wear, what language to speak. The very existence of the gang is a sign, in part, of blocked ambition. Because tensions set in motion by this blockage cannot be resolved by achievement of dominant values, such values are repressed, their importance denied, counter-values affirmed. The gang member is often ambivalent. Thwarted in his desire to achieve higher status by the criteria of the dominant society, he accepts criteria he can meet; but the reaction-formation in this response is indicated by the content of the delinquent norms—non-utilitarian, malicious, and negativistic, in Cohen's terms. This negative polarity represents the need to repress his own tendencies to accept the dominant cultural standards. This is not to say that the values of the gang cannot be explained partially by cultural analysis, by some extension of the idea that "the mores can make anything right." But I suggest that Cohen's multiple-factor analysis might have been clearer, and less subject to misinterpretation, had he introduced the concept of contraculture alongside the concept of subculture. . . .

It should be stressed once more that these are analytic concepts, no one of which is adequate to handle the empirical variations of delinquent behavior. Failure to recognize the abstract quality of our conceptual tools leads to unnecessary disagreements. When Miller describes the "Lower Class Culture as a Generating Milieu of Gang Delinquency," for example, he points to an important series of influences that derive from the value system of the lower-class community.[10] In his effort to emphasize this aspect of the etiology of delinquency, however, he tends to overlook the kind of evidence reported by Sykes and Matza, Cohen,

Finestone, Yablonsky, the McCords, and others concerning collective behavior and personality variables.[11] Surely the evidence is now rich enough for us to state definitively that delinquency is a multi-variable product. The task ahead is not to prove that it stems largely from cultural or subcultural or contracultural influences, but to spell out the conditions under which these and other factors will be found in various empirical mixtures.

CONTRACULTURAL ASPECTS OF CLASS
AND OCCUPATION

The same admixture of the concepts of culture, subculture, and contraculture is found in the extensive literature on occupations and classes. Doubtless all three forces are found in many instances, and the research task is to untangle their various influences. It may stretch the meaning of the term too far to speak of the *position* of the "middle-class member," with its culturally designated role specification; although in relatively stable societies the usage seems appropriate. In such societies, many of the rights and obligations of various status levels are culturally defined. In more mobile class systems, however, subcultural and contracultural norms become important. Our understanding of the American class system has certainly been deepened in the last twenty years by the descriptions of differences, among classes, in value perspectives, time orientations, levels of aspiration, leisure-time styles, and child rearing practices.

The introduction of the concept of subculture has helped to avoid class derived biases in the interpretation of the wide variations in these phenomena. In class analysis as in the study of deviations, however, there may be some over-compensation in the effort to eliminate the distortions of a middle-class and often rural perspective.[12] There is evidence to suggest that differences between classes are based less upon different values and norms than the subcultural approach suggests. The "innovations" of lower-class members, to use Merton's term, are not simply subcultural acts defined as innovative by middle-class persons. They are in part responses to a frustrating situation. They are efforts to deal with the disjunction of means and ends. When the disjunction is reduced, the variations in value and behavior are reduced. Thus Rosen found, "surprisingly," that Negroes in the Northeast made higher scores on an "achievement value" test than his description of Negro "culture" led him to expect. This may indicate that the low achievement response is less the result of a subcultural norm than a protest against a difficult situation. If the situation improves, the achievement value changes.[13] Stephenson's discovery that occupational plans of lower-class youth are considerably below those of higher-class youth, but that their aspirations are only slightly lower, bears on this same point. His data suggest that the classes differ not only in norms, but also in opportunity.[14] Differences in behavior, therefore, are only partly a result of subcultural contrasts. The lower educational aspirations of lower-class members are also found to be in part situationally induced, not simply normatively induced. When the situation changes, values and behavior change, as Mulligan found in his study of the response of the sons of blue-collar workers to the educational opportunities of the GI Bill, and as Wilson reports in his investigation of the aspirations of lower-class boys attending higher-class schools and upper-class boys attending lower-class schools.[15]

In short, our thinking about differences in behavior among social classes will be sharpened if we distinguish among those differences that derive from role influences, those based on subcultural variations, and those that express contracultural responses to deprivation. The proportions will vary from society to society; the research task is to specify the conditions under which various distributions occur. One would expect, to propose one hypothesis, to find more contracultural norms among lower-class members of an open society than in a similar group in a closed society.

The interpretation of differential behavior among the members of various occupational categories can also be strengthened by the distinctions made above. Here the contrast between role and subculture is especially useful. The role of a teacher consists of the rights and duties that *integrate* him into a system of expected and established relationships with others. The teaching subculture, on the other hand, insofar as it exists, *separates* teachers from the cultural world of others. It is either unknown to others or, if known, a source of disagreement and perhaps of conflict with others. There are also contracultural aspects of some occupational styles of life. In interpreting the differences between the values of jazz musicians and "squares," for example, Becker writes: "their rejection of commercialism in music and squares in social life was part of the casting aside of the total American culture by men who could enjoy privileged status but who were unable to achieve a satisfactory personal adjustment within it."[16] Their style of life, in other words, can be understood only by supplementing the cultural and subcultural dimensions with the conflict theme. Cameron develops the same point. Although he makes no use of the term subculture, he describes the differentiating norms of the dance-band group, presumably a result of the "esoteric" aspects of their art, the differences in their time schedule, and the like. But he also describes the *contra* aspects of some of the norms, and suggests that they derive from the fact that early recruitment ties the jazz musician to the adolescence problem.[17]

CONCLUSION

Poorly defined terms plague research in many areas, particularly in the specification of relationships between sociological and social psychological levels of analysis. Thus "anomie" is still used to refer both to a social structural fact and to a personality fact, although this confusion is gradually being reduced. "Role" may refer, alternately, to rights and duties prescribed for the occupants of a position or to individual performance of that position. And subculture, I have suggested, is used to designate both the traditional norms of a sub-society and the emergent norms of a group caught in a frustrating and conflict-laden situation. This paper indicates that there are differences in the origin, function, and perpetuation of traditional and emergent norms, and suggests that the use of the concept contraculture for the latter might improve sociological analysis.

Hypotheses to guide the study of subculture can most profitably be derived from a general theory of culture. As an illustration, it may be hypothesized that a subculture will appear, in the first instance, as a result of mobility or an extension of communication that brings groups of different cultural background into membership in the same society, followed by physical or social isolation or both that prevents full assimilation.

Hypotheses concerning contracultures, on the other hand, can best be derived from social psychological theory—from the study of collective behavior, the frustration-aggression thesis, or the theory of group formation. One might hypothesize, for example, that under conditions of deprivation and frustration of major values (in a context where the deprivation is obvious because of extensive communication with the dominant group), and where value confusion and weak social controls obtain, contracultural norms will appear. One would expect to find, according to these propositions, many subcultural values among southern rural Negroes. Among first and second generation urban Negroes, however, one would expect an increase in contracultural norms. Both groups are deprived, but in the urban situation there is more "value leakage" from the dominant group, more value confusion, and weakened social controls.[18]

The subculture of the sociologist requires sophistication about the full range of human behavior. This desideratum has led to the proposition that the vast diversity of norms believed in and acted upon by the members of a modern society is not a sign of value confusion and breakdown but rather an indication that urban life brings into one system of interaction persons drawn from many cultural worlds. One unanticipated consequence of the sociological subculture may be that we exaggerate the normative insulation and solidarity of these various worlds. An important empirical question concerns the extent and results of their interaction.

NOTES

1. There are a few formal definitions. For example: "The term 'subculture' refers in this paper to 'cultural variants displayed by certain segments of the population.' Subcultures are distinguished not by one or two isolated traits—they constitute relatively cohesive cultural systems. They are worlds within the larger world of our national culture." (Mirra Komarovsky and S. S. Sargent, "Research into

Subcultural Influences upon Personality," in S. S. Sargent and M. W. Smith, editors, *Culture and Personality*, New York: The Viking Fund, 1949, 143.) These authors then refer to class, race, occupation, residence, and region. After referring to sub-group values and language, Kimball Young and Raymond W. Mack state: "Such shared learned behaviors which are common to a specific group or category are called *subcultures.*" (*Sociology and Social Life*, New York: American Book, 1959, 49.) They refer then to ethnic, occupational, and regional variations. Blaine Mercer writes: "A society contains numerous subgroups, each with its own characteristic ways of thinking and acting. These cultures within a culture are called *subcultures.*" (*The Study of Society*, New York: Harcourt-Brace, 1958, 34.) Thereafter he discusses Whyte's *Streetcorner Society.* Although these definitions are helpful, they fail to make several distinctions which are developed below.

2. A. L. Kroeber, "The Concept of Culture in Science," *Journal of General Education* (April, 1949), 187.
3. Ralph Linton, *The Study of Man*, New York: Appleton-Century, 1936, 486.
4. Edward Sapir, "Personality," in *Encyclopedia of the Social Sciences*, New York: Macmillan, 1931, Vol. 12, 86; Charles H. Cooley, *Human Nature and the Social Order*, revised edition, New York: Scribner, 1922.
5. It is possible, of course, for a subculture to specify roles within its own system.
6. Lewis Yablonsky, "The Delinquent Gang as a Near-Group," *Social Problems* (Fall, 1959), 108–17.
7. By the noun in "contraculture" I seek to call attention to the normative aspects of the phenomena under study and by the qualifying prefix to call attention to the conflict aspects.
8. See Robin M. Williams, Jr., "Continuity and Change in Sociological Study," *American Sociological Review* (December, 1958), 619–33.
9. Albert K. Cohen, *Delinquent Boys*, Glencoe, Ill.: Free Press, 1955.
10. Walter B. Miller, "Lower Class Culture as a Generating Milieu of Gang Delinquency," *The Journal of Social Issues* (1958), 5–19.
11. In addition to the studies of Cohen and Yablonsky cited above, see Gresham M. Sykes and David Matza, "Techniques of Neutralization: A Theory of Delinquency," *American Sociological Review* (December, 1957), 664–70; Harold Finestone, "Cats, Kicks, and Color," *Social Problems* (July, 1957), 3–13; and William McCord and Joan McCord, *Origins of Crime. A New Evaluation of the Cambridge-Somerville Youth Study*, New York: Columbia University, 1959.
12. C. Wright Mills, "The Professional Ideology of Social Pathologists," *American Journal of Sociology* (September, 1943), 165–80.
13. Bernard C. Rosen, "Race, Ethnicity, and the Achievement Syndrome," *American Sociological Review* (February, 1959), 47–60.
14. Richard M. Stephenson, "Mobility Orientation and Stratification of 1,000 Ninth Graders," *American Sociological Review* (April, 1957), 204–12.
15. Raymond A. Mulligan, "Socio-Economic Background and College Enrollment," *American Sociological Review* (April, 1951), 188–96; Alan B. Wilson, "Residential Segregation of Social Classes and Aspirations of High School Boys," *American Sociological Review* (December, 1959), 836–45.
16. Howard S. Becker, "The Professional Dance Musician and His Audience," *American Journal of Sociology* (September, 1951), 136–44.
17. W. B. Cameron, "Sociological Notes on the Jam Session," *Social Forces* (December, 1954), 177–82.
18. There are numerous alternative ways in which the protest against deprivation can be expressed. Delinquency and drug addiction often have a contracultural aspect; but somewhat less clearly, political and religious movements among disprivileged groups may also invert the values of the influential but inaccessible dominant group. Thus the concept of contraculture may help us to understand, for example, the Garveyite movement, the Ras Tafari cult, and some aspects of the value schemes of lower-class sects. (See, e.g., Liston Pope, *Millhands and Preachers*, New Haven: Yale University Press, 1942; and George E. Simpson, "The Ras Tafari Movement in Jamaica: A Study of Race and Class Conflict," *Social Forces* [December, 1955], 167–70.)

17. Patterns of Sexual Behavior

Bernard Rosenberg and Harry Silverstein

A common culture presupposes that those who belong to it speak the same language. There is such a language for all Americans as there is an overarching culture that unifies urban dwellers and farmers, the young and the old, the privileged and the underprivileged. Subcultural segmentation produces "special languages" within the larger linguistic community, and they are intelligible only to initiates, that is, members of ethnic, occupational, regional, and religious groups. That the broadly conceptualized culture (or subculture) of poverty is somewhat illusory can be demonstrated by the variegated speech patterns characteristic of poor Appalachian whites, Negroes, and Puerto Ricans. Indeed, for each of our populations it would be possible to assemble a glossary of terms, widely used by insiders but meaningless to most outsiders. How luxuriant local variation (in meaning, accent, and value) takes place is the proper subject matter of a highly technical discipline called ethnolinguistics. It is not our intention to turn that discipline loose on data gathered for other purposes. Nevertheless, this much must be said: each group living in its own slum moves toward a certain linguistic homogeneity, bringing ancestral speech ways, borrowing symbols from the larger society, and synthesizing them into distinctive configurations. Peculiarities of speech are a rough index of differential association and cultural isolation. Unique idioms emerge from intense in-group living, and disappear at the opposite pole of full acculturation. In between, we find a complex mixture reflecting uneven exposure to the wider institutional order, which is itself in constant flux. A few illustrations from the heterosexual sphere may be in order.

In our sample, the adolescent males of New York and Washington are unresponsive to questions about dating. The word does not appear in their lexicon, and, as it turns out, this fact points to a substantive difference in behavior between these boys and those in Chicago. Every respondent in Chicago knows what a date is. One at first defines it as, "Goin' out with a fox," then adds, "you just go out driving, make some love, catch a crib—and that's all." Here indeed are the cadences, the

Reprinted by permission of the publisher from *The Varieties of Delinquent Experience* by Bernard Rosenberg and Harry Silverstein, © 1969 by Xerox Corporation, published by Xerox College Publishing.

inflections and the semantics of a special language in which "fox" means girl and "crib" stands for house or apartment, which in turn signifies a trysting place that one "catches" along with the "fox." Such expressions may have their origin in the hill country of Kentucky and Alabama, whence they were transplanted to the midwest and, merged with much else, produced a dynamic amalgam that cannot be duplicated elsewhere.

There are fuzzy edges around every word that is variously defined not only at different levels of the social hierarchy, but within any one level. For those who generalize in the grand manner, dating is understood to be "an American" phenomenon; the more sophisticated family sociologists who prepare textbooks for college students see it as a peculiar ritual, a courtship pattern, practiced by middle-class youth in the United States. In our sampling of the underclass, only teenagers in Chicago date, and they do so in ways similar to and dissimilar from those of their middle-class counterparts. The telephone for instance plays no great part in their activities, as it does among more privileged adolescents, but the automobile is central. Neither matters much in New York and Washington.

The Chicago boys, who will sometimes commit crimes to get a car and need it to commit other crimes, whose vocabulary is rich with the knowledge they have of car parts, may be said to live in a car complex. This circumstance provides them with a degree of physical mobility far greater than that of any other economically deprived group we have studied. In a crisis, occasioned, say, by the impregnation of a girl friend (by no means a rare occurrence), they can always take to the road, ranging widely over Illinois and adjacent states. The automobile liberates them, up to a point, not only from their constricted neighborhood, but from the metropolis itself. And, given the car, they are able to date girls in a more or less conventional manner. The "portable bedroom" can be used for preliminary sex play most conveniently at drive-in movies where two or three couples commonly occupy one car. Asked what he usually does on a date, a fifteen year old Chicago boy replies in part:

> If your friend's got a girl he's taking to the drive-in, you take her with him. And you take your girl to the show, go out to eat, dance, stuff like that.

On the average, what does a date cost?

> Well, if you go to a show, you won't have to spend but about, at the most, five, maybe six dollars . . . If you go to the drive-in, you spend a dollar and and a half for each one to get in. That's three dollars. Give the kid who's driving the car a buck, split the gas bill, you know, help to pay for some of the gas—and you eat. Oh, it costs you about six dollars.

Bowling and roller-skating are other diversions deemed to be suitable on dates in Chicago. Neither is a popular boy–girl pastime in the other cities—where boys like sports they play with other boys. Pickups are made on the street from a car, in neighborhood movie houses, and teen-age bars which are frequented with great regularity only in Chicago.

All of this sounds a great deal like the textbook account, even to a general preference for double-dating. Yet, the reasons behind that preference give us a clue to something different and specific to the Chicago group, namely that a heavy streak of violence is woven into the texture of their heterosexual behavior. Hence: "I like to go out with other couples because it's better when you travel together. When you're alone, there's always other guys trying to start trouble." You date, but you appear alone with a girl at your own peril, as this little vignette makes clear:

> I saw her walking down the hall with another boy, and I got pretty jealous. I started saying, "If you like that guy so much, go ahead and go out with him," and he walked up and started smartin' off to me. So I hit him, and then I beat him up. She turned around and slapped me. She called me a brute or something . . . So that didn't hit me just right, and I said, "Forget it."

If a date culminates in sexual intercourse, it is also useful to have some-one else along:

> I was going with a girl. She was sixteen. She squealed on me, and they tried to get me on statutory rape. And, oh, she gave 'em a big long story, trying to get me into a lot of trouble. But there was another kid along with me on that date. And she claimed that he held her down and that I held her down. But this boy's stories matched and hers didn't. Otherwise, I would have been sunk.

With dating, there go the lineaments of a rating–dating complex, which does not precisely parallel Willard Waller's famous description of a wide-spread campus phenomenon, but does imply a measure of respect for the girls one dates, by contrast with the disrespect accorded girls and older women who are nothing but sexual objects. The following example is somewhat extreme but highly indicative:

> I consider a girl you go out with and a girl you have intercourse with two different kinds of girls. There's a girl I date. I like to hold hands with her and make out with her, kiss her, but that's as far as I want to go with any girl I take out. If I like the girl, I don't want to mess her up. But then, there is the other girls I just don't care about because they give it to the other guys—which means they don't care too much for theirselves.

The type of boy who makes this provisionally puritanical division be-tween good girls (with lovers who hold back from final consummation) and bad girls who "give it to the other guys," is yet capable of treating "good girls" with greater harshness than their fallen sisters. This double standard means that there are separate norms; less is expected of the promiscuous girl, much more of the girl you date who may after all become your wife. If so, unquestioning submission to male authority is expected:

> What if you married a girl who talked back to you? What would you do? Shut her up.

How?

Well, I'd fix her where she wasn't able to talk too much. Smack!

The respecter of violence is omnipresent. It may issue from association with either type of girl, and although there are always two types, criteria for establishing them vary. (Asked whether he still considers girls decent if they go to bed with him, a Chicago boy answers, "It's a matter of how hard I have to work. If I have to work real hard I think a lot of them. If they give it to me right off I think they're pigs.") Infidelity in a girl friend will ordinarily provoke a physical assault of some sort. What to do if the woman you marry is unfaithful? "Beat the shit out of her," is the semi-automatic response.

Acts of aggression connected with sex no doubt are intensified by heavy consumption of alcohol. Sex, liquor, and violence form a gestalt in Chicago not nearly so discernible in New York or Washington. In another context, whiskey and beer act as a catalyst for serious fighting, possibly with recourse to knives and firearms. In the sexual context, alcohol is also believed to be useful in emboldening the boy and rendering the girl more compliant to his advances.

Do the girls get pretty wild when they've had a few drinks?
Yes.
Do most of the guys try to get the girls loaded?
Yes.
How often are you successful?
We're not very successful at getting them loaded. I mean that takes a little money.

Beer is cheaper than whiskey and favored for that reason; a low alcohol content notwithstanding, it is believed to serve the purpose. Girls plied with beer are considered "better," that is, more available than those who remain unlubricated. They can more easily be "cut"—which is typical and revealing Chicago argot for the sex act.

In New York there is no "cutting." The first few interviews with Puerto Rican youth revealed little about sex, a topic concerning which we had not anticipated that there would be unusual reticence. The breakdown in communication turned out to be no more than terminological. Once in possession of key words and phrases, the interviewers encountered no serious resistance to the free discussion of plain and fancy sex. There are taboo topics, notably religion as it shades off into magic, but sex is not one of them. The linguistic breakthrough occurred in this matter when a resident observer advised us to ask about "scheming." We did so, causing faces to light up that had remained blank as long as we struggled vainly to find the right conventional or unconventional sexual expression. "Scheming" was that expression. Equivalent, in a way, to "cutting" which suggests sex-and-sadism, "scheming" had mild conspiratorial overtones. It stands for kissing, necking, petting, and full sexual consummation, the whole gamut from prepubertal exploration to real coitus, which is secret, explorative, pleasurable, but seldom brutal. With appropriate language, much information can be elicited, and comic misunderstandings are left behind. (To the question, "Did you ever have a girl sexually?" respondent answers by asking, "Did I ever have a girl *sectionally?*" and some minutes are consumed, to no avail, in disentangling the adverbs. We want to know from another boy whether he goes to bed with girls, whether he sleeps with them, and he takes us literally: "No. I sleep by myself, in my own bed.")

Scheming is initiated at parties, and parties are called sets. They function as substitutes for going out, picking up, and dating. Young people at or around twenty may have apartments of their own which, like any of many vacant apartments on the block, can be used for sets, as they can be and are used for private or collective sexual adventures. Boys and girls meet at sets, play records, dance, drink beer or whiskey more or less moderately, smoke cigarettes, and take pot more or less immoderately, and under dim colored lights, engage in uninhibited foreplay. With twenty or more in attendance, sets seem to be fairly large affairs, and while some are organized during the week by hedonistic truants, there are sure to be others around the clock on weekends. Since the youngsters use stimulants and depressants that are costly, and Saturday is the traditional day for pilfering small objects whose sale produces money to buy supplies, the best sets are most likely to occur on Saturday nights. You drink a little, you smoke a lot, you are high, a girl offers to dance with you, and by and by when the dim lights go out altogether, you fondle her. Presently, you step outside with your girl, scheme in the hallway, at her place if no one is at home, on a rooftop, this one or another at the nearby housing project. And:

> If you got a really good friend, and the girl is willing if she's really bad off or somethin', you know what she will do? *She'll pull the train* . . .
> [Pull the train?]
> Yes, that's what we call it: pulling the train. You take one chance. Then another guy takes a chance. You know.
> [Usually, how many guys are there?]
> Two.
> [Not like ten guys with one girl?]
> Oh, depends like on what kind of girl . . . I been in a situation with about six guys.

"Pulling the train" is by no means an everyday occurrence. Sets are. They may be regarded as a spontaneous expression of youth culture, an informal device contrived by teenagers for their own pleasure, a technique for circumventing official and established organizations, an escape from uplift sponsored by benevolent adults. Sets provide an arena—or constitute a preparation—for scheming which, in most cases, means private and secret sexual activity. Boys do boast, with a probable admixture of fantasy and exaggeration, about sexual conquests, but they are loath to name names and thus cause "trouble" for themselves or their girl-

friends. The set in which they begin to participate at about age fifteen
is understood to be somewhat illicit. It may become a pot party or a sex
party (our respondents are ambivalent and divided among themselves
about which they like best)—and either one, if publicized, can lead to
unpleasant sanctions.

Boy–girl relations in Washington are neither as car- and show-centered
as in Chicago nor as party-centered as in New York. In Washington, the
school, despite all its deficiencies, is much more pivotal than we would
have supposed. Young people attend school dances now and then, meet
classmates formally and informally, and, while ungoverned by any particular protocol, they begin to "go out" with one another. Soon there is
sex play, and in many cases, real sexual involvement. Things tend to
begin in school, and there, too, the "facts of life" are transmitted most
frequently and most effectively. Only in our Washington sample do high
school children use technical (now and then garbled) scientific terms for
the sex act and the sex organs. They describe human reproduction as it
has been explained to them by their biology teachers:

> We had it in school. I know how the sperms come down, when a boy is
> having sex relations with a girl; they meet the egg, go up through the vagina,
> stay in the womb and grow month after month. And then after a period of
> time, the woman have a baby.

> We're supposed to do that next half, after we finish with music . . . find
> out where babies come from and things like that.

> Well, I know the process of starting—I mean, you have to have two unions,
> I mean a fusion of, uh, male and female, between the two organs. I mean
> the vulva and the, um, penis. The vulva and the penis. And, um, it takes a
> union of sperm and meeting with the egg. And after that, I know the situa-
> tion of—what do you call it?—the embry—yeah, embry—and that's the first
> stage of the child . . .And the food which the child receives comes from the
> navel of the mother. It's connected to the child, I believe mouth-to-navel,
> something like that. And after a nine month period, the child's supposed to
> be born.

A boy whose parents told him "all about it" at age twelve, says:

> They explained it to me, that it was the entrance of the penis into the
> woman's vulva. I mean, they used other terms, but that's the terms I would
> use because, let's say, I'm more up on it now, on this education.

Again:

> Well, uh, let's see, when the sperm, I think goes into the vagina, something
> like that, then, it meets the other sperm I think, and it starts doing some-
> thing.

However imperfectly they may have absorbed their biology lessons, these
teenagers show a degree of sophistication unavailable to their counterparts in New York and Chicago where sexual knowledge is more likely to
be associated with the street—and its earthy language—than with the
classroom. (In New York a self-taught, semi-demi-social worker has help-

fully taken it upon himself to provide some sex instruction in yet another linguistic style, largely Spanish, partly English argot.) For children to seek or parents to offer information, even when it is urgently needed, seems to be a rare occurrence. (We suspect that parent-youth embarassment on this score is a class phenomenon. There is reason to believe that the middle-class parent now speaks freely to his children about the facts of life while evading questions about the facts of death.) The young mother of two illegitimate children in Washington tells us that she developed early: "At the age of twelve I was as developed as any girl of fourteen or fifteen. Being young, I never paid too much attention to it, but other oider people in the community noticed." As she recounts it, men got fresh, some began to follow her home and she took to making "smart" remarks, and then, after awhile, "I had one man run me home after school." She ran and found sanctuary on a neighbor's porch, and, "The man started to come after me till he looked up and spotted a lady and another man on the porch. After that my mother came over, and we told her about it, and the three of them walked around, but they didn't see him." This incident was but the first of several, including one "proposition" from a preacher, about which the mother was informed. She still divulged nothing to her daughter, and the daughter observes, "I just could not bring myself to look up at my mother and ask her what was happening." The whole story, "the nitty-gritty," came from experience with "fellows" who were judged to be stupid, however, as well as girls on the street and an older sister. From her own account, but never officially, she was a sexual delinquent by age thirteen.

On the other hand, in Washington, a boy may experience sexual initiation under his father's auspices. If there is an older woman who wishes to "come some," that is, who wishes to have a sex partner, the father sometimes encourages his son to cooperate. We have one such case on record:

> She [the older woman] came down to see my sister, and she started liking me. She started paying my way to the movies and all that. So my father told me to go on and do it. So I did . . . He say, "I know you going to do it when I ain't around." So he gave me a protector, and I go on and do it . . . He say we were going to do it behind his back anyhow, and that he just wanted to help me along. I ain't never used the protection, though.

Although he tends to confuse protection against venereal disease with protection against pregnancy, the Washington teenager is generally more knowledgeable about this, too, than his age mate in New York and Chicago. He more often recognizes and applies terms like contraceptive, diaphragm, coil, prophylactic, or rubber—for one reason, because he more often knows what they mean. Not that he or his girlfriend is much inclined to use any of these objects, for their interposition threatens the individual with loss of his "cool"—an important but amorphous quality which must be maintained at all times. Although in all of the three cities only a minority favor contraception, Washington youth understand best, and New York youth least, just what it is they habitually decline to use. And, while amorality or *anomie* tends to prevail in sexual matters, it assumes a degree of egocentricity among Chicago boys unequaled elsewhere. In this exchange, we have an extreme but not a typical expression of the Chicago attitude:

[Do you ever use contraceptives?]
Nope.
[How about women? Do they ever use anything?]
Nope.
[Do you ever think about it?]
Nope.
[Are you afraid of what might happen?]
Nope. *They can't touch me. I'm underage.*

Seeing it exclusively from his own standpoint, and then only insofar as his conduct may lead to legal jeopardy, he is not afraid of making girls pregnant. Later on, when he does come of age, in order to avoid possible charges of statutory rape, such a boy will prefer sexual relations with older women. Even then, this respondent insists, he "ain't gonna use anything." Told by the interviewer about diaphragms and how they work, he vehemently protests against their use. They would interfere with his pleasure, "Might get in my way." To be sure, without contraception, it is possible to spawn an illegitimate child, something he at first claims to have done at least once—before second thoughts cause him to cast doubt on the "mother's" veracity. This is his complete verbatim statement on the matter:

She told me we were gonna have a kid. I said, "Tough." She said, "Ain't it though?" I said, "What you gonna do about it?" She said, "I ain't gonna do nothin' about it. How about you?" I said nothin'. She said, "That's good." I said goodbye and she said goodbye. And that's the last I saw of her. I mean I *saw* her in school. She's still goin' to school. I don't believe that we had a kid, though. She just said we did.

Risk or no risk, boys are generally hostile to the idea of prophylaxis. One objection is phrased purely in terms of the pleasure principle, most colorfully by a Chicago boy who explains why he never uses anything like a rubber, "I tried it once. It's like riding a horse with a saddle instead of bareback." Is he afraid of "knocking a girl up?" Answer: "Sure. *I worry about it afterward.* I guess I'm lucky so far. That's all." The cost factor appears again in Chicago where boys are markedly more reluctant than in Washington and New York to spend money on contraceptive frills. At the climactic moment, their impecuniosity can be frustrating. As a rule in this population girls are no more eager than boys to insure against pregnancy, but once in awhile they are:

Oh, I've used them a couple of times. Like one time, a broad got all worried, and she told us to lay off. . . . We had her pants off and everything. She ask me if I didn't have some rubbers. Uh-uh. "Get off." I had to wait a little longer. I didn't have any money either.

In Chicago there is, then, a minimum of anxiety about the consequences of sexual intercourse, a strong disinclination to take any responsibility for what happens. Most boys are poorly informed and unconcerned about measures taken or not taken by their sex partners. "I wouldn't know if they did or not [use anything to prevent pregnancy]. I don't care if they do or not." Does he know what girls might do to protect themselves? "Well, there's with the hot water, like that. Then, there's, they press on their stomachs someplace . . . on some cords, usually when you get done, the girl has to go to the bathroom. She goes in, she presses here and there, and it all comes out. They claim that's one of the best ways." Ignorance of the facts should not be discounted, but knowledge may or may not be correlative with action. Even if a girl asks for restraint, so that she will not have to cope with unwed motherhood, the boy is likely to refuse:

[Do many girls ask you to stop before you come?]
Most don't. Some do.
[They don't want to get pregnant?]
That's right.
[Do you usually oblige them?]
Well, not usually, no.

Anatomists like Ashley Montagu have established the existence of adolescent sterility, a period after the onset of puberty during which reproduction presumably cannot take place.[1] Widespread premarital sexual experimentation, not always related to courtship, among "primitive peoples" to whom puritanism is unknown, has been noted for over a century. Adolescent sterility helps anthropologists to account for the smoothness with which such relations occur. In ever-larger sectors of our own society, birth control has "sterilized" teenagers, thereby insuring them against the many complications of illegitimacy. Neither of these mechanisms seems to be significantly operative in any of our cities. Adolescent *fertility* is high, and respondents (males only slightly more so than females) express a very nearly uniform distaste for every kind of contraceptive device. Significant differences are in the first instance more attitudinal than behavioral. How much responsibility does a boy feel when he has got his girl with child? Some in New York and Washington; virtually none in Chicago. That unimpeded sexual contact can and does lead to babies is something a transplanted Appalachian white boy is likely to know only too well. For the most part, "He couldn't care less"; the interviewer asks such a boy: "What's stopping you from knocking up girls?" Answer: "Nothin'. I've got four kids, maybe five. Two here in Chicago, two in Wisconsin, and when I left Wisconsin, I heard there was one more." Does he support any of them? "Shit, no." After getting a girl pregnant, "I just take off."

Less able to "take off," as carefree but more likely to be careless, hemmed in on every side, the New York boy generally finds insemination of his girlfriends a worrisome matter. It is seldom a question of direct

responsibility to the "victim"—which would presuppose a kind of socialization or internalization of standards evident neither among "good boys"
nor among "bad boys." What if the girl has a baby? "Maybe the parents
might make him marry her." Coercion under these circumstances into un-
wanted matrimony is a New York nightmare the likes of which no one
in Chicago ever alludes. We pursue the issue one step further: "Suppose
they didn't make you. Would you marry her anyhow?" The response is
a derisive, "Nah!" But then we want to know whether he would support
the baby, and to this the answer is a subculturally typical yes. Even if,
in order to do so, he would have to quit school (and our respondent
values school)? Yes, even so, although, "That would be pretty bad."

The qualitative difference we wish to point up is more than a matter
of nuance. Lloyd Warner and his associates were able to rank people,
whom they interviewed in Yankee City, by class-typed responses to inter-
view questions.[2] We in turn can situate boys and girls (and could do
"blind," that is, without any accompanying data) in one of three impoverished subcultures, by their responses to a variety of straightforward,
nondirective, and projective questions. Thus, a New York boy who presents a tougher "front" than the one just quoted above is still unmistak-
ably a New York, and not a Chicago or Washington boy:

> [Do you try to avoid getting a girl pregnant or don't you care?]
> I try to avoid it.
> [Suppose you did, and she found out where you lived?]
> I'd have to marry the broad.
> [Would you like that?]
> No, that's a hell of a mess.

The less insouciant type, a boy, for instance, whose presentation of self
is somewhat gentler, simply says of the hypothetical girl he has impreg-
nated: "You've got to marry her," leaving implicit why you've got to.

Since precautions to avert childbirth are unpopular, and pregnancy
takes place willy-nilly, abortions should be common. If so, boys in Chicago tend to feel that it is no business of theirs. How different is the
attitude that emerges in New York where, to select one of many examples, an advanced adolescent remarks apropos of a girlfriend who
might get pregnant that, "If I liked the girl enough I would marry her,
or something." Suppose he didn't like her all that much, would he still
feel obligated? "Yeah." In what way, we wonder. Would he arrange for
an abortion? "No. That would mess her up too much . . . Cause some
ladies, they just do it to get money out of it; they don't really do it to
help a person at all."

Nonmedical abortionists, charging about eighty dollars a job, are
said to abound on the street. Nevertheless, boys recoil from availing
themselves of these services, obviously not for financial reasons, which
are important in Chicago, since the stated alternative, assuming marital
or nonmarital responsibility for support, would be so much costlier than
disposition of an undesired fetus.

The differential warmth, involvement, and concern for "the other" in sexual affairs, while significant, should not be exaggerated. It is nonetheless present whatever tack we take. The myth of *machismo*, incorporating an alleged need for constant dramatic assertions of masculinity, notwithstanding, our Puerto Rican teenage boys do not preen themselves on their virility. Most of them accept the code which prohibits tattling "to other guys about girls they have schemed with." Some do engage in invidious talk about "street girls" whose well-known promiscuity makes it impossible to take pride in having "scored" with them. Similarly, the reaction to betrayal is a mild one. Violent assault on a girl may occur if she is suspected of having squealed to the police about stealing or fighting. Not so about sexual defections. When they occur, New York boys say, "I walk away," "I tell her not to do that again," "I call it quits." The gorge does not rise very high, one's manhood is not called into question, and violence flares up but rarely. Likewise, the readiness to spare a girlfriend undue embarrassment—or to share it with her by prematurely shouldering the parental responsibility—is very exceptional. Commenting on the large number of unmarried girls with babies that boys refuse to support, a respondent explains, "Maybe one guy has her, then another, and then another. She doesn't know who the father is." Then what? "The last guy gets the blame." And getting the blame more often than not seems to mean accepting the blame, which in turn (age permitting) means marriage. In this realm, as elsewhere, *fatalismo* apparently counts for more than *machismo*.

Sexual experience, which begins early and mounts in frequency if not intensity, should not be equated with sexual sophistication. Indeed, the manifest naivete is sometimes monumental. So:

[How do you avoid getting girls pregnant?]
(Long pause) I don't really know.
[Nobody ever told you about that?]
Nobody ever told me.
[Well, how do you keep the girl from having a baby?]
I guess you kill the baby.
[Do you know about killing babies?]
I don't know how, but . . .
[Is that what they do around the block?]
If they gonna kill the babies, they gonna kill theirself.
[So you never heard about protection? Like a rubber?]
What did you say? Girdle? Maybe that's the only way. I know a girl lives in my neighborhood. She had a baby, but you couldn't tell, and after awhile they found out she had a girdle on. But she still had a baby. I don't really know how you could stop it. The only way, I suppose, is wearing a girdle.

Another boy reports making a girl pregnant, but there was no baby, "Because she took it out." How, he does not know or will not say. Yet another, asked what he would do if he got his girlfriend pregnant, replies, "There's nothing I could do," and for lack of options, lets it go at that.

Early marriage ensues, in a spirit best described as resignation. This "solution" becomes all the more irrational whenever boys protest, as they do with great vehemence, that it is the one thing they wish above all to avoid. They speak of no marriage or late marriage, drawing the lesson of delay and circumvention from their own experience in unsatisfactory family relations. And, pointing to others all around them, they declaim against too many people marrying too soon, having too many children. It is on this basis that they diagnose most of their own trouble and most of the ills that others encounter in a slum environment. It all starts, they say, when a young man fathers a child he does not want—whose conception he will do nothing to prevent. Here, indeed, for one part of the underclass is the way of all flesh: fully aware of the danger, our young man tumbles headlong into it, doing exactly what he had sworn not to do, classically entering a scene he had resolved to sidestep, with some, no doubt unconscious, propulsion into a trap he professes to abhor.

A finer distinction must be made among Appalachians in Chicago. There, group-affiliated males show a consistent unwillingness to marry, holding out for very long, while among the unaffiliated there is a noticeably higher incidence of early marriage. When it takes place, males tend to be several years older than females, even if both are still in their teens. In the majority of cases, delay is secured through reinforcement of a powerful male peer group that seemingly functions much like the one analyzed by William Foote Whyte in *Street Corner Society*.[3] It is the opinion of two long-time resident observers in Chicago that "Most of the males find it impossible to maintain regular and satisfying experiences with a girl and quickly withdraw their attention and return to the male peer group." They also indicate that despite a well-nigh universal claim to early sexual experience, many of the male youths admit to prolonged periods of disengagement both from overt heterosexual activity and coed sociability. Much of the sexual play that does take place involves a group of boys who exploit one or two females, many of them "young runaways" or disillusioned young wives, viewed as "easy scores" for all. After a week or so of intensified sexuality with one such female, she usually disappears. Then the males resume their involuntary celibacy. Later they embark once again on the same cycle. All of this is absolutely affectless.

Girls in Chicago stress early marriage as a female adjustment. They hope for husbands who "won't be unfaithful," "won't drink," "will be nice," and "will work hard." Demographic findings and intimate observation make it clear that a girl, personal preference apart, often marries the first young male adult with whom she has a steady relationship. Our resident observers also tell us that their "noncodified observations yield another interesting pattern of marital relationship in the next older group," which they feel may have a bearing on "the essentially brittle relations of the teenagers." During our study, a number of marriages have been observed to dissolve into a peculiar pattern of realignments, such that: Male A, aged thirty-five, establishes a liaison with Female X, his own age or older; wife of A establishes a liaison with unmarried Male B, aged twenty-five or thirty or with a formerly married male, aged twenty-five to thirty who in turn has separated from his younger wife. Consequently, for the second marriage, or for sexual adventures after a first marriage, the male is ordinarily younger than the female. We find, in short, that parallel to the traditional form (older husband, younger wife) there is a deviant form that leaves separated, divorced, and unfaithful women with younger husbands and lovers. There is a certain distinctiveness in this duality.

NOTES

1. Ashley Montagu, *Adolescent Sterility: A Study in the Comparative Physiology of the Adolescent Organism in Mammals and Man* (Springfield, Illinois: C. C. Thomas, 1946).
2. W. Lloyd Warner and Paul S. Lunt, *Social Life of a Modern Community* (New Haven: Yale University Press, 1941).
3. William Foote Whyte, *Street Corner Society* (Chicago: University of Chicago Press, 1955).

18. The Saints and the Roughnecks
William J. Chambliss

Eight promising young men—children of good, stable, white upper-middle-class families, active in school affairs, good pre-college students—were some of the most delinquent boys at Hanibal High School. While community residents and parents knew that these boys occasionally sowed a few wild oats, they were totally unaware that sowing wild oats completely occupied the daily routine of these young men. The Saints were constantly occupied with truancy, drinking, wild driving, petty theft and vandalism. Yet not one was officially arrested for any misdeed during the two years I observed them.

This record was particularly surprising in light of my observations during the same two years of another gang of Hanibal High School students, six lower-class white boys known as the Roughnecks. The Roughnecks were constantly in trouble with police and community even though their rate of delinquency was about equal with that of the Saints. What was the cause of this disparity? the result? The following consideration of the

Reprinted from *Society* 11, no. 1 (November–December 1973): 24–31.

activities, social class and community perceptions of both gangs may provide some answers.

THE SAINTS FROM MONDAY TO FRIDAY

The Saints' principal daily concern was with getting out of school as early as possible. The boys managed to get out of school with minimum danger that they would be accused of playing hookey through an elaborate procedure for obtaining "legitimate" release from class. The most common procedure was for one boy to obtain the release of another by fabricating a meeting of some committee, program or recognized club. Charles might raise his hand in his 9:00 chemistry class and ask to be excused—a euphemism for going to the bathroom. Charles would go to Ed's math class and inform the teacher that Ed was needed for a 9:30 rehearsal of the drama club play. The math teacher would recognize Ed and Charles as "good students" involved in numerous school activities and would permit Ed to leave at 9:30. Charles would return to his class, and Ed would go to Tom's English class to obtain his release. Tom would engineer Charles' escape. The strategy would continue until as many of the Saints as possible were freed. After a stealthy trip to the car (which had been parked in a strategic spot), the boys were off for a day of fun.

Over the two years I observed the Saints, this pattern was repeated nearly every day. There were variations on the theme, but in one form or another, the boys used this procedure for getting out of class and then off the school grounds. Rarely did all eight of the Saints manage to leave school at the same time. The average number avoiding school on the days I observed them was five.

Having escaped from the concrete corridors the boys usually went either to a pool hall on the other (lower-class) side of town or to a cafe in the suburbs. Both places were out of the way of people the boys were likely to know (family or school officials), and both provided a source of entertainment. The pool hall entertainment was the generally rough atmosphere, the occasional hustler, the sometimes drunk proprietor and, of course, the game of pool. The cafe's entertainment was provided by the owner. The boys would "accidentally" knock a glass on the floor or spill cola on the counter—not all the time, but enough to be sporting. They would also bend spoons, put salt in sugar bowls and generally tease whomever was working in the cafe. The owner had opened the cafe recently and was dependent on the boys' business which was, in fact, substantial since between the horsing around and the teasing they bought food and drinks.

THE SAINTS ON WEEKENDS

On weekends the automobile was even more critical than during the week, for on weekends the Saints went to Big Town—a large city with a population of over a million 25 miles from Hanibal. Every Friday and

Saturday night most of the Saints would meet between 8:00 and 8:30 and would go into Big Town. Big Town activities included drinking heavily in taverns or nightclubs, driving drunkenly through the streets, and committing acts of vandalism and playing pranks.

By midnight on Fridays and Saturdays the Saints were usually thoroughly high, and one or two of them were often so drunk they had to be carried to the cars. Then the boys drove around town, calling obscenities to women and girls; occasionally trying (unsuccessfully so far as I could tell) to pick girls up; and driving recklessly through red lights and at high speeds with their lights out. Occasionally they played "chicken." One boy would climb out the back window of the car and cross the roof to the driver's side of the car while the car was moving at high speed (between 40 and 50 miles an hour); then the driver would move over and the boy who had just crawled across the car roof would take the driver's seat.

Searching for "fair game" for a prank was the boys' principal activity after they left the tavern. The boys would drive alongside a foot patrolman and ask directions to some street. If the policeman leaned on the car in the course of answering the question, the driver would speed away, causing him to lose his balance. The Saints were careful to play this prank only in an area where they were not going to spend much time and where they could quickly disappear around a corner to avoid having their license plate number taken.

Construction sites and road repair areas were the special province of the Saints' mischief. A soon-to-be-repaired hole in the road inevitably invited the Saints to remove lanterns and wooden barricades and put them in the car, leaving the hole unprotected. The boys would find a safe vantage point and wait for an unsuspecting motorist to drive into the hole. Often, though not always, the boys would go up to the motorist and commiserate with him about the dreadful way the city protected its citizenry.

Leaving the scene of the open hole and the motorist, the boys would then go searching for an appropriate place to erect the stolen barricade. An "appropriate place" was often a spot on a highway near a curve in the road where the barricade would not be seen by an oncoming motorist. The boys would wait to watch an unsuspecting motorist attempt to stop and (usually) crash into the wooden barricade. With saintly bearing the boys might offer help and understanding.

A stolen lantern might well find its way onto the back of a police car or hang from a street lamp. Once a lantern served as a prop for a reenactment of the "midnight ride of Paul Revere" until the "play," which was taking place at 2:00 AM in the center of a main street of Big Town, was interrupted by a police car several blocks away. The boys ran, leaving the lanterns on the street, and managed to avoid being apprehended.

Abandoned houses, especially if they were located in out-of-the-way places, were fair game for destruction and spontaneous vandalism. The boys would break windows, remove furniture to the yard and tear it apart, urinate on the walls and scrawl obscenities inside.

Through all the pranks, drinking and reckless driving the boys managed miraculously to avoid being stopped by police. Only twice in two years was I aware that they had been stopped by a Big City policeman. Once was for speeding (which they did every time they drove whether they were drunk or sober), and the driver managed to convince the policeman that it was simply an error. The second time they were stopped they had just left a nightclub and were walking through an alley. Aaron stopped to urinate and the boys began making obscene remarks. A foot patrolman came into the alley, lectured the boys and sent them home. Before the boys got to the car one began talking in a loud voice again. The policeman, who had followed them down the alley, arrested this boy for disturbing the peace and took him to the police station where the other Saints gathered. After paying a $5.00 fine, and with the assurance that there would be no permanent record of the arrest, the boy was released.

The boys had a spirit of frivolity and fun about their escapades. They did not view what they were engaged in as "delinquency," though it surely was by any reasonable definition of that word. They simply viewed themselves as having a little fun and who, they would ask, was really hurt by it? The answer had to be no one, although this fact remains one of the most difficult things to explain about the gang's behavior. Unlikely though it seems, in two years of drinking, driving, carousing and vandalism no one was seriously injured as a result of the Saints' activities.

THE SAINTS IN SCHOOL

The Saints were highly successful in school. The average grade for the group was "B," with two of the boys having close to a straight "A" average. Almost all of the boys were popular and many of them held offices in the school. One of the boys was vice-president of the student body one year. Six of the boys played on athletic teams.

At the end of their senior year, the student body selected ten seniors for special recognition as the "school wheels"; four of the ten were Saints. Teachers and school officials saw no problem with any of these boys and anticipated that they would all "make something of themselves."

How the boys managed to maintain this impression is surprising in view of their actual behavior while in school. Their technique for covering truancy was so successful that teachers did not even realize that the boys were absent from school much of the time. Occasionally, of course, the system would backfire and then the boy was on his own. A boy who was caught would be most contrite, would plead guilty and ask for mercy. He inevitably got the mercy he sought.

Cheating on examinations was rampant, even to the point of orally communicating answers to exams as well as looking at one another's papers. Since none of the group studied, and since they were primarily dependent on one another for help, it is surprising that grades were so high. Teachers contributed to the deception in their admitted inclination to give these boys (and presumably others like them) the benefit of the doubt. When asked how the boys did in school, and when pressed on specific examinations, teachers might admit that they were disappointed in John's performance, but would quickly add that they "knew that he was capable of doing better," so John was given a higher grade than he had actually earned. How often this happened is impossible to know. During the time that I observed the group, I never saw any of the boys take homework home. Teachers may have been "understanding" very regularly.

One exception to the gang's generally good performance was Jerry, who had a "C" average in his junior year, experienced disaster the next year and failed to graduate. Jerry had always been a little more nonchalant than the others about the liberties he took in school. Rather than wait for someone to come get him from class, he would offer his own excuse and leave. Although he probably did not miss any more classes than most of the others in the group, he did not take the requisite pains to cover his absences. Jerry was the only Saint whom I ever heard talk back to a teacher. Although teachers often called him a "cut up" or a "smart kid," they never referred to him as a troublemaker or as a kid headed for trouble. It seems likely, then, that Jerry's failure his senior year and his mediocre performance his junior year were consequences of his not playing the game the proper way (possibly because he was disturbed by his parents' divorce). His teachers regarded him as "immature" and not quite ready to get out of high school.

The Police and the Saints

The local police saw the Saints as good boys who were among the leaders of the youth in the community. Rarely, the boys might be stopped in town for speeding or for running a stop sign. When this happened the boys were always polite, contrite and pled for mercy. As in school, they received the mercy they asked for. None ever received a ticket or was taken into the precinct by the local police.

The situation in Big City, where the boys engaged in most of their delinquency, was only slightly different. The police there did not know the boys at all, although occasionally the boys were stopped by a patrolman. Once they were caught taking a lantern from a construction site. Another time they were stopped for running a stop sign, and on several occasions they were stopped for speeding. Their behavior was as before: contrite, polite and penitent. The urban police, like the local police, accepted their demeanor as sincere. More important, the urban police were convinced that these were good boys just out for a lark.

THE ROUGHNECKS

Hanibal townspeople never perceived the Saints' high level of delinquency. The Saints were good boys who just went in for an occasional prank. After all, they were well dressed, well mannered and had nice cars. The Roughnecks were a different story. Although the two gangs of boys were the same age, and both groups engaged in an equal amount of wild-oat sowing, everyone agreed that the not-so-well-dressed, not-so-well-mannered, not-so-rich boys were heading for trouble. Townspeople would say, "You can see the gang members at the drugstore, night after night, leaning against the storefront (sometimes drunk) or slouching around inside buying cokes, reading magazines, and probably stealing old Mr. Wall blind. When they are outside and girls walk by, even respectable girls, these boys make suggestive remarks. Sometimes their remarks are downright lewd."

From the community's viewpoint, the real indication that these kids were in for trouble was that they were constantly involved with the police. Some of them had been picked up for stealing, mostly small stuff, of course, "but still it's stealing small stuff that leads to big time crimes." "Too bad," people said. "Too bad that these boys couldn't behave like the other kids in town; stay out of trouble, be polite to adults, and look to their future."

The community's impression of the degree to which this group of six boys (ranging in age from 16 to 19) engaged in delinquency was somewhat distorted. In some ways the gang was more delinquent than the community thought; in other ways they were less.

The fighting activities of the group were fairly readily and accurately perceived by almost everyone. At least once a month, the boys would get into some sort of fight, although most fights were scraps between members of the group or involved only one member of the group and some peripheral hanger-on. Only three times in the period of observation did the group fight together: once against a gang from across town, once against two blacks and once against a group of boys from another school. For the first two fights the group went out "looking for trouble"—and they found it both times. The third fight followed a football game and began spontaneously with an argument on the football field between one of the Roughnecks and a member of the opposition's football team.

Jack had a particular propensity for fighting and was involved in most of the brawls. He was a prime mover of the escalation of arguments into fights.

More serious than fighting, had the community been aware of it, was theft. Although almost everyone was aware that the boys occasionally stole things, they did not realize the extent of the activity. Petty stealing was a frequent event for the Roughnecks. Sometimes they stole as a group and coordinated their efforts; other times they stole in pairs. Rarely did they steal alone.

The thefts ranged from very small things like paperback books, comics and ballpoint pens to expensive items like watches. The nature of the thefts varied from time to time. The gang would go through a period of systematically shoplifting items from automobiles or school lockers. Types of thievery varied with the whim of the gang. Some forms of thievery were more profitable than others, but all thefts were for profit, not just thrills.

Roughnecks siphoned gasoline from cars as often as they had access to an automobile, which was not very often. Unlike the Saints, who owned their own cars, the Roughnecks would have to borrow their parents' cars, an event which occured only eight or nine times a year. The boys claimed to have stolen cars for joy rides from time to time.

Ron committed the most serious of the group's offenses. With an un-identified associate the boy attempted to burglarize a gasoline station. Although this station had been robbed twice previously in the same month, Ron denied any involvement in either of the other thefts. When Ron and his accomplice approached the station, the owner was hiding in the bushes beside the station. He fired both barrels of a double-barreled shotgun at the boys. Ron was severely injured; the other boy ran away and was never caught. Though he remained in critical condition for several months, Ron finally recovered and served six months of the fol-lowing year in reform school. Upon release from reform school, Ron was put back a grade in school, and began running around with a different gang of boys. The Roughnecks considered the new gang less delinquent than themselves, and during the following year Ron had no more trouble with the police.

The Roughnecks, then, engaged mainly in three types of delinquency: theft, drinking and fighting. Although community members perceived that this gang of kids was delinquent, they mistakenly believed that their ille-gal activities were primarily drinking, fighting and being a nuisance to passersby. Drinking was limited among the gang members, although it did occur, and theft was much more prevalent than anyone realized.

Drinking would doubtless have been more prevalent had the boys had ready access to liquor. Since they rarely had automobiles at their disposal, they could not travel very far, and the bars in town would not serve them. Most of the boys had little money, and this, too, inhibited their purchase of alcohol. Their major source of liquor was a local drunk who would buy them a fifth if they would give him enough extra to buy himself a pint of whiskey or a bottle of wine.

The community's perception of drinking as prevalent stemmed from the fact that it was the most obvious delinquency the boys engaged in. When one of the boys had been drinking, even a casual observer seeing him on the corner would suspect that he was high.

There was a high level of mutual distrust and dislike between the Roughnecks and the police. The boys felt very strongly that the police were unfair and corrupt. Some evidence existed that the boys were cor-rect in their perception.

The main source of the boys' dislike for the police undoubtedly stemmed from the fact that the police would sporadically harass the group. From the standpoint of the boys, these acts of occasional enforcement of the law were whimsical and uncalled for. It made no sense to them, for example, that the police would come to the corner occasionally and threaten them with arrest for loitering when the night before the boys had been nowhere in sight. To the boys, the police were stupid on the one hand, for not being where they should have been and catching the boys in a serious offense, and unfair on the other hand, for trumping up "loitering" charges against them.

From the viewpoint of the police, the situation was quite different. They knew, with all the confidence necessary to be a policeman, that these boys were engaged in criminal activities. They knew this partly from occasionally catching them, mostly from circumstantial evidence ("the boys were around when those tires were slashed"), and partly because the police shared the view of the community in general that this was a bad bunch of boys. The best the police could hope to do was to be sensitive to the fact that these boys were engaged in illegal acts and arrest them whenever there was some evidence that they had been involved. Whether or not the boys had in fact committed a particular act in a particular way was not especially important. The police had a broader view: their job was to stamp out these kids' crimes; the tactics were not as important as the end result.

Over the period that the group was under observation, each member was arrested at least once. Several of the boys were arrested a number of times and spent at least one night in jail. While most were never taken to court, two of the boys were sentenced to six months' incarceration in boys' schools.

THE ROUGHNECKS IN SCHOOL

The Roughnecks' behavior in school was not particularly disruptive. During school hours they did not all hang around together, but tended instead to spend most of their time with one or two other members of the gang who were their special buddies. Although every member of the gang attempted to avoid school as much as possible, they were not particularly successful and most of them attended school with surprising regularity. They considered school a burden—something to be gotten through with a minimum of conflict. If they were "bugged" by a particular teacher, it could lead to trouble. One of the boys, Al, once threatened to beat up a teacher and, according to the other boys, the teacher hid under a desk to escape him.

Teachers saw the boys the way the general community did, as heading for trouble, as being uninterested in making something of themselves. Some were also seen as being incapable of meeting the academic standards of the school. Most of the teachers expressed concern for this group of boys and were willing to pass them despite poor performance, in the belief that failing them would only aggravate the problem.

The group of boys had a grade point average just slightly above "C." No one in the group failed either grade, and no one had better than a "C" average. They were very consistent in their achievement or, at least, the teachers were consistent in their perception of the boys' achievement.

Two of the boys were good football players. Herb was acknowledged to be the best player in the school and Jack was almost as good. Both boys were criticized for their failure to abide by training rules, for refusing to come to practice as often as they should, and for not playing their best during practice. What they lacked in sportsmanship they made up for in skill, apparently, and played every game no matter how poorly they had performed in practice or how many practice sessions they had missed.

Two Questions

Why did the community, the school and the police react to the Saints as though they were good, upstanding, nondelinquent youths with bright futures but to the Roughnecks as though they were tough, young criminals who were headed for trouble? Why did the Roughnecks and the Saints in fact have quite different careers after high school—careers which, by and large, lived up to the expectations of the community?

The most obvious explanation for the differences in the community's and law enforcement agencies' reactions to the two gangs is that one group of boys was "more delinquent" than the other. Which group *was* more delinquent? The answer to this question will determine in part how we explain the differential responses to these groups by the members of the community and, particularly, by law enforcement and school officials.

In sheer number of illegal acts, the Saints were the more delinquent. They were truant from school for at least part of the day almost every day of the week. In addition, their drinking and vandalism occurred with surprising regularity. The Roughnecks, in contrast, engaged sporadically in delinquent episodes. While these episodes were frequent, they certainly did not occur on a daily or even a weekly basis.

The difference in frequency of offenses was probably caused by the Roughnecks' inability to obtain liquor and to manipulate legitimate excuses from school. Since the Roughnecks had less money than the Saints, and teachers carefully supervised their school activities, the Roughnecks' hearts may have been as black as the Saints', but their misdeeds were not nearly as frequent.

There are really no clear-cut criteria by which to measure qualitative differences in antisocial behavior. The most important dimension of the difference is generally referred to as the "seriousness" of the offenses.

If seriousness encompasses the relative economic costs of delinquent acts, then some assessment can be made. The Roughnecks probably stole an average of about $5.00 worth of goods a week. Some weeks the figure was considerably higher, but these times must be balanced against long periods when almost nothing was stolen.

The Saints were more continuously engaged in delinquency but their acts were not for the most part costly to property. Only their vandalism and occasional theft of gasoline would so qualify. Perhaps once or twice a month they would siphon a tankful of gas. The other costly items were street signs, construction lanterns and the like. All of these acts combined probably did not quite average $5.00 a week, partly because much of the stolen equipment was abandoned and presumably could be recovered. The difference in cost of stolen property between the two groups was trivial, but the Roughnecks probably had a slightly more expensive set of activities than did the Saints.

Another meaning of seriousness is the potential threat of physical harm to members of the community and to the boys themselves. The Roughnecks were more prone to physical violence; they not only welcomed an opportunity to fight; they went seeking it. In addition, they fought among themselves frequently. Although the fighting never included deadly weapons, it was still a menace, however minor, to the physical safety of those involved

The Saints never fought. They avoided physical conflict both inside and outside the group. At the same time, though, the Saints frequently endangered their own and other people's lives. They did so almost every time they drove a car, especially if they had been drinking. Sober, their driving was risky; under the influence of alcohol it was horrendous. In addition, the Saints endangered the lives of others with their pranks. Street excavations left unmarked were a very serious hazard.

Evaluating the relative seriousness of the two gangs' activities is difficult. The community reacted as though the behavior of the Roughnecks was a problem, and they reacted as though the behavior of the Saints was not. But the members of the community were ignorant of the array of delinquent acts that characterized the Saints' behavior. Although concerned citizens were unaware of much of the Roughnecks' behavior as well, they were much better informed about the Roughnecks' involvement in delinquency than they were about the Saints'.

VISIBILITY

Differential treatment of the two gangs resulted in part because one gang was infinitely more visible than the other. This differential visibility was a direct function of the economic standing of the families. The Saints had access to automobiles and were able to remove themselves from the sight of the community. In as routine a decision as to where to go to have a milkshake after school, the Saints stayed away from the mainstream of community life. Lacking transportation, the Roughnecks could not make it to the edge of town. The center of town was the only practical place for them to meet since their homes were scattered throughout the town and any noncentral meeting place put an undue hardship on some members. Through necessity the Roughnecks congregated in a crowded area where everyone in the community passed frequently, including teachers and law enforcement officers. They could easily see the Roughnecks hanging around the drugstore.

The Roughnecks, of course, made themselves even more visible by making remarks to passersby and by occasionally getting into fights on the corner. Meanwhile, just as regularly, the Saints were either at the cafe on one edge of town or in the pool hall at the other edge of town. Without any particular realization that they were making themselves inconspicuous, the Saints were able to hide their time-wasting. Not only were they removed from the mainstream of traffic, but they were almost always inside a building.

On their escapades the Saints were also relatively invisible, since they left Hanibal and travelled to Big City. Here, too, they were mobile, roaming the city, rarely going to the same area twice.

DEMEANOR

To the notion of visibility must be added the difference in the responses of group members to outside intervention with their activities. If one of the Saints was confronted with an accusing policeman, even if he felt he was truly innocent of a wrongdoing, his demeanor was apologetic and penitent. A Roughneck's attitude was almost the polar opposite. When confronted with a threatening adult authority, even one who tried to be pleasant, the Roughneck's hostility and disdain were clearly observable. Sometimes he might attempt to put up a veneer of respect, but it was thin and was not accepted as sincere by the authority.

School was no different from the community at large. The Saints could manipulate the system by feigning compliance with the school norms. The availability of cars at school meant that once free from the immediate sight of the teacher, the boys could disappear rapidly. And this escape was well enough planned that no administrator or teacher was nearby when the boys left. A Roughneck who wished to escape for a few hours was in a bind. If it were possible to get free from class, downtown was still a mile away, and even if he arrived there, he was still very visible. Truancy for the Roughnecks meant almost certain detection, while the Saints enjoyed almost complete immunity from sanctions.

BIAS

Community members were not aware of the transgressions of the Saints. Even if the Saints had been less discreet, their favorite delinquencies would have been perceived as less serious than those of the Roughnecks.

In the eyes of the police and school officials, a boy who drinks in an alley and stands intoxicated on the street corner is committing a more serious offense than is a boy who drinks to inebriation in a nightclub or a tavern and drives around afterwards in a car. Similarly, a boy who steals a wallet from a store will be viewed as having committed a more serious offense than a boy who steals a lantern from a construction site.

Perceptual bias also operates with respect to the demeanor of the boys in the two groups when they are confronted by adults. It is not simply that adults dislike the posture affected by the boys of the Roughneck ilk; more important is the conviction that the posture adopted by the Roughnecks is an indication of their devotion and commitment to deviance as a way of life. The posture becomes a cue, just as the type of the offense is a cue, to the degree to which the known transgressions are indicators of the youths' potential for other problems.

Visibility, demeanor and bias are surface variables which explain the day-to-day operations of the police. Why do these surface variables operate as they do? Why did the police choose to disregard the Saints' delinquencies while breathing down the backs of the Roughnecks?

The answer lies in the class structure of American society and the control of legal institutions by those at the top of the class structure. Obviously, no representative of the upper class drew up the operational chart for the police which led them to look in the ghettoes and on street-corners—which led them to see the demeanor of lower-class youth as troublesome and that of upper-middle-class youth as tolerable. Rather, the procedures simply developed from experience—experience with irate and influential upper-middle-class parents insisting that their son's vandalism was simply a prank and his drunkenness only a momentary "sowing of wild oats"—experience with cooperative or indifferent, powerless, lower-class parents who acquiesced to the laws' definition of their son's behavior.

ADULT CAREERS OF THE SAINTS AND THE ROUGHNECKS

The community's confidence in the potential of the Saints and the Roughnecks apparently was justified. If anything, the community members underestimated the degree to which these youngsters would turn out "good" or "bad."

Seven of the eight members of the Saints went on to college immediately after high school. Five of the boys graduated from college in four years. The sixth one finished college after two years in the army, and the seventh spent four years in the air force before returning to college and receiving a B.A. degree. Of these seven college graduates, three went on for advanced degrees. One finished law school and is now active in state politics, one finished medical school and is practicing near Hanibal, and one boy is now working for a Ph.D. The other four college graduates entered submanagerial, managerial or executive training positions with larger firms.

The only Saint who did not complete college was Jerry. Jerry had failed to graduate from high school with the other Saints. During his second senior year, after the other Saints had gone on to college, Jerry began to hang around with what several teachers described as a "rough crowd"—the gang that was heir apparent to the Roughnecks. At the end of his second senior year, when he did graduate from high school, Jerry took a job as a used-car salesman, got married and quickly had a child. Although he made several abortive attempts to go to college by attending night school, when I last saw him (ten years after high school) Jerry was unemployed and had been living on unemployment for almost a year. His wife worked as a waitress.

Some of the Roughnecks have lived up to community expectations. A number of them were headed for trouble. A few were not.

Jack and Herb were the athletes among the Roughnecks and their athletic prowess paid off handsomely. Both boys received unsolicited athletic scholarships to college. After Herb received his scholarship (near the end of his senior year), he apparently did an about-face. His demeanor became very similar to that of the Saints. Although he remained a member in good standing of the Roughnecks, he stopped participating in most activities and did not hang on the corner as often.

Jack did not change. If anything, he became more prone to fighting. He even made excuses for accepting the scholarship. He told the other gang members that the school had guaranteed him a "C" average if he would come to play football—an idea that seems far-fetched, even in this day of highly competitive recruiting.

During the summer after graduation from high school, Jack attempted suicide by jumping from a tall building. The jump would certainly have killed most people trying it, but Jack survived. He entered college in the fall and played four years of football. He and Herb graduated in four years, and both are teaching and coaching in high schools. They are married and have stable families. If anything, Jack appears to have a more prestigious position in the community than does Herb, though both are well respected and secure in their positions.

Two of the boys never finished high school. Tommy left at the end of his junior year and went to another state. That summer he was arrested and placed on probation on a manslaughter charge. Three years later he was arrested for murder; he pleaded guilty to second degree murder and is serving a 30-year sentence in the state penitentiary.

Al, the other boy who did not finish high school, also left the state in his senior year. He is serving a life sentence in a state penitentiary for first degree murder.

Wes is a small-time gambler. He finished high school and "bummed around." After several years he made contact with a bookmaker who employed him as a runner. Later he acquired his own area and has been working it ever since. His position among bookmakers is almost identical to the position he had in the gang; he is always around but no one is really aware of him. He makes no trouble and he does not get into any. Steady, reliable, capable of keeping his mouth closed, he plays the game by the rules, even though the game is an illegal one.

That leaves only Ron. Some of his former friends reported that they had heard he was "driving a truck up north," but no one could provide any concrete information.

REINFORCEMENT

The community responded to the Roughnecks as boys in trouble, and the boys agreed with that perception. Their pattern of deviancy was reinforced, and breaking away from it became increasingly unlikely. Once the boys acquired an image of themselves as deviants, they selected new friends who affirmed that self-image. As that self-conception became more firmly entrenched, they also became willing to try new and more extreme deviances. With their growing alienation came freer expression of disrespect and hostility for representatives of the legitimate society. This disrespect increased the community's negativism, perpetuating the entire process of commitment to deviance. Lack of a commitment to deviance works the same way. In either case, the process will perpetuate itself unless some event (like a scholarship to college or a sudden failure) external to the established relationship intervenes. For two of the Roughnecks (Herb and Jack), receiving college athletic scholarships created new relations and culminated in a break with the established pattern of deviance. In the case of one of the Saints (Jerry), his parents' divorce and his failing to graduate from high school changed some of his other relations. Being held back in school for a year and losing his place among the Saints had sufficient impact on Jerry to alter his self-image and virtually to assure that he would not go on to college as his peers did. Although the experiments of life can rarely be reversed, it seems likely in view of the behavior of the other boys who did not enjoy this special treatment by the school that Jerry, too, would have "become something" had he graduated as anticipated. For Herb and Jack outside intervention worked to their advantage; for Jerry it was his undoing.

Selective perception and labelling—finding, processing and punishing some kinds of criminality and not others—means that visible, poor, non-mobile, outspoken, undiplomatic "tough" kids will be noticed, whether their actions are seriously delinquent or not. Other kids, who have established a reputation for being bright (even though underachieving), disciplined and involved in respectable activities, who are mobile and monied, will be invisible when they deviate from sanctioned activities. They'll sow their wild oats—perhaps even wider and thicker than their lower-class cohorts—but they won't be noticed. When it's time to leave adolescence most will follow the expected path, settling into the ways of the middle class, remembering fondly the delinquent but unnoticed fling of their youth. The Roughnecks and others like them may turn around, too. It is more likely that their noticeable deviance will have been so reinforced by police and community that their lives will be effectively channelled into careers consistent with adolescent background.

VI. Urban Communities

Georg Simmel, who died in 1918, was the subtlest of sociologists. A nuance, a hint, a clue on almost any page of his voluminous output still supplies us with productive hypotheses. Although Simmel used no statistics, numbers fascinated him. He was interested in the smallest and the largest groups of people, in two- and three-person groups and in teeming multitudes. His vastly influential essay "The Metropolis and Mental Life" concentrates on size of population and its effects. For where but in the metropolis can one find so large a conglomeration of human beings? In the metropolis, an enormous *number* of people interact; they thereby multiply the *number* of stimuli impinging on every person. Bombarded by sensations, the city dweller runs for cover, and develops "objectivity," "reserve," a "tough hide," and a blasé attitude. He responds to fewer stimuli and responds to them with less than his whole being. He develops a "rational" attitude. The cash nexus tenuously ties him to others. He economizes in the expenditure of money, time, and emotion, responding to symbols as much as to people —or rather to people as symbols. Metropolitan men, women, and children sacrifice depth as they spread themselves thin in human relationships.

It is within this setting that the individual strives to maintain some freedom, autonomy, or independence. Metropolitans have more options than provincials and may in this sense be said to have more freedom. But in the exercise of that freedom they must struggle against being swamped. Their problem is a superabundance of stimuli, a plethora of choices, and an overproduction of culture.

Simmel's approach to the metropolis, which we greatly oversimplify by condensation, was a direct prelude to the emerging field of urban sociology. Robert Park, who studied with Simmel, brilliantly adapted many of his master's ideas. He wrote about and inspired acute studies of the city, especially Chicago, his own city, in the 1920's and 1930's. Successive generations were trained by Park and Park's students.

In *The Moral Order of the Slum*, Gerald Suttles reveals himself to be a most distinguished intellectual descendant of Simmel and Park. Suttles establishes that in our own period, despite urban anomie and disorganization, the city still has a moral order. He finds a patterned social structure even in the most impoverished ghetto, where ethnicity and propinquity form, so to speak, a social glue that holds people together and yet permits them to interact as human beings. Firsthand knowledge, personal loyalty, and a common commitment to group standards counteract the tremendous force of urban anonymity and metropolitan isolation. Not that Suttles sidesteps the difficulties. He knows from his own participatory observation that remorseless political and economic pressure is at work, in the form of urban redevelopment, occupational obsolescence, and a host of related social problems that continually splinter and disperse integral communities within the city. Urbanites fight for survival and for identity. Theirs is not only the struggle of individuals; it is also the struggle of whole social and ethnic groups.

Melvin Webber, a resourceful and provocative writer, brings us to our present anguish. He outlines the circumstances that destabilize society for city dwellers. Webber is particularly sensitive to the impact of mass communication and mass transportation as they draw middle-class people into a national, and even an international, culture. The city as a center of social organization is frequently reduced to an entry-and-exit point for the immense flow of products, messages, and people. Urban expansion and suburban sprawl cause the central city to deteriorate. We have witnessed its dramatic decline not simply as a physical and political entity, but as a focal point for the organization of our lives. As the "city" penetrates the "country," rural migrants come to be a crowded majority inside the central city. They are confronted with the metropolitan malaise at its peak, just when city services and urban opportunities are at a minimum. Private organizations are called upon to take over services and provide opportunities previously, although briefly, supplied by the municipal government.

Webber concludes on a lugubrious note; he is convinced that the metropolis has outgrown all boundaries and that the city as a *political* unit is both too big and yet too small to fulfill its historic functions. Other bases for political and social organization are urgently needed to revive the city. Regional, national, and international factors determine the fate of the city; for all their magnitude, they are nonetheless local and personal in their consequences.

19. The Metropolis and Mental Life

Georg Simmel

The deepest problems of modern life derive from the claim of the individual to preserve the autonomy and individuality of his existence in the face of overwhelming social forces, of historical heritage, of external culture, and of the technique of life. The fight with nature which primitive man has to wage for his *bodily* existence attains in this modern form its latest transformation. The eighteenth century called upon man to free himself of all the historical bonds in the state and in religion, in morals and in economics. Man's nature, originally good and common to all, should develop unhampered. In addition to more liberty, the nineteenth century demanded the functional specialization of man and his work; this specialization makes one individual incomparable to another, and each of them indispensable to the highest possible extent. However, this specialization makes each man the more directly dependent upon the supplementary activities of all others. Nietzsche sees the full development of the individual conditioned by the most ruthless struggle of individuals; socialism believes in the suppression of all competition for the same reason. Be that as it may, in all these positions the same basic motive is at work: the person resists to being leveled down and worn out by a social technological mechanism. An inquiry into the inner meaning of specifically modern life and its products, into the soul of the cultural body, so to speak, must seek to solve the equation which structures like the metropolis set up between the individual and the super-individual contents of life. Such an inquiry must answer the question of how the personality accommodates itself in the adjustments to external forces. This will be my task today.*

The psychological basis of the metropolitan type of individuality consists in the *intensification of nervous stimulation* which results from the swift and uninterrupted change of outer and inner stimuli. Man is a differentiating creature. His mind is stimulated by the difference between

---

* The content of this lecture by its very nature does not derive from a citable literature. Argument and elaboration of its major cultural-historical ideas are contained in my *Philosophie des Geldes* (The Philosophy of Money; München und Leipzig: Duncker und Humblot, 1900).

Reprinted with permission of Macmillan Publishing Co., Inc., from *The Sociology of Georg Simmel*, ed. Kurt Wolff, trans. H. H. Gerth with C. Wright Mills. Copyright 1950 by The Free Press.

a momentary impression and the one which preceded it. Lasting impressions, impressions which differ only slightly from one another, impressions which take a regular and habitual course and show regular and habitual contrasts—all these use up, so to speak, less consciousness than does the rapid crowding of changing images, the sharp discontinuity in the grasp of a single glance, and the unexpectedness of onrushing impressions. These are the psychological conditions which the metropolis creates. With each crossing of the street, with the tempo and multiplicity of economic, occupational, and social life, the city sets up a deep contrast with small town and rural life with reference to the sensory foundations of psychic life. The metropolis exacts from man as a discriminating creature a different amount of consciousness than does rural life.. Here the rhythm of life and sensory mental imagery flows more slowly, more habitually, and more evenly. Precisely in this connection the sophisticated character of metropolitan psychic life becomes understandable—as over against small town life which rests more upon deeply felt and emotional relationships. These latter are rooted in the more unconscious layers of the psyche and grow most readily in the steady rhythm of uninterrupted habituations. The intellect, however, has its locus in the transparent, conscious, higher layers of the psyche; it is the most adaptable of our inner forces. In order to accommodate to change and to the contrast of phenomena, the intellect does not require any shocks and inner upheavals; it is only through such upheavals that the more conservative mind could accommodate to the metropolitan rhythm of events. Thus the metropolitan type of man—which, of course, exists in a thousand individual variants—develops an organ protecting him against the threatening currents and discrepancies of his external environment which would uproot him. He reacts with his head instead of his heart. In this an increased awareness assumes the psychic prerogative. Metropolitan life, thus, underlies a heightened awareness and a predominance of intelligence in metropolitan man. The reaction to metropolitan phenomena is shifted to that organ which is least sensitive and quite remote from the depth of the personality. Intellectuality is thus seen to preserve subjective life against the overwhelming power of metropolitan life, and intellectuality branches out in many directions and is integrated with numerous discrete phenomena.

The metropolis has always been the seat of the money economy. Here the multiplicity and concentration of economic exchange gives an importance to the means of exchange which the scantiness of rural commerce would not have allowed. Money economy and the dominance of the intellect are intrinsically connected. They share a matter-of-fact attitude in dealing with men and with things; and, in this attitude, a formal justice is often coupled with an inconsiderate hardness. The intellectually sophisticated person is indifferent to all genuine individuality, because relationships and reactions result from it which cannot be exhausted with logical operations. In the same manner, the individuality of phenomena is not commensurate with the pecuniary principle. Money is concerned only with what is common to all: it asks for the exchange value, it reduces all quality and individuality to the question: How much? All intimate emotional relations between persons are founded in their individuality, whereas in rational relations man is reckoned with like a number, like an element which is in itself indifferent.

Only the objective measurable achievement is of interest. Thus metropolitan man reckons with his merchants and customers, his domestic servants and often even with persons with whom he is obliged to have social intercourse. These features of intellectuality contrast with the nature of the small circle in which the inevitable knowledge of individuality as inevitably produces a warmer tone of behavior, a behavior which is beyond a mere objective balancing of service and return. In the sphere of the economic psychology of the small group it is of importance that under primitive conditions production serves the customer who orders the good, so that the producer and the consumer are acquainted. The modern metropolis, however, is supplied almost entirely by production for the market, that is, for entirely unknown purchasers who never personally enter the producer's actual field of vision. Through this anonymity the interests of each party acquire an unmerciful matter-of-factness; and the intellectually calculating economic egoisms of both parties need not fear any deflection because of the imponderables of personal relationships. The money economy dominates the metropolis; it has displaced the last survivals of domestic production and the direct barter of goods; it minimizes, from day to day, the amount of work ordered by customers. The matter-of-fact attitude is obviously so intimately interrelated with the money economy, which is dominant in the metropolis, that nobody can say whether the intellectualistic mentality first promoted the money economy or whether the latter determined the former. The metropolitan way of life is certainly the most fertile soil for this reciprocity, a point which I shall document merely by citing the dictum of the most eminent English constitutional historian: through the whole course of English history, London has never acted as England's heart but often as England's intellect and always as her moneybag.

In certain seemingly insignificant traits, which lie upon the surface of life, the same psychic currents characteristically unite. Modern mind has become more and more calculating. The calculative exactness of practical life which the money economy has brought about corresponds to the ideal of natural science: to transform the world into an arithmetic problem, to fix every part of the world by mathematical formulas. Only money economy has filled the days of so many people with weighing, calculating, with numerical determinations, with a reduction of qualitative values to quantitative ones. Through the calculative nature of money a new precision, a certainty in the definition of identities and differences, an unambiguousness in agreements and arrangements has been brought about in the relations of life-elements—just as externally this precision has been effected by the

universal diffusion of pocket watches. However, the conditions of metropolitan life are at once cause and effect of this trait. The relationships and
affairs of the typical metropolitan usually are so varied and complex
that without the strictest punctuality in promises and services the whole
structure would break down into an inextricable chaos. Above all, this
necessity is brought about by the aggregation of so many people with
such differentiated interests, who must integrate their relations and
activities into a highly complex organism. If all clocks and watches in
Berlin would suddenly go wrong in different ways, even if only by one
hour, all economic life and communication of the city would be disrupted
for a long time. In addition an apparently mere external factor: long distances, would make all waiting and broken appointments result in an
ill-afforded waste of time. Thus, the technique of metropolitan life is
unimaginable without the most punctual integration of all activities and
mutual relations into a stable and impersonal time schedule. Here again
the general conclusions of this entire task of reflection become obvious,
namely, that from each point on the surface alone—one may drop a
sounding into the depth of the psyche so that all the most banal external-
ities of life are connected with the ultimate decisions concerning the
meaning and style of life. Punctuality, calculability, exactness are forced
upon life by the complexity and extension of metropolitan existence and
are not only most intimately connected with its money economy and
intellectualistic character. These traits must also color the contents of life
and favor the exclusion of those irrational, instinctive, sovereign traits
and impulses which aim at determining the mode of life from within,
instead of receiving the general and precisely schematized form of life
from without. Even though sovereign types of personality, characterized
by irrational impulses, are by no means impossible in the city, they are,
nevertheless, opposed to typical city life. The passionate hatred of men
like Ruskin and Nietzsche for the metropolis is understandable in these
terms. Their natures discovered the value of life alone in the unsche-
matized existence which cannot be defined with precision for all alike.
From the same source of this hatred of the metropolis surged their hatred
of money economy and of the intellectualism of modern existence.

The same factors which have thus coalesced into the exactness and
minute precision of the form of life have coalesced into a structure of
the highest impersonality; on the other hand, they have promoted a highly
personal subjectivity. There is perhaps no psychic phenomenon which has
been so unconditionally reserved to the metropolis as has the blasé attitude. The blasé attitude results first from the rapidly changing and closely
compressed contrasting stimulations of the nerves. From this, the en-
hancement of the metropolitan intellectuality, also, seems originally to stem.
Therefore, stupid people who are not intellectually alive in the first place
usually are not exactly blasé. A life in boundless pursuit of pleasure makes
one blasé because it agitates the nerves to their strongest reactivity for such
a long time that they finally cease to react at all. In the same way, through

the rapidity and contradictoriness of their changes, more harmless impressions force such violent responses, tearing the nerves so brutally hither and thither that their last reserves of strength are spent; and if one remains in the same milieu they have no time to gather new strength. An incapacity thus emerges to react to new sensations with the appropriate energy. This constitutes the blasé attitude which, in fact, every metropolitan child shows when compared with children of quieter and less changeable milieus.

This physiological source of the metropolitan blasé attitude is joined by another source which flows from the money economy. The essence of the blasé attitude consists in the blunting of discrimination. This does not mean that the objects are not perceived, as is the case with the half-wit, but rather that the meaning and differing values of things, and thereby the things themselves, are experienced as insubstantial. They appear to the blasé person in an evenly flat and gray tone; no one object deserves preference over any other. This mood is the faithful subjective reflection of the completely internalized money economy. By being the equivalent to all the manifold things in one and the same way, money becomes the most frightful leveler. For money expresses all qualitative differences of things in terms of "how much?" Money, with all its colorlessness and indifference, becomes the common denominator of all values; irreparably it hollows out the core of things, their individuality, their specific value, and their incomparability. All things float with equal specific gravity in the constantly moving stream of money. All things lie on the same level and differ from one another only in the size of the area which they cover. In the individual case this coloration, or rather discoloration, of things through their money equivalence may be unnoticeably minute. However, through the relations of the rich to the objects to be had for money, perhaps even through the total character which the mentality of the contemporary public everywhere imparts to these objects, the exclusively pecuniary evaluation of objects has become quite considerable. The large cities, the main seats of the money exchange, bring the purchasability of things to the fore much more impressively than do smaller localities. That is why cities are also the genuine locale of the blasé attitude. In the blasé attitude the concentration of men and things stimulate the nervous system of the individual to its highest achievement so that it attains its peak. Through the mere quantitative intensification of the same conditioning factors this achievement is transformed into its opposite and appears in the peculiar adjustment of the blasé attitude. In this phenomenon the nerves find in the refusal to react to their stimulation the last possibility of accommodating to the contents and forms of metropolitan life. The self-preservation of certain personalities is brought at the price of devaluating the whole objective world, a devaluation which in the end unavoidably drags one's own personality down into a feeling of the same worthlessness.

Whereas the subject of this form of existence has to come to terms with it entirely for himself, his self-preservation in the face of the large city demands from him a no less negative behavior of a social nature. This mental attitude of metropolitans toward one another we may designate, from a formal point of view, as reserve. If so many inner reactions were responses to the continuous external contacts with innumerable people as are those in a small town, where one knows almost everybody one meets and where one has a positive relation to almost everyone, one would be completely atomized internally and come to an unimaginable psychic state. Partly this psychological fact, partly the right to distrust which men have in the face of the touch-and-go elements of metropolitan life, necessitates our reserve. As a result of this reserve we frequently do not even know by sight those who have been our neighbors for years. And it is this reserve which in the eyes of the small-town people makes us appear to be cold and heartless. Indeed, if I do not deceive myself, the inner aspect of this outer reserve is not only indifference but, more often than we are aware, it is a slight aversion, a mutual strangeness and repulsion, which will break into hatred and fight at the moment of a closer contact, however caused. The whole inner organization of such an extensive communicative life rests upon an extremely varied hierarchy of sympathies, indifferences, and aversions of the briefest as well as of the most permanent nature. The sphere of indifference in this hierarchy is not as large as might appear on the surface. Our psychic activity still responds to almost every impression of somebody else with a somewhat distinct feeling. The unconscious, fluid, and changing character of this impression seems to result in a state of indifference. Actually this indifference would be just as unnatural as the diffusion of indiscriminate mutual suggestion would be unbearable. From both these typical dangers of the metropolis, indifference and indiscriminate suggestibility, antipathy protects us. A latent antipathy and the preparatory stage of practical antagonism effect the distances and aversions without which this mode of life could not at all be led. The extent and the mixture of this style of life, the rhythm of its emergence and disappearance, the forms in which it is satisfied—all these, with the unifying motives in the narrower sense, form the inseparable whole of the metropolitan style of life. What appears in the metropolitan style of life directly as dissociation is in reality only one of its elemental forms of socialization.

This reserve with its overtone of hidden aversion appears in turn as the form on the cloak of a more general mental phenomenon of the metropolis: it grants to the individual a kind and an amount of personal freedom which has no analogy whatsoever under other conditions. The metropolis goes back to one of the large developmental tendencies of social life as such, to one of the few tendencies for which an approximately universal formula can be discovered. The earliest phase of social formations found in historical as well as in contemporary social structures is this: a relatively small circle firmly closed against neighboring, strange, or in some way antagonistic circles. However, this circle is

closely coherent and allows its individual members only a narrow field
for the development of unique qualities and free, self-responsible movements. Political and kinship groups, parties and religious associations
begin in this way. The self-preservation of very young associations requires the establishment of strict boundaries and a centripetal unity.
Therefore they cannot allow the individual freedom and unique inner
and outer development. From this stage social development proceeds at
once in two different, yet corresponding directions. To the extent to
which the group grows—numerically, spatially, in significance and in
content of life—to the same degree the group's direct, inner unity loosens,
and the rigidity of the original demarcation against others is softened
through mutual relations and connections. At the same time, the individual gains freedom of movement, far beyond the first jealous de-
limitation. The individual also gains a specific individuality to which
the division of labor in the enlarged group gives both occasion and
necessity. The state and Christianity, guilds and political parties, and
innumerable other groups have developed according to this formula,
however much, of course, the special conditions and forces of the respective groups have modified the general scheme. This scheme seems
to me distinctly recognizable also in the evolution of individuality within
urban life. The small-town life in Antiquity and in the Middle Ages set
barriers against movement and relations of the individual toward the
outside, and it set up barriers against individual independence and
differentiation within the individual self. These barriers were such that
under them modern man could not have breathed. Even today a metropolitan man who is placed in a small town feels a restriction similar,
at least, in kind. The smaller the circle which forms our milieu is, and
the more restricted those relations to others are which dissolve the
boundaries of the individual, the more anxiously the circle guards the
achievements, the conduct of life, and the outlook of the individual,
and the more readily a quantitative and qualitative specialization would
break up the framework of the whole little circle.

The ancient *polis* in this respect seems to have had the very character
of a small town. The constant threat to its existence at the hands of
enemies from near and afar effected strict coherence in political and
military respects, a supervision of the citizen by the citizen, a jealousy
of the whole against the individual whose particular life was suppressed
to such a degree that he could compensate only by acting as a despot in
his own household. The tremendous agitation and excitement, the unique
colorfulness of Athenian life, can perhaps be understood in terms of the
fact that a people of incomparably individualized personalities struggled
against the constant inner and outer pressure of a de-individualizing
small town. This produced a tense atmosphere in which the weaker individuals were suppressed and those of stronger natures were incited
to prove themselves in the most passionate manner. This is precisely
why it was that there blossomed in Athens what must be called, without

defining it exactly, "the general human character" in the intellectual development of our species. For we maintain factual as well as historical validity for the following connection: the most extensive and the most general contents and forms of life are most intimately connected with the most individual ones. They have a preparatory stage in common, that is, they find their enemy in narrow formations and groupings the maintenance of which places both of them into a state of defense against expanse and generality lying without and the freely moving individuality within. Just as in the feudal age, the "free" man was the one who stood under the law of the land, that is, under the law of the largest social orbit, and the unfree man was the one who derived his right merely from the narrow circle of a feudal association and was excluded from the larger social orbit—so today metropolitan man is "free" in a spiritualized and refined sense, in contrast to the pettiness and prejudices which hem in the small-town man. For the reciprocal reserve and indifference and the intellectual life conditions of large circles are never felt more strongly by the individual in their impact upon his independence than in the thickest crowd of the big city. This is because the bodily proximity and narrowness of space makes the mental distance only the more visible. It is obviously only the obverse of this freedom if, under certain circumstances, one nowhere feels as lonely and lost as in the metropolitan crowd. For here as elsewhere it is by no means necessary that the freedom of man be reflected in his emotional life as comfort.

It is not only the immediate size of the area and the number of persons which, because of the universal historical correlation between the enlargement of the circle and the personal inner and outer freedom, has made the metropolis the locale of freedom. It is rather in transcending this visible expanse that any given city becomes the seat of cosmopolitanism. The horizon of the city expands in a manner comparable to the way in which wealth develops; a certain amount of property increases in a quasi-automatical way in ever more rapid progression. As soon as a certain limit has been passed, the economic, personal, and intellectual relations of the citizenry, the sphere of intellectual predominance of the city over its hinterland, grow as in geometrical progression. Every gain in dynamic extension becomes a step, not for an equal, but for a new and larger extension. From every thread spinning out of the city, ever new threads grow as if by themselves, just as within the city the unearned increment of ground rent, through the mere increase in communication, brings the owner automatically increasing profits. At this point, the quantitative aspect of life is transformed directly into qualitative traits of character. The sphere of life of the small town is, in the main, self-contained and autarchic. For it is the decisive nature of the metropolis that its inner life overflows by waves into a far-flung national or international area. Weimar is not an example to the contrary, since its significance was hinged upon individual personalities and died with them; whereas the metropolis is indeed characterized by its essential independence even from the most eminent individual personalities. This is the counterpart to the independence, and it is the price the individual pays for the independence, which he enjoys in the metropolis. The most significant characteristic of the metropolis is this functional extension beyond its physical boundaries. And this efficacy reacts in turn and gives weight, importance, and responsibility to metropolitan life. Man does not end with the limits of his body or the area comprising his immediate activity. Rather is the range of the person constituted by the sum of effects emanating from him temporally and spatially. In the same way, a city consists of its total effects which extend beyond its immediate confines. Only this range is the city's actual extent in which its existence is expressed. This fact makes it obvious that individual freedom, the logical and historical complement of such extension, is not to be understood only in the negative sense of mere freedom of mobility and elimination of prejudices and petty philistinism. The essential point is that the particularity and incomparability, which ultimately every human being possesses, be somehow expressed in the working-out of a way of life. That we follow the laws of our own nature—and this after all is freedom—becomes obvious and convincing to ourselves and to others only if the expressions of this nature differ from the expressions of others. Only our unmistakability proves that our way of life has not been superimposed by others.

Cities are, first of all, seats of the highest economic division of labor. They produce thereby such extreme phenomena as in Paris the remunerative occupation of the *quatorzième*. These are persons who identify themselves by signs on their residences and who are ready at the dinner hour in correct attire, so that they can be quickly called upon if a dinner party should consist of thirteen persons. In the measure of its expansion, the city offers more and more the decisive conditions of the division of labor. It offers a circle which through its size can absorb a highly diverse variety of services. At the same time, the concentration of individuals and their struggle for customers compel the individual to specialize in a function from which he cannot be readily replaced by another. It is decisive that city life has transformed the struggle with nature for livelihood into an inter-human struggle for gain, which here is not granted by nature but by other men. For specialization does not flow only from the competition for gain but also from the underlying fact that the seller must always seek to call forth new and differentiated needs of the lured customer. In order to find a source of income which is not yet exhausted, and to find a function which cannot readily be displaced, it is necessary to specialize in one's services. This process promotes differentiation, refinement, and the enrichment of the public's needs, which obviously must lead to growing personal differences within this public.

All this forms the transition to the individualization of mental and psychic traits which the city occasions in proportion to its size. There is a whole series of obvious causes underlying this process. First, one must meet the difficulty of asserting his own personality within the dimensions of metropolitan life. Where the quantitative increase in importance and the expense of energy reach their limits, one seizes upon qualitative differentiation in order somehow to attract the attention of the social circle by playing upon its sensitivity for differences. Finally, man is tempted to adopt the most tendentious peculiarities, that is, the specifically metropolitan extravagances of mannerism, caprice, and preciousness. Now, the meaning of these extravagances does not at all lie in the contents of such behavior, but rather in its form of "being different," of standing out in a striking manner and thereby attracting attention. For many character types, ultimately the only means of saving for themselves some modicum of self-esteem and the sense of filling a position is indirect, through the awareness of others. In the same sense a seemingly insignificant factor is operating, the cumulative effects of which are, however, still noticeable. I refer to the brevity and scarcity of the inter-human contacts granted to the metropolitan man, as compared with social intercourse in the small town. The temptation to appear "to the point," to appear concentrated and strikingly characteristic, lies much closer to the individual in brief metropolitan contacts than in an atmosphere in which frequent and prolonged association assures the personality of an unambiguous image of himself in the eyes of the other.

The most profound reason, however, why the metropolis conduces to the urge for the most individual personal existence—no matter whether justified and successful—appears to me to be the following: the development of modern culture is characterized by the preponderance of what one may call the "objective spirit" over the "subjective spirit." This is to say, in language as well as in law, in the technique of production as well as in art, in science as well as in the objects of the domestic environment, there is embodied a sum of spirit. The individual in his intellectual development follows the growth of this spirit very imperfectly and at an ever increasing distance. If, for instance, we view the immense culture which for the last hundred years has been embodied in things and in knowledge, in institutions and in comforts, and if we compare all this with the cultural progress of the individual during the same period—at least in high status groups—a frightful disproportion in growth between the two becomes evident. Indeed, at some points we notice a retrogression in the culture of the individual with reference to spirituality, delicacy, and idealism. This discrepancy results essentially from the growing division of labor. For the division of labor demands from the individual an ever more one-sided accomplishment, and the greatest advance in a one-sided pursuit only too frequently means death to the personality of the individual. In any case, he can cope less and less with the overgrowth of objective culture. The individual is reduced to a negligible quantity, perhaps less in his consciousness in his practice and in the totality of his obscure emotional states that are derived from this practice. The individual has become a mere cog in an enormous organization of things and powers which tear from his hands all progress, spirituality, and value in order to transform them from their subjective form into the form of a purely objective life. It needs merely to be pointed out that the metropolis is the genuine arena of this culture which outgrows all personal life. Here in buildings and educational institutions, in the wonders and comforts of space-conquering technology, in the formations of community life, and in the visible institutions of the state, is offered such an overwhelming fullness of crystallized and impersonalized spirit that the personality, so to speak, cannot maintain itself under its impact. On the one hand, life is made infinitely easy for the personality in that stimulations, interests, uses of time and consciousness are offered to it from all sides. They carry the person as if in a stream, and one needs hardly to swim for oneself. On the other hand, however, life is composed more and more of these impersonal contents and offerings which tend to displace the genuine personal colorations and incomparabilities. This results in the individual's summoning the utmost in uniqueness and particularization, in order to preserve his most personal core. He has to exaggerate this personal element in order to remain audible even to himself. The atrophy of individual culture through the hypertrophy of objective culture is one reason for the bitter hatred which the preachers of the most extreme individualism, above all Nietzsche, harbor against the metropolis. But it is, indeed, also a reason why these preachers are so passionately loved in the metropolis and why they appear to the metropolitan man as the prophets and saviors of his most unsatisfied yearnings.

If one asks for the historical position of these two forms of individualism which are nourished by the quantitative relation of the metropolis, namely, individual independence and the elaboration of individuality itself, then the metropolis assumes an entirely new rank order in the history of the spirit. The eighteenth century found the individual in oppressive bonds which had become meaningless—bonds of a political, agrarian, guild, and religious character. They were restraints which, so to speak, forced upon man an unnatural form and outmoded, unjust inequalities. In this situation the cry for liberty and equality arose, the belief in the individual's full freedom of movement in all social and intellectual relationships. Freedom would at once permit the noble substance common to all to come to the fore, a substance which nature had deposited in every man and which society and history had only deformed. Besides this eighteenth-century ideal of liberalism, in the nineteenth century, through Goethe and Romanticism, on the one hand, and through the economic division of labor, on the other hand, another ideal arose: individuals liberated from historical bonds now wished to distinguish themselves from one another. The carrier of man's values is no longer the "general human being" in every individual, but rather man's qualitative uniqueness and irreplaceability. The external and internal history of our time takes its course within the struggle and in the changing entanglements of these two ways of defining the individual's role in the whole of society. It is the function of the metropolis to provide the area for this struggle and its reconciliation. For the metropolis presents the peculiar conditions which are revealed to us as the opportunities and the stimuli for the development of both these ways of allocating roles to men. Therewith these conditions gain a unique place, pregnant with inestimable meanings for the development of psychic existence. The metropolis reveals itself as one of those great historical formations in which opposing streams which enclose life unfold, as well as join one another with equal right. However, in this process the currents of life, whether their individual phenomena touch us sympathetically or anti-pathetically, entirely transcend the sphere for which the judge's attitude is appropriate. Since such forces of life have grown into the roots and into the crown of the whole of the historical life in which we, in our fleeting existence, as a cell, belong only as a part, it is not our task either to accuse or to pardon, but only as a part, it is not our task either to ac-cuse or to pardon, but only to understand.

20. Practicality and Morality
Gerald Suttles

The Addams area is less than one-half square mile in size and contains fewer than 20,000 residents. It is probably a more orderly slum than many others and departs sharply from the common image of an atomized and unruly urban rabble. For all its historical uniqueness, the neighborhood does establish the possibility of a moral order within its population. The reoccurrence of the circumstances that led to its organization is as uncer-tain as the future of the Addams area itself. In spite of all these uncer-tainties, the Addams area shows that slum residents are intent upon finding a moral order and are sometimes successful in doing so.

PROVINCIALISM

The most general characteristics of the Addams area is its provincialism. This provincialism, however, is not total, nor does it constitute an unquali-fied rejection of societal values and norms. A belief in the stereotypes held

Reprinted from *The Social Order of the Slum* by Gerald D. Suttles by permission of The University of Chicago Press. © 1968 by The University of Chicago. All rights reserved.

by the wider society is what arouses so much mutual distrust among the residents and drives them to find another basis for a moral order. Even so, the residents organize themselves on the basis of distinctions that are widely made in American society: age, sex, ethnicity, territoriality, and personal reputation. In the Addams area these distinctions are emphasized to the exclusion of occupational, educational, and other attainments that are more appreciated in the wider society. The process, however, is more nearly one of reversion than inversion or outright rejection.

In the Addams area there are also numerous dependencies and attachments to the wider community. The resident policemen have a strong interest in maintaining stable relations both with the other residents and with their department. The local store owners and managers want the streets safe for their suppliers and customers. The area's politicians take a protective attitude toward the neighborhood and are active in acquiring patronage. Some of the churches are part of a nationwide structure, and street workers have been accepted into the neighborhood since the early days of the Chicago Area Project.[1] Adult crime tends to be organized within an "Outfit" which extends into many portions of the city.

In fact, these structural links between the Addams area and the wider community are essential to its provincialism. Until 1960, the Italians were partially able to fend off the destruction of dwellings preliminary to the development of industry and urban renewal. The control the Italians exercised through the wider community allowed them to become the most provincial ethnic group in the Addams area. The Negroes possess far less control over their ethnic section and are much less provincial than the Italians.

An essential condition to the provincialism of the Addams area is some control over land usage and population movements. This control, however, need not extend over vast areas because of the segmental structure of the neighborhood. The Addams area consists of four ethnic sections in which the residents are dependent primarily upon persons in the same section. Changes in land usage and population shifts, then, tend to disrupt only one section at a time.

The Addams area has been subject to continuous inroads as the Medical Center, the University of Illinois, industry, and the Chicago Housing Authority have occupied contiguous pieces of land at its boundaries. The extent to which this has limited or disrupted the internal organization of each ethnic section has varied a great deal. The location of the Negroes in public housing has made it impossible for them to develop a complement of ethnic institutions; and they remain heavily dependent upon the nearby shopping area, religious establishments, and educational facilities. Public housing is probably the most serious impediment to the developing provincialism in the Addams area. The same effect, however, may be present in other neighborhoods where "absentee" control of land usage makes it impossible for a local group to lay claim to a full complement of the establishments necessary to its day-to-day life.

The Italians in the Addams area have lost several portions of the neighborhood to other ethnic groups and to nonresidential usage. Because they are in private housing, can obtain control over relatively small building spaces, and are not too constrained by zoning laws, the Italians continue to preserve a range of local facilities adequate for daily life. Despite their loss of previous sections of the neighborhood, they are more able than any local ethnic group to restrict their relations to one another.

The Mexicans and Puerto Ricans in the Addams area are also situated in private housing and, like the Italians, they have been able to acquire at least a portion of the facilities to serve their everyday requirements. The success of their efforts is incomplete primarily because of the time it takes Addams area residents to readjust facilities to their own demands and to assimilate themselves to one another. Each ethnic section in the Addams area is able to incorporate a limited number of newcomers in a brief time. The new Puerto Rican and Mexican establishments are only gradually building up a clientele through the credit, informality, and license they permit their patrons. The street groups, named gangs, establishment groups, families, and SAC's are equally slow at accepting a new resident until his personal identity is known. The Mexican and Puerto Rican sections of the Addams area have neither fully developed those groupings which can function to incorporate newcomers nor have they had time to satisfy their doubts about the trustworthiness of many new arrivals.

These variations in the provincialism of each ethnic section reflect gradations in the balance between involvement in the wider community and continued participation in the local neighborhood. Until the beginning of this study, the Italians had maintained enough power in the wider community to protect their ethnic establishments, but they were not so involved with "outsiders" as to detract from their relations with their fellow residents. The Negroes in the housing projects have little voice in the wider community and less to say about how their local facilities are managed. The provincialism of the Addams area qualifies but does not exclude many relations with the wider community. Up to a point, then, an exchange with the wider community is complementary to the provincialism of the Addams area. Moreover, an absence or decline of provincialism in each ethnic section does not mean an increasing compliance with the mores of the wider community. In the Addams area the alternative to provincialism is a pervasive anonymity, distrust, and isolation.

ORDERED SEGMENTATION

Each ethnic section of the Addams area differs from the others in the extent to which it possesses a standardized routine for managing safe social relations. There is, however, a general agreement upon the social categories beyond which associations are not pursued. The boundaries of the neighborhood itself form the outermost perimeter for restricting social relations. Almost all the residents caution their wives, daughters, children, and siblings against crossing Roosevelt, Halsted, Congress, and Ashland. Within each neighborhood, each ethnic section is an additional boundary which sharply restricts movement. Adults cross ethnic boundaries to shop or go to work, while children do so in running errands or attending school. Free time and recreation, however, should be spent within one's own ethnic section.

Further territorial partitions are present in each ethnic section and maintain a degree of segregation between age, sex, and residential groupings. The general pattern is one that fans out from the household and is partitioned according to the age and sex of the residents. Females and children are in closest proximity to the household. Males move progressively beyond this perimeter depending on their age.

These territorial allotments produce only social aggregates which are defined by their spatial proximity. They afford an opportunity for interaction, but each ethnic section differs in how far these face-to-face relations have become a routine basis for association. In all ethnic sections the youngsters form regular play groups, and except for the Puerto Ricans, there are named gangs among the adolescent males. Only among the Italians, however, has this spatial ordering of age and sex aggregates been thoroughly embraced as the basis of group life. The Italian named street corner groups continue into adulthood as a SAC. All of the Italian boys' groups preface their name with either the term "Taylor" or the name of some other street in the area. Italian girls, on the other hand, are kept so close to home that they aggregate in only small unnamed groups. In the evening the Italian adults regularly reassemble at their favorite tavern, doorway, or stoop.

Among the Negroes, the spatial ordering of sex and age groups is not nearly so distinct, and social aggregates are not closely identified with the areas they occupy. Adolescent Negro girls range almost as far from their households as do the boys. The Negro girls also have named street corner groups like those of the boys. Street groupings among the adult Negroes shift a great deal in their membership, and in general, social relations are more transient than elsewhere in the area. The projects themselves seem simply to lack establishments and locations that can be clearly assigned to each age, sex, and residential grouping.

In the Puerto Rican and Mexican sections, spatial aggregation has produced many separate age and sex groups that regularly assemble. The Puerto Rican section is so small that these groups are still known by their membership rather than by some shared title. In the more populous Mexican section both the girls and boys have named groups, but the girls always retreat within the area occupied by an allied boys' group. The adult males and females in both the Puerto Rican and Mexican sections have their regular stoops, taverns, and other places where they expect to congregate in their leisure hours.

Unlike the Italians, the Puerto Ricans and Mexicans have not yet developed any adult SAC's. As they reached adulthood in 1965 both the Erls and the Regents made faltering attempts in this direction but failed when their members were unable to contribute equally to a storefront. The failure of the Mexicans and the Puerto Ricans to follow fully the pattern laid out by the Italians results from some of the same conditions that impede group formation among the Negroes. The Italians are able to command the facilities of their ethnic section; and territorial aggregations repeatedly face one another in the same grocery store, tavern, recreational establishment, and church. The Puerto Ricans and Mexicans cannot always afford a local storefront, and many of their transactions take them outside the local neighborhood. Face-to-face relations among the Negroes are confined largely to the streets; and commercial, religious, and recreational requirements often scatter them beyond their local ethnic section.

CONFLICT AND ORDER

The social order produced in the Addams area is always partial, and there are many occasions for conflict between ethnic sections. When there is trouble with an adjacent neighborhood, all four ethnic groups show their greatest unity. At other times their cohesion is expressed in such limited forms as a common voting pattern, a respect for territorial arrangements, and joint resistance to the clearance for the University of Illinois.

The residential segregation of ethnic groups is compounded by incomplete communication and a number of cultural differences. The older Italians, Mexicans, and Puerto Ricans find their English an embarrassing and inadequate means of handling inter-ethnic relations. Real and inferred differences in dialect, gestures, posture, and eye movements are a continual source of friction and uneasiness. It is doubtful if these communication differences reflect much variation in basic cultural values, and the residents themselves are only perplexed. As one Negro girl put it, "Maybe they [Italian women] don't mean anything by staring at you, but how can you tell?"

These cultural differences are only partially due to separate historical traditions. The provincialism of the Italians creates an expressive order in which they express their solidarity by disregarding the clothing fads, novel language, and new dances of the wider society. The Negroes are very quick to pick up new dances, dress styles, and the novelties of youthful slang. The result is two expressive orders that make it difficult for either ethnic group to accommodate itself to the other. The Puerto Ricans and Mexicans have an especially difficult time since they are neither so "hip" as the Negroes nor so "square" as the Italians.

While these cultural differences are real enough, the major distinctions between these ethnic groups arise from social conditions within the neighborhood itself. The expressive order of the Italians fits into their provincialism, while the Negroes find the recent fads, dances, and linguistic novelties useful in more anonymous circumstances. The variation among ethnic groups is increased by their cultural differences, but it rests essentially on the same conditions that produce varying levels of provincialism within each ethnic section.

The divisions between age, sex, and territorial groups are another source of conflict between and within ethnic sections. Trouble between ethnic sections often starts when peer groups of the same sex confront one another and gradually draw in other age and sex groupings. Within each ethnic section, named groups of about the same age are frequently at odds and occasionally threaten combat. If a girl goes very far out of her territorial confines, she invites the attention of predatory males. The strictness of age ranking in each ethnic section allows the older boys to "push around" the younger ones if they become obstreperous.

All of these instances of conflict, however, are an inevitable and necessary accompaniment to the area's segmental order. Individuals in the Addams area achieve a positive association with coresidents of the same age, sex, and ethnicity primarily because conflict with other persons forces them together into small face-to-face groupings. Otherwise, people might remain almost wholly isolated, associate indiscriminately, or be dependent on such dyadic relations as they could form.

So positive a role for conflict cannot be appreciated unless it is placed in a developmental sequence. At the outset, parents and children in the Addams area do not prescribe a definite set of persons with whom the family are to associate. Instead, they voice a variety of proscriptions: "Don't go out of the neighborhood"; "I thought I told you to stay off Taylor Street"; "Don't you get off the block"; "Stay by the house, like I told you." Injunctions of this sort do not initially produce positive associations but only territorial aggregates confined together in an enduring relationship because of the restrictions on other associations.

The result is a pattern of movement that brings together coresidents of the same age and sex. These small and continuous face-to-face aggregations furnish the occasion for people to get acquainted and to inquire into each other's personal history. In this context they can provide the assurances that relieve their apprehensions. Without some principal of selection, however, the residents could wander from one person to another while failing to establish a firm relation with anyone. Conflict between age, sex, and territorial groups, however, forces the residents to throw their lot in with a definite group of people.

The social order that emerges in these small congregations does not consist of a series of highly standardized role capacities. Addams area residents relate to one another primarily by a personalistic morality in which individual precedent is the major standard for evaluation. The most incongruous of people become associated and continue to remain safe companions. Judgments of worth and social sanctions are individuated and tailored to past commitments. Normative rulings, then, do not apply to a fixed role apart from the incumbent; they can be developed only as individuals have the time and occasion to become familiar with each others' past history and future intentions.

Such a personalistic morality is obviously limited in the number of people it can include because of the time and effort it takes to become so intimately acquainted. Once under way, however, these discrete groupings can be complemented by a growing maze of intergroup relations. The conflict between age, sex, and territorial groups, then, sets the stage so that dyads can relate entire groups of people.

THE EXTENSION OF FACE-TO-FACE RELATIONS

While face-to-face relations and a personalistic morality are the main forms for association, they are extended by a number of other devices. Kinship functions to create an extensive web of connections between informal groups. Children who become closely acquainted seem tacitly to assume some trust and respect for each others' parents. Having a brother, a cousin, or parent in another group is perhaps the most frequent reason given when a resident says, "It's OK, they won't bother me."

Similar intergroup relations are established where different kinds of territorial groups overlap but do not coincide in their membership. This type of connection is most evident among the Italian adults where street groups and establishment groups only partially coincide in the people they include. Since the Negroes have extremely few establishment groups, this type of structural bridge between groups is rare.

There are, however, a variety of ways in which affiliations spread beyond each local group of peers. When people change residences within the neighborhood, they usually become associated with a new street group without, however, losing contact with prior friends. In the Italian section a single church draws people from practically every social grouping and allows for some measure of acquaintance. The local parochial schools serve much the same function among the Italian youngsters. Residents in the other three ethnic sections are more fragmented by the churches and schools they attend; still, these institutions afford some opportunity for association among different street groupings.

The most stable form of intergroup relations occur among the named street corner groups and adult SAC's. Within each ethnic section of the Addams area, the named street corner groups form an age-graded hierarchy with clear dominance relations. The younger groups do not challenge the dominance of their seniors, and the older groups are patronizing toward the younger ones. Shared names and debette groups extend these affiliations and clarify them to other groups. Potential conflict, then, is restricted to groups which are at about the same age level. Even among these groups, however, there are mechanisms that forestall full-scale fights. Among the Italians, the adult SAC's are powerful groups and do not hesitate to quell the youngsters when they get too rowdy or threaten to draw the police into the area. A half dozen or so resident Italian policemen take an equally active role in suppressing disturbances among the youngsters. Local members of the "Outfit" are especially heavy-handed when they think the youngsters will "bring heat on the neighborhood."

The other three ethnic groups in the area do not have these means of dealing with conflict among the youngsters. In part, the area's street workers are able to fill the same role. As among the Italians, however, the pattern of group affiliations is such that most instances of conflict are truncated short of a "gang fight." As grievances and questions of dominance between groups accumulate, other people are notified by a series of rumors. Sometimes this will result in other groups taking sides. Often this process of accretion will progress until the dominant group in the ethnic section becomes implicated. In the Addams area, the Erls, Regents, and Magnificent Gallants were clearly dominant and able to intimidate antagonists within their own ethnic section. If they allied themselves with a particular faction, opponents within their own ethnic section grumbled but gave in.

A far more common pattern was one in which rumors anticipated gang fights and thus became the occasion for intervention from a number of sources. Once altered by these rumors, street workers, the police, parents, shop owners, and priests took a hand in separating the antagonists. As a result, actual conflict was usually restricted to one of two circumstances. First, a few boys might "jump" a member of another group, following rumors of a "gang fight." Second, segments of two groups might unwittingly run into one another and start a row. Full-scale "gang fights" seem very rare, and only two were known to occur in the three years between 1962 and 1965. Both were very brief encounters and left no one seriously injured. In each case two groups had independently strayed out of their local territory and accidentally met.

The discrete groupings and intergroup affiliations that occur in the Addams area produce an ordered segmentation in two senses. First, ethnic, age, sex, and territorial groupings establish an order within which people can be related directly or indirectly to the entire neighborhood. Second, there is a sequential order in which these groupings can be combined through a process of accretion when there is a threat of trouble. Neither of these structural arrangements are fully able to stave off all instances of violence and conflict. The result in the Addams area, however, is a far cry from an atomistic situation in which every person must work out his associations one at a time.

An integral part of the neighborhood's ordered segmentation is its named adolescent street corner groups. Despite widespread apprehension about adolescent gangs, those in the Addams area have gone far toward creating an order which includes a large number of people. Within each ethnic section, age-grading, a dominant group, and explicit alliances establish stable relations between several hundred youngsters, some of who scarcely know one another. Where kinship and friendship might otherwise establish safe relations among those immediately concerned, the street corner group turns these affiliations into a guarantee of safety between entire groups of boys. The adolescent gang, then, may be less an anarchistic rebellion than the first step toward a social solution to individual relations.

REALITY AND MORALITY

The understandings, myths, rumors, gossip, prejudices, and social divisions shared by Addams area residents make up a highly localized subculture. Its content, however, is not easy to characterize with the general concepts of "role," "value," and "norm." The residents themselves tend to describe their relationships in highly personal terms, starting with a series of facts they regard as valid, and then proceeding to detail their behavior as a necessary consequence. Occasionally, reference is made to what people should be like, but a far more common concern is the actual character of people and one's own affiliation with them. There is, then, an explicit recognition of the ideal status of public morality and its undependability when applied to "real people."

The "real people" that Addams area residents are most concerned about are their neighbors. What they know from general sources, however, only furthers their view that public standards of morality are not a safe guideline for conduct. According to general stereotypes and public channels of communication, their neighbors are an urban rabble prone to riot, pillage, disorder, and crime. The residents know such behavior to be the exception rather than the rule. But it is only by going beyond the stereotypes, evaluations, and norms of public conduct that the residents can determine who is the exception and who fits the rule. Thus, cognitive rather than moral considerations dominate the residents' interests.

The resulting subculture consists of a wide range of personal information, shared understandings, ethnic customs, and mutual disclosures. The young boys, the old ladies, men, and adolescent girls all become intimately involved with one another to the point that their omissions and shortcomings are shared and act as pledges to further securities. Ethnic origins are appealed to and kinship is emphasized in the absence of other assurances of affiliation and safety. Gossip, slander, and innuendo are closely attended and serve as a common basis for determining someone else's social character.

Since Addams area residents share many suspicions and common failings, the content of their subculture is limited in the direction it takes. First, there is a great deal of concern about illegal activities, the "Outfit," and criminals. Those involved in these activities are small in number, but the residents are anxious to make peace with them or, if possible, to avoid them. Because they inquire so thoroughly into this issue, the residents are uncommonly aware of each other's illegal activities. The result is a sort of social compact in which respectable residents and those not so respectable are both tolerant and protective of one another.

A second focus of interest is in each other's trustworthiness, sincerity, or loyalty. Addams area residents are very interested in gaining rapport with one another; but they hesitate to reveal too much about themselves, lest they become vulnerable. Thus, "finks," "con-artists," "phonies," and "jitter bugs" are stronger terms of condemnation than "unemployed," "poor" or "felon." By taking each other into their confidence, the residents risk a great deal. Trustworthiness, then, is valued far more than some formal appellation that connotes high morals and good character.

Third, the residents share a number of apprehensions over the exercise of brute force and the physical attributes assumed to divide the weak from the strong. Physical size, age, sex, and numbers enter fully into the residents' calculations and are a strong consideration for assigning super-ordinate or subordinate statuses. Generally these signs of physical prowess are accepted out of hand or settled after a single demonstration. Leadership, social rank, and associations, however, are partially based on shows of strength which, in turn, lead to some measure of violence and force.

The subcultural commonalities of the Addams area consist primarily of a selective search for private information rather than the invention of normative ideals. The residents express admiration for unrelenting respectability, complete frankness, and a general restraint from force. In the real world they live in, however, the residents are willing to settle for a friend of doubtful repute, guarded personal disclosures, and the threat of force to meet force.

The subculture of the Addams area is more nearly a means of gradually discovering a moral order than a set of rules which one mechanically obeys. As the residents fan out from their households, they are very cautious, arranging their social relations to minimize the assumed dangers. The outcome is an ordered segmentation of age, sex, ethnic, and territorial groupings bound together by common disclosures and personal loyalties. Even this order takes time to construct and can be upset by circumstances that continually recur in slum neighborhoods.

SOURCES OF INSTABILITY AND CHANGE

Under very idealized circumstances, it is possible to imagine a social order in the Addams area which is far more inclusive and determinate. Given sufficient control over the facilities in the area, stable boundaries for each ethnic section, and a slow rate of population change, the residents might create a very provincial but also a very orderly neighborhood. So far only the Italians have been able to realize so complete a social order. Looking to the future, it is tempting to predict a convergence between the Italian section and the other three ethnic sections. Such a speculation would be hazardous for a number of reasons.

First, the future of the Addams area itself is uncertain, since urban renewal and institutional building plans threaten to disband its population. Once they are scattered, the residents will have to start anew rather than simply advance from where they stand.

Second, as new economic and political policies gain ground, the entire complex of inner-city life may change its character. Except for the projects, the land and buildings of the Addams area are broken into many small and independent units which allow for the interlarding of religious, commercial, recreational, and domestic life. The growth of public housing and the sale of large blocks of land for special usages is likely to separate these functions. The construction of huge housing developments, uniform in style, size of dwelling unit, and rental costs, may produce a series of residential compounds appropriate to only a period of the family life cycle. If these policies are implemented on a large scale, the centrifugal forces may be so great that slum residents can no longer maintain the integrity of their territorial groups and provincial way of life.

Added uncertainties accumulate as we consider possible changes in the occupational structure and a variety of programs aimed at reacculturation. In the particulars of its ordered segmentation, then, the Addams area may be less a model of the future than a reflection of the past. In a broader sense, however, the Addams area is an example that has direct relevance to the future of all slum neighborhoods. Addams area residents are not engaged in an attempt to create an illusory world that merely denies the one which the wider community has established. The residents are impelled by a far more basic task of finding an order within which they can secure themselves against common apprehensions. So basic is this burden that few slum residents can ignore it or retreat fully into sheer fantasy, opportunism, or defeatism.

The moral order created by Addams area residents does not meet either their own ideals or those of the wider society. The local people recognize as much and view their way of life as a practical exigency. For all its shortcomings, however, the moral order they have developed includes most, if not all, of their neighbors. Within limits, the residents possess a way of gaining associates, avoiding enemies, and establishing each others' intentions. In view of the difficulties encountered, the provincialism of the Addams area has provided a decent world within which people can live.

NOTES

1. Solomon Kobrin, "The Chicago Area Project—A Twenty-five-Year Assessment," *Annals of the American Academy of Political and Social Science*, 322 (March, 1959): 20–29.

21. The Postcity Age

Melvin M. Webber

The pragmatic traditions in American political life have led us to attack the manifest problems of the moment with heavy commitment, but to avoid the longer-term confrontation of underlying issues. The several governmental attempts to undertake long-range problem analysis, forecasting, and planning have never succeeded. We have yet to implant a counter-tradition in America that, by exploring the future, would inform a national development policy. This failing reflects, in part, the current status of the social sciences, which have not developed adequate predictive theory in most fields of national concern. It is sobering that no sociologist predicted the magnitude of the Negro Revolt, that no prewar urbanist anticipated the postwar development patterns in American cities, and that, most troubling of all, no one has yet written systematic alternative futures seeking to chart the possible course of events in these fields.

As one consequence of our political traditions and our inadequate theory, we tend to overreact to events of the day. When a curve turns upward, we expect that it will go off the top of the chart; when it turns down, we despair that it will fall off the bottom. A decade ago we were all assured that America was floating serenely in middle-class affluence and that things could only get better. Then we suddenly changed our national self-image when we discovered a large lower-class population and large-scale poverty. The demonstrations of the past five summers have alternatively been read as signs of a new egalitarianism in America or an impending *apartheid*. We had thought our public school system was unexcelled, until Sputnik shocked us into wholesale reform. We believed that suburban development was going to provide decent homes for all, and now we believe that nothing short of immediate reconstruction of the old cities can save them from disaster.

There can be no doubt about the imperatives for confronting the current crises that are associated with the contemporary city. The outcries from the Negro ghetto must be answered humbly, humanely, and immediately; and that will call for huge investments of intellectual capital and federal money. The scale of the current building and rebuilding enterprise in the cities is unprecedented. We shall have to double the size

From Melvin M. Webber, "The Postcity Age." Reprinted by permission of *Daedalus*, Journal of the American Academy of Arts and Sciences, Boston, Massachusetts, from *Daedalus* 97, no. 4, *The Conscience of the City* (Fall 1968), pp. 1091–1110.

of our physical plant during the next thirty-five years; and that, too, must command full-scale commitment of our intellectual and financial resources. It now appears as though these investments will be forthcoming, largely because the current crisis has captured the nation's conscience and partly because it is our style to respond to emergencies in force.

But it will be an unfortunate mistake, another repetition of our traditional propensities, if we pour our resources into the manifest problems without also dealing with the less visible underlying issues. A deep-swell is shaping those curves on our month-to-month charts—a large historical change that may reshape the character of urban society in the developed world. This, too, must command our attention, for the coming changes may so inhibit future social mobility that our present short-run, ameliorative programs could prove ineffective in retrospect. If so, we had better try to anticipate those changes and then modify our action programs to conform.

URBANIZATION BEYOND THE CITY

We are passing through a revolution that is unhitching the social processes of urbanization from the locationally fixed city and region. Reflecting the current explosion in science and technology, employment is shifting from the production of goods to services; increasing ease of transportation and communication is dissolving the spatial barriers to social intercourse; and Americans are forming social communities comprised of spatially·dispersed members. A new kind of large-scale urban society is emerging that is increasingly independent of the city. In turn, the problems of the city place generated by early industrialization are being supplanted by a new array different in kind. With but a few remaining exceptions (the new air pollution is a notable one), the recent difficulties are not place-type problems at all. Rather, they are the transitional problems of a rapidly developing society-economy-and-polity whose turf is the nation. Paradoxically, just at the time in history when policy-makers and the world press are discovering the city, "the age of the city seems to be at an end."[1]

Our failure to draw the rather simple conceptual distinction between the spatially defined city or metropolitan area and the social systems that are localized there clouds current discussions about the "crisis of our cities."[2] The confusion stems largely from the deficiencies of our language and from the anachronistic thoughtways we have carried over from the passing era. We still have no adequate descriptive terms for the emerging social order, and so we use, perforce, old labels that are no longer fitting. Because we have named them so, we suppose that the problems manifested inside cities are, therefore and somehow, "city problems." Because societies in the past had been spatially and locally structured, and because urban societies used to be exclusively city-based, we seem still to assume that territoriality is a necessary attribute of social systems.

The error has been a serious one, leading us to seek local solutions to problems whose causes are not of local origin and hence are not susceptible to municipal treatment. We have been tempted to apply city-building instruments to correct social disorders, and we have then been surprised to find that they do not work. (Our experience with therapeutic public housing, which was supposed to cure "social pathologies," and urban renewal, which was supposed to improve the lives of the poor, may be our most spectacular failures.) We have lavished large investments on public facilities, but neglected the quality and the distribution of the social services. And we have defended and reinforced home-rule prerogatives of local and state governments with elaborate rhetoric and protective legislation.

Neither crime-in-the-streets, poverty, unemployment, broken families, race riots, drug addiction, mental illness, juvenile delinquency, nor any of the commonly noted "social pathologies" marking the contemporary city can find its causes or its cure there. We cannot hope to invent local treatments for conditions whose origins are not local in character, nor can we expect territorially defined governments to deal effectively with problems whose causes are unrelated to territory or geography. The concepts and methods of civil engineering and city planning suited to the design of unitary physical facilities cannot be used to serve the design of social change in a pluralistic and mobile society. In the novel society now emerging—with its sophisticated and rapidly advancing science and technology, its complex social organization, and its internally integrated societal processes—the influence and significance of geographic distance and geographic place are declining rapidly.

This is, of course, a most remarkable change. Throughout virtually all of human history, social organization coincided with spatial organization. In preindustrial society, men interacted almost exclusively with geographic neighbors. Social communities, economies, and polities were structured about the place in which interaction was least constrained by the frictions of space. With the coming of large-scale industrialization during the latter half of the nineteenth century the strictures of space were rapidly eroded, abetted by the new ease of travel and communication that the industrialization itself brought.

The initial counterparts of industrialization in the United States were, first, the concentration of the nation's population into large settlements and, then, the cultural urbanization of the population. Although these changes were causally linked, they had opposite spatial effects. After coming together at a common place, people entered larger societies tied to no specific place. Farming and village people from throughout the continent and the world migrated to the expanding cities, where they learned urban ways, acquired the occupational skills that industrialization demanded, and became integrated into the contemporary society.

In recent years, rising societal scale and improvements in transportation and communications systems have loosed a chain of effects robbing the city of its once unique function as an urbanizing instrument of society. Farmers and small-town residents, scattered throughout the continent, were once effectively removed from the cultural life of the nation. City folks visiting the rural areas used to be treated as strangers, whose styles of living and thinking were unfamiliar. News of the rest of the world was hard to get and then had little meaning for those who lived the local life. Country folk surely knew there was another world out there somewhere, but little understood it and were affected by it only indirectly. The powerful anti-urban traditions in early American thought and politics made the immigrant city dweller a suspicious character whose crude ways marked him as un-Christian (which he sometimes was) and certainly un-American. The more sophisticated urban upper classes —merchants, landowners, and professional men—were similarly suspect and hence rejected. In contrast, the small-town merchant and the farmer who lived closer to nature were the genuine Americans of pure heart who lived the simple, natural life.[3] Because the contrasts between the rural and the urban ways-of-life were indeed sharp, antagonisms were real, and the differences became institutionalized in the conduct of politics. America was marked by a diversity of regional and class cultures whose followers interacted infrequently, if ever.

By now this is nearly gone. The vaudeville hick-town and hayseed characters have left the scene with the vaudeville act. Today's urbane farmer watches television documentaries, reads the national news magazines, and manages his acres from an office (maybe located in a downtown office building), as his hired hands ride their tractors while listening to the current world news broadcast from a transistor. Farming has long since ceased to be a handicraft art; it is among the most highly technologized industries and is tightly integrated into the international industrial complex.

During the latter half of the nineteenth century and the first third of the twentieth, the traditional territorial conception that distinguished urbanites and ruralites was probably valid: The typical rural folk lived outside the cities, and the typical urbanites lived inside. By now this pattern is nearly *reversed*. Urbanites no longer reside exclusively in metropolitan settlements, nor do ruralites live exclusively in the hinterlands. Increasingly, those who are least integrated into modern society— those who exhibit most of the attributes of rural folk—are concentrating within the highest-density portions of the large metropolitan centers. This profoundly important development is only now coming to our consciousness, yet it points up one of the major policy issues of the next decades.

THE PARTICIPANTS IN THE HIGH-SCALE SOCIETY

Cultural diffusion is integrating immigrants, city residents, and hinterland peoples into a national urban society, but it has not touched all

Americans evenly. At one extreme are the intellectual and business elites, whose habitat is the planet; at the other are the lower-class residents of city and farm who live in spatially and cognitively constrained worlds. Most of the rest of us, who comprise the large middle class, lie somewhere in-between, but in some facets of our lives we all seem to be moving from our ancestral localism toward the unbounded realms of the cosmopolites.

High educational attainments and highly specialized occupations mark the new cosmopolites. As frequent patrons of the airlines and the long-distance telephone lines, they are intimately involved in the communications networks that tie them to their spatially dispersed associates. They contribute to and consume the specialized journals of science, government, and industry, thus maintaining contact with information resources of relevance to their activities, whatever the geographic sources or their own locations. Even though some may be employed by corporations primarily engaged in manufacturing physical products, these men trade in information and ideas. They are the producers of the information and ideas that fuel the engines of societal development. For those who are tuned into the international communications circuits, cities have utility precisely because they are rich in information. The way such men use the city reveals its essential character most clearly, for to them the city is essentially a massive communications switchboard through which human interaction takes place.[4]

Indeed, cities exist *only* because spatial agglomeration permits reduced costs of interaction. Men originally elected to locate in high-density settlements precisely because space was so costly to overcome. It is still cheaper to interact with persons who are nearby, and so men continue to locate in such settlements.[5] Because there *are* concentrations of associates in city places, the new cosmopolites establish their offices there and then move about from city to city conducting their affairs. The biggest settlements attract the most long-distance telephone and airline traffic and have undergone the most dramatic growth during this era of city-building.

The recent expansion of Washington, D.C. is the most spectacular evidence of the changing character of metropolitan development. Unlike the older settlements whose growth was generated by expanding manufacturing activities during the nineteenth and early-twentieth centuries, Washington produces almost no goods whatsoever. Its primary products are information and intelligence, and its fantastic growth is a direct measure of the predominant roles that information and the national government have come to play in contemporary society.

This terribly important change has been subtly evolving for a long time, so gradually that it seems to have gone unnoticed. The preindustrial towns that served their adjacent farming hinterlands were essentially alike. Each supplied a standardized array of goods and services to its neighboring market area. The industrial cities that grew after the Civil

War and during the early decades of this century were oriented to serving larger markets with the manufacturing products they were created to produce. As their market areas widened, as product specialization increased, and as the information content of goods expanded, establishments located in individual cities became integrated into the spatially extensive economies. By now, the large metropolitan centers that used to be primarily goods-producing loci have become interchange junctions within the international communications networks. Only in the limited geographical, physical sense is any modern metropolis a discrete, unitary, identifiable phenomenon. At most, it is a localized node within the integrating international networks, finding its significant identity as contributor to the workings of that larger system. As a result, the new cosmopolites belong to none of the world's metropolitan areas, although they use them. They belong, rather, to the national and international communities that merely maintain information exchanges at these metropolitan junctions.

Their capacity to interact intimately with others who are spatially removed depends, of course, upon a level of wealth adequate to cover the dollar costs of long-distance intercourse, as well as upon the cognitive capacities associated with highly skilled professional occupations. The intellectual and business elites are able to maintain continuing and close contact with their associates throughout the world because they are rich not only in information, but also in dollar income.

As the costs of long-distance interaction fall in proportion to the rise in incomes, more and more people are able and willing to pay the transportation and communication bills. As expense-account privileges are expanded, those costs are being reduced to zero for ever larger numbers of people. As levels of education and skill rise, more and more people are being tied into the spatially extensive communities that used to engage only a few.

Thus, the glue that once held the spatial settlement together is now dissolving, and the settlement is dispersing over ever widening terrains. At the same time, the pattern of settlement upon the continent is also shifting (moving toward long strips along the coasts, the Gulf, and the Great Lakes). These trends are likely to be accelerated dramatically by cost-reducing improvements in transportation and communications technologies now in the research-and-development stages. (The SST, COMSAT communications, high-speed ground transportation with speeds up to 500 m.p.h., TV and computer-aided educational systems, no-toll long-distance telephone service, and real-time access to national computer-based information systems are likely to be powerful ones.) Technological improvements in transport and communications reduce the frictions of space and thereby ease long-distance intercourse. Our compact, physical city layouts directly mirror the more primitive technologies in use at the time these cities were built. In a similar way, the locational pattern of cities upon the continent reflects the technologies available at the time the settlements grew.[6] If currently anticipated technological improvements prove workable, each of the metropolitan settlements will spread out in low-density patterns over far more extensive areas than even the most frightened future-mongers have yet predicted. The new settlement-form will little resemble the nineteenth-century city so firmly fixed in our images and ideologies. We can also expect that the large junction points will no longer have the communications advantage they now enjoy, and smaller settlements will undergo a major spurt of growth in all sorts of now-isolated places where the natural amenities are attractive.

Moreover, as ever larger percentages of the nation's youth go to college and thus enter the national and international cultures, attachments to places of residence will decline dramatically. This prospect, rather than the spatial dispersion of metropolitan areas, portends the functional demise of the city. The signs are already patently clear among those groups whose worlds are widest and least bounded by parochial constraints.

Consider the extreme cosmopolite, if only for purposes of illustrative cartooning. He might be engaged in scientific research, news reporting, or international business, professions exhibiting critical common traits. The astronomer, for example, maintains instantaneous contact with his colleagues around the world; indeed, he is a day-to-day collaborator with astronomers in all countries. His work demands that he share information and that he and his colleagues monitor stellar events jointly, as the earth's rotation brings men at different locales into prime-viewing position. Because he is personally committed to their common enterprise, his social reference group is the society of astronomers. He assigns his loyalties to the community of astronomers, since their work and welfare matter most to him.

To be sure, as he plays out other roles—say, as citizen, parent, laboratory director, or grocery shopper—he is a member of many other communities, both interest-based and place-defined ones. But the striking thing about our astronomer, and the millions of people like him engaged in other professions, is how little of his attention and energy he devotes to the concerns of place-defined communities. Surely, as compared to his grandfather, whose life was largely bound up in the affairs of his locality, the astronomer, playwright, newsman, steel broker, or wheat dealer lives in a life-space that is not defined by territory and deals with problems that are not local in nature. For him, the city is but a convenient setting for the conduct of his professional work; it is not the basis for the social communities that he cares most about.

Indeed, we may not be far from the time when the vernacular meaning of "community" will be archaic and disappear from common usage. It has already lost much of its traditional meaning for a great many of those on the leading edge of the society. If it is retained, it may be restricted to the provisions of children and of those adults who have not gained access to modern society.

The demise of the city is associated with far more subtle and powerful changes than the expansion of market areas for firms and the collaboration among scientists in distant nations. Behind these developments lies the internationalization of society generated by the knowledge explosion.

By its very nature, knowledge is specific to neither cities nor nations. An overriding, largely unanticipated consequence of science is its internationalizing effect—its introduction of common understandings, common libraries of information, common bases for valuation and validation, and, indeed, a common culture for men located in all parts of the world. The same consequences emanate from developments in technology, commerce, the arts, theater, literature, and virtually all areas of creative endeavor. Save for those, like Lyzenko, who hold to certain specialized epistemologies or ideologies, new discoveries and inventions are readily accepted, irrespective of their geographic origins. By now there is a large class of persons around the world who share in the world culture, while simultaneously participating in the idiosyncratic local cultures special to their regions of residence. Their range of opportunity is far larger and far more diverse than the most powerful and wealthy man of past eras could have imagined.

Knowledge is also cumulative; its store can only get larger, and the effects it generates are one-directional. We now know that the recent expansion of knowledge has triggered a rapid explosion of life-space—both geographically and cognitively. We can expect that explosion to continue, further bursting the barriers of geography and ignorance for larger proportions of the population. The counterpart of expanding life-space has been the contracting role of the cities and the nations as the organizing frameworks of societies. This is, of course, a revolutionary development. As Kenneth Boulding has synoptically put it, it portends the end of "civilization" as the culture of the *civitas*.[7] To be sure, the end of civilization has been in sight for a long time; through a telling etymological trick we have become accustomed to speaking of national citizenship, and we even describe some people as "world citizens." This usage is far more prophetic than we had realized.

Although the intellectual and business elites are undoubtedly still a minority among us, the vast middle class is rapidly adopting their styles and their capabilities, and lower-class persons are aspiring to them. About 40 per cent of American youth are now going to college, and the proportion will soon be over half. (In California it is now about 80 per cent.) Television has already supplied a window to a seamless world, a world that the present generation is actively exploring firsthand. If we ever succeed in using television creatively, it could become a more powerful educational force than the public schools have been—extending the classroom to every house and the spectrum of accessible knowledge far beyond the present bounds. Americans may already be consuming more books per capita, more magazines per capita, more music, more lectures, and more art than any population in the world—certainly far more than any peoples in the past. They are traveling widely for recreational and educational purposes; and in the course of their travels, they are absorbing information, ideas, and attitudes, even as they are seeding their own along their paths.

The nationals of other countries are, of course, engaged in the same set of activities. Western Europeans may be the next most-mobile people in the world, although the Japanese probably outpace even them in the rate at which they have been scouting the planet, absorbing and then exploiting the world's knowledge. The signs of this internationalization are clear: the rise of the international business firm, the near-instantaneous diffusion of fashion in dress and the arts, the spectacular spread of the hippie culture, the new international architecture, the Europeans' sense of personal loss at the assassinations of John F. Kennedy, Martin Luther King, and Robert F. Kennedy, the acceptance of the common market idea, and the new-found racial pride among mutually supportive colored peoples.

We have little reason to doubt that the accumulation and dispersion of knowledge will continue, bringing further dissolution of local differences. The economy is expanding in precisely those service industries that demand high educational attainment and sophistication: education, research and development, health, and the information services. Concomitantly, the traditional loci of growth that marked the industrial stage of national development are already on the decline. During the past twenty years, there has been almost no expansion in manufacturing employment in the U.S.; we may soon be seeing an actual decline, despite the fantastic expansion of output. Unskilled jobs are fast disappearing, and physically exhausting work may before long be completely consigned to machines.

The processes have been mutually reinforcing. The service occupations that require high skill have been able to expand because a highly educated labor force has been developing. In turn, these occupations, particularly those within the knowledge industries, have been reproducing their own next-generations of better trained persons and their own next-generations of new knowledge. Thus, we have been riding a rising spiral that is turning the economy upside down, converting it from one in which workers produce physical products to one in which they produce services. Many of the new services are concerned with the management of information, and the information content of most of the new physical products is rising rapidly. (Compare, for example, the information content of a transistor radio with that of a trainload of coal.) In the process, the emphasis on knowledge and information has been increasing dramatically. Already the number of Americans working full time as teachers is over two million. We may now be fast approaching the day, long heralded by the ancient Greek philosophers, when our major occupation will be learning for its own sake.

THE BYPASSED PREINDUSTRIAL LOCALS

As the scale of the society has been rising, carrying the bulk of the national population into the dimly seen post-industrial era, a large segment of the population is being left further and further behind. A short time ago, many of these people were living in rural areas, a high proportion in the southern and Appalachian states; the migration to the cities during the past twenty-five years has by now relocated nearly all of them. Today, they are city dwellers, residing in the most dense sections of the metropolitan areas, but still living in the folk cultures their grandparents knew. Here in the Harlems and South Sides of the nation are some of the last viable remnants of preindustrial societies, where village styles are most nearly intact. Here the turf is the city block, and teenage gangs wage war in its defense. Here in the slum blocks of the central cities may be the only pure place-based social neighborhoods we have left.

American cities have always been magnets for preindustrial migrants searching for access into contemporary society. Like those who preceded them from Europe, the recent migrants are being both pushed by the hardships of their present life and pulled by the promise of opportunities that the city has traditionally held out. And yet the recent migrations occur in a very different setting. Those who now come must bridge a cultural gap far wider than the one their predecessors faced, one that is widening at an exponential rate.

Despite the suffering that accompanied nineteenth-century migration and acculturation, the stage was well set; the paths to social mobility were short and easily traversed. The new manufacturing industries called for large numbers of workers who could easily be trained to perform the standardized tasks. In turn, jobs made for income security that provided relief from the hazards of everyday life, thus fostering a non-fatalistic world-view through which future opportunities could be seen. The physical structure of the city permitted the various ethnic and national groups to settle in colonies within the cities. The transplanted old-world life styles of the ethnic ghettos eased the transition for the adult newcomers, while their children gradually introduced them to the new urban ways. The democratic institutions and the legal rules for acquiring citizenship and voting rights permitted the newcomers to control and then to use local governments instrumentally in accelerating their own development. For some, politics and government provided an important route to social mobility.

Free public schools served as an open doorway through which immigrants' children found access to semiskilled and skilled occupations and thus to higher social status than their parents enjoyed. The public

schools, the free public colleges, the free libraries, the availability of free
or cheap medical services, and the public life of the street became the
major acculturating media. By living the city-based life, the second- and
third-generation Americans acquired the social and cognitive skills and
the internal psychic competencies that modern urbanism demands. In
the school, on the street, and frequently in illicit enterprises, the immigrants' children learned to use the money and credit economy, to defer
gratification, to anticipate future problems and opportunities, to cope
with crises, and to deal with multiple options. The city was, in effect, a
school where peasant migrants learned with incredible speed to be
urbanized Americans. Within single generations, groups that had followed the four-hundred-year-old peasant styles of life and thought were
catapulted into a society of a vastly different kind and scale. Most of
them landed on their feet; some of them shot to the forefront of the society and then led it on to its next stages of development.

The setting for the massive European and Asian migrations to the city
was fortuitous. They arrived just when the national economy was em-
barking upon unprecedented industrial development, and they came into
a social system constrained by few immovable barriers of social class. In
a time when small capitalization was sufficient, some succeeded in establishing small, family-based businesses; in the milieu of a rapidly expanding economy, some of these soon became big businesses. Others entered
the professions, government, and the large corporations where they established themselves as leaders among the intellectual elites.

The way out of the ghetto was fast and easy for a few groups of immigrants. For many Eastern European Jews, the departure from the immigrant ghetto areas in the slums occurred very quickly. Many of the
Jews were culturally urbanized when they came here; in Europe the
legal prohibition against their owning land kept them in towns where
many were small merchants or traders. The relatively unstructured and
open-ended character of their religious doctrines led them as a group to
place high value on scholarship and individual achievement, to adopt a
typically critical intellectual attitude, and to be concerned with the consequences of future events. These characteristics, coupled with a solidly
cohesive family structure, served them well when they reached the
United States. The Chinese and Japanese, with their cohesive, patriarchal family structure and high cultural value on intellectual achievement, were also among the most upwardly mobile groups.

In contrast, mobility has come slower to the Irish, southern Italian,
and Polish immigrants, whose peasant heritage had few of these urbanizing attributes. Only within the past generation or two have their children
been going to college in large numbers, leaving the ethnic ghetto and
the working-class world-view behind them. The rigidity of traditional
practices and beliefs and the emphasis on discipline and conformity
exerted by the Catholic Church had previously discouraged exploration
of wider conceptual worlds than those of the ethnic neighborhoods.

Whatever innate and cultural attributes may have sped social mobility for some of the early migrants to America's cities, their success was just as surely a consequence of the nation's stage of development at the time they arrived. Uneducated migrants to cities were not very far behind those who had arrived long before them. Those of quick mind could master the tasks required by the new factories speedily and then move beyond into the managerial and professional roles.

THE CENTRAL POLICY ISSUE

A far more difficult setting faces the migrants to the cities today. The explosive progress in the arts, sciences, and technologies has triggered an unprecedented rise in the scale of the national society, one marked by ever finer division of labor, calling for ever higher levels of education and training; by the shift from extractive and manufacturing industries to service industries that require long periods of preparation; by increasingly complex organization of the economy and polity; and by the expansion of the spatial and cognitive fields within which human interaction and economic transaction take place. Specialization, interdependence, and integration are the definitive traits of today's urbanism. This new scale of complexity distinguishes modern urbanism from earlier forms and is setting the policy agenda that the nation must now address.

Although it is still easy to migrate to the cities, the demands of large-scale society are making it more and more difficult for newcomers to gain entry into the new urban society. Those city dwellers who are presently least integrated into modern society are facing a series of hurdles far higher than the ones the earlier migrants found. The Appalachians, Negroes, Puerto Ricans, and Mexican Americans now concentrated within the central ghettos of metropolitan areas are not just the most recent wave of newcomers to those districts, as some scholars have suggested. The others were able to pass through, but today's residents could fail to make it.

The editors of *The Economist* saw the situation more clearly from London than did the American commentators who wrote in the days right after the Watts riot. In a brilliant editorial, they observed that Los Angeles symbolizes the frontier of modern society, with the technologically most advanced industries, the large numbers of research-and-development establishments, high-quality public services, and the most widespread distribution of the affluent, modern style of life. With no surprise that the first major riot should occur in Southern California, rather than Chicago or New York, they perceptively interpreted the outcry as a measure of the perceived gap between two juxtaposed populations at widely different stages of development. The Watts rioters were not striking out at the city. After all, the quality of the physical environment in south-central Los Angeles is far superior to that in the metropolitan ghettos of the East. These people were striking out at their plight—at the widening social distance that separates them from their visible neighbors and at the widening differentials in opportunity. The immediate objects of hostility in Watts and in the subsequent riots were whitey's policemen and the physical city. The police and the city were, however, merely convenient symbols of the rioters' frustrating sense of powerlessness and of the many handicaps keeping them from bridging the social gap. They were surely not the real objects of their anger.

By now the message of Watts, Newark, Memphis, and the other violent outcries is beginning to be heard in critical circles, reinforcing the earlier underlying theme of the civil rights movement. Too often the meanings are interpreted simplistically—as racial conflicts between blacks and whites, as rebellion against discriminatory practices, or as protests against the filth and depravity of the slum. The rioters are saying all these things—and more. Their docket of indictments is long and righteous; their dramatic moral censure of American society has by now provoked a crisis of conscience forcing the nation to confront the plight it had been silently ignoring for so long. The nation's response with the new civil rights legislation, new housing programs, and new policing practices is admirable and right; yet none of these is enough. The problems of the poor Negro Americans are not unique to them in America. To be sure, race has been an important exacerbating factor in retarding their progress, but preindustrial status is not a distinctive condition of Negroes. Large Mexican American, Puerto Rican, and domestic Caucasian populations are living in quite similar status, and we should not be surprised when they, too, stage revolts like those of the past three years. If disparities in stages of development are behind the current urbanization crisis, that crisis is far more deep-seated and touches far more people than the current debates recognize. It would then require a much more encompassing effort, one aimed at accelerating the urbanization of all groups whose social mobility has been retarded.

Toward an Urbanization Policy

As the scale of the society has risen, our governmental system has been slowly adapting to it. Almost without deliberate intention, the federal system has been modified to conform to the rise of the nation-state as successor to the city-state. Without an explicit policy decision, the national government has assumed responsibility for confronting the urbanization problems and opportunities, albeit often in the language of localism and home-rule.

The shift in the locus of policy-making in education clearly mirrors this important change. Education has traditionally been one of the most jealously guarded provinces of local governments. People care about their children's educational opportunities and have willingly supported public education through local taxation that permitted local control. And yet when accounted within a larger-system framework, the investment strategies have not always proved prudent. Unlike investments in roads, investments in people are easily lost because, unlike roads, people are movable. Thus, the northern and eastern cities become the beneficiaries of the poor schooling accorded Negro children in the southern states. Similarly they may attract graduates of southern colleges with few direct returns to the southern culture and economy.

Population mobility has raised a difficult dilemma for governments that were initially structured to serve geographically stable peoples. Our adaptive response has been to redistribute revenues and expenditures among geographic regions. Because only the least territorially-bounded of our governments can perform the redistributive function, we have been creating new roles for the federal government and a new set of functional relationships among our various public governments.[8]

At the same time we have been building a vast network of nonpublic organizations having a governmental character and self-assigned responsibilities. Each is organized upon an interest base, rather than a territorial one. Thus, trade associations effectively exert governmental constraints upon their corporation members, and professional associations govern the conduct of physicians, engineers, lawyers, and the rest. Trade unions, churches, and recreational groups have been similarly. structured to serve the special interests of their members. All these groups are governments in the essential meanings of that term; they are regulative agencies with power to exert sanctions and enforce control. Increasingly, they have come to have nationwide realms for they have arisen as manifestations of a society rapidly moving into the post-industrial, post-city stage of its development. Combined with the thousands of "public governments," they contribute to a complex network of policy and decision centers.

With so complex a governing apparatus in this country, it is not possible to formulate a unitary set of policies for national development or a unitary mutually reinforcing set of programs. Nor is it possible to erect a unitary set of controls guided from a central command post. Goals for the nation are surely as pluralistic and competitive as the diverse groups that might formulate them. And yet there may be a national consensus that would permit us to pursue some common objectives in a directed and deliberate fashion. The complexity of contemporary society leaves no group independent of the others, and the welfare of any one group is now unavoidably bound up with the welfare of the others.

The United States has not until recently sensed the need for a national strategy that would accelerate economic and human development, for we have prospered well without one. Moreover, such a development policy has seemed to require far more centralization of authority and control than is tolerable or possible in this nation. Nevertheless, although the nation has prospered, all its members have not. If the left-behinds are to find access to modern society, we are going to have to launch as concerted a programmatic effort as the Latin American attempts to accelerate the social mobility of their *marginalidad.* We now have a considerable intellectual capability for developmental planning that we have so far been exporting. By exploiting those capabilities, while operating within the framework of our contemporary pluralistic governmental system, we should be able to increase the odds that the transition to the post-industrial age can be eased. If we can but use our available intelligence, we should be able to accelerate the social mobility of those who might otherwise never catch up.

"The city" can no longer serve as the central organizing idea behind such a planning effort. The next stage of urbanization planning will be guided by the concept of selective development—by the formulation of tactical programs that conform to strategic plans aimed at bringing the left-behind groups into contemporary urban society.

Some of the programmatic imperatives can be read in the very character of post-industrialism and suggest investment strategies for that human-development effort. The nation is surely rich enough to raise all incomes above the poverty line, and the means for doing so are now being invented at a rising rate. Family allowances and guaranteed minimum incomes appear to be economically feasible.

New jobs are needed in large volumes, particularly for those who are presently the least skilled. The need is most likely to be satisfied in the service occupations, and a wave of social invention under way suggests possibilities for creating new subprofessional careers that carry dignity and status—careers that might serve the recent migrants to cities as the earlier industrial jobs served the earlier arrivals. The poor quality of housing need no longer be the norm for the metropolitan centers. Again some imaginative new schemes are being devised that would merge public and private enterprises in mutually profitable and potentially productive house-building ventures—inside the cities and elsewhere. There is no imperative of the emerging new society so demanding as high-quality educational services, from prekindergarten to postdoctoral levels. Although the nation is now spending heavily in this sector of the economy, large expansion is needed. In parallel, the spectrum of public recreational services—ranging from parks and other outdoor facilities to high-brow museums and low-brow pool halls—are becoming near-necessary attributes of the new style of life. Medical and health services have never been adequate to the standards of health to which we have aspired, so a massive new effort is being aimed at planned improvement of people's physical and mental well-being, whether they live in cities or not.

The designs for such a strategy for national development can never be fitted into coherent and mutually reinforcing wholes. The pluralistic structure of American society would never permit that. Moreover, the dangers are likely to exceed the advantages, and it is wholly unlikely that we would ever know enough even to make such an attempt anyway. Some general policy guides, however, are both economically possible and politically feasible.

NOTES

1. The phrase is Don Martindale's; it closes his "Introduction" to Max Weber's *The City* (New York, 1962), p. 67. The theme is being sounded in many quarters nowadays. See especially, Scott Greer, *The Emerging City* (New York, 1962); Kenneth Boulding, *The Meaning of the Twentieth Century* (New York, 1965); York Willburn, *The Withering Away of the City* (Tuscaloosa, 1964); and Janet Abu-Lhughod, "The City Is Dead—Long Live the City" (Center for Planning and Development Research, University of California, Berkeley, 1966, mimeo.).
2. John Friedman presents a crisp clarification of the distinction in "Two Concepts of Urbanization," *Urban Affairs Quarterly*, Vol. 1, No. 4 (June, 1966), pp. 78–84.
3. Richard Hofstadter, *The Age of Reform* (New York, 1955) and *Anti-Intellectualism in America* (New York, 1963). Morton and Lucia White, *The Intellectuals Against the City* (Cambridge, 1964).
4. Richard L. Meier, *A Communications Theory of Urban Growth* (Cambridge, 1962).
5. I have elaborated this thesis in "Order in Diversity: Community Without Propinquity," in Lowdon Wingo, Jr. (ed.), *Cities and Space* (Baltimore, 1963), pp. 23–54.
6. For example, the first-generation jet airplanes, like the first railroads, accelerated the growth of the largest settlements. The big jets could land at only those airports with long runways and specialized facilities. The second- and third-generation jets are fast equalizing accessibility among settlements, recapitulating the accessibility effects of the railroads and then the highways. ·
7. Boulding, *The Meaning of the Twentieth Century*.
8. See Morton Grodzin's classic essay "The Federal System," in *Goals for Americans: The Report of the President's Commission on National Goals* (Englewood Cliffs, 1960), pp. 265–84.

VII. Social Stratification

The idea of social and economic classes is at least as old as classical Greek philosophy. Many eminent thinkers after Plato and Aristotle re-emphasized the importance of classes in rigidly stratified social systems. They described and supported legally incorporated classes—estates in European feudal society, and religiously defined castes and subcastes in many regions of India. But only Karl Marx, in the *Communist Manifesto, Capital,* and virtually all his other writings, made the notion of class central to an analysis of human society. Since Marx, it has become impossible to slight the class concept or to evade the issue of social stratification. Even American sociologists, raised on the belief that theirs was a classless society, have had to study the system of stratification in which they themselves were embedded. Not that many of them became Marxists. On the contrary, most of these scholars aimed at a refutation of Marx and his followers.

In "Karl Marx's Theory of Social Classes," two famous contemporary sociologists, Reinhard Bendix and Seymour M. Lipset, offer one of the best and most accurate summaries of their subject. They remind us that Marx postulated an unqualified economic basis for social class; that Engels, who outlived his collaborator, later softened the equation; and that Marx conceptualized a transformation of class rooted in economic conditions, positions, and interests (the so-called objective factors) linked to class consciousness or the *recognition* by a class of its common "destiny," its common enemies and common interests—all obviously a matter of subjective social factors.

Max Weber, sometimes referred to as "the bourgeois Marx" and widely regarded as Marx's most formidable antagonist, placed his famous fragment, which we know as "Class, Status, Party," in innumerable essays, studies, and monographs. Excerpts from that fragment appear in this section. They clarify the meaning of such concepts as *objective, class, subjective, status,* and *group interests.* In his exposition of economic class, Weber presents a precise, consistent, and thorough definition of Marx's concept. Marx, who sprinkled his various works with the term, never stated exactly what he meant by it. Weber tells us, and goes on to break with Marx over other forms of stratification, specifically those that are extra-economic. Weber's formulations enable us to analyze any society stratified around honor, style of life, regionalism, or ethnicity. He also indicates that, far from being mere reflections of social reality, political and military variables may be causally related to social stratification. Instead of equating economic and social factors, Weber deals with some of their complex configurations. Ultimately—"*á la long*" is how he puts it—the Marxian and the Weberian conceptions of class itself are not so far apart.

Scores of community studies have been built around class theories. *Black Metropolis* by Horace Cayton and St. Clair Drake is an outstanding case in point. It focuses on "Bronzeville"—a fictitious name for the black slums of Chicago as it was observed in the 1930's. In visceral terms, the study depicts economic-objective and social-subjective factors at work, interpenetrating and commingling to produce a class system, a society, a community, and the individuals caught up in them.

22. Karl Marx's Theory of Social Classes

Reinhard Bendix and Seymour M. Lipset

Karl Marx's theory of social classes was of great importance in his work and it has had a profound influence on modern social thought. Yet the writings of Marx, voluminous as they are, do not contain a coherent exposition of that theory. They contain, instead, many scattered fragments on this topic. We have tried to assemble some of these fragments; and by writing a commentary on this series of quotations we attempt to give a view of the theory as a whole. We should add that such a procedure neglects Marx's own intellectual development, for it treats as part of one theory ideas which he expressed at various times in his career.

Reprinted with permission of Macmillan Publishing Co., Inc., from *Class, Status and Power*, eds., Reinhard Bendix and Seymour Martin Lipset. Copyright 1953 by The Free Press, a Division of Macmillian Publishing Co., Inc.

However, in the case of Marx's theory of social classes this difficulty is not a serious one in our judgment.

According to Marx history may be divided roughly into several periods, for example, ancient civilization, feudalism, and capitalism. Each of these periods is characterized by a predominant mode of production and, based upon it, a class structure consisting of a ruling and an oppressed class. The struggle between these classes determines the social relations between men. In particular, the ruling class, which owes its position to the ownership and control of the means of production, controls also, though often in subtle ways, the whole moral and intellectual life of the people. According to Marx, law and government, art and literature, science and philosophy: all serve more or less directly the interests of the ruling class.

In the period of its revolutionary ascendance each class is "progressive" in two senses of that word. Its economic interests are identical with technical progress and hence with increased human welfare. And its efforts to pursue these interests align this class on the side of liberating ideas and institutions and against all who retard technical progress and human welfare. But in time an ascending class may become a ruling class, such as the feudal lords or the capitalists, and then it comes to play a different role. Its economic interests, which originally favored technical progress, call for opposition to it when further change would endanger the economic dominance which it has won. Upon its emergence as a ruling class, it turns from a champion of progress into a champion of reaction. It resists increasingly the attempts to change the social and economic organization of society, which would allow a full measure of the progress that has become technically possible. Such changes would endanger the entrenched position of the ruling class. Hence, tensions and conflicts are engendered that eventually lead to a revolutionary reorganization of society.

> The means of production and of exchange, which served as the foundation for the growth of the bourgeoisie, were generated in feudal society. At a certain stage in the development of these means of production and of exchange, the conditions under which feudal society produced and exchanged, the feudal organization of agriculture and manufacturing industry, in a word, the feudal relations of property became no longer compatible with the already developed productive forces; they became so many fetters. They had to be burst asunder; they were burst asunder.
>
> Into their place stepped free competition, accompanied by a social and political constitution adapted to it, and by the economic and political sway of the bourgeois class.
>
> A similar movement is going on before our own eyes. Modern bourgeois society with its relations of production, of exchange, and of property, a society that has conjured up such gigantic means of production and of exchange, is like the sorcerer who is no longer able to control the powers of the nether world whom he has called up by his spells. For many a decade past the history of industry and commerce is but the history of the revolt of modern productive forces against modern conditions of production, against the property relations that are the conditions for the existence of the bour-

geoisie and its rule. It is enough to mention the commercial crises that by their periodical return put the existence of the entire bourgeois society on trial, each time more threateningly. In these crises a great part not only of the existing products, but also of the previously created productive forces, are periodically destroyed. In these crises there breaks out an epidemic that, in all earlier epochs, would have seemed an absurdity—the epidemic of over-production. Society suddenly finds itself put back into a state of momentary barbarism; it appears as if a famine, a universal war of devastation had cut off the supply of every means of subsistence; industry and commerce seem to be destroyed. And why? Because there is too much civilization, too much means of subsistence, too much industry, too much commerce. The produc-tive forces at the disposal of society no longer tend to further the develop-ment of the conditions of bourgeois property; on the contrary they have become too powerful for these conditions, by which they are fettered, and no sooner do they overcome these fetters than they bring disorder into the whole of bourgeois society, endanger the existence of bourgeois property. The conditions of bourgeois society are too narrow to comprise the wealth created by them. And how does the bourgeoisie get over these crises? On the one hand by enforced destruction of a mass of productive forces; on the other, by the conquest of new markets, and by the more thorough exploita-tion of the old one. That is to say, by paving the way for more extensive and more destructive crises, and diminishing the means whereby crises are pre-vented.

The weapons with which the bourgeoisie felled feudalism to the ground are now turned against the bourgeoisie itself.

But not only has the bourgeoisie forged the weapons that bring death to itself; it has also called into existence the men who are to wield those weapons—the modern working class—the proletarians.[1]

This conception of class conflict and historical change lent itself to a dogmatic interpretation. In particular, the materialist conception of his-tory was often used in a manner which implied that only technical and economic factors were *really* important and that the whole social, politi-cal and intellectual realm (what Marx called the "superstructure") was of secondary significance. In two letters, written in 1890, Friedrich En-gels, the life-long collaborator of Marx, opposed this "vulgar" interpreta-tion:

Marx and I are ourselves partly to blame for the fact that the younger writers sometimes lay more stress on the economic side than is due it. We had to emphasize this main principle in opposition to our adversaries, who denied it, and we had not always the time, the place or the opportunity to allow the other elements involved in the interaction to come into their own rights. . . .

The materialist conception of history also has a lot of friends nowadays, to whom it serves as an excuse for *not* studying history. . . .

In general the word *materialistic* serves many of the younger writers in Germany as a mere phrase with which anything and everything is labelled without further study; they stick on this label and they think the question disposed of. But our conception of history is above all a guide to study, not a lever for construction after the manner of the Hegelians. All history must be studied afresh, the conditions of existence of the different formations of society must be individually examined before the attempt is made to deduce from them the political, civil-legal, aesthetic, philosophic, religious, etc., notions corresponding to them.[2]

It is well to keep these reservations in mind. They suggest that Marx and Engels often felt compelled by the exigencies of the social and political struggle, to cast their ideas in extremely pointed formulations. Had they been scholars of the traditional type, they might have avoided at least some of the dogmatic interpretations of their work, though they would have had far less success in spreading their ideas and getting them accepted. Much of the difficulty in obtaining a concise view of Marxian theory stems from the fact that it was meant to be a tool for political action. In reviewing briefly Marx's theory of history and his theory of social class, we shall at first disregard this political implication. We shall consider this implication more directly in the concluding paragraphs of this essay.

A social class in Marx's terms is any aggregate of persons who perform the same function in the organization of production. "Freeman and slave, patrician and plebeian, lord and serf, guild-master and journeyman, in a word, oppressor and oppressed" (Communist Manifesto) are the names of social classes in different historical periods. These classes are distinguished from each other by the difference of their respective positions in the economy. Since a social class is constituted by the function which its members perform in the process of production, the question arises why the organization of production is the basic determinant of social class. Marx's answer is contained in his early writings on philosophy, especially in his theory of the division of labor.

Fundamental to this theory is Marx's belief that work is man's basic form of self-realization. Man cannot live without work; hence the way in which man works in society is a clue to human nature. Man provides for his subsistence by the use of tools; these facilitate his labor and make it more productive. He has, therefore, an interest in, and he has also a capacity for, elaborating and refining these tools, and in so doing he expresses himself, controls nature and makes history. *If* human labor makes history, then an understanding of the conditions of production is essential for an understanding of history. There are four aspects of production, according to Marx, which explain why man's efforts to provide for his subsistence underlie all change in history.

> a. . . . Life involves before everything else eating, and drinking, a habitation, clothing and many other things. The first historical act is thus the production of the means to satisfy these needs, the production of material life itself.[3]
> b. The second fundamental point is that as soon as a need is satisfied (which implies the action of satisfying, and the acquisition of an instrument), new needs are made.[4]
> c. The third circumstance which, from the very first, enters into historical development, is that men, who daily remake their own life, begin to make other men, to propagate their kind: the relation between man and wife, parents and children, the FAMILY. The family, which to begin with is the only social relationship, becomes later, when increased needs create new social relations and the increased population (creates) new needs, a subordinate one. . . .[5]

d. The production of life, both of one's own in labor and of fresh life in procreation, now appears as a double relationship: on the one hand as a natural, on the other as a social relationship. By social we understand the cooperation of several individuals, no matter under what conditions, in what manner and to what end. It follows from this that a certain mode of production, or industrial stage, is always combined with a certain mode of cooperation, or social stage, and this mode of cooperation is itself a "productive force." Further, that the multitude of productive forces accessible to men determines the nature of society, hence that the "history of humanity" must always be studied and treated in relation to the history of industry and exchange.[6]

There is a logical connection between these four aspects. The satisfaction of man's basic needs makes work a fundamental fact of human life, but it also creates new needs. The more needs are created the more important is it that the "instruments" of production be improved. The more needs are created and the more the technique of production is improved, the more important is it that men cooperate, first within the family, then also outside it. Cooperation implies the division of labor and the organization of production (or in Marx's phrase "the mode of cooperation" as a "productive force") over and above the techniques of production which are employed. It is, therefore, the position which the individual occupies in the social organization of production, that indicates to which social class he belongs. The fundamental determinant of class is the way in which the individual cooperates with others in the satisfaction of his basic needs of food, clothing, and shelter. Other indexes such as income, consumption patterns, educational attainment, or occupation are so many clues to the distribution of material goods and of prestige-symbols. This distribution is a more or less revealing consequence of the organization of production; it is not identical with it. Hence, the income or occupation of an individual is *not*, according to Marx, an indication of class-position, that is, of his position in the production process. For example, if two men are carpenters, they belong to the same occupation, but one may run a small shop of his own, while another works in a plant manufacturing pre-fabricated housing; the two men belong to the same occupation, but to different social classes.

Marx believed that a man's position in the production process provided the crucial life experience, which would determine, either now or eventually, the beliefs and the actions of that individual. The experience gained in the effort of making a living, but especially the experience of economic conflict, would prompt the members of a social class to develop common beliefs and common actions. In analyzing the emergence of these beliefs and actions Marx specified a number of variables which would facilitate this process:

1. Conflicts over the distribution of economic rewards between the classes
2. Easy communication between the individuals in the same class-position so that ideas and action-programs are readily disseminated

3. Growth of class-consciousness in the sense that the members of the class have a feeling of solidarity and understanding of their historic role

4. Profound dissatisfaction of the lower class over its inability to control the economic structure of which it feels itself to be the exploited victim

5. Establishment of a political organization resulting from the economic structure, the historical situation and maturation of class-consciousness

Thus, the organization of production provides the necessary but not a sufficient basis for the existence of social classes. Repeated conflicts over economic rewards, ready communication of ideas between members of a class, the growth of class-consciousness, and the growing dissatisfaction with exploitation which causes suffering in psychological as much as in material terms: these are the conditions which will help to overcome the differences and conflicts between individuals and groups within the class and which will encourage the formation of a class-conscious political organization.

Marx's discussions of the development of the bourgeoisie and of the proletariat give good illustrations of the manner in which he envisages the emergence of a social class.

In the Middle Ages the citizens in each town were compelled to unite against the landed nobility to save their skins. The extension of trade, the establishment of communications, led the separate towns to get to know other towns, which had asserted the same interests in the struggle with the same antagonist. Out of the many local corporations of burghers there arose only gradually the burgher *class*. The conditions of life of the individual burghers became, on account of their antagonism to the existing relationships and of the mode of labor determined by these conditions which were common to them all and independent of each individual. The burghers had created the conditions in so far as they had torn themselves free from feudal ties, and were created by them in so far as they were determined by their antagonism to the feudal system which they found in existence. When the individual towns began to enter into associations, these common conditions developed into class conditions. The same conditions, the same antagonism, the same interests necessarily called forth on the whole similar customs everywhere. The bourgeoisie itself, with its conditions, develops only gradually, splits according to the division of labor into various fractions and finally absorbs all earlier possessing classes (while it develops the majority of the earlier non-possessing, and a part of the earlier possessing, class into a new class, the proletariat) in the measure to which all earlier property is transformed into industrial or commercial capital.

The separate individuals form a class only in so far as they have to carry on a common battle against another class; otherwise they are on hostile terms with each other as competitors. On the other hand, the class in its turn achieves an independent existence over against the individuals, so that the latter find their conditions of existence predestined, and hence have their position in life and their personal development assigned to them by their class, become subsumed under it. This is the same phenomenon as the subjection of the separate individuals to the division of labor and can only be removed by the abolition of private property and of labor itself.[7]

This passage makes it apparent that Marx thought of social class as a condition of group-life which was constantly generated (rather than simply given) by the organization of production. Essential to this formation of a class was the existence of a common "class enemy," because without it competition between individuals would prevail. Also, this is a gradual process, which depends for its success upon the development of "common conditions" and upon the subsequent realization of common interests. But the existence of common conditions and the realization of common interests are in turn only the necessary, not the sufficient bases for the development of a social class. Only when the members of a "potential" class enter into an association for the organized pursuit of their common aims, does a class in Marx's sense exist.

In discussing the development of the proletariat under capitalism Marx described a process which was essentially similar to that which he had described for the development of the modern bourgeoisie.

> The first attempts of the workers to *associate* among themselves always take place in the form of combinations (unions).
>
> Large-scale industry concentrates in one place a crowd of people unknown to one another. Competition divides their interests. But the maintenance of wages, this common interest which they have against their boss, unites them in a common thought of resistance—combination. Thus combination always has a double aim, that of stopping the competition among themselves, in order to bring about a general competition with the capitalist. If the first aim of the general resistance was merely the maintenance of wages, combinations, at first isolated, constitute themselves into groups as the capitalists in their turn unite in the idea of repression, and in the face of always united capital, the maintenance of the association becomes more necessary to them than that of wages. This is so true that the English economists are amazed to see the workers sacrifice a good part of their wages in favor of associations, which in the eyes of the economists, are established solely in favor of wages. In this struggle—a veritable civil war—are united and developed all the elements necessary for the coming battle. Once it has reached this point association takes on a political character.
>
> Economic conditions had first transformed the mass of the people of the country into workers. The domination of capital has created for this mass a common situation, common interests. This mass is thus already a class as against capital, *but not yet for itself*. In this struggle, of which we have noted only a few phases, this mass becomes united, and constitutes itself as a class for itself. The interests it defends become class interests. But the struggle of class against class is a political struggle.[8]

Thus in the case of the proletariat, as in the case of the bourgeoisie, Marx cited several conditions which were essential for the development of a social class: conflict over economic rewards, physical concentration of masses of people and easy communication among them, the development of solidarity and political organization (in place of competition between individuals and organization for purely economic ends).

The antagonism of the workers to the capitalist class and to the prevailing economic system was to Marx not simply a consequence of the struggle for economic advantage. In addition to the conditions mentioned he laid great stress on the human consequences of machine production under capitalism. The social relations which capitalist industry imposed deprived the workers of all opportunities to obtain psychological satisfaction from their work. This complete want of satisfaction Marx called the alienation of human labor. He attributed it to the division of labor in modern industry, which turned human beings into the appendages of the machine.

The knowledge, the judgment and the will, which though in ever so small a degree, are practiced by the independent peasant or handicraftsman, in the same way as the savage makes the whole art of war consist in the exercise of his personal cunning—these faculties (?) are now required only for the workshop as a whole. Intelligence in production expands in one direction, because it vanishes in many others. What is lost by the detail laborers, is concentrated in the capital that employs them. It is a result of the division of labor in manufactures, that the laborer is brought face to face with the intellectual potencies of the material process of production, as the property of another, and as a ruling power. This separation begins in simple cooperation, where the capitalist represents to the single workman, the oneness and the will of the associated labor. It is developed in manufacture which cuts down the laborer into a detail laborer. It is completed in modern industry, which makes science a productive force distinct from labor and presses it into the service of capital.

In manufacture, in order to make the collective laborer, and through him capital, rich in social productive power, each laborer must be made poor in individual productive powers. "Ignorance is the mother of industry as well as of superstition. Reflection and fancy are subject to err; but a habit of moving the hand or the foot is independent of either. Manufactures, accordingly, prosper most where the mind is least consulted, and where the workshop may . . . be considered as an engine, the parts of which are men." (A. L. Ferguson, p. 280.)[9]

. . . Within the capitalist system all methods for raising the social productiveness of labor are brought about at the cost of the individual laborer; all means for the development of production transform themselves into means of domination over, and exploitation of the producers; they mutilate the laborer into a fragment of a man, degrade him to the level of an appendage of a machine, destroy every remnant of charm in his work and turn it into a hated toil; they estrange from him the intellectual potentialities of the labor-process in the same proportion as science is incorporated in it as an independent power; they distort the conditions under which he works, subject him during the labor-process to a despotism the more hateful for its meanness; they transform his life time into working-time and drag his wife and child under the wheels of the Juggernaut of capital. But all methods for the accumulation of surplus value are at the same time methods of accumulation; *and every extension of accumulation becomes again a means for the development of those methods. It follows therefore that in proportion as capital accumulates, the lot of the laborer, be his payments high or low, must grow worse.*[10]

Marx believed that the alienation of labor was inherent in capitalism and that it was a major psychological deprivation, which would lead eventually to the proletarian revolution. This theory of why men under capitalism would revolt was based on an assumption of what prompts men to be satisfied or dissatisfied with their work. Marx contrasted the modern industrial worker with the medieval craftsman, and—along with many other writers of the period—observed that under modern conditions of production the worker had lost all opportunity to exercise his "knowledge, judgment and will" in the manufacture of his product. To Marx this psychological deprivation seemed more significant even than the economic pauperism to which capitalism subjected the masses of workers. At any rate, two somewhat conflicting statements can be found in his work. In one he declared that the physical misery of the working classes would increase with the development of capitalism.

> Accumulation of wealth at one pole is, therefore, at the same time accumulation of misery, agony of toil, slavery, ignorance, brutality, mental degradation, at the opposite pole.[11]

But in the other he maintained, that capitalism could result in an absolute increase of the standard of living for the workers, but that it would result nevertheless in the experience of mounting personal deprivation.

> When capital is increasing fast, wages may rise, but the profit of capital will rise much faster. The material position of the laborer has improved, but it is at the expense of his social position. The social gulf which separates him from the capitalist has widened.[12]

And, as we have seen, Marx summarized his analysis of the oppressive effects of capitalism with a long list of striking phrases, only to conclude this eloquent recital with the sentence: "It follows therefore that in proportion as capital accumulates, the lot of the laborer, *be his payment high or low,* must grow worse."

It will be apparent from the preceding discussion that Marx did not simply identify a social class with the fact that a large group of people occupied the same objective position in the economic structure of a society. Instead, he laid great stress on the importance of subjective awareness as a precondition of organizing the class successfully for the economic and the political struggle. Marx felt certain that the pressures engendered by capitalism would determine its development in the future. And he believed it to be inevitable that the masses of industrial workers would come to a conscious realization of their class-interests. Subjective awareness of class interests was in his view an indispensable element in the development of a social class, but he believed that his awareness would inevitably arise along with the growing contradictions inherent in capitalism. In the preceding discussion we have cited two of the conditions which made Marx feel sure of his prediction: the concentration of workers in towns and the resulting ease of communication between them, and the psychological suffering engendered by the alienation of labor. By way of summarizing Marx's theory of class we cite his views on the French peasants, who occupy a similar position in the economic structure but do not thereby provide the basis for the formation of a social class.

> The small peasants form a vast mass, the members of which live in similar conditions, but without entering into manifold relations with one another. Their mode of production isolates them from one another, instead of bringing them into mutual intercourse. . . . In so far as millions of families live under economic conditions of existence that divide their mode of life, their interests and their culture from those of other classes, and put them into hostile contrast to the latter, they form a class. In so far as there is merely a local interconnection among these small peasants, and the identity of their interests begets no unity, no national union, and no political organization, they do not form a class.[13]

That is to say, the peasants occupy the same position in the economic structure of their society. But in their case this fact itself will *not* create similar attitudes and common actions. The peasants do not form a social class in Marx's sense, because they make their living on individual farms in isolation from one another. There is no objective basis for ready communication between them.

In the case of the industrial workers, however, such an objective basis for ready communication existed. They were concentrated in the large industrial towns, and the conditions of factory production brought them into close physical contact with one another. Yet, even then Marx did not believe that the political organization of the working class and the development of class-consciousness in thought and action would be the automatic result of these objective conditions. In his view these objective conditions provided a favorable setting for the development of political agitation. And this agitation was in good part the function of men who were not themselves workers, but who had acquired a correct understanding of historical change, and who were willing to identify themselves with the movement of those who were destined to bring it about.

> In times when the class struggle nears the decisive hour, the process of dissolution going on within the ruling class, in fact within the whole range of old society, assumes such a violent, glaring character, that a small section of the ruling class cuts itself adrift and joins the revolutionary class, the class that holds the future in its hands. Just as, therefore, at an earlier period, a section of the nobility went over to the bourgeoisie, so now a portion of the bourgeoisie goes over to the proletariat, and in particular, a portion of the bourgeois ideologists, who have raised themselves to the level of comprehending theoretically the historical movement as a whole.[14]

There is little question that Marx conceived of his own work as an example of this process. The scientific analysis of the capitalist economy, as he conceived of it, was itself an important instrument by means of which the class-consciousness and the political organization of the workers could be furthered. And because Marx conceived of his own work in these terms, he declared that the detachment of other scholars was spurious, was merely a screen thrown up to disguise the class-interests which their work served. Hence he denied the possibility of a social science in the modern sense of that word. The "proof" of his theory was contained in the actions of the proletariat.

It is apparent that Marx's theory of social classes, along with other parts of his doctrine, involved a basic ambiguity which has bedevilled his interpreters ever since. For, on the one hand, he felt quite certain that the contradictions engendered by capitalism would inevitably lead to a class-conscious proletariat and hence to a proletarian revolution. But on the other hand, he assigned to class-consciousness, to political action, and to his scientific theory of history a major role in bringing about this result. In his own eyes this difficulty was resolved because such subjective elements as class-consciousness or a scientific theory were themselves a by-product of the contradictions inherent in capitalism. The preceding discussion has sought to elucidate the meaning of this assertion by specifying the general philosophical assumptions and the specific environmental and psychological conditions on the basis of which Marx felt able to predict the *inevitable* development of class-consciousness.[15] To the critics this claim to predict an inevitable future on the basis of assumptions and conditions, which may or may not be valid, has always seemed the major flaw in Marxian theory.

NOTES

1. Karl Marx and Friedrich Engels, *Manifesto of the Communist Party* (New York: International Publishers, 1932), pp. 14–15.
2. Karl Marx and Friedrich Engels, *Selected Correspondence, 1846–1895* (New York: International Publishers, 1942), pp. 477, 472–73.
3. Karl Marx and Friedrich Engels, *The German Ideology* (New York: International Publishers, 1939), p. 16.
4. *Ibid.,* pp. 16–17.
5. *Ibid.,* p. 16.
6. *Ibid.,* p. 18.
7. *Ibid.,* pp. 48–49.
8. Karl Marx, *The Poverty of Philosophy* (New York: International Publishers, n.d.), pp. 145–46.
9. Karl Marx, *Capital* (New York: Modern Library, 1936), pp. 396–97.
10. Marx, *op. cit.,* pp. 708–9. (Our emphasis.)
11. *Ibid.,* p. 709.
12. Karl Marx, "Wage, Labor and Capital," in *Selected Works,* vol. 1 (Moscow: Cooperative Publishing Society of Foreign Workers in the U.S.S.R., 1936), p. 273.
13. Karl Marx, *The Eighteenth Brumaire of Louis Bonaparte* (New York: International Publishers, n.d.), p. 109.
14. Marx and Engels, *Manifesto of the Communist Party,* p. 19.
15. On a few occasions Marx allowed for the possibility that the development from capitalism to socialism might occur without a proletarian revolution, especially in England, Holland, and the United States. Properly understood the statement to this effect did not mean that this development was a mere possibility, but that it might take several forms, depending upon the historical situation of each country. By his analysis of the capitalist economy Marx sought to predict major changes, not specific occurrences; but while he allowed for the latter he did not expect them to alter the central tendency of the former.

23. Class, Status, Party
Max Weber

I   ECONOMICALLY DETERMINED POWER AND THE SOCIAL ORDER

Law exists when there is a probability that an order will be upheld by a specific staff of men who will use physical or psychical compulsion with the intention of obtaining conformity with the order, or of inflicting sanctions for infringement of it.* The structure of every legal order directly influences the distribution of power, economic or otherwise, within its respective community. This is true of all legal orders and not only that of the state. In general, we understand by "power" the chance of a man or of a number of men to realize their own will in a communal action even against the resistance of others who are participating in the action.

"Economically conditioned" power is not, of course, identical with "power" as such. On the contrary, the emergence of economic power may be the consequence of power existing on other grounds. Man does not strive for power only in order to enrich himself economically. Power, including economic power, may be valued "for its own sake." Very frequently the striving for power is also conditioned by the social "honor" it entails. Not all power, however, entails social honor: The typical American Boss, as well as the typical big speculator, deliberately relinquishes social honor. Quite generally, "mere economic" power, and especially "naked" money power, is by no means a recognized basis of social honor. Nor is power the only basis of social honor. Indeed, social honor, or prestige, may even be the basis of political or economic power, and very frequently has been. Power, as well as honor, may be guaranteed by the legal order, but, at least normally, it is not their primary source. The legal order is rather an additional factor that enhances the chance to hold power or honor; but it cannot always secure them.

The way in which social honor is distributed in a community between typical groups participating in this distribution we may call the "social order." The social order and the economic order are, of course, similarly related to the "legal order." However, the social and the economic order are not identical. The economic order is for us merely the way in which

---

* *Wirtschaft und Gesellschaft,* part III, chap. 4, pp. 631–40. The first sentence in paragraph one and the several definitions in this chapter which are in brackets do not appear in the original text. They have been taken from other contexts of *Wirtschaft und Gesellschaft.*

From *Max Weber: Essays in Sociology,* edited and translated by H. H. Gerth and C. Wright Mills. Copyright 1946 by Oxford University Press, Inc.; renewed 1973 by Dr. Hans H. Gerth. Reprinted by permission of the publisher.

economic goods and services are distributed and used. The social order is of course conditioned by the economic order to a high degree, and in its turn reacts upon it.

Now: "classes," "status groups," and "parties" are phenomena of the distribution of power within a community.

II Determination of Class-Situation by Market-Situation

In our terminology, "classes" are not communities; they merely represent possible, and frequent, bases for communal action. We may speak of a "class" when (1) a number of people have in common a specific causal component of their life chances, in so far as (2) this component is represented exclusively by economic interests in the possession of goods and opportunities for income, and (3) is represented under the conditions of the commodity or labor markets. [These points refer to "class situation," which we may express more briefly as the typical chance for a supply of goods, external living conditions, and personal life experiences, in so far as this chance is determined by the amount and kind of power, or lack of such, to dispose of goods or skills for the sake of income in a given economic order. The term "class" refers to any group of people that is found in the same class situation.]

It is the most elemental economic fact that the way in which the disposition over material property is distributed among a plurality of people, meeting competitively in the market for the purpose of exchange, in itself creates specific life chances. According to the law of marginal utility this mode of distribution excludes the non-owners from competing for highly valued goods; it favors the owners and, in fact, gives to them a monopoly to acquire such goods. Other things being equal, this mode of distribution monopolizes the opportunities for profitable deals for all those who, provided with goods, do not necessarily have to exchange them. It increases, at least generally, their power in price wars with those who, being propertyless, have nothing to offer but their services in native form or goods in a form constituted through their own labor, and who above all are compelled to get rid of these products in order barely to subsist. This mode of distribution gives to the propertied a monopoly on the possibility of transferring property from the sphere of use as a "fortune," to the sphere of "capital goods"; that is, it gives them the entrepreneurial function and all chances to share directly or indirectly in returns on capital. All this holds true within the area in which pure market conditions prevail. "Property" and "lack of property" are, therefore, the basic categories of all class situations. It does not matter whether these two categories become effective in price wars or in competitive struggles.

Within these categories, however, class situations are further differentiated: on the one hand, according to the kind of property that is usable for returns; and, on the other hand, according to the kind of services that can be offered in the market. Ownership of domestic buildings; productive establishments; warehouses; stores; agriculturally usable land, large and small holdings—quantitative differences with possibly qualitative consequences—; ownership of mines; cattle; men (slaves); disposition over mobile instruments of production, or capital goods of all sorts, especially money or objects that can be exchanged for money easily and at any time; disposition over products of one's own labor or of others' labor differing according to their various distances from consumability; disposition over transferable monopolies of any kind—all these distinctions differentiate the class situations of the propertied just as does the "meaning" which they can and do give to the utilization of property, especially to property which has money equivalence. Accordingly, the propertied, for instance, may belong to the class of rentiers or to the class of entrepreneurs.

Those who have no property but who offer services are differentiated just as much according to their kinds of services as according to the way in which they make use of these services, in a continuous or discontinuous relation to a recipient. But always this is the generic connotation of the concept of class: that the kind of chance in the *market* is the decisive moment which presents a common condition for the individual's fate. "Class situation" is, in this sense, ultimately "market situation." The effect of naked possession *per se*, which among cattle breeders gives the nonowning slave or serf into the power of the cattle owner, is only a forerunner of real "class" formation. However, in the cattle loan and in the naked severity of the law of debts in such communities, for the first time mere "possession" as such emerges as decisive for the fate of the individual. This is very much in contrast to the agricultural communities based on labor. The creditor-debtor relation becomes the basis of "class situations" only in those cities where a "credit market," however primitive, with rates of interest increasing according to the extent of dearth and a factual monopolization of credits, is developed by a plutocracy. Therewith "class struggles" begin.

Those men whose fate is not determined by the chance of using goods or services for themselves on the market, e.g. slaves, are not, however, a "class" in the technical sense of the term. They are, rather, a "status group."

III   Communal Action Flowing from Class Interest

According to our terminology, the factor that creates "class" is unambiguously economic interest, and indeed, only those interests involved in the existence of the "market." Nevertheless, the concept of "class-interest" is an ambiguous one: even as an empirical concept it is ambiguous as soon as one understands by it something other than the factual direction of interests following with a certain probability from the class situation for a certain "average" of those people subjected to the class situation. The class situation and other circumstances remaining the same, the direction in which the individual worker, for instance, is likely to pursue his interests may vary widely, according to whether he is constitutionally qualified for the task at hand to a high, to an average, or to a low degree. In the same way, the direction of interests may vary according to whether or not a *communal* action of a larger or smaller portion of those commonly affected by the "class situation," or even an association among them, e.g. a "trade union," has grown out of the class situation from which the individual may or may not expect promising results. [Communal action refers to that action which is oriented to the feeling of the actors that they belong together. Societal action, on the other hand, is oriented to a rationally motivated adjustment of interests.] The rise of societal or even of communal action from a common class situation is by no means a universal phenomenon.

The class situation may be restricted in its effects to the generation of essentially *similar* reactions, that is to say, within our terminology, of "mass actions." However, it may not have even this result. Furthermore, often merely an amorphous communal action emerges. For example, the "murmuring" of the workers known in ancient oriental ethics: the moral disapproval of the work-master's conduct, which in its practical significance was probably equivalent to an increasingly typical phenomenon of precisely the latest industrial development, namely, the "slow down" (the deliberate limiting of work effort) of laborers by virtue of tacit agreement. The degree in which "communal action" and possibly "societal action," emerges from the "mass actions" of the members of a class is linked to general cultural conditions, especially to those of an intellectual sort. It is also linked to the extent of the contrasts that have already evolved, and is especially linked to the *transparency* of the connections between the causes and the consequences of the "class situation." For however different life chances may be, this fact in itself, according to all experience, by no means gives birth to "class action" (communal action by the members of a class). The fact of being conditioned and the results of the class situation must be distinctly recognizable. For only then the contrast of life chances can be felt not as an absolutely given fact to be accepted, but as a resultant from either (1) the given distribution of property, or (2) the structure of the concrete economic order. It is only then that people may react against the class structure not only through acts of an intermittent and irrational protest, but in the form of rational association. There have been "class situations" of the first category (1), of a specifically naked and transparent sort, in the urban centers of Antiquity and during the Middle Ages; especially then, when great fortunes were accumulated by factually monopolized trading in industrial products of these localities or in foodstuffs. Furthermore, under certain circumstances, in the rural economy of the most diverse periods, when agriculture was increasingly exploited in a profit-making manner. The most important historical example of the second category (2) is the class situation of the modern "proletariat."

IV   TYPES OF "CLASS STRUGGLE"

Thus every class may be the carrier of any one of the possibly innumerable forms of "class action," but this is not necessarily so. In any case, a class does not in itself constitute a community. To treat "class" conceptually as having the same value as "community" leads to distortion. That men in the same class situation regularly react in mass actions to such tangible situations as economic ones in the direction of those interests that are most adequate to their average number is an important and after all simple fact for the understanding of historical events. Above all, this fact must not lead to that kind of pseudo-scientific operation with the concepts of "class" and "class interests" so frequently found these days, and which has found its most classic expression in the statement of a talented author, that the individual may be in error concerning his interests but that the "class" is "infallible" about its interests. Yet, if classes as such are not communities, nevertheless class situations emerge only on the basis of communalization. The communal action that brings forth class situations, however, is not basically action between members of the identical class; it is an action between members of different classes. Communal actions that directly determine the class situation of the worker and the entrepreneur are: the labor market, the commodities market, and the capitalistic enterprise. But, in its turn, the existence of a capitalistic enterprise presupposes that a very specific communal action exists and that it is specifically structured to protect the possession of goods per se, and especially the power of individuals to dispose, in principle freely, over the means of production. The existence of a capitalistic enterprise is preconditioned by a specific kind of "legal order." Each kind of class situation, and above all when it rests upon the power of property per se, will become most clearly efficacious when all other determinants of reciprocal relations are, as far as possible, eliminated in their significance. It is in this way that the utilization of the power of property in the market obtains its most sovereign importance.

Now "status groups" hinder the strict carrying through of the sheer market principle. In the present context they are of interest to us only from this one point of view. Before we briefly consider them, note that not much of a general nature can be said about the more specific kinds of antagonism between "classes" (in our meaning of the term). The great shift, which has been going on continuously in the past, and up to our times, may be summarized, although at the cost of some precision: the struggle in which class situations are effective has progressively shifted from consumption credit toward, first, competitive struggles in the commodity market and, then, toward price wars on the labor market. The "class struggles" of antiquity—to the extent that they were genuine class struggles and not struggles between status groups—were initially carried on by indebted peasants, and perhaps also by artisans threatened by debt bondage and struggling against urban creditors. For debt bondage is the normal result of the differentiation of wealth in commercial cities, especially in seaport cities. A similar situation has existed among cattle breeders. Debt relationships as such produced class action up to the time of Cataline. Along with this, and with an increase in provision of grain for the city by transporting it from the outside, the struggle over the means of sustenance emerged. It centered in the first place around the provision of bread and the determination of the price of bread. It lasted throughout antiquity and the entire Middle Ages. The propertyless as such flocked together against those who actually and supposedly were interested in the dearth of bread. This fight spread until it involved all those commodities essential to the way of life and to handicraft production. There were only incipient discussions of wage disputes in antiquity and in the Middle Ages. But they have been slowly increasing up into modern times. In the earlier periods they were completely secondary to slave rebellions as well as to fights in the commodity market.

The propertyless of antiquity and of the Middle Ages protested against monopolies, pre-emption, forestalling, and the withholding of goods from the market in order to raise prices. Today the central issue is the determination of the price of labor.

This transition is represented by the fight for access to the market and for the determination of the price of products. Such fights went on between merchants and workers in the putting-out system of domestic handicraft during the transition to modern times. Since it is quite a general phenomenon we must mention here that the class antagonisms that are conditioned through the market situation are usually most bitter between those who actually and directly participate as opponents in price wars. It is not the rentier, the share-holder, and the banker who suffer the ill will of the worker, but almost exclusively the manufacturer and the business executives who are the direct opponents of workers in price wars. This is so in spite of the fact that it is precisely the cash boxes of the rentier, the share-holder, and the banker into which the more or less "unearned" gains flow, rather than into the pockets of the manufacturers or of the business executives. This simple state of affairs has very frequently been decisive for the role the class situation has played in the formation of political parties. For example, it has made possible the varieties of patriarchal socialism and the frequent attempts—formerly, at least—of threatened status groups to form alliances with the proletariat against the "bourgeoisie."

V STATUS HONOR

In contrast to classes, *status groups* are normally communities. They are, however, often of an amorphous kind. In contrast to the purely economically determined "class situation" we wish to designate as "status situation" every typical component of the life fate of men that is determined by a specific, positive or negative, social estimation of *honor*. This honor may be connected with any quality shared by a plurality, and, of course, it can be knit to a class situation: class distinctions are linked in the most varied ways with status distinctions. Property as such is not always recognized as a status qualification, but in the long run it is, and with extraordinary regularity. In the subsistence economy of the organized neighborhood, very often the richest man is simply the chieftain. However, this often means only an honorific preference. For example, in the so-called pure modern "democracy," that is, one devoid of any expressly ordered status privileges for individuals, it may be that only the families coming under approximately the same tax class dance with one another. This example is reported of certain smaller Swiss cities. But status honor need not necessarily be linked with a "class situation." On the contrary, it normally stands in sharp oppositions to the pretensions of sheer property.

Both propertied and propertyless people can belong to the same status group, and frequently they do with very tangible consequences. This "equality" of social esteem may, however, in the long run become quite precarious. The "equality" of status among the American "gentlemen," for instance, is expressed by the fact that outside the subordination determined by the different functions of "business," it would be considered strictly repugnant—wherever the old tradition still prevails—if even the richest "chief," while playing billiards or cards in his club in the evening, would not treat his "clerk" as in every sense fully his equal in birthright. It would be repugnant if the American "chief" would bestow upon his "clerk" the condescending "benevolence" marking a distinction of "position," which the German chief can never dissever from his attitude. This is one of the most important reasons why in America the German "clubby-ness" has never been able to attain the attraction that the American clubs have.

VI Guarantees of Status Stratification

In content, status honor is normally expressed by the fact that above all else a specific *style of life* can be expected from all those who wish to belong to the circle. Linked with this expectation are restrictions on "social" intercourse (that is, intercourse which is not subservient to economic or any other of business's "functional" purposes). These restrictions may confine normal marriages to within the status circle and may lead to complete endogamous closure. As soon as there is not a mere individual and socially irrelevant imitation of another style of life, but an agreed-upon communal action of this closing character, the "status" development is under way.

In its characteristic form, stratification by "status groups" on the basis of conventional styles of life evolves at the present time in the United

States out of the traditional democracy. For example, only the resident of a certain street ("the street") is considered as belonging to "society," is qualified for social intercourse, and is visited and invited. Above all, this differentiation evolves in such a way as to make for strict submission to the fashion that is dominant at a given time in society. This submission to the fashion also exists among men in America to a degree unknown in Germany. Such submission is considered to be an indication of the fact that a given man *pretends* to qualify as a gentleman. This submission decides, at least *prima facie*, that he will be treated as such. And this recognition becomes just as important for his employment chances in "swank" establishments, and above all, for social intercourse and marriage with "esteemed" families, as the qualification for dueling among Germans in the Kaiser's day. As for the rest: certain families resident for a long time, and, of course, correspondingly wealthy, for instance, "F. F. V., i.e. First Families of Virginia," or the actual or alleged descendants of the "Indian Princess" Pocahontas, of the Pilgrim fathers, or of the Knickerbockers, the members of almost inaccessible sects and all sorts of circles setting themselves apart by means of any other characteristics and badges . . . all these elements usurp "status" honor. The development of status is essentially a question of stratification resting upon usurpation. Such usurpation is the normal origin of almost all status honor. But the road from this purely conventional situation to legal privilege, positive or negative, is easily traveled as soon as a certain stratification of the social order has in fact been "lived in" and has achieved stability by virtue of a stable distribution of economic power.

VII   "Ethnic" Segregation and "Caste"

Where the consequences have been realized to their full extent, the status group evolves into a closed "caste." Status distinctions are then guaranteed not merely by conventions and laws, but also by *rituals*. This occurs in such a way that every physical contact with a member of any caste that is considered to be "lower" by the members of a "higher" caste is considered as making for a ritualistic impurity and to be a stigma which must be expiated by a religious act. Individual castes develop quite distinct cults and gods.

In general, however, the status structure reaches such extreme consequences only where there are underlying differences which are held to be "ethnic." The "caste" is, indeed, the normal form in which ethnic communities usually live side by side in a "societalized" manner. These ethnic communities believe in blood relationship and exclude exogamous marriage and social intercourse. Such a caste situation is part of the phenomenon of "pariah" peoples and is found all over the world. These people form communities, acquire specific occupational traditions of handicrafts or of other arts, and cultivate a belief in their ethnic community. They live in a "diaspora" strictly segregated from all personal intercourse, except that of an unavoidable sort, and their situation is legally precarious. Yet, by virtue of their economic indispensability, they are tolerated, indeed, frequently privileged, and they live in interspersed political communities. The Jews are the most impressive historical example.

A "status" segregation grown into a "caste" differs in its structure from a mere "ethnic" segregation: the caste structure transforms the horizontal and unconnected coexistences of ethnically segregated groups into a vertical social system of super- and subordination. Correctly formulated: a comprehensive societalization integrates the ethnically divided communities into specific political and communal action. In their consequences they differ precisely in this way: ethnic coexistences condition a mutual repulsion and disdain but allow each ethnic community to consider its own honor as the highest one; the caste structure brings about a social subordination and an acknowledgment of "more honor" in favor of the privileged caste and status groups. This is due to the fact that in the caste structure ethnic distinctions as such have become "functional" distinctions within the political societalization (warriors, priests, artisans that are politically important for war and for building, and so on). But even pariah people who are most despised are usually apt to continue cultivating in some manner that which is equally peculiar to ethnic and to status communities: the belief in their own specific "honor." This is the case with the Jews.

Only with the negatively privileged status groups does the "sense of dignity" take a specific deviation. A sense of dignity is the precipitation in individuals of social honor and of conventional demands which a positively privileged status group raises for the deportment of its members. The sense of dignity that characterizes positively privileged status groups is naturally related to their "being" which does not transcend itself, that is, it is to their "beauty and excellence." Their kingdom is "of this world." They live for the present and by exploiting their great past. The sense of dignity of the negatively privileged strata naturally refers to a future lying beyond the present, whether it is of this life or of another. In other words, it must be nurtured by the belief in a providential "mission" and by a belief in a specific honor before God. The "chosen people's" dignity is nurtured by a belief either that in the beyond "the last will be the first," or that in this life a Messiah will appear to bring forth into the light of the world which has cast them out the hidden honor of the pariah people. This simple state of affairs, and not the "resentment" which is so strongly emphasized in Nietzsche's much admired construction in the *Genealogy of Morals*, is the source of the religiosity cultivated by pariah status groups. In passing, we may note that resentment may be accurately applied only to a limited extent; for one of Nietzsche's main examples, Buddhism, it is not at all applicable.

Incidentally, the development of status groups from ethnic segregations is by no means the normal phenomenon. On the contrary, since objective "racial differences" are by no means basic to every subjective sentiment of an ethnic community, the ultimately racial foundation of status structure is rightly and absolutely a question of the concrete individual case. Very frequently a status group is instrumental in the production of a thoroughbred anthropological type. Certainly a status group is to a high degree effective in producing extreme types, for they select personally qualified individuals (for instance, the Knighthood selects those who are fit for warfare, physically and psychically). But selection is far from being the only, or the predominant, way in which status groups are formed: Political membership or class situation has at all times been at least as frequently decisive. And today the class situation is by far the predominant factor, for of course the possibility of a style of life expected for members of a status group is usually conditioned economically.

VIII   Status Privileges

For all practical purposes, stratification by status goes hand in hand with a monopolization of ideal and material goods or opportunities, in a manner we have come to know as typical. Besides the specific status honor, which always rests upon distance and exclusiveness, we find all sorts of material monopolies. Such honorific preferences may consist of the privilege of wearing special costumes, of eating special dishes taboo to others, of carrying arms—which is most obvious in its consequences—the right to pursue certain non-professional dilettante artistic practices, e.g., to play certain musical instruments. Of course, material monopolies provide the most effective motives for the exclusiveness of a status group; although, in themselves, they are rarely sufficient, almost always they come into play to some extent. Within a status circle there is the question of intermarriage: the interest of the families in the monopolization of potential bridegrooms is at least of equal importance and is parallel to the interest in the monopolization of daughters. The daughters of the circle must be provided for. With an increased inclosure of the status group, the conventional preferential opportunities for special employment grow into a legal monopoly of special offices for the members. Certain goods become objects for monopolization by status groups. In the typical fashion these include "entailed estates" and frequently also the possessions of serfs or bondsmen and, finally, special trades. This monopolization occurs positively when the status group is exclusively entitled to own and to manage them; and negatively when, in order to maintain its specific way of life, the status group must *not* own and manage them.

The decisive role of a "style of life" in status "honor" means that status groups are the specific bearers of all "conventions." In whatever way it may be manifest, all "stylization" of life either originates in status groups or is at least conserved by them. Even if the principles of status conventions differ greatly, they reveal certain typical traits, especially among those strata which are most privileged. Quite generally, among privileged status groups there is a status disqualification that operates against the performance of common physical labor. This disqualification is now "setting in" in America against the old tradition of esteem for labor. Very frequently every rational economic pursuit, and especially "entrepreneurial activity," is looked upon as a disqualification of status. Artistic and literary activity is also considered as degrading work as soon as it is exploited for income, or at least when it is connected with hard physical exertion. An example is the sculptor working like a mason in his dusty smock as over against the painter in his salon-like "studio" and those forms of musical practice that are acceptable to the status group.

IX ECONOMIC CONDITIONS AND EFFECTS OF STATUS STRATIFICATION

The frequent disqualification of the gainfully employed as such is a direct result of the principle of status stratification peculiar to the social order, and of course, of this principle's opposition to a distribution of power which is regulated exclusively through the market. These two factors operate along with various individual ones, which will be touched upon below.

We have seen above that the market and its processes "knows no personal distinctions": "functional" interests dominate it. It knows nothing of "honor." The status order means precisely the reverse, viz.: stratification in terms of "honor" and of styles of life peculiar to status groups as such. If mere economic acquisition and naked economic power still bearing the stigma of its extra-status origin could bestow upon anyone who has won it the same honor as those who are interested in status by virtue of style of life claim for themselves, the status order would be threatened at its very root. This is the more so as, given equality of status honor, property *per se* represents an addition even if it is not overtly acknowledged to be such. Yet if such economic acquisition and power gave the agent any honor at all, his wealth would result in his attaining more honor than those who successfully claim honor by virtue of style of life. Therefore all groups having interests in the status order react with special sharpness precisely against the pretensions of purely economic acquisition. In most cases they react the more vigorously the more they feel themselves threatened. Calderon's respectful treatment of the peasant, for instance, as opposed to Shakespeare's simultaneous and ostensible disdain of the *canaille* illustrates the different ways in which a firmly structured status order reacts as compared with a status order that has become economically precarious. This is an example of a state of affairs that recurs everywhere. Precisely because of the rigorous reactions against the claims of property *per se*, the "parvenu" is never accepted, personally and without reservation, by the privileged status groups, no matter how completely his style of life has been adjusted to theirs. They will only accept his descendants who have been educated in the conventions of their status group and who have never besmirched its honor by their own economic labor.

As to the general *effect* of the status order, only one consequence can be stated, but it is a very important one: the hindrance of the free development of the market occurs first for those goods which status groups directly withheld from free exchange by monopolization. This monopolization may be effected either legally or conventionally. For example, in many Hellenic cities during the epoch of status groups, and also originally in Rome, the inherited estate (as is shown by the old formula for indiction against spendthrifts) was monopolized just as were the estates of knights, peasants, priests, and especially the clientele of the craft and merchant guilds. The market is restricted, and the power of naked property *per se,* which gives its stamp to "class formation," is pushed into the background. The results of this process can be most varied. Of course, they do not necessarily weaken the contrasts in the economic situation. Frequently they strengthen these contrasts, and in any case, where stratification by status permeates a community as strongly as was the case in all political communities of antiquity and of the Middle Ages, one can never speak of a genuinely free market competition as we understand it today. There are wider effects than this direct exclusion of special goods from the market. From the contrariety between the status order and the purely economic order mentioned above, it follows that in most instances the notion of honor peculiar to status absolutely abhors that which is essential to the market: higgling. Honor abhors higgling among peers and occasionally it taboos higgling for the members of a status group in general. Therefore, everywhere some status groups, and usually the most influential, consider almost any kind of overt participation in economic acquisition as absolutely stigmatizing.

With some over-simplification, one might thus say that "classes" are stratified according to their relations to the production and acquisition of goods; whereas "status groups" are stratified according to the principles of their *consumption* of goods as represented by special "styles of life."

An "occupational group" is also a status group. For normally, it successfully claims social honor only by virtue of the special style of life which may be determined by it. The differences between classes and status groups frequently overlap. It is precisely those status communities most strictly segregated in terms of honor (viz. the Indian castes) who today show, although within very rigid limits, a relatively high degree of indifference to pecuniary income. However, the Brahmins seek such income in many different ways.

As to the general economic conditions making for the predominance of stratification by "status," only very little can be said. When the bases of the acquisition and distribution of goods are relatively stable, stratification by status is favored. Every technological repercussion and economic transformation threatens stratification by status and pushes the class situation into the foreground. Epochs and countries in which the naked class situation is of predominant significance are regularly the periods of technical and economic transformations. And every slowing down of the shifting of economic stratifications leads, in due course, to the growth of status structures and makes for a resuscitation of the important role of social honor.

24. The Measure of the Man
St. Clair Drake and Horace Cayton

STANDARD OF LIVING

Money and a job are important primarily because they offer a base upon which a "standard of living" may be erected.* In the final analysis, the way in which people spend their money is the most important measuring rod in American life, particularly among people *within* the same general income range. In Bronzeville, where most incomes are comparatively low, a man's style of living—what he does with his money —becomes a very important index to social status. It is through the expenditure of money that his educational level and ultimate aspirations for himself and his family find expression. Stockyards Worker A may spend his $150 a month on flashy clothes and plenty of liquor, while his wife and children live in squalor. Stockyards Worker B brings his pay check home, his wife and children are well clothed and fed, and a bank account for the children's education is piling up. Bronzeville puts A and B in quite distinct *social* classes. Difference in occupation and income sets the broad lines of status division, but standard of living marks off the social strata within the broad income groups.

This emphasis upon standard of living is apparent in the two statements quoted below from interviews with Bronzeville's professional group:

These people are just common ordinary people having no intellectual inclina-

* The term "standard of living" is used here in its popular sense to apply to the actual level of living. It is customary in some academic circles to reserve this term for the level on which a family would like to live, and to use the term "plane of living" for the actual state of affairs.

From *Black Metropolis* copyright, 1945, by St. Clair Drake and Horace R. Cayton; renewed, 1973, by St. Clair Drake and Susan C. Woodson. Reprinted by permission of Harcourt Brace Jovanovich, Inc.

tion whatsoever. I have known them for approximately a year, and I find they spend a large sum of money on food and don't bother so much about clothes. They are not affiliated with any club or social group. I should put them in the middle class so far as income is concerned, but socially in a class slightly lower.

Now take that house next door. Why, for three years people lived over there who were the nastiest folks I have ever seen. The building was condemned and they didn't have to pay any rent so they just lived there like pigs or dogs. The water was cut off. The man who had the garage in back used to let them come over and get water. They brought their pails. You should have seen them go in droves after the water. They reminded me of people in the South. . . . Most of them were working, but they were just a bunch of no-good Negroes.

During the Depression, the masses of the people were operating on a "subsistence budget" which allowed little surplus for savings or "culture."* Within the community were thousands of clients on direct relief, each visited periodically by a case-worker who gave him a small check for rent and food; for other commodities he went to a government depot. When he was sick he got free treatment at a public clinic. Others had WPA jobs netting an average of $55 a month. Obviously the standard of living for all such was rather rigidly limited, dependent as it was on a meager income plus what little could be gleaned from policy winnings or earned by occasional domestic service. Many people on relief had been used to something better during the Fat Years, but had been gradually reduced to "subsistence level." They lived in hope that prosperity would return. Thousands of people on relief and WPA were drawn back into productive employment by the industries of the Second World War. With plenty of money in their hands some concentrated on "getting ahead," while others devoted their time and money to a round of immediate gratification. The business of selecting a pattern of expenditure and saving became vital.

All during the Depression, at least a third of Bronzeville's families could be classified as "strainers" and "strivers." These were people who were determined to maintain what America generally regards as "the middle-class way of life." They were interested in a well-furnished home, adequate clothing, a car, and membership in a few organizations of their choice. Their ideal was to be what Bronzeville calls "good livers." Wartime jobs allowed them to realize some of these goals.

Those members of the business and professional group who weathered the Depression, and those with stable incomes from civil service jobs, formed the status bearers of Bronzeville. They were likely to look down somewhat on "strainers" and "strivers" who had accumulated

---

* In 1935, the standard emergency budget as set up by the WPA for the family of a manual laborer with two children under 16 was $973 per year. At least 40 per cent of Bronzeville's families were existing on or below this level, supported by WPA or relief. Of the families with jobs in private industry or domestic service, only a third received an income greater than the WPA minimum.

money but didn't know how to spend it with taste. Thus one physician ridiculed the pretensions of the climbers:

A person who has little or no background usually feels that it is necessary to have a high-priced car, loud in color with flashy gadgets that will single him out. Such persons seek houses and apartments in good neighborhoods, but their furnishings are not always in good taste. Yet some of the "strivers" are smart enough to have an interior decorator when they realize that their knowledge is limited. Now a person who has education, family connections, and background will satisfy himself with a modest and comfortable home and an inexpensive car.

Bronzeville's more conservative well-to-do people—"those who are used to something"—were particularly critical of the rapidly mobile, especially if the latter had got money through "shady" enterprises. One man who had a long criminal record, but who opened a successful business, managed to get into an exclusive apartment house. A resident with "education, background, and family connections" belabored him for his "crudeness":

All individuals like J——— feel a need for elevating themselves socially, you know. Well, he's gone in for display in dress with his loud suits. He's dressing a bit better now. I think he must have started buying his things from some good clothing store downtown, and he must be taking its suggestions about his clothes because they are more conservative now.

Standard of living is decisive in measuring the status of a family, and standard of living is one aspect of that important characteristic—"front."

THE IMPORTANCE OF "FRONT"

Over and over, people in Bronzeville told interviewers that "it's not what you do that counts, but how you do it." This dictum is applied to varied aspects of behavior—dancing, liquor-drinking, wife-beating, church-going—by those who maintain a rather stable and relatively high standard of living. There is a very sharp division, as we shall see later, between those who value "front"—who stress decorous *public* behavior—and those who don't.

Because of the stress that the "dicties" place upon correct *public* behavior they are often the target of the less sophisticated people who dub them "hypocrites." They are constantly gossiped about by people who do not value front and who exult at finding a chink in the "stuck-ups" armor. But one of the most fundamental divisions in Bronzeville is that between people who stress conventional, middle-class "American" public behavior and those who ignore it. Professional men, postal workers, clerical workers and others with "position" rail constantly at the "loud," "boisterous," "uncouth" behavior of other segments of the society. The "respectable," "educated," and "refined" believe in "front," partly because it is their accustomed way of life and partly in order to impress the white world.

The decisive measure of the man is how he acts in public.

FAMILY, CLIQUE, AND CLASS

All the measures of the man that we have described are either objective traits or types of behavior. More important, however, in placing people are their social relationships. People not only ask, "What kind of person is he?" They also want to know, "What kind of family does he come from?" "Who's in his crowd?" "What kind of organizations does he belong to?" Occupation, income, education, standard of living, and public behavior ultimately find their reflection in social groupings.

Family background is not too important in Bronzeville. Three generations ago nearly all Negroes were slaves, and "getting ahead" by education and the acquisition of wealth have gone on at too fast a pace to allow any tradition of "old families" to mean much. But contemporary family *behavior* is very important in placing people.

Far more important in "placing" people than their family connections are their clique affiliations. The rough rule that "birds of a feather flock together" is used to stratify people in Bronzeville. A man takes on the reputation of his crowd. In a rapidly changing society, clique affiliations become important for social mobility also. People may change their cliques easily, and thus change their social personalities. The cliques become "selectors," and at the top of the society the small high-status cliques become the social arbiters for the community.

It has become fashionable for a broad section of Bronzeville's people to formalize their small cliques as social clubs devoted to card-playing and dancing. Between "Society" at the top and the disorganized masses at the bottom are several thousand of these social clubs. To belong to any of them a person must discipline his behavior, keep up a front, and spend his money for socially approved types of clothing, entertainment, and whatever other appurtenances the social ritual requires. These social clubs are a distinctive feature of Bronzeville's middle class. . . .

In a very limited sense, churches, too, are ranked in a system of social prestige. Congregational and Episcopal churches are considered high-status; Holiness and Spiritualist churches low-status. Most churches, however, include people of all status levels. Neither the question "What church does he belong to?" nor the question "Does he go to church?" is important in placing a man, except at the very top and the very bottom of the social scale.

For persons "on the make" or "on the rise," getting the proper "connections" becomes extremely important. People change their status by acquiring money and education, and then changing their "set." The dynamics of social mobility in Bronzeville can only be understood by observing individuals actually shifting from clique to clique, church to church, and club to club in the struggle to get ahead. The people who are "in" control this upward mobility by setting the standards and holding the line against those who don't make the grade. They also limit the number of persons who are "accepted." At the same time the socially ambitious are able to copy the behavior of the strata above them and to bring *new* cliques, churches, and clubs into existence with the desired pattern. After a time such new increments are accepted and the ambitious rise as a group.

THE SYSTEM OF SOCIAL CLASSES

Everybody in Bronzeville recognizes the existence of social classes, whether called that or not. People with slight education, small incomes, and few of the social graces are always referring to the more affluent and successful as "dicties," "stuck-ups," "muckti-mucks," "high-toned folks," "tony people." The "strainers" and "strivers" are well-recognized social types, people whose whole lives are dominated by the drive to get ahead and who show it by conspicuous consumption and a persistent effort to be seen with the right people and in the right places. People at the top of the various pyramids that we have described are apt to characterize people below them as "low-class," "trash," "riff-raff," "shift-less." The highly sensitive professional and business classes, keenly aware of the estimate which the white world puts on Negro behavior, frequently complain that white people do not recognize the class distinctions within the Negro community.

Class-thinking is essentially a way of sizing up individuals in terms of whether they are social equals, fit for acceptance as friends, as intimate associates, and as marriage partners for one's self or one's children. It differs from caste-thinking (which dominates Negro-white relations) in that the people in the upper strata expect some of the people below them to enter the upper levels of society once they have qualified. The individual measures of the man are weighed and combined in such a way as to strike a rough average of position. According to these estimates, and out of the cliques, families, and voluntary associations that arise from them, people in Bronzeville become grouped into several broad, social classes.

A Negro social worker is referring to this class system when she says to an interviewer:

> I think education gives social status. And of course money talks. After a person gets an education I think he should try to get money so as to be able to live at a certain standard. Of course there are different classes of people. The educated won't go with the ignorant and those with money won't go with poor people.

The Upper Class. At the top of the social pyramid is a scant 5 per cent of the population—an articulate social world of doctors, lawyers, schoolteachers, executives, successful business people, and the frugal and fortunate of other occupational groups who have climbed with difficulty and now cling precariously to a social position consonant with what money, education, and power the city and the castelike controls allow them. They are challenged at every point, however, by the same forces that condemn the vast majority of the people to poverty and restricted opportunities.

Carrying the responsibilities of the major Negro institutions and co-operating with sympathetic and liberal whites who give them financial and moral support, this Negro upper class becomes symbolic of racial potentialities, and, despite the often caustic criticisms leveled at them from the classes below, they go their way supplying goods and services to the Negro community; seeking to maintain and extend opportunities for themselves and their children; snatching some enjoyment from the round of bridge and dancing; seeking cultural development from the arts and sciences; and displaying all of the intraclass conflicts which a highly competitive social and economic system has made characteristic of any group in an insecure position—as this upper class certainly is. Yet they have a measure of satisfactory adjustment which makes their life pattern fruitful if measured by any of the objective standards of "success," except for certain disabilities that *all* Negroes share.

The Lower Class. The Chicago adult world is predominantly a working-class world. Over 65 per cent of the Negro adults earn their bread by manual labor in stockyard and steel mill, in factory and kitchen, where they do the essential digging, sweeping, and serving which make metropolitan life tolerable. During the Depression, whether on public projects or in private industry, the bulk of the employed adult Negroes, with a minimum of education and still betraying their southern origin, were toilers, working close to the soil, the animals, and the machinery that undergird Chicago's economy. Many of them also were forced to "only stand and wait" at relief stations, on street corners, in poolrooms and taverns, in policy stations and churches, for op-portunities that never came and for the work which eluded both them and their white fellow-hopers.

A part of this working class constitutes the backbone of Bronzeville's "middle" *social* class, identified by its emphasis on the symbols of "respectability" and "success." The largest part of this working class is in a "lower" *social* position, however, characterized by less restraint and without a consuming drive for the symbols of higher social prestige. Desertion and illegitimacy, juvenile delinquency, and fighting and roistering are common in lower-class circles.

Not alone by choice, but tossed by the deep economic tides of the modern world, pressed and molded by a usually indifferent and occa-sionally unkind white world, and hounded by an often unsympathetic Law, the lower social classes in Bronzeville have their being in a world apart from both white people and other Negroes.

The Middle Class. About a third of Bronzeville is in a social position between the "uppers" and the "lowers"—an amorphous, sandwich-like middle class. Trying with difficulty to maintain respectability, they are caught between the class above into which they (or at least their children) wish to rise and the group below into which they do not wish to fall. Some of them are in white-collar pursuits; many of them must do manual labor; a few of them are secure in civil service jobs. Released somewhat from the restraints of poverty, they have not found it necessary to emphasize the extremes of religious or recreational behavior, or to tie their lives to the rhythm of the policy drawings or the very occasional relief or WPA check as has the lower class. Life to them has some stability and order; expectations for their children and for their own future can be predominantly this-worldly; and the individual psyche is given form by the church and associations whose dues they are able to pay with some regularity and from whose functions they are not barred by inadequate clothing or by lack of education, formal or informal.

The "Shadies." But the class structure of Bronzeville is not a simple tripartite system through which individuals move by attaining the class-behavior pattern which their occupational and educational position permits and their training stimulates. Within each class there is a group, proportionately smallest in the upper class and largest in the lower class, which has secured and maintained its position by earning its income in pursuits not generally recognized by the community as "respectable." The marginal position of the Negro in the economic system and the traditional role of the Negro community as an area for exploitation and risqué recreation by the white community have brought into existence and maintained the whole complex of "protected business" —illegal enterprises winked at and preyed upon by cooperative politicians. This complex is composed of the "policy" business, prostitution, and allied pursuits, and is intimately connected with the legal but none-the-less "shady" liquor interests and cabarets. Thus a considerable proportion of each class is connected at some points with these businesses, and the more mobile individuals are able to rise even to the top where they challenge the position of the upper "respectables" who, as one student has phrased it, "find it politic to accord them some measure of social recognition." These "upper shadies," in turn, are by no means entirely scornful of the opinions of the "upper respectables." They seek to secure prestige in the eyes of this group by assuming many aspects of its behavior patterns, and by attempting to become Race Leaders even to the extent of supporting the organizations of the upper and middle classes, becoming the patrons of the arts, and entering legitimate business.

Bronzeville's upper class is oriented around a *secular* pattern of living, with emphasis on "culture" and "refinement" as well as "racial advancement." A smaller group within the upper class is church-centered, and a very small but powerful group earns its living in "shady" pursuits. As we leave the top of society, however, and move toward the bottom, the proportion of "church minded" people and of "shadies" increases, and the group of "non-church" respectables decreases.

VIII. Race and Ethnicity

Since its inception in the nineteenth century, race as a quasi-scientific concept has plagued society—and sociology. Biologists and physical anthropologists have hardly fared better than laymen with the concept. They agree that we are a single interbreeding species that may be subdivided for purposes of classification in the Linnaean but, so far, not in the Mendelian mode. That is to say, criteria for establishing "the races of mankind" have been superficial (phenotypes), not fundamental (genotypes). Well into the twentieth century, biologists knew much more about the heredity of fruit flies than about the heredity of human beings.

Meanwhile, genocide—systematic mass murder—continues to be perpetrated in the name of race; entire peoples are exterminated while others are unjustifiably exalted. Since we now know a great deal more, though still too little, about the infinite biological variation of *Homo sapiens*, perverse political use of race is less defensible than ever. And yet it persists. The biologist Theodosius Dobzhansky is a distinguished student of the subject. Notice that in his discussion of gene frequencies and gene flows Dobzhansky feels called upon to acknowledge culture as a decisive factor in the human species. Like some of his predecessors, he disposes once again—but this time with admirable sophistication—of the IQ controversy, which nevertheless still rages.

Why does the question of race and intelligence continue to be so hotly contested? Because racism—the prejudicial attribution of certain allegedly innate psychological, social, and intellectual traits—has not yet been eradicated. In the long war on racism, few leaders have been more conscientious and scholarly than Bayard Rustin, a black activist who was closely associated with the late Dr. Martin Luther King, Jr.

Rustin shared the general exhilaration that was felt among many in 1954, the year in which the legal foundations of racism were destroyed; but in 1964, a decade after the United States Supreme Court had ordered the desegregation of all public schools, he looked back and found "mounting frustration." His essay was prophetic, for shortly thereafter the civil rights movement began to falter and "Black Power" became the slogan of black separatists. By 1970 Rustin could, with some justification, declare the separatist movement a failure and call for radical renovation of the American economy as a solution to racism.

If black separatism failed in the overall sense, it nevertheless produced a shift from shame to pride in an oppressed ethnic group. For many social scientists, that shift shattered the myth of the melting pot and replaced it with the new ethnicity. Thus, Peter Schrag, a clear-eyed observer of the scene before us, sees the United States as a "nation of strangers." He not only chronicles the decline of white Anglo-Saxon domination, but points to the rise of ethnic consciousness in subcultures comprised of seemingly unassimilable ethnics. The new ethnics, he concludes, are struggling over the corpse of the WASP establishment.

25. Genetics and the Races of Man

Theodosius Dobzhansky

RACIAL DIFFERENCES AND RACES NAMED

The apparently endless variety of living beings is as fascinating as it is perplexing. There are no two identical humans, as there are no two identical pine trees, or two Drosophila flies, or two infursoria. The runaway diversity of our perceptions is made manageable by means of human language. Classifying and giving names to classes of things is perhaps the primordial scientific activity. It may antedate the appearance of *Homo sapiens,* and it is bound to continue as long as symbol-forming animals will exist. Biologists and anthropologists describe and name the complexes of organisms which they study in order to identify for themselves, and let others know, what they are talking and writing about.

Human beings whom we meet, and about whose existence we learn

Reprinted from Bernard G. Campbell, *Sexual Selections and the Descent of Man* (Chicago: Aldine Publishing Company, 1972); copyright © 1972 by Aldine Publishing Company. Reprinted by permission of the author and Aldine Publishing Company.

from others, are numerous and diversified. We have to classify them and attach recognition labels to the classes. So we distinguish the speakers of English, Russian, Swahili, and other languages; college students, industrial workers, and farmers; intellectuals and the "silent majority," and so on. Those who study human physical, physiological, and genetic variations among men find it convenient to name races. Races can be defined as arrays of Mendelian populations belonging to the same biological species, but differing from each other in incidence of some genetic variants.

The question is often posed: Are races objectively ascertainable phenomena of nature, or are they mere group concepts invented by biologists and anthropologists for their convenience? Here we must make unequivocally clear the duality of the race concept. First, it refers to objectively ascertainable genetic differences among Mendelian populations. Second, it is a category of classification which must serve the pragmatic function of facilitating communication. One can specify the operational procedures whereby any two populations can be shown to be racially different or racially identical. The populations contain different arrays of genotypes if racially different, or similar arrays if racially identical.

Racial differences exist between populations regardless of whether or not somebody is studying them. Yet this does not mean that any two genetically different populations must receive different race names. For example, Cavalli-Sforza (1959) has found no significant genetic differentiation between inhabitants of villages on the densely settled Parma plain; he did find such a differentiation between the villages in the more sparsely settled mountains. . . . Racial differences are, therefore, ascertained among the latter but not among the former. It would nevertheless not occur to anyone to give race names to the populations of every mountain village. The village names are adequate labels for the populations that live in them.

How many arrays of populations in the human species should be provided with race names is a matter of expediency. Already, Darwin noted that "Man has been studied more carefully than any other organic being, and yet there is the greatest possible diversity among capable judges" concerning the number of races recognized and named. Different authors referred to by Darwin named from 2 to as many as 63 races. The incertitude is undiminished today. Hardly any two independently working classifiers have proposed identical sets of races. This lack of unanimity has driven some modern "capable judges" to desperation. They claim that mankind has no races, and that the very word "race" should be expunged from the lexicon. This proposal is often motivated by a laudable desire to counteract notorious racist propaganda. But will this be achieved by denying the existence of races? Or will such denials only impair the credibility of the scientists making them? Is it not better to make people understand the nature of the race differences, rather than to pretend that such differences are nonexistent?

To give an example of a race classification by an author fully conversant with modern biology and anthropology, Garn (1965) recognizes 9 "geographical races" and 32 "local races," some of the latter being subdivisions of the former. The geographical races are as follows:

1. Amerindian
2. Polynesian
3. Micronesian
4. Australian
5. Melanesian-Papuan
6. Asiatic
7. Indian
8. European
9. African

Among the local races not included in his major geographical list, Garn distinguishes three interesting categories—Ainu and Bushmen are "long-isolated marginal," Lapps, Pacific Negritos, African Pygmies, and Eskimos are "puzzling, isolated, numerically small," and American Blacks, Cape Colored, Ladinos, and Neo-Hawaiians are hybrid local races of recent origin." On the other hand, Lundman (1967) recognizes only 4 main races—white, yellow, red (Amerindian), and black; his 16 subraces correspond only in part to Garn's local races. If one of these classifications is accepted as correct, must the other necessarily be incorrect? This, I believe, need not be so; we should rather ask which classification is more convenient, and for what purpose.

In sexually reproducing and outbreeding organisms, every individual can usually be recognized as a member of one and only one species, or else as a hybrid of two species. Adherents to the typological race concepts believed that the same should be true of races. Every individual, excepting only the progeny of interracial crosses, should be classifiable as belonging to a certain race. This is not so, because species are genetically closed, while races are gentically open systems. For example, there is no individual whose belonging to the species man or the species chimpanzee could be called in question. These species do not exchange genes. There are, however, many local populations in northwestern Asia intermediate between the white and the yellow, and in northern Africa intermediate between the white and the black races. This does not mean that individual members of these intermediate populations necessarily have two parents belonging to different "pure" white, black, or yellow races. Whole populations are intermediate. Sometimes this is due to secondary intergradation (Mayr, 1963), that is, to interbreeding of populations which became genetically distinct in a near or remote past. This is, in fact, the origin of Garn's "hybrid local races." More often the intermediate populations are autochthonous; primary intergradation is a result of gene diffusion taking place while the racial divergence of the populations is in progress, as well as after the populations have diverged. The gene

gradients or clines result from both primary and secondary intergrada-
tions.

Gene gradients make it only rarely possible to draw a line on the map
to divide the regions of different races. Race boundaries are more often
blurred than sharp. Worse still, gradients of the frequencies of different
genes and traits may be only weakly or not at all correlated. This can
easily be seen on maps that show the frequencies of various traits in
human populations, such as different blood antigens, pigmentation, and
stature (see, for example, the maps in Lundman, 1967). Human races are
not discrete units imagined by typologists, so some disappointed typologists have seen fit to draw the radical conclusion that races do not
exist.

Let us take a closer look at the situation. If gene or character gradients
were uniform, gene frequencies would increase or decrease regularly by
so many percentages per so many miles traveled in a given direction.
With uniform gradients, race boundaries could only be arbitrary. However, often the gradients are steeper in some places and are more gentle
or absent elsewhere. Consider two gene alleles, A_1 and A_2 in a species with
a distribution area 2,100 miles across. Suppose that for 1,000 miles the
frequency of A_1 declines from 100 to 90 percent; for the next 100 miles
from 90 to 10 percent; and for the remaining 1,000 miles from 10 to 0
percent. It is then reasonable and convenient to divide the species into
two races, characterized by the predominance of A_1 and A_2, respectively,
and to draw the geographic boundary between the races where the cline
is steep.

Why are the gene frequency gradients gentle in some and steep in
other places? The steepening of the gradients usually coincides with
geographic and environmental barriers that make travel difficult. Barriers
to travel are also barriers to gene diffusion. Newman (1963) has analyzed
the human racial taxonomy in a thoughtful article. His general conclusion
is that ". . . . there are valid races among men, but that biology is only
beginning to properly discover and define them. . . . I consider some of
Garn's races probably valid, others probably invalid, with still others in
the 'suspense' category for lack of adequate data." He validates Garn's
Asiatic, African, and Amerindian races as showing good trait correlations
in such visible traits as pigmentation, hair form and quantity, nose and lip
form, cheek bone prominence, eyelid form, and general body shape.
European, Indian, and Australian are "unwarranted abstractions," on
account of the high variability and discordance (lack of correlation) in
the geographical distribution of many traits. Melanesian, Polynesian,
and Micronesian are in the "suspense" category.

Adherents of the "no races" school argue that one should study the
geographic distributions of genes and character frequencies, rather than
attempt to delimit races. The truth is that both kinds of studies are
necessary. Gene and character geography is the basis of the biological
phenomenon of racial variation; classification and naming are indispensa-

ble for information storage and communication. The fact that races are not always or even usually discrete, and that they are connected by transitional populations, is in itself biologically meaningful. This is evidence of gene flow between races being not only potentially possible but actually taking place. Gene flow between species, however, is limited or prevented altogether. To hold that because races are not rigidly fixed units they do not exist is a throwback to typological thinking of the most misleading kind. It is about as logical as saying that towns and cities do not exist because the country intervening between them is not totally uninhabited, or that youth and old age do not exist because there is also middle age. . . .

Are Races of Man Genetically Adapted to Different Ways of Life?

The species mankind, in common with many, perhaps a majority of, animal and plant species, is genetically differentiated into major races (subspecies), minor races, and local populations of various orders. Because man is the only animal species having culture, certain kinds of differentiation are peculiar to him—linguistic, religious, and socioeconomic isolates, some of which may not be genetically identical. As pointed out above, most or all of this genetic differentiation is quantitative rather than qualitative. Racially distinct populations of *Homo sapiens* usually differ in frequencies of variable genes, rather than one race having 100 percent of a gene variant which another race lacks altogether. The genetic differences between human races can therefore be said to be relatively minor; in many species of animals the races have diverged genetically much further, and are on the threshold of becoming derived independent species.

All men are genetically "brothers under the skin." It is nevertheless legitimate to inquire to what extent genetic differences between populations are reflected in their health, environmental preferences, and capacity for mental development and for becoming members of different cultures. What is the biological, evolutionary function of race formation in the living world as a whole? It is differential adaptedness of subdivisions of a species for living in different geographic and ecological circumstances. Does this apply to human races?

We have discussed the roles of natural selection and of random genetic drift in the origination of race differences. Differences induced by selection make the population adaptively different in some respects, at least where and when the selective process operates. The random drift may, as a first approximation, be regarded as "noise" in evolutionary adaptive processes. It is most likely that race differentiation in man arose neither by selection nor by drift alone, but by interaction of these evolutionary forces. It would nevertheless be foolhardy to attempt to dichotomize racial differences into adaptively meaningful and adaptively neutral ones.

The possibility must be considered that genetic differences between the races and populations were adaptive in the past but are neutral at present. They may have been induced by natural selection in response to the environments in which the populations lived. But human environments change radically because of the adoption of different ways of life, particularly because of cultural and technological innovations. The selection may act in a different way, or may no longer be effective in changed environments. The skin color differences are a case in point. As shown above, it is most probable that skin pigmentation was adjusted by natural selection to the climatic characteristics of the territories in which the human races were formed. But how much adaptive importance does the skin pigmentation have at present, when most people have most of their body surfaces covered with clothes, and live in artificial dwellings rather than outdoors? It may well be that for most people skin pigmentation is now an adaptively neutral characteristic.

Other examples of changing selection pressures may be found among genetic defenses against infectious diseases. Such genetic defenses become racial traits in territories in which a given infectious disease is pandemic. A classical example is the gene for the sickle red blood cell condition (hemoglobin S). Though this gene results in fatal anemia when homozygous, the heterozygous carriers not only survive but are relatively protected against some tropical forms of malarial fevers. The gene is absent in countries where these fevers do not occur, but reaches high frequencies (up to 30 percent) in some populations of tropical Africa exposed to malarial infections. Here, then, is a racial trait which was maintained by natural selection as an aid for survival in malarial environments. With malaria brought under control and perhaps approaching eradication, the S gene has lost its adaptive function. Of course, no population was ever homozygous for this gene, since it is lethal when homozygous; in the absence of malaria it is at best neutral, or mildly deleterious, when heterozygous. Its frequencies are dwindling, and it may eventually be eliminated altogether.

By far the greatest attention, and also some violent emotional reactions, are aroused by studies on possible race differences in mental traits, especially in the so-called "intelligence." Are people of all racial stocks born equal, or are some intrinsically superior and others inferior? [There are] arguments . . . to show that the emotional reactions unleashed by studies on the "intelligence" of human races are due to sheer misunderstanding. We [present here] the highlights of these arguments. Equality should not be confused with biological identity, or genetic diversity with inequality. Human equality and inequality are not statements of observable biological conditions. They are policies adopted by societies, ethical principles, and religious commandments.

People can be made equal before the law, equality of opportunity may be promoted or guaranteed, human dignity equally recognized, and human beings can be regarded equally God's sons and daughters. To be equal, people need not be identical twins, that is, need not be genetically alike. And vice versa, regardless of how similar or different they are genetically, individuals can be treated unequally, as social superiors and inferiors, masters and servants, aristocrats and plebeians. There is no reason why monozygotic twins must necessarily be social equals, even though they are genetically as nearly identical as two individuals can be. People can be made equal or unequal by the societies in which they live; they cannot be made genetically or biologically identical, even if this were desirable. In principle, human diversity is as compatible with equality as it is with inequality.

Any two human individuals, identical twins excepted, carry different sets of genes. This has traditionally been stressed by partisans of social inequalities, and deemphasized by champions of equality. It should be the reverse—equality is meaningful only because people are not identical. Like illness, genetic lottery is no respecter of the social position or rank of the parents. Owing to gene recombination in the progeny of highly heterozygous individuals, genetically well-and poorly-endowed children are born to parents of either kind. This does not deny the existence of some positive correlations between the genetic endowments of parents and offspring. The fact that these correlations are far from complete is, however, socially and ethically no less important than that the correlations are there.

The above is a necessary preamble to the substantive issue: Is there incontrovertible evidence of genetic differences between human populations, such as major and minor races, in mental traits, particularly in their capacities for intellectual development? The literature of the subject is as formidable in bulk as it is uncritical and unreliable. Most of it deals with ostensibly a single trait, the IQ, which in reality is a compound of several abilities that may well be genetically independent in various degrees. Furthermore, only a small minority of racial stocks have been studied, perhaps because of insuperable difficulties of devising intelligence tests that would be applicable to people speaking different languages and brought up in different cultural traditions. Whether such culture-free, or culture-fair, tests can be constructed is an open question, but it is certain that existing ones fall short of this desideratum in various degrees. There is always a danger that the tests will be biased in favor of the race, social class, culture, and subculture to which the test constructors themselves belong. A fair comparison becomes less and less possible as the groups tested differ more and more in socioeconomic, linguistic, traditional, and attitudinal backgrounds. Attempts have been made to correct for these sources of error, but with scant success.

By far the greatest number of studies deal with only two population groups—the blacks and the whites in the United States. The so-called Coleman Report (1966) is exceptional in also including IQ statistics for American Indians, Puerto Ricans, Mexican-Americans, and Oriental populations living in the United States. The plethora of papers comparing the IQ test results of whites and blacks have been uncritically compiled by Shuey (1966), and analyzed by Jensen (1969). There is no doubt that the average IQ scores of the blacks tend to be lower than those of the whites.

The means for either race vary in different parts of the country, obviously depending on the socioeconomic and educational opportunities of the inhabitants of different states. In some northern states the blacks have shown higher mean scores than the whites in some southern states. However, most often the black mean is found to be 10 to 20 IQ points below the white. Jensen takes 15 points as a fair estimate of the average difference. It happens that the standard deviation (square root of variance) for the white populations is also close to 15 points. Of course, the black and white distributions overlap, and about 15 percent of the individual blacks score above the white average, while many whites score below the black average. According to the Coleman Report, the American Indians, Puerto Ricans, and Mexican-Americans are intermediate between blacks and whites, and Orientals are about equal to whites in the mean IQ score (the amount of data concerning these "ethnic" populations is a small fraction of those for the blacks and whites).

The key problem is, of course, whence comes the observed difference between the IQ means for blacks and whites? This problem has provoked ample polemics, which show no sign of subsiding. . . . Differences in IQ scores between individuals within a population have an impressively high heritability, estimated by Jensen to be about 0.8 (80 percent). Racists have seized upon this figure as evidence of racial superiorities and inferiorities, arguing that since the heritability of the IQ variations is so high, differences in the IQ averages between races are fixed and irremediable. This is certainly unproven and unconvincing.

Jensen (1969) is fully aware of the fact that a heritability estimate for *intra*populational variability does not necessarily tell us anything about the magnitude of the genetic component in an *inter*populational difference of means. Environments in which the racial groups live in the same country or state are appreciably and often drastically different. Even if the intrapopulational heritability were 100 percent, the interracial differences could be wholly environmental. Nevertheless Jensen argues, and rightly in my opinion, that it is not valid to attribute the interracial differences in IQ averages to undefinable differences between environments. For interpopulational, as well as for intrapopulational, differences in mean IQs, one should be able to specify just what environmental factors produce a specific effect. He appeals to studies which have tried to equate the environments of the blacks and the whites by comparing population samples of ostensibly equal socioeconomic status. When this is done, the IQ average differences diminish but do not disappear entirely. Jensen takes this as evidence of a strong genetic component in the differences between the black and white populations.

Bodmer and Cavalli-Sforza (1970), among others, have pointed out the inadequacies of equalization of the socioeconomic status as a way toward equating the total environments in which the races live. In their words:

It is difficult to see, however, how the status of blacks and whites can be compared. The very existence of a racial stratification correlated with a relative socioeconomic deprivation makes this comparison suspect. Black schools are well known to be generally less adequate than white schools, so that equal numbers of years of schooling certainly do not mean equal educational attainments. Wide variation in the level of occupation must exist within each occupational class. Thus one would certainly expect, even for equivalent occupational classes, that the black level is on the average lower than the white. No amount of money can buy a black person's way into a privileged upper-class white community, or buy off more than 200 years of accumulated racial prejudice on the part of the whites, or reconstitute the disrupted black family, in part culturally inherited from the days of slavery. It is impossible to accept the idea that matching for status provides an adequate, or even substantial, control over most important environmental differences between black and white.

One can only conclude that the degree to which differences in the IQ arrays between races are genetically conditioned is at present an unsolved problem. I fully agree with Bodmer and Cavalli-Sforza that "we do not by any means exclude the possibility that there could be a genetic component in the mean difference in IQ between races. We simply maintain that currently available data are inadequate to resolve this question in either direction." Assume for the sake of argument that some part of the average difference between the IQs of the blacks and the whites is genetic. Would it follow that the blacks are an inferior and the whites a superior race? Would it be a vindication of the racists in Alabama, South Africa, and elsewhere? Certainly not. Two basic facts refute the racists: the broad overlap of the variation curves for IQs and other human abilities, and the universal educability, and hence capacity for improvement, however that be defined.

We may accordingly agree with Darwin (1871), that "Although the existing races of man differ in many respects . . . yet if their whole organization be taken into consideration they are found to resemble each other closely in a multitude of points. . . . The same remark holds good with equal or greater force with respect to the numerous points of mental similarity between the most distinct races of man. The American aborigines, negroes and Europeans differ as much from each other in mind as any three races that can be named; yet I was incessantly struck, whilst living with the Fuegians on board the 'Beagle,' with the many little traits of character, shewing how similar their minds were to ours; and so it was with a full-blooded negro with whom I happened once to be intimate."

RACES OF MAN AND BREEDS OF DOMESTIC ANIMALS

In conclusion, consideration must be given to the argument which is the more misleading since it is superficially so plausible. Races of animal and plant species, of free-living as well as domesticated forms, develop differential adaptedness to the environments in which they live, or to the employments for which they are used. In particular, breeds of domestic animals differ, often quite strikingly, in their structural as well as behavioral characteristics.

Consider the numerous and diverse breeds of dogs, many of them specialized for different uses, with behaviors suitable for their employment. Thus shepherd dogs learn to herd sheep and cattle, scent hounds and bird dogs to find game, hunting dogs are used for pursuit, terriers for attack, and toy and lap dogs for companionship with humans. There is no doubt that these very different forms of behavior are genetically conditioned, although at the same time not only dogs but even wolves, which are their wild ancestors, possess the potentiality of being trained in different ways and of changing their behaviors accordingly (Scott and Fuller, 1965; Scott, 1968; Woolpy and Ginsburg, 1967). If the behavior of dog breeds and of breeds of other domesticated species is very strongly conditioned, why would man's races not follow this rule of genetic conditioning? Even some eminent geneticists who should have known better have been led astray by such reasoning (for example, Darlington, 1969, 1972). Modern technologically advanced societies have been invented and built by a minority of human breeds. It is likely that the "lesser" breeds do not possess genetic aptitudes sufficient not only to create and manage but even to be members of these advanced societies.

The above argument is fallacious because it fails to take into consideration the unique and basic characteristics of human evolution (Dobzhansky, 1962, 1972). The cardinal distinction between mankind and all other forms of life is that man's adaptedness depends primarily on his cultural rather than on his genetic inheritance. Culture is acquired by each individual through learning, and is transmitted by instruction, chiefly, though not exclusively, by means of a language consisting of socially agreed-upon symbols. To adapt to new environments, mankind changes mainly its cultural inheritance, rather than its genes, as other organisms do. Of course, genes and culture are not independent but interdependent. It is man's genetic endowment which makes him able to think in symbols, abstractions, and generalizations. The potentiality of cultural evolution, which is uniquely human, has developed through the evolution of his gene pool. But the contents of his gene pool do not determine the contents of his culture. By way of analogy, genes give man his ability to speak, but do not decide just what he shall say on a given occasion.

The basic, and unique, capacity of man is his genetically established educability by means of symbolic language. This educability is a species trait common to all races and all nonpathological individuals. Its universality is no more surprising than that all people have body temperature and the pH of the blood varying only within narrow limits. Both educability and symbolic language became universal human traits because survival and success in man-made environments depended on possession of these traits. Nothing of the sort happened in any other wild or domesticated animal species. By contrast, genetically fixed specializations in both body structure and behavior have often been deliberately built into different domestic breeds.

In sum: breeds of domestic animals often differ in behavior, and the differences are genetically more or less rigidly fixed. Their behavior is a part of the complex of characteristics which make a given breed suitable for performance of a certain kind of work or function. The kind of behavior exhibited, as well as its degree of fixity, are induced by the artificial selection which the owners or masters of the animals practiced, deliberately or unwittingly, in the process of formation of a given breed. The evolutionary pattern of the human species is quite different. Natural selection has unrelentingly favored the ability of human beings to learn and to modify their behavior depending on the circumstances of their upbringing and social conditions in the midst of which they find themselves. This is precisely the opposite of selection in breeds of domesticated animals. Furthermore, selection for trainability and cultural receptivity has been going on not in some populations and races but in the whole human species, and uninterruptedly ever since the inception of humanity and of its dependence on culture as a method of adaptation to and control of the environment. Two million years and one hundred thousand generations are probably conservative estimates of the duration of this selective process. The evolutionary uniqueness of the human species should not be underestimated.

References

1. Bodmer, W. F., and Cavalli-Sforza, L. L. 1970. "Intelligence and Race." *Scientific American* 223:19–29.
2. Cavalli-Sforza, L. L. 1959. "Some Data on the Genetic Structure of Human Populations." *Proceedings of the International Congress of Genetics* 1:389–407.
3. Coleman, J. S. 1966. *Equality of Educational Opportunity.* Washington, D.C.: U.S. Office of Education.
4. Darlington, C. D. 1969. *The Evolution of Man and Society.* London: Allen & Unwin.
5. Darlington, C. D. 1972. "Race, Class, and Culture," in J. W. S. Pringle, ed., *Biology and the Human Sciences,* pp. 95–120. Oxford: Clarendon Press.
6. Darwin, Charles. 1871. *The Descent of Man, and Selection in Relation to Sex.* 2 vols. London: John Murray.
7. Dobzhansky, Theodosius. 1962. *Mankind Evolving.* New Haven, Conn.: Yale University Press.
8. Dobzhansky, Theodosius. 1972. "Unique Aspects of Human Evolution," in J. W. S. Pringle, ed., *Biology and the Human Sciences.* Oxford: Clarendon Press.
9. Garn, S. M. 1965. *Human Races.* Springfield, Ill.: Charles C. Thomas.
10. Jensen, A. R. 1969. "How Much Can We Boost IQ and Scholastic Achievement?" *Harvard Educational Review* 31:1–123.
11. Lundman, B. 1967. *Geographische Anthropologie.* Stuttgart: Gustav Fischer.
12. Mayr, E. 1963. *Animal Species and Evolution.* Cambridge, Mass.: Harvard University Press.
13. Newman, M. T. 1963. "Geographic and Microgeographic Races." *Current Anthropology* 4:189–91, 204–5.
14. Scott, J. P. 1968. "Evolution and Domestication of the Dog." *Evolutionary Biology* 2:243–75.
15. Scott, J. P., and Fuller, J. L. 1965. *Genetics and the Social Behavior of the Dog.* Chicago: University of Chicago Press.
16. Shuey, A. M. 1966. *The Testing of Negro Intelligence.* New York: Social Science Press.
17. Woolpy, J. H., and Ginsburg, B. E. 1967. "Wolf Socialization: A Study of Temperament in a Wild Social Species." *American Zoologist* 7:357–63.

26. From Protest to Politics: The Future of the Civil Rights Movement

Bayard Rustin

I

The decade spanned by the 1954 Supreme Court decision on school de-segregation and the Civil Rights Act of 1964 will undoubtedly be re-corded as the period in which the legal foundations of racism in America were destroyed. To be sure, pockets of resistance remain; but it would be hard to quarrel with the assertion that the elaborate legal structure of segregation and discrimination, particularly in relation to public accom-modations, has virtually collapsed. On the other hand, without making light of the human sacrifices involved in the direct-action tactics (sit-ins, freedom rides, and the rest) that were so instrumental to this achieve-ment, we must recognize that in desegregating public accommodations, we affected institutions which are relatively peripheral both to the Ameri-can socio-economic order and to the fundamental conditions of life of the Negro people. In a highly industrialized, 20th-century civilization, we hit Jim Crow precisely where it was most anachronistic, dispensable, and vulnerable—in hotels, lunch counters, terminals, libraries, swimming pools, and the like. For in these forms, Jim Crow does impede the flow of commerce in the broadest sense: it is a nuisance in a society on the move (and on the make). Not surprisingly, therefore, it was the most mobility conscious and relatively liberated groups in the Negro community—lower-middle-class college students—who launched the attack that brought down this imposing but hollow structure.

The term "classical" appears especially apt for this phase of the civil rights movement. But in the few years that have passed since the first flush of sit-ins, several developments have taken place that have compli-cated matters enormously. One is the shifting focus of the movement in the South, symbolized by Birmingham; another is the spread of the revolution to the North; and the third, common to the other two, is the expansion of the movement's base in the Negro community. To attempt to disentangle these three strands is to do violence to reality. David Danzig's perceptive

Reprinted from *Commentary* 39 (February 1965):25–31.

article, "The Meaning of Negro Strategy," correctly saw in the Birmingham events the victory of the concept of collective struggle over individual achievement as the road to Negro freedom. And Birmingham remains the unmatched symbol of grass-roots protest involving all strata of the black community. It was also in this most industrialized of Southern cities that the single-issue demands of the movement's classical stage gave way to the "package deal." No longer were Negroes satisfied with integrating lunch counters. They now sought advances in employment, housing, school integration, police protection, and so forth.

Thus, the movement in the South began to attack areas of discrimination which were not so remote from the Northern experience as were Jim Crow lunch counters. At the same time, the interrelationship of these apparently distinct areas became increasingly evident. What is the value of winning access to public accommodations for those who lack money to use them? The minute the movement faced this question, it was compelled to expand its vision beyond race relations to economic relations, including the role of education in modern society. And what also became clear is that all these interrelated problems, by their very nature, are not soluble by private, voluntary efforts but require government action—or politics. Already Southern demonstrators had recognized that the most effective way to strike at the police brutality they suffered from was by getting rid of the local sheriff—and that meant political action, which in turn meant, and still means, political action within the Democratic party where the only meaningful primary contests in the South are fought.

And so, in Mississippi, thanks largely to the leadership of Bob Moses, a turn toward political action has been taken. More than voter registration is involved here. A conscious bid for *political power* is being made, and in the course of that effort a tactical shift is being effected: direct-action techniques are being subordinated to a strategy calling for the building of community institutions or power bases. Clearly, the implications of this shift reach far beyond Mississippi. What began as a protest movement is being challenged to translate itself into a political movement. Is this the right course? And if it is, can the transformation be accomplished?

II

The very decade which has witnessed the decline of legal Jim Crow has also seen the rise of *de facto* segregation in our most fundamental socio-economic institutions. More Negroes are unemployed today than in 1954, and the unemployment gap between the races is wider. The median income of Negroes has dropped from 57 per cent to 54 per cent of that of whites. A higher percentage of Negro workers is now concentrated in jobs vulnerable to automation than was the case ten years ago. More Negroes attend *de facto* segregated schools today than when the Supreme Court handed down its famous decision; while school integration proceeds at a snail's pace in the South, the number of Northern schools with an excessive proportion of minority youth proliferates. And behind this is the continuing growth of racial slums, spreading over our central cities and trapping Negro youth in a milieu which, whatever its legal definition, sows an unimaginable demoralization. Again, legal niceties aside, a resident of a racial ghetto lives in segregated housing, and more Negroes fall into this category than ever before.

These are the facts of life which generate frustration in the Negro community and challenge the civil rights movement. At issue, after all, is not *civil rights*, strictly speaking, but social and economic conditions. Last summer's riots were not race riots; they were outbursts of class aggression in a society where class and color definitions are converging disastrously. How can the (perhaps misnamed) civil rights movement deal with this problem?

Before trying to answer, let me first insist that the task of the movement is vastly complicated by the failure of many whites of good will to understand the nature of our problem. There is a widespread assumption that the removal of artificial racial barriers should result in the automatic integration of the Negro into all aspects of American life. This myth is fostered by facile analogies with the experience of various ethnic immigrant groups, particularly the Jews. But the analogies with the Jews do not hold for three simple but profound reasons. First, Jews have a long history as a literate people, a resource which has afforded them opportunities to advance in the academic and professional worlds, to achieve intellectual status even in the midst of economic hardship, and to evolve sustaining value systems in the context of ghetto life. Negroes, for the greater part of their presence in this country, were forbidden by law to read or write. Second, Jews have a long history of family stability, the importance of which in terms of aspiration and self-image is obvious. The Negro family structure was totally destroyed by slavery and with it the possibility of cultural transmission (the right of Negroes to marry and rear children is barely a century old). Third, Jews are white and have the *option* of relinquishing their cultural-religious identity, intermarrying, passing, and so forth. Negroes, or at least the overwhelming majority of them, do not have this option. There is also a fourth, vulgar reason. If the Jewish and Negro communities are not comparable in terms of education, family structure, and color, it is also true that their respective economic roles bear little resemblance.

This matter of economic role brings us to the greater problem—the fact that we are moving into an era in which the natural functioning of the market does not by itself ensure every man with will and ambition a place in the productive process. The immigrant who came to this country during the late nineteenth and early twentieth centuries entered a society which was expanding territorially and/or economically. It was then possible to start at the bottom, as an unskilled or semi-skilled worker, and move up the ladder, acquiring new skills along the way. Especially was this true when industrial unionism was burgeoning, giving new dignity and higher wages to organized workers. Today the situation has changed. We are not expanding territorially, the western frontier is settled, labor organizing has leveled off, our rate of economic growth has been stagnant for a decade. And we are in the midst of a technological revolution which is altering the fundamental structure of the labor force, detroying unskilled and semiskilled jobs—jobs in which Negroes are disproportionately concentrated.

Whatever the pace of this technological revolution may be, the *direction* is clear: the lower rungs of the economic ladder are being lopped off. This means that an individual will no longer be able to start at the bottom and work his way up; he will have to start in the middle or on top, and hold on tight. It will not even be enough to have certain specific skills, for many skilled jobs are also vulnerable to automation. A broad educational background, permitting vocational adaptability and flexibility, seems more imperative than ever. We live in a society where, as Secretary of Labor Williard Wirtz puts it, machines have the equivalent of a high school diploma. Yet the average educational attainment of American Negroes is 8.2 years.

Negroes, of course, are not the only people being affected by these developments. It is reported that there are now 50 per cent fewer unskilled and semi-skilled jobs than there are high school dropouts. Almost one-third of the 26 million young people entering the labor market in the 1960's will be dropouts. But the percentage of Negro dropouts nationally is 57 per cent, and in New York City, among Negroes 25 years of age or over, it is 68 per cent. They are without a future.

To what extent can the kind of self-help campaign recently prescribed by Eric Hoffer in the *New York Times Magazine* cope with such a situation? I would advise those who think that self-help is the answer to familiarize themselves with the long history of such efforts in the Negro community, and to consider why so many foundered on the shoals of ghetto life. It goes without saying that any effort to combat demoralization and apathy is desirable, but we must understand that demoralization in the Negro community is largely a common-sense response to an objective reality. Negro youths have no need of statistics to perceive, fairly accurately, what their odds are in American society. Indeed, from the point of view of motivation, some of the healthiest Negro youngsters I know are juvenile delinquents: vigorously pursuing the American Dream of material acquisition and status, yet finding the conventional means of attaining it blocked off, they do not yield to defeatism but resort to illegal (and often ingenious) methods. They are not alien to American culture. They are, in Gunnar Myrdal's phrase, "exaggerated Americans." To want a Cadillac is not unAmerican; to push a cart in the garment center is. If Negroes are to be persuaded that the conventional path (school, work, and so on) is superior, we had better provide evidence which is now sorely lacking. It is a double cruelty to harangue Negro youth about education and training when we do not know what jobs will be available for them. When a Negro youth can reasonably foresee a future free of slums, when the prospect of gainful employment is realistic, we will see motivation and self-help in abundant enough quantities.

Meanwhile, there is an ironic similarity between the self-help advocated by many liberals and the doctrine of the Black Muslims. Professional sociologists, psychiatrists, and social workers have expressed amazement at the Muslims' success in transforming prostitutes and dope addicts into respectable citizens. But every prostitute the Muslims convert to a model of Calvinist virtue is replaced by the ghetto with two more. Dedicated as they are to maintenance of the ghetto, the Muslims are powerless to affect substantial moral reform. So too with every other group or program which is not aimed at the destruction of slums, their causes and effects. Self-help efforts, directly or indirectly, must be geared to mobilizing people into power units capable of effecting social change. That is, their goal must be genuine self-help, not merely self-improvement. Obviously, where self-improvement activities succeed in imparting to their participants a feeling of some control over their environment, those involved may find their appetites for change whetted; they may move into the political arena.

III

Let me sum up what I have thus far been trying to say: the civil rights movement is evolving from a protest movement into a full-fledged *social movement*—an evolution calling its very name into question. It is now concerned not merely with removing the barriers to full *opportunity* but with achieving the fact of *equality*. From sit-ins and freedom rides we have gone into rent strikes, boycotts, community organizations, and political action. As a consequence of this natural evolution, the Negro today finds himself stymied by obstacles of far greater magnitude than the legal barriers he was attacking before: automation, urban decay, *de facto* school segregation. These are problems which, while conditioned by Jim Crow, do not vanish upon its demise. They are more deeply rooted in our socio-economic order; they are the result of the total society's failure to meet not only the Negro's needs, but human needs generally.

These propositions have won increasing recognition and acceptance, but with a curious twist. They have formed the common premise of two apparently contradictory lines of thought which simultaneously nourish and antagonize each other. On the one hand, there is the reasoning of the New York *Times* moderate who says that the problems are so enormous and complicated that Negro militancy is a futile irritation, and that the need is for "intelligent moderation." Thus, during the first New York school boycott, the *Times* editorialized that Negro demands, while abstractly just, would necessitate massive reforms, the funds for which could not realistically be anticipated; therefore the just demands were also foolish demands and would only antagonize white people. Moderates of this stripe are often correct in perceiving the difficulty or impossibility of racial progress in the context of present social and economic policies. But they accept the context as fixed. They ignore (or perhaps see all too well) the potentialities inherent in linking Negro demands to broader pressures for radical revision of existing policies. They apparently see nothing strange in the fact that in the last twenty-five years we have spent nearly a trillion dollars fighting or preparing for wars, yet throw up our hands before the need for overhauling our schools, clearing the slums, and really abolishing poverty. My quarrel with these moderates is that they do not even envision radical changes; their admonitions of moderation are, for all practical purposes, admonitions to the Negro to adjust to the status quo, and are therefore immoral.

The more effectively the moderates argue their case, the more they convince Negroes that American society will not or cannot be reorganized for full racial equality. Michael Harrington has said that a successful war on poverty might well require the expenditure of a $100 billion. Where, the Negro wonders, are the forces now in motion to compel such a commitment? If the voices of the moderates were raised in an insistence upon a reallocation of national resources at levels that could not be confused with tokenism (that is, if the moderates stopped being moderates), Negroes would have greater grounds for hope. Meanwhile, the Negro movement cannot escape a sense of isolation.

It is precisely this sense of isolation that gives rise to the second line of thought I want to examine—the tendency within the civil rights movement which, despite its militancy, pursues what I call a "no-win" policy. Sharing with many moderates a recognition of the magnitude of the obstacles to freedom, spokesmen for this tendency survey the American scene and find no forces prepared to move toward radical solutions. From this they conclude that the only viable strategy is shock; above all, the hypocrisy of white liberals must be exposed. These spokesmen are often described as the radicals of the movement, but they are really its moralists. They seek to change white hearts—by traumatizing them. Frequently abetted by white self-flagellants, they may gleefully applaud (though not really agreeing with) Malcolm X because, while they admit he has no program, they think he can frighten white people into doing the right thing. To believe this, of course, you must be convinced, even if unconsciously, that at the core of the white man's heart lies a buried affection for Negroes—a proposition one may be permitted to doubt. But in any case, hearts are not relevant to the issue; neither racial affinities nor racial hostilities are rooted there. It is institutions—social, political, and economic institutions —which are the ultimate molders of collective sentiments. Let these institutions be reconstructed *today*, and let the ineluctable gradualism of history govern the formation of a new psychology.

My quarrel with the "no-win" tendency in the civil rights movement (and the reason I have so designated it) parallels my quarrel with the moderates outside the movement. As the latter lack the vision or will for fundamental change, the former lack a realistic strategy for achieving it. For such a strategy they substitute militancy. But militancy is a matter of posture and volume and not of effect.

I believe that the Negro's struggle for equality in America is essentially revolutionary. While most Negroes—in their hearts—unquestionably seek only to enjoy the fruits of American society as it now exists, their quest cannot *objectively* be satisfied within the framework of existing political and economic relations. The young Negro who would demonstrate his way into the labor market may be motivated by a thoroughly bourgeois ambition and thoroughly "capitalist" considerations, but he will end up having to favor a great expansion of the public sector of the economy. At any rate, that is the position the movement will be forced to take as it looks at the number of jobs being generated by the private economy, and if it is to remain true to the masses of Negroes.

The revolutionary character of the Negro's struggle is manifest in the fact that this struggle may have done more to democratize life for whites than for Negroes. Clearly, it was the sit-in movement of young Southern Negroes which, as it galvanized white students, banished the ugliest features of McCarthyism from the American campus and resurrected political debate. It was not until Negroes assaulted *de facto* school segregation in the urban centers that the issue of quality education for *all* children stirred into motion. Finally, it seems reasonably clear that the civil rights movement, directly and through the resurgence of social conscience it kindled, did more to initiate the war on poverty than any other single force.

It will be—it has been—argued that these by-products of the Negro struggle are not revolutionary. But the term revolutionary, as I am using it, does not connote violence; it refers to the qualitative transformation of fundamental institutions, more or less rapidly, to the point where the social and economic structure which they comprised can no longer be said to be the same. The Negro struggle has hardly run its course; and it will not stop moving until it has been utterly defeated or won substantial equality. But I fail to see how the movement can be victorious in the absence of radical programs for full employment, abolition of slums, the reconstruction of our educational system, new definitions of work and leisure. Adding up the cost of such programs, we can only conclude that we are talking about a refashioning of our political economy. It has been estimated, for example, that the price of replacing New York City's slums with public housing would be $17 billion. Again, a multi-billion dollar federal public-works program, dwarfing the currently proposed $2 billion program, is required to reabsorb unskilled and semi-skilled workers into the labor market—and this must be done if Negro workers in these categories are to be employed. "Preferential treatment" cannot help them.

I am not trying here to delineate a total program, only to suggest the scope of economic reforms which are most immediately related to the plight of the Negro community. One could speculate on their political implications—whether, for example, they do not indicate the obsolescence of state government and the superiority of regional structures as viable units of planning. Such speculations aside, it is clear that Negro needs cannot be satisfied unless we go beyond what has so far been placed on the agenda. How are these radical objectives to be achieved? The answer is simple, deceptively so: *through political power.*

There is a strong moralistic strain in the civil rights movement which would remind us that power corrupts, forgetting that the absence of power also corrupts. But this is not the view I want to debate here, for it is waning. Our problem is posed by those who accept the need for political power but do not understand the nature of the object and therefore lack sound strategies for achieving it; they tend to confuse political institutions with lunch counters.

A handful of Negroes, acting alone, could integrate a lunch counter by strategically locating their bodies so as *directly* to interrupt the operation of the proprietor's will: their numbers were relatively unimportant. In politics, however, such a confrontation is difficult becauses the interests involved are merely *represented.* In the execution of a political decision a direct confrontation may ensue (as when federal marshals escorted James Meredith into the University of Mississippi—to turn from an example of non-violent coercion to one of force backed up with the threat of violence). But in arriving at a political decision, numbers and organizations are crucial, especially for the economically disenfranchised. (Needless to say, I am assuming that the forms of political democracy exist in America, however imperfectly, that they are valued, and that elitist or putschist conceptions of exercising power are beyond the pale of discussion for the civil rights movement.)

Neither that movement nor the country's twenty million black people can win political power alone. We need allies. The future of the Negro struggle depends on whether the contradictions of this society can be resolved by a coalition of progressive forces which becomes the *effective* political majority in the United States. I speak of the coalition which staged the March on Washington, passed the Civil Rights Act, and laid the basis for the Johnson landslide—Negroes, trade unionists, liberals, and religious groups.

There are those who argue that a coalition strategy would force the Negro to surrender his political independence to white liberals, that he would be neutralized, deprived of his cutting edge, absorbed into the Establishment. Some who take this position urged last year that votes be withheld from the Johnson-Humphrey ticket as a demonstration of the Negro's political power. Curiously enough, these people who sought to demonstrate power through the non-exercise of it, also point to the Negro "swing vote" in crucial urban areas as the source of the Negro's independent political power. But here they are closer to being right: the urban Negro vote will grow in importance in the coming years. If there is anything positive in the spread of the ghetto, it is the potential political power base thus created, and to realize this potential is one of the most challenging and urgent tasks before the civil right movement. If the movement can wrest leadership of the ghetto vote from the machines, it will have acquired an organized constituency such as other major groups in our society now have.

But we must also remember that the effectiveness of a swing vote depends solely on "other" votes. It derives its power from them. In that sense, it can never be "independent," but must opt for one candidate or the other, even if by default. Thus coalitions are inescapable, however tentative they may be. And this is the case in all but those few situations in which Negroes running on an independent ticket might conceivably win. "Independence," in other words, is not a value in itself. The issue is which coalition to join and how to make it responsive to your program. Necessarily there will be compromise. But the difference between expediency and morality in politics is the difference between selling out a principle and making smaller concessions to win larger ones. The leader who shrinks from this task reveals not his purity but his lack of political sense.

The task of molding a political movement out of the March on Washington coalition is not simple, but no alternatives have been advanced. We need to choose our allies on the basis of common political objectives. It has become fashionable in some no-win Negro circles to decry the white liberal as the main enemy (his hypocrisy is what sustains racism); by virtue of this reverse recitation of the reactionary's litany (liberalism leads to socialism, which leads to Communism) the Negro is left in majestic isolation, except for a tiny band of fervent white initiates. But the objective fact is that *Eastland and Goldwater* are the main enemies—they and the opponents of civil rights, of the war on poverty, of medicare, of social security, of federal aid to education, of unions, and so forth. The labor movement, despite its obvious faults, has been the largest single organized force in this country pushing for progressive social legislation. And where the Negro-labor-liberal axis is weak, as in the farm belt, it was the religious groups that were most influential in rallying support for the Civil Rights Bill.

The durability of the coalition was interestingly tested during the election. I do not believe that the Johnson landslide proved the "white backlash" to be a myth. It proved, rather, that economic interests are more fundamental than prejudice; the backlashers decided that loss of social security was, after all, too high a price to pay for a slap at the Negro. This lesson was a valuable first step in re-educating such people, and it must be kept alive, for the civil rights movement will be advanced only to the degree that social and economic welfare gets to be inextricably entangled with civil rights.

The 1964 elections marked a turning point in American politics. The Democratic landslide was not merely the result of a negative reaction to Goldwaterism; it was also the expression of a majority liberal consensus.

The near unanimity with which Negro voters joined in that expression was, I am convinced, a vindication of the July 25th statement by Negro leaders calling for a strategic turn toward political action and a temporary curtailment of mass demonstrations. Despite the controversy surrounding the statement, the instinctive response it met with in the community is suggested by the fact that demonstrations were down 75 per cent as compared with the same period in 1963. But should so high a percentage of Negro voters have gone to Johnson, or should they have held back to narrow his margin of victory and thus give greater visibility to our swing vote? How has our loyalty changed things? Certainly the Negro vote had higher visibility in 1960, when a switch of only 7 per cent from the Republican column of 1956 elected President Kennedy. But the slimness of Kennedy's victory—of his "mandate"—dictated a go-slow approach on civil rights, at least until the Birmingham upheaval.

Although Johnson's popular majority was so large that he could have won without such overwhelming Negro support, that support was important from several angles. Beyond adding to Johnson's total national margin, it was specifically responsible for his victories in Virginia, Florida, Tennessee, and Arkansas. Goldwater took only those states where fewer than 45 per cent of eligible Negroes were registered. That Johnson would have won those states had Negro voting rights been enforced is a lesson not likely to be lost on a man who would have been happy with a unanimous electoral college. In any case, the 1.6 million Southern Negroes who voted have had a shattering impact on the Southern political party structure, as illustrated in the changed composition of the Southern congressional delegation. The "backlash" gave the Republicans five House seats in Alabama, one in Georgia, and one in Mississippi. But on the Democratic side, seven segregationists were defeated while all nine Southerners who voted for the Civil Rights Act were re-elected. It may be premature to predict a Southern Democratic party of Negroes and white moderates and a Republican Party of refugee racists and economic conservatives, but there certainly is a strong tendency toward such a relignment; and an additional 3.6 million Negroes of voting age in the eleven Southern state are still to be heard from. Even the *tendency* toward disintegration of the Democratic party's racist wing defines a new context for Presidential and liberal strategy in the congressional battles ahead. Thus the Negro vote (North as well as South), while not *decisive* in the Presidential race, was enormously effective. It was a dramatic element of a historic mandate which contains vast possibilities and dangers that will fundamentally affect the future course of the civil rights movement.

The liberal congressional sweep raises hope for an assault on the seniority system, Rule Twenty-two, and other citadels of Dixiecrat-Republican power. The overwhelming of this conservative coalition should also mean progress on much bottlenecked legislations of profound interest to the movement (for instance, bills by Senators Clark and Nelson on planning, manpower, and employment). Moreover, the irrelevance of the South to

Johnson's victory gives the President more freedom to act than his predecessor had and more leverage to the movement to pressure for executive action in Mississippi and other racist strongholds.

None of this *guarantees* vigorous executive or legislative action, for the other side of the Johnson landslide is that it has a Gaullist quality. Goldwater's capture of the Republican party forced into the Democratic camp many disparate elements which do not belong there, Big Business being the major example. Johnson, who wants to be President "of all people," may try to keep his new coalition together by sticking close to the political center. But if he decides to do this, it is unlikely that even his political genius will be able to hold together a coalition so inherently unstable and rife with contradictions. It must come apart. Should it do so while Johnson is pursuing a centrist course, then the mandate will have been wastefully dissipated. However, if the mandate is seized upon to set fundamental changes in motion, then the basis can be laid for a new mandate, a new coalition including hitherto inert and dispossessed strata of the population.

Here is where the cutting edge of the civil rights movement can be applied. We must see to it that the reorganization of the "consensus party" proceeds along lines which will make it an effective vehicle for social reconstruction, a role it cannot play so long as it furnishes Southern racism with its national political power. (One of Barry Goldwater's few attractive ideas was that the Dixiecrats belong with him in the same party). And nowhere has the civil rights movement's political cutting edge been more magnificently demonstrated than at Atlantic City, where the Mississippi Freedom Democratic Party not only secured recognition as a bona fide component of the national party, but in the process routed the representatives of the most rabid racists—the white Mississippi and Alabama delegations. While I still believe that the FDP made a tactical error in spurning the compromises, there is no question that they launched a political revolution whose logic is the displacement of Dixiecrat power. They launched that revolution within a major political institution and as part of a coalitional effort.

The role of the civil rights movement in the reorganization of American political life is programmatic as well as strategic. We are challenged now to broaden our social vision, to develop functional programs with concrete objectives. We need to propose alternatives to technological unemployment, urban decay, and the rest. We need to be calling for public works and training, for national economic planning, for federal aid to education, for attractive public housing—all this on a sufficiently massive scale to make a difference. We need to protest the notion that our integration into American life, so long delayed, must now proceed in an atmosphere of competitive scarcity instead of in the security of abundance which technology makes possible. We cannot claim to have answers to all the complex problems of modern society. That is too much to ask of a movement still battling barbarism in Mississippi. But we can agitate the right questions by probing at the contradictions which still stand in the way of the "Great Society." The questions having been asked, motion must begin in the larger society, for there is a limit to what Negroes can do alone.

27. The Failure of Black Separatism

Bayard Rustin

We are living in an age of revolution—or so they tell us. The children of the affluent classes pay homage to their parents' values by rejecting them; this, they say, is a youth revolution. The discussion and display of sexuality increases—actors disrobe on stage, young women very nearly do on the street—and so we are in the midst of a sexual revolution. Tastes in music and clothing change, and each new fashion too is revolutionary. With every new social phenomenon now being dubbed a "revolution," the term has in fact become nothing more than a slogan which serves to take our minds off an unpleasant reality. For if we were not careful, we might easily forget that there is a conservative in the White House, that our country is racially polarized as never before, and that the forces of liberalism are in disarray. Whatever there is of revolution today, in any meaningful sense of the term, is coming from the Right.

But we are also told—and with far greater urgency and frequency— that there is a black revolution. If by revolution we mean a radical escalation of black aspirations and demands, this is surely the case. There is a new assertion of pride in the Negro race and its cultural heritage, and although the past summer was marked by the lack of any major disruptions, there is among blacks a tendency more pronounced than at any time in Negro history to engage in violence and the rhetoric of violence. Yet if we look closely at the situation of Negroes today, we find that there has been not the least revolutionary reallocation of political or economic power. There is, to be sure, an increase in the number of black elected officials throughout the United States and particularly in the South, but this has largely been the result of the 1965 Voting Rights Act, which was passed before the "revolution" reached its height and the renewal of which the present Administration has not advocated with any

Reprinted from *Harper's* 240 (January 1970): 25–32 ff.

noticeable enthusiasm. Some reallocation of political power has indeed taken place since the Presidential election of 1964, but generally its beneficiaries have been the Republicans and the anti-Negro forces. Nor does this particular trend show much sign of abating. Nixon's attempt to reverse the liberal direction of the Supreme Court has just begun. Moreover, in the 1970 Senate elections, 25 of the 34 seats to be contested were originally won by the Democrats in the great liberal surge of 1964, when the political picture was quite different from that of today. And if the Democrats only break even in 1970, the Republicans will control the Senate for the first time since 1954. A major defeat would leave the Democrats weaker than they have been at any time since the conservative days of the 1920's.

There has been, it is true, some moderate improvement in the economic condition of Negroes, but by no stretch of the imagination could it be called revolutionary. According to Andrew Brimmer of the Federal Reserve System, the median family income of Negroes between 1965 and 1967 rose from 54 per cent to 59 per cent of that for white families. Much of that gain reflected a decrease in the rate of Negro unemployment. But between February and June of 1969, Negro unemployment rose again by 1.3 per cent and should continue to rise as Nixon presses his crusade against inflation. The Council of Economic Advisers reports that in the past eight years the federal government has spent $10.3 billion on metropolitan problems while it has spent $39.9 billion on agriculture, not to mention, of course, $507.2 billion for defense. In the area of housing, for instance, New York City needs at the present time as many new subsidized apartments—780,000—as the federal housing program has constructed *nationally* in its entire thirty-four years. The appropriations for model cities, rent supplements, the Job Corps, the Neighborhood Youth Corps, and other programs have been drastically reduced, and the Office of Economic Opportunity is being transformed into a research agency. Nixon's welfare and revenue-sharing proposals, in addition to being economically stringent, so that they will have little or no effect on the condition of the Northern urban poor, are politically and philosophically conservative.

Any appearance that we are in the grip of a black revolution, then, is deceptive. The problem is not whether black aspirations are outpacing America's ability to respond but whether they have outpaced her willingness to do so. Lately it has been taken almost as axiomatic that with every increase in Negro demands, there must be a corresponding intensification of white resistance. This proposition implies that only black complacency can prevent racial polarization, that any political action by Negroes must of necessity produce a reaction. But such a notion ignores entirely the question of what *kind* of political action, guided by what *kind* of political strategy. One can almost assert as a law of American politics that if Negroes engage in violence as a tactic they will be met with repression, that if they follow a strategy of racial separatism they will be isolated, and that if they engage in anti-democratic activity, out of the deluded wish to skirt the democratic process, they will provoke a reaction. To the misguided, violence, separatism, and minority ultimatums may seem revolutionary, but in reality they issue only from the desperate strivings of the impotent. Certainly such tactics are not designed to enhance the achievement of progressive social change. Recent American political history has proved this point time and again with brutal clarity.

The irony of the revolutionary rhetoric uttered in behalf of Negroes is that it has helped in fact to promote conservatism. On the other hand, of course, the reverse is also true: the failure of America to respond to the demands of Negroes has fostered in the minds of the latter a sense of futility and has thus seemed to legitimize a strategy of withdrawal and violence. Other things have been operating as well. The fifteen years since *Brown versus Topeka* have been for Negroes a period of enormous dislocation. The modernization of farming in the South forced hundreds of thousands of Negroes to migrate to the North where they were confronted by a second technological affliction, automation. Without jobs, living in cities equipped to serve neither their material nor spiritual needs, these modern-day immigrants responded to their brutal new world with despair and hostility. The civil-rights movement created an even more fundamental social dislocation, for it destroyed not simply the legal structure of segregation but also the psychological assumptions of racism. Young Negroes who matured during this period witnessed a basic challenge to the system of values and social relations which had presumed the inferiority of the Negro. They have totally rejected this system, but in doing so have often substituted for it an exaggerated and distorted perception both of themselves and of the society. As if to obliterate the trace of racial shame that might be lurking in their souls they have embraced racial chauvinism. And as if in reply to past exclusions (and often in response to present insecurities), they have created their own patterns of exclusiveness.

The various frustrations and upheavals experienced recently by the Negro community account in large part for the present political orientation of some of its most vocal members: seeing their immediate self-interest more in the terms of emotional release than in those of economic and political advancement. One is supposed to think black, dress black, eat black, and buy black without reference to the question of what such a program actually contributes to advancing the cause of social justice. Since real victories are thought to be unattainable, issues become important in so far as they can provide symbolic victories. Dramatic confrontations are staged which serve as outlets for radical energy but which in no way further the achievement of radical social goals. So that, for instance, members of the black community are mobilized to pursue the "victory" of halting construction of a state office building in Harlem, even though it is hard to see what actual economic or social benefit will be conferred on the impoverished residents of that community by their success in doing so.

Such actions constitute a politics of escape rooted in hopelessness and further reinforced by government inaction. Deracinated liberals may romanticize this politics, nihilistic New Leftists may imitate it, but it is ordinary Negroes who will be the victims of its powerlessness to work any genuine change in their condition.

The call for Black Power is now over three years old, yet to this day no one knows what Black Power is supposed to mean and therefore how its proponents are to unite and rally behind it. If one is a member of CORE, Black Power posits the need for a separate black economy based upon traditional forms of capitalist relations. For SNCC the term refers to a politically united black community. US would emphasize the unity of black culture, while the Black Panthers wish to impose upon black nationalism the philosophies of Marx, Lenin, Stalin, and Chairman Mao. Nor do these exhaust all the possible shades and gradations of meaning. If there is one common theme uniting the various demands for Black Power, it is simply that blacks must be guided in their actions by a consciousness of themselves as a separate race.

Now, philosophies of racial solidarity have never been unduly concerned with the realities that operate outside the category of race. The adherents of these philosophies are generally romantics, steeped in the traditions of their own particular clans and preoccupied with the simple biological verities of blood and racial survival. Almost invariably their rallying cry is racial self-determination, and they tend to ignore those aspects of the material world which point up divisions within the racially defined group.

But the world of black Americans is full of divisions. Only the most supine of optimists would dream of building a political movement without reference to them. Indeed, nothing better illustrates the existence of such divisions within the black community than the fact that the separatists themselves represent a distinct minority among Negroes. No reliable poll has ever identified more than 15 per cent of Negroes as separatists; usually the percentage is a good deal lower. Nor, as I have already indicated, are the separatists unified among themselves, the differences among them at times being so intense as to lead to violent conflict. The notion of the undifferentiated black community is the intellectual creation of both whites—liberals as well as racists to whom all Negroes are the same—and of certain small groups of blacks who illegitimately claim to speak for the majority.

The fact is that like every other racial or ethnic group in America, Negroes are divided by age, class, and geography. Young Negroes are at least as hostile toward their elders as white New Leftists are toward their liberal parents. They are in addition separated by vast gaps in experience, Northern from Southern, urban from rural. And even more profound are the disparities in wealth among them. In contrast to the white community, where the spread of income has in recent years remained unchanged or has narrowed slightly, economic differentials among blacks have increased. In 1965, for example, the wealthiest 5 per cent of white and non-white families each received 15.5 per cent of the total income in their respective communities. In 1967, however, the percentage of white income received by the top 5 per cent of the white families had dropped to 14.9 per cent while among non-whites the share of income of the top 5 per cent of the families had risen to 17.5 per cent. This trend probably reflects the new opportunities which are available to black professionals in industry, government, and academia, but have not touched the condition of lower-class and lower-middle-class Negroes.

To Negroes for whom race is the major criterion, however, divisions by wealth and status are irrelevant. Consider, for instance, the proposals for black economic advancement put forth by the various groups of black nationalists. These proposals are all remarkably similar. For regardless of one's particular persuasion—whether a revolutionary or a cultural nationalist or an unabashed black capitalist—once one confines one's analysis to the ghetto, no proposal can extend beyond a strategy for ghetto development and black enterprise. This explains in part the recent popularity of black capitalism and, to a lesser degree, black cooperatives: once both the economic strategy and goal are defined in terms of black self-determination, there is simply not much else available in the way of ideas.

There are other reasons for the popularity of black capitalism, reasons having to do with material and psychological self-interest. E. Franklin Frazier has written that Negro business is "a social myth" first formulated toward the end of the nineteenth century when the legal structure of segregation was established and Negro hopes for equality destroyed. History has often shown us that oppression can sometimes lead to a rationalization of the unjust conditions on the part of the oppressed and following on this, to an opportunistic competition among them for whatever meager advantages are available. This is, according to Frazier, exactly what happened among American Negroes. The myth of Negro business was created and tied to a belief in the possibility of a separate Negro economy. "Of course," wrote Frazier, "behind the idea of the separate Negro economy is the hope of the black bourgeoisie that they will have the monopoly of the Negro market." He added that they also desire "a privileged status within the isolated Negro community."

Nor are certain Negro businessmen the only ones who stand to gain from a black economy protected by the tariff of separatism. There are also those among the white upper class for whom such an arrangement is at least as beneficial. In the first place, self-help projects for the ghetto, of which black capitalism is but one variety, are inexpensive. They in-

volve no large-scale redistribution of resources, no "inflationary" government expenditures, and above all, no responsibility on the part of whites.
These same upper-class whites may have been major exploiters of black
workers in the past, they may have been responsible for policies which
helped to create ghetto poverty, but now, under the new dispensations
of black separatism, they are being asked to do little more by way of
reparation than provide a bit of seed money for a few small ghetto enterprises.

Moreover, a separate black economy appears to offer hope for what
Roy Innis has called "a new social contract." According to Innis's theory,
the black community is essentially a colony ruled by outsiders: there
can be no peace between the colony and the "mother country" until the
former is ruled by some of its own. When the colony is finally "liberated"
in this way, all conflicts can be resolved through negotiation between
the black ruling class and the white ruling class. Any difficulties within
the black community, that is, would become the responsibility of the
black elite. But since self-determination in the ghetto, necessitating as it
would the expansion of a propertied black middle class, offers the advantage of social stability, such difficulties would be minimal. How could
many whites fail to grasp the obvious benefit to themselves in a program
that promises social peace without the social inconvenience of integration
and especially without the burden of a huge expenditure of money?
Even if one were to accept the colonial analogy—and it is in many ways
an uninformed and extremely foolish one—the strategy implied by it is
fatuous and unworkable. Most of the experiments in black capitalism
thus far have been total failures. As, given the odds, they should continue to be. For one thing, small businesses owned and run by blacks
will, exactly like their white counterparts, suffer a high rate of failure.
In fact, they will face even greater problems than white small businesses
because they will be operating in predominantly low income areas where
the clientele will be poor, the crime rate and taxes high, and the cost of
land, labor, and insurance expensive. They will have to charge higher
prices than the large chains, a circumstance against which "Buy Black"
campaigns will in the long or even the short run have little force. On
the other hand, to create large-scale black industry in the ghetto is unthinkable. The capital is not available, and even if it were, there is no
vacant land. In Los Angeles, for example, the area in which four-fifths
of the Negroes and Mexican-Americans live contains only 0.5 per cent
of all the vacant land in the city, and the problem is similar elsewhere.
Overcrowding is severe enough in the ghetto without building up any
industry there.

Another current axiom of black self-determination is the necessity for
community control. Questions of ideology aside, black community control
is as futile a program as black capitalism. Assuming that there were a
cohesive, clearly identifiable black community (which, judging by the

factionalism in neighborhoods like Harlem and Ocean Hill-Brownsville, is a far from safe assumption), and assuming that the community were empowered to control the ghetto, it would still find itself without the money needed in order to be socially creative. The ghetto would still be faced with the same poverty, deteriorated housing, unemployment, terrible health services, and inferior schools—and this time perhaps with the exacerbation of their being entailed in local struggles for power. Furthermore, the control would ultimately be illusory and would do no more than provide psychological comfort to those who exercise it. For in a complex technological society there is no such thing as an autonomous community within a large metropolitan area. Neighborhoods, particularly poor neighborhoods, will remain dependent upon outside suppliers for manufactured goods, transportation, utilities, and other services. There is, for instance, unemployment in the ghetto while the vast majority of new jobs are being created in the suburbs. If black people are to have access to those jobs, there must be a metropolitan transportation system that can carry them to the suburbs cheaply and quickly. Control over the ghetto cannot build such a system nor can it provide jobs within the ghetto.

The truth of the matter is that community control as an idea is provincial and as a program is extremely conservative. It appears radical to some people because it has become the demand around which the frustrations of the Negro community have coalesced. In terms of its capacity to deal with the social and economic causes of black unrest, however, its potential is strikingly limited. The call for community control in fact represents an adjustment to inequality rather than a protest against it. Fundamentally, it is a demand for a change in the racial composition of the personnel who administer community institutions: that is, for schools, institutions of public and social service, and political organizations—as all of these are presently constituted—to be put into the keeping of a new class of black officials. Thus in a very real sense, the notion of community control bespeaks a fervent hope that the poverty-stricken ghetto, once thought to be a social problem crying for rectification, might now be deemed a social good worthy of acceptance. Hosea Williams of SCLC, speaking once of community control, unwittingly revealed the way in which passionate self-assertion can be a mask for accommodation: "I'm now at the position Booker T. Washington was about sixty or seventy years ago," Williams said. "I say to my brothers, 'Cast down your buckets where you are'—and that means there in the slums and ghettos."

There is indeed profound truth in the observation that people who seek social change will, in the absence of real substantive victories, often seize upon stylistic substitutes as an outlet for their frustrations.

A case in point is the relation of Negroes to the trade-union movement. In their study *The Black Worker*, published in 1930. Sterling D.

Spero and Abraham L. Harris describe the resistance to separatism among economically satisfied workers during the heyday of Marcus Garvey:

> spokesmen of the Garvey movement went among the faction-torn workers preaching the doctrine of race consciousness. Despite the fact the Garvey-ism won a following everywhere at this time, the Negro longshoremen of Philadelphia were deaf to its pleas, for their labor movement had won them industrial equality such as colored workers nowhere else in the industry enjoyed.

The inverse relation of black separatism and anti-unionism to the quality of employment available to Negroes holds true today also. In the May 1969 UAW elections, for example, black candidates won the presidency and vice-presidency of a number of locals. Some of the most interesting election victories were won at the Chrysler Eldon Gear and Axle Local 961 and at Dodge #3 in Hamtramck where the separatist Eldon Revolutionary Union Movement (ELRUM) and Dodge Revolutionary Union Movement (DRUM) have been active. At both locals the DRUM and ELRUM candidates were handily defeated by black trade unionists who campaigned on a program of militant integrationism and economic justice.

This is not to say that there are not problems within the unions which have given impetus to the separatist movements. There are, but in the past decade unions have taken significant steps toward eliminating discrimination against Negroes. As Peter Henle, the chief economist of the Bureau of Labor Statistics, has observed:

> Action has been taken to eliminate barriers to admission, abolish discrimination in hiring practices, and negotiate changes in seniority arrangements which had been blocking Negro advances to higher-paying jobs. At the same time, unions have given strong support to governmental efforts in this same direction.

Certainly a good deal is left to be done in this regard, but just as certainly the only effective pressure on the unions is that which can be brought by blacks pressing for a greater role *within* the trade-union movement. Not only is separatism not a feasible program, but its major effect will be to injure black workers economically by undermining the strength of their union. It is here that ignorance of the economic dimension of racial injustice is most dangerous, for a Negro, whether he be labeled a moderate or a militant, has but two alternatives open to him. If he defines the problem as primarily one of race, he will inevitably find himself the ally of the white capitalist against the white worker. But if, though always conscious of the play of racial discrimination, he defines the problem as one of poverty, he will be aligned with the white worker against management. If he chooses the former alternative, he will become no more than a pawn in the game of divide-and-conquer played by, and for the benefit of, management—the result of which will hardly be self-determination but rather the depression of wages for all workers. This path was followed by the "moderate" Booker T. Washington who disliked unions because they were "founded on a sort of enmity to the man by whom he [the Negro] is employed" and by the "militant" Marcus Garvey who wrote:

> It seems strange and a paradox, but the only convenient friend the Negro worker or laborer has in America at the present time is the white capitalist. The capitalist being selfish—seeking only the largest profit out of labor—is willing and glad to use Negro labor wherever possible on a scale reasonably below the standard union wage . . . but if the Negro unionizes himself to the level of the white worker, the choice and preference of employment is given to the white worker.

And it is being followed today by CORE, which collaborated with the National Right to Work Committee in setting up the Black Workers Alliance.

If the Negro chooses to follow the path of interracial alliances on the basis of class, as almost two million have done today, he can achieve a certain degree of economic dignity, which in turn offers a genuine, if not the only, opportunity for self-determination. It was this course which A. Philip Randolph chose in his long struggle to build a Negro-labor alliance, and it was also chosen by the black sanitation workers of Memphis, Tennessee, and the black hospital workers of Charleston, South Carolina.

Not that I mean here to exonerate the unions of their responsibility for discrimination. Nevertheless, it is essential to deal with the situation of the black worker in terms of American economic reality. And as long as the structure of this reality is determined by the competing institutions of capital and labor (or government and labor, as in the growing public sector of the economy), Negroes must place themselves on one side or the other. The idea of racial self-determination within this context is a delusion.

There are, to be sure, sources beyond that of economic discrimination for black separatism within the unions. DRUM, ELRUM, and similar groups are composed primarily of young Negroes who, like whites their age, are not as loyal to the union as are older members, and who are also affected by the new militancy which is now pervasive among black youth generally. This militancy has today found its most potent form of expression on campus, particularly in the predominantly white universities outside of the South. The confusion which the movement for programs in black studies has created on campus almost defies description. The extremes in absurdity were reached this past academic year at Cornell, where, on the one hand, enraged black students were demanding a program in black studies which included Course 300c, Physical Education: "Theory and practice in the use of small arms and hand combat. Discussion sessions in the proper use of force," and where, on the other hand, a masochistic and pusillanimous university president placed his airplane at the disposal of two black students so that they could go to New York City and purchase, with $2,000 in university funds, some bongo drums for Malcolm X Day. The foolishness of the students was surpassed only by the public-relations manipulativeness of the president.

The real tragedy of the dispute over black studies is that whatever truly creative opportunities such a program could offer have been either ignored or destroyed. There is, first, the opportunity for a vastly expanded scholastic inquiry into the contribution of Negroes to the American experience. The history of the black man in America has been scandalously distorted in the past, and as a field of study it has been relegated to a second-class status, isolated from the main themes of American history and omitted in the historical education of American youth. Yet now black students are preparing to repeat the errors of their white predecessors. They are proposing to study black history in isolation from the mainstream of American history: they are demanding separate black-studies programs that will not be open to whites, who could benefit at least as much as they from a knowledge of Negro history; and they hope to permit only blacks (and perhaps some whites who toe the line) to teach in these programs. Unwittingly they are conceding what racist whites all along have professed to believe, namely that black history is irrelevant to American history.

In other ways black students have displayed contempt for black studies as an academic discipline. Many of them, in fact, view black studies as not an academic subject at all, but as an ideological and political one. They propose to use black-studies programs to create a mythologized history and a system of assertive ideas that will facilitate the political mobilization of the black community. In addition, they hope to educate a cadre of activists whose present training is conceived of as a preparation for organizational work in the ghetto. The Cornell students made this very clear when they defined the purpose of black-studies programs as enabling "black people to use the knowledge gained in the classroom and the community to formulate new ideologies and philosophies which will contribute to the development of the black nation."

Thus faculty members will be chosen on the basis of race, ideological purity, and political commitment—not academic competence. Under such conditions, few qualified black professors will want to teach in black-studies programs, not simply because their academic freedom will be curtailed but their obligation to adhere to the revolutionary "line" of the moment, but because their professional status will be threatened by their association with programs of such inferior quality.

Black students are also forsaking the opportunity to get an education. They appear to be giving little thought to the problem of teaching or learning those technical skills that all students must acquire if they are to be effective in their careers. We have here simply another example of the pursuit of symbolic victory where a real victory seems too difficult to achieve. It is easier for a student to alter his behavior and appearance than to improve the quality of his mind. If engineering requires too much concentration, then why not a course in soul music. If Plato is both "irrelevant" and difficult, the student can read Malcolm X instead. Class will be a soothing, comfortable experience, somewhat like watching television. Moreover, one's image will be militant and, therefore, acceptable by current college standards. Yet one will have learned nothing, and the fragile sense of security developed in the protective environment of college will be cracked when exposed to the reality of competition in the world.

Nelson Taylor, a young Negro graduate of Morehouse College, recently observed that many black students "feel it is useless to try to compete. In order to avoid this competition, they build themselves a little cave to hide in." This "little cave," he added, is black studies. Furthermore, black students are encouraged in this escapism by guilt-ridden New Leftists and faculty members who despise themselves and their advantaged lives and enjoy seeing young Negroes reject "white middle class values" and disrupt the university. They are encouraged by university administrators who prefer political accommodation to an effort at serious education. But beyond the momentary titillation some may experience from being the center of attention, it is difficult to see how Negroes can in the end benefit from being patronized and manipulated in this way. Ultimately, their only permanent satisfaction can come from the certainty that they have acquired the technical and intellectual skills that will enable them upon graduation to perform significant jobs competently and with confidence. If they fail to acquire these skills, their frustration will persist and find expression in ever-newer forms of antisocial and self-destructive behavior.

The conflict over black studies, as over other issues, raises the question of the function in general served by black protest today. Some black demands, such as that for a larger university enrollment of minority students, are entirely legitimate; but the major purpose of the protest through which these demands are pressed would seem to be not so much to pursue an end as to establish in the minds of the protesters, as well as in the minds of whites, the reality of their rebellion. Protest, therefore, becomes an end in itself and not a means toward social change. In this sense, the black rebellion is an enormously *expressive* phenomenon which is releasing the pent-up resentments of generations of oppressed Negroes. But expressiveness that is oblivious to political reality and not structured by instrumental goals is mere bombast.

James Forman's *Black Manifesto*, for instance, provides a nearly perfect sample of this kind of bombast combined with positive delusions of grandeur. "We shall liberate all the people in the U.S.," the introduction to the *Manifesto* declares, "and we will be instrumental in the liberation of colored people the world around. . . . We are the most humane people within the U.S. . . . . Racism in the U.S. is so pervasive in the mentality of whites that only an armed, well-disciplined, black-controlled government can insure the stamping out of racism in this country. . . . We say think in terms of the total control of the U.S."

One might never imagine from reading the *Manifesto* that Forman's organization, the National Black Economic Development Conference, is politically powerless, or that the institution it has chosen for assault is not the government or the corporations, but the church. Indeed, the exaggeration of language in the *Black Manifesto* is directly proportional to the isolation and impotence of those who drafted it. And their actual achievements provide an accurate measure of their strength. Three billion dollars in reparations was demanded—and $20,000 received. More important, the effect of this demand upon the Protestant churches has been to precipitate among them a conservative reaction against the activities of the liberal national denominations and the National Council of Churches. Forman's failure, of course, was to be expected: the only effect of an attack upon so organizationally diffuse and nonpolitical an institution as the church can be the deflection of pressure away from the society's major political and economic institutions and, consequently, the weakening of the black movement for equality.*

The possibility that his *Manifesto* might have exactly the opposite effect from that intended, however, was clearly not a problem to Forman, because the demands he was making upon white people were more moral than political or economic. His concern was to purge white guilt far more than to seek social justice for Negroes. It was in part for this reason that he chose to direct his attack at the church, which, as the institutional embodiment of our society's religious pretensions, is vulnerable to moral condemnation.

Yet there is something corrupting in the wholesale release of aggressive moral energy, particularly when it is in response to the demand for reparations for blacks. The difficulty is not only that as a purely racial demand its effect must be to isolate blacks from the white poor with whom they have common economic interests. The call for three billion dollars in reparations demeans the integrity of blacks and exploits the self-demeaning guilt of whites. It is insulting to Negroes to offer them reparations for past generations of suffering, as if the balance of an irreparable past could be set straight with a handout. In a recent poll, *Newsweek* reported that "today's proud Negroes, by an overwhelming 84 to 10 per cent, reject the idea of preferential treatment in hiring or college admissions in reparation for past injustices." There are few controversial issues that can call forth greater uniformity of opinion than this in the Negro community.

---

* Forman is not the only militant today who fancies that his essentially reformist program is revolutionary. Eldridge Cleaver has written that capitalists regard the Black Panther Breakfast for Children program (which the Panthers claim feeds 10,000 children) "as a threat, as cutting into the goods that are under their control." He also noted that it "liberates" black children from going to school hungry each morning. I wonder if he would also find public-school lunch programs liberating.

I also question both the efficacy and the social utility of an attack that impels the attacked to applaud and debase themselves. I am not certain whether or not self-flagellation can have a beneficial effect on the sinner (I tend to doubt that it can), but I am absolutely certain it can never produce anything politically creative. It will not improve the lot of the unemployed and the ill-housed. On the other hand, it could well happen that the guilty party, in order to lighten his uncomfortable moral burden, will finally begin to rationalize his sins and affirm them as virtues. And by such a process, today's ally can become tomorrow's enemy. Lasting political alliances are not built on the shifting sands of moral suasion.

On his part, the breast-beating white makes the same error as the Negro who swears that "black is beautiful." Both are seeking refuge in psychological solutions to social questions. And both are reluctant to confront the real cause of racial injustice, which is not bad attitudes but bad social conditions. The Negro creates a new psychology to avoid the reality of social stagnation, and the white—be he ever so liberal—professes his guilt precisely so as to create the illusion of social change, all the while preserving his economic advantages.

The response of guilt and pity to social problems is by no means new. It is, in fact, as old as man's capacity to rationalize or his reluctance to make real sacrifices for his fellow man. Two hundred years ago, Samuel Johnson, in an exchange with Boswell, analyzed the phenomenon of sentimentality:

> Boswell: "I have often blamed myself, Sir, for not feeling for others, as sensibly as many say they do."
> Johnson: "Sir, don't be duped by them any more. You will find these very feeling people are not very ready to do you good. They *pay* you by *feeling*."

Today, payments from the rich to the poor take the form of "Giving a Damn" or some other kind of moral philanthropy. At the same time, of course, some of those who so passionately "Give a Damn" are likely to argue that full employment is inflationary.

We are living in a time of great social confusion—not only about the strategies we must adopt but about the very goals these strategies are to bring us to. Only recently whites and Negroes of good will were pretty much in agreement that racial and economic justice required an end to segregation and the expansion of the role of the federal government. Now it is a mark of "advancement," not only among "progressive" whites but among the black militants as well, to believe that integration is passé. Unintentionally (or as the Marxists used to say, objectively), they are lending aid and comfort to traditional segregationists like Senators Eastland and Thurmond. Another "advanced" idea is the notion that government has gotten too big and that what is needed to make the society more humane and livable is an enormous new move toward local participation and decentralization. One cannot question the value or importance of democratic participation in the government, but just as misplaced sympathy for Negroes is being put to use by segregationists, the liberal preoccupation with localism is serving the cause of conservatism. Two years of liberal encomiums to decentralization have intellectually legitimized the concept, if not the name, of states' rights and have set the stage for the widespread acceptance of Nixon's "New Federalism."

The new anti-integrationism and localism may have been motivated by sincere moral conviction, but hardly by intelligent political thinking. It should be obvious that what is needed today more than ever is a political strategy that offers the real possibility of economically uplifting millions of impoverished individuals, black and white. Such a strategy must of necessity give low priority to the various forms of economic and psychological experimentation that I have discussed, which at best deal with issues peripheral to the central problem and at worst embody a frenetic escapism. These experiments are based on the assumption that the black community can be transformed from within when, in fact, any such transformation must depend on structural changes in the entire society. Negro poverty, for example, will not be eliminated in the absence of a total war on poverty. We need therefore, a new national economic policy. We also need new policies in housing, education, and health care which can deal with these problems as they relate to Negroes within the context of a national solution. A successful strategy, therefore, must rest upon an identification of those central institutions which, if altered sufficiently, would transform the social and economic relations in our society; and it must provide a politically viable means of achieving such an alteration.

Surely the church is not a central institution in this sense. Nor is Roy Innis's notion of dealing with the banking establishment a useful one. For the banks will find no extra profit—quite the contrary—in the kind of fundamental structural change in society that is required.*

Moreover, the recent flurry of excitement over the role of private industry in the slums seems to have subsided. A study done for the Urban Coalition has called the National Alliance of Businessmen's claim to have hired more than 100,000 hard-core unemployed a "phony numbers game." Normal hiring as the result of expansion or turnover was in some cases counted as recruitment. Where hard-core workers have been hired and trained, according to the study, "The primary motivation . . . is the need for new sources of workers in a tight labor market. If and when the need for workers slackens, so will industry's performance." This has already occurred. The *Wall Street Journal* reported in July of 1969 that

---

* Innis's demand that the white banks deposit $6 billion in black banks as reparations for past injustices should meet with even less success than Forman's ill-fated enterprise. At least Forman had the benefit of the white churchman's guilt, an emotion not known to be popular among bankers.

the Ford Motor Company, once praised for its social commitment, was forced to trim back production earlier in the year and in the process "quietly closed its two inner-city hiring centers in Detroit and even laid off some of the former hard cores it had only recently hired." There have been similar retrenchments by other large companies as the result of a slackening in economic growth, grumblings from stockholders, and the realization by corporate executives that altruism does not make for high profits. Yet even if private industry were fully committed to attack the problem of unemployment, it is not in an ideal position to do so. Private enterprise, for example, accounted for only one out of every ten new jobs created in the economy between 1950 and 1960. Most of the remainder were created as the result of expansion of public employment.

While the church, private enterprise, and other institutions can, if properly motivated, play an important role, finally it is the trade-union movement and the Democratic party which offer the greatest leverage to the black struggle. The serious objective of Negroes must be to strengthen and liberalize these. The trade-union movement is essential to the black struggle because it is the only institution in the society capable of organizing the working poor, so many of whom are Negroes. It is only through an organized movement that these workers, who are now condemned to the margin of the economy, can achieve a measure of dignity and economic security. I must confess I find it difficult to understand the prejudice against the labor movement currently fashionable among so many liberals. These people, somehow for reasons of their own, seem to believe that white workers are affluent members of the Establishment (a rather questionable belief, to put it mildly, especially when held by people earning over $25,000 a year) and are now trying to keep the Negroes down. The only grain of truth here is that there *is* competition between black and white workers which derives from a scarcity of jobs and resources. But rather than propose an expansion of those resources, our stylish liberals underwrite that competition by endorsing the myth that the unions are the worst enemy of the Negro.

In fact it is the program of the labor movement that represents a genuine means for reducing racial competition and hostility. Not out of a greater tenderness of feeling for black suffering—but that is just the point. Unions organize workers on the basis of common economic interests, not by virtue of racial affinity. Labor's legislative program for full employment, housing, urban reconstruction, tax reform, improved health care, and expanded educational opportunities is designed specifically to aid both whites and blacks in the lower- and lower-middle classes where the potential for racial polarization is most severe. And only a program of this kind can deal simultaneously and creatively with the interrelated problems of black rage and white fear. It does not placate black rage at the expense of whites, thereby increasing white fear and political reaction. Nor does it exploit white fear by repressing blacks.

Either of these courses strengthens the demagogues among both races who prey upon frustration and racial antagonism. Both of them help to strengthen conservative forces—the forces that stand to benefit from the fact that hostility between black and white workers keep them from uniting effectively around issues of common economic interest.

President Nixon is in the White House today largely because of this hostility; and the strategy advocated by many liberals to build a "new coalition" of the affluent, the young, and the dispossessed is designed to keep him there. The difficulty with this proposed new coalition is not only that its constituents comprise a distinct minority of the population, but that its affluent and youthful members—regardless of the momentary directions of their rhetoric—are hardly the undisputed friends of the poor. Recent Harris polls, in fact, have shown that Nixon is most popular among the college educated and the young. Perhaps they were attracted by his style or the minimal concessions he has made on Vietnam, but certainly their approval cannot be based upon his accomplishments in the areas of civil rights and economic justice.

If the Republican ascendancy is to be but a passing phenomenon, it must once more come to be clearly understood among those who favor social progress that the Democratic party is still the only mass-based political organization in the country with the potential to become a majority movement for social change. And anything calling itself by the name of political activity must be concerned with building precisely such a majority movement. In addition, Negroes must abandon once and for all the false assumption that as 10 per cent of the population they can by themselves effect basic changes in the structure of American life. They must, in other words, accept the necessity of coalition politics. As a result of our fascination with novelty and with the "new" revolutionary forces that have emerged in recent years, it seems to some the height of conservatism to propose a strategy that was effective in the past. Yet the political reality is that without a coalition of Negroes and other minorities with the trade-union movement and with liberal groups, the shift of power to the Right will persist and the democratic Left in America will have to content itself with a well-nigh permanent minority status.

The bitterness of many young Negroes today has led them to be unsympathetic to a programs based on the principles of trade unionism and electoral politics. Their protest represents a refusal to accept the condition of inequality, and in that sense it is part of the long, and I think, magnificent black struggle for freedom. But with no comprehensive strategy to replace the one I have suggested, their protest, though militant in rhetoric and intention, may be reactionary in effect.

The strategy I have outlined must stand or fall by its capacity to achieve political and economic results. It is not intended to provide some new wave of intellectual excitement. It is not intended to suggest a new style of life or a means to personal salvation for disaffected members of the middle class. Nor is either of these the proper role of politics. My strategy is not meant to appeal to the fears of threatened whites, though it would calm those fears and increase the likelihood that someday we shall have a truly integrated society. It is not meant to serve as an outlet for the terrible frustrations of Negroes, though it would reduce those frustrations and point a way to dignity for an oppressed people. It is simply a vehicle by which the wealth of this nation can be redistributed and some of its more grievous social problems solved. This in itself would be quite enough to be getting on with. In fact, if I may risk a slight exaggeration, by normal standards of human society I think it would constitute a revolution.

28. The Decline of the WASP
Peter Schrag

For most of us who were born before World War II, America was a place to be discovered: it was imperfect, perhaps—needed some reform, some shaping up—but it did not need to be reinvented. It was all given, like a genetic code, waiting to unfold. We all wanted to learn the style, the proper accent, agreed on its validity, and while our interpretations and our heroes varied, they were all cut from the same stock. Cowboys, pioneers, athletes, entrepreneurs, men of letters: whatever we were offered we took pretty much as our own. Whether we were small-town boys or the children of urban immigrants, we shared an eagerness to become apprentices in the great open democracy, were ready to join up, wanting only to be accepted according to the terms that history and tradition had already established. It never occurred to us to think otherwise.

What held that world together was not just a belief in some standardized version of textbook Americanism, a catalogue of accepted values, but a particular class of people and institutions that we identified with our vision of the country. The people were white and Protestant; the institutions were English; American culture was WASP. We paid lip service to the melting pot, but if, for instance, one's grandmother asked, "Is it good for the Jews?" there wasn't any question in her mind about who was running the country. The critics, the novelists, the poets, the social theorists, the men who articulated and analyzed American ideas, who governed our institutions, who embodied what we were or hoped to be—

Reprinted from *Harper's* 240 (April 1970):85–91. Reprinted by permission of Curtis Brown Ltd. Copyright © 1972 by Simon and Schuster.

nearly all of them were WASPs: Hemingway, Fitzgerald, Eliot, MacLeish, Sandburg, Lewis, Steinbeck, Dewey, Santayana, the Jameses, Beard, Parrington, Edmund Wilson, Van Wyck Brooks, Lester Frank Ward, Oliver Wendell Holmes: *The Saturday Evening Post* under George Horace Lorimer (with covers by Norman Rockwell); *The Atlantic* under Edward Weeks; *Harper's* in the days of Frederick Lewis Allen—to name only a few, and only from the twentieth century. Of all the major figures discussed by Henry Steele Commager in *The American Mind*, not one is a Jew, a Catholic, or a Negro. The American mind was the WASP mind.

We grew up with them; they surrounded us: they were the heroes of the history we studied and of the fantasy life we sought in those Monday-through-Friday radio serials. Even Hollywood, after all the creation of Jewish producers, never did much for pluralism. The stars were often ethnics—show business and sports constituting two major avenues for "outsiders" to make it into the mainstream—but their names and the roles they played rarely, if ever, acknowledged the existence of anything beyond that mainstream. The Hyman Kaplans were joyable jerks, immigrant Sambos; Rochester said, "Yassuh, Mr. Benny" (did we realize that Benny was a Jew?) and anything beginning with Mike, Pat, or Abie was set up for a laugh. Hollywood's Jews sold the American dream strictly in WASP terms.

They—the WASPs—never thought of themselves as anything but Americans, nor did it occur to others to label them as anything special until, about twenty-five years ago, their influence began to decline and they started to lose their cultural initiative and preeminence. There were, to be sure, regional distinctions, but whatever was "American" was WASP. Indeed, there was no "other"—was, that is, no domestic base of social commentary, no voice except their voice, for the discussion of "American" problems. The ethnics had their place and their strong loyalties, but insofar as that place was *American* it was defined by WASPs. We could distinguish Jews, Irishmen, Italians, Catholics, Poles, Negroes, Indians, Mexican-Americans, Japanese-Americans, but not WASPs. When WASPs were alienated it was because, as in the case of Henry Adams, the country had moved away from them, not because, as with the others, they regarded themselves as alien in heritage or tradition. (Southerners who had lost their war and their innocence were—in that respect—alien, ethnically WASPs but also in some sense unwilling immigrants; they were among the first to be out of place in their own country.) For most WASPs, their complaints were proprietary. That is, the old place was going down because the tenants weren't keeping it up properly. They were the landlords of our culture, and their values, with rare exceptions, were those that defined it: hard work, perseverance, self-reliance, puritanism, the missionary spirit, and the abstract rule of law.

They are, of course, still with us—in corporations and clubs, in foundations and universities, in government and the military, maintaining the interlocking directorates that make sociologists salivate and that give the

Establishment its ugly name: the Power Structure, the Military-Industrial Complex; the rulers of America. But while they still hold power, they hold it with less assurance and with less legitimacy than at any time in history. They are hanging on, men living off their cultural capital, but rarely able or willing to create more. One can almost define their domains by locating the people and institutions that are chronically on the defensive: university presidents and trustees; the large foundations; the corporations; government; the military. They grew great as initiators and entrepreneurs. They invented the country, its culture and its values; they shaped the institutions and organizations. Then they drew the institutions around themselves, moved to the suburbs, and become org-men.

Who and what has replaced them, then, in the invention and production of our culture? Jews and Negroes, Catholics and immigrants. "Of the Americans who have come into notice during the past fifty years as poets, as novelists, as critics, as painters, as sculptors, and in the minor arts," wrote Henry Mencken in 1924, "less than half bear Anglo-Saxon names. . . . So in the sciences, so in the higher reaches of engineering and technology. . . ." Mencken's declaration was premature then; it is an understatement now: Mailer and Roth; Malamud and Bellow; Ellison and Baldwin; Edward Teller and Robert Oppenheimer and Wernher von Braun; Ralph Nader and Cesar Chavez; Noam Chomsky and Allen Ginsberg; John Rock and Jonas Salk; Paul Goodman and Herbert Marcuse; Bruno Bettelheim and Erik Erikson; Eldridge Cleaver and Malcolm X and Martin Luther King. The 1969 Pulitzer Prize for nonfiction was divided between a Jew from Brooklyn (Mailer) and a French immigrant (René Dubos); the Pulitzer Prize for fiction was awarded to an American Indian (Scott Momaday). The spokesmen of American literature and culture tend increasingly to represent the pluralistic residues of a melting pot that—for better or worse—never worked as well as some Americans had hoped. It is not simply that many of the major postwar journals of criticism—*Commentary, The New York Review of Books, The New American Review*—are edited by Jews, or that *Time* is edited by a Jewish refugee from Hitler, or that *The Saturday Evening Post* is dead, or that the function of radical muckraking was revitalized by *Ramparts,* originally established as a Catholic magazine, or that William Buckley, a Catholic, is the most articulate conservative in America; we do, after all, still have WASP writers and journals—*Foreign Affairs,* for example, and *The Atlantic* (not to mention *Life* or *Reader's Digest*). It is, rather, that the style, ideas, traumas, perplexities, and passions tend to reflect other backgrounds and interests, and that the integrative capabilities of the WASP style have plunged into precipitous decline. The cultural issues of the 1960s' enjoying the greatest cachet were not only ethnic and pluralistic, but also disintegrative—Alienation, the Identity Crisis, Black Power, Doing Your Own Thing, Dropping Out, the White Negro—and it seemed that any kind of material was acceptable as long as it was distinguishable from the old WASP mainstream: the life of the black ghetto, rock music and long hair and pot, Hindu gurus and Zen philosophers, Cuban guerrillas and Catholic radicals, black hustlers and Jewish anarchists. (The first thing I learned, coming from Brooklyn to Amherst in 1949 was that you didn't say "Bullshit" when you disagreed with someone, even your roomate. You said "Yes, but . . ." Now bullshit is back in style.) For the young, the chief villainy of the age is to be uptight, and who seems to them more uptight than WASPs, or the Jews and Irishmen trying to be like them? The 1960's was the decade of gaps—missile gaps, credibility gaps, generation gaps—when we became, in many respects, a nation of outsiders, a country in which the mainstream, however mythic, lost its compelling energy and its magnetic attraction. Now that the New Frontier and the Great Society have failed (not only as programs but as verbal rituals) so, at least for the moment, has the possibility of integration and, with it, traditional Americanism. The Average Man has become the Silent Majority. Both of these, of course, are merely convenient political fiction, but the change in labels points to a far deeper crisis of belief.

It is not that WASPs lack power and representation—or numbers—but that the once-unquestioned assumptions on which that power was based have begun to lose their hold. The foundation of WASP dominance in national politics and culture rested on the supposition that WASPdom was the true America, no subculture or special group. Now WASPs are beset by the need to enforce allegiance to something that their very place in power is supposed to take for granted. The problem is then compounded: government can become increasingly gray, trying to represent (or not to offend) "all the people," or it can begin to act as the voice of a distinctive group (the Forgotten Man, the Silent Majority)—in other words, to represent the majority as if it were a minority. (There is a third alternative, which I'll discuss later.) Nixon, characteristically, is trying to do both. When he was first elected in 1968 he brought to Washington a Cabinet of nonentities selected, it seemed, to illustrate the fix we were in: Winton Blount, Clifford Hardin, Maurice Stans, Walter Hickel, the old Agnew. (The exceptions—neither was then a regular Cabinet member— were Daniel Patrick Moynihan, an Irishman, and Henry Kissinger, a Central European immigrant.) They were men without visible personality, class, or place. Something of the same was true in Washington under Eisenhower, but then the Eisenhower atmosphere was tempered by an older lingering sense of independence, of region, a sense—finally—of principle. John Foster Dulles may have been a dangerous moralist, a stubborn Puritan, but he was not plastic. Nixon brought with him no John McCloy, no John Gardner, no Nelson Rockefeller (let alone a George C. Marshall or a Henry Stimson from an even earlier era of WASP assertion) nor does he carry Eisenhower's aura of small-town decency. (Eisenhower's men, like Nixon's, were or are institutional men, but many of them came from a tradition of "service" in which the social purposes of institutions tended to be more important than the problems of management.) We now have a government of "low profiles," gray men who represent no identifiable place, no region, no program. The security of the historic WASP position made regional roots and styles attractive; you weren't just an American but an American from a specific place, with a personality, with foibles and prejudices and attitudes. You didn't have to prove you were a WASP. But where is Nixon from? In what accent does he speak? What is his style, what are his convictions, even his hobbies? Nixon's campaign, his public conduct, and his tastes reflect not only the corporate-organization-man residue of WASPishness; they also symbolize the new insecurity of the mainstream culture.

There are advantages in all this: gray men are not crusaders; they don't speak about massive retaliation or final solutions (or, on the other hand, to be sure, the Great Society). But they are likely to regard any sort of noise as offensive and possibly dangerous. For a moment this afforded us some fun (Spiro Who?), but then Nixon, through the offices of Agnew and Mitchell, turned this quality of his Administration into a serious matter. The noise (of students, of Black Power, of protest) was, and is, scaring them. And for the first time in history—certainly for the first time since the 1920's—the majority has begun to act like a minority, like an ethnic group. The powerful are paranoid about the weak. (And needless to say, many ethnic groups are acting more like ethnic groups than they have at any time since the melting pot was pronounced a success.) This is what makes Agnew potentially more dangerous than Joe McCarthy. McCarthy's quarrels, finally, were those of an outsider attacking the Establishment, and the Establishment, which was still running the country, despite a bad case of nerves, ultimately put him down. But Agnew, Mitchell, and Nixon *are* the government, and among their most important targets are people who have no money, little organization, and access to nothing except the streets. The threat represented by Nixon's targets is not that of a foreign power, but that of a culture or cultures at odds with the mainstream. Inquisitions and witch-hunts generally mark the end, or the beginning of the end, of an age.

One of the major attributes of the WASP idiom was its self-confidence in its own Americanism. In following the ethic of the small town, in trying to make it, the WASP was operating in a system designed by his people, operated by his people, and responsive to his people. He wasn't trying to stand somebody else's ground or beat somebody else's game. But what is there for a nation that is urban (or suburban), in which the majority has (presumably) already made it, and where size and technology are rendering much of the system impersonal and unresponsive? It is no longer possible for anyone to control the country (or the world) as we once believed we could. With the exception of the balanced ticket (in politics or employment) we have no urban ethic. And so somewhere the self-confidence froze: what in the national spirit and imagery was expansive became conservative and restrictive, enterprise turned to management, ebullience to caution. Most of all, it tended to become dull. One of the most graphic illustrations of these differences in spirit is to be found in a book by John McPhee, *Levels of the Game*, an account of a tennis match between the Negro Arthur Ashe (then the highest-ranking American) and the WASP Clark Graebner (Shaker Heights suburban, churchy, the son of a dentist). Graebner speaks:

> I've never been a flashy stylist, like Arthur. I'm a fundamentalist. Arthur is a bachelor. I am married and a conservative. I'm interested in business, in the market, in children's clothes. It affects the way you play the game. He's not a steady player. He's a wristy slapper. Sometimes he doesn't even know where the ball is going. . . . I've never seen Arthur really discipline himself. He plays the game with the lackadaisical, haphazard mannerisms of a liberal. He's an underprivileged type who worked his way up. . . . There is something about him that is swashbuckling, loose. He plays the way he thinks. My style is playmaking—consistent, percentage tennis—and his style is shotmaking.

Ashe speaks:

> There is not much variety in Clark's game. It is steady, accurate, and conservative. He makes few errors. He plays stiff, compact Republican tennis.

Blacks, of course, can be disciplined grubbers as much as anyone else, and WASPs certainly never used to lack for swashbuckling types—soldiers, tycoons, ball players, frontiersmen, outlaws. Ashe, obviously, had to grub a lot harder than any white man to break into the big time, or to become a player at all, but he now manages his games with an aristocratic flair, not with what seems to be bourgeois lack of grace. But Graebner's description is otherwise right: he plays percentage tennis, Ashe takes chances. WASPs have learned to live by percentages "steady" (as Ashe says), "accurate, stiff, compact." A little uptight. In taking risks there is more to lose than to gain.

A lot of people, needless to say, have only barely made it, or haven't made it at all: prominent among them Negroes, Puerto Ricans, Poles, Irishmen, Italians, and a good number of underclass WASPs.

For them the decline in confidence tends to be traumatic. At the very moment that they are persuaded, of forced to believe, that the system will work for them—that they can make it, that their children must go to college, and all the rest—the signals from headquarters become confused and indistinct, and the rules seem to change. The children of the affluent march in the streets; long hair and at least the outward signals of sexual freedom are acceptable; hard work, stoicism, and perseverance aren't the ultimate values; individual initiative is not sufficient; the schools are "in trouble." The cultural colonies, forced by "modernization" (the supermarket, urban renewal, automated equipment, Vatican II) to abandon their own styles of life—the hierarchical family, ward politics, closed unions, old neighborhoods, religion, language, food—become witnesses to behavior indicating that the (perhaps mythic) mainstream has begun to stagnate, that a lot of people no longer believe in it, or no longer believe in the old ways of getting there. Those on the move upward and outward have, in other words, no attractive place to go. Which is to say that the underclass tenants have discovered the neglect of the landlord.

Blacks are alienated because they have been kept out of the running. The white ethnics are frustrated because public attention, in defiance of the rhetoric of individual initiative and equality, has gone to blacks. (And because affluent WASPs, who had discriminated against all minorities, are trying to shift the burden of blame on the white underclass.) All of them, sensing the decline of WASP self-confidence and leadership, are left with choices among law and order (meaning militant normalcy, the old ethic), a return to their own cultural and political resources, or exotic combinations of the two. Following the lead, and to their eyes, success of Black Power and Black Studies, a lot of minorities are trying to re-develop or to invent some exactly corresponding form of ethnic con-sciousness for themselves. Most of the whites, however, are or in the end will be content to cheer on the cops. For the first time we have Polish vigilantes and a Hebrew posse (the Jewish Defense League). Blacks and honkies, talking like frontiersmen, are buying guns. If the old WASP ethic was the ethic of making it, it isn't surprising that the most militant contemporary exponents of that ethic—those inclined to take its legends of force and action literally—should be among people outside the system trying to break in.

A measure of the decline of the WASP style—perhaps the best measure we have—is the conquest of space. From Lindbergh to NASA (or from Jack Armstrong to Neil Armstrong), from the man who was still a con-queror trusting his own bets and his own skills, and therefore an underdog (no dry runs, no simulators, no mission control) to the org-man, pro-grammed and computerized to the last $24-billion step and the last tele-vised statement, betting his life on the competence and devotion of anonymous technicians: courageous yes, underdog never. A symbol of modern man, to be sure (what if the trains stop or the electricity fails, what if the water becomes polluted and poisonous?), but also a sign of the decline of the great old WASP virtues of self-reliance, initiative, ir-reverence. Lindbergh was free enterprise; Apollo was the work of a crowd. No ape could have flown the *Spirit of St. Louis* from New York to Paris. But we could have sent an ape to the moon. Or a robot. With a fake flag artificially distended for a dead place where there is no wind.

It was a WASP enterprise all the way. Is it possible to conceive of NASA sending a Negro, a Jew—or a woman? Muhammad Ali perhaps? Joe Namath? Norman Mailer (who wanted to go)? Can one conceive of an astronaut who does not fit absolutely congruously into the background, like Muzak in a supermarket or Spiro Agnew at a picnic of Legionnaires? Can one conceive of an astronaut's wife living in a Jewish section of the Bronx, or expressing an opinion critical of the Vietnam war, or not taking the children to church on Sunday, or having a career of her own? Was it not inevitable that one of the wives would get down on her knees in front of the television set to pray for a safe reentry? (One can imagine, in that setting, that Walter Cronkite *is* God.) Can one expect Richard Nixon not to say that the mission was the greatest thing since the Creation—or Billy Graham not to suggest, in reply, that perhaps the Resurrection was more important?

What made the moonshot interesting was its unbelievably bad taste, the taste of a cultural style that has lost its juice: suburbs and corporation offices, network television and the electric toothbrush, airline pilots and airline hostesses, "the whole mechanical consolidation of force," as Henry Adams wrote in the *Education*, "which ruthlessly stamped out the life of the class into which Adams was born, but created monopolies capable of controlling the new energies that America adored." Clearly space travel is technologically impossible except as a collective enterprise. But that is precisely the point. There is no role for the American (*i.e.* WASP) hero. Heroes presumably defy great odds alone. Gary Cooper has been replaced by Dustin Hoffman.

You ask yourself: Does the Establishment live? And the answer, clearly, is Yes. And yet it does not live in the style to which it was accustomed. Ever since the development of large bureaucracies and tenure systems there has been a tendency among outside intellectuals to overestimate the influence of elites. Not that corporations and institutions are going out of style (and they may, in case of a recession, regain some of their allure to the ambitious because they offer security), but that they have become so large, so stiff, and so beset by critics and complexity as to have lost considerable influence and all the romance of their former connection to success. (In Nixon's Republican party there are disparaging references to "The Eastern Establishment" which suggest that there might now be more than one—meaning, of course, that there is none at all.) Here is Francis T. P. Plimpton, the former Deputy U.S. Ambassador to the U.N., and one of the finest representatives of the old style of WASP culture in America. A gentleman, a man of parts. From *Who's Who in America* (1964–1965):

PLIMPTON, Francis T. P., diplomat; b. N.Y.C., N.Y., Dec. 7, 1900; s. George Arthur and Frances Taylor (Pearsons) P.; grad. Phillips Exeter Acad., 1917; A.B., magna cum laude, Amherst Coll., 1922: LL.B., Harvard University, 1925; LL.D., Colby College, 1960; married Pauline Ames, June 4, 1926; children—George Ames, Francis T. P., Jr., Oakes Ames, Sarah Gay. Admitted to bar, 1926; asso. with Root, Clark, Buckner & Ballantine, N.Y. City, 1925–32, in charge of Paris office, 1930–31; gen. solicitor, Reconstruction Finance Corp., Washington, D.C., 1932–33; partner Debevoise, Plimpton & McLean, N.Y.C., and predecessor firms, 1933–61; dep. U.S. rep. to UN with rank ambassador E. and P., 1961–. Trustee U.S. Trust Co. of N.Y., Bowery Savs. Bank. Mem. U.S. delegation UN 15th–17th gen. assemblies. Trustee Tchrs. Ins. and Annuity Assn. (pres. trustees of stock), Coll. Retirement Equities Fund Corp., Amherst Coll., Barnard Coll. (vice chmn. bd.). Phillips Exeter Acad. (chmn. bd.), Union Theol. Sem., Athens Coll. (Greece), Lingnan U. (China), Dir. Philharmonic-Symphony Soc. N.Y., Roosevelt Hosp., Am—Italy

Soc. Fellow Am. Bar Found.; mem. Am., N.Y. State bar assns., Am. Law
Inst., Bar Assn. City N.Y., Fgn. Policy Assn.

The style is responsible, worldly involvement, directing institutions which
nourished and arbitrated the culture; schools, universities, hospitals, the
Council on Foreign Relations, the United Nations, the Church Peace
Union, the missionary college in China, the Philharmonic. They were
good institutions all, and many of them still do their good works, but with
the possible exception of the federal courts, most of them are no longer
sanctified as sources of social and cultural initiative, or even as mediators
of conflict. There must have been a time when it was fun to be a university trustee.

The interest and action tend to come from others. George Plimpton, the
son of Francis T. P. and probably the best-known WASP dealer in living
culture, operates like a Paris salonist among Interesting People (Capote,
Mailer, the Kennedys), writing brilliantly of his amateur involvement in
The Real Stuff: fighting Archie Moore, playing quarterback for the
Detroit Lions, pitching to the Yankees. (All sports are now saturated with
ethnics.) It is a new role for the children of privilege. Is there a redeeming
social utility in this work? Had Plimpton been Jewish he might have
played *schlemiel* in a jockstrap, but as an upper-class WASP perhaps all
he can do is represent the man whose dreams of command have turned to
fantasy and whose greatest moments of glory come from watching other
people do something well. A WASP playing honkie and nigger to find out
how it feels to be upward bound. Does the aspiring WASP hero have a
choice other than that between Apollo and *Paper Lion?*

The enervation of WASP culture may derive, more than anything, from
a loss of place. The geographic and psychic worlds of the old mainstream
become less distinct, but certain special neighborhoods, even if they are
a generation away, survive as regions of the mind. The sense of place:
Salem and Boston and Concord; Zenith and Winesburg; Yoknapatawpha
County. It produced people with accents and fashions and biases—personalities—that they carried around as overtly as parasols and walking sticks.
And because they knew who they were, they were quite willing to be
eccentric and crazy. Now much of that material is gone. The black ghetto
still remains as a real place, and so does the memory, if not the fact, of
South Boston, of Brooklyn, of rural Mississippi and small-town Texas. But
how much of a sense of place can grow in a bedroom suburb? What is the
inner sense of Bronxville or Winnetka?

Because WASPs regarded themselves as the proprietors of history and
the managers of destiny, there was a double displacement. While they
were losing their regions they also began to lose their special role as the
intrinsic Americans. When we discovered that the country and the world
were no longer easily manageable—when we lost our innocence—it was
the WASP role which was most affected. No matter how enthusiastically
the ethnics waved the flag, they had always been partial outsiders. (Or

perhaps better to say that they enjoyed dual citizenship.) In any case, their culture never depended on the assurance that they were running the show. They were tenants, had learned to survive as minorities. Obviously this produced problems, but it also created the tensions and identities of which modern literature (for example) is made. And these conditions of tenancy haven't yet been destroyed, may, indeed, have been strengthened through the mass media, which have nationalized isolated pockets of minority culture. Moreover, the media help create new minorities, new constituencies: students, for example, and women. What kids or blacks do in one town is now immediately communicated to others. Normalcy doesn't make good television, happenings do. The greatest effect of the melting pot, ironically, may not have been on immigrants and minorities, but on the mainstream.

The vacuum left by the old arbiters of the single standard—Establishment intellectuals, literary critics, English professors, museum directors, and all the rest—has produced a sort of cultural prison break. And not only by ethnics, by blacks and Indians, or by kids, but by a lot of others, including all sorts of WASPs themselves, who behave as if they have been waiting for this freedom all their lives. That a lot of what results from this new breakout is bad (and who, these days, can get away with saying that?), and that a lot will be transitory is hardly surprising. In a decade hundreds of thousands of "creative" people proclaimed themselves artists and poets, a million amateurs entered the culture biz, and God knows how many gurus, cultists, swamis, and T-group trainers hung out their shingles. No one could expect most of them to be good, or perhaps even to be serious. The wildcatters are working new territory and a lot are going to go bust. But for the moment they're thriving: the Stones and the Beatles, the groups and groupies, Polish Power and Black Studies, liberation schools and free universities, Norman Mailer's ego and Alexander Portnoy's mother, *The Graduate* and *Alice's Restaurant,* rebellious nuns and protesting priests, *Rat* and *Screw* and a hundred other underground papers, mixed-media shows and the Living Theater, bookstores of the occult, Taro cards and freaks and hipsters, miniskirts and maxi coats, beads and joss sticks . . . all coexisting (barely, uneasily) with Lyndon Johnson's cornpone, Norman Vincent Peale's sermons, *I Love Lucy, Reader's Digest,* and Apollo 12. If the 1960s produced the beginning of any sort of renaissance, its characteristic instruments are the hand-held movie camera, the electric guitar, and the mimeograph machine, and if its efforts survive in nothing else, they will undoubtedly be remembered by the greatest outpouring of poster art in all history: peace doves and protest proclamations, the face of John Lennon, the pregnant Girl Scout over the motto "Be Prepared," and the pregnant black woman over the 1968 campaign slogan. "Nixon's The One." This is a counterculture—not high, not low or middle—but eclectic.

Until recently, when encounter groups, public therapy, and other psychic ceremonies became fashionable, reason had been more or less successfully keeping the dark night of the soul within the hidden closets of the mind. And WASPs were the most reasonable people of all. There were, obviously, advantages in that. Most people, I suspect, prefer dispassionate men for airline pilots, surgeons, and commanders of nuclear-armed strategic bombers. Moreover, we may have survived the last twenty-five years precisely because we kept hot men from taking charge. But their style didn't do much for cultural enrichment. Now everything that a graying, nervous civilization kept jammed in those closets is coming out, whether it deserves to or not: sex in all forms, feelings, emotions, self-revelation, and forms of religion and ritual long condemned as superstition. "Honesty" replaces stoicism, and "love," however understood, overwhelms "work." It may well be that the kids are mining McLuhan's non-linear culture, that print and cool reason (and WASPs) will go under together. So far there is no way of knowing. What is certain is that the old media—books, newspapers, magazines—can no longer claim a monopoly on urgent cultural articulation, and that people who work the new territories have moved a long way from the old mainstream.

WASPs seem to have been crippled by their own sanity. They have become too levelheaded. Having confused their particular social order with the Immutability of Things (and with their own welfare), they have defaulted on their birthright of cussedness and irreverence. "This took courage, this took prudence, this took stoutheartedness," thinks Arthur Winner, Jr., James Gould Cozzens' hero, at the end of *By Love Possessed*. (He has just covered up—to his and Cozzens' satisfaction—some $200,000 worth of ledger-de-main perpetrated by one of his partners.) "In this life we cannot have everything for ourselves we might like to have. . . . Victory is not in reaching certainties or solving mysteries; victory is making do with uncertainties, in supporting mysteries." WASPs are willing to be "sick"—meaning that they can have their neuroses and their "reason" too—but never crazy. People who are willing to be crazy are almost invariably Something Else. We no longer have, or seem to have the possibility of having, a figure like Bertrand Russell; we no longer even have an Everett Dirksen or a John L. Lewis.

WASP crimes these days are invariably dull—price fixing, antitrust capers, tax fraud—which is why we are so fascinated by Jimmy Hoffa, Roy Cohn, and the Mafia, why we need the Mafia, would have to invent it were we ever to suspect (as has Daniel Bell) that it doesn't really exist.

Beyond the formal institutions of business and government—the banks, the corporations, the State Department, and Congress—the unique provinces of WASP domination tend to be conservative (in the pure sense) and mediating. WASPs, I think, still regard themselves as the principal heirs of an estate in which the streams flowed clear, the air was clean, and the language pure. In the growing number of conservation societies, and in their almost exclusive dominion over libraries, dictionary-making, and (surprising as it may seem to those familiar with only the current "celeb-

rities" in the profession) the teaching of English, they are trying to preserve some of that estate. But as "the environment" becomes a national
issue, they are going to lose ground (you should pardon the pun) even as
conservationists. There are going to be new men—technicians, population
planners, engineers—who will move in on the Audubon Society, the Sierra
Club, and the Izaak Walton League. The urban environment (John
Lindsay versus the New York legislature and Nelson Rockefeller) will
demand parity with the environment of Daniel Boone and the bald eagle.
On some issues urban and rural conservationists can make common cause,
but on others (mass transit, housing, street cleaning, and garbage collection) they cannot.

But it would unfortunate, perhaps even fatal, if the WASP's mediating
function (through courts and other institutions) were also to be seriously
eroded. It is inconceivable that America could ever be integrated on
ethnic terms. Can one imagine this country as essentially Negro or Italian
or Polish; or believe that the Republican party would nominate anyone
named Spiro Agnopopoulos for Vice President; or visualize a trial in
which the defendant is white and all the other participants—judge, jurors,
lawyers, witnesses—are black? (It did, in fact, happen—in the preliminary
proceedings against the Klansmen charged with plotting to murder
Charles Evers, the black mayor of Fayette, Mississippi—but it may never
happen again.) For if the minorities no longer accept the new style of the
mainstream, they are even further from accepting each other. And somebody is going to have to help keep them from tearing each other apart:
cops and kids, blacks and blue-collar whites, freaks and squares. Robert
Kennedy, I think, recognized this need before he was killed (significantly
by a crazy ethnic resenting Kennedy's sympathy with other ethnics). This
is also what made the reelection of John Lindsay possible—and significant. The Jews and Negroes of New York may have distrusted him, but
they trusted the Italians even less.

Even mediation, however, is no longer feasible on the old standard
rigid WASP terms. For the first time, any sort of settlement among competing group interests is going to have to do more than pay lip service to
minorities and to the pluralism of styles, beliefs, and cultures. The various
commissions on violence and urban riots struggled with that problem but
couldn't see beyond their assumptions to the logical conclusion. America
is not on the verge of becoming two separate societies, one rich and white,
the other poor and black. It is becoming, in all its dreams and anxieties, a
nation of outsiders for whom no single style or ethic remains possible. The
Constitutional prohibition against an established state religion was
adopted because the Jeffersonians understood the destructive consequences of imposing a single set of cultural beliefs beyond the guarantees
of freedom and due process.

The Establishment in America has, in part, lost its grip because it
devoted itself too much to the management of its game, rather than to the
necessary objective of making it possible for everyone to play his own.

Minorities—cultural, ethnic, even minorities of one—are fighting over the wreckage of the WASP-abandoned cities and the WASP-forsaken culture. If the WASP Establishment is to act as umpire in this contest—and if we are not to become a police state—it will have to recognize the legitimacy of the contenders. One of the reasons that growing up in America is absurd and chaotic is that the current version of Americanization—what the school people call socializing children—has lost its appeal. We will now have to devise ways of recognizing and assessing the alternatives. The mainstream is running thin.

IX. Bureaucracy

Bureaucratic predominance is perhaps the outstanding feature of modern society. American social scientists recognize this fact, even if they shy away from the term. Many refer to "large-scale organization" instead of bureaucracy—a word that in our popular tradition simply means red tape, inefficiency, and the abuse of power.

However we designate it, there is nothing new about bureaucracy, which to some extent existed in ancient Egypt, classical China, and feudal Europe. But presence is not the same as predominance. Bureaucracy began to achieve ascendancy in the Western world only two or three centuries ago. The origins of that ascendancy lie in the modern army and the state civil service. Eventually, bureaucracy was adapted to the industrial process and the mass production of goods, and by now it predominates in virtually all our institutions.

In 1920 Max Weber presented the first adequate technical description and definition of bureaucracy, the most essential part of which is to be found in this section. More than anyone else, Weber alerted sociologists and political scientists to the importance of a phenomenon they had insufficiently studied. He underscored two critical dimensions: (1) that as a system of *mass* administration, bureaucracy provides the same speed, precision, clarity, and low-unit cost that technology provides in industrial production, and (2) that bureaucracy centralizes the apparatus of organizations that direct and order human life. In so doing, bureaucracy generates a feeling of isolation, impersonality, and powerlessness among both its members and its subjects. The apparatus may develop a high degree of autonomy, or when manageable, it may be controlled by special interests inimical to the democratic process.

Bureaucracy embodies hierarchically arranged pyramids of authority in which categorical obedience is taken for granted. Modern democracy is its antithesis. Their coexistence plagues us with contradictions and dilemmas. Impersonal efficiency is one thing, human concern is another—and they are mutually exclusive. How to reconcile bureaucracy and democracy is a constant problem. It is a bone of contention in nearly every public issue, a canker in nearly every institution, and a source of conflict in broad sectors of private life. Few students of the subject see it as anything but a permanent problem of modern society.

In *The New Industrial State*, John Kenneth Galbraith chronicles the triumph of bureaucratic control in industrial organizations. His terminology is not the same as ours, but the substance of Galbraith's ideas does not differ from that of sociologists. These ideas are foreshadowed in Weber's reflections; Galbraith extends them to our economy. He observes that centralized government and corporate planning have to a large extent replaced the decentralized market. Advanced technology makes such planning possible, but long periods of "lead time" and control of markets are necessary to implement the planning. Given these conditions, increasingly complex technology is both a result and a cause of mass production for mass markets.

Galbraith's thesis states that technological imperatives culminate in a technostructure composed of high-level bureaucrats who are also technicians or engineers. Through an interlocking system of committees, the technostructure plans, controls, and coordinates a sizable part of the economy. It raises capital, manipulates the market, and neutralizes the influence of outsiders. In Galbraith's opinion, the intricacy of this operation is such that it disarms stockholders and financial backers. In his view, the technostructure, unhampered by external control, has become self-recruiting and self-perpetuating. Galbraith's thesis is most applicable to a prosperous, late-capitalistic industrial economy.

Arthur K. Davis is best known for his perceptive study of the Navy Officers Corps during World War II. In it he vividly portrays the negative side of military bureaucracy. Peacetime functions of the Army and Navy interfere with their wartime functions. Consequently, various bureaucratic practices developed that *in toto* are the very opposite of Weber's ideal type. Legalism and conformism supersede actual performance of prescribed tasks; ritualism and ceremonialism, with a concomitant reward and status system, replace achievement. The buck is passed; responsibility is avoided.

The Weberian model postulates efficiency. Davis revealed inefficiency, and his study was merely the first of many. Those who observe the working of a bureaucracy at close quarters are bound to find inefficiency, incompetence, and inhumanity. The pertinent questions to be asked are: Are the negative aspects of bureaucracy worse than the negative aspects of earlier administrative systems? Do the advantages of present-day bureaucracy outweigh the disadvantages? Can contemporary society escape from the toils of bureaucracy once the bureaucracy has become predominant? Finally, a more pragmatic question is: How can we preserve the technical advantages of bureaucracy without being victimized by the inherent disadvantages?

29. Bureaucracy
Max Weber

I   CHARACTERISTICS OF BUREAUCRACY

Modern officialdom functions in the following specific manner:

I. There is the principle of fixed and official jurisdictional areas, which are generally ordered by rules, that is, by laws or administrative regulations.

1. The regular activities required for the purposes of the bureaucratically governed structure are distributed in a fixed way as official duties.

2. The authority to give the commands required for the discharge of these duties is distributed in a stable way and is strictly delimited by rules concerning the coercive means, physical, sacerdotal, or otherwise, which may be placed at the disposal of officials.

3. Methodical provision is made for the regular and continuous fulfilment of these duties and for the execution of the corresponding rights; only persons who have the generally regulated qualifications to serve are employed.

In public and lawful government these three elements constitute "bureaucratic authority." In private economic domination, they constitute bureaucratic "management." Bureaucracy, thus understood, is fully developed in political and ecclesiastical communities only in the modern state, and, in the private economy, only in the most advanced institutions of capitalism. Permanent and public office authority, with fixed jurisdiction, is not the historical rule but rather the exception. This is so even in large political structures such as those of the ancient Orient, the Germanic and Mongolian empires of conquest, or of many feudal structures of state. In all these cases, the ruler executes the most important measures through personal trustees, table-companions, or court-servants. Their commissions and authority are not precisely delimited and are temporarily called into being for each case.

II. The principles of office hierarchy and of levels of graded authority mean a firmly ordered system of super- and subordination in which there is a supervision of the lower offices by the higher ones. Such a system offers the governed the possibility of appealing the decision of a

Wirtschaft und Gesellschaft, part III, chap. 6, pp. 650–78.
From Max Weber: Essays in Sociology, edited and translated by H. H. Gerth and C. Wright Mills. Copyright 1946 by Oxford University Press, Inc.; renewed 1973 by Dr. Hans H. Gerth. Reprinted by permission of the publisher.

lower office to its higher authority, in a definitely regulated manner. With the full development of the bureaucratic type, the office hierarchy is monocratically organized. The principle of hierarchical office authority is found in all bureaucratic structures: in state and ecclesiastical structures as well as in large party organizations and private enterprises. It does not matter for the character of bureaucracy whether its authority is called "private" or "public."

When the principle of jurisdictional "competency" is fully carried through, hierarchical subordination—at least in public office—does not mean that the "higher" authority is simply authorized to take over the business of the "lower." Indeed, the opposite is the rule. Once established and having fulfilled its task, an office tends to continue in existence and be held by another incumbent.

III. The management of the modern office is based upon written documents ("the files"), which are preserved in their original or draft form. There is, therefore, a staff of subaltern officials and scribes of all sorts. The body of officials actively engaged in a "public" office, along with the respective apparatus of material implements and the files, make up a "bureau." In private enterprise, "the bureau" is often called "the office."

In principle, the modern organization of the civil service separates the bureau from the private domicile of the official, and, in general, bureaucracy segregates official activity as something distinct from the sphere of private life. Public monies and equipment are divorced from the private property of the official. This condition is everywhere the product of a long development. Nowadays, it is found in public as well as in private enterprises; in the latter, the principle extends even to the leading entrepreneur. In principle, the executive office is separated from the household business from private correspondence, and business assets from private fortunes. The more consistently the modern type of business management has been carried through the more are these separations the case. The beginnings of this process are to be found as early as the Middle Ages.

It is the peculiarity of the modern entrepreneur that he conducts himself as the "first official" of his enterprise, in the very same way in which the ruler of a specifically modern bureaucratic state spoke of himself as "the first servant" of the state.[1] The idea that the bureau activities of the state are intrinsically different in character from the management of private economic offices is a continental European notion and, by way of contrast, is totally foreign to the American way.

IV. Office management, at least all specialized office management—and such management is distinctly modern—usually presupposes thorough and expert training. This increasingly holds for the modern executive and employee of private enterprises, in the same manner as it holds for the state official.

V. When the office is fully developed, official activity demands the

full working capacity of the official, irrespective of the fact that his obligatory time in the bureau may be firmly delimited. In the normal case,
this is only the product of a long development, in the public as well as
in the private office. Formerly, in all cases, the normal state of affairs
was reversed: official business was discharged as a secondary activity.

VI. The management of the office follows general rules, which are
more or less stable, more or less exhaustive, and which can be learned.
Knowledge of these rules represents a special technical learning which
the officials possess. It involves jurisprudence, or administrative or business management.

The reduction of modern office management to rules is deeply embedded in its very nature. The theory of modern public administration,
for instance, assumes that the authority to order certain matters by decree—which has been legally granted to public authorities—does not en-
title the bureau to regulate the matter by commands given for each case,
but only to regulate the matter abstractly. This stands in extreme contrast to the regulation of all relationships through individual privileges
and bestowals of favor, which is absolutely dominant in patrimonialism,
at least in so far as such relationships are not fixed by sacred tradition.

II THE POSITION OF THE OFFICIAL

All this results in the following for the internal and external position
of the official:

I. Office holding is a "vocation." This is shown, first, in the requirement of a firmly prescribed course of training, which demands the entire
capacity for work for a long period of time, and in the generally prescribed and special examinations which are prerequisites of employment.
Furthermore, the position of the official is in the nature of a duty. This
determines the internal structure of his relations, in the following manner: Legally and actually, office holding is not considered a source to be
exploited for rents or emoluments, as was normally the case during the
Middle Ages and frequently up to the threshold of recent times. Nor is
office holding considered a usual exchange of services for equivalents,
as is the case with free labor contracts. Entrance into an office, including
one in the private economy, is considered an acceptance of a specific
obligation of faithful management in return for a secure existence. It is
decisive for the specific nature of modern loyalty to an office that, in the
pure type, it does not establish a relationship to a *person*, like the vassal's
or disciple's faith in feudal or in patrimonial relations of authority. Modern loyalty is devoted to impersonal and functional purposes. Behind the
functional purposes, of course, "ideas of culture-values" usually stand.
These are *ersatz* for the earthly or supra-mundane personal master:
ideas such as "state," "church," "community," "party," or "enterprise" are
thought of as being realized in a community; they provide an ideological
halo for the master.

The political official—at least in the fully developed modern state—is not considered the personal servant of a ruler. Today, the bishop, the priest, and the preacher are in fact no longer, as in early Christian times, holders of purely personal charisma. The supra-mundane and sacred values which they offer are given to everybody who seems to be worthy of them and who asks for them. In former times, such leaders acted upon the personal command of their master; in principle, they were responsible only to him. Nowadays, in spite of the partial survival of the old theory, such religious leaders are officials in the service of a functional purpose, which in the present-day "church" has become routinized and, in turn, ideologically hallowed.

II. The personal position of the official is patterned in the following way:

1. Whether he is in a private office or a public bureau, the modern official always strives and usually enjoys a distinct *social esteem* as compared with the governed. His social position is guaranteed by the prescriptive rules of rank order and, for the political official, by special definitions of the criminal code against "insults of officials" and "contempt" of state and church authorities.

The actual social position of the official is normally highest where, as in old civilized countries, the following conditions prevail; a strong demand for administration by trained experts; a strong and stable social differentiation, where the official predominantly derives from socially and economically privileged strata because of the social distribution of power; or where the costliness of the required training and status conventions are binding upon him. . . . The possession of educational certificates is usually linked with qualification for office. Naturally, such certificates or patents enhance the "status element" in the social position of the official. For the rest this status factor in individual cases is explicitly and impassively acknowledged; for example, in the prescription that the acceptance or rejection of an aspirant to an official career depends upon the consent ("election") of the members of the official body. This is the case in the German army with the officer corps. Similar phenomena, which promote this guild-like closure of officialdom, are typically found in patrimonial and, particularly, in prebendal officialdoms of the past. The desire to resurrect such phenomena in changed forms is by no means infrequent among modern bureaucrats. For instance, they have played a role among the demands of the quite proletarian and expert officials (the *tretyj* element) during the Russian revolution.

Usually the social esteem of the officials as such is especially low where the demand for expert administration and the dominance of status conventions are weak. This is especially the case in the United States; it is often the case in new settlements by virtue of their wide fields for profit-making and the great instability of their social stratification.

2. The pure type of bureaucratic official is *appointed* by a superior authority. An official elected by the governed is not a purely bureaucratic figure. Of course, the formal existence of an election does not by itself

mean that no appointment hides behind the election—in the state, especially, appointment by party chiefs. Whether or not this is the case does not depend upon legal statutes but upon the way in which the party mechanism functions. Once firmly organized, the parties can turn a formally free election into the mere acclamation of a candidate designated by the party chief. As a rule, however, a formally free election is turned into a fight, conducted according to definite rules, for votes in favor of one of two designated candidates.

In all circumstances, the designation of officials by means of an election among the governed modifies the strictness of hierarchical subordination. In principle, an official who is so elected has an autonomous position opposite the superordinate official. The elected official does not derive his position "from above" but "from below," or at least not from a superior authority of the official hierarchy but from powerful party men ("bosses"), who also determine his further career. The career of the elected official is not, or at least not primarily, dependent upon his chief in the administration. The official who is not elected but appointed by a chief normally functions more exactly, from a technical point of view, because, all other circumstances being equal, it is more likely that purely functional points of consideration and qualities will determine his selection and career. As laymen, the governed can become acquainted with the extent to which a candidate is expertly qualified for office only in terms of experience, and hence only after his service. Moreover, in every sort of selection of officials by election, parties quite naturally give decisive weight not to expert considerations but to the services a follower renders to the party boss. This holds for all kinds of procurement of officials by elections, for the designation of formally free, elected officials by party bosses when they determine the slate of candidates, or the free appointment by a chief who has himself been elected. The contrast, however, is relative: substantially similar conditions hold where legitimate monarchs and their subordinates appoint officials, except that the influence of the followings are then less controllable.

Where the demand for administration by trained experts is considerable, and the party followings have to recognize an intellectually developed, educated, and freely moving "public opinion," the use of unqualified officials falls back upon the party in power at the next election. Naturally, this is more likely to happen when the officials are appointed by the chief. The demand for a trained administration now exists in the United States, but in the large cities, where immigrant votes are "corraled," there is, of course, no educated public opinion. Therefore, popular elections of the administrative chief and also of his subordinate officials usually endanger the expert qualification of the official as well as the precise functioning of the bureaucratic mechanism. It also weakens the dependence of the officials upon the hierarchy. This holds at least for the large administrative bodies that are difficult to supervise. The superior qualification and integrity of federal judges, appointed by the

President, as over against elected judges in the United States is well known, although both types of officials have been selected primarily in terms of party considerations. The great changes in American metropolitan administrations demanded by reformers have proceeded essentially from elected mayors working with an apparatus of officials who were appointed by them. These reforms have thus come about in a "Caesarist" fashion. Viewed technically, as an organized form of authority, the efficiency of "Caesarism," which often grows out of democracy, rests in general upon the position of the "Caesar" as a free trustee of the masses (of the army or of the citizenry), who is unfettered by tradition. The "Caesar" is thus the unrestrained master of a body of highly qualified military officers and officials whom he selects freely and personally without regard to tradition or to any other considerations. This "rule of the personal genius," however, stands in contradiction to the formally "democratic" principle of a universally elected officialdom.

3. Normally, the position of the official is held for life, at least in public bureaucracies; and this is increasingly the case for all similar structures. As a factual rule, *tenure for life* is presupposed, even where the giving of notice or periodic reappointment occurs. In contrast to the worker in a private enterprise, the official normally holds tenure. Legal or actual life-tenure, however, is not recognized as the official's right to the possession of office, as was the case with many structures of authority in the past. Where legal guarantees against arbitrary dismissal or transfer are developed, they merely serve to guarantee a strictly objective discharge of specific office duties free from all personal considerations. In Germany, this is the case for all juridical and, increasingly, for all administrative officials.

Within the bureaucracy, therefore, the measure of "independence," legally guaranteed by tenure, is not always a source of increased status for the official whose position is thus secured. Indeed, often the reverse holds, especially in old cultures and communities that are highly differentiated. In such communities, the stricter the subordination under the arbitrary rule of the master, the more it guarantees the maintenance of the conventional seigneurial style of living for the official. Because of the very absence of these legal guarantees of tenure, the conventional esteem for the official may rise in the same way as, during the Middle Ages, the esteem of the nobility of office[2] rose at the expense of esteem for the freemen, and as the king's judge surpassed that of the people's judge. In Germany, the military officer or the administrative official can be removed from office at any time, or at least far more readily than the "independent judge," who never pays with loss of his office for even the grossest offense against the "code of honor" or against social conventions of the salon. For this very reason, if other things are equal, in the eyes of the master stratum the judge is considered less qualified for social intercourse than are officers and administrative officials, whose greater dependence on the master is a greater guarantee of their conformity with status conventions. Of course, the average official strives for a civil-service law, which would materially secure his old age and provide increased guarantees against his arbitrary removal from office. This striving, however, has its limits. A very strong development of the "right to the office" naturally makes it more difficult to staff them with regard to technical efficiency, for such a development decreases the career-opportunities of ambitious candidates for office. This makes for the fact that officials, on the whole, do not feel their dependency upon those at the top. This lack of a feeling of dependency, however, rests primarily upon the inclination to depend upon one's equals rather than upon the socially inferior and governed strata. The present conservative movement among the Badenia clergy, occasioned by the anxiety of a presumably threatening separation of church and state, has been expressly determined by the desire not to be turned "from a master into a servant of the parish."[3]

4. The official receives the regular *pecuniary* compensation of a normally fixed *salary* and the old age security provided by a pension. The salary is not measured like a wage in terms of work done, but according to "status," that is, according to the kind of function (the "rank") and, in addition, possibly, according to the length of service. The relatively great security of the official's income, as well as the rewards of social esteem, make the office a sought-after position, especially in countries which no longer provide opportunities for colonial profits. In such countries, this situation permits relatively low salaries for officials.

5. The official is set for a *"career"* within the hierarchical order of the public service. He moves from the lower, less important, and lower paid to the higher positions. The average official naturally desires a mechanical fixing of the conditions of promotion: if not of the offices, at least of the salary levels. He wants these conditions fixed in terms of "seniority," or possibly according to grades achieved in a developed system of expert examinations. Here and there, such examinations actually form a character *indelebilis* of the official and have lifelong effects on his career. To this is joined the desire to qualify the right to office and the increasing tendency toward status group closure and economic security. All of this makes for a tendency to consider the offices as "prebends" of those who are qualified by educational certificates. The necessity of taking general personal and intellectual qualifications into consideration, irrespective of the often subaltern character of the educational certificate, has led to a condition in which the highest political offices, especially the positions of "ministers," are principally filled without reference to such certificates. . . .

III THE CONCENTRATION OF THE MEANS OF ADMINISTRATION

The bureaucratic structure goes hand in hand with the concentration of the material means of management in the hands of the master. This concentration occurs, for instance, in a well-known and typical fashion, in the development of big capitalist enterprises, which find their essential characteristics in this process. A corresponding process occurs in public organizations.

The bureaucratically led army of the Pharaohs, the army during the later period of the Roman republic and the principate, and, above all, the army of the modern military state are characterized by the fact that their equipment and provisions are supplied from the magazines of the war lord. This is in contrast to the folk armies of agricultural tribes, the armed citizenry of ancient cities, the militias of early medieval cities, and all feudal armies; for these, the self-equipment and the self-provisioning of those obliged to fight was normal.

War in our time is a war of machines. And this makes magazines technically necessary, just as the dominance of the machine in industry promotes the concentration of the means of production and management. In the main, however, the bureaucratic armies of the past, equipped and provisioned by the lord, have risen when social and economic development has absolutely or relatively diminished the stratum of citizens who were economically able to equip themselves, so that their number was no longer sufficient for putting the required armies in the field. They were reduced at least relatively, that is, in relation to the range of power claimed for the polity. Only the bureaucratic army structure allowed for the development of the professional standing armies which are necessary for the constant pacification of large states of the plains, as well as for warfare against far-distant enemies, especially enemies overseas. Specifically, military discipline and technical training can be normally and fully developed, at least to its modern high level, only in the bureaucratic army.

Historically, the bureaucratization of the army has everywhere been realized along with the transfer of army service from the propertied to the propertyless. Until this transfer occurs, military service is an honorific privilege of propertied men. Such a transfer was made to the native-born unpropertied, for instance, in the armies of the generals of the late Roman republic and the empire, as well as in modern armies up to the nineteenth century. The burden of service has also been transferred to strangers, as in the mercenary armies of all ages. This process typically goes hand in hand with the general increase in material and intellectual culture. The following reason has also played its part everywhere: the increasing density of population, and therewith the intensity and strain of economic work, makes for an increasing "indispensability" of the acquisitive strata[4] for purposes of war. Leaving aside periods of strong ideological fervor, the propertied strata of sophisticated and especially of urban culture as a rule are little fitted and also little inclined to do the coarse war work of the common soldier. Other circumstances being equal, the propertied strata of the open country are at least usually better qualified and more strongly inclined to become professional officers. This difference between the urban and the rural propertied is balanced only where the increasing possibility of mechanized warfare requires the leaders to qualify as "technicians."

The bureaucratization of organized warfare may be carried through in the form of private capitalist enterprise, just like any other business. Indeed, the procurement of armies and their administration by private capitalists has been the rule in mercenary armies, especially those of the Occident up to the turn of the eighteenth century. During the Thirty Years' War, in Brandenburg the soldier was still the predominant owner of the material implements of his business. He owned his weapons, horses, and dress, although the state, in the role, as it were, of the merchant of the "putting-out system," did supply him to some extent. Later on, in the standing army of Prussia, the chief of the company owned the material means of warfare, and only since the peace of Tilsit has the concentration of the means of warfare in the hands of the state definitely come about. Only with this concentration was the introduction of uniforms generally carried through. Before then, the introduction of uniforms had been left to a great extent to the arbitrary discretion of the regimental officer, with the exception of individual categories of troops to whom the king had "bestowed" certain uniforms, first, in 1620, to the royal bodyguard, then, under Frederick II, repeatedly.

Such terms as "regiment" and "battalion" usually had quite different meanings in the eighteenth century from the meanings they have today. Only the battalion was a tactical unit (today both are); the "regiment" was then a managerial unit of an economic organization established by the colonel's position as an "entrepreneur." "Official" maritime ventures (like the Genoese *maonae*) and army procurement belong to private capitalism's first giant enterprises of far-going bureaucratic character. In this respect, the "nationalization" of these enterprises by the state has its modern parallel in the nationalization of the railroads, which have been controlled by the state from their beginnings.

In the same way as with army organizations, the bureaucratization of administration goes hand in hand with the concentration of the means of organization in other spheres. The old administration by satraps and regents, as well as administration by farmers of office, purchasers of office, and, most of all, administration by feudal vassals, decentralize the material means of administration. The local demand of the province and the cost of the army and of subaltern officials are regularly paid for in advance from local income, and only the surplus reaches the central treasure. The enfeoffed official administers entirely by payment out of his own pocket. The bureaucratic state, however, puts its whole administrative expense on the budget and equips the lower authorities with the current means of expenditure, the use of which the state regulates and controls. This has the same meaning for the "economics" of the administration as for the large centralized capitalist enterprise.

In the field of scientific research and instruction, the bureaucratization of the always existing research institutes of the universities is a function of the increasing demand for material means of management. Liebig's laboratory at Giessen University was the first example of big enterprise in this field. Through the concentration of such means in the hands of the privileged head of the institute, the mass of researchers and docents are separated from their "means of production," in the same way as capitalist enterprise has separated the workers from theirs.

In spite of its indubitable technical superiority, bureaucracy has everywhere been a relatively late development. A number of obstacles have contributed to this, and only under certain social and political conditions have they definitely receded into the background.

NOTES

1. Frederick II of Prussia.
2. "Ministerialen."
3. Written before 1914. (German editor's note.)
4. *Erwerbende Schichten.*

---

30. The Nature of Industrial Planning

John Kenneth Galbraith

I

Until the end of World War II, or shortly thereafter, planning was a moderately evocative word in the United States. It implied a sensible concern for what might happen in the future and a disposition, by forehanded action, to forestall avoidable misfortune. As persons won credit for competent planning of their lives, so communities won credit for effective planning of their environment. It was thought good to live in a well-planned city. The United States government had a National Resources Planning Board. During the war, postwar planning acquired the status of a modest industry in both the United States and the United Kingdom; it was felt that it would reassure those who were fighting as to their eventual utility as civilians.

From *The New Industrial State* by John Kenneth Galbraith. Copyright © 1967, 1971 by John Kenneth Galbraith. Reprinted by permission of the publisher Houghton Mifflin Company.

With the cold war, however, the word planning acquired ideological overtones. The Communist countries not only socialized property, which seemed not a strong likelihood in the United States, but they planned, which somehow seemed more of a danger. Since liberty was there circumscribed, it followed that planning was something that the libertarian society should avoid. Modern liberalism carefully emphasizes tact rather than clarity of speech. Accordingly it avoided the term and conservatives made it one of opprobrium. For a public official to be called an economic planner was less serious than to be charged with Communism or imaginative perversion, but it reflected adversely nonetheless. One accepted and cherished whatever eventuated from the untrammeled operation of the market. Not only concern for liberty but a reputation for economic hardihood counseled such a course.

For understanding the economy and polity of the United States and other advanced industrial countries, this reaction against the word planning could hardly have been worse timed. It occurred when the increased use of technology and the accompanying commitment of time and capital were forcing extensive planning on all industrial communities. This has now been sensed. And, in many quarters, the word planning is again acquiring a measure of respectability.

Still what is not supposed to exist is often imagined not to exist. In consequence, the role of planning in the modern industrial society remains only slightly appreciated. Additionally, it is the sound instinct of conservatives that economic planning involves, inevitably, the control of individual behavior. The denial that we do any planning has helped to conceal the fact of such control even from those who are controlled.

II

In the market economy the price that is offered is counted upon to produce the result that is sought. Nothing more need be done. The consumer, by his offer to pay, obtains the necessary responding action by the firm that supplies his needs. By offering to pay yet more he gets more. And the firm, in its turn, by similar offers gets the labor, materials and equipment that it requires for production.

Planning exists because this process has ceased to be reliable. Technology, with its companion commitment of time and capital, means that the needs of the consumer must be anticipated—by months or years. When the distant day arrives the consumer's willingness to buy may well be lacking. By the same token, while common labor and carbon steel will be forthcoming in response to a promise to pay, the specialized skills and arcane materials required by advanced technology cannot similarly be counted upon. The needed action in both instances is evident: in addition to deciding what the consumer will want and will pay, the firm must take every feasible step to see that what it decides to produce is wanted by the consumer at a remunerative price. And it must see that the labor, materials and equipment that it needs will be available at a cost consistent with the price it will receive. It must exercise control over what is sold. It must exercise control over what is supplied. It must replace the market with planning.

That, as more time elapses and more capital is committed, it will be increasingly risky to rely on the untutored responses of the consumer needs no elaboration. And this will be increasingly so the more technically sophisticated the product. There is a certain likelihood that even two or three years hence there will be a fairly reliable consumer demand for strawberries, milk and fresh eggs. There is no similar assurance that people will want, so spontaneously, an automobile of particular color or contour, or a transistor of particular size or design.

The effect of technology, and related change, in reducing the reliability of the market for labor or equipment and in making imperative the planning of their procurement, is equally clear and can be seen in the simplest case.[1] If men use picks and shovels to build a road, they can be called out on the same morning that the decision is taken to do the job. The picks and shovels serve a variety of purposes; accordingly, the market stocks them in readily available quantities. It will help in getting manpower if, as Marx thought necessary, there is an industrial reserve army of the unemployed. But an equally prompt beginning is possible by raiding the work force of another employer of unskilled labor with the simple market promise of more pay.

When specifications are raised to modern superhighway standards and heavy machinery is introduced, the market no longer works as well. Engineers, draftsmen, drainage experts and those who arrange the elimination of trees, grass, parkland, streams and the other environmental amenities may not be readily available even in response to a substantial advance in pay. Bulldozers and heavy earth-moving equipment cannot be bought with the same facility as picks and shovels. In all of these cases anticipatory steps must be taken to insure that the necessary supply is available at an appropriate wage or price. Market behavior must be modified by some measure of planning.[2]

For inertial systems engineers, digital circuit design specialists, superconductivity research specialists, aeroelasticity investigators and radio test and evaluation engineers as also for titanium alloys in comparison with steel, and space vehicles as compared with motorcycles, the market is greatly less dependable. Need must be elaborately anticipated and arranged. The language of both industry and government reflects the modern fact. Civil War quartermasters went into the market for their needs. So, in turn, did the contractors who filled these orders. The equivalent procurement would now be programmed.

As viewed by the industrial firm, planning consists in foreseeing the actions required between the initiation of production and its completion and preparing for the accomplishment of these actions. And it consists also of foreseeing, and having a design for meeting, any unscheduled developments, favorable or otherwise, that may occur along the way.[3] As planning is viewed by the economist, political scientist or pundit, it consists of replacing prices and the market as the mechanism for determining what will be produced, with an authoritative determination of what will be produced and consumed and at what price. It will be thought that the word planning is being used in two different senses.

In practice, however, the two kinds of planning, if such they may be called, are inextricably associated. A firm cannot usefully foresee and schedule future action or prepare for contingencies if it does not know what its prices will be, what its sales will be, what its costs including labor and capital costs will be and what will be available at these costs. If the market is unreliable, it will not know these things. Hence it cannot plan. If, with advancing technology and associated specialization, the market becomes increasingly unreliable, industrial planning will become increasingly impossible unless the market also gives way to planning. Much of what the firm regards as planning consists in minimizing or getting rid of market influences.

III

A variety of strategies are available for dealing with the increasing unreliability of markets. Not all, in fact, require their replacement. If the item is unimportant, market uncertainty can be ignored. For General Electric it is a matter of considerable interest to know the price at which it will be able to buy high alloy steel or sell large generators, and the quantities that will be forthcoming or which can be sold. No similar urgency attaches to knowledge of the price at which flatware will be available for the plant cafeterias. And size is a solvent for uncertainty that cannot otherwise be eliminated. In the late nineteen-fifties and early nineteen-sixties, the Convair Division of General Dynamics Corporation lost $425 million on the manufacture of jet transports. Part of this was the result of uncertainties associated with research and development; its 880 and 990 passenger jets cost more to bring into being than expected. But a major factor was the failure of the market—or more precisely default on or failure to obtain the contracts that were meant to reduce market uncertainty. The company did not fail (although it was a near thing) because it had annual revenues of around $2 billion from —in addition to aircraft—such diverse artifacts as missiles, building materials, submarines and telephones.[4] None of these was affected by the misfortunes of Convair. For a smaller company, with one product, a $425 million loss would have been uncomfortable. We have here an important explanation of one of the more notable corporate developments of recent times, the growth of the so-called polyglot corporation. It combines great size with highly diverse lines of manufacture. Thus it can absorb the adverse consequences of uncertainty that cannot otherwise be eliminated. Uncontrolled aversion of customers to one product, such as aircraft, is unlikely to affect telephones or building materials. The effects of market uncertainty are thus contained in what will often be a relatively small part of the total planning unit.

But the more common strategies require that the market be replaced by an authoritative determination of price and the amounts to be sold or bought at these prices. There are three ways of doing this:

1. The market can be superseded.
2. It can be controlled by sellers or buyers.
3. It can be suspended for definite or indefinite periods by contract between the parties to sale and purchase.

All of these strategies are familiar features of the industrial system.

IV

The market is superseded by what is commonly called vertical integration. The planning unit takes over the source of supply or the outlet; a transaction that is subject to bargaining over prices and amounts is thus replaced with a transfer within the planning unit. Where a firm is especially dependent on an important material or product—as an oil company on crude petroleum, a steel firm on ore,[5] an aluminum company on bauxite or Sears, Roebuck on appliances—there is always danger that the requisite supplies will be available only at inconvenient prices. To have control of supply—to rely not on the market but on its own sources of supply—is an elementary safeguard. This does not eliminate market uncertainty; rather, the large and unmanageable uncertainty as to the price of ore or crude is replaced by the smaller, more diffuse and more manageable uncertainties as to the costs of labor, drilling, ore transport and yet more remote raw materials. But this is a highly beneficial exchange. For Socony-Vacuum or Sohio, a change in the cost of crude is a serious matter, a change in the cost of drilling equipment a detail.

As viewed by the firm, elimination of a market converts an external negotiation and hence a partially or wholly uncontrollable decision to a matter for purely internal decision. Nothing, we shall see, better explains modern industrial policy in regard to capital and labor than the desire to make these highly strategic cost factors subject to purely internal decision.

Markets can also be controlled. This consists in reducing or eliminating the independence of action of those to whom the planning unit sells or from whom it buys. Their behavior being subject to control, uncertainty as to that behavior is reduced. At the same time the outward form of the market, including the process of buying and selling, remains formally intact.

This control of markets is the counterpart of large size and large size in relation to the particular market. A Wisconsin dairy farm cannot influence the price that it pays for fertilizer or machinery. Being small, its decision to purchase or not to purchase is of no appreciable significance to the supplier. The same is true of its sales. Having no control over its suppliers or its customers it pays and receives the going prices.

Not so with General Motors. Its decision to buy or not to buy will usually be very important to its suppliers; it may be a matter of survival. This induces a highly cooperative posture. So with any large firm.[6] Should it be necessary to press matters, General Motors, unlike the dairyman, has always the possibility of supplying a material or component to itself. The option of eliminating a market is an important source of power for controlling it.

Similarly, size allows General Motors as a seller to set prices for automobiles, diesels, trucks, refrigerators and the rest of its offering and be secure in the knowledge that no individual buyer, by withdrawing its custom, can force a change. The fact that GM is one of a few sellers adds to its control. Each seller shares the common interest in secure and certain prices; it is to the advantage of none to disrupt this mutual security system. Competitors of General Motors are especially unlikely to initiate price reductions that might provoke further and retributive price-cutting. No formal communication is necessary to prevent such actions; this is considered naïve and arouses the professional wrath of company counsel. Everyone knows that the survivor of such a contest would be not the aggressor but General Motors. Thus do size and small numbers of competitors lead to market regulation.

Control of prices is only a part of market control; if uncertainty is to be eliminated there must also be control of the amount sold. But size also makes this possible. It allows advertising, a well-nurtured sales organization and careful management of product design which can help to insure the needed customer response. And since General Motors produces some half of all the automobiles, its designs do not reflect the current mode, but are the current mode. The proper shape of an automobile, for most people, will be what the automobile majors decree the current shape to be. The control of demand, as we shall see later, is not perfect. But what is imperfect is not unimportant for reducing market uncertainty.

Finally, in an economy where units are large, firms can eliminate market uncertainty for each other. This they do by entering into contracts specifying prices and amounts to be provided or bought for substantial periods of time. A long-term contract by a Wisconsin dairy farmer to buy fertilizer or sell milk accords no great certainty to the fertilizer dealer or the dairy receiving the milk. It is subject to the capacity of the farmer to fulfill it; death, accident, drought, high feed costs and contagious abortion can all supervene. But a contract with the United States Steel Corporation to supply sheet steel or to take electric power is extremely reliable. In a world of large firms, it follows, there can be a matrix of contracts by which each firm eliminates market uncertainty for other firms and, in turn, gives to them some of its own.

Outside of the industrial system, most notably in agriculture, the government also intervenes extensively to set prices and insure demand and thus to suspend the operation of the market and eliminate market uncertainty. This it does because the participating units—the individual farms—are not large enough to control prices. Technology and the associated commitment of capital and time require nonetheless that there be stable prices and assured demand. But within the industrial system, similar action is also required where exacting technology, with extensive research and development, mean a very long production period and a very large commitment of capital. Such is the case in the development and supply of modern weapons, in the exploration of space and in the development of a growing range of modern civilian products or services including transport planes, high-speed ground transport and various applied uses of nuclear energy. Here the state guarantees a price sufficient, with suitable margin, to cover costs. And it undertakes to buy what is produced or to compensate fully in the case of contract cancellation. Thus, effectively, it suspends the market with all associated uncertainty. One consequence, as we shall see, is that in areas of most exacting and advanced technology the market is most completely replaced and planning is therefore most secure. As a further consequence this has become for the participants a very attractive part of the industrial system. The fully planned economy, so far from being unpopular, is warmly regarded by those who know it best.

V

Two things of some interest are evident from this analysis. It is clear, first of all, that industrial planning is in unabashed alliance with size. The large organization can tolerate market uncertainty as a smaller firm cannot. It can contract out of it as the smaller firm cannot. Vertical integration, the control of prices and consumer demand and reciprocal absorption of market uncertainty by contracts between firms all favor the large enterprise. And while smaller firms can appeal to the state to fix prices and insure demand, this security is also provided by the state to the big industrial firm when it is most needed. Those circumstances—the exacting technology, large commitments of time and capital—make it fairly certain that most of this government work will be done by large organizations.[7]

By all but the pathologically romantic, it is now recognized that this is not the age of the small man. But there is still a lingering presumption among economists that his retreat is not before the efficiency of the great corporation, or even its technological proficiency, but before its monopoly power. It has superior capacity to extract profits. Therein lies its advantage. "Big business will undertake only such innovations as promise to enhance its profits and power, or protect its market position . . . free competitive men have always been the true innovators. Under the stern discipline of competition they must innovate to prosper and to survive."[8]

This, by the uncouth, would be called drivel. Size is the general servant of technology, not the special servant of profits. The small firm cannot be restored by breaking the power of the larger ones. It would require, rather, the rejection of the technology which since earliest consciousness we are taught to applaud. It would require that we have simple products made with simple equipment from readily available materials by unspecialized labor. Then the period of production would be short; the market would reliably provide the labor, equipment and materials required for production; there would be neither possibility nor need for managing the market for the finished product. If the market thus reigned there would be, and could be, no planning. No elaborate organization would be required. The small firm would then, at last, do very well. All that is necessary is to undo nearly everything that, at whatever violence to meaning, has been called progress in the last half century. There must be no thought of supersonic travel, or exploring the moon, and there will not be many automobiles.

We come thus to the second conclusion which is that the enemy of the market is not ideology but the engineer. In the Soviet Union and the Soviet-type economies, prices are extensively managed by the state. Production is not in response to market demand but given by the overall plan. In the western economies, markets are dominated by great firms. These establish prices and seek to insure a demand for what they have to sell. The enemies of the market are thus to be seen, although rarely in social matters has there been such a case of mistaken identity. It is not socialists. It is advanced technology and the specialization of men and process that this requires and the resulting commitment of time and capital. These make the market work badly when the need is for greatly enhanced reliability—when planning is essential. The modern large corporation and the modern apparatus of socialist planning are variant accommodations to the same need. It is open to every freeborn man to dislike this accommodation. But he must direct his attack to the cause. He must not ask that jet aircraft, nuclear power plants or even the modern automobile in its modern volume be produced by firms that are subject to unfixed prices and unmanaged demand. He must ask instead that they not be produced.

NOTES

1. In technical terms the supply price of highly specialized materials, components and labor is inelastic. So is the demand for highly technical products. In the first instance large (and punishing) increases in prices will bring no added supply. In the second case large (and equally punishing) decreases will bring no added customers.

2. That planning is necessary does not mean that it is well done. At any given time on any particular construction site, as everyone has observed, nothing much is happening. Planning, to anticipate and arrange material, machinery, manpower and subcontractor requirements, is necessary. But, in context, it is done with great imprecision or incompetence. Accordingly, something is normally being awaited.

3. "In practice [business management] . . . aims to minimize uncertainty, minimize the consequences of uncertainty, or both." Robin Marris, *The Economic Theory of "Managerial" Capitalism* (New York: The Free Press of Glencoe, 1964), p. 232.

4. Richard Austin Smith, *Corporations in Crisis* (New York: Doubleday, 1963), pp. 91 *et seq.* The company's misfortunes in the sale of aircraft were intimately bound up with the contemporary difficulties of Howard Hughes at TWA.

5. This problem has been of importance in the difficulties experienced in recent years by Wheeling Steel, a non-integrated producer. "Thus under its contracts Wheeling in the late 1950's and early 1960's, found itself powerless to trim ore supplies as sales fluctuated. . . . Moreover by the early 1960's the operating efficiencies of using beneficiated ores . . . were fully apparent, but Wheeling, tied to out-moded sources of supply, lagged behind many in the industry in using such ores." *Fortune*, June, 1965.

6. Economists, in the past, have been at pains to disassociate large absolute size from large size in relation to the particular market. "Concentration [i.e. small numbers and hence large size in relation to the market] has nothing to do with size of firms, no matter by what resounding name it is called—big business, colossal corporation, financial giantism, etc. . . . most of my fellow economists would agree that 'absolute size is absolutely irrelevant.'" M. A. Adelman, Hearings before the Subcommittee on Antitrust and Monopoly of the Committee on the Judiciary, United States Senate, Eighty-Eighth Congress, Second Session, Pursuant to S. Res. 262, Part I. *Economic Concentration. Overall and Conglomerate Aspects* (1964), p. 228. This contention, although wrong, is deeply grounded in contemporary economic attitudes.

   Market power is associated by economists not with planning but with monopoly. Market concentration or monopoly in the conventional view is inimical to efficient employment of resources by the market and has strong overtones of illegality. If big business and monopoly power tend to be identical, then all big business is inefficient and presumptively illegal. This, however, given the evident role of large firms in the modern economy is absurd. So disassociation of absolute from relative size is important if traditional antipathy to monopoly is to seem sensible and big business is to be legitimate. In fact, large absolute size and large size relative to the market do go together. Great firms—General Motors, Standard Oil, Ford, United States Steel—are invariably large in relation to their principal markets. On this see the sensible remarks of Carl Kaysen, "The Corporation: How Much Power? What Scope?" in *The Corporation in Modern Society*, Edward S. Mason, ed. (Cambridge: Harvard University Press, 1959), p. 89.

7. In 1960, 384 firms with 5,000 employees or more accounted for an estimated 85 per cent of all industrial research-and-development expenditure. Firms employing fewer than 1,000 people, though numbering 260,000, accounted for only 7 per cent of such expenditure. An estimated 65 per cent of these funds were supplied by the Federal Government. (M. A. Adelman, Hearings before the Subcommittee on Antitrust and Monopoly of the Committee on the Judiciary, United States Senate, Eighty-Ninth Congress, First Session, Pursuant to S. Res. 70, Part III. *Economic Concentration. Concentration, Invention and Innovation* [1965], pp. 1137, 1140.) In recent years the high degree of market security in the use of Federal funds—a secure coverage of all costs and a secure market for the product—has allowed a considerable number of small firms to enter the manufacture of highly technical products. These firms line highways adjacent to major educational centers, most notably in Massachusetts and California, and have encouraged the belief that the small firm has a major foothold in the manufacture of highly technical products and components particularly for defense and space exploration. Their share of the total is, in fact, negligible.

8. Horace M. Gray, Hearings before the Subcommittee on Antitrust and Monopoly of the Committee on the Judiciary, United States Senate, Eighty-Ninth Congress, First Session, Pursuant to S. Res. 70, Part III. *Economic Concentration. Concentration, Invention and Innovation* (1965), p. 1164.

31. Bureaucratic Patterns in the Navy Officer Corps

Arthur K. Davis

This paper concerns the sociology of occupations. Within the general framework of the occupational system, reference is made first to Max Weber's concept of bureaucracy. The military variant of this ideal type is then outlined to set the stage for our central interest: some structural strains inherent in military bureaucracy.[1]

Our specific hypothesis is: *the effective performance of the manifest functions of a military bureaucracy requires a certain type of occupational discipline and formal organization; these in turn tend to create inherent pressures toward recession of goals, occupational ritualism, and professional insulation; which in turn may alter the actor's definition of the situation so as to impair systematically his effectiveness in carrying out the manifest functions of the bureaucracy.*

Concrete data for this paper, which in no way represents the official views of the Navy Department, are based on three years in the Naval Reserve as an Air Combat Intelligence Officer with two Fleet Air Wings. Observations are limited to four aspects of naval social organization: (1) the tendency to avoid responsibility; (2) legalism; (3) the Navy as an insulated occupation; (4) ceremonialism. These aspects are functionally related to each other and to the ideal (normative) pattern of military bureaucracy, whence they issue and upon which they profoundly react. This study relates the ideal pattern or "manifest structure" of a military bureaucracy to concrete social reality. It points to unintended "latent structures" which necessarily emerge from attempts to realize in practice an abstract ideal pattern.[2]

For scientific relevance, participant-observer studies like this one depend on integration with a more highly generalized theoretical system. Empirical observation can thus gain support and validity from the body of older propositions, which in turn it may confirm or refine. In this way a series of such observations may form a significant element of cumulative, systematic and therefore compelling scientific knowledge, though each investigation by itself may provide merely plausible "post factum" sociological interpretations, "proving" nothing.[3] This study is accordingly

Reprinted from *Social Forces* 27 (1948):143–53, by permission of the author and the publisher. Copyright, 1948, by the Williams and Wilkins Company.

oriented to the work of Weber and Parsons on institutional structure and to the significant contributions made by Merton and Barnard in the field of large-scale organization.[4]

Our growing concern with such dynamic processes as goal-recession and the development of latent structures points up what seems to be a serious weakness of Parsons' institutional approach—its preoccupation with ideal types which are identified essentially with institutional or normative patterns.[5] On the theoretical level this approach does provide explicitly for non-normative elements in action.[6] These are called situational or conditional elements, and are treated in effect as a residual category. Whether that conception is adequate is debatable: residual categories usually indicate unfinished areas in scientific systems. On its empirical level, however, the institutional approach may be criticized for dealing almost exclusively with the normative elements of social systems and with that deviance which arises from the conflict of such elements. A considerable degree of institutional integration is clearly a functional imperative of any social system, and conflict among institutions is sometimes a source of deviance. But institutional theory is not a comprehensive theory of social systems. On its most abstract level it is at least potentially comprehensive. But as currently used it slights many functional prerequisites[7] which every social system must meet—problems of recruitment, handling frustration, socialization, etc. Action is only partly a function of ideal patterns.

Moreover preoccupation with institutional patterns, by definition the most stable normative elements in a society, may lend itself to a static and unrealistic view of concrete social organization. It is but a short step thence to the pitfall of ideological affirmation of the traditional social order. This would be unfortunate, to say the least. The danger can be avoided by directing attention toward more explicit analytical formulation of non-normative action structures and situational elements. A theoretically integrated conception of social deviation and of social change will probably depend on the formulation of a mature theory of social systems.

THE NAVY AS A MILITARY VARIANT OF BUREAUCRACY

In terms of occupational functions the Navy corresponds to the general occupational pattern of modern industrial economics. On an ideal-typical level, this pattern may be conceived as large-scale organization, the upper and smaller division of which is a steep hierarchy of executive and technical-expert functions ("line" and "staff"), roughly equivalent to Weber's concept of bureaucracy. The lower division is a broad mass of easily learned "labor" roles (operatives, enlisted men), usually classified as skilled, semi-skilled, and unskilled. The "foreman" role (army noncom, navy Chief Petty Officer) is a subsidiary link between the two divisions. Executive, technical-expert and labor functions as used here are analytical abstractions. Any specific job usually includes elements of all three, with one predominating. The "foreman" role alone is a fairly balanced blend.

Our present concern is with the upper division, the Navy Officer Corps, the social structure of which is highly bureaucratized. A label and not an epithet, bureaucracy denotes an integrated hierarchy of specialized offices defined by systematic rules—an impersonal routinized structure wherein legitimized authority rests in the office and not in the person of the incumbent. Founded on technical competence, the bureaucratic career begins with successful examination or appointment to office, and it proceeds by regular stages of promotion, often based largely on seniority, to honorable and pensioned retirement. Salary is better conceived as a means of maintaining requisite social status than as a wage for irksome labor. We do not "pay" military men to risk their lives in war. Rather, we give them high social status and tacitly invoke extraordinary service on the principle of *noblesse oblige*. Officers are gentlemen by common consent as well as by legal fiat, as is shown by their frequent admission to exclusive clubs regardless of their social origins.

Achieving any high occupational status usually involves a probationary ordeal which inculcates the requisite technical skills sometimes, and the necessary social attitudes and behavior patterns always. Examples are an Annapolis education or getting a Ph.D. Such apprenticeship devices are often ritual rather than rational.

The key to understanding the military variant of bureaucracy probably lies in (1) its ultimate purpose of winning battles; (2) the highly "seasonal" nature of combat operations; (3) the consequently acute problem of maintaining a battle organization during long stand-by periods. Sociologically, a Navy is a bureaucratic organization designed to operate under battle conditions which rarely occur. Civilian groups can usually operate in terms of probabilities calculated from their everyday experience. But in military groups the dire consequences of defeat preclude routines based to the same degree on the weight of experience, that is, on non-combat conditions. A Navy can never exist entirely in the present. It must keep in view a future moment which rarely comes, but which must be assumed as constantly impending. Hence it builds its routines on the abnormal, its expectations on the unexpected. This procedure affords a rational technique for war and an equally necessary rationale for peacetime.

The extreme uncertainty of the battle situation directly affects the social organization of the Navy. Size alone would impose the bureaucratic pattern on Naval organization. Coordination of masses of men and material clearly requires those properties of precision, impersonality, and reliability which make bureaucracy the most efficient form of large-scale organization. The battle premise greatly intensifies the need for those same qualities. This pressure is met by an extraordinary emphasis on authority and tradition which also serves the need for peacetime self-maintenance.

The essence of any military organization is its structure of authority, the ultimate source of which is the enormous file of written regulations. Military groups carry the normal bureaucratic stress on authority to its extreme development. It is the function of a multitude of practices—drills, musters, inspections, deference to superiors—to minimize uncertainty by instilling habits of automatic response that will survive the distractions of combat and the *ennui* of peace. Reducing the jobs of officers and men to the simplest possible operations permits rapid substitution of personnel on the principle of the interchangeability of standardized parts. Uniforms and insignia, by "telegraphing" the wearer's status in the hierarchy of authority and his job in the division of labor, facilitate communication, coordination and impersonality.

Against the hazards of sea and battle, a mass of rules is designed for every possible occasion. Men must come to attention at the approach of an officer. This is partly because he may announce an emergency wherein split-second response is the only alternative to destruction. Such a consideration will be irrelevant 999 times, but navies are more prone than other groups to take the thousandth chance as their norm. The other 999 cases symbolically reaffirm and "exercise" the Navy's basic social structure—its system of authority. Both as rehearsal for battle and as a device for self-perpetuation of the organization, deference is an instrumental pattern. Yet its endless repetition tends to build up the pattern as an end in itself so that hierarchy comes to be an ultimate value far beyond its instrumental requirements.[8]

Carrying out his prime function of military command may require a line officer to order men to death. Impersonality is often a prerequisite to maximum efficiency both in issuing and obeying the order; hence the institutionalizing of the "caste line" between officers and enlisted men. Within the Officer Corps the danger from particularism is minimized partly by the secondary caste lines which exist between all commissioned ranks, especially between Ensign and Lieutenant (junior grade), between Lieutenant-Commander and Commander, and between Captain and Flag Officers. It is also restricted by the Navy's pervasive formality and ritual, both vocational and social. But even more important in reinforcing impersonality is the intensive indoctrination of the Officer Corps with the idea of duty—with such sentiments as "Don't give up the ship." The instrument of this indoctrination is the four-year Annapolis course. On the enlisted level there is nothing corresponding to this indoctrination. Petty Officers have less need of it since they merely administer the hazardous orders which commissioned officers issue.

The military variant of bureaucracy may thus be viewed as a skewing of Weber's ideal type by the situational elements of uncertainty and standing by. Detailed description of the Navy's "blueprint" organization[9] would tell us how the Navy ought to work without always showing how it actually does work. We turn therefore to some concrete material. Clearly our analysis must be far from comprehensive. The limited empirical uniformities described below, since they are recurrent, may be conceived as structural pressures or tendencies—sometimes overt, sometimes latent—subject in any particular instance to modification by other basic tendencies, by local circumstances, and by the effect of individual personalities. Attention is focussed on the Regular Officer Corps. Although by 1945 there were more than five times as many Reserve Officers as there were Regulars, the latter defined the situation to which the others were indoctrinated to conform.[10]

Some Characteristics of Naval Organization

A. *Avoiding responsibility: the philosophy of do-the-least.* So pervasive a tendency must be explained primarily in terms of social organization and only secondarily on the basis of particular personalities and local conditions. The "buck-passing" pattern includes (a) minimizing responsibility for making decisions, especially those for which no precedent exists; (b) getting out of doing work (carrying out decisions). Responsibility tends to be passed upward; work, downward.[11] Whenever it is practiced in primary groups, whether in the context of large-scale organization or not, it is generally sanctioned by the primary group as a whole. Sentiments of solidarity together with informal sanctions like ridicule usually keep the members in line. The basic explanation of avoiding responsibility must therefore lie outside the informal organization. It must be sought in the pressures generated by the formal organization or by the situation. Five propositions are submitted.

1. Shunting responsibility upward stems partly from the universal fact that a functionary's area of responsibility invariably exceeds that of his control. No official can direct or even recognize all the complex social, personal, and technical factors operating in his department. Yet he is generally accountable for whatever befalls there, and most strictly and necessarily so in military organizations. For adequate performance and a successful career the official must rely heavily upon favorable attitudes on the part of his superiors. Consequently, he is strongly tempted to slide his problems into his superior's lap by asking advice, requesting instructions, securing approval in advance. And he will accept for decision some of his subordinates' problems to minimize uncertainty in his own sphere of accountability. Responsibility for making decisions tends to move upward. This does not apply to authority to carry out decisions. Interference by superiors in the routine execution of work is strongly resented.

The discrepancy between control and responsibility makes for avoiding responsibility particularly in the lower and middle levels of a bureaucracy. For the man at the top there is no such escape from the strains of decision except by a do-nothing policy.[12] Another pressure on top executives is to find subordinates who will get things done.[13]

2. A second incentive for buck-passing is the latent conflict between

authority and specialization. When organizations involve elements as dynamic as science and technology, officials sometimes lack the specialized knowledge prerequisite to making adequate decisions. The temptation is strong to get rid of such problems as soon as possible. The rapidity of wartime technological and organizational changes made for an extraordinary circulation of these hot potatoes among military units.

The two tendencies just outlined are in some degree common to all bureaucratic hierarchies. Business corporations partly counteract these pressures by making status and rewards depend heavily on individual initiative. These incentives and sanctions are less available to the Navy, where seniority is primary and competition often operates negatively. Officer personnel are seldom dismissed, and then usually for offences against discipline rather than for incompetence. "Misfits" are often transferred to posts where they can do no harm. In military organizations the rewards for assuming responsibility and the penalties for failing to do so seem less extreme than in the business world.

Moreover, cost reduction is a constant pressure in modern capitalism. No such compulsion operates on military organizations, whose competition for income is lobbying for a larger share of the federal budget. Lobbying is confined to a few top officers, whereas the cost-consciousness of many business firms permeates their entire hierarchy.

3. Bureaucracies often develop an *esprit de corps* which congeals individual initiative. They present two conflicting goal-orientations: (a) the tangible and intangible rewards for efficient performance in the formally defined role; (b) the informal social satisfactions from harmonious in-group relations, which are prerequisite to (*a*) yet incompatible with the invidious sentiments aroused by (*a*). For the "eager beaver" often appears to his fellows as a threat to their status and self-esteem. Epithets such as "sucking around" and "brown-nosing" operate as informal sanctions.[14] The resultant *esprit* protects in-group solidarity by restraining competition and resists change by intrenching vested interests.

The "sucker philosophy" of the Armed Forces grew partly from this conflict. The widespread sentiments against volunteering for special tasks were tacitly recognized and conciliated by "compulsory volunteering" ("Three volunteers—you and you and you!"). Enlisted men seeking commissions were observed to conceal the fact from their fellows, although they discussed it freely with their officers. Trainees at the Quonset Officers Indoctrination School were invariably eager beavers until they got out on a billet. The zeal of trainees at the Navy Air Combat Intelligence School contrasted sharply with the later indifference of the same officers back for a refresher course. Instructors without field experience loaded graduating student officers with intelligence publications. But instructors who had seen field duty advised the graduates to stow such paraphernalia in the nearest furnace and to carry whisky instead. It was the writer's observation that the latter advice was the more functional.

4. Structuralized discrepancies between individual effort and reward

in military systems restrain initiative in both war and peace, though for different reasons. The wartime Services expanded so rapidly that they could attend only to categories and not to individuals. The imputed needs of the organization at the moment determined the disposition of resources. Most of the individual's vital interests—his work, friends, rewards, punishments—were largely outside his control. Uncertainty evokes many responses, including "griping," scapegoating, magic, and religious conversion. Here we will indicate only its relation to buck-passing.

Zeal could bring undesirable results as often as not. An "eager beaver" might be held overseas or in rank longer than less valuable personnel. Sudden transfer to another unit could deprive a man of the fruits of prestige hard-earned in his old outfit. Unearned rewards might fall into his lap. Everyone knew of such cases if he did not experience them himself. Many basic needs which are major incentives in civilian occupations are furnished automatically in the Service. All this contributed to fatalism and inertia. The individual naturally sought refuge in his primary-group relationships. If clique behavior did not modify one's formal situation, it did at least make it more endurable.

Competitive achievement officially counted for promotion in the Army Officer Corps but not in the Navy, except for rare "spot" promotions and for ranks above Lieutenant Commander. But the Army system aroused more discontent. Its capriciousness was due to (1) the exigencies of the organization; (2) lack of standardized competitive criteria; (3) invidiousness aroused by competition. And non-competitive criteria (for instance, seniority) drew resentment because they contradicted official ideology. Navy promotions, based on seniority, evoked less resistance, although the fact that some incompetents went up with everyone else was disliked because of the implied downward levelling.

In time of peace unpredictability is minimized, but a ritualism stemming from minute observance of routine and regulation submerges initiative more than ever. Military organizations between wars, in terms of their wartime *raison d'etre*, are relatively lacking in manifest functions. To maintain their organization they must fall back on routine for its own sake. Security and every possible comfort are provided, unhampered by wartime hazards and improvisations. The philosophy of Do-the-least rules unchallenged.[15]

5. The unofficial conception of a Regular Navy career often minimizes assumption of responsibility. Promotions below and to Lieutenant Commander are *en bloc*, based on seniority, examination, and quotas authorized by Congress. Higher appointments are filled by individual selection. Elaborate "fitness reports" on each officer are periodically filed with the Navy Department by his superior. During the war these examination and quota rules were suspended, and mass promotions in the junior grades became in effect automatic on completion of the specified months in rank. The ranks above Lieutenant Commander continued to be filled by individual selection. Despite the large element of seniority the naval career

is competitive in important respects, and it thus conforms roughly to the basic occupational pattern of the United States. In peacetime the "up or out" principle is applied to all ranks.

But this is often a negative competition to avoid departure from precedent. If an officer makes a decision unsupported by regulation or custom he is sticking out his neck, because he is officially responsible for his acts and nothing will save him if things go wrong. Deviation from routine may pull down his fitness report and cause him to be passed over years later by the Selection Board. It is difficult indeed to escape indoctrination with a psychology of affirm-and-conform. Minimizing responsibility is simply playing it safe. This is reinforced by the inherent exaltation of authority-obedience relationships in military organizations, by the relatively greater role of seniority in the early and formative stages of the career, and by strong tendencies toward ritualism and legalism.

An apparent exception to the buck-passing philosophy was the Construction (Seabee) Branch. Its slogan, "Can Do," seems to have been a realistic index of attitudes toward work and responsibility. Instances on Okinawa were observed where Seabee outfits consistently volunteered for additional *routine* tasks—a sharp contrast to the atmosphere in the writer's own attachment, a relatively elite combat command. A partial explanation may be the fact that the Seabees were drawn from the construction industry with a minimum of occupational reorientation. They could give maximum scope to the industry's best traditions of visible achievement and ingenious improvisation.

B. *Legalism: the psychology of affirm-and-conform.* This results from the characteristic bureaucratic tendency toward displacement or recession of goals whereby instrumental patterns become ends in themselves. A Navy's hierarchy of authority is necessarily overemphasized because of (a) the primacy of authority-obedience relationships in military groups; (b) the necessity for bureaucracies to proliferate and to refine rule-systems so as to minimize role-conflict; (c) the prevalence of the "play-it-safe" attitude toward the naval career. Regulation becomes a sacred cow.

Military systems do not countenance debate about orders. The severest sanctions enforce compliance because of the need for countering the proven fallibility of military commanders with the assumption and trappings of infallibility. Otherwise, the precision and coördination essential in battle would be lost.

The minimizing of role-conflicts in a complex organization requires a clear definition of jurisdictions. Because of the need for standardization, new situations bring a ceaseless flow of new regulations.[16] *Navy Regulations* specifies detailed behavior for thousands of situations. If trouble results from failure to observe these directions, responsibility can be pinned on someone. Against the pressure of authority from above, the sole defense of the individual lies in strictly observing regulations—an outcome reinforced by the endless routine in naval life.[17]

Bureaucratic personnel suffer from chronic status-anxiety. Everyone focuses his attention on his superior, whose slightest display of pleasure or displeasure is magnified and distorted downward. The mildest criticism from a superior is often viewed by the recipient as a crushing attack. Praise may bring an accusation of "brown-nosing" from one's colleagues. To counteract both these tensions is one function of the Navy's extraordinarily emphasized norm of "loyalty upward."

As examples of the disfunctional tendency of formal organizations to overemphasize their main instrumental devices, we cite two cases. For efficient coördination, official communications must travel by the chain of command. In one large air unit, even the most trivial correspondence was routed up to the Chief of Staff and often to the Admiral, then down to the appropriate department for action. Here the reply was drafted, typed, routed back to the top for approval and signature (often refused, pending minor changes) and finally routed down to the dispatching office. Mail which a clerk should have handled in and out in 24 hours was thus sent to the top and back two or three times, drawing attention from eight to twelve persons over a ten-day period.

We cite next the behavior of certain heavy-bomber crews on anti-submarine patrols. Because of their short tour of duty, the infrequency of submarine sightings, and the complexity of anti-submarine tactics, these air crews usually made several errors in the course of an attack. For this they would be sharply criticized by their superiors. Hence arose a serious morale problem. At least three flight crews in one squadron began going out for "quiet patrols" by their own admission. Observing the letter of their instructions legalistically, they flew their patrols exactly as charted. If a suspicious object appeared a few miles abeam, their course lay straight ahead.

Combining legalism and avoidance of unnecessary responsibility, we arrive at the golden rule for the professional military career: Follow the book or pass the buck. . . .

Beginning with Weber's ideal bureaucratic type, we have discussed the military variant of bureaucracy chiefly in terms of its special emphasis on authority and tradition. These elements require such emphasis because of the situational pressures of uncertainty and organizational self-maintenance. Devices for meeting those pressures were shown to be disfunctional at times as well as functional for the organization. Significant latent structures, such as those making for legalism and avoidance of responsibility, were outlined. Points of articulation between this paper and other studies of large-scale organization, particularly those by Merton and Barnard, were indicated as part of the generalized theoretical system upon which the present observations depend for much of their scientific relevance.

This study suggests the great plasticity of individual behavior in response to occupational discipline. What was it that almost overnight made us all buckpassers? that steeped us in a psychology of affirm-and-conform? The answer—in this case, bureaucracy—may be sought in the structure of the action situation. In industrial society the occupational pattern is a primary aspect of that situation.

Further light would be shed on the problems of this paper by investigation of the following hypothesis: the effectiveness of military leaders tends to vary inversely with their exposure to a conventionally routinized military career. Some outstanding military leaders were men who (1) had had experience in non-military occupations; or (2) rose with phenomenal rapidity through the ranks; or (3) belonged to military organizations newly created or renovated—for instance, the German and Soviet armies and the several air forces. Conventional career soldiers on the other hand have frequently resisted essential innovations like automatic firearms in the nineteenth century, tanks in World War I, the modern conception of air power, the unified command.

NOTES

1. *Cf.* Robert K. Merton, "Bureaucratic Structure and Personality," in *Social Forces* 27 (1948).
2. The terms *manifest structure* and *latent structure*, credit for which belongs to Professor Marion Levy of Princeton University, resemble Merton's well known concepts of manifest and latent function. In this study latent structure is viewed as an emergent property of the manifest structure. Manifest structure is the abstract formal organization consciously taken as a model or normative ideal pattern to realize the manifest (intended) functions of a group. Latent structure is that structure, originally unintended but prone to become increasingly "manifest" over time, which results from the concrete activation of the manifest structure, by virtue of the influence of other elements in the situation not foreseen or not provided for in the manifest structure. Structure of course cannot be equated with function, since a given structure may serve several functions.
3. *Cf.* Merton, "Sociological Theory," *American Journal of Sociology* 50 (1945), 467–73.
4. *Cf.* Weber, *Theory of Social and Economic Organization*, (New York: Oxford University Press, 1947); and *Essays in Sociology* (New York: Oxford University Press, 1946), ch. 8; Parsons, *Structure of Social Action* (New York: McGraw-Hill, 1937), and miscellaneous papers (bibliography in *Psychiatry* 10, May, 1947); Merton, "Bureaucratic Structure and Personality," *Social Forces* 27 (1948), and "Role of the Intellectual in Public Bureaucracy," *Social Forces* 23 (1945), 504–15; Barnard, *Functions of the Executive* (Cambridge: Harvard University Press, 1938), and "Functions and Pathology of Status Systems in Formal Organizations," in W. F. Whyte, ed., *Industry and Society* (New York: McGraw-Hill, 1946), 46–83.
5. *Cf.* Parsons, "Sociological Theory," in Gurvitch and Moore, eds., *Twentieth Century Sociology* (New York: Philosophical Library, 1945), pp. 61–62.
6. *Ibid.*, pp. 60–62.
7. This concept is discussed by Albert K. Cohen, "Themes and Kindred Concepts in Social Theory," *American Anthropologist* 50 (1948), 436–43, a paper highly relevant to the problem of developing a more adequate theory of social systems.
8. *Cf.* Merton, "Bureaucratic Structure and Personality," *Social Forces* 27 (1948), on the displacement of goals; also G. W. Allport, *Personality* (New York: Henry Holt, 1937), ch. 7 on "functional autonomy" as the motivational aspect of goal-displacement. The tendency of formal organization sometimes to defeat its own ends by overemphasizing the elements most essential to its success is a recurrent theme of this paper.
9. *Cf. U. S. Navy Regulations* (Washington: Government Printing Office, 1932); A. A. Ageton, *Naval Officer's Guide* (New York: McGraw-Hill, 1943), and *Naval*

Leadership (New York: McGraw-Hill, 1944); R. P. Erdmann, *Reserve Officer's Manual* (Washington: Government Printing Office, 1932); L. P. Lovette, *Naval Customs* (Annapolis: U.S. Naval Institute, 1934); *The Watch Officer's Guide* (Annapolis: U.S. Naval Institute, 1935); *The Bluejacket's Manual* (Annapolis: U.S. Naval Institute, 1940).

10. R. L. Warren, "The Naval Reserve Officer: A Study in Assimilation," *American Sociological Review*, XI (1946), 202–11; R. Lewis, "Officer-Enlisted Men's Relationships," *American Journal of Sociology* 52 (1947), 410–19.

11. But sometimes an officer, ignorant of his job and unable to shift responsibility upward, had to shift it downward to his Petty Officers. This was probably easier to do in the Navy, which gave more attention than the Army did to technical competence in enlisted men's assignments. Unlike the Army, Navy enlisted ratings specify technical function (gunner, radioman) as well as rank.

12. Apparently this was the course of the 1941 Hawaiian commanders with respect to proposals for improved reconnaissance around Oahu and warnings of Japanese aggression. *Cf.* W. B. Huie, *The Case Against the Admirals* (New York: E. P. Dutton, 1946), pp. 92–99. Accession to august rank does not change overnight the habits of a lifetime.

13. Mr. B. Barber of Harvard University has suggested that the buck-passing tendency is related to the great popularity of Hubbard's story, "A Message to Garcia," among top executives. Rowan in the Garcia story was a man to get things done. He was almost blindly obedient as well as strikingly competent. The point also illustrates the authoritarian character of bureaucracy.

14. These epithets are primarily related to the violation of universalistic norms, but rationalization easily distorts others' success into unfair competition. The "sucker philosophy" is also closely linked to other aspects of naval organization such as legalism and wartime fatalism. It is not a simple function of the conflict between manifest and latent functions of formal and informal organizations.

15. *Cf.* E. Larrabee, "The Peacetime Army: Warriors Need Not Apply," *Harper's* (March, 1947), pp. 240–47.

16. *Cf.* the development of gunnery safety precautions, 1818–1924, as a result of the lessons from fatal accidents, by W. H. P. Blandy in H. F. Cope, *Command at Sea* (New York: Norton, 1943), pp. 159–74.

17. In wartime the predominance of Reservists and the pressure of situational necessities resulted in systematic rule-breaking. This could be done safely where in-group solidarity and/or approval of superiors gave such practices a secondary or *ad hoc* institutionalization. Their contribution to winning the war was probably very great, although there were disfunctional aspects too.

X. Art and Mass Culture

In section I, Tylor, Laird, and White differentiated man from non-man on the basis that *Homo sapiens* is most distinctively *Homo symbolicus*. We are social animals capable of communicating in a way that is unique to us. Our species is the one that manipulates symbols, creates culture, re-creates the physical environment, invents tools, and devises its own social organization.

In an age of science, we are inclined to think of language as the primary form of human expression, and of conceptual, abstract, general, and precise language as the highest form. The late Herbert Read, a seminal art historian and critic of lasting influence, presents us with a useful corrective to that bias. His "Art as a Symbolic Language" is a brilliant restatement of the argument that art may be regarded not merely as a symbolic representation of reality, but as a vehicle for the definition and redefinition of reality itself. As much as science or philosophy, art *interprets* human existence. In so doing, it often provides entertainment, which in and of itself can transport us from our immediate reality. But art is more than entertainment. The aesthetic experience brings us closer to reality. Art, by defining reality and refining the sensibility of those exposed to it, helps us to confront, if not to surmount, the human condition.

While discursive language is sometimes used to heighten cognitive perception and to attain greater precision and more clarity of a logical and abstract nature, poetry, drama, music, painting, and sculpture unfold in concrete manifestations capable of fusing with sensuous and emotional realities. Since all of the arts are expressive *and* communicative, they are *ipso facto* social phenomena that have to do with the formation of character and personality.

Ian Watt, a man of letters with sociological insight, deals tellingly with the influence of technology on art and of art on social life. All art is dependent upon technology, both with respect to its craftmanship, as in writing, sculpture, and painting, and with respect to its dissemination, as in printing, broadcasting, and recording. One could say that without Gutenberg's invention of movable type and "the Gutenberg galaxy" to which it led, there would be no novel. That particular form of fiction has its technological base in modern printing, an advance that vastly reduced the cost of literature and made it available to an even larger public. The mass production and consumption of books occurred simultaneously with the rise of mass education. Literacy and leisure intensified the mass desire for printed matter. In the process, new populations slowly and selectively entered the realm of literary culture. But when this happened, literature began to change (as did all the fine arts). Writers accommodated themselves to new levels and types of taste as they geared their output to a larger and larger mass of people. To some, this change heralded a disastrous decline in the quality of high aesthetic expression, while to others it signaled a welcome end to the aristocratic monopoly of art.

For better or worse, every technological innovation—from that of Gutenberg through Edison and Marconi to the inventors of television—has extended mass culture. The pervasiveness of what we today call "mass media" was encountered first in printing, then in rotogravure, stereotyping, photography, telegraphy, telephony, color reproduction, and then, in rapid succession, sound transmission via the phonograph and radio, and sound-and-image transmission via the movies and world-wide television. In an apparently irreversible progression, more effective media are producing more and more mass culture.

A professional media expert, Gerhart Wiebe, has devoted much of his time to research and reflection on this subject. He asks: Why has ubiquitous mass media so signally failed to raise the level of public taste? His answer is ingenious. It involves a contrast between highly demanding personal relations and wholly undemanding impersonal reactions. To Wiebe, the mass media serves principally to *preserve and maintain* existing attitudes in audiences that select familiar messages to which they can effortlessly respond. Also, the audiences use media content to discharge anger, resentment, and other powerful emotions that they accumulate in private life. The crude depiction of conflict, violence, and sadism caters to this propensity. The mass media thus become a device by which diverted and distracted audiences can avoid possibly painful human encounters. Wiebe's analysis gives us a picture of non-art amounting to anti-art. Mass culture exacerbates the condition that art alleviates. We would only add that broadcasters and other media managers are usually aware of what they are doing. They intentionally design programs that will yield the effects described by Wiebe, since these effects increase the size of their audience.

32. Art as a Symbolic Language

Herbert Read

> Art may be defined as symbolic language
> —CASSIRER

A renewed interest in symbolism is one of the characteristics of our time. It is due partly to those social sciences, like anthropology, which have emphasized the great and necessary rôle of symbolism in the life of primitive communities; and partly to the science of psychology which has shown the great and necessary (but often unacknowledged) rôle of symbolism in the mental life of civilized communities. Stemming from these studies there have been more specialized investigations into linguistics and aesthetics which have again assigned a predominant rôle to symbolism. The rationalists of the eighteenth century, or the historical materialists of the nineteenth century, were of the opinion that mankind in its intellectual development had transcended the symbol; today we not only admit the continuing force of symbolic modes of thought, but are even compelled to make a plea for their revival and extension.

"Man is primarily a communicating animal"—such is the opinion of Professor J. Z. Young, an English biologist who has made a special study of the human brain and nervous system.[1] Human beings communicate with one another by means of a great variety of signs, the most obvious being the signs systematized in language, spoken or written. But they also communicate by gesture (in which we may include the subtle but expressive movements of the face and eyes), by sounds that are not linguistic (music, for example), and by visual images.

A science which goes back to ancient Greek medicine and philosophy has been devoted to the study of these various sign-processes—it is known as *semiotic*. The ancient Stoics, we are told, made semiotic "a basic division of knowledge co-ordinate with physics and ethics, and included within it logic and the theory of knowledge."[2]

A related science, which has been given the name of *semantics*, is concerned more specifically with a study of the meaning of signs. In modern times these two overlapping sciences, semiotic and semantics, have become highly organized disciplines, with their own technical terminology, and are associated with some of the greatest names in

Reprinted from *The Form of Things Unknown* by Herbert Read, copyright 1960, by permission of the publisher, Horizon Press, New York.

modern philosophy: Charles Peirce and Mead, Dewey and Russell, Cassirer and Carnap. More specialized studies are due to Ogden and Richards, to Susanne Langer and Charles Morris, and to many others whose names would only be familiar to a specialist in the subject.

It is far from my intention, or capacity, to contribute to this discussion on a technical level. I shall rely on these sciences for a few definitions, but in the main I shall be concerned with the fact that there exist two competing systems of communication, one based on *sound*, the other on *sight*. I shall argue that the system based on sight has been underrated and sadly neglected by modern society, and that any satisfactory social integration or personal intelligence requires the full development of both systems of communication.

In general, semioticians have confined themselves to the study of the various types of discourse which make use of language. Charles Morris has classified discourse, firstly according to use as *informative, valuative, incitive,* and *systemic;* and secondly according to mode as *designative, appraisive, prescriptive* and *formative*. The various combinations of these modes and uses give sixteen major types of discourse—scientific, fictive, legal, mythical, poetic, moral, critical, religious, and so on, and a good deal can be said about the characteristics of each type of discourse. Scientific discourse, for example, illustrates (according to Charles Morris) "the most specialized form of designative-informative discourse. In it the designative mode of signifying is freed to the maximum degree from the other modes and developed in ways which most adequately perform the task of conveying true information about what has been, does, or will exist. In this respect, it merely elaborates and refines such statements as occur in common speech. As science advances, its statements become more purely designative, more general, better confirmed, and better systematized . . . Science is especially concerned with the search for reliable signs."[3] Poetic discourse, on the other hand, is primarily appraisive-valuative. According to Morris, it "signifies by signs which are appraisive in mode and its primary aim is to cause the interpreter to accord to what is signified the preferential place in his behavior signified by the appraisors"—surely the most unpoetic description of poetry ever tapped out on a typewriter. But Dr. Morris makes his meaning clearer when he states that "the great significance of poetic discourse lies in the vivid and direct way that it records and sustains achieved valuations, and explores and strengthens novel valuations".[4] To contrast extreme types of discourse such as these is to emphasize the general distinction, first established by Ogden and Richards in *The Meaning of Meaning,* between referential and emotive types of discourse, and our whole discussion might have centered on this conflict which is inherent in language itself, did not a more fundamental conflict—that between linguistic and non-linguistic modes of communication—call for more urgent consideration.

I ought to confess, before proceeding any further, that the title of this essay does not indicate accurately the subject with which I am concerned. At any rate, I ought to begin with a distinction, the one that Susanne Langer makes between the symbol "which lets us *conceive* its object," and the sign, "which causes us to *deal with* what it means." Strictly speaking, as Charles Morris has argued, all symbols are signs, and the true contrast to the symbol is not the sign, but the *signal*. I do not think I need introduce such a refinement, because I am about to substitute another distinction which is more relevant to the discussion. But briefly it is now "scientific" to use the word "sign" for any vehicle of meaning, anything that directs behavior and is not at the moment a physical stimulus; signs can then be divided into "signals" and "symbols" according to whether they are direct responses of the organism to its environment, or substitutes for such direct responses. To quote an illustration from Morris: "A person may interpret his pulse as a sign of his heart condition or certain sensations as a sign that he needs food; such signs are simply signals; his resulting words—when substituted for such signals—would however be symbols." A neater definition is C. F. von Weizsäcker's: "A sign which cannot be made superfluous simply by pointing to the object simplified, we shall call a symbol."[6]

It is the contention of a semiotician like Charles Morris that our understanding of symbols is now always dependent in some degree on language, and symbols are distinguished as prelanguage, language, and post-language. But a whole group of non-vocal signs—"signs other than those produced by the vocal cords and heard by the ear," is recognized. Spoken-heard language, Dr. Morris admits, "has never supplanted its great rival—visual signs." And he goes on to say:

"An age in which printing, photography, painting, film and television have an important place will call for a semiotic which has not neglected the visual sign; music lovers will rightly ask the sign status of musical sounds; and students of human nature will seek insight into the rôle of those signs which play such a prominent place [*sic*] in 'thinking' and yet which are not spoken or heard." That is precisely the problem I am concerned with now. But it is not merely a problem of whether the science of semiotic or semantics can afford to neglect non-vocal signs; the question is whether in any sphere of human activity, and more especially in the sphere of education and social discourse, we can afford to neglect those systems of non-vocal signs, known more familiarly as the plastic arts, which constitute modes of communication as essential as the modes of communication embodied in vocal (spoken-heard) language.

Let us first note that there is a good deal of ground common to the vocal and non-vocal languages. A painting may convey information, or evaluate a situation, with the same accuracy as a spoken description of that situation. Morris admits that "a portrait of a person, together with the name of the person, is, as Peirce held, no less a statement than the verbal description of a person."[7] Music can convey information about a situation or a mood. Morris further admits that:

"Such arts as music and painting may then signify in any of the modes of signifying. And since they can be put to various uses, they can illustrate in various degrees all the types of discourse which have been distinguished. Painting or music, for example, can be designatively informative, appraisively valuative, and so on. Hence a painting or a piece of music can in principle be scientific, poetic, mythological, religious, and the like, terms which we do in fact frequently (and correctly) employ in this way."

The most that a scientist like Charles Morris will admit—and among scientists I think he would classify himself as a behaviorist—is that nonvocal signs, organized as arts, are "indispensable for appraisive-valuative discourse, since they can embody vividly and concretely in their icons the very characteristics of the objects which in their appraisive capacity they signify as valuata." This seems to be an admission, jargon apart, that works of art can have an effect on human behavior without necessarily being translated into linguistic signs. They can act as substitutes for speech. There is nowhere an admission, as far as I can gather, that works of art have a special rôle in social discourse—that they can express, and communicate, knowledge or values altogether beyond the scope of language.

For an assertion of this truth we must go to the philosophers and to the poets. I think almost all the great poets have been aware that they were in some sense the possessors of what Leone Vivante has described as "a principle of inward light—an original, self-active principle, which characterizes life and spontaneity as contrasted with mechanism."[8] What we have to assert, and attempt to prove, is that art is a cognitive activity —that it is not merely an embellishment or intensification of linguistic types of discourse: it is not even a substitute for those types of discourse: it is a unique mode of discourse, giving access to areas of knowledge that are closed to other types of discourse.

This truth, although always evident to philosopher-poets like Goethe and Shelley, was first given full philosophical status by Cassirer in his *Philosophy of Symbolic Forms*, the first volume of which was published in 1923. It is true that fifty years earlier the symbolic nature of the plastic arts had been clearly recognized by another German philosopher, Conrad Fiedler, but his fragmentary writings have been neglected and even Cassirer seems to have been unaware of them. But Cassirer's recognition, not in the *Philosophy of Symbolic Forms* but in the shorter and later *Essay on Man*,[9] that art "is not the mere reproduction of a ready-made, given reality . . . not an imitation but a discovery of reality" is identical with Fiedler's recognition of the same truth, and when Cassirer goes on to affirm that "art may be defined in symbolic language," he is using phraseology identical with Fiedler's.

It would simplify our discussion at this stage if we were to follow Fiedler's example and confine ourselves to the visual arts. The very fact that poetry makes use of words, the material also of rational discourse, complicates any discussion of its non-rational uses; though I believe that the kind of illumination that comes to the consciousness of the poet, and is expressed in words, is not essentially different from the kind of illumination that comes to the painter or sculptor and is expressed in visual images; nor is it essentially different from the kind of illumination that comes to the musician and is expressed in tonal images.[10]

A poem, like a picture or a musical composition, has its unique form, which is a complex of images and cadences, and this form is an embodiment of the artist's feelings and conveys a meaning which is not necessarily co-extensive with the discursive or rational meaning of the words employed. A poem not only *is* different, but *means* more, than its prose paraphrase. It has a physical shape (the black words as they lie on the white page); it has a musical configuration that in itself, as sound, is expressive. At the simplest such a musical configuration is a meaningless refrain, a "hey nonny no," or a "fara diddle dyno." But every line and verse has this sound-pattern that can be abstracted from the literal content of the statement made in the poem, and when abstracted this sound-pattern would have an expressive function, just as the visual composition of a painting has an expressive function when abstracted from its figurative content. The whole purpose of art, of course, is to make these two functions reinforce one another, so that form comes in aid of feeling—the sound is *responsive* to an unconscious need for expressiveness, for emphasis. A poet can establish, for a particular poem, a pattern of musical expression, and then subtly vary it. Poe's lines "To Helen" owe part of their mysterious beauty to this principle of variation. A regular pattern is established in the first verse—a steady iambic beat corresponding to the sweep of oars over "a perfumed sea." Then the quickened rhythm of the second verse, describing how Helen has brought the poet home over "desperate seas."

> To the glory that was Greece
> And the grandeur that was Rome

and finally an invocation in slow rhythm and a last line which ends two voiceless but evocative syllables short of the established pattern:

> Ah, Psyche, from the regions which
> Are Holy Land!

This is a simple example of symbolic form in poetry, of sound-pattern established almost visually, like musical notation, but at any rate as an aural composition, for the ear, superimposed, as it were, on the literal meaning, an accompaniment in another medium.

The form of the poem, that is to say, is a non-vocal sign, even when it is a shape of words which express meaning in the ordinary semantic sense by their syntax. But let us avoid the formal ambiguities of linguistic art and confine ourselves to the visual arts. We can then more confidently affirm, with Conrad Fiedler, that "artistic activity is an entirely original and absolutely independent mental activity."[11]

Fiedler was the first philosopher to suggest that the knowledge of reality given by the visual arts is *sui generis* and in no necessary degree coincident with the knowledge of reality which we owe to science or philosophical speculation. Works of art embody an independent and free development of perceptual experience. "It is the rare privilege of highly organized, sensitive persons," says Fiedler, "that they can achieve immediate contact with nature. Their relation to an object does not arise from single effects; on the contrary, they grasp its very existence, and they feel the object as a whole before they break up this general feeling into many separate sensations."[12]

The artist, Fiedler goes on to say, "becomes an artist by virtue of his ability to rise above his sensations." Fiedler contrasts "the conceptual mastery of the world," which is given in abstract cognition, with the perceptual mastery of the world given in artistic creation. He points out that the scientist, and we might add the educationist, habitually considers a perceptual activity inferior if it does not lead to clear concepts dominating perception. But the scientist and educationist are wrong in believing that "through abstract thinking alone all the intellectual capacities of human nature have been recognized and fulfilled. To remain at the stage of perception rather than to pass onward to the stage of abstraction does not mean remaining on a level which does not lead to cognition; on the contrary, *it means to keep open other roads that also arrive at cognition*. But if cognition attained by perceptual experience is different from cognition reached by abstract thinking, it can nevertheless be a true and final cognition."[13]

Fiedler's description of the artistic process as "a holding on to perceptual experiences in spite of both sensation and abstraction" has been corroborated by the statements of many artists, notably, since Fiedler's time, by Cézanne. Here, for example, is a quotation from a letter of Cézanne's to Emile Bernard (12th May 1904):

"I am progressing very slowly, for nature reveals herself to me in very complex forms; and the progress needed is incessant. One must see one's model correctly and experience it in the right way; and furthermore express oneself forcibly and distinctly.

"The artist must scorn all judgment that is not based on an intelligent observation of character. He must beware of the literary spirit which so often causes painting to deviate from its true path—the concrete study of nature—to lose itself all too long in intangible speculations."

Or again (26th May 1904):

"Literature expresses itself by abstractions, whereas painting, by means of drawing and color, gives concrete shape to sensations and perceptions. One is neither too scrupulous nor too sincere nor too submissive to nature; but one is more or less master of one's model, and, above all, of the means of expression. Get to the heart of what is before you and continue to express yourself as logically as possible."[14]

Cézanne also said, in a phrase which summarizes much that Fiedler had to say: "All things, particularly in art, are theory developed and applied in contact with nature." In other words, there can be no divorce between the artist's modes of thought and his perceptual experience. Though he had no command of philosophical discourse, Cézanne was always trying to state that the practice of art, making an object to embody and at the same time define a feeling, is in itself a mode of cognition distinct from scientific or philosophical cognition, and sufficient unto the artist as a principle of reality.

I could quote many other statements made by artists themselves which show that they are always aware, if they reflect on their creative experience, that they are using a language which has nothing to do with literary language, the language of concepts, but which, in its own way, can express the profoundest truths about reality, truths that are not readily expressed in concepts. If we ask what the artist is trying to do we can reply with Fiedler that he is trying to achieve clarity of consciousness. "Artistic activity begins when man finds himself face to face with the visible world as with something immensely enigmatical; when, driven by an inner necessity and applying the powers of his mind, he grapples with the twisted mass of the visible which presses in upon him and gives it creative form. In the creation of a work of art, man engages in a struggle with nature not for his physical but for his mental existence . . . the beginning and the end of artistic activity reside in the creation of forms which only thereby attain existence. What art creates is no second world alongside the other world which has an existence without art; what art creates is the world, made by and for the artistic consciousness . . . Art creates the form for that which does not yet exist for the human mind and for which it contrives to create forms on behalf of the human mind. Art does not start from abstract thought in order to arrive at forms; rather, it climbs up from the formless to the formed, and in the process is found its entire mental meaning.

"In the artist's mind a peculiar consciousness of the world is in process of development."[15]

I am making too generous a use of one author, but no one who has ever written on art has made these points so clearly as Fiedler. Indeed, it is not until comparatively recently that these truths have been rediscovered or re-expressed. A modern philosopher like Susanne Langer, without reference to Fiedler, can suggest that "the limits of language are not the last limits of experience, and things inaccessible to language may have their own forms of conception, that is to say, their own symbolic devices;"[16] and this same philosopher elsewhere admits that artistic expression is "the verbally ineffable, yet not inexpressible law of vital experience, the pattern of affective and sentient being."[17] I find the same admission in a recent work by Karl Jaspers, all the more significant in that it comes from such a typically conceptual thinker. "The fine arts," says Jaspers, "make our visible work speak to us. We see things as art teaches us to see them. We experience space through the form that the architect has imposed upon it; we experience a landscape as it has been epitomized in its religious architecture, shaped by human labor, and made a part of life by constant use. We experience nature and man only as they are reduced to their essence in sculpture, drawing and painting. In a sense, it is when this is done, and only when this is done, that things assume their characteristic form and reveal their visible quality and soul which had previously seemed hidden."[18]

Jaspers would make a distinction, as we must do too, between "art as a code of symbols for metaphysical reality," and "art in the sense of technical cleverness with no relation to philosophy." It is the distinction we usually make between art and entertainment, and the failure to maintain this distinction will inevitably lead to a misunderstanding of the symbolic function of art. All "great art," Jaspers says, is metaphysical art—that is to say, "an art whose visible creations reveal the underlying reality." The word "great" begs the question: let us rather say that art is either *metaphysical*, an activity aiming at the comprehension of reality, or it is *divertive*, an activity that aims at escaping from reality. But we must then make it very clear that metaphysical art is in no sense a philosophical activity; it is as Fiedler says; "an entirely original and absolutely independent mental activity."[19]

I hope that I have now made clear this absolute distinction between two activities, one working through non-vocal or iconic signs, the other working through intellectual concepts or logic, but both having as their aim the development of consciousness of reality. Let us now ask what relative attention is paid, by society, to these distinct modes of communication.

The answer is, on the one hand *everything*; on the other hand *nothing*. Everything is done to develop and perfect linguistic modes of communication; to encourage the formation of logical signs and to erect the products of the various types of discourse into systems of knowledge. Our whole civilization is based on the assumption that scientific, legal, technological, political, moral, religious and all the other modes of discourse are not merely adequate, but exclusively adequate, for the acquisition of knowledge and the discovery of truth. On the other hand, so little in general are we aware of non-vocal modes of experience and comprehension that we now conceive them as the special function of an artistic minority, of little relevance to mankind in general. Education is regarded almost exclusively as a system for developing a capacity for forming concepts, and any idea that education should devote at least as much attention to developing a capacity for concrete perceiving has hardly ever occurred to those who formulate and direct our educational ideals.

Over the whole course of human development in historic times there has no doubt been a bias in favor of conceptual thought, and the higher reaches of human thought would never have been possible without the power of conceiving abstract, universal and problematic objects. But the superiority of conceptualization as a mental process can be exaggerated. As William James pointed out:

"Our meanings are of singulars, particulars, indefinites, problematics, and universals, mixed together in every way. A singular individual is as much *conceived* when he is isolated and identified away from the rest of the world in my mind, as is the most rarified and universally applicable quality he may possess—*being*, for example, when treated in the same way. From every point of view, the overwhelming and portentous character ascribed to universal conceptions is surprising. Why, from Socrates downwards, philosophers should have vied with each other in scorn of the knowledge of the particular, and of adoration of that of the general, is hard to understand, seeing that the more adorable knowledge ought to be that of the more adorable things, and that the *things* of worth are all concretes and singulars. The only value of universal characters is that they help us, by reasoning, to know new truths about individual things. The restrictions of one's meaning, moreover, to an individual thing, probably requires even more complicated brain-processes than its extension to all the instances of a kind; and the mere mystery, as such, of the knowledge, is equally great, whether generals or singulars be the things known. In sum, therefore, the traditional Universal-worship can only be called a bit of perverse sentimentalism, a philosophic 'idol of the cave.' "[20]

James thus supports my whole argument, if we add to his observations the fact that by the conception of concretes and singulars we imply the process of the perceptual or visual comprehension of the world. The apprehension of singulars, in any complete sense, is the artistic process itself. It is the comprehending of the things of worth, of adorable concretes and singulars, but it is a process that has been wholly neglected not only by philosophy, but also by all the systems of education ever established by human societies.

Such an unbalanced development was made possible by the invention of sign-systems, usually linguistic. There is no reason to assume, as some behaviorist psychologists do, that thought has always been linguistic; there is plenty of evidence to prove that, in the earliest stages of writing, meaning was expressed by visual signs that did not correspond to linguistic signs.[21] In its early stages, writing only loosely expressed the spoken language. "At the basis of all writing lies the picture," says Professor Gelb, the latest and perhaps the foremost authority on the subject. "Just as speech developed out of imitation of sounds, so writing developed out of imitation of the forms of real objects or beings." The evolution of writing from primitive drawings by way of descriptive-representational and identifying-mnemonic devices to word-syllabic systems, and so on to alphabetic systems, has been studied in great detail by modern philologists, who have shown how writing only gradually lost its visual or representational quality, and even its sub-vocal or speech forms, to become a system of signs for the transmission of abstract concepts.

A developed system of writing of any kind did not appear before 3,000 B.C. Writing, therefore, and the whole conceptual mode of reasoning which depends upon it, is of very recent origin compared with man's use of visual symbols—the earliest cave-drawings are perhaps 40,000 years old. I do not make this comparison with any disparaging intention: I merely want to show how basic is the attempt to comprehend the world visually. Now if, on the invention of alphabetic writing, man had dispensed with the representation of visual perceptions altogether, and had discarded art as a useless method of comprehension, then the bias in favor of conceptual thought would be understandable. But on the contrary, driven by the necessities of comprehension and expression, man went on refining his visual consciousness and art became, in every great civilization, the embodiment of his finest feelings and deepest intuitions. By unreflecting consent all men would accord equal honor to Plato and the architect of the Parthenon; to St. Thomas Aquinas and the architect of Chartres; to Bacon and Michelangelo; to Spinoza and Rembrandt; to Bergson and Cézanne—not that philosophers and artists should be paired off as contemporaries in this way. We honor our great artists, and count them as among the most enlightening spirits of history. But we deny the faculties by virtue of which they become great artists— we deny, in our education and in our social estimation of capabilities, any recognition of the fruits of perceptual experience in ordinary people.

So long as civilization was based on handcrafts, there always existed, in the actual mode of living, some counterpoise to abstract conceptual thought. But during the course of the last two centuries millions of people have become divorced from all perceptual effort. Of course, people still have to use their eyes (automatically, with the same kind of reactions that we might expect from a calculating machine, but with less reliability); but there is little need for any positive co-ordination of hand and eye, for any visual exploration of the world, for any constructive use of perceptual experience. A whole method of communication, the language of non-vocal signs, has been thoughtlessly jettisoned by modern society.[22]

But not without protest, of course. Some of the shrillness of modern art is due to its sense of dereliction. It no longer belongs to the people; it is no longer an acceptable mode of communication The artist has to adopt shock-tactics, in an attempt to reawaken the visual responses of an apathetic public. He is trying to communicate by visual signs with people who are blind. In such a situation it is not the art that should be reformed, but the people that should be given eyes to see. And if they are given eyes to see, they in their turn will wish to express themselves in this distinct and necessary fashion. In learning to use visual signs, to conceive the world symbolically and to create artistic form, they will correct the bias of an exclusively linguistic mode of thought, and, what is equally important, correct the bias of a mechanized mode of life.

NOTES

1. *Doubt and Certainty in Science*. A Biologist's Reflections on the Brain. Oxford, Clarendon Press, 1951, p. 58.
2. Charles Morris, *Signs, Language and Behavior*, New York, Prentice-Hall, 1946. In an Appendix Dr. Morris gives a history of the development of semiotic.
3. *Op. cit.*, p. 126.
4. *Philosophy in a New Key*, Harvard University Press, 1951, p. 223.
5. Morris, *op. cit.*, p. 26.
6. *The World View of Physics*, London, Routledge & Kegan Paul, 1952, p. 140.
7. Morris, *op. cit.*, p. 194.
8. *English Poetry*, London, Faber, 1950, p. 1.
9. Yale University Press, 1944.
10. The particular way in which a poem functions symbolically is well described in Rosemund Tuve's book, *A Reading of George Herbert*, London, Faber, 1952, p. 93: "The meanings of a poem carried to its author often lie too deep for formulation without the aid of metaphor; that is why they must be symbolized. . . . A work of art is a highly conscious achievement; perhaps the human consciousness is seen functioning at its highest when it tries thus to give form to the formless. The welter has its interests, too, but the excitement of literature is that a mind has shaped into loveliness that which otherwise would lie unshaped and dumb. The business of criticism is likewise not with the word unspoken, not with the thing unheard, unshaped, unknown, unmeant, but with the beauty and the power which is taken on by that to which a maker gives form."
11. *On Judging Works of Visual Art*, trans, by Henry Schaefer-Simmern and Fulmer Mood, University of California Press, 1949, p. 61.
12. *Op. cit.*, p. 28. It is not entirely a question of sensation—although sensation cannot be experienced without perception, nevertheless, Fiedler points out, "sensation does not stimulate and further, but rather hinders, the growth of our visual conceptions. Our feeling is something else than our visual conceiving, and if the former dominates, then the latter must step back. For example, in sensing the beauty of a particular object, we may occupy ourselves with this sensation entirely, without proceeding a single step towards the *perceptual mastering of the object*. However, at that moment when interest based on visual conception takes hold of us again, we must be able to forget every sensation in order to further our perceptual grasp of the object for its own sake. Because many persons are all too quick to transform perceptual experience into feeling, their perceptual abilities remain on a low level of development." *Op. cit.*, pp. 29–30. (My italics.)
13. *Op. cit.*, pp. 34–35.
14. Paul Cézanne, *Letters*, edited by John Rewald, London, Cassirer, 1941, pp. 235–6, 237.
15. *Op. cit.*, pp. 48–49.
16. *Philosophy in a New Key*, p. 265.
17. *Op. cit.*, p. 257.
18. *Tragedy is not Enough*, trans. by Harold Reiche, Harry T. Moore, and Karl W. Deutsch. Boston, Beacon Press, 1952.
19. *Op. cit.*, p. 61.
20. *Psychology* (Briefer Course), London, Macmillan, 1892, pp. 242–43.
21. *Cf.* I. J. Gelb, *A Study of Writing*, London, Routledge & Kegan Paul, 1952, p. 10 and *passim*.
22. To be salvaged, of course, by the publicity men, the practitioners in advertising, who are well aware of the "subliminal" appeal of visual signs.

33. The Reading Public
and the Rise of the Novel
Ian Watt

The novel's formal realism, we have seen, involved a many-sided break with the current literary tradition. Among the many reasons which made it possible for that break to occur earlier and more thoroughly in England than elsewhere, considerable importance must certainly be attached to changes in the eighteenth-century reading public. In his *English Literature and Society in the Eighteenth Century,* for example, Leslie Stephen long ago suggested that "the gradual extension of the reading class affected the development of the literature addressed to them,"[1] and he pointed to the rise of the novel, together with that of journalism, as prime examples of the effect of changes in the audience for literature. The nature of the evidence is such, however, that a reasonably full analysis would be inordinately long and yet fall far short of completeness in some important matters where information is scanty and difficult to interpret; what is offered here, therefore, is only a brief and tentative treatment of a few of the possible connections between changes in the nature and organization of the reading public, and the emergence of the novel.

Many eighteenth-century observers thought that their age was one of remarkable and increasing popular interest in reading. On the other hand, it is probable that although the reading public was large by comparison with previous periods, it was still very far from the mass reading public of today. The most convincing evidence of this is statistical, although it must, of course, be remembered that all the numerical estimates available are, to varying but always considerable degrees, both untrustworthy in themselves and problematic in their application.

The only contemporary estimate of the size of the reading public was made very late in the century: Burke estimated it at 80,000 in the nineties.[2] This is small indeed, out of a population of at least six millions, and would probably imply an even smaller figure for the earlier part of the century with which we are most concerned. Such is certainly the implication of the most reliable evidence available on the circulation

From *The Rise of the Novel* by Ian Watt. Originally published by the University of California Press; reprinted by permission of The Regents of the University of California.

of newspapers and periodicals: one figure, that of 43,800 copies sold weekly in 1704,[3] implies less than one newspaper buyer per hundred persons per week; and another later figure, of 23,673 copies sold daily in 1753,[4] suggests that although the newspaper-buying public tripled in the first half of the century, it remained a very small percentage of the total population. Even if we accept the highest contemporary estimate of the number of readers per copy, that of twenty made by Addison in the *Spectator*,[5] we are left with a maximum newspaper-reading public of less than half a million—at most one in eleven of the total population; and since the estimate of twenty readers per copy seems a wild (and not disinterested) exaggeration, the real proportion was probably no more than half of this, or less than one in twenty.

The sale of the most popular books in the period suggests a book-buying public that is still numbered only in tens of thousands. Most of the very few secular works with sales of over ten thousand were top-ical pamphlets, such as Swift's *Conduct of the Allies* (1711), with a sale of 11,000 copies,[6] and Price's *Observations on the Nature of Civil Liberty* (1776), with a sale of 60,000 in a few months.[7] The highest figure recorded for a single work, that of 105,000, for Bishop Sherlock's 1750 *Letter from the Lord Bishop of London to the Clergy and People of London on the Occasion of the Late Earthquakes . . .*,[8] was for a some-what sensational religious pamphlet, many of which were distributed free for evangelical purposes. Sales of full-length, and therefore more expensive, works were much smaller, especially when they were of a secular nature.

Figures showing the growth of the reading public are an even more unreliable guide than those indicating its size; but two of the least dubious suggest that a very considerable increase occurred during the period. In 1724 Samuel Negus, a printer, complained that the number of printing presses in London had increased to 70;[9] but by 1757 another printer, Strahan, estimated that there were between 150 and 200 "constantly employed."[10] A modern estimate of the average annual pub-lication of new books, excluding pamphlets, suggests that an almost four-fold increase occurred during the century; annual output from 1666 to 1756 averaging less than 100, and that from 1792 to 1802, 372.[11]

It is likely, therefore, that when, in 1781, Johnson spoke of a "nation of readers,"[12] he had in mind a situation which had to a large extent arisen after 1750, and that, even so, his phrase must not be taken literally: the increase in the reading public may have been sufficiently marked to justify hyperbole, but it was still on a very limited scale.

A brief survey of the factors which affected the composition of the reading public will show why it remained so small by modern standards.

The first and most obvious of these factors was the very limited distribution of literacy; not literacy in its eighteenth-century sense—knowledge of the classical languages and literatures, especially Latin—

but literacy in the modern sense of a bare capacity to read and write the mother-tongue. Even this was far from universal in eighteenth-century England. James Lackington, for example, towards the end of the century reported that "in giving away religious tracts I found that some of the farmers and their children, and also three-fourths of the poor could not read";[13] and there is much evidence to suggest that in the country many small farmers, their families, and the majority of laborers, were quite illiterate, while even in the towns certain sections of the poor—especially soldiers, sailors and the rabble of the streets—could not read.

In the towns, however, it is likely that semi-literacy was much commoner than total illiteracy. In London especially: the general spread of shop names instead of signs, which struck a Swiss visitor, Carl Philipp Moritz, as unusual, in 1782,[14] surely implies that it was being increasingly assumed that written communications would be understood by a large enough proportion even of the denizens of Gin Lane to be worth addressing to them.

Opportunities for learning to read seem to have been fairly widely available, although the evidence strongly suggests that popular schooling was at best casual and intermittent. An educational system as such hardly existed; but a miscellaneous network of old endowed grammar schools and English schools, charity schools and non-endowed schools of various kinds, notably dame schools, covered the country, with the exception of some outlying rural areas and some of the new industrial towns of the north. In 1788, the first year for which adequate figures are available, about a quarter of the parishes of England had no school at all, and nearly a half had no endowed schools.[15] The coverage earlier in the century was probably a little, but not much, greater.

Attendance at these schools was usually too short and irregular to give the poor anything but the rudiments of reading. Children of the lower classes often left school at the age of six or seven, and if they continued, it was only for a few months in the year when there was no work in the fields or the factories. The fees of 2d. to 6d. a week charged at the commonest type of elementary school, the dame schools, would be a considerable drain on many incomes, and completely beyond the normal range of the million or more persons who were regularly on poor relief throughout the century.[16] For some of these, especially in London and the larger towns, Charity Schools provided free educational facilities; but their main emphasis was on religious education and social discipline; the teaching of reading, writing and arithmetic—the "three R's"—was a secondary aim and it was rarely pursued with much expectation of success:[17] for this and other reasons it is very unlikely that the Charity School movement made any considerable contribution to the effective literacy of the poor, much less to the growth of the reading public.

There was in any case no general agreement that this would be desirable. Throughout the eighteenth century utilitarian and mercantilist objections to giving the poor a literate education increased. The current attitude was expressed by Bernard Mandeville with his usual forthrightness in his *Essay on Charity and Charity Schools* (1723): "Reading, writing and arithmetic, are . . . very pernicious to the Poor . . . Men who are to remain and end their days in a laborious, tiresome and painful station of life, the sooner they are put upon it at first, the more patiently they'll submit to it for ever after."[18]

This point of view was widely held, not only by employers and economic theorists, but by many of the poor themselves, both in the town and the country. Stephen Duck, the thresher poet, for example, was taken away from school at the age of fourteen by his mother "lest he become too fine a gentleman for the family that produced him";[19] and many other children of the country poor attended school only when they were not needed for work in the fields. In the towns there was one factor at least which was even more hostile to popular education: the increasing employment of children from the age of five onwards to offset the shortage of industrial labor. Factory work was not as subject to seasonal factors, and the long hours left little or no time for schooling; and as a result it is likely that in some textile and other manufacturing areas the level of popular literacy tended to fall throughout the eighteenth century.[20]

There were, then, as is shown by the lives of the uneducated poets and self-made men, such as Duck, James Lackington, William Hutton and John Clare, many serious obstacles in the way of those members of the laboring classes who wanted to be able to read and write; while the most pervasive factor of all in restricting literacy was probably the lack of positive inducement to learn. Being able to read was a necessary accomplishment only for those destined to the middle-class occupations —commerce, administration and the professions; and since reading is inherently a difficult psychological process and one which requires continual practice, it is likely that only a small proportion of the laboring classes who were technically literate developed into active members of the reading public, and further, that the majority of these were concentrated in those employments where reading and writing were a vocational necessity.

Many other factors tended to restrict the reading public. Perhaps the most significant of them from the writer's point of view was the economic one.

Two of the most reliable estimates of the average incomes of the main social groups, those of Gregory King in 1696 and of Defoe in 1709,[21] show that more than half of the population was short of the bare necessities of life. King specifies that some 2,825,000 people out of a total population of 5,550,500, constituted an "unprofitable majority" who were "decreasing the wealth of the kingdom" This majority of the population was mainly composed of cottagers, paupers, laboring people and

outservants; and King estimated that their average incomes ranged from
£6 to £20 per annum per family. All these groups, it is clear, lived so
close to subsistence level that they can have had little to spare for such
luxuries as books and newspapers.

Both King and Defoe speak of an intermediate class, between the
poor and the well-to-do. King lists 1,990,000 people with family incomes
of between £38 and £60 per annum. They comprised: 1,410,000 "free-
holders of the lesser sort, and farmers" with annual incomes of £55 and
£42:10s.; 225,000 "shopkeepers and tradesmen", at £45 per annum;
and 240,000 "artisans and handicrafts," with average incomes of £38 a
year. None of these incomes would allow a large surplus for book-buying, especially when one considers that the income given is for a whole
family; but some money would be available among the richer farmers,
shopkeepers and tradesmen; and it is probable that changes within this
intermediate class account for the main increases in the eighteenth-
century reading public.

This increase was probably most marked in the towns, for the number
of small yeoman farmers is thought to have diminished during the period,
and their incomes probably either stayed stationary or decreased,[22]
whereas there was a marked rise in the numbers and wealth of shopkeepers, independent tradesmen and administrative and clerical employees throughout the eighteenth century.[23] Their increasing affluence
probably brought them within the orbit of the middle-class culture, previously the reserve of a smaller number of well-to-do merchants, shopkeepers and important tradesmen. It is probably from them that the most
substantial additions to the book-buying public were drawn, rather than
from the impoverished majority of the population.

The high cost of books in the eighteenth century emphasizes the severity of economic factors in restricting the reading public. Prices were
roughly comparable with those today, whereas average incomes were
something like one-tenth of their present monetary value, with 10s. a
week an average laborer's wage, and £1 a week a decent income for
skilled journeymen or small shopkeepers.[24] Charles Gildon sneered that
"there's not an old woman that can go to the price of it, but buys
Robinson Crusoe":[25] there can surely have been few poor women who
were buyers of the original edition at five shillings a copy.

Just as there was a much greater contrast than today between the
incomes of different classes, so there was a much greater range between
the prices of different types of books. Magnificent folios for the libraries
of the gentry and the rich merchants would cost a guinea a volume or
more, whereas a duodecimo, with perhaps the same amount of reading,
ranged from one to three shillings. Pope's *Iliad,* at six guineas the set, was
far beyond the reach of many members of the book-buying public; but
very soon a pirated Dutch duodecimo and other cheaper versions were
provided "for the gratification of those who were impatient to read what
they could not yet afford to buy."[26]

These less affluent readers would not have been able to afford the French heroic romances, usually published in expensive folios. But—significantly—novels were in the medium price range. They gradually came to be published in two or more small duodecimo volumes, usually at 3s. bound, and 2s. 3d. in sheets. Thus *Clarissa* appeared in seven and later eight volumes, *Tom Jones* in six. The prices of novels, then, though moderate compared to larger works, were still far beyond the means of any except the comfortably off: *Tom Jones,* for example, cost more than a laborer's average weekly wage. It is certain, therefore, that the novel's audience was not drawn from such a wide cross-section of society as, for example, that of the Elizabethan drama. All but the destitute had been able to afford a penny occasionally to stand in the pit of the Globe; it was no more than the price of a quart of ale. The price of a novel, on the other hand, would feed a family for a week or two. This is important. The novel in the eighteenth century was closer to the economic capacity of the middle-class additions to the reading public than were many of the established and respectable forms of literature and scholarship, but it was not, strictly speaking, a popular literary form.

For those on the lower economic fringes of the book-buying public there were, of course, many cheaper forms of printed entertainment; ballads at a halfpenny or a penny; chapbooks containing abbreviated chivalric romances, new stories of criminals, or accounts of extraordinary events, at prices ranging from a penny to sixpence; pamphlets at three-pence to a shilling; and, above all, newspapers at the price of one penny until a tax was imposed in 1712, rising to three-halfpence or twopence until 1757, and eventually to threepence after 1776. Many of these newspapers contained short stories, or novels in serialized form—*Robinson Crusoe,* for example, was thus reprinted in the *Original London Post,* a thrice-weekly journal, as well as in cheap duodecimos and chapbooks. For our particular purposes, however, this poorer public is not very important; the novelists with whom we are concerned did not have this form of publication in mind, and the printers and publishers who specialized in it normally used works that had already been published in more expensive form, often without payment.

The extent to which economic factors retarded the expansion of the reading public, and especially that for the novel, is suggested by the rapid success of the non-proprietary or circulating libraries, as they were called after 1742 when the term was invented.[27] A few such libraries are recorded earlier, especially after 1725, but the rapid spread of the movement came after 1740, when the first circulating library was established in London, to be followed by at least seven others within a decade. Subscriptions were moderate: the usual charge was between half a guinea and a guinea a year, and there were often facilities for borrowing books at the rate of a penny a volume or threepence for the usual three-volume novel.

Most circulating libraries stocked all types of literature, but novels were widely regarded as their main attraction: and there can be little doubt that they led to the most notable increase in the reading public for fiction which occurred during the century. They certainly provoked the greatest volume of contemporary comment about the spread of reading to the lower orders. These "slop-shops in literature"[28] were said to have debauched the minds of schoolboys, ploughboys, "servant women of the better sort,"[29] and even of "every butcher and baker, cobbler and tinker, throughout the three kingdoms."[30] It is likely, therefore, that until 1740 a substantial marginal section of the reading public was held back from a full participation in the literary scene by the high price of books; and further, that this marginal section was largely composed of potential novel readers, many of them women.

The distribution of leisure in the period supports and amplifies the picture already given of the composition of the reading public; and it also supplies the best evidence available to explain the increasing part in it played by women readers. For, while many of the nobility and gentry continued their cultural regress from the Elizabethan courtier to Arnold's "Barbarians," there was a parallel tendency for literature to become a primarily feminine pursuit.

As so often, Addison is an early spokesman of a new trend. He wrote in the *Guardian* (1713): "There are some reasons why learning is more adapted to the female world than to the male. As in the first place, because they have more spare time on their hands, and lead a more sedentary life. . . . There is another reason why those especially who are women of quality, should apply themselves to letters, namely, because their husbands are generally strangers to them."[31] For the most part quite unashamed strangers, if we can judge by Goldsmith's busy man of affairs, Mr. Lofty, in *The Good Natur'd Man* (1768), who proclaims that "poetry is a pretty thing enough for our wives and daughters; but not for us."[32]

Women of the upper and middle classes could partake in few of the activities of their menfolk, whether of business or pleasure. It was not usual for them to engage in politics, business or the administration of their estates, while the main masculine leisure pursuits such as hunting and drinking were also barred. Such women, therefore, had a great deal of leisure, and this leisure was often occupied by omnivorous reading.

Lady Mary Wortley Montagu, for example, was an avid novel reader, asking her daughter to send a list of novels copied down from newspaper advertisements, and adding: "I doubt not that at least the greater part of these are trash, lumber, etc. However, they will serve to pass away the idle time. . . ."[33] Later, and at a definitely lower social level, Mrs. Thrale recounted that by her husband's orders she "was not to *think of the kitchen*" and explained that it was as a result of this enforced leisure that she was "driven . . . on literature as [her] sole resource."[34]

Many of the less well-to-do women also had much more leisure than previously. B. L. de Muralt had already found in 1694 that "even among the common people the husbands seldom make their wives work";[35] and another foreign visitor to England, César de Saussure, observed in 1727 that tradesmen's wives were "rather lazy, and few do any needle-work."[36] These reports reflect the great increase in feminine leisure which had been made possible by an important economic change. The old household duties of spinning and weaving, making bread, beer, candles and soap, and many others, were no longer necessary, since most necessities were now manufactured and could be bought at shops and markets. This connection between increased feminine leisure and the development of economic specialization was noted in 1748 by the Swedish traveler, Pehr Kalm, who was surprised to find that in England "one hardly ever sees a woman here trouble herself in the least about outdoor duties"; even indoors, he discovered, "weaving and spinning is also in most houses a rare thing, because their many manufactures save them from the necessity of such."[37]

Kalm probably conveys a somewhat exaggerated impression of the change, and he is in any case speaking only of the home counties. In rural areas further from London the economy changed much more slowly, and most women certainly continued to devote themselves almost entirely to the multifarious duties of a household that was still largely self-supporting. Nevertheless a great increase in feminine leisure certainly occurred in the early eighteenth century, although it was probably mainly restricted to London, its environs and the larger provincial towns.

How much of this increased leisure was devoted to reading is difficult to determine. In the towns, and especially in London, innumerable competing entertainments offered themselves: during the season there were plays, operas, masquerades, ridottos, assemblies, drums, while the new watering-places and resort towns catered for the summer months of the idle fair. However, even the most ardent devotees of the pleasures of the town must have had some time left for reading; and the many women who did not wish to partake of them, or could not afford to, must have had much more. For those with puritan backgrounds, especially, reading would be a much more unobjectionable resource. Isaac Watts, a very influential early eighteenth-century Dissenter, dwelt luridly on "all the painful and dismal consequences of lost and wasted time,"[38] but he encouraged his charges, very largely feminine, to pass their leisure hours in reading and literary discussions.[39]

There is in the early eighteenth century a good deal of outraged comment about how the laboring classes were bringing ruin upon themselves and the country by aspiring to the leisure pursuits of their betters. The implications of these jeremiads, however, must be largely discounted. Not only because genteel dress and fashionable entertainments were much more expensive in relation to the standard of living than they are today, but because a very slight increase in the leisure of a few fortunate or improvident members of the populace would have been enough to arouse alarm and hostility of a kind we find difficult to understand today. The traditional view was that class distinctions were the basis of social order, and that consequently leisure pursuits were only proper for the leisure classes; and this outlook was strongly reinforced by the economic theory of the day which opposed anything which might keep the laboring classes away from their tasks. There was therefore considerable agreement among the spokesmen both of mercantilism and of traditional religious and social thought that even reading constituted a dangerous distraction from the proper pursuits of those who worked with their hands. Robert Bolton, Dean of Carlisle, for instance, in his *Essays on the Employment of Time* (1750), mentions the possibility of reading as a pastime for the peasant and mechanic, only to reject it summarily: "No, the advice to him is, Observe what passes."[40]

The opportunities of the poor for any extensive impropriety in this direction were in any case very small. Hours of work for laborers in the country included all the hours of daylight, and even in London they were from six in the morning to eight or nine at night. The usual holidays were only four—Christmas, Easter, Whitsun and Michaelmas, with the addition, in London, of the eight hanging days at Tyburn. It is true that laborers in favored occupations, especially in London, could and did absent themselves from work fairly freely. But in the main conditions of work were not such as to give appreciable leisure except on Sundays; and then six days of *labor ipse voluptas* usually led to the seventh's being devoted to activities more extrovert than reading. Francis Place thought that drink was almost the only working-class recreation during the eighteenth century;[41] and it must be remembered that cheap gin made drunkenness available for less than the cost of a newspaper.

For those few who might have liked to read there were other difficulties besides lack of leisure and the cost of books. There was little privacy, as, in London especially, housing was appallingly overcrowded; and there was often not enough light to read by, even by day. The window tax imposed at the end of the seventeenth century had reduced windows to a minimum, and those that remained were usually deepset, and covered with horn, paper or green glass. At night lighting was a serious problem, since candles, even farthing dips, were considered a luxury. Richardson was proud of the fact that as an apprentice he bought them for himself,[42] but others could not, or were not allowed to. James Lackington, for example, was forbidden to have light in his room by his employer, a baker, and claims to have read by the light of the moon![43]

There were, however, two large and important groups of relatively poor people who probably did have time and opportunity to read—apprentices and household servants, especially the latter. They would normally have leisure and light to read by; there would often be books in the house; if there were not, since they did not have to pay for their food and lodging, their wages and vails could be devoted to buying them if they chose; and they were, as ever, peculiarly liable to be contaminated by the example of their betters.

It is certainly remarkable how many contemporary declamations against the increased leisure, luxury and literary pretensions of the lower orders specifically refer to apprentices and domestic servants, especially footmen and waiting-maids. In assessing the literary importance of this latter group it must be remembered that they constituted a very large and conspicuous class, which in the eighteenth century probably constituted the largest single occupational group in the country, as was the case, indeed, until within living memory. Pamela, then, may be regarded as the culture-heroine of a very powerful sisterhood of literate and leisured waiting-maids. We note that her main stipulation for the new post she envisaged taking up after leaving Mr. B. was that it should allow her "a little Time for Reading."[44] This emphasis prefigured her triumph when, following a way of life rare in the class of the poor in general but less so in her particular vocation, she stormed the barriers of society and of literature alike by her skillful employment of what may be called conspicuous literacy, itself an eloquent tribute to the extent of her leisure.

Evidence on the availability and use of leisure thus confirms the previous picture given of the composition of the reading public in the early eighteenth century. Despite a considerable expansion it still did not normally extend much further down the social scale than to tradesmen and shopkeepers, with the important exception of the more favored apprentices and indoor servants. Still, there had been additions, and they had been mainly recruited from among the increasingly prosperous and numerous social groups concerned with commerce and manufacture. This is important, for it is probable that this particular change alone, even if it was of comparatively minor proportions, may have altered the center of gravity of the reading public sufficiently to place the middle class as a whole in a dominating position for the first time.

In looking for the effects of this change upon literature, no very direct or dramatic manifestations of middle-class tastes and capacities are to be expected, for the dominance of the middle class in the reading public had in any case been long preparing. One general effect of some interest for the rise of the novel, however, seems to follow from the change in the center of gravity of the reading public. The fact that literature in the eighteenth century was addressed to an ever-widening audience must have weakened the relative importance of those readers with enough education and leisure to take a professional or semi-professional interest in classical and modern letters; and in return it must have increased the relative importance of those who desired an easier form of literary entertainment, even if it had little prestige among the literati.

People have always, presumably, read for pleasure and relaxation, among other things; but there seems to have arisen in the eighteenth century a tendency to pursue these ends more exclusively than before. Such, at least, was Steele's view, put forward in the *Guardian* (1713); he attacked the prevalence of:

> this unsettled way of reading . . . which naturally seduces us into as un-determined a manner of thinking. . . . That assemblage of words which is called a style becomes utterly annihilated. . . . The common defence of these people is, that they have no design in reading but for pleasure, which I think should rather arise from reflection and remembrance of what one had read, than from the transient satisfaction of what one does, and we should be pleased proportionately as we are profited.[45]

"The transient satisfaction of what one does" seems a peculiarly appropriate description of the quality of the reading which was called for by most examples of those two new eighteenth-century literary forms, the newspaper and the novel—both obviously encourage a rapid, inattentive, almost unconscious kind of reading habit. The effortlessness of the satisfaction afforded by fiction, indeed, had been urged in a passage from Huet's *Of the Origin of Romances* which prefaced Samuel Croxall's *Select Collection of Novels and Histories* (1720):

> those discoveries which engage and possess [the mind] most effectually are such as are obtained with the least labour, wherein the imagination has the greatest share, and where the subject is such as is obvious to our senses . . . And of this sort are *romances;* which are to be comprehended without any great labour of the mind, or the exercise of our rational faculty, and where a strong fancy will be sufficient, with little or no burthen to the memory.[46]

The new literary balance of power, then, probably tended to favor ease of entertainment at the expense of obedience to traditional critical standards, and it is certain that this change of emphasis was an essential permissive factor for the achievements of Defoe and Richardson. That these achievements were also related to other and more positive features of the tastes and attitudes of the main accessions to the reading public during the period also seems likely: the outlook of the trading class, for instance, was much influenced by the economic individualism and the somewhat secularized puritanism which finds expression in the novels of Defoe; and the increasingly important feminine component of the public found many of its interests expressed by Richardson.

NOTES

1. London, 1904, p. 26. See also Helen Sard Hughes, "The Middle Class Reader and the English Novel," *JEGP*, XXV (1926):362–78.
2. *Cit.* A. S. Collins, *The Profession of Letters* (London, 1928), p. 29.
3. J. Sutherland, "The Circulation of Newspapers and Literary Periodicals, 1700–1730," *Library*, 4th ser., XV (1934):111–13.
4. A. S. Collins, *Authorship in the Days of Johnson* (London, 1927), p. 255.
5. No. 10 (1711).
6. Swift, *Journal to Stella*, Jan. 28, 1712.
7. Collins, *Profession of Letters*, p. 21.
8. E. Carpenter, *Thomas Sherlock* (London, 1936), pp. 286–87.
9. Collins, *Authorship*, p. 236.

10. R. A. Austen-Leigh, "William Strahan and His Ledgers," *Library*, 4th ser., III (1923):272.
11. Marjorie Plant, *The English Book Trade* (London, 1939), p. 445.
12. *Lives of the Poets*, ed. Hill (Oxford, 1905), III, p. 19.
13. *Confessions* (London, 1804), p. 175.
14. *Travels*, ed., Matheson (London, 1924), p. 30.
15. M. G. Jones, *The Charity School Movement* . . . (Cambridge, 1938), p. 332.
16. Dorothy Marshall, *The English Poor in the Eighteenth Century* (London, 1926), pp. 27–29, 76–77.
17. Jones, *Charity School Movement*, pp. 80, 304.
18. "Essay on Charity and Charity Schools," *The Fable of the Bees*, ed. Kaye (Oxford, 1924), I, p. 288.
19. *Poems on Several Occasions: Written by Stephen Duck . . .*, 1730, p. iv.
20. Jones, *Charity School Movement*, p. 332; J. L. and Barbara Hammond, *The Town Labourer, 1760–1832* (London, 1919), pp. 54–55, 144–47.
21. In *Natural and Political Observations and Conclusions upon the State and Condition of England*, 1696; and in *Review*, VI no. 36 (1709).
22. H. J. Habakkuk, "English Land Ownership, 1680–1740," *Economic History Review*, X (1940):2–17.
23. M. D. George, *London Life in the 18th Century* (London, 1926), p. 2.
24. On this difficult subject, see E. W. Gilboy, *Wages in 18th Century England* (Cambridge, Mass., 1934), pp. 144 ff.
25. *Robinson Crusoe Examin'd and Criticis'd*, ed. Dottin (London and Paris, 1923), pp. 71–72.
26. Johnson, "Pope," *Lives of the Poets*, ed. Hill. III, p. 111.
27. See especially Hilda M. Hamlyn, "Eighteenth Century Circulating Libraries in England," *Library*, 5th ser., I (1946): 197.
28. Mrs. Griffith, *Lady Barton*, 1771, Preface.
29. *Cit.* John Tinnon Taylor, *Early Opposition to the English Novel* (New York, 1943), p. 25.
30. Fanny Burney, *Diary*, March 26, 1778.
31. No. 155.
32. Act II.
33. *Letters and Works*, ed. Thomas (London, 1861), I, p. 203; II, pp. 225–26, 305.
34. *A Sketch of Her Life . . .*, ed. Seeley (London, 1908), p. 22.
35. *Letters Describing the Character and Customs of the English and French Nations*, 1726, p. 11.
36. *A Foreign View of England*, trans. Van Muyden (London, 1902), p. 206.
37. *Kalm's Account of His Visit to England . . .*, trans. Lucas (London, 1892), p. 326.
38. 'The End of Time', *Life and Choice Works of Isaac Watts*, ed. Harsha (New York, 1857), p. 322.
39. *Improvement of the Mind* (New York, 1885), pp. 51, 82.
40. P. 29.
41. George, *London Life*, p. 289.
42. A. D. McKillop, *Samuel Richardson: Printer and Novelist* (Chapel Hill, 1936), p. 5.
43. *Memoirs*, 1830, p. 65.
44. *Pamela*, Everyman Edition, I, p. 65.
45. No. 60.
46. 1729 ed., I, p. xiv.

34. The Social Effects of Broadcasting

Gerhart D. Wiebe

THE PROBLEM

The central problem to be explored may be introduced by reference to two familiar observations. The first is that the broadcast media in the United States generate huge audiences. The second is that the content of very popular programs is generally regarded by members of the intellectual community as being light, superficial, trivial, and in some cases, as vulgar and even harmful. That is, it is regarded as of little use, or even as being negative in its effects on the quality of people's lives.

The remarkable size of audiences is regularly documented by the rating services, and the calibre of program content is deplored by critics and scholars with comparable regularity. The situation is documented and deplored, but it is not explained. The implications for broadcasters devoted to education, the arts, and religion are serious and perplexing. The media seem to open the way to intellectual, cultural, and spirited refinement for the millions, but the millions elude the proffered enlightenment, preferring the light, the superficial, the trivial.

The problem is familiar. So also are several prescriptions for improvement. It is frequently argued that tastes would improve if people were exposed to programs of high calibre. But the record is discouraging. Consider for example, the twenty-year history of Sunday afternoon concerts by the New York Philharmonic Orchestra, broadcast by the Columbia Broadcasting System. Despite vigorous promotion, a good and unchanged position in the schedule, and excellent production, the audience for these concerts did not grow nor did it ever achieve a size considered minimal for successful commercial programs. Similar examples can be cited in other content areas. Opportunity is apparently not enough.

A second proposal for improving public taste would restrict program offerings to those of high intellectual, moral, and artistic quality for a period of time long enough so that discriminating taste would become habitual and normative among the public. Given twenty years of consis-

From *Mass Culture Revisited* edited by Bernard Rosenberg and David White. © 1971 by Litton Educational Publishing, Inc. Reprinted by permission of Van Nostrand Reinhold Company.

tently high quality programming, it is suggested, people would not tolerate programs of comparatively low quality. This proposal, like the earlier one, finds rough going in the light of experience. After some twenty years of programming in England, controlled exclusively by the BBC, commercial television came to England. With it came some commercial entertainment series from the United States which, according to the present hypothesis, should have found a very chilly reception. But that isn't what happened.

The appetite in the United States for light diversion on television is perhaps most thoroughly and authoritatively documented in the late Dr. Steiner's book, *The People Look at Television* (New York: Alfred A. Knopf, 1963, especially chap. 6).

Steiner studied both attitudes toward television and actual viewing behavior by the same respondents. He found that people verbalized more interest in fine programming than their viewing behavior demonstrated. And further, that although the college educated respondents differed in their program preferences from the less well educated in expected ways, the degree of difference was remarkably small. For example, during periods when cultural entertainment, public information programming, and light entertainment were available simultaneously, a random distribution of the audience would allocate 33 per cent to each type. Since light entertainment predominates most of the time, the simultaneous availability of the three types constitutes an unusual opportunity for those with discriminating tastes to tune in quality programming. Still, even during these periods, 40 per cent of those with college education chose the light entertainment (Steiner, p. 201).

The impact of broadcasting ranges from slight to sweeping appeal and we have no explanation for this phenomenon beyond the descriptive observation that in general there is a tendency toward an inverse relationship between audience size and the cultural merit of the program.

This observation is not peculiar to our time nor is it observed exclusively with reference to the broadcast media. With the introduction of printing in the fifteenth century the treasures of learning, which had been severely restricted, were henceforth as widely available as was literacy. But instead of grasping the unprecedented opportunities for enlightenment, the public appetite, from the first decades of printing, was for the light, the superficial, the trivial, and it may be added for the scandalous, the seditious, and the vulgar. H. A. Innis, in his book, *Empire and Communication,* quotes a seventeenth century observation that "The slightest pamphlet is nowadays more vendable than the works of learnedest men." This pattern even appears to pre-date the press. A pre-Gutenberg example appears in the relation of the wandering minstrel to the public appetite for messages that offend refined taste.

I share the concern expressed by musicians, scientists, poets, dramatists, educators, critics, and others of comparable intellectual accomplishment regarding the apparent waste, the loss of opportunity in the general preference for the trivial while the mass media make it practical for the peoples of the earth to advance their education, to refine the quality of their experience, and to share in the finest achievements of human intellect. But I no longer believe that what has been called "the taste for trash" can be remedied by scholarly exhortation or by attempting to teach good taste or by increasing budgets for cultural offerings. The best hope of understanding this problem, and then perhaps improving the situation in some degree, seems to lie in posing the hypothesis that the observed behavior has positive psychological utility. If this utility can be identified, then perhaps, as we learn to understand it, we may be able to apply this knowledge to the general welfare. In pursuing this path I have set aside observations on the media themselves, turning instead to patterns of psychological and sociological behavior that are independent of the media.

Two such patterns will be discussed. Both appear to contribute to a theoretical understanding of media audience behavior. The first is the apparent difficulty with which we humans acquire the *concept of the other*. By "the other," I mean simply a person other than oneself.

RELUCTANCE TO COPE WITH THE OTHER

We begin with findings relating to infant egocentrism. The term egocentrism is used here, not in the pejorative sense of selfishness or conceit, but simply in nonvalued reference to preoccupation with self. The psychologist Piaget has contributed much to our understanding of infant egocentrism. His ingenious experiments indicate that when an object at which an infant had been looking is screened from his view, it is not just hidden. For the infant, it apparently ceases to exist. (Jean Piaget, *The Construction of Reality in the Child.* New York: Basic Books, 1954, pp. 20–40.) There is a learning process that precedes the child's recognition that objects and persons actually occupy space and exist as permanent and substantial entities.

The child's early preoccupation is in the discovery and maintenance of self. His success in this early learning obviously depends on the solicitude of the mother or her substitute, but the relationship is not reciprocal. The human infant levies demands on the outside, and apparently perceives the objects and persons that make up the outside as ephemera among which he seeks satisfaction—primarily nourishment and comfort.

Unlike some animals, human young do not mature without elaborate care. Studies of the so-called feral children and others raised in near isolation demonstrate the dependence of the maturation process on association with others. I believe, however, that developmental psychologists have tended, until recently, to underemphasize the unilateral, taking orientation of the young child's interaction with the outside.

The traditional concept of the mother-child relationship during the first year as one of reciprocal love must be re-examined. Findings suggest that in the normal process of maturation during the first year, a child cannot be said to perceive another person as an individual, autonomous, other. The psychoanalyst Rene Spitz has recently reported experiments showing that the treasured smiling response, observed at about six months, is elicited equally well by mother or stranger, male or female, old or young, even by a person in a mask, so long as the face presented to the baby is animated, and is presented head on. (Rene Spitz, *The First Year of Life*. New York: International Universities Press, Inc., 1965, p. 86.)

The crucial period of the infant's dependence on solicitous care by a specific individual during the last part of the first year appears to be largely a need for stimulation and nourishment in accustomed ways as the child práctices his early and precarious attempts to cope with the substantial outside.

Mothers know that a two-year-old, left in reach of an age mate treats him as if he were a thing rather than as another person. The concept of *the other* has not yet emerged.

Margaret Greene, in her charming and informative book, entitled *Learning to Talk* (New York: Harper and Brothers, 1960) reports this incident: "Heather," she writes, "when three, enjoyed building a snow-man, and when he was complete, . . . begged him to talk to her. . . . But he didn't and her eyes filled with tears of disappointment. Quickly I made some kind of remark in a gruff snowman-sort-of voice. Immediately, she laughed and in a moment was impersonating him herself."

The point here is that the bright child of three who probably had a vocabulary of some 600 or 800 words was still so vague in her perception of other people *as people* that she thought the snowman she had just helped to make would be able to talk. And then after momentary disappointment, she didn't mind that he couldn't.

Moving along in time, we come to a series of findings on six-year-olds reported by Piaget. He observed and then studied what he called egocentric language among six-year-olds. He divides egocentric speech into three subgroups—repetition, monologue, and collective monologue. The point in common among these three categories is that the speech is not addressed to anyone. Although the presence of others sometimes seems to serve as a general sort of stimulus, the child during egocentric speech apparently does not actually address other persons. He seems rather to "talk past them."

Piaget found that something over a third of the speech of the six-year-olds he studied fell into this category of egocentric language. (Jean Piaget, *The Language and Thought of the Child*. London: The Humanities Press, 1952, chap. 1.) Thus, even in groups of six-year-olds where language would seem so obviously to be a tool of interaction, much of their behavior contradicts this expectation, and consciousness of the other is only inconsistently observed.

More recently the work of Dr. Melvin H. Fiffer (*Journal of Personality*

28, 1960, pp. 383–96) proceeding from that of Piaget indicates that the ability to assume different social perspectives is only gradually developed, that it is correlated with chronological age, and that its measurement, still far from precise, may well turn out to be an important index to psychological maturation.

These findings from developmental psychology document the relatively slow emergence of the concept of *the other* in contrast with the precocious development observed in what might be called the unilateral achievement of self-expression and need gratification.

Such concepts as sharing, mutuality, reciprocal relationships, empathy, service, interaction, all of these positively valued concepts, endlessly stressed in the process of socialization, turn out, on examination, to refer to rather sophisticated, psychologically demanding processes which call for a well-developed sense of *the other*. They are essentially *social* processes which require the surrender or at least the inhibiting of the early deep-seated pattern of egocentrism.

How does this late developing sense of *the other* relate to media behavior? The relationship seems quite direct when it is recalled that the media, by definition, remove *the other*. The media present printed symbols or sounds or images, but never persons. The media reinstate the opportunity to enjoy the early pattern of taking, without deference to the reciprocal needs of the giver. The media offer immediate need gratification without "paying the piper." They provide the sense of experience without the accommodation required in true participation. One may weep or laugh or hate or fear and escape the necessity of acknowledging the physical existence and the reciprocal demands of those others who arouse the emotion. The media allow the audience member to resume the infantile posture observed by Piaget in which, when the stimulus is removed, it ceases to exist. Reality, on the other hand is beset with people and things that resist, react, counterthrust, encroach, demand. Small wonder then, if when people are weary, frustrated, and crowded, they embrace the media where people and things are ephemera—as they once were for each of us. It is characteristic of popular media content that it maximizes immediate need gratification, minimizes intellectual effort, and excuses the audience member from acknowledging a substantial *other*.

But the point appears to have reference to broadcasters as well as to audiences. Broadcasters tend to consider their mission accomplished when their message is released. The sequel is seldom investigated except by commercial broadcasters who are disciplined by the buying responses of those others out there. Perhaps this deep-seated reluctance to cope with *the other* influences behavior on both the sending and the receiving sides of the media.

It is often said that the media bring people into contact with each other. We must be more literal. The media only transport symbols. They do not bring people together. On the contrary, the media stand between people. The media may *invite* subsequent interaction, but they do not and cannot provide it.

This is the first idea that seems to merit careful study. Facility in personal interaction comes late in the developmental sequence. The phenomenon of talking past people rather than with them is familiar. Interpersonal frictions plague adult life. The fact that media messages provide the illusion of interaction together with immunity from *the other* seems to relate a basic psychological factor to media audience behavior.

THREE ASPECTS OF SOCIALIZATION

The second point relates to the process of socialization, and particularly to the individual's resistance to this process.

Socialization has been defined by the Hartleys as "the process by which an individual becomes a member of a given social group." (Eugene L. and Ruth E. Hartley, *Fundamentals of Social Psychology*. New York: Alfred A. Knopf, 1952, p. 202.) The identity of the "actor" and the "acted-upon" in this process is clear. The group requires. The individual adjusts. Ruth Benedict says "culture exists in the habituated bodies and minds of the people who belong to the culture." Margaret Mead reminds us of the extent and pervasiveness of this habituating process in observing "that the growing child is systematically patterned in every detail, in posture as well as in gesture, in tempo as well as in speech, in his way of thinking as well as in the content of his thinking, in his capacity to feel as well as in the forms which his feelings take." (Hartley and Hartley, pp. 202, 203.) Professor George Herbert Mead built an entire school of thought around the concept of the individual as a cumulative composite of the environmental feedback he himself experiences.

The Hartleys add to this "nature-nurture" discussion what they call a psychological truism, namely "that all development depends on both the innate qualities of the organism and the external environment in which the organism exists" (p. 203). This recognition that both the innate nature of the individual and the demands of a structured environment are involved in the process of socialization may indeed be self-evident, but its importance has perhaps been underestimated. Each human being has inherent tendencies, innate patterns, which would direct growth in ways different from those that actually occur if this growth were uninfluenced by the requirements of the group.

It follows that the socializing process does not simply mold inert stuff. It is rather the modifying and changing of a dynamic system, deflecting it from the course it would otherwise follow. Socialization is alteration of forces in motion, and when one alters the direction of forces in motion, he encounters resistance. This resistance to socialization is familiar, but it has received rather little attention from social psychologists except as an inconvenience that must be handled in order to proceed with the essential business of qualifying the individual for group membership.

The typical example of socialization is the parent training the child. The child's changing toward normative behavior is seen as the essential content of socialization. Seen from the child's point of view, however, the process of socialization is a series of defeats and compromises in which what he wants to do must bow to what he is required to do. In a good parent-child relationship, the child's sacrifice is in some degree compensated by praise and other rewards. Even so, however, viewed as the child sees it, the process is coercive. Impulse is inhibited. Spontaneity is modified. The individual must adapt to the group prescription.

It would be remarkable indeed if all of this compromising, substituting, bending, changing, and giving up to which the growing human is subjected during socialization did not generate a deep and persistent pattern of counteraction. Behavior that fits this expectation is, of course, familiar. In addition to their outright opposition against prescribed behavior, the young retreat and restore themselves somewhat through secret retaliation against authority figures. In solitude and with peers, in both manifest and symbolic behavior, in their play and their fantasy, children assuage the discomforts of the socializing process and find some degree of psychic face-saving that makes the losing battle tolerable.

From the child's point of view, socialization can be seen as consisting of three sorts of behavior. The first includes learning, refinement, or improvement in the direction of prescribed behavior. The second includes the relatively stable and acceptable everyday behavior at one's achieved level of socialization. The third includes the retaliatory, assuaging, and indemnifying counterstrokes just discussed. These three phases of socialization may be referred to as *directive, maintenance,* and *restorative.* For convenience these labels will be used as if they referred to discrete categories. Actually I see them as zones in a continuum.

The process of socialization is inconceivable without communication. Professor Merton calls communication the instrument of social process. If we view socialization in terms of the messages involved, we find the *directive, maintenance,* and *restorative* aspects of socialization clearly identifiable in corresponding categories of messages.

Directive messages come from authority figures. They command, exhort, instruct, persuade, and urge in the direction of learning and new understanding that represent progress in the estimation of authority figures. Directive messages call for substantial and conscious intellectual effort on the part of the learner.

Maintenance messages include all the every-day messages sent and received in the customary business of living. They call for relatively little conscious intellectual effort.

Restorative messages, including individual fantasies, are those with which the individual refreshes himself from the strain of adapting, the weariness of conforming. They provide an interim for the reasserting of impulse. The child, seemingly with perverse precociousness, articulates his restorative messages as he screams, complains, jeers, taunts, defies, says forbidden words, and gleefully plays out cruel and destructive fantasies.

The socializing process is concentrated in childhood and youth, but it continues in adult society. Many elements of media audience behavior seem to fit into a coherent pattern if they are viewed as responsive to *directive, maintenance,* and *restorative* messages in the context of adult socialization.

In beginning this exploration we must differentiate between the purpose a message is meant to perform by the sender, and the purpose it actually performs for the receiver. Communicators tend to speak primarily in terms of the sender's intention. But much of the following discussion is couched in terms of the receiver's reaction. Certainly the two points of view cannot be assumed to be identical. We will frequently refer to a message that is intended as *directive,* but received as *maintenance,* or one that is intended as *maintenance* but is received as *restorative.*

DIRECTIVE MEDIA MESSAGES

Directive messages call for learning, for changed behavior, new differentiations, refined perceptions. Such responses require the expenditure of intellectual effort on the part of the neophyte. In childhood, these changes customarily take place, whether in home, church, or school, in a disciplined face-to-face relationship. This pattern appears to extend beyond childhood. If a person can read and has access to a good library, the prerequisites for a college education would appear to be present. But professors who command the respect of their students continue to be required. The printed Bible has not made the church obsolete nor has it reduced the role of the clergy. Granting the existence of the exceptional few with unusually high motivation, it seems to be true that the large majority of people do not move to higher spiritual, artistic, or intellectual levels except within the disciplined context of face-to-face pupil-teacher relationship.

The media do not provide this relationship. Certainly they can supplement and enrich the learning process. But I find no evidence that by themselves they will bring about substantial learning among the rank and file of a society—presumably because most people will not expend the required intellectual effort in the absence of an authority figure. This generalization finds strong support in Dr. Wilbur Schramm's book *The New Media* (UNESCO, International Institute for Educational Planning, 1967). In this survey of education by radio and television in many nations, Dr. Schramm reviews twenty-three projects. He reports many reasons for failure or success. But in no instance does he report success in the absence of a face-to-face relationship between the learner and a teacher, monitor, parent, or comparable authority figure.

Once an individual has achieved a unit of learning within such a structured situation, he may voluntarily enter the audience for broadcasts featuring these recently acquired concepts and insights, but he then experiences such programs as *maintenance* messages rather than as *directive*.

MAINTENANCE MEDIA MESSAGES

Who then among the general public, tunes in media messages intended to educate, to elevate, to present substantial new insights, to refine? Even though such programs do not command very large audiences, people do tune them in. The answer, in substantial degree, seems to lie in the familiar observation that the large majority of those who tune in religious programs are already religious. Most of those who tune in a science series already understand science at about the level presented in the series. I believe Dr. Paul Lazarsfeld first documented this pattern of media audience behavior years ago when he found that the audience for a radio series entitled "Americans All, Immigrants All," changed significantly from program to program, each nationality group tending to tune in the program about itself, but being less faithful in listening to the programs about other nationality groups where more learning would have been achieved. *Thus, given a range of choice, media audiences, through a self-selecting process, tend to turn messages intended to be directive into maintenance messages.*

Stated differently, given a permissive situation with available alternatives, people avoid the intellectual effort required in a true learning situation, preferring messages that review or embellish or elaborate what they already know. This, in essence, is what *maintenance* messages do. News programs will serve as the prototype of media *maintenance* messages. They are intended to extend or up-date the audience member's information about the world he already knows, and they seem, in general, to perform that function. They do not call for disciplined intellectual effort.

There is a second way in which messages intended as *directive* are transformed into a *maintenance* function. Child psychologists have long known that children, exposed to programs intended for adults, perceive what they are ready to perceive, but miss many points that seem quite obvious to adults. I hypothesize that this same pattern persists in adult audiences so that in listening to a news program, a political speech, or a sermon, people hear what they can comfortably accommodate in the context of their present knowledge, and very little more.

When do media messages move audience members to subsequent action? The answer, in terms of the present hypothesis, must be sought in a combination of at least three factors. First, in the existing readiness, the present predisposition among audience members to react. Secondly, in the social provisions for facilitating such action, and third, in the appeal of the message. Media messages themselves are only one of at least three factors. Seen in this way, the limitations as well as the power of media messages become less obscure. By way of illustration, consider the general experience in the United States regarding advertising on the one hand and sermons about brotherhood on the other. Successful advertising, if my observations are correct, succeeds not by the power of the medium and the message alone. Its success depends on these elements in combination with at least two other factors, namely a favorable predisposition among the audience and a retail establishment that facilitates the completion of the requested behavior. Sermons on brotherhood, on the other hand, though they have been numerous, and often eloquent, as in the case of the late Dr. King, bring very little positive change in behavior. Why? Our hypothesis suggests that audience members are not favorably disposed toward changing accustomed ways, and further, that social and institutional arrangements tend to impede rather than to facilitate changed behavior in this area.

Perhaps an interim summary is appropriate here.
1. Broadcasts seldom move audience members to substantially new and higher levels of intellectual, artistic, or spiritual experience except when such messages are received in the context of a face-to-face teacher-pupil relationship.
2. Given a permissive situation with available alternatives, media audiences avoid *directive* messages which require disciplined intellectual effort.
3. Those who choose programs intended to be *directive* are in many cases those who already know all or most of what is presented so that the program is *perceived*, not as *directive*, but as *maintenance*.
4. Others with less understanding who attend to *directive* messages tend to hear only what can easily be accommodated in the context of present knowledge, and so, again, experience the *directive* message as *maintenance*.
5. Programs *intended* as *maintenance* messages, for example news shows, and in religious broadcasting, programs of familiar hymns and sermons that stay on ground familiar to the general public— such programs are received as *maintenance*, and are preferred over *directive* messages.
6. *Maintenance* media messages are the counterpart of everyday conversation. They review, elaborate, extend the audience member's experience at approximately his achieved level of sophistication and accordingly do not demand the disciplined intellectual effort characteristic of substantial learning experiences.
7. Maintenance media messages like conversations with acquaintances lead to responsive behavior provided the suggested behavior is a feasible and convenient extension of an existing predisposition.

RESTORATIVE MEDIA MESSAGES

What of the *restorative* category? The adult counterpart of youthful protest and retaliation against authority figures appears spontaneously and apparently inevitably as an antidote for the strictures of organized living. Mimicry, caricature, pantomime, satire, gossip, ribald ballads, malicious rhymes, broad humor, and scandalous drama were popular before the days of Gutenberg. They have appeared persistently through history and have withstood the most harsh attempts at suppression. Their counterparts in media content fit our expectations for *restorative* messages and lend strong support to the hypothesis that the *restorative* aspect of socialization is served copiously, though of course not exclusively, by the kinds of media content that seem so deplorable to those with discriminating taste.

Restorative media messages feature crime, violence, disrespect for authority, sudden and unearned wealth, sexual indiscretion, and freedom from social restraints. The themes of these most popular media messages seem to make up a composite reciprocal of the values stressed in adult socialization.

Because the very essence of restorative messages is their token retaliation against the establishment, the likely effect of well-intentioned attempts by proponents of high standards to "improve" popular *restorative* content is clear. Let's take out the violence, we say, and substitute a theme of cooperative problem solving. The *restorative* essence is removed and *directive* content is substituted. The psychological utility of the message is altered and its popularity is correspondingly reduced.

It was observed earlier that messages intended as *directive* are often received as *maintenance*. There is a similar mechanism that appears regarding the *maintenance* and *restorative* categories. News messages, for example, are supposed to inform the audience about happenings of significance so that audience members will be better able to maintain a clear view of the world in which they live. But if we examine the contents of news programs or of newspapers, it is hard to escape the conclusion that other criteria have also gotten into the picture. Crime, scandal, sports, accidents, fires, and comics receive more attention than would seem to be justified by their true importance in shaping our concept of the reality in which we live. I believe their prominence can be better understood by seeing them as *restorative* messages in a *maintenance* format.

The *restorative* mechanism hypothesized here, has as perhaps its chief merit the characteristic of releasing hostility in small amounts. Seen in quantitative terms, it follows that if an individual or members of a subgroup or indeed of a whole society perceive themselves as oppressed or frustrated in nearly intolerable ways, the *restorative* mechanism may not suffice to accommodate the required relief. In such cases, messages intended as *restorative* may trigger overt retaliatory behavior in grossly antisocial forms. The pattern suggested here is familiar in its childhood version where, among inhibited children, fun often escalates into fighting.

Throughout history, authority figures, and particularly those in autocratic hierarchies have kept anxious watch on popular satire, comedy, songs, rhymes, stories, dramas, and festivals. There is always the question of whether retaliation against the establishment will remain token, and so, restorative, or whether it will override social restraints. The answer is appropriately sought, less in analysis of message content than in the psychological condition of audience members. Perhaps one measure of a society's health is the degree to which it can tolerate the *restorative* mechanism without risking escalation into action that threatens some segment of the social structure.

Should a society regulate the amount of restorative content to which adults have access? In childhood the amount of make-believe, petty sadism, and noisy play is limited by authority figures. But in adulthood, given a permissive situation and available alternatives among media offerings, no comparable institutionalized regulation exists. Whether such regulation should exist is a matter of momentous significance, but it is beyond the scope of the present discussion.

The two mechanisms discussed here interact with each other and, no doubt, with many other factors too. In concluding, I will attempt to relate *reluctance to cope with the other,* successively with *directive, maintenance,* and *restorative messages,* and to do this with reference to the current and crucial problem of race relations in the United States.

RELUCTANCE TO COPE WITH THE OTHER
AND DIRECTIVE MESSAGES

We have observed that *directive* media messages, that is messages intended to bring about substantial learning, do not generally succeed unless they tie in to a structured, face-to-face teacher-pupil relationship. This observation even applies to the teaching of content that does not call for changes in interpersonal behavior, such as mathematics, or the understanding of serious music. If in addition to the intellectual work required, the lesson also requires greater refinement and discipline in interpersonal relationships, reluctance to cope with the other intervenes to further reduce the chances of success.

If Dr. Martin Luther King had expected whites who heard his broadcast messages to substantially increase their understanding of Christianity and also to reflect this understanding in their behavior toward blacks, he would have been unrealistic according to the present hypotheses. But apparently he had no such expectations. He did not stay in the broadcasting studio. Even though he had no special liking for the hurly-burly of the pavements, he carried his mission into face-to-face interaction and it is there that changed behavior was accomplished.

The present formulation appears to accommodate the remarkable and tragic fact that in a nation where Christianity has been the dominant religion for three centuries, and where few living adults have not heard Dr. King and others of like mind via the media, behavior patterns toward blacks have not changed substantially except as such behavior has been compelled by law or in physical confrontations.

RELUCTANCE TO COPE WITH THE OTHER AND MAINTENANCE MESSAGES

We have mentioned two ways in which messages intended as *directive* are transformed into *maintenance* messages at the receiving end. Although I do not have specific data to prove it, it seems highly likely that both mechanisms have transpired with regard to media messages on civil rights. First, the media audiences for civil rights leaders, I speculate, have included a much larger proportion of those already favorable to the civil rights campaign than of those who oppose it. Secondly, among those who favor the civil rights campaign, such exhortations as those of Dr. King have been selectively perceived so that, for example, northern audience members could sincerely agree that blacks should be served in southern restaurants while still feeling no need to take specific steps in breaking through established patterns of discriminatory housing in their own northern neighborhoods.

Maintenance messages provide additional information that extends, updates, and elaborates one's view of reality at approximately his achieved level of socialization. The media perform this function in the United States with remarkable success. By doing so, audience members with a predisposition or readiness to behave in a given manner may be notified of a new or improved social situation in which such behavior is facilitated. Thus the announcement of a civil rights protest demonstration, according to our hypothesis, will activate that small proportion of audience members who have reached the conviction that they must participate in such an activity, and the probably somewhat larger number of those who like to go as spectators to see what happens while avoiding the personal commitment of actual participation. The very large majority, however, receive the news, perceive it in a manner consonant with their existing view of things, and then continue behaving very much as they ordinarily do.

RELUCTANCE TO COPE WITH THE OTHER AND RESTORATIVE MESSAGES

The function of the *restorative* mechanism is to provide token retaliation against authority figures. It reverses deference lines so that the acted upon becomes the actor. In order to insure victory in these forays of the weak against the strong, *restorative* messages typically involve symbolism, metaphor, or fantasy. Institutionalized ceremonies, often featuring costumes and masks, provide occasions in many societies where the weak are guaranteed immunity in acts that would bring stern punishment in everyday life. Either by social or by individual devices, the *restorative* mechanism evades the danger of a forthright test of power with established authority figures. The *restorative* mechanism thus accommodates reluctance to cope with the other.

We have hypothesized a tendency on the part of media audience members to transform messages intended as *directive* or *maintenance* into *restorative* messages if content lends itself to such transformation. This opportunity is certainly present in the case of speeches, documentaries, and televised news reports on the civil rights campaign. In one way or another, these messages say "we are oppressed and we appeal for justice." But the white audience member, preoccupied with his own frustrations, can easily perceive such a message as symbolic reference to his own problems, and so, treat such reports of social reality as if they were drama. Black audience members, on the other hand, many of whom carry nearly explosive accumulations of resentment, are more likely to experience such messages in a personal and literal rather than metaphorical sense, and in some cases are stimulated to gross antisocial behavior.

The hypothesis that civil rights media messages are intuitively transformed for purposes of individual psychological utility seems to contribute toward an understanding of several perplexing and tragic reactions to the assassination of Dr. King; for example:

1. The fact that a significant number of blacks reacted to the death of this disciple of nonviolence with violence.
2. The fact that a significant number of whites reacted to this tragic event by asking, "What can *I* do?"—a question sincerely asked by many whites, but heard as the ultimate in hypocrisy by blacks.
3. The fact that capable and resourceful leaders in the white community preach the efficacy of orderly and peaceful appeals for change, but seem to respond only to the destruction of property or the dislocation of commerce.

The media offer the illusion of participation together with immunity from interaction with the other. The media make it easy to look and pass on, a pattern that has been familiar since ancient times:

A certain man went down from Jerusalem to Jericho, and fell among thieves, which stripped him of his raiment, and wounded him, and departed, leaving him half dead. And by chance there came down a certain priest that way: and when he saw him, he passed by on the other side. And likewise a Levite, when he was at the place, came and looked on him, and passed by on the other side. But a certain Samaritan, as he journeyed, came where he was: and when he saw him, he had compassion on him, and went to him, and bound up his wounds. St. Luke: 10.

The media make it easy to pass by on the other side.

XI. Economic Institutions

Quite apart from any question of its validity, the *Communist Manifesto*, published by Karl Marx and Friedrich Engels in 1848, haunts us in the same way that the specter of communism was said to be haunting Europe over a century ago. It ranks in importance with only a few other political declarations in the history of the world. Not only was this manifesto converted into the communist creed as a rationale for revolution; it also became the theology of repressive regimes forcibly installed in the name of communist revolution. Furthermore, the *Communist Manifesto* advanced a theory of society that the masses could not have grasped in Marx's more esoteric writings. In clear, demagogic prose, Marx and Engels encompassed all of human history, which they saw as a perpetual class war that would culminate in an apocalyptic communist revolution.

According to Marx and Engels, precapitalist and capitalist society form a vast superstructure based on an economic substructure that is comprised of material conditions, property relations, and "the relations of production." They believed that these relations ultimately determined all other social relations. Once capitalism began to emerge, it swept away feudalism just as feudalism had swept away the classical slave system. They confidently predicted that capitalism, with its "inner contradictions," would soon be similarly swept away by communism.

Marx (the giant) and Engels (his junior partner) anatomized most of the essential features of capitalism. They stressed the separation of workers from the means of production, the concentration of the means —and therefore of industry itself—in the hands of a single class (the *haute bourgeoisie*), the expansion of domestic and international mar-

375

kets, and the steady growth of a proletariat and an entrepreneurial middle class.

Marx also predicted disastrous economic crises coupled with increasing misery and unemployment. As capitalism ripened and rotted, its collapse would be hastened by the inevitable secession of industrial workers who would overthrow capitalism, "expropriate the expropriators," and form a classless communist society. Nowhere has this utopian vision of "scientific socialism" come close to realization. Communist revolutions have succeeded, but almost always in precapitalist societies such as Russia, China, the Balkan states, and Cuba. Capitalism, while changing in both predictable and unpredictable fashion, has endured.

Although Marx had some idea of what was to come, neither he nor his collaborator could have foreseen in 1848 that corporate capitalism would become the dominant force in world economics. In *The New Industrial State*, John Kenneth Galbraith, institutional economist and statesman, describes modern corporations that are more powerful economically than nineteenth-century societies. In the chapter excerpted here, Galbraith shows how the largest of these corporations attempt to free themselves from the fluctuations of the market and other capitalistic controls. He posits a technostructure—that is, a technological elite—neither "capitalist" nor "proletarian," that is responsible only to the logic of its technology, the long-term planning imposed by that logic, and attendant managerial functions.

In "The State-Management," from *Pentagon Capitalism*, Seymour Melman, one of America's foremost authorities on industrial engineering and management, illuminates the nature of state capitalism, another phenomenon that Marx could not have foreseen. Under this form of capitalism, the state guarantees and underwrites an exceedingly large sector of private industry. In the period following World War II, federal budgetary support of this sort amounted to well over $1 trillion. The growth of Pentagon capitalism, with its military-industrial establishment (a vast politicoeconomic administrative apparatus), constitutes a direct threat to individual freedom. Moreover, in Melman's opinion, this complex fosters vested interests in government and business that greatly impede the efficient use of human, economic, and natural resources. When the Pentagon and the corporation loom that large, they reduce classic models of capitalism to caricature.

35. From *The Communist Manifesto:* Bourgeois and Proletarians[*]

Karl Marx

The history of all hitherto existing society† is the history of class struggles.

Freeman and slave, patrician and plebeian, lord and serf, guild-master‡ and journeyman, in a word, oppressor and oppressed, stood in constant opposition to one another, carried on an uninterrupted, now hidden, now open fight, a fight that each time ended, either in a revolutionary reconstitution of society at large, or in the common ruin of the contending classes.

In the earlier epochs of history, we find almost everywhere a complicated arrangement of society into various orders, a manifold gradation of social rank. In ancient Rome we have patricians, knights, plebeians, slaves; in the Middle Ages, feudal lords, vassals, guild-masters, journeymen, apprentices, serfs; in almost all of these classes, again, subordinate gradations.

---

[*] By bourgeoisie is meant the class of modern Capitalists, owners of the means of social production and employers of wage labor. By proletariat, the class of modern wage-laborers who, having no means of production of their own, are reduced to selling their labor power in order to live. [*Note by Engels to the English edition of 1888.*]

† That is, all *written* history. In 1847, the pre-history of society, the social organization existing previous to recorded history, was all but unknown. Since then, Haxthausen discovered common ownership of land in Russia, Maurer proved it to be the social foundation from which all Teutonic races started in history, and by and by village communities were found to be, or to have been the primitive form of society everywhere from India to Ireland. The inner organization of this primitive Communistic society was laid bare, in its typical form, by Morgan's crowning discovery of the true nature of the *gens* and its relation to the *tribe.* With the dissolution of these primeval communities society begins to be differentiated into separate and finally antagonistic classes. I have attempted to retrace this process of dissolution in: *Der Ursprung der Familie, des Privateigenthums und des Staats* (*The Origin of the Family, Private Property and the State*), 2nd edition, Stuttgart 1886. [*Note by Engels to the English edition of 1888.*]

‡ Guild-master, that is, a full member of a guild, a master within, not a head of a guild. [*Note by Engels to the English edition of 1888.*]

From *The Communist Manifesto* by Karl Marx. Translation by Samuel Moore (1888).

The modern bourgeois society that has sprouted from the ruins of feudal society has not done away with class antagonisms. It has but established new classes, new conditions of oppression, new forms of struggle in place of the old ones.

Our epoch, the epoch of the bourgeoisie, possesses, however, this distinctive feature: it has simplified the class antagonisms. Society as a whole is more and more splitting up into two great hostile camps, into two great classes directly facing each other: Bourgeoisie and Proletariat.

From the serfs of the Middle Ages sprang the chartered burghers of the earliest towns. From these burgesses the first elements of the bourgeoisie were developed.

The discovery of America, the rounding of the Cape, opened up fresh ground for the rising bourgeoisie. The East Indian and Chinese markets, the colonization of America, trade with the colonies, the increase in the means of exchange and in commodities generally, gave to commerce, to navigation, to industry, an impulse never before known, and thereby, to the revolutionary element in the tottering feudal society, a rapid development.

The feudal system of industry, under which industrial production was monopolized by closed guilds, now no longer sufficed for the growing wants of the new markets. The manufacturing system took its place. The guild-masters were pushed on one side by the manufacturing middle class; division of labor between the different corporate guilds vanished in the face of division of labor in each single workshop.

Meantime the markets kept ever growing, the demand ever rising. Even manufacture no longer sufficed. Thereupon, steam and machinery revolutionized industrial production. The place of manufacture was taken by the giant, Modern Industry, the place of the industrial middle class, by industrial millionaires, the leaders of whole industrial armies, the modern bourgeois.

Modern industry has established the world market, for which the discovery of America paved the way. This market has given an immense development to commerce, to navigation, to communication by land. This development has, in its turn, reacted on the extension of industry; and in proportion as industry, commerce, navigation, railways extended, in the same proportion the bourgeoisie developed, increased its capital, and pushed into the background every class handed down from the Middle Ages.

We see, therefore, how the modern bourgeoisie is itself the product of a long course of development, of a series of revolutions in the modes of production and of exchange.

Each step in the development of the bourgeoisie was accompanied by a corresponding political advance of that class. An oppressed class under the sway of the feudal nobility, an armed and self-governing association in the medieval commune;* here independent urban republic (as in Italy and Germany), there taxable "third estate" of the monarchy (as in France), afterwards, in the period of manufacture proper, serving either the semi-feudal or the absolute monarchy as a counterpoise against the nobility, and, in fact, corner-stone of the great monarchies in general, the bourgeoisie has at last, since the establishment of Modern Industry and of the world market, conquered for itseif, in the modern representative State, exclusive political sway. The executive of the modern State is but a committee for managing the common affairs of the whole bourgeoisie.

The bourgeoisie, historically, has played a most revolutionary part.

The bourgeoisie, wherever it has got the upper hand, has put an end to all feudal, patriarchal, idyllic relations. It has pitilessly torn asunder the motley feudal ties that bound man to his "natural superiors" and has left remaining no other nexus between man an man than naked self-interest, than callous "cash payment." It has drowned the most heavenly ecstasies of religious fervor, of chivalrous enthusiasm, of philistine sentimentalism, in the icy water of egotistical calculation. It has resolved personal worth into exchange value, and in place of the numberless indefeasible chartered freedoms, has set up that single, unconscionable freedom—Free Trade. In one word, for exploitation, veiled by religious and political illusions, it has substituted naked, shameless, direct, brutal exploitation.

The bourgeoisie has stripped of its halo every occupation hitherto honored and looked up to with reverent awe. It has converted the physician, the lawyer, the priest, the poet, the man of science, into its paid wage-laborers.

The bourgeoisie has torn away from the family its sentimental veil, and has reduced the family relation to a mere money relation.

The bourgeoisie has disclosed how it came to pass that the brutal display of vigor in the Middle Ages, which Reactionists so much admire, found its fitting complement in the most slothful indolence. It has been the first to show what man's activity can bring about. It has accomplished wonders far surpassing Egyptian pyramids, Roman aqueducts, and Gothic cathedrals; it has conducted expeditions that put in the shade all former Exoduses of nations and crusades.

The bourgeoisie cannot exist without constantly revolutionizing the

---

* "Commune" was the name taken, in France, by the nascent towns even before they had conquered from their feudal lords and masters local self-government and political rights as the "Third Estate." Generally speaking, for the economical development of the bourgeoisie, England is here taken as the typical country; for its political development, France. [*Note by Engels to the English edition of 1888.*]

This was the name given their urban communities by the townsmen of Italy and France, after they had purchased or wrested their initial rights of self-government from their feudal lords. [*Note by Engels to the German edition of 1890.*]

instruments of production, and thereby the relations of production, and with them the whole relations of society. Conservation of the old modes of production in unaltered form, was, on the contrary, the first condition of existence for all earlier industrial classes. Constant revolutionizing of production, uninterrupted disturbance of all social conditions, everlasting uncertainty and agitation distinguish the bourgeois epoch from all earlier ones. All fixed, fast-frozen relations, with their train of ancient and venerable prejudices and opinions are swept away, all new formed ones become antiquated before they can ossify. All that is solid melts into air, all that is holy is profaned, and man is at last compelled to face with sober senses, his real conditions of life, and his relations with his kind.

The need of a constantly expanding market for its products chases the bourgeoisie over the whole surface of the globe. It must nestle everywhere, settle everywhere, establish connections everywhere.

The bourgeoisie has through its exploitation of the world market given a cosmopolitan character to production and consumption in every country. To the great chagrin of Reactionists, it has drawn from under the feet of industry the national ground on which it stood. All old-established national industries have been destroyed or are daily being destroyed. They are dislodged by new industries, whose introduction becomes a life and death question for all civilized nations, by industries that no longer work up indigenous raw material, but raw material drawn from the remotest zones; industries whose products are consumed, not only at home, but in every quarter of the globe. In place of the old wants, satisfied by the productions of the country, we find new wants, requiring for their satisfaction the products of distant lands and climes. In place of the old local and national seclusion and self-sufficiency, we have intercourse in every direction, universal inter-dependence of nations. And as in material, so also in intellectual production. The intellectual creations of individual nations become common property. National one-sidedness and narrow-mindedness become more and more impossible, and from the numerous national and local literatures, there arises a world literature.

The bourgeoisie, by the rapid improvement of all instruments of production, by the immensely facilitated means of communication, draws all, even the most barbarian, nations into civilization. The cheap prices of its commodities are the heavy artillery with which it batters down all Chinese walls, with which it forces the barbarians' intensely obstinate hatred of foreigners to capitulate. It compels all nations, on pain of extinction, to adopt the bourgeois mode of production; it compels them to introduce what it calls civilization into their midst, that is, to become bourgeois themselves. In one word, it creates a world after its own image.

The bourgeoisie has subjected the country to the rule of the towns. It has created enormous cities, has greatly increased the urban population as compared with the rural, and has thus rescued a considerable part of the population from the idiocy of rural life. Just as it has made the country dependent on the towns, so it has made barbarian and semi-barbarian countries dependent on the civilized ones, nations of peasants on nations of bourgeois, the East on the West.

The bourgeoisie keeps more and more doing away with the scattered state of the population, of the means of production, and of property. It has agglomerated population, centralized means of production, and has concentrated property in a few hands. The necessary consequence of this was political centralization. Independent, or but loosely connected, provinces with separate interests, laws, governments and systems of taxation, became lumped together into one nation, with one government, one code of laws, one national class-interest, one frontier and one customs-tariff.

The bourgeoisie, during its rule of scarce one hundred years, has created more massive and more colossal productive forces than have all preceding generations together. Subjection of Nature's forces to man, machinery, application of chemistry to industry and agriculture, steam-navigation, railways, electric telegraphs, clearing of whole continents for cultivation, canalization of rivers, whole populations conjured out of the ground—what earlier century had even a presentiment that such productive forces slumbered in the lap of social labor?

We see then: the means of production and of exchange, on whose foundation the bourgeoisie built itself up, were generated in feudal society. At a certain stage in the development of these means of production and of exchange, the conditions under which feudal society produced and exchanged, the feudal organization of agriculture and manufacturing industry, in one word, the feudal relations of property became no longer compatible with the already developed productive forces; they became so many fetters. They had to be burst asunder; they were burst asunder.

Into their place stepped free competition, accompanied by a social and political constitution adapted to it, and by the economical and political sway of the bourgeois class.

A similar movement is going on before our own eyes. Modern bourgeois society with its relations of production, of exchange and of property, a society that has conjured up such gigantic means of production and of exchange, is like the sorcerer, who is no longer able to control the powers of the nether world whom he has called up by his spells. For many a decade past the history of industry and commerce is but the history of the revolt of modern productive forces against modern conditions of production, against the property relations that are the conditions for the existence of the bourgeoisie and of its rule. It is enough to mention the commercial crises that by their periodical return put on its trial, each time more threateningly, the existence of the entire bourgeois society. In these crises a great part not only of the existing products, but also of the previously created productive forces, are periodically destroyed. In these crises there breaks out an epidemic that, in all earlier epochs, would have seemed an absurdity—the epidemic of overproduction. Society suddenly finds itself put back into a state of momentary barbarism; it appears as if a famine, a universal war of devastation had cut off the supply of every means of subsistence; industry and commerce seem to be destroyed; and why? Because there is too much civilization, too much means of subsistence, too much industry, too much commerce. The productive forces at the disposal of society no longer tend to further the development of the conditions of bourgeois property; on the contrary, they have become too powerful for these conditions, by which they are fettered, and so soon as they overcome these fetters, they bring disorder into the whole of bourgeois society, endanger the existence of bourgeois property. The conditions of bourgeois society are too narrow to comprise the wealth created by them. And how does the bourgeoisie get over these crises? On the one hand by enforced destruction of a mass of productive forces; on the other, by the conquest of new markets, and by the more thorough exploitation of the old ones. That is to say, by paving the way for more extensive and more destructive crises, and by diminishing the means whereby crises are prevented.

The weapons with which the bourgeoisie felled feudalism to the ground are now turned against the bourgeoisie itself.

But not only has the bourgeoisie forged the weapons that bring death to itself; it has also called into existence the men who are to wield those weapons—the modern working class—the proletarians.

In proportion as the bourgeoisie, that is, capital, is developed, in the same proportion is the proletariat, the modern working class, developed —a class of laborers, who live only so long as they find work, and who find work only so long as their labor increases capital. These laborers, who must sell themselves piecemeal, are a commodity, like every other article of commerce, and are consequently exposed to all the vicissitudes of competition, to all the fluctuations of the market.

Owing to the extensive use of machinery and to division of labor, the work of the proletarians has lost all individual character, and, consequently, all charm for the workman. He becomes an appendage of the machine, and it is only the most simple, most monotonous, and most easily acquired knack, that is required of him. Hence, the cost of production of a workman is restricted, almost entirely, to the means of subsistence that he requires for his maintenance, and for the propagation of his race. But the price of a commodity, and therefore also of labor, is equal to its cost of production. In proportion, therefore, as the repulsiveness of the work increases, the wage decreases. Nay more, in proportion as the use of machinery and division of labor increases, in the same proportion the burden of toil also increases, whether the prolongation of the working hours, by increase of the work exacted in a given time or by increased speed of the machinery, and so on.

Modern industry has converted the little workshop of the patriarchal master into the great factory of the industrial capitalist. Masses of laborers, crowded into the factory, are organized like soldiers. As privates of the industrial army they are placed under the command of a perfect hierarchy of officers and sergeants. Not only are they slaves of the bourgeois class, and of the bourgeois State; they are daily and hourly enslaved by the machine, by the overlooker, and, above all, by the individual bourgeois manufacturer himself. The more openly this despotism proclaims gain to be its end and aim, the more petty, the more hateful and the more embittering it is.

The less the skill and exertion of strength implied in manual labor, in other words, the more modern industry becomes developed, the more is the labor of men superseded by that of women. Differences of age and sex have no longer any distinctive social validity for the working class. All are instruments of labor, more or less expensive to use, according to their age and sex.

No sooner is the exploitation of the laborer by the manufacturer, so far, at an end, that he receives his wages in cash, than he is set upon by the other portions of the bourgeoisie, the landlord, the shopkeeper, the pawnbroker, and so on.

The lower strata of the middle class—the small tradespeople, shopkeepers, and retired tradesmen generally, the handicraftsmen and peasants—all these sink gradually into the proletariat, partly because their diminutive capital does not suffice for the scale on which Modern Industry is carried on, and is swamped in the competition with the large capitalists, partly because their specialized skill is rendered worthless by new methods of production. Thus the proletariat is recruited from all classes of the population.

The proletariat goes through various stages of development. With its birth begins its struggle with the bourgeoisie. At first the contest is carried on by individual laborers, then by the work-people of a factory, then by the operatives of one trade, in one locality, against the individual bourgeois who directly exploits them. They direct their attacks not against the bourgeois conditions of production, but against the instruments of production themselves; they destroy imported wares that compete with their labor, they smash to pieces machinery, they set factories ablaze, they seek to restore by force the vanished status of the workman of the Middle Ages.

At this stage the laborers still form an incoherent mass scattered over the whole country, and broken up by their mutual competition. If anywhere they unite to form more compact bodies, this is not yet the consequence of their own active union, but of the union of the bourgeoisie, which class, in order to attain its own political ends, is compelled to set the whole proletariat in motion, and is moreover yet, for a time, able to do so. At this stage therefore, the proletarians do not fight their enemies, but the enemies of their enemies, the remnants of absolute monarchy, the landowners, the non-industrial bourgeois, the petty bourgeoisie. Thus the whole historical movement is concentrated in the hands of the bourgeoisie; every victory so obtained is a victory for the bourgeoisie.

But with the development of industry the proletariat not only increases in number; it becomes concentrated in greater masses, its strength grows, and it feels that strength more. The various interests and conditions of life within the ranks of the proletariat are more and more equalized, in proportion as machinery obliterates all distinctions of labor, and nearly everywhere reduces wages to the same low level. The growing competition among the bourgeois, and the resulting commercial crises, make the wages of the workers ever more fluctuating. The unceasing improvement of machinery, ever more rapidly developing, makes their livelihood more and more precarious; the collisions between individual workmen and individual bourgeois take more and more the character of collisions between two classes. Thereupon the workers begin to form combinations (Trades Unions) against the bourgeois; they club together in order to keep up the rate of wages; they found permanent associations in order to make provisions beforehand for these occasional revolts. Here and there the contest breaks out into riots.

Now and then the workers are victorious, but only for a time. The real fruit of their battles lies, not in the immediate result, but in the ever-expanding union of the workers. This union is helped on by the improved means of communication that are created by modern industry and that place the workers of different localities in contact with one another. It was just this contact that was needed to centralize the numerous local struggles, all of the same character, into one national struggle between classes. But every class struggle is a political struggle. And that union, to attain which the burghers of the Middle Ages, with their miserable highways, required centuries, the modern proletarians, thanks to railways, achieve in a few years.

This organization of the proletarians into a class, and consequently into a political party, is continually being upset again by the competition between the workers themselves. But it ever rises up again, stronger, firmer, mightier. It compels legislative recognition of particular interests of the workers, by taking advantage of the division among the bourgeoisie itself. Thus the Ten Hours bill in England was carried.

Altogether collisions between the classes of the old society further, in many ways, the course of development of the proletariat. The bourgeoisie finds itself involved in a constant battle. At first with the aristocracy; later on, with those portions of the bourgeoisie itself, whose interests have become antagonistic to the progress of industry; at all times, with the bourgeoisie of foreign countries. In all these battles it sees itself compelled to appeal to the proletariat, to ask for its help, and thus, to drag it into the political arena. The bourgeoisie itself, therefore, supplies the proletariat with its own elements of political and general education, in other words, it furnishes the proletariat with weapons for fighting the bourgeoisie.

Further, as we have already seen, entire sections of the ruling classes are, by the advance of industry, precipitated into the proletariat, or are at least threatened in their conditions of existence. These also supply the proletariat with fresh elements of enlightenment and progress.

Finally, in times when the class struggle nears the decisive hour, the process of dissolution going on within the ruling class, in fact within the whole range of old society, assumes such a violent, glaring character, that a small section of the ruling class cuts itself adrift, and joins the revolutionary class, the class that holds the future in its hands. Just as, therefore, at an earlier period, a section of the nobility went over to the bourgeoisie, so now a portion of the bourgeoisie goes over to the proletariat, and in particular, a portion of the bourgeois ideologists, who have raised themselves to the level of comprehending theoretically the historical movement as a whole.

Of all the classes that stand face to face with the bourgeoisie today, the proletariat alone is a really revolutionary class. The other classes decay and finally disappear in the face of modern industry; the proletariat is its special and essential product.

The lower middle class, the small manufacturer, the shopkeeper, the artisan, the peasant, all these fight against the bourgeoisie, to save from extinction their existence as fractions of the middle class. They are therefore not revolutionary, but conservative. Nay more, they are reactionary, for they try to roll back the wheel of history. If by chance they are revolutionary, they are so only in view of their impending transfer into the proletariat, they thus defend not their present, but their future interests, they desert their own standpoint to place themselves at that of the proletariat.

The "dangerous class," the social scum, that passively rotting mass thrown off by the lowest layers of old society, may, here and there, be swept into the movement by a proletarian revolution; its conditions of life, however, prepare it far more for the part of a bribed tool of reactionary intrigue.

In the conditions of the proletariat, those of old society at large are already virtually swamped. The proletarian is without property, his relation to his wife and children has no longer anything in common with the bourgeois family relations; modern industrial labor, modern subjection to capital, the same in England as in France, in America as in Germany, has stripped him of every trace of national character. Law, morality, religion, are to him so many bourgeois prejudices, behind which lurk in ambush just as many bourgeois interests.

All the preceding classes that got the upper hand sought to fortify their already acquired status by subjecting society at large to their conditions of appropriation. The proletarians cannot become masters of the productive forces of society, except by abolishing their own previous mode of appropriation, and thereby also every other previous mode of appropriation. They have nothing of their own to secure and to fortify; their mission is to destroy all previous securities for, and insurances of, individual property.

All previous historical movements were movements of minorities, or in the interest of minorities. The proletarian movement is the self-conscious, independent movement of the immense majority, in the interest of the immense majority. The proletariat, the lowest stratum of our present society, cannot stir, cannot raise itself up, without the whole superincumbent strata of official society being sprung into the air.

Though not in substance, yet in form, the struggle of the proletariat with the bourgeoisie is at first a national struggle. The proletariat of each country must, of course, first of all settle matters with its own bourgeoisie.

In depicting the most general phases of the development of the proletariat, we traced the more or less veiled civil war, raging within existing society, up to the point where that war breaks out into open revolution, and where the violent overthrow of the bourgeoisie lays the foundation for the sway of the proletariat.

Hitherto, every form of society has been based, as we have already seen, on the antagonism of oppressing and oppressed classes. But in order to oppress a class, certain conditions must be assured to it under which it can, at least, continue its slavish existence. The serf, in the period of serfdom, raised himself to membership in the commune just as the petty bourgeois, under the yoke of feudal absolutism, managed to develop into a bourgeois. The modern laborer, on the contrary, instead of rising with the progress of industry, sinks deeper and deeper below the conditions of existence of his own class. He becomes a pauper, and pauperism develops more rapidly than population and wealth. And here it becomes evident, that the bourgeoisie is unfit any longer to be the ruling class in society, and to impose its conditions of existence upon society as an overriding law. It is unfit to rule because it is incompetent to assure an existence to its slave within his slavery, because it cannot help letting him sink into such a state, that it has to feed him, instead of being fed by him. Society can no longer live under this bourgeoisie, in other words, its existence is no longer compatible with society.

The essential condition for the existence, and for the sway of the bourgeois class, is the formation and augmentation of capital; the condition for capital is wage labor. Wage labor rests exclusively on competition between the laborers. The advance of industry, whose involuntary promoter is the bourgeoisie, replaces the isolation of the laborers, due to competition, by their revolutionary combination, due to association. The development of Modern Industry, therefore, cuts from under its feet the very foundation on which the bourgeoisie produces and appropriates products. What the bourgeoisie, therefore, produces, above all, is its own grave-diggers. Its fall and the victory of the proletariat are equally inevitable.

36. The Corporation
John Kenneth Galbraith

I

Few subjects of earnest inquiry have been more unproductive than study of the modern large corporation. The reasons are clear. A vivid image of what *should* exist acts as a surrogate for reality. Pursuit of the image then prevents pursuit of the reality.

For purposes of scholarly inquiry, the corporation has a sharp legal image. Its purpose is to do business as an individual would but with the added ability to assemble and use the capital of several or numerous persons. In consequence, it can undertake tasks beyond the reach of any single person. And it protects those who supply capital by limiting their liability to the amount of their original investment, insuring them a vote on the significant affairs of the enterprise, defining the powers and the responsibilities of directors and officers, and giving them access to the courts to redress grievance. Apart from its ability to mobilize capital and its lessened association with the active life of any individual, the corporation is not deemed to differ functionally from the individual proprietorship or partnership. Its purpose, like theirs, is to conduct business on equitable terms with other businesses and make money for the owners.

Such corporations do exist and in large numbers. But one wonders if the natural interest of the student of economics is the local paving firm or body repair shop. Or is it General Motors and Standard Oil of New Jersey and General Electric?

But these firms depart sharply from the legal image. In none of these firms is the capital pooled by original investors appreciable; in each it could be paid off by a few hours' or a few days' earnings. In none does the individual stockholder pretend to power. In all three cases, the corporation is far more influential in the markets in which it buys materials, components and labor and in which it sells its finished products than is commonly imagined to be the case with the individual proprietorship.

In consequence, nearly all study of the corporation has been concerned with its deviation from its legal or formal image. This image—that of "an association of persons into an autonomous legal unit with a distinct legal personality that enable it to carry on business, own property and

From *The New Industrial State* by John Kenneth Galbraith. Copyright © 1967, 1971 by John Kenneth Galbraith. Reprinted by permission of the publisher Houghton Mifflin Company.

contract debts"[1]—is highly normative. It is what a corporation should be. When the modern corporation disenfranchises its stockholders, grows to gargantuan size, expands into wholly unrelated activities, is a monopoly where it buys and a monopoly where it sells, something is wrong.

That the largest and most famous corporations, those whose names are household words and whose heads are accorded the most distinguished honors by their fellow businessmen, should be considered abnormal must seem a little dubious.

Additionally, it must be evident that General Motors does not have much in common with the Massachusetts Institute of Technology professors who pool their personal funds and what they can borrow from the banks and their friends to supply some erudite item to the Department of Defense and thus, in their modest way, help to defend the country and participate in capital gains. Their enterprise, created, owned and directed by themselves and exploiting the advantages of the corporate form, approaches the established image. General Motors as clearly does not.

The answer is that there is no such thing as *a* corporation. Rather there are several kinds of corporations all deriving from a common but very loose framework. Some are subject to the market; others reflect varying degrees of adaptation to the requirements of planning and the needs of the technostructure. The person who sets out to study buildings on Manhattan on the assumption that all are alike will have difficulty in passing from the surviving brownstones to the skyscrapers. And he will handicap himself even more if he imagines that all buildings should be like brownstones and have load-carrying walls and that others are abnormal. So with corporations.

II

The most obvious requirement of effective planning is large size. This, we have seen, allows the firm to accept market uncertainty where it cannot be eliminated; to eliminate markets on which otherwise it would be excessively dependent; to control other markets in which it buys and sells; and it is very nearly indispensable for participation in that part of the economy, characterized by exacting technology and comprehensive planning, where the only buyer is the Federal Government.

That corporations accommodate well to this need for size has scarcely to be stressed. They can, and have, become very large. But because of the odor of abnormality, this adaptation is not stressed. The head of the largest corporation is automatically accorded precedence at all business conventions, meetings and other business rites and festivals. He is complimented for his intelligence, vision, courage, progressiveness and for the remarkable rate of growth of his firm under his direction. But the great size of his firm—the value of its assets or the number of its employees—is not praised although this is its most striking feature.

Nothing so characterizes the industrial system as the scale of the modern corporate enterprise. In 1962 the five largest industrial corporations in the United States, with combined assets in excess of $36 billion, possessed over 12 per cent of all assets used in manufacturing. The fifty largest corporations had over a third of all manufacturing assets. The 500 largest had well over two-thirds. Corporations with assets in excess of $10,000,000, some 2,000 in all, accounted for about 80 per cent of all the resources used in manufacturing in the United States.[2] In the mid nineteen-fifties, 28 corporations provided approximately 10 per cent of all employment in manufacturing, mining and retail and wholesale trade. Twenty-three corporations provided 15 per cent of all the employment in manufacturing. In the first half of the decade (June 1950–June 1956) a hundred firms received two-thirds by value of all defense contracts; ten firms received one-third.[3] In 1960 four corporations accounted for an estimated 22 per cent of all industrial research and development expenditure. Three hundred and eighty-four corporations employing 5,000 or more workers accounted for 85 per cent of these expenditures; 260,000 firms employing fewer than 1,000 accounted for only 7 per cent.[4]

Planning is a function that is associated in most minds with the state. If the corporation is the basic planning unit, it is appropriate that the scale of operations of the largest should approximate those of government. This they do. In 1965, three industrial corporations, General Motors, Standard Oil of New Jersey and Ford Motor Company, had more gross income than all of the farms in the country. The income of General Motors, of $20.7 billion, about equaled that of the three million smallest farms in the country—around ninety per cent of all farms. The gross revenues of each of the three corporations just mentioned far exceed those of any single state. The revenues of General Motors in 1963 were fifty times those of Nevada, eight times those of New York and slightly less than one-fifth those of the Federal Government.[5]

Economists have anciently quarreled over the reasons for the great size of the modern corporation. Is it because size is essential in order to reap the economies of modern large scale production?[6] Is it, more insidiously, because the big firm wishes to exercise monopoly power in its markets? The present analysis allows both parties to the dispute to be partly right. The firm must be large enough to carry the large capital commitments of modern technology. It must also be large enough to control its markets. But the present view also explains what the older explanations don't explain. That is, why General Motors is not only large enough to afford the best size of automobile plant but is large enough to afford a dozen or more of the best size; and why it is large enough to produce things as diverse as aircraft engines and refrigerators, which cannot be explained by the economies of scale; and why, though it is large enough to have the market power associated with monopoly, consumers do not seriously complain of exploitation. The size of General Motors is in the service not of monopoly or the economies of scale but of planning. And for this planning—control of supply, control of demand, provision of capital, minimization of risk—there is no clear upper limit to the desirable size. It could be that the bigger the better. The corporate form accommodates to this need. Quite clearly it allows the firm to be very, very large.

III

The corporation also accommodates itself admirably to the needs of the technostructure. This, we have seen, is an apparatus for group decision—for pooling and testing the information provided by numerous individuals to reach decisions that are beyond the knowledge of any one. It requires, we have also seen, a high measure of autonomy. It is vulnerable to any intervention by external authority for, given the nature of the group decision-making and the problems being solved, such external authority will always be incompletely informed and hence arbitrary. If problems were susceptible to decision by individuals, no group would be involved.

One possible source of such intervention is the state. The corporate charter, however, accords the corporation a large area of independent action in the conduct of its affairs. And this freedom is defended as a sacred right. Nothing in American business attitudes is so iniquitous as government interference in the *internal* affairs of the corporation. The safeguards here, both in law and custom, are great. There is equally vehement resistance to any invasion by trade unions of the prerogatives of management.

There is also, however, the danger of intervention by the owners—by the stockholders. Their exclusion is not secured by law or sanctified by custom. On the contrary, either directly or through the agency of the Board of Directors, their power is guaranteed. But being legal does not make it benign. Exercise of such power on substantive questions requiring group decisions would be as damaging as any other. So the stockholder too must be excluded.

In part this has been accomplished by the simple attrition of the stockholder's power as death and the distribution of estates, the diversifying instincts of trusts and foundations, the distributional effects of property settlements and alimony, and the artistic, philanthropic and social enjoyments of non-functional heirs all distribute the stock of any corporation to more and more hands. This process works rapidly and the distribution need by no means be complete to separate the stockholder from all effective power. In the mid nineteen-twenties, in the first case to draw wide public attention to this tendency, it became known that Colonel Robert W. Stewart, the Chairman of the Board of Directors of the Standard Oil Company of Indiana, had, in concert with some of the men who later won immortality as the architects of the Teapot Dome and Elk Hills transactions, organized a highly specialized enterprise in Canada called the Continental Trading Company. This company had the sole function of buying crude oil from Colonel E. A. Humphreys, owner of the rich Mexica field in east central Texas, and reselling it to companies controlled by the same individuals, including Standard Oil of Indiana, at a markup of twenty-five cents a barrel. It was an excellent business. No costs were involved, other than a small percentage to the Canadian lawyer who served as a figurehead and went hunting in Africa whenever wanted for questioning, and for mailing back the proceeds after they had been converted into Liberty Bonds. (If some of these had not been used, carelessly, to bribe Secretary of the Interior Albert B. Fall and others to pay the deficit of the Republican National Committee, Continental might have forever remained unknown as was unquestionably intended.) It was Colonel Stewart's later contention that he had always intended to turn over the profit to Standard Oil of Indiana. But, absentmindedly, he had allowed the bonds to remain in his own possession for many years and had cashed some of the coupons. In 1929 Standard of Indiana was only eighteen years distant from the decree which had broken up the Standard Oil empire of John D. Rockefeller of which it had been an important part. The Rockefellers still owned 14.9 per cent of the voting stock of the Indiana Company and were deemed to have the controlling interest. They reacted sternly to the outrage; the elder Rockefeller had, on notable occasions, imposed a somewhat similar levy on his competitors, but never on his own company. With the aid of the publicity generated by the Teapot Dome scandal, his own high standing in the financial community, his brother-in-law Winthrop W. Aldrich, who solicited proxies, and a very large expenditure of money, John D. Rockefeller, Jr., was able to oust the Colonel, although not by a wide margin.[7] (The latter had the full support of his Board of Directors.) In the absence of the scandal and his ample resources, Rockefeller, it was realized with some shock, would have had little hope.

In most other large corporations, the chance for exerting such power would have been less and it has become increasingly less with the passage of time. Professor Gordon's prewar study of the 176 largest corporations showed that at least half of their stock was held in blocks of less than one per cent of the total outstanding. In less than a third of the companies was there a stockholder interest large enough to allow of potential control, i.e., the election of a Board of Directors, and "the number of companies in which any large degree of *active* leadership is associated with considerable ownership is certainly even smaller."[8] That was a quarter of a century ago, the dispersion of stock ownership, which was then much greater for the older railroad corporations than for newer industrial corporations, has almost certainly continued.[9] It means that to change control more stockholders must be persuaded, against the advice of management, to vote their stock for someone whom, in the nature of the case, they do not know and will not be disposed to trust. The effort must also contend with the tendency of the indifferent to give proxies to management. It is also in face of the requirement that the loser of a proxy battle, if he is an outsider, must pay the cost. And it must contend finally with the alternative, always available to the dissatisfied stockholder, of simply selling his stock. Corporate size, the passage of time and the dispersion of stock ownership do not disenfranchise the stockholder. Rather, he can vote but his vote is valueless.

IV

To be secure in its autonomy, the technostructure also needs to have a source of new capital to which it can turn without having, as a *quid pro quo*, to surrender any authority over its own decisions. Here capital abundance enters as a factor. A bank, insurance company or investment banker cannot make control of decision, actual or potential, a condition of a loan or security underwriting if funds are readily available from another and more permissive source and if there is vigorous competition for the business.

The complexity of modern technological and planning decisions also protects the technostructure from outside interference. The country banker, out of his experience and knowledge of the business, can readily interpose his judgment, as against that of a farmer, on the prospects for feeder cattle—and does. Not even the most self-confident financier would wish to question the judgment of General Electric engineers, product planners, stylists, market researchers and sales executives on the culturally advanced toaster taken up in the last chapter. By taking decisions away from individuals and locating them deeply within the technostructure, technology and planning thus remove them from the influence of outsiders.

But the corporation accords a much more specific protection to the technostructure. That is by providing it with a source of capital, derived from its own earnings, that is wholly under its own control. No banker can attach conditions as to how retained earnings are to be used. Nor can any other outsider. No one, the normally innocuous stockholder apart, has the right to ask about an investment from retained earnings that turns out badly. It is hard to overestimate the importance of the shift in power that is associated with availability of such a source of capital. Fewer other developments can have more fundamentally altered the character of capitalism. It is hardly surprising that retained earnings of corporations have become such an overwhelmingly important source of capital.

V

There remains one final source of danger to the autonomy of the technostructure. That arises with a failure of earnings. Then there are no retained earnings. If new plant is needed or working capital must be replenished, there will have to be appeal to bankers or other outsiders. This will be under circumstances, that is, the fact that the firm is showing losses, when the right of such outsiders to inquire and to intervene will have to be conceded. They cannot be told to mind their own business. Thus does a shortage of capital, though limited in time and place, promptly revive the power of the capitalist. And it is in times of such failure of earnings, and then only, that the stockholder of the large corporation can be aroused. In large corporations, battles for control have been rare in recent times. And in all notable cases involving large corporations—the New York Central, Loew's, TWA, the New England railroads, Wheeling Steel, Curtis Publishing—the firm in contention was doing badly at the time. If revenues are above some minimum—they need not be at their maximum for no one will know what that is— creditors cannot intervene and stockholders cannot be aroused.

Here too the corporation, and the industrial system generally, have adapted effectively to the needs of the technostructure, though, surprisingly, the nature of the adaptation has been little noticed. The adaptation is, simply, that big corporations do not lose money. In 1957, a year of mild recession in the United States, not one of the one hundred largest industrial corporations failed to return a profit. Only one of the largest two hundred finished the year in the red. Seven years later in 1964, a prosperous year by general agreement, all of the first hundred again made money; only two among the first two hundred had losses and only seven among the first five hundred. None of the fifty largest merchandising firms—Sears, Roebuck, A & P, Safeway *et al.*—failed to return a profit. Nor, predictably, did any of the fifty largest utilities. And among the fifty largest transportation companies only three railroads and the momentarily unfortunate Eastern Airlines, failed to make money.[10]

The American business liturgy has long intoned that this is a profit and loss economy. "The American competitive enterprise system is an acknowledged profit and loss system, the hope of profits being the incentive and the fear of loss being the spur."[11] This may be so. But it is not true of that organized part of the economy in which a developed technostructure is able to protect its profits by planning. Nor is it true of the United States Steel Corporation, author of the sentence just cited, which has not had losses for a quarter of a century.

VI

As always, no strong case is improved by overstatement. Among the two hundred largest corporations in the United States—those that form the heart of the industrial system—there are few in which owners exercise any important influence on decisions. And this influence decreases year by year. But there are exceptions. Some owners—the du Pont, and in lesser measure the Firestone and Ford, families are examples—participate, or have participated, actively in management. Thus they earn influence by being part of the technostructure and their influence is unquestionably increased by their ownership. Others, through position on the Board of Directors, have power in the selection of management—in decision on those who make decisions. And yet others may inform themselves and intervene substantively on individual decisions—a merger, a plant acquisition or the launching of a new line.

In the last case, however, there must always be question as to how much the individual is deciding and how much has been decided for him by the group which has provided the relevant information; the danger of confusing ratification with decision must again be emphasized. And in all circumstances it is important to realize that corporate ceremony more or less deliberately disguises the reality. This deserves a final word.

Corporate liturgy strongly emphasizes the power of the Board of Directors and ultimately, thus, of the stockholders they are assumed to represent. The rites which attest this point are conducted with much solemnity; no one allows himself to be cynical as to their substance. Heavy dockets, replete with data, are submitted to the Board. Time is allowed for study. Recommendations are appended. Given the extent and group character of the preparation, rejection would be unthinkable. The Board, nonetheless, is left with the impression that it has made a decision.

Corporate procedure also allows the Board to act on financial transactions—changes in capital structure, declaration of dividends, authorization of lines of credit. These, given the control by the technostructure of its sources of savings and capital supply, are frequently the most routine and derivative of decisions. But as elsewhere noted, any association with large sums of money conveys an impression of power. It brings it to mind for the same traditional reasons as does a detachment of soldiers.

With even greater unction although with less plausibility, corporate ceremony seeks also to give the stockholders an impression of power. When stockholders are (or were) in control of a company, stockholders' meetings are an occasion of scant ceremony. The majority is voted in and the minority is voted out, with such concessions as may seem strategic, and all understand the process involved. As stockholders cease to have influence, however, efforts are made to disguise this nullity. Their convenience is considered in selecting the place of meeting. They are presented with handsomely printed reports, the preparation of which is now a specialized business. Products and even plants are inspected. During the proceedings, as in the report, there are repetitive references to *your* company. Officers listen, with every evidence of attention, to highly irrelevant suggestions of wholly uninformed participants and assure them that these will be considered with the greatest care. Votes of thanks from women stockholders in print dresses owning ten shares "for the excellent skill with which you run *our* company" are received by the management with well-simulated gratitude. All present show stern disapproval of critics. No important stockholders are present. No decisions are taken. The annual meeting of the large American corporation is, perhaps, our most elaborate exercise in popular illusion.

In 1956 upwards of 100,000 stockholders of Bethlehem Steel returned proxies to a management committee. These were voted routinely for a slate of directors selected by management exclusively from among its own members. The following colloquy occurred in Washington the following year:

> Senator Kefauver: The exhibit shows that the members of the Board of Directors paid themselves $6,499,000 in 1956.
> Mr. Homer (President of Bethlehem Steel Corporation): I wish to interpose there, Senator, we did not pay ourselves. I wish that term would not be used.
> Senator Kefauver: Very well, approved by the stockholders.
> Mr. Homer: That is better.[12]

NOTES

1. Harry G. Guthmann and Herbert E. Dougall, *Corporation Financial Policy,* Second Edition (New York: Prentice-Hall, Inc., 1948), p. 9.
2. Hearings before the Subcommittee on Antitrust and Monopoly of the Committee of the Judiciary, United States Senate, Eighty-Eighth Congress, Second Session, Pursuant to S. Res. 262. Part I. *Economic Concentration. Overall and Conglomerate Aspects* (1964), p. 113. Data on the concentration of industrial activity in the hands of large firms, and especially any that seem to show an increase in concentration, sustain a controversy in the United States that, at times, reaches mildly pathological proportions. The reason is that much of the argument between those who see the market as a viable institution and those who feel that it is succumbing to monopolistic influences has long turned on these figures. These figures are thus defended or attacked according to predilection. However, the general orders of magnitude given here are not subject to serious question.
3. Carl Kaysen, "The Corporation: How Much Power? What Scope?" in *The Corporation in Modern Society,* Edward S. Mason, ed. (Cambridge: Harvard University Press, 1959), pp. 86–87.
4. M. A. Adelman, Hearings before the Subcommittee on Antitrust and Monopoly of the Committee on the Judiciary, United States Senate. Eighty-Ninth Congress, First Session, Pursuant to S. Res. 70, Part III. *Economic Concentration. Concentration, Invention and Innovation* (1965), pp. 1139–40.
5. Data from *Fortune,* U.S. Department of Agriculture and *Statistical Abstract of the United States.*
6. Cf. Joe S. Bain, "Economics of Scale, Concentration and the Condition of Entry in Twenty Manufacturing Industries," *The American Economic Review,* Vol. XLIV, No. 1. (March, 1954).
7. Cf. Adolf A. Berle, Jr. and Gardiner C. Means, *The Modern Corporation and Private Property* (New York: Macmillan, 1934), pp. 82–83. Of the 8,465,299 shares represented, Rockefeller got the votes of 5,510,313. Stewart retired on a pension of $75,000 a year. M. R. Werner and John Starr, *Teapot Dome* (New York: The Viking Press, Inc., 1959), pp. 274–75.
8. R. A. Gordon, *Business Leadership in the Large Corporation* (Washington: Brookings, 1945), Chapter II. The median holdings of management were 2.1 per cent of the stock. In 56 per cent of the companies, management owned less than one per cent; in only 16 of the companies did it own as much as 20 per cent of the stock outstanding. A more recent study by Mabel Newcomer, *The Big Business Executive* (New York: Columbia University Press, 1955), showed that by 1952 there had been a further reduction in management holdings.

9. This is explicitly confirmed by a study by R. J. Larner, "The 200 Largest Non-financial Corporations," *The American Economic Review*, Vol. LVI, No. 4, Part 1 (September 1966), pp. 777–87, which appeared just as this book was going to press.
10. *The Fortune Directory*, August, 1958, August, 1965.
11. United States Steel Corporation. *Annual Report, 1958*.
12. U.S. Congress, Hearings on Administered Prices, Part II. *Steel*, p. 562.

37. The State-Management

Seymour Melman

In the name of defense, and without announcement or debate, a basic alteration has been effected in the governing institutions of the United States. An industrial management has been installed in the federal government, under the Secretary of Defense, to control the nation's largest network of industrial enterprises. With the characteristic managerial propensity for extending its power, limited only by its allocated share of the national product, the new state-management combines peak economic, political, and military decision-making. Hitherto, this combination of powers in the same hands has been a feature of statist societies—communist, fascist, and others—where individual rights cannot constrain central rule.

This new institution of state-managerial control has been the result of actions undertaken for the declared purposes of adding to military power and economic efficiency and of reinforcing civilian, rather than professional, military rule. Its main characteristics are institutionally specific and therefore substantially independent of its chief of the moment. The effects of its operations are independent of the intention of its architects, and may even have been unforeseen by them.

The creation of the state-management marked the transformation of President Dwight Eisenhower's "military-industrial complex," a loose collaboration, mainly through market relations, of senior military officers, industrial managers, and legislators. Robert McNamara, under the direction of President John Kennedy, organized a formal central-management office to administer the military-industrial empire. The market was replaced by a management. In place of the complex, there is now a defined administrative control center that regulates tens of thousands of subordinate managers. In 1968, they directed the production of $44 billion of goods and services for military use. By the measure of the scope and

From *Pentagon Capitalism* by Seymour Melman. Copyright © 1972 by Seymour Melman. Used with permission of McGraw-Hill Book Company.

scale of its decision-power, the new state-management is by far the largest and most important single management in the United States. There are about 15,000 men who arrange work assignments to subordinate managers (contract negotiation), and 40,000 who oversee compliance of submanagers of subdivisions with the top management's rules. This is the largest industrial central administrative office in the United States—perhaps in the world.

The state-management has also become the most powerful decision-making unit in the United States government. Thereby, the federal government does not "serve" business or "regulate" business. For the new management is the largest of them all. Government *is* business. That is state capitalism.

The normal operation, including expansion, of the new state-management has been based upon preemption of a lion's share of federal tax revenue and of the nation's finite supply of technical manpower. This use of capital and skill has produced parasitic economic growth—military products which are not part of the level of living and which cannot be used for further production. All this, while the ability to defend the United States, to shield it from external attack, has diminished.

From 1946 to 1969, the United States government spent over $1,000 billion on the military, more than half of this under the Kennedy and Johnson administrations—the period during which the state-management was established as a formal institution. This sum of staggering size (try to visualize a billion of something) does not express the cost of the military establishment to the nation as a whole. The true cost is measured by what has been foregone, by the accumulated deterioration in many facets of life, by the inability to alleviate human wretchedness of long duration.

Here is part of the human inventory of depletion:

1. By 1968, there were 6 million grossly substandard dwellings, mainly in the cities.
2. Ten million Americans suffered from hunger in 1968–1969.
3. The United States ranked 18th at last report (1966) among nations in infant mortality rate (23.7 infant deaths in first year per 1,000 live births). In Sweden (1966) the rate was 12.6.
4. In 1967, 40.7 percent of the young men examined were disqualified for military service (28.5 percent for medical reasons).
5. In 1950, there were 109 physicians in the United States per 100,000 population. By 1966 there were 98.
6. About 30 million Americans are an economically underdeveloped sector of the society.

The human cost of military priority is paralleled by the industrial-technological depletion caused by the concentration of technical manpower and capital on military technology and in military industry. For example:

1. By 1968, United States industry operated the world's oldest stock of metal-working machinery; 64 percent was 10 years old and over.
2. No United States railroad has anything in motion that compares with the Japanese and French fast trains.
3. The United States merchant fleet ranks 23rd in age of vessels. In 1966, world average-age of vessels was 17 years, United States 21, Japan 9.
4. While the United States uses the largest number of research scientists and engineers in the world, key United States industries, such as steel and machine tools, are in trouble in domestic markets: in 1967, for the first time, the United States imported more machine tools than it exported.

As civilian industrial technology deteriorates or fails to advance, productive employment opportunity for Americans diminishes.

All of this only begins to reckon the true cost to America of operating the state military machine. (The cost of the Vietnam war to the Vietnamese people has no reckoning.) Clearly, no mere ideology or desire for individual power can account for the colossal costs of the military machine. A lust for power has been at work here, but it is not explicable in terms of an individual's power drive. Rather, the state-management represents an institutionalized power-lust. A normal thirst for more managerial power within the largest management in the United States gives the new state-management an unprecedented ability and opportunity for building a military-industry empire at home and for using this as an instrument for building an empire abroad. This is the new imperialism.

The magnitude of the decision-power of the Pentagon management has reached that of a state. After all, the fiscal 1970 budget plan of the Department of Defense—$83 *billion*—exceeds the gross national product (GNP) of entire nations: in billions of dollars for 1966—Belgium, $18.1; Italy $61.4; Sweden $21.3. The state-management has become a parastate, a state within a state.

In its beginning, the government of the United States was a political entity. The managing of economic and industrial activity was to be the province of private persons. This division of function was the grand design for American government and society, within which personal and political freedom could flourish alongside of rapid economic growth and technological progress. After 1960, this design was transformed. In the name of ensuring civilian control over the Department of Defense and of obtaining efficiencies of modern management, Secretary of Defense Robert McNamara redesigned the organization of his Department to include, within the office of the Secretary, a central administrative office. This was designed to control operations in thousands of subsidiary industrial enterprises undertaken on behalf of the Department of Defense. Modeled after the central administrative offices of multi-division industrial firms—such as the Ford Motor Company, the General Motors Corporation, and the General Electric Company—the new top management in the Department of Defense was designed to control the activities of subsidiary managements of firms producing, in 1968, $44 billion of goods and services for the Department of Defense.

By the measure of industrial activity governed from one central office, this new management in the Department of Defense is beyond compare the largest industrial management in the United States, perhaps in the world. Never before in American experience has there been such a combination of economic and political decision-power in the same hands. The senior officers of the new state-management are also senior political officers of the government of the United States. Thus, one consequence of the establishment of the new state-management has been the installation, within American society, of an institutional feature of a totalitarian system.

The original design of the American government was oriented toward safeguarding individual political freedom and economic liberties. These safeguards were abridged by the establishment of the new state-management in the Department of Defense. In order to perceive the abridgement of traditional liberties by the operation of the new managerial institution, one must focus on its functional performance. For the official titles of its units sound like just another government bureaucracy: Office of the Secretary of Defense, Defense Supply Agency, and so on.

The new industrial management has been created in the name of defending America from its external enemies and preserving a way of life of a free society. It has long been understood, however, that one of the safeguards of individual liberty is the separation of roles of a citizen and of an employee. When an individual relates to the same person both as a citizen and as an employee, then the effect is such—regardless of intention—that the employer-government official has an unprecedented combination of decision-making power over the individual citizen-employee.

In the Soviet Union, the combination of top economic and political decision-power is a formal part of the organization and ideology of that society. In the United States, in contrast, the joining of the economic-managerial and top political power has been done in an unannounced and, in effect, covert fashion. In addition to the significance of the new state-management with respect to individual liberty in American society, the new organization is significant for its effects in preempting resources and committing the nation to the military operations that the new organization is designed to serve. Finally, the new power center is important because of the self-powered drive toward expansion that is built into the normal operation of an industrial management.

The preemption of resources takes place because of the sheer size of the funds that are wielded by the Department of Defense. Its budget, amounting to over $80 billion in 1969, gives this organization and its industrial-management arm unequalled decision-power over manpower, materials, and industrial production capacity in the United States and abroad. It is, therefore, predictable that this organization will be able to get the people and other resources that it needs whenever it needs them, even if this requires outbidding other industries and other organizations —including other agencies of the federal and other governments.

Regardless of the individual avowals and commitments of the principal officers of the new industrial machine, it is necessarily the case that the increased competence of this organization contributes to the competence of the parent body—the Department of Defense. This competence is a war-making capability. Hence, the very efficiency and success of the new industrial-management, unavoidably and regardless of intention, enhances the war-making capability of the government of the United States. As the war-making department accumulates diverse resources and planning capability, it is able to offer the President blueprint-stage options for responding to all manner of problem situations—while other government agencies look (and are) unready, understaffed, and underequipped. This increases the likelihood of recourse to "solutions" based upon military power.

Finally, the new government management, insofar as it shares the usual characteristics of industrial management, has a built-in propensity for expanding the scope and intensity of its operations—for this expansion is the hallmark of success in management. The chiefs of the new state-management, in order to be successful in their own eyes, strive to maintain and extend their decision-power—by enlarging their activities, the number of their employees, the size of the capital investments which they control, and by gaining control over more and more subsidiary managements. By 1967–1968, the scope of the state-management's control over production had established it as the dominant decision-maker in U.S. industry. The industrial output of $44 billion of goods and services under state-management control in 1968 exceeded by far the reported net sales of American industry's leading firms (in billions of dollars for 1968): A.T.&T., $14.1; Du Pont, $3.4; General Electric, $8.4; General Motors, $22.8; U.S. Steel, $4.6. The giants of United States industry have become small- and medium-sized firms, compared with the new state-management—with its conglomerate industrial base.

The appearance of the new state-managerial machine marks a transformation in the character of the American government and requires us to re-examine our understanding of its behavior. Various classic theories of industrial capitalist society have described government as an essentially political entity, ideally impartial. Other theories depict government as justifiably favoring, or even identifying with, business management, while the theories in the Marxist tradition have depicted government as an arm of business. These theories require revision.

Theories of Government—Business Power

The classic theory of imperialism explained the behavior of government, in part, as the result of the influence of private industrial managers and chiefs of financial organizations. In this view, a ruling class, located in private enterprise, used the political instruments of government in the service of private gain. Thereby, the central government's political, legal, and military powers were utilized at home and abroad to maintain and extend the decision-power of this ruling class, through sponsoring and protecting private property rights, foreign trade, and foreign investment.

These classic theories of imperialism do not help us understand one of the most important of recent United States government policies—participation in the war in Vietnam and preparation for a series of such wars. At the time of this writing, the United States government had expended not less than $100 billion in military and related activities in connection with the Vietnam war. This excludes the economic impacts of an indirect sort within the United States caused by this war.

No one has demonstrated any past, present, or foreseeable volume of trade or investment in Vietnam and/or adjacent areas that would justify an outlay of $100 billion. The accompanying data on location and size of United States foreign investments speak for themselves.

U.S. Private Direct Long-Term Investments Abroad,
1966* (In billions of dollars)

Total	$54.2
Canada	$16.8
Western Europe	16.2
Latin American republics	9.8
Other Western hemisphere	1.6
Africa	2.0
Middle East	1.6
Far East	2.2
Oceania	2.0
Miscellaneous international	2.0

* SOURCE: *Statistical Abstract of the United States, 1968,* U.S. Department of Commerce, 1968, p. 792.

Indeed, there is substantial evidence to indicate that an important segment of the industrial corporations of the United States are not beneficiaries of participation by the American industrial system in military and allied production. (Thus, a Marxist political economist, Victor Perlo, has judged that about one-half of the major American industrial firms would gain materially from a cessation of military production.) Moreover, criticism of the Vietnam war by important institutions of the American establishment, such as *The Wall Street Journal* and *The New York Times,* is not consistent with the idea that the war has been conducted to suit the requirements of private finance and industry.

However, the operation of Vietnam war policies by the federal government is quite consistent with the maintenance and extension of decision-power by the new industrial management centered in the Department of Defense—for the management of the Vietnam war has been the occasion of major enlargement of budgets, facilities, manpower, capital investment and control over an additional million Americans in the labor force and more than one-half million additional Americans in the armed forces.

In his notable volume *The Power Elite,* C. Wright Mills, writing in 1956, perceived a three-part system of elites in the United States: economic, military, and political. At different times in American history, Mills wrote, this elite has been variously composed. That is, one or another of these three principals exercised primary decision-power. Mills concluded:

> The shape and the meaning of the power elite today can be understood only when these three sets of structural trends are seen at their point of coincidence: the military capitalism of private corporations exists in a weakened and formal democratic system containing a military order already quite political in outlook and demeanor.

Mills stated further:

> Today all three are involved in virtually all ramifying decisions. Which of the three types seems to lead depends upon the tasks of the period as they, the elite, define them. Just now, these tasks center upon defense and international affairs. Accordingly, as we have seen, the military are ascendent in two senses: as personnel and as justifying ideology. That is why, just now, we can most easily specify the unity and the shape of the power elite in terms of the military ascendency.

In a similar vein, Robert L. Heilbroner, writing of *The Limits of American Capitalism,* supports the Mills analysis that a system of elites wields primary decision-power in American society: the military, professionals—including technical experts—and government administrators. "There is little doubt," Heilbroner wrote,

> that a military-industrial-political interpenetration of interests exists to the benefit of all three. Yet in this alliance I have seen no suggestion that the industrial element is the dominant one. It is the military or the political branch that commands, and business that obeys: . . . the role of business in the entire defense effort is essentially one of jockeying for favor rather than initiating policy.

The analysis by C. Wright Mills was a reasonable one for his time. It was appropriate to a period of transition, whose closing was marked by the famous farewell address of President Dwight Eisenhower.

In his final address as President, Eisenhower gave his countrymen a grave message. "In the councils of government we must guard against the acquisition of unwarranted influence, whether sought or unsought, by the military-industrial complex. The potential for the disastrous rise of misplaced power exists and will persist. . . ." Here and in subsequent addresses, Eisenhower did not offer a precise definition of what he meant by military-industrial complex. It is reasonable, however, to see the meaning of this category in the context in which it was stated. Military-industrial complex means a loose, informally defined collection of firms producing military products, senior military officers, and members of the executive and legislative branches of the federal government—all of them limited by the market relations of the military products network and having a common ideology as to the importance of maintaining or enlarging the armed forces of the United States and their role in American politics.

The military-industrial complex has as its central point an informality of relationships, as befits the market form which underpins its alliances. The understanding, therefore, is that the main interest groups concerned tend to move together, each of them motivated by its own special concerns, but with enough common ground to produce a mutually reinforcing effect. It is noteworthy that neither Eisenhower nor anyone else has suggested that there was a formal organization, or directorate, or executive committee of the military-industrial complex. The new industrial management in the federal government is, by contrast, clearly structured and formally organized, with all the paraphernalia of a formal, centrally managed organization, whose budget draws upon 10 percent of the Gross National Product of the richest nation in the world.

The formal organization and powers of the new state-management also bear on the meaning of the various elite theories. It is true that various groups in society obviously have greater power over the course of events than ordinary citizens. But the elites are not equal. Some are "more equal than others." Primacy in decision-power among major elites is determined by the extent of control over production and by the ability to implement policies whose consequences are favorable to some elites, even while being hurtful to the others. By these tests the new state-management dominates the field. It manages more production than any other elite. Its policies of military priority, military buildups, and the Vietnam wars program have been damaging to the decision-power of other elites. . . . In sum, an understanding of the normal operation of the new state-management and its consequences is essential for a meaningful theory of contemporary American economy, government, and society.

During recent years, many writers have been intrigued by the panoply of technological power displayed by the immense and complicated stockpile of weapons fashioned for the Department of Defense. There has been a tendency in some quarters to focus on control over weaponry rather than on decision-power over people. In December, 1967, Arthur I. Waskow told the American Historical Association, "The first major trend event of the last generation in America has been the emergence of what could almost be seen as a new class, defined more by its relation to the means of total destruction than by a relation to means of production."

In a somewhat similar vein, Ralph E. Lapp, in his recent volume *The Weapons Culture*, concluded: "It is no exaggeration to say that the United States has spawned a weapons culture which has fastened an insidious grip on the entire nation." While I admire the excellence of Lapp's analyses of military organization and weaponry and the consequences of their use, it seems to me that to emphasize the idea of a weapons culture, implying a kind of weapons-technological Frankenstein, is less than helpful for appreciating the sources of recent changes in the American government and its policy.

Lapp declared: "The United States has institutionalized its arms-making to the point that there is grave doubt that it can control this far-flung apparatus." He may be correct in his judgment that the whole affair has gone beyond the point of being halted or reversed. But in order to make this judgment, it seems altogether critical to define exactly what it is that has been institutionalized. Where is the location of critical decision-power over "the weapons culture," with several million Americans involved directly or indirectly in military organization and in its support? Should we understand that one person, or one part, of this network is as important as any other?

In my estimate, it is important to identify the crucial decision-makers of the largest military organization (including its industrial base) in the world. Apart from these considerations, I am uneasy about theories viewing man as the captive of his weapons. This is a self-defeating mode of understanding, rather different from identifying the top decision-makers and their mode of control. Men may be captives, but only of other men. The concept of man in the grip of a Frankenstein weapons system has a severely limiting effect on our ability to do anything about it, if that is desired.

Recently, two writers have developed theories of convergence between military industry and government. Better-known are the ideas of John Kenneth Galbraith, as formulated in his volume *The New Industrial State*. Galbraith states: "Increasingly, it will be recognized that the mature corporation, as it develops, becomes part of the larger administrative complex associated with the state. In time the line between the two will disappear." In this perspective, the major military-industrial firms, as part of the larger family of major enterprises, merges with governmental organization. But this theory does not specify which of the managerial groups involved becomes more important than the other. Indeed, one of the theoretical contributions of *The New Industrial State* is the idea of a "technostructure," a community of technically trained managers operating on behalf of enterprises, public and private, with their movements among these enterprises serving as a bond between public and private institutions. But the technostructure idea homogenizes the men of the managerial-industrial occupations on the basis of their skills and work tasks. This bypasses the fact that an accountant, for example, in the state-management participates in a power-wielding institution of incomparably greater scope than the management of any private firm. Being in the state-management amplifies the significance of his work tasks, which may be qualitatively undifferentiable from those in a private firm.

In a similar vein, a former economist for Boeing, Murray L. Weidenbaum (now Professor of Economics at Washington University), presented another convergence hypothesis before the American Economic Association in December, 1967. In Weidenbaum's view,

> The close, continuing relationship between the military establishment and the major companies serving the military establishment is changing the nature of both the public sector of the American economy and a large branch of American industry. To a substantial degree, the government is taking on the traditional role of the private entrepreneur while the companies are becoming less like other corporations and acquiring much of the characteristics of a government agency or arsenal. In a sense, the close, continuing relationship between the Department of Defense and its major suppliers is resulting in a convergence between the two, which is blurring and reducing much of the distinction between public and private activities in an important branch of the American economy.

The Weidenbaum thesis is close to the analyses which I am presenting in this book. My purpose here, however, is to underscore not convergence but the managerial primacy of the new managerial control institution in the Department of Defense, and the consequences for the character of American economy and society that flow from this.

When the Kennedy-Johnson administration took office in 1961, the President's aides were impressed with the problem of ensuring civilian White House control over the armed forces. From this vantage point, one of the main accomplishments of Robert S. McNamara was to reorganize the Department of Defense so as to give top decision-power to the newly enlarged and elaborated office of the Secretary of Defense—clearly a civilian control office superior to and separate from the Joint Chiefs of Staff. McNamara obviously drew upon his experience as a top manager of the Ford Company central office to design a similar organization under the Office of the Secretary of Defense. There is a similarity between these two central offices, but the difference in decision-power is very great. The Pentagon's management is by far the more powerful in the industrial sphere, and is tied to top decision-power in the military and political spheres as well.

It is true that the top echelons of the Department of Defense were reorganized in a manner consistent with the goal of establishing firmer civilian control. This result, however, was achieved by methods that also established an industrial management of unprecedented size and decision-power within the federal government. One result is that it is no longer meaningful to speak of the elites of industrial management, the elites of finance, and the elites of government and how they relate to each other. The elites have been merged in the new state-management.

This development requires a review of many of our understandings of the role of the federal government in relation to individual freedom in our society. For example, antitrust laws, and their enforcement by the executive branch of the government, have been designed to preserve individual freedom by limiting combinations and preventing conspiracies in the economic realm. The laws have been enforced with varying intensity, but have pressed in particular on the largest firms by restraining them in their growth relative to small firms in the same industry.

These laws exempted government because government, in particular its executive branch, was seen as acting for the nation as a whole. With the new development of the state-management, the government-management is now acting for the extension of its own managerial power.

It is worth recalling that Eisenhower warned against the acquisition of unwarranted influence by the military-industrial complex, *"whether sought or unsought."* One of the controlling features of the new industrial management is that, like other managements, it may be expected to act for the acquisition of additional influence; such behavior is normal for all managements. . . .

In the present case, the drive for improvement of their standing as managers requires them to maintain and enlarge the military-industry and military organizations of the United States; that is precisely what the state-management has done. From 1960 to 1970, the budget of the Department of Defense has been enlarged by 80 percent—from $45 to $83 billion. All large managerial organizations, whether private or governmental, carry on planning and calculate choices among alternatives. When confronted with an array of different ways to solve a particular problem, members of a managerial team are impelled by their particular professional-occupational requirements to select those options that will maintain and extend the decision-power of the managerial group, and improve their own professional standing in the managerial hierarchy. This sort of selective preference by managers is operative in industrial management whether private or public.

An enterprise is private when its top decision-making group is not located in a government office. For this analysis of the Pentagon, what is crucial is whether the top decision-making group is a true management. A management is defined by the performance of a set of definable functions which give management its common character, whether the enterprise is private or public. A management accumulates capital for making investments. Management decides what to produce, how to carry on production, how much to produce, and where to dispose of the product at the acceptable price. It is the performance of these functions by the new organizations in the industrial directorate of the Department of Defense which defines it as a bona fide industrial management. In addition, the operating characteristics of this new management are comparable to those of other industrial managements. The special characteristics of the state-management are associated with its location in the government and its control over military production.

While the industrial-management in the Department of Defense actually owns only a minority part of the industrial capital that is used for military production, it exercises elaborate control over the use of *all* resources in thousands of enterprises. This differentiation between ownership and control is the classic one of the modern industrial corporation. Ever since Berle and Means did their classic study on *The Modern Corporation and Private Property*, it is well understood that the top managers of an industrial corporation do not necessarily wield property rights over the assets used in production, but do control the use of these assets. The differentiation between ownership and control is a central feature of the new state-management.

The Pentagon management also displays the other characteristic features of corporate organization. Management decision-making usually includes a hierarchical organization of the administration group and built-in pressures for expanding the decision-making sphere of the management. Hierarchical organization means the separation of decision-making on production matters from the performance of the work itself, and the investment of final decision-power in the men at the top of the management organization. This sort of organization structure is visible in the Pentagon's organization charts and in the key role played by the Secretary of Defense and his closest aides in controlling the enlargement of nuclear and conventional forces from 1961 to 1969.

Success of management is ordinarily shown by growth in decision-power, measured by size of investment, number of employees, volume of sales, or quantity of goods produced. Such criteria indicate a true competitive gain only when they reflect a differential increase as against other management; thus, what is critical in defining the importance of a management at any one moment is not simply the absolute quantity of sales, but more importantly, the proportion of an industry's activity controlled by the management. Similarly, an increase in the volume of sales or the size of investment or the number of employees is significant only in terms of a proportional increase. In a military organization, for example, if everyone is promoted at the same time by one grade, then no one has been promoted. Similarly, promotion in a hierarchical organization must be relative promotion, and a gain in managerial position must be a relative gain. If we are competitors, then your gain must include my relative loss or you have not gained. This idea of relative gain in managerial position applies not only within a single managerial-hierarchical organization, but also applies *among* managerial organizations.

Within and among managements, the controlling criterion of managerial success is, therefore, competitive gain in decision-making position. From 1960 to 1970, the Defense Department budget rose from $45 to

$83 billion, with industrial procurement roughly 50 percent of these amounts. No other management, private or public, has enjoyed such growth. The military-managerial machine is in a class by itself.

I have emphasized here the idea of enlarging decision-power as the occupational imperative, the operative end-in-view of modern corporate management—as against the more traditional idea that profit-making is the avowed central purpose of management. Profit-making, as a step in the recoupment of invested money, has diminished in importance as an independent measure of managerial performance. This stems from the fact that modern industrial operations increasingly involve classes of "fixed" or "regulated" costs, which are subject to substantial managerial control during a given accounting period. For example, a management must decide how it assigns the cost, year by year, of a new factory or a road that it has constructed. There is nothing in the nature of the factory that determines whether its capital investment shall be allocated to the costs of operations in one year, two years, or twenty years, or varied each year according to degree of use. This decision is an entirely arbitrary one, subject to the convenience of the management, within the limits allowed by the tax authorities. Since such assignment of costs is managerially controlled and has substantial effect on the size of profits that remain after costs, profits *per se* have a lessened importance as an autonomous indicator of managerial success. Moreover, there is accumulating evidence that some industrial costs, notably the costs of administration and of selling operations, are enlarged even where that involves reduction in the size of profits that would otherwise be available in a given accounting period. Such reductions in profit are ordinarily made and justified in the name of long-term maintenance or extension of the relative decision-power of the management and its enterprise.

One of the characteristic processes in industrial managements during the twentieth century has been an elaboration in the scope and intensity of managerial controlling. This has been accompanied by growing management costs and a growing ratio of managerial to production employees. All this has meant higher costs and, necessarily, diminished profits. But the choice of options in industrial management has systematically been toward enlarging the scope and intensity of managerial control, rather than toward management methods which would minimize costs and thereby enlarge profits or allow a reduction in prices. The state-management has also been piling on managerial controls, obviously giving priority to the consequent growth in its decision-power, as against possible economies that might be effected in its own central offices or in the operation of subsidiary enterprises of the Pentagon empire.

All this is no mere theoretical exercise for understanding the operation of the state-management. This organization skips over the customary processes of industrial capitalism for enlarging control via an intervening mechanism of investing and recouping money with a gain-profit, then reinvesting more money and, thereby, adding to decision-power. Instead, the state-management, drawing on its unique capital resource—an annual portion of the nation's product—applies this directly to increasing either the scope or the intensity of its decision-power. The usual processes of marketing products and recouping capital are leapfrogged by the state-management.

One of the characteristic features of private industrial management has been a sustained pressure to minimize cost in production. In modern industry, this effort is institutionalized by making it the special province of industrial engineers, cost accountants and others. The state-management . . . includes various professional groups that are identified as acting to control costs. But that does not necessarily produce cost-minimization. For cost control can be focused mainly on controlling the people in various occupations.

The Pentagon record—before, during, and after Robert McNamara—includes obvious cost excesses. Before McNamara, average prices on major weapons systems were 3.2 times their initial cost estimates. Under McNamara, the famous F-111 airplane was costing $12.7 million per plane by December, 1969, as compared to one first cost estimate of $3.9 million—or 3.25 times the initial estimate. Such performance under the well-advertised regime of the state-management's "cost effectiveness" programs was characteristic of this era as well. . . . This pattern of cost excesses during the rule of "cost effectiveness" is explicable, not as aberrant behavior, but as a pattern that is normal to the state-management. The state-management's control system . . . includes monitoring for so-called cost overruns as a regular function. Payment for the cost overruns by the Pentagon has been the functional equivalent of a grant of capital from a central office to a division of its firm, serving to enlarge the assets of the larger enterprise.

Owing to the basic difference between private industrial management and the state-management with respect to the role of conversion of capital through the market place, there is a parallel, distinguishing interest in the stability and instability of industrial operations. Stability means operating within predictable and acceptable limits of variation in output. For private industrial management, this is a highly desirable condition, because this makes possible predictability in the ongoing processes of conversion of money from investment funds to products sold on the market place and to new capital funds for further investment. Where costs, prices, and the value of the dollar in purchasing power are highly unstable, the investment-recoupment process of capital for private management is rendered extremely difficult to operate—it is put "out of control." These limiting conditions are not operative for the administrators of the state-management, for they deal directly with the conversion of capital funds into decision-orders on industrial operation. Also, their products need not be designed to be salable at a price producing a profit which they may accumulate for further investment. Their investment funds have been constantly acquired in the name of defense from a willing

Congress and nation. Accordingly, instability in costs, prices, and profits are no major constraint for the managers of the state machine. And so, when military outlays at home and abroad become the traceable cause of danger to the value of the dollar relative to other currencies, it is not a source for alarm among the Pentagon managers. Some measures are taken to slow down the outflow of Treasury gold, but no major policy changes are introduced.

Mythology that Supports the State-Management

The size of the United States Gross National Product, approaching $900 billion for 1969, makes it difficult to absorb the fact that while the nation is rich, it is not indefinitely rich. An important part of the nation's productive resources are being used for growth that is parasitic rather than productive. Parasitic growth refers to products which are not part of the current level of living and cannot be used for further production. Productive growth refers to products that are part of the current level of living, or that can be used for further production. The activities of producing for and operating the military establishment fall in the category of parasitic growth. This holds despite the fact that the people who do the work are paid wages and salaries, and that these are used, in turn, to supply their own level of living. The crucial point is that the product of the military-serving workers, technicians, and managers is a product that does not enter the market place, is not bought back, and cannot be used for current level of living or for future production. This economic differentiation is independent of the worth which may be assigned to military activity for other reasons. With $900 billion per year, a military budget of $83 billion appears as less than 10 percent of the GNP. Such arithmetic, however, conceals the fact that the lion's share of the nation's research and development manpower is used for military purposes, that this manpower is present in finite supply even in a rich society, and that this imposes severe constraints on what can be done in the many spheres of civilian life that require the services of this class of skilled manpower. The long-standing military priority for skilled manpower, financial and other resources was the final constraint on the ability of the Johnson administration to implement its "Great Society" programs. Many of the programs looked fine on paper. The preambles to the various laws of the Johnson administration's legislative program read as admirable descriptions of conditions in American society and as statements of intent. Only one thing was lacking: the commitment of men and money to make the work possible. This commitment was restrained by the fact that priority was given to military and related work.

This is not to say that the effects from giving priority to the military cannot be surmounted. This could be done in two ways: first, the drastic regrouping, under central control, of civilian production and other resources; or, second, changing the whole national priorities schedule away from military emphasis. Regrouping of industrial resources could mean, for example, the arbitrary conversion of two of the three major automobile firms, allowing the auto market to be supplied by the remaining firm. Thereby, an enormous block of industrial resources, manpower, and so forth, would be made available for other uses. This is technically conceivable, but it is not socially conceivable as long as the country wishes to have something other than a rigorously state-controlled economy and society. A garrison society, in which the state is empowered to dispose of resources at will, would be able to make this sort of regrouping. But such a regrouping of industrial resources under state control has not been acceptable to the American people except in a war crisis. Within the present political-economic framework, fresh resources for productive economic growth could only be made available by a basic change in national priorities. In detail, that would mean utilizing the federal public-responsibility budget of the nation for other than military priority purposes, which would necessarily involve a major reduction in the decision-power of the state-management. This is why the managers and apologists for the state-management are vigorous in maintaining the mythology of unlimited wealth, unlimited growth, and the absence of a priorities problem in American society.

The American people and the Congress have accepted decision-making by the state-management in the belief that it possesses critical expertise, not only in military matters, but also in the management of industry and the economy. In its 1966 Report, the Joint Economic Committee of the Congress declared:

> Let no one, at home or abroad, doubt the ability of the United States to support, if need be, simultaneous programs of military defense of freedom and economic and social progress for our people, or (2) our capacity and preference to live and grow economically without the stimulus of government spending on defense or a competitive arms race.

Here the Committee affirmed that government spending for military purposes is an economic stimulus and that the country can afford guns and butter at the same time. This assurance among the members of the Joint Economic Committee of Congress reflects repeated assertions in a similar vein made by the President and by the Secretary of Defense, the two senior executives of the state-management. Accordingly, in the presentation of the federal budget, the accompanying analyses of economic growth characteristically show no differentiation between parasitic and productive growth.

Against this background, the mayors of principal American cities have formulated varying estimates of the capital investment needed to bring material conditions of life up to a reasonable standard. In 1966, the mayor of Detroit, Jerome P. Cavanaugh, estimated that $242 billion would be required to solve the plight of the cities. The chief officers and ideologists of the state-management respond to such proposals in two ways. First, they say, there is no reason why such money could not be made available, if the nation only had the will to do it. Second, they say, there is no reason why this cannot be done while maintaining military priority in the federal government's budget, the largest pool of tax funds in the land. In a similar vein, many editors have written during the last years on the theme that "Cities Cannot Wait" (for example, *The New York Times*, August 22, 1966). But these writers show no readiness to come to grips with the military budget and the scale of the military organization and management in the federal government, both of which preempt the money, men, and materials needed to establish decent conditions in many areas of civilian life. In a memorable address at the University of Connecticut, Senator Fulbright stated the contradiction:

> There is a kind of madness in the facile assumption that we can raise the many billions of dollars necessary to rebuild our schools and water while also spending tens of billions to finance an open-ended war in Asia.

Even in the wealthiest economy, war expenditures change from economic stimulus to economic damage: first, when the military activity preempts production resources to a degree that limits the ability of the society to supply necessities such as shelter; second, when the military spending causes rapid price inflation, thereby depressing the level of living of all who live on limited incomes; and third, when price inflation disrupts the process of civilian capital investment which requires capability for predicting the worth of a nation's currency.

During the last years, there has been more than a beginning of an understanding that the nation does, in fact, have a priorities problem. But there has been hardly a beginning in preparing for the conversion of resources from military to civilian use. The official economic advisors of the federal government have repeatedly counseled that if there is sufficient advance planning, and the will in Washington to establish a clear set of priorities, then a transition from war to peace activity can be made without great upheaval (*The New York Times*, April 14, 1968). The point is precisely that until now, there has been no advance planning or a will in Washington to establish peace-time priorities, and the lack of will in this realm contrasts sharply with the clear will and the openhanded dedication of resources to the requirements of the state-managerial machine.

Many lines of evidence contribute to the conclusion that both recognition and denial of a national priorities problem cuts across conventional political lines. Support of the state-management and its functioning in the name of defense is independent not only of party, but also of personalities. The Kennedy administration was formally Democratic, but the architect of the present military machine, and its operating chief from 1961 to 1968, was a Republican, Robert McNamara. Support for the plans and the budgets of the state-management have come from both major parties in the Congress. At the same time, there has been a fair amount of turnover in the persons holding key posts at the top of the state-management.

Indeed, the very openness of operations of the state machine is one of its great sources of strength. Thus, no conspiracy, in the ordinary sense of the word, was required to get the American people to accept the myth of the missile gap and the subsequent major capital outlays for an overkill nuclear war program. The American people were sold on the myth and thought they were buying defense. Nor is a conspiracy required to secure fresh capital funds of unprecedented size for further expansion of the state-management. This is agreed to by a Congress and a public that has been taught to believe that all this activity is for defense and that it stimulates the economy of a society that can enjoy both guns and butter. In all of this, the controlling factor is not a political party or a single political theory, not a personality, not a conspiracy: the existence and normal operation of the Pentagon's management-institution dominates and gives continuity of direction.

The government of the United States now includes a self-expanding war machine that uses military power for diverse political operations and is based upon an industrial management that has priority claims to virtually unlimited capital funds from the federal budget. The state-management is economically parasitic, hence exploitative, in its relation to American society at home. The military-political operations of the Pentagon chieftains abroad, following the pattern of the Vietnam wars program, are parasitic there as well. To the older pattern of exploitative imperialism abroad, there is now added an institutional network that is parasitic at home. This combination is the new imperialism.

XII. Politics

The state may be defined as that institution which "legitimately" monopolizes the legal use of violence both at home and abroad. In fact, no state can sustain itself exclusively through the exertion of military and police power, or by resorting to prisons, concentration camps, and execution chambers. Since coercion alone does not work, rulers seek compliance. Those in charge of government must somehow "legitimize" themselves. Thus, social and political theorists formulate ideologies to justify the use of violence and the presence of authority. Legitimacy implies acceptance of a reigning ideology that expresses a general willingness to be ruled by those who claim that right. When achieved, legitimacy means that the underlying population voluntarily obeys state law or submits to "just" punishment for its violation.

We are indebted to Max Weber for many of the major concepts in this area. Like other thinkers, he traced the origins and described the operations of state power. As a sociologist, he studied politics within a social and institutional context. Weber's analysis of legitimacy has proved to be particularly enlightening. Its three-fold division (into "traditional, charismatic, and rational-legal"), as set forth in the pages that follow, is crucial to an understanding of the sociological perspective in government and politics.

Weber's interpretation of bureaucracy—presented in section IX—is also germane. It fits big government as well as any other large-scale organization. All discussion of the subject, whether critical or not, begins with Weber. Philip Selznick, a contemporary sociologist, follows Weber and Weber's student, Roberto Michels. In "An Approach to a Theory of Bureaucracy," Selznick demonstrates how the "imperatives" of bureaucracy produce strains toward centralization and authoritarianism in accordance with Michels's famous "Iron Law of Oligarchy." The Law, although not the *Iron* Law, is equally applicable to public and private organizations, including those that are formally democratic. A conflict between leaders and led, between rulers and ruled appears to be inherent even in democratic societies and polities *if* their administrative branches come to be large in number, size, or authority.

Benjamin S. Kleinberg, a brilliant young sociologist, elucidates the extension of this principle in post-World War II America—a task undertaken by Seymour Melman from another point of view in the previous section. Kleinberg draws our attention to experts and technicians in the Department of Defense who develop autonomous world views. At the same time, businessmen, chiefly contractors, are simultaneously bound together by their common interest and flung apart in bitter competition as they vie for benefits from the "contract state." These benefits confer enormous favors on certain corporations headed by executives who are clever or lucky enough to secure defense contracts. The technicians, managers, and bureaucrats representing these corporations have interests and perspectives that they often share with their counterparts in the Defense Department.

Since President Eisenhower's "Farewell Address," this merger of contracts, contacts, interests, and perspectives has been called "the military-industrial complex." Out of that complex, Americans confront a serious challenge to their system of democratic legitimacy: In a contract state, how do elected representatives control vested interests and an unelected elite that maintains both the public and private bureaucracies of our society?

38. Types of Authority
Max Weber

All ruling powers, profane and religious, political and apolitical, may be considered as variations of, or approximations to, certain pure types. These types are constructed by searching for the basis of *legitimacy*, which the ruling power claims. Our modern "associations," above all the political ones, are the type of "legal" authority. That is, the legitimacy of the power-holder to give commands rests upon rules that are rationally established by enactment, by agreement, or by imposition. The legitimation for establishing these rules rests, in turn, upon a rationally enacted

From Max Weber: Essays in Sociology, edited and translated by H. H. Gerth and C. Wright Mills. Copyright 1946 by Oxford University Press, Inc.; renewed 1973 by Dr. Hans H. Gerth. Reprinted by permission of the publisher.

or interpreted "constitution." Orders are given in the name of the impersonal norm, rather than in the name of a personal authority; and even
the giving of a command constitutes obedience toward a norm rather
than an arbitrary freedom, favor, or privilege.

The "official" is the holder of the power to command; he never exercises this power in his own right; he holds it as a trustee of the impersonal and "compulsory institution" [*Anstalt*]. This institution is made up
of the specific patterns of life of a plurality of men, definite or indefinite,
yet specified according to rules. Their joint pattern of life is normatively
governed by statutory regulations.

The "area of jurisdiction" is a functionally delimited realm of possible
objects for command and thus delimits the sphere of the official's legitimate power. A hierarchy of superiors, to which officials may appeal and
complain in an order of rank, stands opposite the citizen or member of
the association. Today this situation also holds for the hierocratic association that is the church. The pastor or priest has his definitely limited
"jurisdiction," which is fixed by rules. This also holds for the supreme
head of the church. The present concept of [papal] "infallibility" is a
jurisdictional concept. Its inner meaning differs from that which preceded
it, even up to the time of Innocent III.

The separation of the "private sphere" from the "official sphere" (in the
case of infallibility: the *ex cathedra* definition) is carried through in the
church in the same way as in political, or other, officialdoms. The legal
separation of the official from the means of administration (either in
natural or in pecuniary form) is carried through in the sphere of political
and hierocratic associations in the same way as is the separation of the
worker from the means of production in capitalist economy: it runs fully
parallel to them.

No matter how many beginnings may be found in the remote past, in
its full development all this is specifically modern. The past has known
other bases for authority, bases which, incidentally, extend as survivals
into the present. Here we wish merely to outline these bases of authority
in a terminological way.

1. In the following discussions the term "charisma" shall be understood
to refer to an *extraordinary* quality of a person, regardless of whether this
quality is actual, alleged, or presumed. "Charismatic authority," hence,
shall refer to a rule over men, whether predominantly external or predominantly internal, to which the governed submit because of their belief
in the extraordinary quality of the specific *person*. The magical sorcerer,
the prophet, the leader of hunting and booty expeditions, the warrior
chieftain, the so-called "Caesarist" ruler, and, under certain conditions,
the personal head of a party are such types of rulers for their disciples,
followings, enlisted troops, parties, and so on. The legitimacy of their
rule rests on the belief in and the devotion to the extraordinary, which
is valued because it goes beyond the normal human qualities, and which

was originally valued as supernatural. The legitimacy of charismatic rule thus rests upon the belief in magical powers, revelations and hero worship. The source of these beliefs is the "proving" of the charismatic quality through miracles, through victories and other successes, that is, through the welfare of the governed. Such beliefs and the claimed authority resting on them therefore disappear, or threaten to disappear, as soon as proof is lacking and as soon as the charismatically qualified person appears to be devoid of his magical power or forsaken by his god. Charismatic rule is not managed according to general norms, either traditional or rational, but, in principle, according to concrete revelations and inspirations, and in this sense, charismatic authority is "irrational." It is "revolutionary" in the sense of not being bound to the existing order: "It is written—but I say unto you . . . !"

2. "Traditionalism" in the following discussions shall refer to the psychic attitude-set for the habitual workaday and to the belief in the everyday routine as an inviolable norm of conduct. Domination that rests upon this basis, that is, upon piety for what actually, allegedly, or presumably has always existed, will be called "traditionalist authority."

Patriarchalism is by far the most important type of domination the legitimacy of which rests upon tradition. Patriarchalism means the authority of the father, the husband, the senior of the house, the sib elder over the members of the household and sib; the rule of the master and patron over bondsmen, serfs, freed men; of the lord over the domestic servants and household officials; of the prince over house- and court-officials, nobles of office, clients, vassals; of the patrimonial lord and sovereign prince [*Landesvater*] over the "subjects."

It is characteristic of patriarchical and of patrimonial authority, which represents a variety of the former, that the system of inviolable norms is considered sacred; an infraction of them would result in magical or religious evils. Side by side with this system there is a realm of free arbitrariness and favor of the lord, who in principle judges only in terms of "personal," not "functional," relations. In this sense, traditionalist authority is irrational.

3. Throughout early history, charismatic authority, which rests upon a belief in the sanctity or the value of the extraordinary, and traditionalist (patriarchical) domination, which rests upon a belief in the sanctity of everyday routines, divided the most important authoritative relations between them. The bearers of charisma, the oracles of prophets, or the edicts of charismatic war lords alone could integrate "new" laws into the circle of what was upheld by tradition. Just as revelation and the sword were the two extraordinary powers, so were they the two typical innovators. In typical fashion, however, both succumbed to routinization as soon as their work was done.

With the death of the prophet or the war lord the question of successorship arises. This question can be solved by *Kürung*, which was originally not an "election" but a selection in terms of charismatic quali-

fication; or the question can be solved by the sacramental substantiation
of charisma, the successor being designated by consecration, as is the case
in hierocratic or apostolic succession; or the belief in the charismatic
qualification of the charismatic leader's sib can lead to a belief in hereditary charisma, as represented by hereditary kingship and hereditary
hierocracy. With these routinizations, *rules* in some form always come
to govern. The prince or the hierocrat no longer rules by virtue of
purely personal qualities, but by virtue of acquired or inherited qualities,
or because he has been legitimized by an act of charismatic election. The
process of routinization, and thus traditionalization, has set in.

Perhaps it is even more important that when the organization of
authority becomes permanent, the staff supporting the charismatic ruler
becomes routinized. The ruler's disciples, apostles, and followers became
priests, feudal vassals and, above all, officials. The original charismatic
community lived communistically off donations, alms, and the booty of
war: they were thus specifically alienated from the economic order. The
community was transformed into a stratum of aids to the ruler and
depended upon him for maintenance through the usufruct of land, office
fees, income in kind, salaries, and hence, through prebends. The staff
derived its legitimate power in greatly varying stages of appropriation,
infeudation, conferment, and appointment. As a rule, this meant that
princely prerogatives became *patrimonial* in nature. Patrimonialism can
also develop from pure patriarchalism through the disintegration of the
patriarchical master's strict authority. By virtue of conferment, the prebendary or the vassal has as a rule had a personal *right* to the office bestowed upon him. Like the artisan who possessed the economic means of
production, the prebendary possessed the means of administration. He
had to bear the costs of administration out of his office fees or other
income, or he passed on to the lord only part of the taxes gathered from
the subjects, retaining the rest. In the extreme case he could bequeath
and alienate his office like other possession. We wish to speak of *status*
patrimonialism when the development by appropriation of prerogatory
power has reached this stage, without regard to whether it developed
from charismatic or patriarchical beginnings.

The development, however, has seldom stopped at this stage. We
always meet with a *struggle* between the political or hierocratic lord and
the owners or usurpers of prerogatives, which they have appropriated as
status groups. The ruler attempts to expropriate the estates, and the estates attempt to expropriate the ruler. The more the ruler succeeds in
attaching to himself a staff of officials who depend solely on him and
whose interests are linked to his, the more this struggle is decided in
favor of the ruler and the more the privilege-holding estates are gradually expropriated. In this connection, the prince acquires administrative
means of his own and he keeps them firmly in his own hands. Thus we
find political rulers in the Occident, and progressively from Innocent III
to John XXII, also hierocratic rulers who have finances of their own,

as well as secular rulers who have magazines and arsenals of their own for the provisioning of the army and the officials.

The *character* of the stratum of officials upon whose support the ruler has relied in the struggle for the expropriation of status prerogatives has varied greatly in history. In Asia and in the Occident during the early Middle Ages they were typically clerics; during the Oriental Middle Ages they were typically slaves and clients; for the Roman Principate, freed slaves to a limited extent were typical; humanist literati were typical for China; and finally, jurists have been typical for the modern Occident, in ecclesiastical as well as in political associations.

The triumph of princely power and the expropriation of particular prerogatives has everywhere signified at least the possibility, and often the actual introduction, of a rational administration. As we shall see, however, this rationalization has varied greatly in extent and meaning. One must, above all, distinguish between the *substantive* rationalization of administration and of judiciary by a patrimonial prince, and the *formal* rationalization carried out by trained jurists. The former bestows utilitarian and social ethical blessings upon his subjects, in the manner of the master of a large house upon the members of his household. The trained jurists have carried out the rule of general laws applying to all "citizens of the state." However fluid the difference has been—for instance, in Babylon or Byzantium, in the Sicily of the Hohenstaufen, or the England of the Stuarts, or the France of the Bourbons—in the final analysis, the difference between substantive and formal rationality has persisted. And, in the main, it has been the work of *jurists* to give birth to the modern Occidental "state" as well as to the Occidental "churches." We shall not discuss at this point the source of their strength, the substantive ideas, and the technical means for this work.

With the triumph of *formalist* juristic rationalism, the legal type of domination appeared in the Occident at the side of the transmitted types of domination. Bureaucratic rule was not and is not the only variety of legal authority, but it is the purest. The modern state and municipal official, the modern Catholic priest and chaplain, the officials and employees of modern banks and of large capitalist enterprises represent, as we have already mentioned, the most important types of this structure of domination.

The following characteristic must be considered decisive for our terminology: in legal authority, submission does not rest upon the belief and devotion to charismatically gifted persons, like prophets and heroes, or upon sacred tradition, or upon piety toward a personal lord and master who is defined by an ordered tradition, or upon piety toward the possible incumbents of office fiefs and office prebends who are legitimized in their own right through privilege and conferment. Rather, submission under legal authority is based upon an *impersonal* bond to the generally defined and functional "duty of office." The official duty—like the corresponding right to exercise authority: the "jurisdictional competency"—is fixed by *rationally established* norms, by enactments, decrees, and regulations, in such a manner that the legitimacy of the authority becomes the legality of the general rule, which is purposely thought out, enacted, and announced with formal correctness.

The differences between the types of authority we have sketched pertain to all particulars of their social structure and of their economic significance. Only a systematic presentation could demonstrate how far the distinctions and terminology chosen here are expedient. Here we may emphasize merely that by approaching in this way, we do not claim to use the only possible approach nor do we claim that all empirical structures of domination must correspond to one of these "pure" types. On the contrary, the great majority of empirical cases represent a combination or a state of transition among several such pure types. We shall be compelled again and again to form expressions like "patrimonial bureaucracy" in order to make the point that the characteristic traits of the respective phenomenon belong in part to the rational form of domination, whereas other traits belong to a traditionalist form of domination, in this case to that of estates. We also recognize highly important forms that have been universally diffused throughout history, such as the feudal structure of domination. Important aspects of these structures, however, cannot be classified smoothly under any one of the three forms we have distinguished. They can be understood only as combinations involving several concepts, in this case the concepts of "status group" and "status honor." There are also forms that have to be understood partly in terms of principles other than those of "domination," partly in terms of peculiar variations of the concept of charisma. Examples are: the functionaries of *pure* democracy with rotations of honorific offices and similar forms, on the one hand, and plebiscitarian domination, on the other hand, or certain forms of notable rule that are special forms of traditional domination. Such forms, however, have certainly belonged to the most important ferments for the delivery of political rationalism. By the terminology suggested here, we do not wish to force schematically the infinite and multifarious historical life, but simply to create concepts useful for special purposes and for orientation.

39. An Approach to a Theory of Bureaucracy

Philip Selznick

This analysis will consider bureaucracy as a special case of the general theory of purposive organization. Recent sociological research has made explicit several conceptions which must serve as essential background for any analysis such as that to follow. Based upon that research, three hypotheses may be introduced here:

A. Every organization creates an informal structure.
B. In every organization, the goals of the organization are modified (abandoned, deflected, or elaborated) by processes within it.
C. The process of modification is effected through the informal structure.

Three recent sociological studies have elucidated these hypotheses.

1. In an intensive examination of a shop department, Roethlisberger and Dickson found clear evidences of an informal structure. This structure consisted of a set of procedures (binging, sarcasm, ridicule) by means of which control over members of the group was exercised, the formation of cliques which functioned as instruments of control, and the establishment of informal leadership. "The men had elaborated, spontaneously and quite unconsciously, an intricate social organization around their collective beliefs and sentiments."[1]

The informal structure of the worker group grew up out of the day-to-day practices of the men as they groped for ways of taking care of their own felt needs. There was no series of conscious acts by which these procedures were instituted, but they were no less binding on that account. These needs largely arose from the way in which the men defined their situation within the organization. The informal organization served a triple *function*: (a) it served to control the behavior of the members of the worker group; (b) within the context of the larger organization (the plant), it was an attempt on the part of the particular group to control the conditions of its existence; (c) it acted as a mechanism for the expression of personal relationships for which the formal organization did not provide. Thus the informal structure provided those avenues of aggression, solidarity, and prestige-construction required by individual members.

Reprinted from *American Sociological Review* 8, no. 1 (1943):47–54, with permission of The American Sociological Association and the author.

The *consequence* of the activity of the men through the informal organization was a deleterious effect upon the professed goal of the organization as a whole: it resulted in the restriction of output. In asserting its control over the conditions of the job, the group wanted above all to protect itself from outside interference, exhibiting a strong resistance to change.

Thus the facts in this empirical investigation illustrate the hypotheses noted above: the creation of an informal organization, the modification of the professed goal (maximum output), and the effectuation of this modification through the informal structure. In addition, three important characteristics of the informal structure were observed in the study: (a) it arises spontaneously; (b) the bases of the relationships are personal, involving factors of prestige, acceptance within the group, friendship ties, etc.; and (c) the relationships are *power* relationships, oriented toward techniques of *control*. These characteristics are general, and they are important for conceiving of the theory of bureaucratic behavior as a special case of the general theory of organization.

2. C. I. Barnard, in his theoretical analysis of organizational structure, concerned mainly with the problems of the executive discusses explicitly the character and function of informal structures which arise out of the attempts to solve those problems. By informal structures he means "the aggregate of the personal contacts and interactions and the associated groupings of people" which do not have common or joint purposes, and which are, in fact, "indefinite and rather structureless."[2] He says, further, that "though common or joint purposes are excluded by definition, common or joint results of an important character nevertheless come from such organization."[3]

Barnard lists three functions of informal structures as they operate in formal organizations: (a) as a means of communication, establishing norms of conduct between superordinates and subordinates; (b) "maintenance of cohesiveness in formal organizations through regulating the willingness to serve and the stability of objective authority"; (c) "the maintenance of the feeling of personal integrity, of self-respect, of independent choice."[4] The last mentioned function means simply that the individual's "integrity" is protected by the *appearance* of choice, at the same time that subtle group pressures guarantee control of his actions. Barnard's view of the function of the informal structure is primarily in terms of the needs of the executive (control through friendship ties, personal authority, a "grape-vine" system, etc.), but it is clear that his analysis agrees with the hypothesis that the informal organization is oriented essentially toward the techniques of control. In the Roethlisberger and Dickson study, it was the worker group which was attempting to control the conditions of its existence; in this case, it is the executive who is doing the same thing.

3. A discussion by Waller and Henderson[5] based on the study of institutions of segregative care, gives further evidence for the theses pre-

sented here. The general hypotheses about organizational processes are confirmed by the examination of such structures as private schools, transient camps, prisons, flophouses, reformatories and military organizations. The authors set the problem in this way:

> Each of our institutions has an idea or purpose—most of them have several purposes more or less compatible with one another—and this idea or purpose gives rise to an institutional structure. The institutional structure consists of a system of organized groups. The interaction of these elements is a principal clue to the understanding of institutions of segregative care. Without a structure, the purpose of an institution would be an empty form of words, and yet the process of translating the purpose into an institutional structure always somehow deflects and distorts it.
>
> It is thus the iron necessity of an organizational structure for the achievement of group goals which creates the paradox to which we have referred. The ideals of those who construct the organization are one thing; the "facts of life" operating independently of and often against those ideals are something else again.

Professed and Operational Goals. Running an organization, as a specialized and essential activity, generates problems which have no necessary (and often an opposed) relationship to the professed or "original" goals of the organization. The day-to-day behavior of the group becomes centered around specific problems and proximate goals which are primarily an internal relevance. Then, since these activities come to consume an increasing proportion of the time and thoughts of the participants, they are—from the point of view of actual behavior—*substituted* for the professed goals.

The day-to-day activity of men is ordered by those specific problems which have a direct relevance to the materials with which they have to deal. "Ultimate" issues and highly abstract ideas which do not specify any concrete behavior have therefore little direct influence on the bulk of human activities. (The general ideas, of course, may influence action by setting its context and, often, defining its limits.) This is true not because men are evil or unintelligent, but because the "ultimate" formulations are not *helpful* in the constant effort to achieve that series of equilibria which represents behavioral solutions to the specific problems which day-to-day living poses. Besides those professed goals which do not specify any concrete behavior, which are analogous to non-procedural formulations in science, there are other professed goals which require actions which conflict with what must be done in the daily business of running an organization. In that conflict the professed goals will tend to go down in defeat, usually through the process of being extensively ignored. This phenomenon may be introduced as a fourth hypothesis in the general theory of organization:

> D. The actual procedures of every organization tend to be molded by action toward those goals which provide operationally relevant solutions for the daily problems of the organization as such.

This hypothesis does not deny that operational goals may be, and very often are, specified in the formulation of the professed goals of the organization. But in any case it is the operational goals which must be looked to for an understanding of the conduct of the organization.

What is meant by the "daily problems"? Consider a boys' reformatory.[6] The institution is organized on the basis of progressive ideals as specified in social work literature. But the processes of constructing and operating the organization create problems and demands, effective daily, to which the general ideals give no adequate answer. Since, however, the existence of the organization depends upon such answers, and since the way of life of everyone concerned depends on the continued existence of the organization, a set of procedural rules is worked out which *is helpful* in solving these problems. These rules are, in practice, substituted for the professed ideals. "The social work ideals are fine, but how can we do otherwise than use techniques of discipline, regimentation, spying, etc.?" This is the cry of those who must meet daily crises in the institutions of segregative care. "Holiday speech," "lip-service," "we've got to be practical" are expressions which confirm from ordinary experience, repeated over and over again, the validity of this hypotheses.

The "Tragedy of Organization." Beyond such specific sociological investigations as have been mentioned, it is necessary only to point to the fact of organizational frustration as a persistent characteristic of the age of relative democracy. The tragedy of organization is evident precisely in the fact and in the consequences of increased participation in associational endeavor.

There have been many critics of democracy, but relatively few have ventured to support the sweeping judgment of Robert Michels that democracy leads inevitably to oligarchy.[7] It must be admitted, however, that in this discussion the thesis of Michels finds much comfort. For this theory (taken in its sociological rather than in its psychological context) stands or falls, in terms of its lasting significance, with the possibility of establishing that there are processes inherent in and internal to organization as such which tend to frustrate action toward professed goals. The burden of research, on the plane of organizations in general, indicates quite clearly that such is the case.

Bearing in mind the hypotheses stated above, and the specified character of the informal structure (spontaneity, network of personal relationships, orientation toward control), we may turn to the problem of bureaucracy itself.

The Term Bureaucracy. If the ideas developed above have been clear, it will be readily evident that the approach which identifies bureaucracy with any administrative system based on professionalization and on hierarchical subordination is not accepted here. Such a point of view is maintained in the work of Friedrich and Cole[8] on the Swiss Civil Service; the interest of the authors is clearly in the *formal* structure of the administrative apparatus as a mechanism of, in this case, popular government. The structure is related to the asserted, professed purposes of the administration; and *bureaucratization* is conceived of as the tendency toward the complete achievement of the formal system.

The same point of view is evident in Max Weber's long and careful essay on bureaucracy—the outstanding work in the literature we have at present:[9] The main burden of Weber's work is devoted to an examination of the roots, conditions, and dominant features of the formal organization of an administrative hierarchy. The development of this structure with its dominant features of authoritative jurisdiction, hierarchy of office, specialized training and general abstract rules of procedure, is a process of the *depersonalization* of administrative relationships. Weber's main interest was in the development of rational bureaucratic behavior as a break from the ties of seignorial leadership set up under the feudal system. The development of centralized hierarchical administration did in fact involve a tendency to vitiate that particular kind of personal influence. But what Weber seems to have only partly understood is that the dynamics of the administrative apparatus itself created new personal influences—those of the administrators themselves seeking their own ends and engaging, as newly powerful participants, in power relationships. That Weber did not overlook the facts of the case is clear from his final pages, in which he discusses the power-role of the bureaucracy. Although recognizing them, he seems to have neglected their theoretical importance.

The use of the term bureaucracy, not as designating an administrative organization as such, but rather some special characteristics of that organization, is common in the literature. Thus Laski's[10] definition of bureaucracy emphasizes the *de facto* power relationships and their consequences. Again, although Dimock and Hyde[11] *define* bureaucracy in terms of the subdivision of jurisdiction, hierarchy and professionalization of personnel, their *use* of the term indicates an interest in such phenomena as "organizational resistance," with the formal structure operating as simply the environment of the bureaucratic tendencies.

The idea of bureaucracy proposed here is consonant although not identical with the usage of Laski and Dimock-Hyde. It will be considered in terms of the hypotheses suggested above. "Bureaucratic behaviour" will designate that behavior of *agents in social action* which:

1. tends to create the organization-paradox, that is, the modification of the professed aims of the organization—aims toward which the agent is formally supposed to strive; this process obtains

2. through such behavior patterns in the informal organization as are centered primarily around the ties of influence among the functionaries, and as tend to concentrate the locus of power in the hands of the officials; and

3. through such patterns as develop through the displacement of the functionaries' motives on the habit level, e.g., routinization.

This does not mean that every situation in which the organization-paradox is found is a bureaucratic one. Bureaucracy is concerned with the behavior of officials, while the action of, say, worker groups, may also lead to deflection of an organization. It is clear from this definition that the emphasis is on the *informal* structure as the mechanism or manifestation of bureaucratic patterns; it does not follow, of course, that those patterns are uninfluenced by the character of the formal organization.

A final point is the question of size. For the most part, the existence of bureaucracy in any sense is associated with large organizations. For Dimock and Hyde, for example, "The broadest structural cause of bureaucracy, whether in business or in government, is the tremendous size of the organization."[12] Indeed, there seems to be little doubt that the factor of sheer size is a very important element in concrete bureaucratic structures. However, because of the patterns exhibited in the behavior of agents in small organized groups and because of the implications for greater generality, the formulation used here does not make the factor of size crucial for the existence of bureaucratic behavior patterns.

Bureaucratization: A General Formulation. A brief analytical formula stating the general character of the process of bureaucratization may here be introduced:

1. Co-operative effort, under the conditions of increasing number and complexity of functions, requires the *delegation of functions*. Thus action which seeks more than limited, individual results becomes *action through agents*. It is the activity of officials acting as agents with which the discussion of bureaucracy is concerned.

2. The use of intermediaries creates a tendency toward a *bifurcation of interest* between the initiator of the action and the agent employed. This is due to the creation of two sets of problems: for the initiator, the achievement of the goal which spurred him to action, and for the intermediary, problems which are concerned chiefly with his social position as agent. The character of the agent's new values are such as to generate actions whose objective consequences undermine the professed aims of the organization. This conflict need not be between the employer as a person or a group and the agent, for the latter may be able to manipulate the ideas of the former, but between the actual course of the organization and those aims formally asserted, whether the employer recognizes the conflict or not.

3. This bifurcation of interest makes dominant, for initiator and agent alike, the issue of *control*. What is at stake for each is the control of the conditions (the organizational mechanism) which each group will want to manipulate (not necessarily consciously) toward solving its special problems. In this struggle for control, an *informal structure* is created, based largely on relationships involving personal influences rather than formal rules.

4. Because of the concentration of skill and the control of the organ-

izational mechanism in the hands of the intermediaries, it becomes possible for the problems of the officials as such to become those which operate *for the organization.* The action of the officials tends to have an increasingly *internal relevance,* which may result in the deflection of the organization from its original path, which, however, usually remains as the formally professed aim of the organization.

The Bureaucratic Leader versus the Rank and File Which Employs Him. Utilizing the scheme outlined above, let us examine a concrete type of bureaucratic situation, that which opposes a bureaucratic leader to the rank and file for which he is formally an agent. This situation tends to arise whenever a group of people organize for the attainment of shared objectives, with the additional aim of conducting their organization along democratic lines. Common examples are political parties, trade unions, a national political democracy.

1. The need for the delegation of functions to a leader arises from the pressure of the wide range of problems, with which every individual must deal in his social existence, against strictly limited time and ability as well as against the social pressures which limit the exercise of certain functions to only some personality types and to members of only some classes. Even in the small group, individual differences in terms of aptitude for the various functions of organized effort (speaker, writer, record-keeper, etc.) play an important role in creating a leader-ranks relationship.

2. Another bifurcation of problems arises from the fact that the problems and interests which impel men to organization are of a quite different kind from those which occur in running the organization. Whenever the ranks are needed to carry out the work of the organization, this gap becomes of real importance. Spurts in organizational effort on the part of the members occur when a direct connection can be seen between this organizational work and the reason for allegiance to the organization. Thus a political party can get "activity" when it carries on direct political propaganda—but the day-to-day task of keeping the party together, shaping its character, and strengthening its roots in various centers of power are tasks too far divorced from the original problems to stir most people from their ordinary way of living. In a political democracy, too, only heated contests over broad issues can really "bring out the vote," while the day-to-day changes which in the long run are decisive remains uninfluenced by the mass.

3. There is a hierarchy of values attached to *kinds of work.* Thus even equality between a worker in a unionized plant and the union organizer, in terms of money, does not alter the situation. It is the kind of work involved which is valued above the work of the ordinary members. Not only is there the fact of being well-known (the prestige of bare celebrity), but the facts of having certain powers, however small, of being associated with the incumbent leadership and of being acquainted with

the "mysteries" of organization are important. There are always men who *want* to be officials.

4. Positive valuation of the office as such raises new problems for the bureaucrat. His interest in the ultimate purpose of the organization, or in the "common good," becomes subordinate to his preoccupation with the problems involved in the *maintenance* of his post. This is not the same thing as the attempt to hold on to an official sinecure; for in this case, the post is primarily a source of social prestige and power. In many cases, the leaders could obtain better positions financially in another field. The leader of a women's club who, *because she has a following*, is treated with respect by political or other socially important forces, has more than a merely well-paid position. A. J. Muste, in his discussion of factional fights in trades unions[13] deals with the problem of why a leadership seeks to maintain its status. He points to reasons such as those already mentioned: the positions are pleasant, the return to the shop is humiliating, the official tends to become less efficient in his old trade. In addition there are motives connected with what they honestly consider to be the good of the union. They feel that they are better (more competent, have a better policy) than the opposition and that they have given more to the union and deserve to be left in power. This is often quite sincere and even *objectively a correct appraisal*. For our purposes that changes nothing: whether honest or corrupt, the tendency is for leaders, to use the same general procedures for the maintenance of their power. This ought not to be surprising: if the question of organizational dominance as such becomes directive in action, and the available means are limited, it is to be expected that the characters of their procedures would converge toward a common type, regardless of their ultimate reasons for desiring dominance.

5. The delegation of functions introduces a relation of *dependence*. This is enforced by and perhaps directly dependent upon the *professionalization* of the work of the officialdom. To the extent that the necessary knowledge and skill are increased, the possibilities for replacement of the leadership are diminished. The existence of the organization itself becomes dependent on the continued functioning of the incumbent leadership. And so long as this is true, and the ranks still require the organization (or think they require it), their dependence upon the leaders become firmly established. This has nothing to do with the existence of formal (*e.g.*, constitutional) procedures for replacing leaders; these may continue to exist, but they are relatively harmless to the intrenched leaders (because functionless) so long as the ranks fear the consequences of using them.

6. In order to be secure in his position, the leader-bureaucrat must strive to make himself as independent as possible from the ranks. He must seek a power-base which is not controlled by them. He may attempt to derive his strength from an electorate more general than the party or union membership. Thus he will be able to follow independent

policies by claiming that he has a responsibility to a broader base than the party ranks; and the ranks cannot do without his influence on outside groups. In a nation, an independent politician tends to cultivate those forces, such as a ruling economic group, which control the instruments which shape mass opinion as well as the electoral machinery, but which are not themselves controlled by the mass. It is a well-established political principle that a politician reacts most sensitively to those forces to which he owes the maintenance of his position; to the extent that forces can be developed apart from the electorate, he can—and often must, because he becomes dependent upon the new force—assert his independence from his formal constituency.

7. The leader-bureaucrat must seek a personal base *within* a group itself: some mechanism directly dependent on, devoted to, or in alliance with him which can be used to maintain his organizational fences. A class base in a nation, a political faction in a trade union, paid gangsters, an elite guard, a secret police force, protégés and confidants—these are the weapons which he must use in order to be independent of the shifting sands of public favor.

8. Because of this series of problems which the bureaucrat must face, his action in the name of the group, that is, that activity carried on to further its professed purposes, comes to have more and more a chiefly *internal relevance*. Actions are taken, policies adopted, with an eye more to the effect of the action or policy on the power-relations *inside* the organization than to the achievement of its professed goals. An organization drive in a trade union, party activity, legislative action, even the "activities program" of a club—all come to be oriented toward the problem of self-maintenance before possible onslaughts from the membership. Factors of "morale"—the condition wherein the ranks support the incumbent leadership—become dominant. *Bureaucratization is in a sense the process of transforming this set of procedures from a minor aspect of organization into a leading consideration in the behavior of the leadership.*

9. Struggles within a group tend to become exclusively struggles *between leaders*. The masses (rank and file) play the role of manipulable weapons in the conflict between the controlling groups. The struggle for control between the initiators and the agent-officials is a very complex problem. The rank and file as a group (and in an important sense the leader, too, because he has to build an apparatus which creates new problems for him) cannot exercise *direct* control. Even a struggle against an incumbent leadership must be carried on through intermediaries. When a faction is formed, it being an organization too, the relations which operated for the organization as a whole come to be effective within the faction. The faction leaders assert their dominance over their groups and come to grips with one another as leaders whose strength is measured by the forces they can deploy. There are, however, three ways in which the influence of the rank and file is felt in a democratic

organization: (a) the threat of spontaneous rank and file action and of a consequent internal revolt makes the construction of bureaucratic power-relationships necessary as a preventive measure; (b) opposing faction leaders tend to champion the professed aim of the organization against the leaders who abandoned it, thus expressing, if temporarily, the desires of the rank and file; and (c) pressure groups, often spontaneous, which do not seek the seizure of the organizational reins, may influence the course of the leadership in directions desired by the mass. This last, however, has usually a limited measure of success precisely because no direct threat to the power of the leadership is offered. It is significant that tolerance of these groups is a function of the extent to which they are interested in "new leadership."

10. The bureaucrats, like every other social type with a power-position to maintain, *construct an ideology* peculiar to their social position. The following general characteristics may be noted.

a. By the identification of the particular administration with the group as a whole: playing upon the known desire of the ranks for the maintenance of the organization (national, state, party, union, and so on), the leadership attempts to spread the idea that any opposition immediately places the very existence of the organization in jeopardy. In defending itself from attack, it tends to identify its opposition with enemies of the group as such. Thus opponents are "disrupters," "foreign agents," "agents of an alien class," and so on.

b. An incumbent leadership tends to adopt the ideology of *centralization*, while those out of office call for *autonomy*. The opposition wants to retain its dominance over the local groups or factions which it controls and in general desires to avoid increasing the power of the central authority; the concentration of the control of the organizational mechanism (jobs, equipment, finances) is especially to be avoided, although the minority may not object to that within its own domain. For the ruling group, on the other hand, it is convenient that its power, *especially* over the organizational mechanism, be increased; it is also desirable that the central powers have the right to step into the affairs of a local group dominated by the opposition, in order to be able to take the offensive against it within the center of its own power. Each side attempts to defend its view by appealing to the professed aims of the group as a whole. In an action organization, the leadership will stress the military aspect and the importance of centralization for discipline action; the opposition will stress the importance of democracy. Although this rule is often broken, there is a tendency for *neither* side to discuss the matter on the basis of the power-motives involved, either in defense of their own view or in criticism of their opponents. This is not surprising, for that would create the danger of exposing the irrelevance of the struggle to the overt aims of the group, which would inevitably result in alienating some of the ranks from both. They therefore sometimes form a pact of silence on these matters, carrying the discussion forward on the level of general principles, at the same time waging furious battle in the shadow-land of informal maneuver.

c. The leadership creates the ideology of the "collective submission to the collective will."[14] The obvious necessity for the delegation of certain functions is generalized, and democracy is interpreted sufficiently broadly to include the notion that the group has the democratic right to abdicate its power. The leader, it is proclaimed, represents the "general will," and every action that he takes is justifiable on the ground that he is merely exercising the desires of the collective. Thus the symbol of democracy itself becomes an ideological bulwark of autocracy within the group.

d. An existing leadership tends to don the mantle of *conservatism*, with its many variant expressions justifying the maintenance of existing conditions. Since, having the power they are responsible for the exercise of the basic functions of the group or state, they must abandon slogans which are characteristic of irresponsible minorities. The latter need not be considered merely a term of opprobrium; the fact is that a minority *can* be irresponsible because its function as an opposition is radically different from its function as an administrative leadership, manning and responsible for the conduct of the chief posts of a party or a state. In small groups too, the function of the critic may change, and with that his ideas as well, when he is faced with the *new* problem of carrying out a program.[15] It is also important to note that a party can be deeply conservative in some aspects and revolutionary in others: thus in the Marxist parties, factors in conservative ideology such as dependence on tradition, depreciation of youth, and rigidity in organizational procedure may go hand in hand with a thoroughly revolutionary program with respect to *outside* political events. Needless to say, the internal character of such an organization plays an important rôle if that organization achieves any great social influence.

The above discussion emphasizes certain characteristic tendencies in the organization process. These tendencies are, however, analytical: they represent abstractions from concrete organizational patterns. To state these tendencies is merely to *set* a problem, for although they ascribe to organizations in general an *initial presumption of bureaucratic consequence*, it always remains to be determined to what degree the bureaucratic tendencies have become dominant. It may be said, indeed, that this is the way organizations will develop if they are permitted to follow the line of least resistance. That is what does happen, often enough. But in the real world of living organizations there is always the possibility of counter-pressure, of devising techniques for blocking the bureaucratic drift. The study of these techniques, which must be based on a clear understanding of the general nature of the problem involved, is one of the most pressing intellectual tasks of our time.

NOTES

1. F. J. Roethlisberger, and W. J. Dickson, *Management and the Worker,* Cambridge: Harvard University Press, 1941, p. 524.
2. C. I. Barnard, *The Functions of the Executive,* Cambridge: Harvard University Press, 1940, p. 115.
3. *Ibid.*
4. *Loc. cit.,* pp. 122–23.
5. W. Waller and W. Henderson, "Institutions of Segregative Care and the Organized Group" (unpublished manuscript), 1941.
6. From a description by Mr. F. E. Robin.
7. *Political Parties,* Hearst's International Library Co., New York, 1915.
8. C. J. Friedrich, and T. Cole, *Responsible Bureaucracy,* Cambridge: Harvard University Press, 1932, p. 84.
9. Max Weber, "Bürokratie," Ch. 7, Pt. 3 of *Wirtschaft und Gesellschaft.* Since translated in *The Theory of Economic and Social Organization.*
10. H. J. Laski, "Bureaucracy" in *Encyclopedia of the Social Sciences,* v. 3, p. 70.
11. M. E. Dimock, and H. Hyde, *Bureaucracy and Trusteeship in Large Corporations,* TNEC Monograph No. 11, p. 31.
12. *Ibid.,* p. 36.
13. "Factional Fights in Trade Unions," *American Labor Dynamics,* ed. by J. B. S. Hardman, New York, Harcourt, Brace, 1928.
14. See Robert Michels' excellent chapter on "Bonapartist Ideology" in his *Political Parties.*
15. For material on the metamorphosis of leaders see Michels, *op. cit.,* and J. B. S. Hardman, "Problems of a Labor Union Somewhere in the U.S.," pp. 163–66, in his *American Labor Dynamics.*

40. Postindustrial America and the "Contract State"

Benjamin S. Kleinberg

In this chapter we trace the basic development of a unique American politicoeconomic subsystem which was initiated during World War II and which has crystallized during the postwar period around the large-scale production of military hardware and technology, with profound effect on the overall society. This subsystem, often popularly described as the "military-industrial complex" (and here referred to as the "Contract State"), incorporates major productive units of the regular civilian

From *American Society in the Postindustrial Age: Technocracy, Power, and the End of Ideology* by Benjamin S. Kleinberg. Copyright © 1973 by Charles E. Merrill Publishing Company. Reprinted by permission of the publisher.

economy as well as more narrowly specialized defense and research firms, linking them together with political-organizational allies in related government agencies and the broader polity. By way of illustrating the larger dynamics of growth of this state-within-a-state, we will briefly review the specific case of the Air Force in promoting the growth of a defense-industrial complex related to its military operations, and in using nominally civilian-controlled agencies such as the National Aeronautics and Space Agency to foster these aims. Finally, pursuing these developments, we can identify the "Contract State" as the essential matrix of military-industrial relations within which there has in recent years been established an explicitly centralized political-technical system of coordination, located in the Pentagon.

THE EVOLUTION OF THE CONTRACT STATE

As a result of the postwar growth of defense-industrial contracting empires, there exists today an interlocking structure of federal agencies, their industrial constituents, and their joint political allies, which has come to constitute a significant political economy within the larger society. This internal political economy, a virtual state within the larger state, has come to be referred to as the "Contract State," owing to the central role played within it by the government contract as the binding element between the different interests included in it.[1] It is this structure which serves as the relevant context for the political-technical role of the scientists and technocrats connected with government-sponsored programs involving technical research and development.

From the launching of the first Russian "Sputnik" satellite in 1957 to the end of the Kennedy regime, the military services engaged in a free-wheeling competition in the newly developing aerospace field. Through the power to choose industrial contractors in states across the country, the military services came to develop their own widespread and powerful industrial and political constituencies, which returned the favor through political and technical support for further space and missile development. The system of delegating various management responsibilities to prime contractors in overseeing the work of a host of subcontractors in a pyramid-like contracting structure enabled favored corporations to become powerful industrial brokers in their own right in the R & D sector. By virtue of the authority vested in them by government contract, they could now disburse vast public funds through the award of subcontracts, thereby strengthening their economic position, and enhancing their own local political influence, through the building of subcontracting constituencies. Moreover, operating under a largely noncompetitive system of negotiated contracts, and in the absence of any objective economic yardstick, industrial contractors could safely inflate costs and charge contract overruns to the contracting agency, thereby permitting many levels of hidden profits.

Since the bulk of government contracting to date has been directed toward the purchase of military supplies, weapons, and related research, the background to the Contract State may be traced through a brief review of government policy in this area.

Following a series of contracting scandals involving profiteering during World War I, federal legislation established that government would henceforth seek to provide its own military supplies through public-owned facilities, whenever economically feasible. The aim was to maintain a system of "in-house" capability which would serve as a yardstick by which to measure the performance of industrial contractors, as well as to provide expert advice on weapon-systems development. (Much the same concept was involved in the later creation of the TVA as a yardstick for the performance of private power companies during the New Deal.) This led to the establishment of shipyards, arsenals, and research laboratories by the military services after World War I, continuing through World War II and the early Fifties.[2] The military emergency of World War II led the government once again to depend on private contractors for weapons development, as reflected in major changes in contracting procedures which became basic features of much of postwar military contracting. In order to encourage prompt industrial response to the government's vastly enlarged war needs, military agencies were freed from procurement practices based strictly on competitive bidding among contractors.[3] Instead the cost-plus-fixed-fee contract, with contractor's fee calculated on the basis of estimated costs, became the typical mode of military contracting until almost the mid-1960's. In this system, unrealistically low initial cost estimates frequently led to renegotiation of contracts to cover contractors' cost overruns, with an additional fee added. This in effect provided an inflatable "sliding fee" for contractors similar to that which led in the first place to establishment of in-house facilities.[4]

The initial intent of the in-house system to strengthen the hand of government in industrial contracting has further been weakened by the employment of private corporations as "systems managers" for weapons development. In the postwar period, the traditional practice of contracting specialized components to subcontractors was transformed into a means by which "prime contractors," subsidized by government funds, were given many powers formerly reserved to government agencies. Through this management approach, private firms designated as prime contractors took on the role of "systems engineers and technical directors for multibillion dollar R & D and production activities involving hundreds of other corporations."[5] In this role the primes have exercised many of the functions of government itself, in relation to subcontractors and supplies. According to a report of the House Committee on Governmental Operations:

These companies establish procurement organizations and methods which proximate those of the government. Thus large prime contractors will invite design competition, establish source selection bids, send out industrial survey teams, make subcontract awards on a competitive or a negotiated basis, appoint small business administrators, designate plant resident representatives, develop reporting systems to spot bottlenecks, make cost analyses of subcontractor operations, and request monthly progress and cost reports from subcontractors.[6]

In consequence, the granting of prime contract status to a relative handful of large corporations has given them a position of enormous discretionary power and managerial leverage over their numerous subcontractors. Under the terms of its contract status, the prime contractor is granted power over the fortunes of dozens of subcontractors, investors, bankers, businessmen, and employees, often entailing the economic well-being of whole geographic areas. As an officially designated "systems manager" it has the power to contract out or do work itself, to acquire subcontractors' proprietary information, to exert pressures on subcontractors to sell out, and even to create dummy subcontractors which can be useful in concealing profits or proprietary information from the government. In general, the prime will use its subcontracting power to stabilize its operations by expanding or curtailing subcontracts in phase with swings in government business. In addition, the prime contractor, standing at the top of its "system-management" hierarchy, can buttress its own economic position among other large corporations by "mergers, acquisitions, and investments in the flock of companies dependent upon them for government largess."[7] In this light, the government contract can be viewed as a cushion which helps secure and enhance the economic position of the favored corporations whose productive capacities and political influence qualify them for prime status.

The trend toward the employment of private contractors for government work on a system-management basis first became pronounced during the Eisenhower administration.[8] Its most important stimulus was the expanding need of the rapidly growing Air Force for R & D capability. Unlike the Army, of which it was only a post-World War II offspring, the Air Force lacked the in-house facilities for research, engineering, or management which were integral to the Army's system. Thus the Air Force resorted to private contractors to perform what would normally have been in-house functions. In the intense interservice competition for jurisdiction over new weapons systems which marked the 1950's, the Air Force promoted the growth of private companies which ultimately took over a substantial segment of regular military operations, from routine aircraft maintenance to the technical management of a host of military-related subcontractors. The Air Force's lack of in-house capacity, far from hindering its competitive efforts, gave it a major advantage, allowing it to pare down personnel levels in keeping with administrative policies, and at the same time to put together a huge industrial and political constituency with a stake in the continued heavy funding of its weapons systems. So successful was this approach that other federal agencies,

including the other services with heavy R & D requirements, soon began
employing it, and this encouraged a new era of intimacy in government-
corporate relations, embodied in the notion of the Contract State.

PROFIT AND POWER IN THE CONTRACT STATE

One major result of these developments was that the government's capacity to independently evaluate private R & D performance was seriously
reduced, while a procurement system highly vulnerable to abuse by
private interests came into being. Though the firms which do the bulk of
their business on government contract are organized as private enterprises, they have rather special and unprecedented relations with government, through which the mechanism of an open competitive market has
been replaced by the complex and obscure processes of government
agency contracting. Low performance standards have been facilitated by
the permissive nature of much of government contracting, as embodied in
such practices as the tolerance of overspending, failure to meet schedules,
lack of adequate product specifications, faulty cost estimates, charging
of private overhead to the contract, and so forth.[9] In addition, the complexities of multiple subcontracting constitute a "labyrinth" largely
impervious to government inspection, so that the average contractor fee
of about six percent does not indicate the various layers of overhead
and concealed profit in hierarchic subcontracting by prime contractors,
who can charge the total subcontracting costs, "including profit fee for
the sub," to their own costs.[10]

Under the Eisenhower administration, the abandonment of government
in-house facilities was openly encouraged as part of the move back to
"free enterprise" in reaction to the excursions of government under the
New Deal into the private domain. During this administration, many installations and factories built during World War II were sold to industry,
usually at a fraction of cost; TVA itself came close to being dismembered
and sold to private power companies in the Tennessee Valley area, under
the Dixon-Yates scheme. Other installations were leased at nominal fees
to contractors who then received government contracts to make their use
profitable; in some cases new facilities were built and then leased by the
government at low fees. Contractors were also allowed to use leased facilities for commercial production outside their contract obligations, at no
cost to themselves. These publicly encouraged arrangements were consistent with practices already well under way during the Truman administration.

Over half of the fifteen hundred government-financed industrial plants
built during World War II at a cost of almost $13 billion by 1949, were
either sold to private industry at nominal cost or held by the military
services under the National Security Act, reserved for their original use;
the value of the plants involved is estimated at "over nine billion dollars."
In this way the government was able to directly and indirectly subsidize

"extensive capital expansion" sought by political leaders, while at the same time the military establishment was assured the war-built defense plants "would remain oriented to military production."[11] The Eisenhower administration merely stepped up the process of selling or leasing these facilities to private industry. Though the intention was ostensibly to cut military expenditures by substituting private contractors for government in-house work, the cost of military R & D quadrupled over the course of the Eisenhower administration.[12] The costs of R & D increased not merely because there was considerably more of it by the late 1950s than at the beginning of the decade; also contributing to this precipitous rise was the inflation of costs under negotiated contracts which often permitted overpricing, duplicate billings, technical errors, mismanagement, and overhead charges to the government for costs actually applicable to the contractors' private commercial work.[13] In large part this was the consequence of the great discretionary authority allowed by negotiated awards to federal agencies and their contract officers,[14] allowing them to commit large sums to contractors on the basis of often inadequate specifications, estimates, and reviews.[15] Yet, despite these drawbacks, with the emergence of the Contract State, negotiated contracting had come to comprise almost nine-tenths of the dollar volume of government contracts by the mid-1960s.[16]

The prevailing system of government contracting has to date contributed not only to inflationary trends, but also to the acceleration of corporate concentration in a variety of ways. In the whole economy, only 300 major corporations perform 97 percent of all federal R & D; at the same time they also account for 91 percent of all private R & D, much of which is a means of maintaining capability for government work, and is generally paid for by government in the form of overhead on other contracts. But even this does not give an adequate idea of the degree of concentration in the R & D sector. In the 1960's prime contracts accounting for more than half the total R & D and production business in the aerospace field were held by a few giant corporations, such as North American, Lockheed, General Dynamics, and Thompson-Ramo Wooldridge, which specialize in aerospace work; together with a small number of old established commercial giants such as GE, GM, Westinghouse, Chrysler, Ford, Socony, Firestone, Philco, Goodyear, and so on, which moved into the field. In this way, the private corporate sector and the government contract sector have become closely interconnected.[17] In fact some of the newer aerospace corporations seem to be merely legal fictions, facades for interlocking arrangements between established industrial corporations. Thus the House Judiciary Committee cited the five largest aerospace firms in 1965 as examples of corporate interlock. In one case an aerospace firm had interlocking directorships with 18 financial institutions and 28 industrial corporations; it was also found that companies in the field frequently hold stock in nominal competitors. According to the antitrust subcommittee staff, interlocking directorships are

today as widespread as when the Clayton Act of 1914 was passed prohibiting such interlocks; in about 75 major corporations it was found that
approximately 1500 officers and directors held a total of about 4500 positions.[18]

Recently a number of observers have remarked that there are in effect
two economies in America today: one dominated by the huge corporations which command advanced technology and are relatively independent of the traditional commercial market, and the old-fashioned market
economy consisting of small and middle-sized entrepreneurs, characterized by an increasingly outmoded technology and depressed or marginal
labor conditions.[19] Clearly it is the corporate economy which is now the
dominant and determinant element in the overall economy, and its ongoing development is closely linked to our movement into a "postindustrial" era. Moreover, the most dynamic element of the corporate economy
is the R & D sector, funded by huge sums of government money each
year, and increasingly interlocked with government through contractual
relations. Thus, through the government contract, private corporations
have become the agents of an essentially new economic subsystem which
combines features of private enterprise such as private ownership and
profits, with state-monopoly aspects of the "corporate state" which
achieved fullest development under European systems of fascism little
more than a generation ago. A handful of corporate giants, acting as
"systems managers," have been granted government authority to oversee R & D and production activities costing billions of dollars and involving hundreds of smaller firms. In dealing with these subcontractors, the
prime contractors take on the role of government itself, from the making
of subcontract awards to the supervision and cost analysis of subcontract
operations. In the process, the corporate prime contractor has become a
quasi-public organization, a veritable "arm of the state."

In this perspective, the government contract can be viewed as a significant instrument for linking up that complex of organizations and institutions (both defense and nondefense oriented) which are the structural
core of the postindustrial society. Government and corporate industry
are the focal institutions of this society, commanding its major economic
and administrative resources, deciding its major public policies and their
administration, employing most of the technocrats who are its most vital
manpower and its scarcest resource. Alongside them, the universities play
an extremely important ancillary role in doing much of the research and
training most of the manpower required by this system. Today these
three institutional areas are interconnected as never before through integrative relations which increasingly take the form of government contracts. Government agencies employ major corporations to engage in
functions formerly reserved to in-house facilities: NASA employs GE to
integrate and test its space equipment, and Bellcomm (an AT & T subsidiary) to manage its R & D and engineering operations; the Air Force
employs a single corporation, Aerospace, to do both.[20] Major universities

do the greatest part of their research for federal agencies under government contract; government labs are operated for government by industry or universities under government contract; "nonprofit" institutions such as Rand and the Hudson Institute conduct computer studies of policy matters for federal agencies, under government contract.[21]

In this way, the new, highly integrated political economy of the Contract State is embodied in large-scale organizations operated most frequently on a profit basis (but also, particularly in the academic world, on a nonprofit basis), which have officially been granted the power to dispose of enormous resources, often holding sway over a host of economic dependents. At the inner core of the postindustrial society in America, earlier distinctions between "public sector" and "private sector" have increasingly tended to lose their meaning while private economic interests have come to enjoy a highly intimate relationship with the agencies of government, largely without the knowledge or consent of the general public.

INTEREST INVESTMENT IN THE CONTRACT STATE

The contemporary loss of distinction between the "public" and the "private" sector appears not only in terms of the interlocking functions of organizations once functionally quite distinct, but also in terms of the growth of structural interrelations between organizations. One important mode of interorganizational linkage is provided by those who have leadership roles in different organizations; Nieburg suggests that connecting the organizations that stand at the core of the Contract State is a group of probably no more than few thousand men, predominantly industrial managers and brokers, with closely related roles in the system. Moving between private corporations and government tours of duty, sitting on boards of directors, consulting with government agencies, serving on agency advisory committees, and acting as managers on behalf of government in the distribution and supervision of subcontractors, this managerial elite constitutes an essential element in the structure of the Contract State.[22]

Though Nieburg is certainly correct in naming industrial broker-managers as a crucial and powerful interest group in the system, his own discussion of the Contract State indicates that, in singling them out as the strategic elite, he is focusing on but one side of the contract relation. The point which needs to be made, it seems, is that the Contract State is built around a structure of relations between a number of strategic elites; that it is based, in fact, on an evolving reciprocity of elite interests which have by now come to formal expression in the government contract itself. In this respect, the core of the Contract State is both elitist and pluralist; rather than a monolithic ruling class at the center, we have a pluralism of powerful elites. Who are these elites? In the professional as well as the popular literature, there are a number of favorite candidates for this role, besides the industrial managers:[23] the agency heads and bureau chiefs in the government agencies; the leading figures in office and in the political parties; the chairmen and senior members of congressional committees responsible for agency oversight; and the scientific-technical advisors to government agencies and the executive office (though in light of our discussion in preceding chapters, we would tend to discount the latter as a group having significant power in the making of basic policy).[24]

In order to develop a model of the relations between these elites that reflects the manner in which their interests bear on the making and administration of policy in the Contract State, we begin with the formal structure of government to which we then relate the ongoing structure of elite interests. The structure of government can be looked upon as simultaneously an investment firm and an investment market. In the first instance it is by now something of a commonplace to note that the government is the largest firm in the nation. However, it is not basically a production firm; its productive output is relatively small compared to GNP and ha's been cut back since the 1950's with the closing of various in-house government facilities. It does in a sense engage in "productive" activities; these, however, are political rather than economic, though they do have ultimately significant economic impact: the "production" of policy for achieving and maintaining social standards in a wide range of public concerns, from public health to public order. Its major economic function is making socially sanctioned (politically legitimated) investments and purchases out of public revenues through a variety of programs, in accordance with the broad outlines of its policy. Those investments take on the form of subsidies, grants, contracts, and so on, from which a "return" of some kind is expected, from agricultural price stability to the stimulation of scientific research, to the actual production of governmentally required goods or services, in the case of the government contract. The return, as in the cooling of "long hot summers" *via* poverty grants, is not always measurable primarily in economic terms, though there may be economic as well as social, political, or cultural benefits that flow from any given government investment, such as the assurance of a normal level of small business activity in riot-threatened slums.

Viewed as a market for investment, the formal structure of government represents a differential structure of opportunities for "interest investment." This type of investment has both an economic and a political component; for example, the industrial contractors interested in obtaining defense contracts are extremely active employers of retired ex-military officers. This is surely the kind of economic investment which it is also "politic" to make, and which has real political consequences in the sense of the influence it brings to bear in the competition for contracts. We find that the level of "interest investments" of this kind in fact correlate fairly closely with the granting of contracts by given agencies.[25] The contractor "invests" politically in such-and-such an agency or several agencies by way of lobbying, securing personal contacts with agency administrators because they offer contracts in areas related to his general productive capability. He may find himself, after having done business with a given agency, invested more heavily in it than in others and not inclined to invest in the others; on the other hand, if a given agency's appropriations are cut, or particular programs on which his contracts depend are cut back, he will have to redirect his political "investments" to other agencies relevant to his interest in government contracts. In either case, the executive branch, composed of these various agencies, appears to him as a structure of various investment opportunities of differing attractiveness and risk, somewhat like the conventional investment market. In this context, the formal meeting ground for the industrial contractor and the government agency is the negotiating table. The formal negotiating process is, however, typically preceded by numerous informal managerial contacts and explorations, and supplemented by formal contracts such as are provided by agency meetings with industrial advisory committees on which favored contractor representatives sit. Such at any rate is a simplified version of the reciprocal entrepreneurial relations between contractor and agency—each facing an investment "field" or market, either in the spectrum of agencies, or in the array of contractors, which confront it at any given time, each choosing to make an investment in a given agency or market based on the maximization of its own particular interests.

In this way, the "military-industrial complex," whose major actors were the chief elements of the Contract State until almost the mid-1960's (prior to the development of central budgetary control elements in the Defense Department), constituted itself as a new kind of market, in which contemporary economic-entrepreneurial relationships with all their own complexity (involving "administered" prices and "integrated" markets), were embedded in a political context marked by its own peculiar intricacies. At least in part this owed to the fact that the executive branch of government, from which contracts are to be obtained, had itself become an enormously complex apparatus, standing at the center of a number of political conflict relations—on one hand, the conflict between presidential and congressional authority; on the other, the conflict of presidential and agency authority, which is closely related to conflict between agencies. In each of these instances, the Presidency, as symbol of the central political authority and of the public interest, is under challenge. But there is something else in common between these challenges to presidential authority; typically, those who are the central actors in offering the challenge are members of what has been called the "bureaucratic subsystem" of government.[26]

The bureaucratic subsystem is the structure of relations between the leading members of the Congress—the chairmen and senior members of the standing committees, as well as the party leaders in each house—and the leading members of the executive bureaucracy, the agency chiefs, and bureau heads. Moreover, as Charles Jacob points out, both sets of actors in the policy process are "specialists, technicians with wide experience in a particular area of policy,"[27] both enjoy considerable continuity of position, often outlasting the regime of one or more presidents, and both have a good deal of autonomy in the formulation of policy relevant to their special area of competence. It may come as no surprise to hear the agency person referred to as a technician, but the conception of the politician as a technical specialist is of particular interest in light of the sharp distinction which [Daniel] Bell has drawn between the politician and the technocrat, and makes that contrast appear rather overdrawn. In any event, in the context of the growing technicality of government affairs, these capacities qualify their possessors as leading actors in the administration below the surface of a succession of changing presidential administrations. Thus, any given interest group, such as the corporation seeking government contracts to secure its influence in the policy process, will have to make interest investments in both sectors of this infrasystem.

Of course, it is to be expected that Congress will present itself as a focus for interest investment; its formal role of representation invites its various constituencies to vie for influence which may bear upon their fortunes in the policy process. On the other hand, the only interest of the executive agencies is, theoretically, the execution of policy in terms of the "functional rationality" of which Bell speaks, that is, the efficient execution and administration of broad government policy. Even if Congress or the executive tend to favor particular constituents because of the political value of their support, the agencies of the executive are no more than operating arms, and should ostensibly themselves have no particular favorites, no "constituents." The autonomy and expertise which agency officials possess should insure their political neutrality and their indifference to attempts at interest investment by groups seeking influence or benefits with regard to agency programs.

In practice, however, it is the nature not only of the Congress but also of the executive agencies to invite a kind of "interest investment" by the various interests found in contemporary society. As a matter of course, a variety of interests, not merely economic, but also social, cultural, and ethnic are drawn to these agencies to insure that they will not be excluded from the beneficence of the state. The fact that government agencies are often in conflict themselves, tends to invite the involvement of various interests, and vests these interests with considerable influence in the making of agency policy in return for their support in the Congress and the broader polity.

Since World War I, and particularly since the New Deal, there has been a proliferation of agencies with overlapping functions whose roughly equal status has made for interagency conflict over their respective lines of authority. Theoretically, of course, the President has the constitutional power as the chief executive to impose his concept of policy on the executive departments; in reality, however, the President finds himself limited to formulating general principles of policy which he hopes will not suffer too much in the process of execution. The result is a system of policy formation in which the ostensible technical instruments of policy take on a policy role of their own; rather than merely executing public policy, the executive agencies become in practice independent centers of decision to which there have fallen important segments of the executive's authority to make public policy. As Hans Morgenthau observes:

> The executive agency, competing for the determination of policy with other agencies, more and more resembles a feudal fief that owes its existence to the delegation of powers by higher authority but becomes an active operation and autonomous center of power, defending itself against other centers of power and trying to increase its power at the expense of others.[28]

In the process of acquiring autonomy, the executive agency takes on characteristics typical of elected centers of decision, including the development of constituencies within those groups in the society interested in its activities; these are its primary constituency. Moreover, due to the importance of these constituencies to the Congress, the agency takes on segments of the Congress itself as a secondary constituency.

ADMINISTRATIVE AUTONOMY VERSUS
CENTRALIZATION IN THE CONTRACT STATE

It is within this framework that we can briefly examine the establishment of NASA and its administrative capture by the Air Force in the late 1950's. In the opening phase of these developments, prior to the Russian launching of "Sputnik," there was already an on-going relationship of reciprocal interest investment between the Air Force and its industrial contractors. At the same time, there existed another such relationship between strategic members of Congress and these same industrial constituents, who have generally represented prominent elements in the economies of those states which are locations of aircraft and missile production. Shortly after Sputnik, the administration bill for NASA, incorporating the recommendations of the President's Science Advisory Committee, came down for congressional action. Despite strong service opposition to a civilian space agency, the bill had too much public support (owing in some measure to the prestige of the President's science advisors) to be rejected outright by the Congress. Instead, the Department of the Air Force, together with its constituents in the missile industry and Congress, obtained important modifications of the bill so that a civilian NASA would not have jurisdiction over the space programs of the Defense Department. In the legislative process, the executive military agency, through its expert testimony to the Congress and through propaganda aimed at public support and claiming special military-technical knowledge of the requirements and opportunities of international space competition, acted as a technocratic voice for the economic and political space interests which were at the same time its own constituents. But this is not where Air Force action ended. Next, apparently through its industrial constituent Thompson-Ramo-Woodridge Corporation and its congressional allies, the Air Force affected the choice of the NASA administrator thus facilitating the use of the agency as a magnet to draw away the programs and facilities of its service competitors. Finally, having prevented NASA from becoming a possible lever for reducing its influence over space programs, the Air Force, partly through its enhanced influence at NASA, bypassed the Defense Department's Advanced Research Projects Agency and stripped it of working authority over military space programs, thus neutralizing the very instrument of centralization by which its own autonomy might have been curbed.[29]

The possibility of even beginning to correct such a situation did not really present itself until the Kennedy administration, with the advent of Defense Secretary McNamara, committed itself to the establishment of effective centralized controls over the military agencies, particularly in the matter of imposing a central managerial perspective and appropriate operating controls on the process of military planning and budgeting.

Coming from the presidency of a major industrial corporation with a reputation for modernizing efficiency, McNamara represented the administrative technocrat par excellence, and he lived up to his reputation on many counts. Ultimately, he forced the services to define and justify their military strategies within a comprehensive framework, and to relate strategic requirements to weapons systems and budgetary requests. In addition, he took steps toward enforcing a new code of ethics designed to eliminate any gratuities from individual contractors to Defense Department personnel engaged in R & D contracting, and toward reforming the instruments of R & D contracting themselves. Yet, in the final analysis, McNamara's reforms may have failed at the level which the technocrat perhaps cannot really understand—the level of politics. It is, therefore, the story of the political struggle within the context of technocratic reforms which is of most interest here.

Prior to McNamara, military planning and budgeting had been treated as independent entities, divided between the Joint Chiefs of Staff and civilian budget officials. While planning for military forces and weapons systems was projected over a number of years, budgeting was based on a single fiscal year, so that military plans were prepared without regard to limitations of resources, with little in the way of external controls.[30] The resulting military budgets represented compromises between the longer-range ambitions of the different services, rather than actual strategic requirements. As a result, serious imbalances in service capabilities developed, hampering integrated service deployment; for example, while the Air Force's strategic bombing capacity was highly developed, its capability for tactical support to Army ground forces was grossly inadequate.

McNamara attacked these deficiencies through a rigorous program of cost-effectiveness analysis. Fighting strength was reconceptualized in "program packages" which treated functionally related budget items as unit categories. Thus, Polaris submarines were considered part of the same strategic package as Air Force B-52's, Skybolts, and ICBM's. This made clear the strategic redundancy of some of the services' pet projects, and forced the military to calculate the cost and effectiveness of every available alternative, or to lay out R & D projects to help establish such knowledge. By defining each project in steps which spelled out the scope, technical requirements, and probable cost of given weapons programs at levels of commitment prior to full-scale development, premature commitment to redundant, irrelevant, or overly costly programs could be averted. In this way, the tendencies of run-away military technology, driven by service ambitions and rivalries, could at least be contained, if not halted.[31] Much, of course, depends on the character of the civilian leadership, particularly the defense secretary and the president, on the firmness of their commitment to technocratic control over service ambitions, and on the nature of their relations to Congress and other sources of political support in the society. Moreover, it should not be assumed that functional cost analysis and its contractual concomitants are a technically self-contained system. Like other governmental procedures, they are open to the pressures of domestic political interests and to changes in the international political situation, where the relaxation or escalation of crisis can provide opportunities either for strengthening or bypassing central controls over domestic military development.

The Problems of Central Control in the Contract State

The cost-effectiveness procedures introduced by Defense Secretary McNamara ultimately made possible the cancellation of a number of costly weapons programs, such as the Skybolt missile, the Dynasoar space glider, and the B-70 bomber, as well as a "bomb-in-orbit" proposal.[32] However, this came only after several changes in the domestic and international political context. As matters went during the Kennedy administration, a recalcitrant Congress was able successfully to bargain in the interest of its contractor constituents, using its traditional power over legislation and appropriations to dilute the impact of the defense secretary's policies. By the third year of Kennedy's term, when the delaying tactics of the Contract State interests began wearing thin, technological substitutes for programs subject to cancellation began to appear, such as the Manned Orbiting Laboratory (MOL), which reflected continuing Air Force determination to create military missions for outer space, and the luxury Supersonic Transport, which was aimed at satisfying aircraft contractor interests.[33]

Significantly from our viewpoint, it was not until after the Kennedy administration that McNamara's reforms began to show any sign of real effect. It should be recalled that Kennedy came to the presidency with a fairly sophisticated managerial orientation, was able to accept the implications of the "new economics" much more fully than his predecessor, and brought to Washington representatives of the technocratic mentality who would put these new economic and organizational perspectives to work. In addition, Kennedy explicitly put forward a pragmatic "end-of-ideology" position which pictured major political problems as being of an essentially technical nature and too complex to be settled by the clash of militant creeds, but ultimately yielding to the patient search for workable compromise by technicians and experts.[34] If any American president could, as of the 1960's, be said to express the technocratic orientation toward politics, it was John Kennedy. His successor, on the other hand, was the very image of the wheeler-dealer politician, trading favors and votes with aplomb, promising and cajoling, making alliances and creating a politics of "consensus" based on old-fashioned interest bargaining. Yet it was Lyndon Johnson, the traditional politician's politician, under whose regime McNamara's reforms finally were provided with enough effective political support to take hold, as reflected in estimated savings of over $4 billion in the Defense Department during 1964, which provided the model for Johnson's much publicized "war on waste," the government-wide cost reduction program instituted in October of that year. The great irony is that Johnson, as Senate Majority Leader during the 1950's, had been the key broker of the complex military-industrial-political coalition which emerged in the context of the opportunities provided by the crash missile programs of that decade, and which was nourished from the system of government contracting that burgeoned so rapidly in the military R & D sector. This was a role which linked up with similar roles played by Senators Robert Kerr, Clinton Anderson, Stuart Symington, and others, among whom Johnson became *primus inter pares;* moreover, it was a role which he maintained under Kennedy as head of NASA's Space Policy Board, which he had personally helped bring into being during the Eisenhower regime. In this role, Johnson was a central figure among the interests who sought to perpetuate and extend the system of the military oriented Contract State which took shape during the 1950's, fed by the panic of the nuclear missile race.

The first possibility of a break in the nuclear arms race came only near the end of the Kennedy administration with the signing of the nuclear test ban treaty. With the passage of the treaty, the context was provided for cutting-back on redundant strategic weapons development. Hence the series of weapons program cancellations over which Defense Secretary McNamara presided around this time. In addition, McNamara's managerial programs seemed now to have the possibility of going beyond the integration of the military services and the cutting of contract costs, to the control of the basic direction of R & D investments in strategic weaponry. Basing himself on the Bell Committee Report,[35] as well as on reports of the government's General Accounting Office (GAO), McNamara moved to rebuild government in-house capability and to exert greater control over contractor fees. In this way, the basis would be laid for switching from cost-plus contracts to open competitive fixed-price bidding for Defense Department procurement. In those cases where negotiated contracts might be unavoidable, the department would invite multiple-source proposals, and provide incentive fees, rather than the old system of fixed fees. If the contractor's performance was excellent, his fee would correspond with the maximum, or incentive figure; on the other hand, to the extent that he deviated from target costs, scheduling, or performance objectives, he would suffer penalties in the fee, down to a minimum figure.

McNamara scored some considerable successes with this program to reform the contract instrument. Cost-plus-fixed-fee contracts, for example, for building Titan III launch vehicles were converted to an incentive-fee basis; as a result, spending on the program was claimed to be one percent below the original cost estimates, entailing the lowest number of engineering changes relative to comparable procurements, and the program was unprecedentedly on schedule. In the case of the "Bull Pup" air-to-surface missile, introduction of a second contractor source for follow-on production led to competitive negotiated bidding and dropped the missile's price by about twenty percent, or over $40 million. The same procedure was then applied, with similar cost reductions, for procurement of the antisubmarine torpedo ASTOR, the air defense missile TALOS, and several other weapons systems.[36]

By the mid-sixties, McNamara's system had undoubtedly begun to have an important effect on contracting procedures and the resulting costs of procurement; yet the objects of the system, the agencies and their contractor constituents, were again beginning to find their way around it. Through a kind of collusion between agencies and contractors, contractors were nominally converted to the new system on the basis of grossly inflated cost figures containing provisions for rather unlikely contingencies. In this way incentive fee schedules tended to become safeguards against risk, rather than motives for quality performance. Furthermore, contractors soon realized that fixed-price contracts provided legal protection against GAO and Defense Department scrutiny, so that they could safely enter into such contracts, relying on the permissive attitude of contract officers and the lack of governmental yardsticks. In one case the contractor overran the negotiated target by almost $15 million, and was seriously behind schedule as well, yet NASA indicated that the final fee would be above the minimum, providing the equivalent of a performance bonus. The very instruments of the McNamara system—competitive procurement, incentive fees, and fixed prices—were turned to the purpose of the R & D contractors.[37]

While the contractors were learning to evade the new system of cost effectiveness, their congressional allies were busy attacking one of its major institutions, the General Accounting Office. Established by Congress shortly after World War I as a response to dubious contracting practices during the war, the GAO has functioned as a kind of inspector-general, with gradually expanding powers to examine records pertinent to negotiated awards and to suspend payments to contractors in questionable cases. Using these powers, GAO in 1965 detected the trend toward subversion of the McNamara reforms and reported a large number of cases in which conversion to incentive and fixed-price contracts had added millions of dollars of cost above what would have been required on the basis of the initial contract arrangements. As a result, Congress turned on its own creature and launched an investigation of the GAO in response to contract complaints about its rigorous use by McNamara as a management tool. The investigation, conducted by the House Military Operations Subcommittee, gave contractors testifying an opportunity to vent their displeasure with McNamara's reforms as well as the GAO audits which supported them. In these reforms, which were based upon a long series of GAO reports and recommendations, contractors thought they discerned a philosophy contrary to the rights of free enterprise, one which viewed them as regulated agents of government rather than private businesses. Underlying their complaints about this philosophy was the more mundane concern, in the words of Boeing's Howard Neffner, that

> the increasing number of audit reports, the scope and uncompromising nature of GAO criticism, and the efforts made to enforce its recommendations are already dominating factors in procurement policy and practice.[38]

While the subcommittee's members were openly friendly to the contractors who testified, making cordial invitations to them to move their businesses to their respective home states, they acted more like adversaries in relation to the GAO officials. Thus, even before the hearings had ended in specific recommendations for limiting the GAO's investigative powers, they served notice to the agency that the vigorous pursuit of its role would surely lead to further difficulties.

The expansion of the scale of the Vietnam War in 1965 brought with it an insistent clamoring for increased appropriations for defense contracts; often coupled with attacks on McNamara's "short-sighted," "penny-wise" attitudes, to which were attributed the nation's inadequate state of military preparedness. The congressional assault on McNamara's cost-cutting activities came to a head in the fall of that year, when it passed the Military Construction Act as a kind of congressional veto of military base shutdowns by the defense secretary. For the first time in his dealings with this Congress, President Johnson found it necessary to use the veto, signifying a breakdown of the formerly smooth working relationship between this master politician and his ex-colleagues. Again, as in the case of the GAO investigation, Congress served notice that it would defend the institution of the Contract State against incursions by the executive authority; the struggle over central government control was by no means over, and the Vietnam War has served as the context of a continuing conflict over the powers of legislature *versus* executive.[39]

As the economy's largest consumer today, government is no longer a passive referee of the rules of the economic game. The government contract, an improvised, inadequately understood, but basic instrument of the new political economy, has become an increasingly important device for intervention in the economy and in the larger society. In this chapter, we have explored some of its implications. We have observed that the government contract serves not only the ends of economic stability and growth; it becomes a basic means of achieving important ends of government policy, involving the allocation of major resources and the mobilization of manpower for specific programs of development deemed vital to the national well-being. Concomitantly, it has become an important means for the distribution of wealth and the reordering of social status and power in various states and regions of the country. As such it becomes the object of a new kind of political activity with important effect on the relations of public and private power.

Using the concept of "interest investment" we have sought to specify the key policy makers in postindustrial America and the binding relations between them, over and above their common interest in "maintaining the system." The government contract, by subsidizing major elements of the corporate economy and at the same time strengthening these elements as constituencies of the grantor agencies and their political allies, has achieved both the maintenance of the system as a whole and the satisfaction of the respective investing interests.[40]

Though the government contract has been important as a tool for the central guidance of both military and non-military economic development since World War II, there was until the late 1960's little general consciousness of this trend. The result has been a kind of covert economic federalism in which specially-privileged constituencies have participated, shielded from the surrounding society by a combination of political ambiguity and technical complexity. In the process, the allocation of government contracts to "private" enterprises and organizations has tended to blur the distinctions between private and governmental objectives, blending them into a system of interpenetrating corporate bureaucratic interests which stand beyond the critical scrutiny or control of the general public. In this power context, we have described how the role of the scientific-knowledge elite (one segment of Bell's "technocratic class") has proved to be subsidiary to the coalition of military agencies, industrial contractors, and political officials with interests in the development and application of the military and extra-terrestrial technologies of the new society. Finally in reviewing the establishment of NASA and the related actions of the Air Force we have traced an important instance of the way in which these interest relations have in the postwar era taken the shape of institutional arrangements best described as the "Contract State," over which the assertion of central governmental control was for a long time a difficult and uncertain objective.

Notes

1. Harold L. Nieburg, *In the Name of Science*, ch. 10, "The Contract State," pp. 184–99. In the present chapter we are indebted to this excellent work which has recently begun to receive the wide recognition it deserves for its thorough investigation of the military-industrial "R & D" complex and its development. See also John K. Galbraith, *New Industrial State*, chs. 26, 27, "The Industrial System and The State, II," esp. pp. 296–302, 309–14.

2. Examples are the establishment of Navy Yards after World War I, the Naval Research Lab and the Army Electronics Lab between World War I and World War II, the expansion of the Jet Propulsion Lab (JPL) of Cal Tech during World War II, and the establishment and growth of the Army's Redstone Arsenal after World War II. (Cf. Nieburg, *In the Name of Science*, pp. 218–19, 230–35.)

3. Cf. Robert Borosage, "The Making of the National Security State," in Leonard S. Rodberg and Derek Shearer, eds., *The Pentagon Watchers* (Garden City, N.Y.: Doubleday, 1970), pp. 3–63. As Borosage indicates, the contracting authority of the services "was delineated in the Armed Services Procurement Act of 1947." Though the act stipulated that military contracts with industrial suppliers or university researchers should proceed on the basis of advertising and bidding, "any one of sixteen exceptions" could allow for a negotiated contract instead; the effect was to release the services from competitive bidding requirements, whenever it was deemed in the "defense interest"; and this was more often than not, i.e., in about two-thirds of the dollar value of postwar contracts. (*Ibid.*, pp. 24–25.)

4. While the cost plus fixed-fee contract was a more liberal arrangement than the fixed-price contract requirements established after World War I, it seemed at the time less open to abuse than the practice during that war of determining profit as a percentage of total cost, which was often conducive to cost inflation. In the course of World War II the cost-plus contract became the major instrument for military procurement of aircraft, ordnance equipment, and ammunition; over one-third of all procurement was arranged through cost-plus contracts, totalling over $50 billion. Despite the fact that Senator Truman's World War II defense-spending committee uncovered widespread profiteering under these contracting arrangements, the cost-plus contract became a basic instrument for government procurement during the ensuing Cold War. (*Ibid.*, pp. 201–2.) Cf. House Committee on Government Operations, *Systems Development and Management*, Hearings, 87th Cong. 2d sess., 1962, esp. Part 3, pp. 231–32, and House Committee on Government Operations, *Comptroller General Reports to Congress on Audits of Defense Contracts*, Hearings, 89th Cong., 1st sess., 1965, pp. 170–71.

5. Nieburg, *In the Name of Science*, p. 190.

6. House Committee on Government Operations, *Eleventh Report, Organization and Management of Missile Programs*, House Report No. 1121, 86th Cong., 1st sess., 1959, pp. 129–30.

7. Nieburg, *In the Name of Science*, pp. 190–91.

8. *Ibid.*, p. 220. Contracting out government work was construed by the Eisenhower administration as a means of preventing "unfair competition" by government in-house facilities *vis-à-vis* private contractors. Cf. *Bureau of Budget Bulletin 60–2*, September 21, 1959, which emphasized maximizing R & D performance by private contractors. This approach was adhered to in spite of admonitions from the president's own Science Advisory Committee, which cautioned against pursuit of such a policy, noting that "government laboratories are vital national assets whose activities will need to keep pace" with expanding R & D programs and that "undue reliance on outside laboratories . . . could greatly impair the morale and vitality of needed government laboratories." (U.S., President, Science Advisory Committee, Report, *Strengthening American Science* [Washington: Government Printing Office, 1959], p. 425.)

9. See Nieburg, *In the Name of Science*, pp. 269–77, 284–85. Cf. House Committee

on Government Operations, *Comptroller General Reports,* 89th Cong., 1st sess., 1965, Appendices 2A–E, pp. 735–835. See also House Armed Services Committee, *Overpricing of Government Contracts,* Hearings, 87th Cong., 1st sess., 1961, pp. 14–16.

10. *Ibid.,* p. 278. The idea that defense contracting has meant "super-profits" for favored contractors has been challenged in an article by George E. Berkley, a political scientist. (See "The Myth of War Profiteering," *The New Republic,* December 20, 1969, pp. 15–18). Berkley notes that while defense contractors have often derived much of their annual revenue from war contracts, their highest profits have come from nondefense sales. He refers to a study made in 1969 by the Logistics Management Institute, which showed that "the average profit margin for all U.S. sales industry was 8.7 percent of sales, but that the average profit margin on defense work was only 4.2 percent of sales." (Apparently these figures apply to 1968 though Berkley does not make this explicitly clear.) In fact, he notes that the actual nondefense to defense profits ratio may be higher than this one-to-one rate, since "low-profit defense work" was included in the overall industrial average profit. (*Ibid.,* p. 16.) He does note, however, that the data for this study came from the contractors themselves and "was attacked in some quarters" on that account, but he reassures the reader that for the sake of stock market appearances and the politics of corporate mergers, defense contractors had probably tended to overstate rather than understate profits. (*Ibid.,* pp. 17–18.) One critic of the study cited by Berkley notes that the Logistics Management Institute (a "think tank" working under contract to the Pentagon) used "unverified, unaudited data obtained on a voluntary basis from a sample of defense contractors" and that nearly half of this sample (42 percent) returned no data on their profit situation. See Richard F. Kaufman, "The Military-Industrial Complex," in Jerome H. Skolnick and Eliott Currie, eds., *Crisis in American Institutions* (Boston: Little, Brown, 1970), p. 185. Furthermore, since the Institute's study was made for the Pentagon rather than the stock market, it seems plausible that those suffering *lowest* profits under the Defense Department's "cost-effectiveness" contract reforms of recent years, would be most motivated to respond; at the least we must agree with Kaufman that "there is no way of knowing whether the contractors who refused to participate . . . included the ones making the highest profits." (*Ibid.*) Kaufman also cites a General Accounting Office study which compared average profits negotiated in defense contracts during the last half of 1966 with those for the period 1959 through 1963, finding an increase of 26 percent; moreover, he notes that these profit rates, calculated as a percentage of costs, tend to understate the "true profit level." He cites in this regard a 1962 tax case in which North American Aviation claimed profits of 8 percent as a percentage of costs, whereas "the tax court found that the company had realized profits of 612 percent and 803 percent on its investment in two succeeding years." (*Ibid.*) He further cites a study by Murray Weidenbaum which measured profit rate as a percentage of investment and found that from 1962 to 1965 "a sample of *large* defense contractors earned 17.5 percent net profit . . . while companies of similar size doing business in the commercial market earned 10.6 percent." (*Ibid.,* our emphasis.) This finding of higher defense profits, based on investment, is confirmed by David E. Sims, "Spoon-Feeding the Military—How New Weapons Come to Be," Rodberg and Shearer, eds., *Pentagon Watchers,* pp. 225–65. Sims observes that "if profits are measured as a percentage of sales, then they have been low . . . but . . . a more accurate measure of profit is the return on net investment." The profit margin as a percent of sales for 1962–65 was only 2.6 percent for a sample of defense firms as against 4.6 percent for industrial firms (close to the two-to-one ratio cited by Berkley), but profits calculated as a return on net investment were 17.5 percent as against 10.6 percent for the defense *versus* industrial sample, as reported by Wiedenbaum. (Figures presented to the Subcommittee on Antitrust and Monopoly, Summer 1968, and quoted in *ibid.,* p. 229.) This apparent discrepancy is explained by the fact that the Defense Department has made a "policy of providing government-owned property and federal working capital to defense contractors," and that this has particularly been true in the case of larger contractors. (*Ibid.*)

11. Borosage, "National Security State," p. 26. These interlocking relationships between military, political, and industrial interests first crystallized during World War II, through the medium of *ad hoc* governmental and quasi-governmental agencies set up to promote continuing contact between leaders in these several institutional sectors. Both military and political leaders established regular communication with industrial leaders through industrial and technical advisory committees and boards. Secretary Forrestal (then Secretary of the Navy, later to become the first Secretary of Defense), brought together defense contractors to found the National Security Industrial Association in 1944. By 1948 there were over a dozen industrial advisory committees to the government's R & D Board; by 1949 the government's Munitions Board was receiving assistance from almost a score of advisory committees, made up of approximately 400 top industrial executives. As Borosage notes, "These advisory committees greatly influenced the contracting process." (*Ibid.*, p. 29.) He goes on to quote the Steelman report on advisory committees issued in 1947, which observed that advisory committees "are influential in awarding contracts commonly negotiated without competitive bidding." This would tend to favor the largest enterprises or universities seeking contracts, since such institutions often have associations with the "outstanding scientists of the country," who along with their officers, "often . . . sit upon the program-planning and evaluating committees." (Quoted in *ibid.*)

12. Don K. Price, *The Scientific Estate* (Cambridge, Mass.: Harvard University Press, The Belknap Press, 1967), p. 11.

13. Nieburg, *In the Name of Science*, pp. 254–55. Some idea of the scale of excessive pricing and profit in the R & D sector is provided by a 1961 GAO sample of about 5 percent of contract awards, by dollar value, which revealed overcharges of $60 million, or over $1 billion projected to 100 percent; by 1964, the size of ascertainable overpricing in a 5 percent sample had multiplied almost tenfold to about half a billion dollars, or $10 billion projected to 100 percent. (*Ibid.*, p. 269.)

14. The danger of untoward influence has been compounded by the fact that the industrial contractor often employs as contract negotiators corporate officials who can significantly affect the contract officer's career; many negotiators are ex-military or government agency officials who retain friendly ties with members of congressional committees responsible for overseeing agency operations. Charles E. Jacob, *Policy and Bureaucracy* (Princeton, N.J.: Van Nostrand, 1966), pp. 178–79.

15. House Committee on Government Operations, *Comptroller General Reports to Congress on Audits of Defense Contracts*, 89th Cong., 1st sess., 1965, p. 46.

16. Cf. Sims, "Spoon-feeding the Military," p. 228.

17. Nieburg, *In the Name of Science*, pp. 190–95. See also Richard J. Barber, "The New Partnership: Big Government and Big Business," in Robert Perucci and Marc Pilisuk, eds., *The Triple Revolution*, pp. 224–26; and John K. Galbraith, "The Big Defense Firms are Really Public Firms," *New York Times*, Section 6, November 16, 1969, pp. 164, 167.

18. Nieburg, *In the Name of Science*, p. 196; cf. Barber, "The New Partnership," pp. 218–24; Jacob, *Policy and Bureaucracy*, p. 117.

19. See Galbraith, *New Industrial State*, pp. 8–10 and Robert L. Heilbroner, *The Limits of American Capitalism* (New York: Harper & Row, 1967), pp. 8–14.

20. House Committee on Government Operations, *Systems Development and Management*, Hearings, 87th Cong., 2d sess., 1962, pp. 1103–1228.

21. For a detailed discussion, see Nieburg, *In the Name of Science*, ch. 13, "The New Braintrusters," pp. 244–67.

22. *Ibid.*, p. 190.

23. Cf. Jacob, *Policy and Bureaucracy*, pp. 77–81, 182–86; Heilbroner, *Limits of American Capitalism*, pp. 49–58; and Price, *Scientific Estate*, pp. 227–42.

24. Cf. Jacob, *Policy and Bureaucracy*, p. 185.

25. *Ibid.*, p. 178.

26. *Ibid.*, p. 77.

27. *Ibid.*

28. Hans Morgenthau, *The Purpose of American Politics* (New York: Vintage Books, 1960), p. 277.

29. Cf. Sanford Lakoff, ed., *Knowledge and Power, Essays on Science and Government* (New York: Free Press, 1966), pp. 242, 253; and Nieburg, *In the Name of Science*, pp. 46–49.

30. As Borosage points out, the military budget has been shielded from congressional control by virtue of a number of factors, including the secrecy and complexity of the national security establishment and the dependency of many congressmen and their home districts on the largess of the military complex. ("National Security State," pp. 50–53.) Add to this the climate of postwar public opinion stirred by "war-scares" emanating from the Congress, the executive, and the military establishment, with its numerous public information facilities. (*Ibid.*, pp. 45–51.) As a result, the public tended without much question to support requests for military expenditures during the first two postwar decades, until the "credibility gaps" of the late 1960's, which were largely related to the visible failure of administration promises regarding the course of the war in Vietnam.

31. Alain C. Enthoven and K. Wayne Smith, *How Much is Enough? Shaping the Defense Program, 1961–1969* (New York: Harper & Row, 1971).

32. Nieburg, *In the Name of Science*, pp. 20–21. As Nieburg indicates, "The key symbol of the change was the formal cancellation in December of the Air Force Dynasoar program." (*Ibid.*, p. 53.) In place of the cancelled Dynasoar program, the Air Force soon put forward a proposal for a manned orbiting laboratory (MOL) which it had nurtured for almost five years as a project of the first importance.

33. Among their tactics for evading McNamara's new budgetary controls, the Air Force and its supporters sought to assign MOL to NASA "where Congress could find it uninhibited by McNamara's scrutiny." (*Ibid.*, p. 59.) In the case of the Supersonic Transport, Nieburg indicates that government support for development of a commercial SST came as a "substitute means for maintaining the financial health . . . of the private carriers," in view of the displacement of supersonic bombers such as the B-70 by the shift to strategic missiles. (*Ibid.*, p. 325.)

34. In an article on the "end of ideology," Stephen Rousseas and James Farganis have observed how committed the late President Kennedy was to the Bell-Lipset thesis. To this effect, they cite his address before the Economic Conference in Washington in May 1962: "The fact of the matter is that most of the problems, or at least many of them that we now face, are technical problems, are administrative problems. They are very sophisticated judgments which do not lend themselves to the great sort of 'passionate movements' which have stirred this country so often in the past. Now they deal with questions which are beyond the comprehension of most men." And a month later, at his 1962 commencement address at Yale, he observed: "What is at stake in our economic decisions today is not some grand warfare of rival ideologies which will sweep the country with passion but the practical management of a modern economy . . . ." Cited in "American Politics and the End of Ideology," in Irving Louis Horowitz, *The New Sociology* (New York: Oxford University Press, 1946), p. 284.

35. This report, written under the name of David Bell, Kennedy's Budget Director, and including McNamara himself as one of the committee's participants, expressed concern that government management capabilities had been reduced because of Defense Department's overdependence on interested contractors for technical advice relevant to weapons, development policy, and for management functions more appropriately performed by government agencies. See Nieburg, *In the Name of Science*, p. 334–50.

36. *Ibid.*, p. 364.

37. *Ibid.*, pp. 369–73. Cf. House Committee on Armed Services, *The Aerospace Corporation*, 89th Cong., 1st sess., 1965, pp. 149–50; House Committee on Government Operations, *Comptroller General Reports*, Hearings, 89th Cong., 1st sess., 1965, pp. 170–71, 640–41.

38. House Committee on Government Operations, *Comptroller General Reports*, p. 452.

39. Increasing centralization of control over military budget has not necessarily meant the elimination of programs involving massive waste of resources. Thus the C-5A, with cost overruns of over $2 billion, was authorized by Secretary McNamara and

endorsed by his successor Clark Clifford, despite "internal Defense Department studies questioning the cost-effectiveness of the huge military transport plane." Cf. Tom Klein, "The Capacity to Intervene," in Rodberg and Shearer, eds., *The Pentagon Watchers*, pp. 195–98, 207–8. It appears that the Pentagon's political commitment, established under McNamara, to a capability for rapid deployment of armed forces anywhere in the world, consonant with a global "interventionist" policy, clearly outweighed the technical questions of cost-effectiveness. (With respect to its use as an instrument of executive "interventionist" policy, Senator Fulbright noted "the C–5A does not itself represent a commitment to anybody, but it represents a significant new facility for the making of commitments in the hands of the executive." Quoted in Klein, "Capacity," p. 207).

40. See C. Wright Mills, *The Power Elite*, esp. pp. 269–97. Cf. Daniel Bell, *End of Ideology*, pp. 55–56.